Hands On: Practical Tips and Useful Programs for IBM Personal Computers from the Pages of PC World

Edited by the Editors of PC World
Joe Matazzoni, Project Editor

PC World Books
Published by
Computer Book Division
Simon & Schuster, Inc.
New York

Published by the Computer Book Division
Simon & Schuster, Inc.
Simon & Schuster Building
Rockefeller Center
1230 Avenue of the Americas
New York, New York 10020

A complete listing of trademarks and their holders appears on page 314.

Manufactured in the United States of America

10 9 8 7 6 5 4 3 2 1

Library of Congress Cataloging in Publication Data

Main entry under title:

Hands on.

1. IBM microcomputers. 2. IBM microcomputers—
programming. I. PC World Communications, Inc.
QA76.8.I1015H36 1985 001.64 85-2061

ISBN 0-671-49285-3

Contents

Preface ix
Introduction 1

1

Spreadsheets 3
Hands On 3
Tracking Bulls and Bears, *Andrew T. Williams* 4
Formulas for Profit, *Donald Hunt* 12
/X Marks the Macro, *Eric Weiss* 20
Linking Worksheets with Multiplan, *Andrew T. Williams* 28
. Star-Dot-Star 33
Automatic 1-2-3 Subdirectories 33
Worksheet Printer Controls 33
Legendary Graphs 34
1-2-3 As a Calculator 34
1-2-3 Break 34

2

Word Processing 37
Hands On 37
WordStar Made to Order, *Emil Flock* 38
First-Class MailMerge, *Bobbie Ray Leach* 49
Enhancing the IBM Personal Editor, *Steven J. Lagreca* 52
Getting the Word, *Burton L. Alperson* 62
. Star-Dot-Star 71
DOS to WordStar to DOS 71
Strip Ease 72
Faster Searches 73
The WordStar WIP File 73
pfs:write with DOS 2.00 74
More PATH and PeachText 74
VW in Overdrive 75

3

Data Base Management 77
Hands On 77
Tracking Your Expenses with dBASE II or dBASE III, *Lawrence J. Magid* 78
The dBase.report, *David Jenkins* 84
The Little Black Book, *Paul McDermott* 90
The Little Black Book II, *Paul McDermott* 97
. Star-Dot-Star 102
dBASE II SORT Magic 102
dBoxes 102
dBASE Displays 103
dBASE Video 103

4

Graphics 107
Hands On **107**
A World for Your PC, *Karl Koessel* **108**
1-2-3 Graphics Made Easy, *Joseph P. Celentano* **112**
Pixel to Printer, *Peter Baenziger* **117**
Character Construction, *J.G. Vaughan* **130**
Screen Shots, *Alan J. Fridlund* **145**
. Star-Dot-Star **148**
Colorful Tip 148
ASCII Graphics Chart **148**
VCR as RF Modulator **148**
PC Cartography **149**
Secret Graphics Mode **149**

5

Entertainment 155
Hands On **155**
Video Game Graphics, *Dan Illowsky and Michael Abrash* **156**
A Snake in the Glass, *Peter Quinn* **164**
Digital Deduction, *Karl Koessel* **168**
Programming Sound in BASIC, *Lon Poole* **170**
. Star-Dot-Star **178**
Mine Field **178**

6

Communications 181
Hands On **181**
Smartmodem 450, *Larry Jordan* **182**
Smartmodem Gets Smarter, *Burton L. Alperson* **184**
PC CTTY, *Richard Steck* **191**
. Star-Dot-Star **194**
PC-Beep III **194**
PC-Talk III and Microcom Marriage **194**
Built-In Assembler **194**

7

Enhancing the Operating System 199
Hands On **199**
Menus Made Easy, *Tom Sheldon* **200**
Changing Keys, *Brian Mann* **207**
Macro Mastery, *Burton L. Alperson* **210**
. Star-Dot-Star **220**
File Finder **220**
Hard Disk Organization **220**
Defensive Disk Driving **222**
Greasing the Pipe **222**
Build a Better Blanker **223**
Say What You Mean **226**
Key Reassignments with DEBUG **227**
Flip Lock **228**

8

BASIC Programming 233
Hands On **233**
Building a BASIC Program, *Donald B. Trivette* **234**
Disk Data Files, *Lon Poole* **239**
Optimizing for BASCOM, *Dan Rollins* **251**
BASIC Block Moves, *Stuart Greenberg* **260**
. Star-Dot-Star **274**
BASIC Cross-Reference **274**
BASIC Variable Reference **274**
Cross-Reference Checker **274**
Making 'Em Pause **276**
Save the Keys **277**
XMAKER **277**
DATAMKR **277**

9

Hardware 281
Hands On **281**
How the PC Thinks, *Peter Norton* **282**
Getting Started with an 8087, *Walter Cooke* **291**
The Cassette Port Lives!, *Michael A. Covington* **297**
. Star-Dot-Star **304**
ProWriter Switches **304**
Star Fix **304**
Okidata MODE Fix **304**
Printer Check Perfected **305**
Half-Height Fix **305**
Cassette Port Control Compiled **306**

Appendix **309**

Index **315**

Preface

In one respect, *Hands On* is a departure from other books published in the PC World book series. It departs by being a collection of 35 Hands On articles and 46 Star-Dot-Star vignettes reprinted from the pages of *PC World* magazine; each of the other books in the series is individually authored or coauthored.

However, *Hands On* also continues the tradition of the series. This volume presents a host of practical, precise, and often hard-won methods to faster and more efficient personal computing. On the one hand, you benefit from distilled results, tried and tested methods, and exact answers of expert users. The Hands On authors are professionals who have crafted nifty solutions to testy problems they have encountered in their everyday work.

On the other hand, you also benefit from creative and inspired responses of *PC World* readers who contribute insights from every nook and cranny of the personal computer world. The Star-Dot-Star (*.*) tidbits, hints, and suggestions come directly from the readership of the magazine. These short topics focus on specific answers to specific problems.

Hands On and Star-Dot-Star articles included here have something for everyone. Many of the articles are gems of wizardry. Most have received high praise from an appreciative audience. And taken together, they vividly demonstrate the art, skill, and joy of the personal computer enthusiasts who wrote them.

The Editors of PC World are indebted to all these authors and readers for their creativity, enthusiasm, and willingness to share their personal computer craftsmanship.

Introduction

This anthology takes its title and contents from the "Hands On" section of *PC World* magazine. The premise of the "Hands On" section has always been that the best way to learn about personal computing on the IBM PC is by doing, and that premise is now the theme of this book.

The articles reprinted here fall into two general types: some are tutorials that take you through the steps of solving a particular problem, in the process demonstrating some software feature, programming technique, or new piece of hardware; the others are projects, which are designed to be instructive, but which also leave you with a valuable end-product such as a utility or spreadsheet template. In either case, what distinguishes these pieces is that each encourages you to get your "hands on" the keyboard and do some computing.

In addition to the full-length articles reprinted here we've culled some 46 chestnuts from *PC World*'s "Star-Dot-Star" column. The name "Star-Dot-Star" comes from the DOS global wildcard characters *.*; most commonly used in copy commands to mean "copy all," the characters suggest the column's function—a kind of anything-goes exchange. "Star-Dot-Star" comes out of the spirit of the early days of personal computing; like the free bulletin board services that sprang up as a means for early computer users to communicate with each other, "Star-Dot-Star" is a medium for readers to publish their personal computer discoveries. In the "Star-Dot-Star" section at the end of each chapter you can harvest the often hard-won fruits of our readers' experience—a rich crop of pointers, programs, warnings and recommendations.

Of the scores of "Hands On" articles from which to choose, we decided on the 35 included here not only because they seemed the most widely applicable and well written, but because together they form a well-balanced collection that should have something for everyone. The first five chapters focus on the ways in which people use their computers, covering the most common PC application areas—spreadsheets, word processing, data base management, graphics, and entertainment. Many of the articles in these chapters are built around popular applications programs, such as *dBASE II, 1-2-3,* and *WordStar,* and show you how to use those pieces of software to their fullest. The last four chapters—"Communications," "Enhancing the Operating System," "BASIC Programming," and "Hardware"— take a step back, from the PC's applications to the system itself and from using programs to writing them. While the subjects of these last chapters may sound more advanced, many of the articles are designed to introduce beginners into these sometimes-intimidating areas.

We bring these articles and "Star-Dot-Star" items together to make them available to new or non-subscribers. Our authors, your guides, bring to bear an array of talent and expertise that would be difficult to duplicate.

IBM
Personal
Computer
Display

1

Spreadsheets

Hands On

What's the single event that computer historians generally credit with having launched personal computers out of hobbyist circles and into the mass market? It isn't the development of CP/M—the first workable personal computer operating system—nor the advent of the Apple II or the IBM PC; rather it's the release of *VisiCalc,* the first electronic spreadsheet. Spreadsheet programs transformed personal computers from toys into business machines because they answered a real business need: for the first time they gave small businesses and individuals the means to make complex calculations automatically. Virtually any job that involves numbers and calculation can be done more quickly and easily with a computer and spreadsheet program than by hand. Applications can be created that automatically perform such involved processes as finding information, carrying out mathematical and logical operations on it, and using the results to create a formatted report. Spreadsheets reduce drudgery and give you the capability to use numbers in more creative ways.

The following articles are built around three popular spreadsheet programs for the PC. If you're a spreadsheet novice, following the step-by-step instructions in the articles will familiarize you with the basic commands and logic of this type of program and give you a sense of what spreadsheets can do. If you've used a spreadsheet before, these projects will give you a workout on advanced concepts and program features.

"Tracking Bulls and Bears" shows how to link three *SuperCalc* worksheets to form a system that assesses the performance of your stock portfolio in a matter of minutes—including such calculations as how much you've made or lost since you bought the stocks and the commission you'd pay if you sold. The article also serves as a good tutorial on the use of IF and LOOKUP statements.

The next two articles use Lotus Development's *1-2-3*. "Formulas for Profit" provides a template for doing cost-volume- profit analyses, a calculation performed by financial planners to model the impact of changes in costs, sales volume, and other variables on bottom-line profits. In "/X Marks the Macro" you can learn about *1-2-3*'s advanced macro capabilites, including the little-known use of macros within macros, while you create a program that produces loan-amortization schedules.

The last article, "Linking Worksheets in Multiplan," is a tutorial on one of *Multiplan*'s most useful—but somewhat tricky—features: its ability to link worksheets so that changes in one are carried over into the others. Building the spreadsheet in the tutorial will show you how to avoid getting caught in the snarl of interdependencies that can develop in a complex worksheet.

Tracking Bulls and Bears

Andrew T. Williams

Owning common stocks means watching their movements like a hawk. Casting a sharp eye on each morning's financial page, you find out your stocks' current prices as well as how much the prices have changed since the previous day.

But the newspaper can't tell you how much you've made or lost since you bought the stocks. Nor can it tell you how much commission to subtract from the gross sale price if you want to sell a holding. You might also want to calculate the percentage change on an annualized basis so you can see how stocks you've owned for different periods of time are doing. And by the way, how long have you owned that stock? Does it qualify for treatment as a long-term capital gain?

If you own a portfolio of common stocks, these important analyses should be made every day. With a calculator, portfolio tracking is tedious and time consuming. But with a PC and an electronic spreadsheet package, you can transform this task into a matter of a few minutes of data entry and a push of the recalculation key.

By recreating the worksheets in this article you can easily monitor the performance of your stock portfolio. These worksheets are arranged on a single *SuperCalc* spreadsheet in three descending steps (see Figure 1.1). Figure 1.2, which is dependent on Figures 1.3 and 1.4, is the main worksheet on which your portfolio is tracked. Figure 1.3 is a work space where many calculations are performed and summarized. Figure 1.4 contains five lookup tables: the top two are used when calculating the commission, and the bottom three are used when calculating the number of days between dates.

By constructing these worksheets separately, you can insert or delete rows and expand or contract column widths in any table without affecting entries in the other two tables. This layout demonstrates a cardinal rule of electronic worksheet construction: use the entire worksheet; don't be constrained by the small portion displayed on the screen.

The Electronic Worksheet

You can see how much you've invested in each of your stocks and how much they're worth each day with the help of the electronic worksheet in Figure 1.2. The worksheet shows how much the value of each stock has changed since it was purchased and how much the stock's value has changed since you last evaluated your portfolio. The value of your holdings is summarized at the bottom of the worksheet, and the portfolio's performance is compared with the change in the Dow Jones Industrial Average (DJIA) over the same period. With this worksheet you can track changes in your portfolio value quickly and easily, enabling you to act fast when required.

The worksheet shown in Figure 1.2 uses several special features of *SuperCalc,* although you could duplicate the worksheet with other spreadsheet programs designed to run on the IBM PC. This worksheet uses *SuperCalc*'s ability to copy values from one part of the worksheet to another without copying the underlying formulas. It also uses *SuperCalc*'s variable column widths, which enable you to place as much material as possible on a single page.

Formulas

Before entering formulas into the worksheet, turn off *SuperCalc*'s automatic recalculation feature by typing **/GM**. With recalculation off, the computer won't calculate the formulas on the worksheet after each entry; type an exclamation mark when you want to recalculate the worksheet.

To create Figure 1.2, position the cursor at cell AA45. Set column widths as indicated in row 45, and copy the title material and column headings in the lower rows. Set the dollars and cents format to the global format with the command **/FG$**. Set the columns AB and AE and the date cells (AA56 to AC56) to the integer format.

The formulas entered into each cell of row 62 of the worksheet and the formulas from cells AO55 and AO56 are listed in the lower left of the worksheet. Most of the formulas are straightforward. Those in AD62 and AJ62 calculate the value of each holding, while those in AK62 and AN62 calculate the difference between yesterday's value and the purchase price. The formulas in row 73 total the overall value of the portfolio.

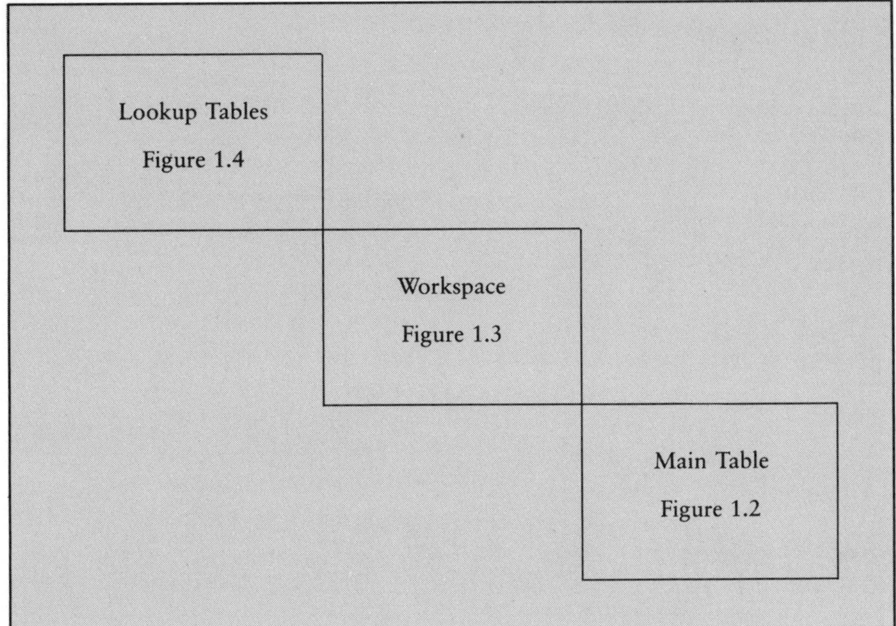

Figure 1.1 *Arrange Figures 1.2, 1.3, and 1.4 in this stepwise manner.*

Enter the formulas for columns AE and AF, even though these formulas are dependent on information from Figure 1.3. Once we construct Figure 1.3, the information in columns AE and AF will be calculated.

The four IF functions in cells AL62, AO62, AQ62, and AO55 prevent error messages from appearing on the worksheet when division by zero is attempted. These IF functions, like all other IF functions, consist of a comparison and two alternatives. If the comparison is true, the IF function calculates the first alternative; if the comparison is false, the IF function calculates the second alternative.

In cell AL62 the comparison "Is AH62 equal to zero?" is true if AH62 equals zero. In this case, 'Error' would be displayed if division by zero were attempted. To prevent this from happening, when the comparison is true the IF function calculates the first alternative, placing a zero instead of an error message in the cell. If the comparison is false, the second alternative performs the division.

Completing the Table

Complete the worksheet by replicating the formulas in the first row of Figure 1.2 down their respective columns. Before you do the replication, however, enter dots (. . . .) into those columns where you'll be entering information, move the cursor to AF62, and set the graph format by typing **/F***. Enter percent signs into columns AM, AP, and AR. The dots remind you where you need to make entries when filling out the worksheet, and the percent signs signify the values that are percentages rather than dollars and cents. The columns containing the percent signs are so narrow that their column letters don't appear at the top of the *SuperCalc* screen, but the columns can be viewed by moving the worksheet cursor across row 62.

Replicate row 62 down the worksheet, allowing all the formula references to adjust, except the one in column AE that refers to cell X31. Today's Date is the same for each stock, so the reference in column AE to cell X31 is not relative. (Remember that until we construct Figure 1.3, which contains the information for cell X31, column AE will contain zeros and AF will be blank.) Figure 1.2 has ten rows for ten stocks, but you should make the table large enough to hold your portfolio, plus some room to grow.

The formulas in the Total line (row 73) are listed in the lower right of Figure 1.2. These are simple summation functions and formulas to calculate percentage changes. Notice that the range of the summation functions includes the row of dashes at the top and the row of double dashes at the bottom. These are evaluated as zeros; using them means that you can insert or delete any row in the table—including the first or the last—and not have to worry about upsetting the range of a summation function.

Using the Worksheet

Constructing this electronic worksheet is an exacting task, but the result is worthwhile. You can update the table quickly and add new purchases and remove sales easily. By the way, if you haven't saved a copy of the worksheet on disk, do so now.

To use the worksheet the first time, enter the symbol, the number of shares, and the purchase price per share for each of your stocks into the first three columns of the table. Enter the day's date into cells AA56, AB56, and AC56. Enter today's DJIA into cell AO53, and the day before's DJIA into cell AO54. Enter

```
   | AA || AB||  AC  ||  AD  || AE ||   AF   ||  AG  ||  AH  ||  AI  ||  AJ  || AK || AL | |   AN   ||  AO  | | AQ |
42|
43|                                                      COLUMN WIDTH SETTINGS
44|==========================================================================================================================
45|  6     5     9        9      6      11       9       9       9       9      8     7  1   10       9   1   7   1
46|==========================================================================================================================
47|
48|PRINT:AA50:AQ75   [CTRL]-[O]
49|Work Space IS LOCATED AT: J33
50|
51|                                         KEEPING TRACK OF YOUR STOCKS
52|                                              (c) Williams 1983
53|                                                                              TODAY'S DJIA:                  1088.91
54|    TODAY'S DATE                                                              YESTERDAY'S DJIA:              1087.43
55|    MO  DAY YEAR                                                              % CHANGE IN DJIA:                  .14%
56|     2   17     1983                                                          % CHANGE IN PORTFOLIO:             .96%
57|
58|                                                                               CHANGE FROM      OVERALL   OVERALL  ANNUAL
59| STOCK # OF       PURCHASE       DAYS  LONG TERM    YESTERDAY'S         TODAY'S           YESTERDAY     $ GAIN OR        %        %
60|SYMBOL SHS.  PRICE        VALUE OWNED   ??????? PRICE        VALUE   PRICE     VALUE        $        %   LOSS (-)   CHANGE  CHANGE
61|--------------------------------------------------------------------------------------------------------------------------
62|IBM     100     88.25  8870.00    44              98.875  9804.03  98.875  9804.03      .00     .00%     934.03    10.53%  87.35%
63|CSC     400    20.625  8331.75   848 *******        21.5  8517.20    21.5  8517.20      .00     .00%     185.45     2.23%    .96%
64|UAL     125    29.875  3790.63   620 *******       31.75  3912.50      33  4068.75   156.25    3.99%     278.13     7.34%   4.32%
65|DEC     200   104.375 20965.00    76              123.75 24660.00  126.25 25160.00   500.00    2.03%    4195.00    20.01%  96.10%
66|BUD      75      51.5  3896.25   410 *******      64.875  4806.45  65.375  4843.95    37.50     .78%     947.70    24.32%  21.65%
67|AAPL    250     19.75  5003.13    77              44.375 11003.47      44 10910.00   -93.47    -.85%    5906.88   118.06% 559.65%
68|...     ...     .....      .00     0                 ...    .....     ...      .00      .00     .00%        .00      .00%    .00%
69|...     ...     .....      .00     0                 ...    .....     ...      .00      .00     .00%        .00      .00%    .00%
70|...     ...     .....      .00     0                 ...    .....     ...      .00      .00     .00%        .00      .00%    .00%
71|...     ...     .....      .00     0                 ...    .....     ...      .00      .00     .00%        .00      .00%    .00%
72|==========================================================================================================================
73|TOTAL                    50856.75                          62703.64          63303.93   600.28     .96%   12447.18    24.47%
74|
75|
76|CONTENTS OF                                          CONTENTS OF
77|CELLS IN ROW 62                                      CELLS IN ROW 73
78|
79|AD62   (AB62*AC62)+R38                               AJ73     SUM(AJ61:AJ72)
80|
81|AE62   IF(AB62=0,0,X31-X38)                          AK73     SUM(AK61:AK72)
82|
83|AF62   IF(AE62>=365,7,0)                             AL73     IF(AH73=0,0,(AK73/AH73)*100)
84|
85|AJ62   (AI62*AB62)-W38                               AN73     SUM(AN61:AN72)
86|
87|AK62   AJ62-AH62                                     AO73     IF(AD73=0,0,((AJ73/AD73)-1)*100)
88|
89|AL62   IF(AH62=0,0,((AJ62-AH62)/AH62)*100)
90|
91|AN62   AJ62-AD62
92|
93|AO62   IF(AD62=0,0,(AN62/AD62)*100)
94|
95|AQ62   IF(AE62=0,0,(AO62/AE62)*365)
96|
97|
98|CONTENTS OF
99|CELLS AO55 AND AO56
100|
101|AO55   IF(AO54=0,0,(((AO53-AO54)/AO54)*100))
102|
103|AO56   AL73
104|
105|
```

Figure 1.2 *The stock tracking worksheet.*

```
  |  J  ||K|| L || M ||  N ||  O  ||  P  ||  Q  ||  R  || S ||  T  ||  U  ||  V  ||  W  ||  X  |
21|
22|                                              COLUMN WIDTH SETTINGS
23|==================================================================================================
24|   9     3   5    5     6      9       9       9       9       9   9       9       9       9       9
25|==================================================================================================
26|         PRINT J28:X49   [CTRL]-[O]
27|         MAIN TABLE IS LOCATED AT:AA50
28|
29|            WORK SPACE                                  WORK SPACE                         WORK SPACE
30|
31|                                                                                # OF TODAY'S DAY:  2943
32|
33|                                      PURCHASE VALUES                          TODAY'S VALUES
34|                          ----------------------------------------- ---------------------------------------      # OF
35|STOCK    PURCHASE DATE  COM.    VALUE     MIM.     MAX.  CORRECT  COM.    VALUE     MIM.     MAX.  CORRECT PURCHASE
36|SYMBOL     MO  DAY YEAR  RATE     COM.     COM.     COM.     COM.  RATE     COM.     COM.     COM.     COM.      DAY
37|------------------------------------------------------------------------------------------------------------------------
38|IBM         1    4 1983  .003    83.48     8.00    45.00    45.00  .003    86.66     8.00    83.48    83.48     2899
39|CSC        10   23 1980  .003    81.75    32.00   180.00    81.75  .003    82.80    32.00   180.00    82.80     2095
40|UAL         6    7 1981  .006    58.41    10.00    56.25    56.25  .006    60.75    10.00    56.25    56.25     2323
41|DEC        12    3 1982  .003   119.63    16.00    90.00    90.00  .003   132.75    16.00    90.00    90.00     2867
42|BUD         1    3 1982  .006    59.18     6.00    33.75    33.75  .006    65.42     6.00    59.18    59.18     2533
43|AAPL       29    2 1982  .006    65.63    20.00   112.50    65.63  .003    90.00    20.00   112.50    90.00     2866
44|  ...      ..  ... ....     0      .00      .00      .00      .00     0      .00      .00      .00      .00        0
45|  ...      ..  ... ....     0      .00      .00      .00      .00     0      .00      .00      .00      .00        0
46|  ...      ..  ... ....     0      .00      .00      .00      .00     0      .00      .00      .00      .00        0
47|  ...      ..  ... ....     0      .00      .00      .00      .00     0      .00      .00      .00      .00        0
48|========================================================================================================================
49|
50|         CONTENTS OF
51|         CELL...
52|
53|         N38     LOOKUP(AB62*AC62,B10:B14)
54|
55|         O38     LOOKUP(N38,E10:E13)+AB62*AC62*N38
56|
57|         P38     IF(AB62<600,AB62*.08,((AB62-600)*.04)+42)
58|
59|         Q38     IF(AB62>0,AB62*.45,O38)
60|
61|         R38     IF(P38>O38,P38,IF(Q38<O38,Q38,O38))
62|
63|         S38     LOOKUP(AB62*AI62,B10:B14)
64|
65|         T38     LOOKUP(S38,E10:E13)+AB62*AI62*S38
66|
67|         U38     IF(AB62<600,AB62*.08,((AB62-600)*.04)+42)
68|
69|         V38     IF(AB62>100,AB62*.45,O38)
70|
71|         W38     IF(U38>T38,U38,IF(V38<T38,V38,T38))
72|
73|         X38     L38+LOOKUP(K38,B21:B33)+LOOKUP(M38,E21:E32)+IF(K38>2,LOOKUP(M38,H21:H32),0)
74|
75|
76|         X31     AB56+LOOKUP(AA56,B21:B33)+LOOKUP(AC56,E21:E32)+IF(AA56>2,LOOKUP(AC56,H21:H32),0)
77|
78|
```

Figure 1.3 *Calculations and formulas for stock commissions.*

```
  |  A  ||  B  ||  C  ||  D  ||  E  ||  F  ||  G  ||  H  ||  I  |
 1|
 2|
 3|              LOOKUP TABLES FOR STOCK TRANSACTIONS
 4|                 CHARLES SCHWAB AND COMPANY
 5|
 6|          COMMISSION RATE            DOLLAR COMMISSION
 7|
 8|                         COM.            COM.        $
 9|          AMOUNT         RATE            RATE     AMT.
10|               0            0               0        0
11|            .001         .012            .003       57
12|            3000         .006            .006       36
13|            7000         .003            .012       18
14|           56000          N/A
15|
16|                       LOOKUP TABLES FOR DAYS BETWEEN DATES
17|
18|   MONTH'S TABLE                     YEAR'S TABLE                   YEAR'S TABLE
19|
20| MONTH        #       DAYS        YEAR    # OF DAYS               LEAP YEARS
21|              0          0           0          0                    0      0
22| January      1          0        1975          0                 1975      0
23| February     2         31        1976        365                 1976      1
24|    March     3         59        1977        731                 1977      0
25|    April     4         90        1978       1096                 1978      0
26|      May     5        120        1979       1434                 1979      0
27|     June     6        151        1980       1799                 1980      1
28|     July     7        181        1981       2165                 1981      0
29|   August     8        212        1982       2530                 1982      0
30|September     9        243        1983       2895                 1983      0
31|  October    10        273        1984       3260                 1984      1
32| November    11        304        1985       3626                 1985      0
33| December    12        334
34|
35|
36|
37|
38|
39|
40|
```

Figure 1.4 *Lookup tables.*

yesterday's stock prices into the column labeled Today's Price, and press the exclamation mark to calculate the values on the worksheet. After the values have been calculated, move the entries in columns AI and AJ (Today's Price and Today's Value) to columns AG and AH (Yesterday's Price and Yesterday's Value). Do this by using the *SuperCalc* copy command (/C). When you are asked for the range of the cells you wish to copy, type **AI62:AJ71**.

When you press <Enter> after the last cell address of the source range, *SuperCalc* asks for the cell address of the upper-left corner of the target range. Type **AG62**, the first cell in the Yesterday's Price column, but don't press <Enter> yet. Pressing <Enter> transfers all the formulas in the source range, but you want to transfer only the values, so type a comma. *SuperCalc* asks if you want N (no adjust), A (ask for adjust), or V (values). To copy values only, type a V.

Now you're ready to enter today's prices into column AI and press the exclamation mark to evaluate your portfolio. Each day, when you update the table, all you have to do is enter the date, move the entries in Today's DJIA down to Yesterday's DJIA, enter the current day's DJIA, move the figures for Today's Price and Value into Yesterday's Price and Value, enter the current day's prices into the the appropriate cells, and press the exclamation mark to recalculate the worksheet. The updating procedure takes only a few moments.

The worksheet in Figure 1.2 is changeable, so adapt it to your needs. You may want to calculate percentage distributions or compare a stock's value to certain predetermined values. Some experts, for example, recommend selling if a stock drops 10 percent. If you wish, dividends can be included and total returns (capital gains plus dividends) calculated for each stock.

Laying Out the Work Space

The work space in Figure 1.3 is where commissions are calculated and numbers are assigned to the purchase date and to the current day's date so that the number of days between dates can be calculated.

Before laying out the work space, adjust the column widths as indicated at the top of Figure 1.3. Copy the titles and row headings and the formulas listed at the bottom of Figure 1.3 into the appropriate cells. Use /C to copy the list of stock symbols in column AA into column J, beginning with cell J38. Enter the purchase date for each stock into columns K, L, and M.

Days Owned

When the information in Figure 1.3 is filled in, columns AE and AF in Figure 1.2 will also be complete. Let's return briefly to that table to review the two simple formulas for these columns. Column AE displays the number of days you've owned each stock. Look at the formula in cell AE62:

IF(AB62 = 0,0,X31-X38)

The last part, X31-X38, subtracts the purchase date number (cell X38) from the number assigned to Today's Day (X31). The IF function prevents the number for Today's Day from appearing whenever an entry is not made in a row. Instead, the IF function assigns a zero to the cell.

With the help of an IF function and the graph format we set when we constructed Figure 1.2, column AF sets a flag (a row of seven asterisks) if the Days Owned column value is 365 or greater. The formula that sets the asterisks in cell AF62 is:

IF(AE62> = 365,7,0)

This IF function asks, "Is the value in AE62 (the number of days you've owned a stock) greater than or equal to 365?" If the value is greater than or equal to 365, then the comparison is true and the first alternative of the IF function is executed. This alternative places a 7 into the cell, and the graph format converts the 7 into asterisks. If the comparison is false, the second alternative is executed and a zero is entered into the cell. (Note: The holding period for long term capital gains changed on June 22, 1984. For stocks purchased after that date replace 365 in the formula with 180.)

Calculating the Commission

For a better understanding of how to use the work space, look at how the commission rates are calculated. Stock commissions are made up of a combination of a flat fee and a percentage fee based on the value of the transaction. Each stock sale is subject to a minimum and maximum commission based on the number of shares traded. The commission schedule in Figure 1.5 is for Charles Schwab and Co., Inc., the largest discount brokerage firm in the United States. Schwab's commission schedule is typical of what you would find at other brokerage houses. At Schwab the minimum commission is 8 cents per share on trades of up to 600 shares and 4 cents per share thereafter. The maximum commission, on trades of 100 shares or more, is 45 cents per share.

The easiest way to find a commission rate is to use the LOOKUP functions in this worksheet. Every LOOKUP function consists of a search argument and a range of cells that gives the location of the LOOKUP table. The LOOKUP function in cell N38, for example, looks up the commission rate based on the value of the transaction:

LOOKUP (AB62*AC62,B10:B14)

In this formula, AB62*AC62 is the search argument and B10:B14 is the location of the lookup table. The search argument is the value of the transaction. Check cells B10 to B14 in the lookup table in Figure 1.4 for the search argument.

A LOOKUP function looks through a table to find the largest value that is less than or equal to the value of the search argument. After the largest value is found, the function returns the corresponding percentage value and puts it in the cell containing the LOOKUP function. In this case, the search argument is $8825 and the largest value in the lookup table less than or equal to this value is $7001. Thus, the LOOKUP function returns .003 and puts it in the appropriate cell in the Com. Rate column in Figure 1.3. This means that for a transaction of $8825 there is a commission rate of 3 percent.

Once you've found the commission rate, you can calculate the total commission based on the value of the trade. Remember that each commission is made up of a flat dollar amount and a percentage of the value of the trade. Using a LOOKUP function, you can find the appropriate amount for each transaction. In Figure 1.3 the formulas entered into

Reprinted with permission of Charles Schwab and Co., Inc., 1983, Rates Subject to Change

Dollar Range Per Transaction	Commission Rates
$ 0–3000	$18 + 1.2% of principal amount
$3001–7000	$36 + 0.6% of principal amount
$7001–56,000*	$57 + 0.3% of principal amount

*Over $56,000 principal amount the commission charge is 72% below fixed rates in effect prior to 5/1/75 but not less than $225.

The above rates are subject to minimums and maximums. Minimum charge is 8 cents per share for the first 600 shares and 4 cents per share thereafter. Maximum commission is 45 cents per share for orders of 100 or more shares.

Figure 1.5 *Charles Schwab and Co., Inc., stock transaction commission schedule. Reprinted with permission of Charles Schwab and Co., Inc., 1983; rates subject to change.*

column O under the heading Value Com. calculate this amount for each stock in your portfolio.

Recall that the Schwab commission schedule also specifies a minimum and maximum commission based on the number of shares traded. These commissions are figured in columns P (Min. Com.) and Q (Max. Com.). The following formula is entered in cell P38 and calculates the minimum commission for the first entry in the workspace table:

```
IF(AB62<600,AB62*0.08,
   ((AB62-600)*0.4)+42)
```

The comparison in the IF function asks, "Is the number of shares in AB62 less than 600?" If the number of shares is less than 600, the comparison is true and the first alternative, which calculates the commission at the rate of 8 cents per share, is calculated. If the number of shares is 600 or more, the second alternative is calculated. This alternative adds $42 (the commission on 600 shares at 8 cents per share) to 4 cents times the number of shares over 600.

The maximum commission, listed in column Q under the title Max. Com., is calculated by a similar formula.

The Correct Commission

There are three commissions that might apply to the sale of a stock: the commission based on value, the minimum commission, and the maximum commmission. Use an IF function to find the correct one. The IF function entered into cell R38 is:

```
IF(P38>O38,P38,
   IF(Q38<O38,Q38,O38))
```

In this formula O38 is the commission based on value, P38 is the minimum commission, and Q38 is the maximum commission. The comparison asks, "Is the minimum commission larger than the commission based on value?" If so, the first alternative is executed and the minimum commission is the correct commission. If the comparison is false, the second alternative is executed, in which case another IF function asks, "Is the maximum commission less than the commission based on value?" If so, this function's first alternative is executed and the maximum commission is the correct commission. If this comparison is false, the second alternative of this IF function is executed and the commission based on the transaction value is the correct value.

The work space must also calculate the various commissions that apply to each stock's current value. The formulas to do this are entered into columns S through W.

To complete this part of the work space, replicate the formulas in the first row of the table, columns N to W, down to the bottom of the table. Include enough rows to accommodate your current portfolio and, in anticipation of a bullish market, your future portfolio.

When replicating the formulas, keep all references except the ones to the locations of various lookup tables relative to their current locations. Ask *SuperCalc* to specify each reference individually, or the program will automatically make all references relative.

Days Between Dates

For tax purposes, a stock held for more than 1 year (6 months for shares purchased after June 22, 1984) is a long-term capital asset. Gains on long-term assets are taxed at substantially lower rates than ordinary income, while long-term losses result in substantially less tax savings than their short-term counterparts. Consequently, knowing the number of days since you purchased a stock can be helpful with your taxes.

Before examining the formula that assigns a number to a specific date, review the numbering system in the bottom half of Figure 1.4. The Months Table shows the numbers assigned to each month (e.g., January, 1; February, 2). Beside the month numbers are the numbers of days that have elapsed since the first of the year up to the first day of each month (e.g., February, 31; March, 59).

The Years Table indicates the number of days that have elapsed each year. In the example, the numbering system begins with zero on January 1, 1975. Start this part of your lookup table with the year in which you purchased your oldest stock.

Finally, to make amends for leap years, there is a leap year lookup table. Next to each year listed is a zero or a one; zeros indicate normal years and ones indicate leap years.

Once you understand the numbering system, you can examine the formula in cell X31 of Figure 1.3 that assigns the number to Today's Day:

```
AB56+LOOKUP(AA56,B21:B33)
  +LOOKUP(AC56,E21:E32)
  +IF(AA56>2,LOOKUP
  (AC56,H21:H32),0)
```

This formula is made up of a series of simple LOOKUP functions. The number assigned to Today's Day is the sum of the number of the day of the month, the number of days between the first day of the current year and the first day of the current month, the number of days elapsed since the beginning of the numbering system and the first day of the current year, and the leap year adjustment.

On Your Own

The worksheet in this article uses IF and LOOKUP functions extensively and can serve as an example of how to use these functions to make other electronic worksheets. Once the worksheet is constructed, it can perform a large number of calculations quickly and easily. With a minimum of effort you can know just how well your stock portfolio is doing each day.

Use this worksheet as a starting point for your own modifications. One of the great strengths of electronic worksheets is that they can be modified to suit the user's needs. Take advantage of this flexibility to build in the comparisons you need and to omit the ones you don't need.

Then, with the help of this worksheet, just keep on trackin'.

Andrew T. Williams is a Contributing Editor for PC WORLD. *This article was published in* PC World, *Volume 1, Number 4. It was adapted from his book* WHAT IF? A User's Guide to Spreadsheets on the IBM PC *(New York, John Wiley & Sons, 1984) with permission from the publisher.*

If you want a copy of this worksheet enhanced with a dividend tracking worksheet but don't feel like constructing it yourself, send your address and a check for $15 to cover the cost of a disk, postage, and handling to Andrew T. Williams, Keeping Track of Your Stocks, P.O. Box 9563, Berkeley, CA 94709. Please specify whether you would like the model to run on an IBM PC, in SuperCalc, SuperCalc II, SuperCalc III, 1-2-3, *or* VisiCalc *form. To use the worksheet disk you'll need your own copy of the appropriate spreadsheet program.*

Formulas for Profit

Donald Hunt

To a gunfighter of the Old West, reaction time often meant life or death. To a professional baseball player, response time can make the difference between being a hero or a bum. And to today's business executive, quick action can ensure profit instead of loss, success rather than failure.

Business conditions change rapidly and affect virtually every aspect of the bottom line: price increases for materials, labor negotiations, commission schedules, advertising trends, and pricing strategies. Not only must you stay on top of the changes you know about, you must also attempt to predict tomorrow's changes.

With a PC, a spreadsheet package, and a few key concepts, you can develop a powerful tool to help you fine-tune your reaction time and perhaps even improve your aim.

Eyeing the Bottom Line

For many years financial planners have used cost-volume-profit (CVP) analysis to determine the impact that changes in cost and volume have on their profits. What happens to the bottom line if material costs go up 5 percent and selling price goes down 2 percent? If your company sells multiple products and operates from several locations, analyzing the bottom-line impact of changes in cost or sales volume of a single product can be difficult and time-consuming. When fixed overhead is high, a small change in sales volume can mean the difference between profit and loss.

CVP analysis is used to model the profit impact of changes in raw material or service costs, overhead expenses, and sales volume. Once you define and develop the CVP model, you can modify any cost or volume variable to reflect the profit impact of changes. Good or bad news comes quickly.

CVP analysis works with any type of business. It has been used primarily in manufacturing companies, where production or sales fluctuations can significantly affect the profitability of a product line, an individual plant, or the company as a whole. CVP analysis can also be used creatively in distribution, retail, service, and construction businesses.

A distribution company, for example, usually has high fixed costs for warehouse facilities, salaried personnel, and delivery equipment. Since those costs do not vary directly with sales volume, they do not conveniently disappear in a slow sales month. If the distributor relies on smart promotional planning such as discounts, purchasing incentives, and contests, additional volume can be generated in an otherwise slow month. CVP analysis can be used to gauge the profit impact of the increased volume and the increased costs resulting from scheduled promotions. Various combinations of advertising, price cuts, and other volume- boosting techniques can be modeled and compared.

CVP analysis is also an effective budgeting tool. Rather than change the CVP variables to reflect day-to-day activity in the marketplace, you can manipulate variables to test profit- maximizing strategies or operating assumptions prior to formalizing plans and budgets. (For a detailed discussion of the theory behind CVP analysis, see "The Mechanics of CVP.")

You may already have used one facet of CVP analysis called break-even analysis. But since most companies strive to do more than break even, you'll need to take a broader view of CVP analysis as a means of achieving profit objectives. The method can be used by anyone with a pad, a pencil, and a calculator, but it takes time to recalculate the numbers each time variables change. A *1-2- 3* spreadsheet equipped with keyboard macros can put CVP analysis to work for you.

The XYZ Story

To try your hand at building a *1-2-3* template for CVP analysis, use the hypothetical XYZ Company. XYZ manufactures sheet metal parts for aircraft, truck, and other large manufacturing companies. Because XYZ doesn't have products of its own, production volume is often difficult to predict. Both volume and profits vary substantially from month to month. Because XYZ has high fixed costs, a low-volume month can have a big impact on cash flow.

XYZ Company could use CVP analysis to help it make better decisions about what contracts to bid on and at what prices. In some months CVP analysis would help maximize profits, while in others it would help minimize losses.

The *1-2-3* template described here enables you to enter monthly manufacturing, sales, and overhead cost information easily. The input component of the template contains five sections (see Figure 1.6).

XYZ's industrial engineer has set normal capacity (line 7) for the plant at 7400 direct labor hours per month. Normal capacity is the production volume that XYZ should achieve in an average sales month. (It is neither the best nor the worst the firm can do.) This capacity assumes no changes in equipment or plant layout. It also assumes a single-shift operation. XYZ can produce in excess of normal capacity in peak months by working the first shift overtime or by bringing in a second shift. The template could easily be changed to reflect increased labor costs. Since virtually no costs are absolutely fixed, it's necessary to have a working concept of fixed costs that falls within a "relevant range" of sales or production volume. That range then becomes this model's normal capacity—the approximate volume at which certain costs are considered fixed. If actual volume changed significantly, these cost estimates would have to be revised.

The average amount paid for all direct labor (line 8) at XYZ is $5.55 per hour. This figure does not include fringe benefits, which are added to variable indirect manufacturing costs.

The fixed indirect manufacturing costs (line 9) include plant supervision, depreciation of building and equipment, and other production costs that do not vary with production volume. These are costs at normal capacity, and they total $55,000 per month.

The variable rate for indirect manufacturing costs (line 10) is computed for manufacturing costs that fluctuate. This rate includes plant electricity, fringe benefits for plant employees, and labor for handling material. It is expressed as a percentage of sales dollars. At XYZ, indirect manufacturing costs equal 8 percent of sales per month.

XYZ's sales expenses (line 12) encompass fixed and variable outlays. Fixed outlays include the sales manager's salary, advertising materials, and sales travel and entertainment. Fixed selling expenses are estimated at $10,000 (line 13). XYZ also hires manufacturers' representatives who pay their own expenses and are compensated by a 3½ percent commission (line 14).

For each product sold or expected to be sold, XYZ enters figures in several columns under the product sales forecast and cost data category (line 16). Sales units include the number of units sold or expected to be sold. Selling price is the average selling price per unit, which reflects sales made to different customers at different price levels. Direct labor (DL) hours/unit conveys the number of direct labor hours per unit calculated by XYZ's industrial engineer, assuming normal efficiency. Material/$ unit is the amount of material in dollars that each product unit requires. Standard prices and a normal scrap allowance are assumed.

General and administrative expenses (line 23) have both fixed and variable cost elements. Fixed general and administrative expenses are those fixed costs not allotted to manufacturing or sales activities. At XYZ, those costs include executive and clerical salaries, office rent and expenses, and insurance. The fixed cost element is $40,000. The only variable general and administrative expenses at XYZ are for part-time clerical workers and temporary office help whose hours per month vary according to sales volume. The variable expense averages 4 percent of sales.

The projection modifier information section (beginning on line 27) shows the impact on profit made by certain percentage changes in various sales, cost, and expense categories. In this section a value of 1 lets you easily manipulate variables without changing a given formula, making data entry a snap. If a factor is less than 1, the normal amount will be reduced. If the factor is greater than 1, the normal amount will be increased. To see the profit impact of an overall 5 percent sales price increase, for example, you would enter 1.05 in the Selling Price Modifier (line 28). Costs that do not have a modifier can be changed directly at their cell locations.

Setting Up a CVP Template

Now that you know the basic structure of XYZ, you can set up the *1-2-3* template and several quick keyboard macros that make the template easy to use.

Start by entering the top portion of the spreadsheet format shown in

```
       A       B       C       D       E         F          G
1
3    ====================================================================
4     PROJECTION ASSUMPTIONS AND FACTORS
5    --------------------------------------------------------------------
6     MANUFACTURING INFORMATION
7      Normal Capacity-Direct Labor Hours                 7400
8      Average Labor Rate Per Direct Labor Hour           5.55
9      Indirect Manufacturing Costs-Fixed                55000
10     Indirect Manufacturing Costs-Variable Rate         0.08
11
12    SELLING EXPENSE INFORMATION
13     Fixed Expenses                          10000
14     Commission Rate Per Sales Dollar        0.035
15
16    PRODUCT SALES FORECAST AND COST DATA
17                              Sales    Selling DL Hours/ Materials/
18                              Units     Price    Unit     $ Unit
19     Product A                 2000      26       0.5       12
20     Product B                 4000      32       0.6       14
21     Product C                 3000      38       0.5       18
22
23    GENERAL AND ADMINISTRATIVE EXPENSES INFORMATION
24     Fixed Expenses                          40000
25     Variable Rate Per Sales Dollar           0.04
26
27    PROJECTION MODIFIER INFORMATION
28     Selling Price Modifier         1
29     Labor Rate Modifier            1
30     Material Cost Modifier         1
31     Fixed IMC Modifier             1
32     Variable IMC Modifier          1
33   ===================================================================
34
35
36    COST-VOLUME-PROFIT ANALYSIS
37     Analysis Title: Preliminary Forecast
38     For Month:      February 1984       Fixed  Variable    Total
39
40    Sales                                                  294000
41
42   Manufacturing Costs:
43     Direct Material                              134000   134000
44     Direct Labor                                  27195    27195
45     Indirect Manufacturing              55000     23520    78520
46                                        -------   -------  -------
47       Total Manufacturing Costs         55000    184715   239715
48
49    Selling Expenses                     10000     10290    20290
50    General and Administrative           40000     11760    51760
51                                        -------   -------  -------
52       Total Costs and Expenses         105000    206765   311765
53                                                           ------
54    Profit Before Income Taxes                             -17765
55                                                          =======
56    Percent of Sales                      0.36      0.70    -0.06
57
```

Figure 1.6 *This template for CVP analysis permits easy entry of monthly sales, manufacturing, and overhead cost data.*

Figure 1.6 (Projection Assumptions and Factors). If you have any problems building the template, you can refer to the complete cell-by-cell description of the template as shown in Figure 1.7. The range of cells from F40 to G54 should be formatted to display only integers with the command */Range Format Fixed* **0** <**Enter**> **F40..G54** <**Enter**>.

Enter the numbers as shown so you can check your results with the figures shown in the next section of the template, Cost-Volume-Profit Analysis. Later you can build keyboard macros and easily change the variables.

The lower portion of the template displays the results of the CVP calculations. After you have completed this portion of the template, your calculated amounts should match the results shown.

Data Input Macros

Figure 1.8 shows three input macros for use with the CVP template. Although you don't have to use keyboard macros, they facilitate data entry. Macros automatically move to the cell pointer at various input cells and eliminate time-consuming manual keying.

The input macros are named ranges. The sales forecast input macro is named \A; when you press <Alt>-A, the cell pointer automatically moves to the proper cells for entering the sales forecast information. The title input macro (<Alt>-B) moves the cell pointer so you can enter the template title, date, and period covered by the model. You can change the projection modifiers by using the modifier input macro (<Alt>-C).

Template in Action

You can use the CVP template to analyze each month's anticipated production volume. First analyze the anticipated contract sales by product; then enter the volume, cost, and sales price. You can do this on a preliminary basis at least one month in advance to determine how much capacity will be used based on the number of contracts already sold. If the anticipated volume is low, you'll know that a sales push is in order.

As potential new contracts are identified, you can use the template to evaluate various alternative bid prices and estimate an overall profit or loss position. The closer you get to the actual month, the more competitive your pricing will be. If a month looks bad, you can try to generate enough production to cover variable costs and make some contribution to the fixed costs to minimize loss.

You can also use the template to analyze the profit impact of real or anticipated changes in the marketplace. For example, if labor costs increase 5 percent due to a scheduled union contract raise, how much will profits be eroded? By entering a labor rate modifier of 1.05, you can quickly determine the profit impact of the labor increase. If a 3 percent increase in raw material costs was not anticipated during bidding, you can calculate the profit impact of having to absorb the total increase by entering a material cost modifier of 1.03. And if spending $10,000 per month on new equipment would yield a 5 percent labor cost improvement, you can determine whether an increase in profits will result. Simply enter the fixed cost increase and a labor rate modifier of .95 to obtain your answer.

You can use the template to pose a variety of questions. If the company hires an industrial engineer at $2500 per month and cuts labor costs by 5 percent, what is the effect on profit? Does it make sense to accept a contract below the usual margins if the resulting production level exceeds normal capacity? How much of a loss will be sustained in a month of very low volume? (For demonstration purposes, assume a layoff of some plant supervision personnel at a $10,000 savings in fixed costs and a 2 percent increase in variable manufacturing costs.)

Once you have mastered basic CVP concepts, you can easily augment the template. By adding some *1-2-3* data table functions, you can automatically test numerous other "what if" assumptions. Using the *1-2-3* graph functions, you can build an *X-Y* graph of your company's CVP curves. The number of questions that a CVP template can answer is virtually infinite. You'll gain a significant amount of information from a small investment in time.

Donald Hunt is a CPA and a data processing consultant in Atlanta, Georgia. He specializes in personal computer training for top- and middle-management executives. This article was originally published in PC World, *Volume 2, Number 13.*

```
A3: (T) '=================================================================
A4: (T) ' PROJECTION ASSUMPTIONS AND FACTORS
A5: (T) "
A6: (T) ' MANUFACTURING INFORMATION
A7: (T) '  Normal Capacity-Direct Labor Hours
F7: (T) 7400
A8: (T) '  Average Labor Rate Per Direct Labor Hour
F8: (T) 5.55
A9: (T) '  Indirect Manufacturing Costs-Fixed
F9: (T) 55000
A10: (T) '  Indirect Manufacturing Costs-Variable Rate
F10: (T) 0.08
A12: (T) ' SELLING EXPENSE INFORMATION
A13: (T) '  Fixed Expenses
E13: (T) 10000
A14: (T) '  Commission Rate Per Sales Dollar
E14: (T) 0.035
A16: (T) ' PRODUCT SALES FORECAST AND COST DATA
D17: (T) ^Sales
E17: (T) ^Selling
F17: (T) ^DL Hours
G17: (T) ^Materials
D18: (T) ^Units
E18: (T) ^Price
F18: (T) ^Unit
G18: (T) ^$ Unit
A19: (T) '  Product A
D19: (T) 2000
E19: (T) 26
F19: (T) 0.5
G19: (T) 12
A20: (T) '  Product B
D20: (T) 4000
E20: (T) 32
F20: (T) 0.6
G20: (T) 14
A21: (T) '  Product C
D21: (T) 3000
E21: (T) 38
F21: (T) 0.5
G21: (T) 18
A23: (T) ' GENERAL AND ADMINISTRATIVE EXPENSES INFORMATION
A24: (T) '  Fixed Expenses
E24: (T) 40000
A25: (T) '  Variable Rate Per Sales Dollar
E25: (T) 0.04
A27: (T) ' PROJECTION MODIFIER INFORMATION
A28: (T) '  Selling Price Modifier
D28: (T) 1
A29: (T) '  Labor Rate Modifier
D29: (T) 1
A30: (T) '  Material Cost Modifier
D30: (T) 1
A31: (T) '  Fixed IMC Modifier
D31: (T) 1
```

Figure 1.7 *Cell-by-cell breakdown of CVP template.*

```
A32: (T) '  Variable IMC Modifier
D32: (T) 1
A33: (T) '=============================================================
A36: (T) ' COST-VOLUME-PROFIT ANALYSIS
A37: (T) '  Analysis Title:
C37: (T) 'Preliminary Forecast
A38: (T) '  For Month:
C38: (T) 'February 1984
E38: (T) ^Fixed
F38: (T) ^Variable
G38: (T) ^Total
A40: (T) ' Sales
G40: (F0) +D19*E19+D20*E20+D21*E21*D28
A42: (T) 'Manufacturing Costs:
A43: (T) '  Direct Material
F43: (F0) (+D19*G19+D20*G20+D21*G2)*(D30)
G43: (F0) +F43
A44: (T) '  Direct Labor
F44: (F0) (D19*F19+D20*F20+D21*F21)*F8*D29
G44: (F0) +F44
A45: (T) '  Indirect Manufacturing
E45: (F0) +F9*D31
F45: (F0) +G40*F10*D32
G45: (F0) @SUM(E45..F45)
E46: (T) "-------
F46: (T) "-------
G46: (T) "-------
A47: (T) '    Total Manufacturing Costs
E47: (F0) @SUM(E43..E45)
F47: (F0) @SUM(F43..F45)
G47: (F0) @SUM(G43..G45)
A49: (T) ' Selling Expenses
E49: (T) +E13
F49: (F0) +G40*E14
G49: (F0) @SUM(E49..F49)
A50: (T) ' General and Administrative
E50: (T) +E24
F50: (F0) +G40*E25
G50: (F0) @SUM(E50..F50)
E51: (T) "-------
F51: (T) "-------
G51: (T) "-------
A52: (T) '    Total Costs and Expenses
E52: (T) @SUM(E47..E50)
F52: (F0) @SUM(F47..F50)
G52: (F0) @SUM(G47..G50)
G53: (T) "------
A54: (T) ' Profit Before Income Taxes
G54: (F0) +G40-G52
G55: (T) "=======
A56: (T) '    Percent of sales
E56: (F2) +E52/G40
F56: (F2) +F52/G40
G56: (F2) +G54/G40
```

Figure 1.7 *(continued)*

```
Sales Forecast Input Macro   Alt A
          /WGRM{GOTO}A16~
          {GOTO}D19~{?}{RIGHT}{?}{RIGHT}{?}{RIGHT}{?}~
          {GOTO}D20~{?}{RIGHT}{?}{RIGHT}{?}{RIGHT}{?}~
          {GOTO}D21~{?}{RIGHT}{?}{RIGHT}{?}{RIGHT}{?}~
          /WGRA
          {GOTO}A37~

Title Input Macro   Alt B
     {GOTO}A36~{GOTO}C37~{?}{GOTO}H37~{?}{GOTO}C38~{?}{HOME}

Modifier Input Macro  Alt C
     {GOTO}A27~{GOTO}D28~{?}{DOWN}{?}{DOWN}{?}{DOWN}{?}{DOWN}{?}{HOME}
```

Figure 1.8 *Input macros.*

The Mechanics of CVP

To develop a CVP model, you must identify all the costs of doing business. If you're a manufacturer, you must deal with raw materials, production labor, and plant overhead. Service businesses have to monitor labor and materials costs. Wholesalers and retailers need to factor in the costs of items bought for resale.

In addition to these product- or service-related costs, businesses incur expenses such as sales administration, office rent, printing, and product liability insurance.

Your next step is to classify each cost as being either fixed or variable. Fixed costs generally do not change directly in relation to sales or production volume. Few costs are totally fixed, but in a practical sense, many are almost fixed. Most general and administrative corporate expenses are fixed costs, at least in the short run. Office rent, for example, is fixed until you move or expand your facilities.

Variable costs change in direct relation to sales or production volume. Labor and raw materials costs should vary according to the number of units produced. Sales commissions expressed as a percentage of sales volume represent another variable cost. As sales or production volume rises or falls, so do variable costs.

Once costs have been classified as either fixed or variable, you can compute a "contribution" amount per unit of sales. Contribution is not necessarily the same as profit; it is the amount remaining when total variable costs are subtracted from total sales. Because variable costs such as sales commissions increase or decrease directly with sales or production volume, the contribution per dollar or unit of sales remains the same. Suppose, for example, that your company buys one style of rain umbrella for $4 apiece (a variable cost) and retails them for $12 apiece. The only other variable cost is the $3 per unit sales commission paid to vendors who sell the umbrellas. To determine your contribution per umbrella, subtract the variable cost (product and commission) from the sales price to end up with a contribution of $5.

For each umbrella sold you will have $5 available to pay for the fixed expenses of running your business. But the $5 is contribution, not profit, because you have some large fixed costs to cover. If these fixed costs total $80,000 per year, divide that figure by 5; the company will break even at a sales volume of 16,000 umbrellas.

But there is more to the umbrella business than breaking even. How about a little profit? The marginal profit per unit after the company reaches break-even volume is equal to the contribution per unit. If the break-even figure is 16,000 umbrellas, and the company sells 20,000 umbrellas in 1984, multiply the difference (4000) by the contribution ($5); the profit should be $20,000.

Any time you try to represent the real world as a model, you encounter problems. In CVP analysis not all costs are strictly fixed or strictly variable, and you may have to make some difficult decisions to classify a cost as being one or the other. You may even want to separate the individual costs into fixed and variable components.

Keep in mind the following observations: All planning depends to a certain degree on your ability to make assumptions about your business. Using CVP analysis involves making some assumptions about cost and volume. The real world is so complex that you may have to simplify things a little to make CVP analysis work for you. If you are careful, your assumptions and simplifications will not greatly affect the value of the information that CVP analysis provides.

/X Marks the Macro

Eric Weiss

Although electronic spreadsheets are time-savers compared to pencil, paper, and calculator, they can still be tedious to use. Labels and numbers must be entered cell by cell, and cell formulas, which specify calculations and the relationships between cells, may be lengthy, confusing, and difficult to write. Any method of automating spreadsheet functions, from label and formula entry to worksheet formatting and printing, is highly desirable.

Keyboard macros store a sequence of keystrokes representing labels, formulas, or commands that perform a specific function. Novices and intermediate users of *1-2-3* often write macros to automate report printing from frequently used spreadsheets or to handle file and graphics operations. But *1-2-3* contains a special set of commands, accessible only from within a macro, that enable the user to extend the capabilities of *1-2-3* and customize its operation.

Defining Macros

A keyboard macro is a series of *1-2-3* commands and text that is entered as a label in any range of cells. In a sense, making a macro is like recording some keystrokes so that you can "play them back" later. You must name the range containing the macro (a single cell is still considered a range) using the */Range Name Create* command. The name must be two characters long; the first character must be a backslash, and the second can be any letter from A to Z. Once the range is named, the commands in the macro will be executed whenever you hold down the <Alt> key and press the letter used in the range name.

1-2-3's keyboard macro facility can be used simply to minimize typing keystrokes by storing the text of frequently used labels. For example, if you want to insert the months of the year in several labels, you can create 12 single-cell macros starting with JANUARY in a cell that you name \J. The labels can then be entered by typing:

<Alt>-J SALES
<Alt>-J COST OF SALES

to produce:

JANUARY SALES
JANUARY COST OF SALES

This limited application requires more effort to set up than is saved by using it. Command sequences that automate repetitive operations, such as the one shown in Figure 1.9, are more common. Figure 1.9 is a short macro that prints the contents of three ranges whenever the <Alt>-P key combination is pressed. This macro is a range of cells containing stored character equivalents of the keystrokes used to control printing. To create the macro use the command:

/Range Name Create
\P <Enter> N4. .N12 <Enter>

in which N4 and N12 are the first and last cells of the macro, respectively.

With a little practice this type of macro can be written easily. You can apply the same concept to many cursor movement, file-handling, and graphing operations.

But macros are capable of much more. The *1-2-3* user manual briefly describes the /X commands, which are not accessed from the keyboard and can be used only in macros. Table 1.1 is a list of advanced macro commands for *1-2-3* versions 1.0 and 1A. These commands enable users to create memory-efficient macros to handle complex modeling tasks. The master macro shown later in this article (see Figure 1.10) takes up only 6.8K of memory when first loaded. A formatted spreadsheet performing the same function takes up over 100K. As the macro version of the application is executed, the macro dynamically allocates memory in direct proportion to the number of iterations performed, something a formatted spreadsheet cannot do.

Templates vs. Macros

A formatted spreadsheet is known as a template; cell formulas are already established and perform calculations on input values. A user loads the template file into *1-2-3*, enters values, and lets the computer do the necessary calculations. Though a template is easy to use, it is hard to alter and takes up a lot of space in memory and on disk.

A macro can, in most cases, perform the same functions as a template, but it takes up less memory

```
 ||   M     ||   N   ||  O  ||    P     ||    Q     ||    R     ||    S     ||    T   |
 1 PROCEDURE  PROCEDURE
 2 NAME       STATEMENTS        COMMENTS
 3 -----------------------------------------
 4 \P         '/ppcf            Print, to printer--clear format
 5            oml2~mr77~        Options:  left margin = 2, right margin = 77
 6            s\018\0272~       Send setup string for normal print size
 7            qral.al4~         Quit options menu--set first print range to Al..A14
 8            g                 Go--print the specified range
 9            rbl.e8~           Set new print range to Bl..E8
10            g                 Go--print the new range
11            ral5.a20          Set the last print range to Al5..A20
12            gpq               Go--print the last range, send a "page feed" signal,
13                              and quit the print menu
```

Figure 1.9 *Sample print macro.*

Version 1.0 /X commands are:

/XM (location)~	invoke a menu in the control panel
/XG (location)~	branch to the indicated macro cell
/XI (formula)~(t-action)~	if-then
/XQ~	done; return to READY mode

Version 1A includes these additional commands:

/XC (location)~	call subroutine (GOSUB)
/XR~	return from subroutine
/XL (message)~(location)~	prompted label input
/XN (message)~(location)~	prompted number input

Table 1.1 *Macro commands for* 1-2-3 *versions 1.0 and 1A.*

and is easier to understand and modify. However, you must spend more time planning, writing, testing, and correcting macros. A macro runs more slowly, too, since each instruction requires at least one additional cycle to be read and executed besides the cycles needed to read and execute cell formulas.

So when should you use a macro? Generally, macros are best when a template requires complex cell formulas and many decisions, the data resides in several files, and the application is very large or its size varies from run to run.

A Sample Macro

The macro developed for the loan amortization schedule in the following example might be better suited for a template, but it is sufficiently complex to illustrate all the capabilities of a properly structured macro. This macro is composed of smaller, self-sufficient macros that are linked together, in much the same way that source code modules are combined to form a large, complex computer program.

The first objective in writing a macro is knowing exactly what it should do when it's completed. The example macro should accept input from the keyboard (the loan note's principal, pro rata annual interest, as a whole number, and term in years). At the user's option, it should accept a payment as input or compute the payment from other keyboard input. From these inputs, it should produce a full amortization schedule, by period, in a desired format (see Figure 1.11). When the macro is completed, the user should be guided through the input procedure, and the computer should control everything except entry of the actual values.

The macro can be placed in any worksheet cell that cannot be written over, copied to, deleted, or otherwise affected by using the worksheet. Be especially careful not to locate macros where they may be altered by the effects of sorting data or inserting columns. Many users prefer to locate print and file-handling macros for an existing worksheet in the lower right corner. In my example, however, a worksheet does not yet exist and data will not be sorted, so

```
   ||   A        ||   B       ||   C       ||   D       ||   E       ||   F       ||   G       |
 1 PROCEDURE     PROCEDURE                  COMMENTS
 2 NAME          STATEMENTS
 3 -----------------------------------------------
 4 PROC          '/xgsetup~                 Format worksheet
 5 STORE         '/xgds~                    Define storage
 6 INPUT         '/xg\i~                    Accept inputs
 7 STEP2         '/xgpaycomp~               Compute payment
 8 STEP3         '/xgbuild~                 Create amortization schedule
 9 STEP4         '/xgsummary~               Do totals
10 DONE          '/xq~                      Return to ready mode
11
12
13
14 \S            '/wgcl2~                   Set global column width to 12 characters
15               '/wgf,2~                   Set global format to "," with 2 decimals
16               {goto}il~                  Position cursor at labels column (cell I1)
17               '/wcs20~                   Set column width to 20 characters
18               '/xgproc~                  Branch to macro called PROC
19
20
21
22
23 SETUP         {goto}i5~                  Set up labels
24               PRINCIPAL~{down}
25               RATE~{down}
26               TERM (IN YEARS)~{down}
27               PAYMENT~{down}{down}
28               {right}                    Set up column headings
29               "PERIOD #~{right}
30               "PAYMENT~{right}
31               "INTEREST~{right}
32               "PRINCIPAL~{right}
33               "O/S BALANCE~{end}{left}{down}
34               '\=~
35               '/c~kll.nll~
36               '/xgstore~                 Branch to define storage procedure
37
38
39
40 DS            '/rncinareal~j5~           Principal input area
41               '/rncinarea2~j6~           Annual rate input area
42               '/rncinarea3~j7~           Term input area
43               '/rncinarea4~j8~           Payment input area
44               '/xginput~                 Branch to input procedure
45
46
47
```

(continues)

Figure 1.10 *Loan amortization schedule—example macro system.*

the macro can start at the upper left corner.

The entire macro could be contained in one cell of the worksheet (up to 240 characters), but that would make it difficult to edit or change. You could write a macro using one column, but the procedures would not be easy to read. It is preferable to use smaller macros and at least three columns (see Figure 1.10). Column C is left blank to make the other columns more readable.

In writing any macro, remember that each statement is contained in one cell and entered as a label. Use a single quote as the label prefix for any macro cell that begins with a slash, backslash, or "at sign" character. Type the labels as they appear in cells A1 to D2. Type a backslash and a hyphen to create a repeating label in cell A3. Then use the /Copy <Enter> B3..D3 command to extend the dashed line to column D.

Next type in the set of macros that start with PROC. These macros are simply a series of commands that call other macro procedures. This group is called the linking macro; it

```
  ||   A      ||   B     ||    C    ||    D     ||    E     ||    F     ||    G     |
 48
 49 \I          {goto}inarea1~
 50             {left}{right}           Adjust window position
 51             {?}~                    Input principal
 52             {down}
 53             {?}~                    Input rate
 54             {down}
 55             {?}~                    Input term
 56             '/xgstep2~              Branch to step2 procedure
 57
 58
 59
 60 PAYCOMP     {down}{left}
 61             '/cprompt1~~            Copy PROMPT1
 62             {right}
 63             {?}~                    Input payment or 0
 64             '/xi$inarea4<>0~/xgstep3~
 65             '@pmt($inarea1,(($inarea2/100)/12),($inarea3*12))~
 66             {left}
 67             PAYMENT~
 68             {right}
 69             '/xgstep3~              Branch to step3 procedure
 70
 71
 72
 73 BUILD       {goto}n13~              Position cursor
 74             $inarea1~               Get beginning balance
 75             {goto}j14~              Position cursor
 76             {up}{up}{up}{up}        Adjust window position
 77             {down}{down}{down}{down}
 78             '+{up}+1~{right}        First period
 79             $inarea4~               Get payment amount
 80             {right}                 Compute interest paid
 81             '+n13*(($inarea2/100)/12)~
 82             {right}
 83             '+{left}{left}-{left}~  Point and compute principal paid
 84             {right}
 85             '+{up}-{left}~          Compute o/s balance
 86             {end}{left}
 87 LOOP        '/c{end}{right}~        Copy logic
 88             {down}~{down}
 89             '/rnccount~~            Name count range
 90             '/xicount<($inarea3*12)~/rndcount~/xgloop~
 91             '/xgstep4~
 92
 93
 94
 95 SUMMARY     {down}{down}{right}
 96             '@sum({end}{up}{end}{up}.{end}{down})~
 97             '/c~{right}.{right}~
 98             {end}{right}{right}+{up}{up}~{up}
 99             '\-~
100             '/c~{left}.{left}{left}~
101             {down}{down}
102             '\=~
103             '/c~{left}.{left}{left}~
104             '/xgdone~
105
106
107 PROMPT1     PAYMENT AMOUNT, -->  __________  <-- OR 0 TO HAVE ME COMPUTE IT.
108
109
110 \D          '/fs~r                  File save and replace
```

Figure 1.10 *(continued)*

```
    |     I        ||    J       ||      K       ||      L      ||      M       || N ||    O    |
  5 PRINCIPAL          10,000.00
  6 RATE                   15.00
  7 TERM (IN YEARS)         1.00
  8 PAYMENT               902.58
  9
 10                    PERIOD #          PAYMENT       INTEREST      PRINCIPAL    O/S BALANCE
 11                    ========================================================================
 12
 13                                                                                  10,000.00
 14                         1.00          902.58         125.00         777.58        9,222.42
 15                         2.00          902.58         115.28         787.30        8,435.11
 16                         3.00          902.58         105.44         797.14        7,637.97
 17                         4.00          902.58          95.47         807.11        6,830.86
 18                         5.00          902.58          85.39         817.20        6,013.66
 19                         6.00          902.58          75.17         827.41        5,186.25
 20                         7.00          902.58          64.83         837.75        4,348.50
 21                         8.00          902.58          54.36         848.23        3,500.27
 22                         9.00          902.58          43.75         858.83        2,641.44
 23                        10.00          902.58          33.02         869.57        1,771.87
 24                        11.00          902.58          22.15         880.43          891.44
 25                        12.00          902.58          11.14         891.44             .00
 26                         ------------------------------------------------------------------
 27                                    10,831.00         831.00      10,000.00             .00
 28                         ==================================================================
```

Figure 1.11 *Completed amortization schedule.*

will determine the order of execution of the other procedures. Of course, none of the statements in this section will work until the macros they call are created and activated by the /Range Name Create command.

The macro called \S formats a workspace and sets up a column to hold labels up to 20 characters long. It then invokes the PROC linking macro. This, in turn, invokes SETUP, which types labels into several cells. Type in the SETUP macro as shown in Figure 1.10 starting at cell A23. In addition to the single-quote label prefix, the words entered as labels may have single or double quotes for left or right justification and are followed by a tilde (~), the macro symbol for <Enter>. At this point you should save the worksheet including the macros you've created so far. Use the /File Save command and type in the file name (you might call it "amortize").

To save time you may want to create a file-saving macro: /fs~r will save the file under the current file name and replace the old version of the file. On the worksheet, enter the text of the macro at cell B110 and call it \D using the /Range Name Labels Right <Enter> command with the cursor on cell A110 (see Figure 1.10).

Before the macros can be executed, range names must be assigned to each of them. The best way to do this is to type in all the macros first and then make the procedure name in column A the range name of the procedure in column B. Use the command /Range Name Labels Right and then use the cursor control keys to highlight column A, from the cell containing PROC to the one containing \D. In one operation a range name has been created for each macro and made part of the macro.

However, if you want to test one of the macros independently, you can temporarily change the name of the range to a backslash and a single letter. You should also temporarily add an extra label prefix (a single or double quotation mark) to the last statement in the group (the one that starts /XG . . .). The extra label prefix will cause the statement to be printed on the screen rather than executed.

If you test the \S macro independently, for example, the screen should display the labels formatted as shown in Figure 1.12. If you hear a beep, check the control panel at the top of the screen to see what command was executing when the error occurred. One or more macro statements may be missing a tilde, or a label or bracket could be out of place.

Macro Statements

In the \S macro, a series of /Worksheet commands format the workspace. In SETUP there are several bracket symbols that indicate cursor movement keys. Where a word is followed by a tilde, *1-2-3* types that word into the cell at which the cursor is located. The \S macro also contains two statements ({goto}I1 and /xgsetup) that are very similar. {goto} is a cursor control command, the macro equivalent of pressing the <F5> key; /XG, however, is a macro branching instruction. When *1-2-3* encounters such a statement, it tells

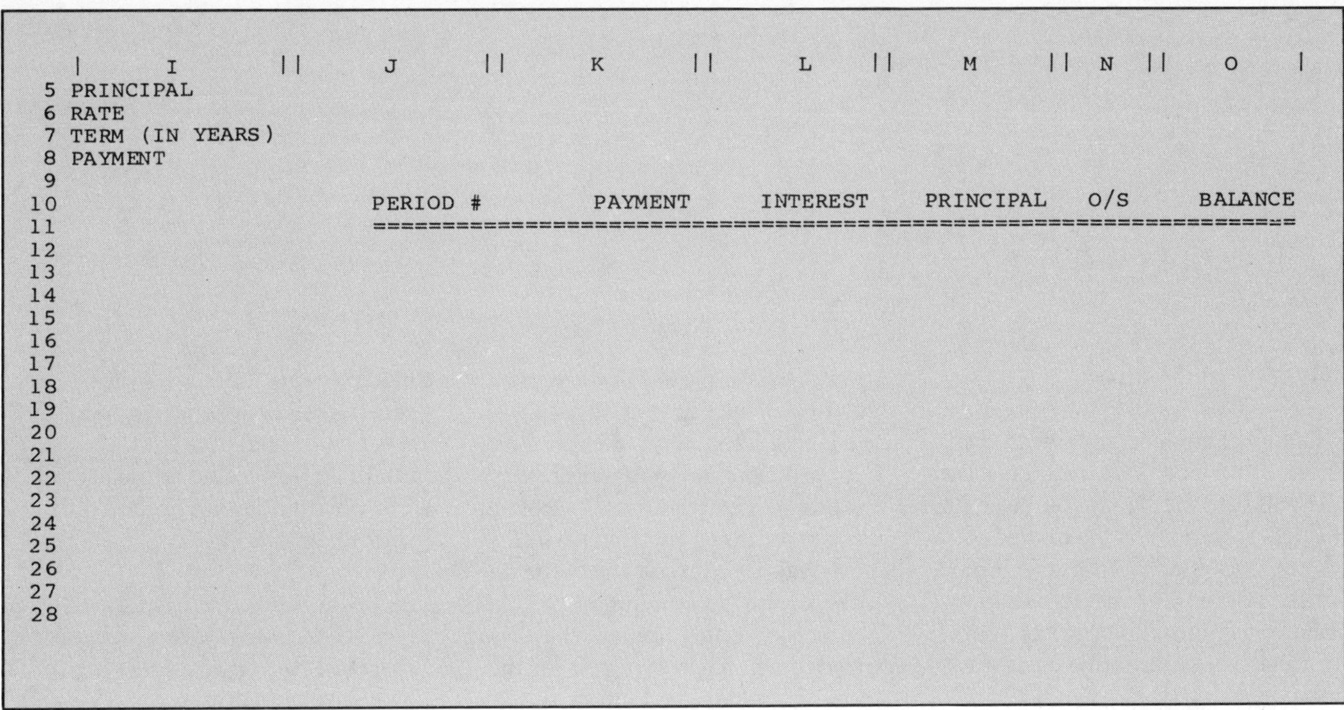

Figure 1.12 *Results of SETUP macro.*

the computer the cell in which it will find its next instruction. This command works with range names or cell addresses, but using range names improves the portability of macros.

When you write your own macros, after you have done a SETUP you should at least sketch out how cell formulas will be placed in the worksheet. From Figure 1.12, you can see that column J will show the period numbers from 1 to *n,* where *n* is the last payment in the term. Column K will be for the payment amount; columns L and M will contain formulas to compute portions of the payment attributable to interest and principal respectively. Column N will consist of formulas to reduce the outstanding balance by the amount of principal paid each period.

A macro must then be written that takes the input data, places it in the worksheet, and uses it to build the entries and formulas for each row in columns J through N. The steps in this process are:

1) Get the beginning outstanding balance and put it in N13.

2) Assign a number to the first payment in J14.

3) Put the payment amount in K14.

4) Multiply the amount in N13 by the pro rata annual percentage rate (APR), or interest, and put the result in L14.

5) Subtract the interest in L14 from the payment in K14 and put the result in M14.

6) Subtract M14 from N13 to get the new outstanding balance.

7) Repeat up to and including the last payment in the term.

To make the macro system more portable and flexible, substitute range names for absolute cell references. The macro group named DS uses the /Range Name Create command to define four such ranges. These cells will be used to accept the input data. It is not important that the first input cell is J5, but that the first input cell be named INAREA1. If you wanted to change the location of the first input cell, you'd have to change only one macro, and all the formulas that used INAREA1 would automatically know where to look.

Type in the DS and \I macros now. \I is the macro that actually accepts and stores the input. Key this macro in using the four-column format, beginning with the name \I in cell A49. Save the file using the <**Alt**>**-D** command.

Using the PAYCOMP macro, you can enter a payment or have the computer calculate it. There are two new commands in this section: /C and /XI. /C (for copy) displays the named range called PROMPT1 in the current cursor location. This prompt tells the user the options for entering the payment amount. Type in the PAYCOMP macro now, starting at cell A60.

/XI is a conditional statement. *1-2-3* acts on the user's response, so if a payment amount is keyed in, the remainder of the macro will be ignored. Otherwise, the payment will be computed using the @PMT formula.

Macros in Macros

The BUILD macro is where the real work of the note amortization schedule will be done. First, you place the LOOP procedure in the middle of the BUILD macro. This label indicates the start of a macro within a macro, technically known as a subroutine. This subroutine creates a temporary variable name (COUNT), which moves down a column testing the value of a cell. Once the comparison is done, the variable COUNT is deleted; it will be recreated on the next pass through the loop.

Before entering the loop, BUILD makes extensive use of cursor control key sequences to create the cell formulas for the first two rows of the note amortization schedule. The two ways to set up cell formulas with a macro are through cursor movements or cell references. Each method has its advantages and drawbacks, which are discussed in detail in the *1-2-3* user manual.

Type in the SUMMARY macro now. SUMMARY takes column totals and prints them at the bottom of the worksheet. Finally, reset the range names and recreate the names this macro needs in order to run by typing /Range Name Labels Right, and highlight column A from PROC to \D. Press <**Enter**> and save the file using the <Alt>-D command; press <**Alt**>-**S** and it should run. If the computer beeps, make sure that all tildes are in place, no labels are omitted, labels are aligned with the first cell of each macro, and /RNC statements are not omitted from DS.

When you press <Alt>-S, the cursor will stop at cell J5, next to the label PRINCIPAL. Key in the loan principal amount and press <Enter>. The cursor will automatically move down the column to cell J6 to wait for you to type in the annual percentage rate (interest). When you press <Enter> again, the cursor moves down to prompt you for the term of the loan, and finally the macro will ask if you want to specify a payment. If not, type a zero and the system will calculate a payment amount for you. When you're finished, the worksheet should resemble Figure 1.11.

If you are using *1-2-3* version 1A, you have the option of replacing /XG with the /XC and /XR command pair in the linking macro. /XG is a GOTO (cell location) command and is less flexible than the /XC and /XR commands, which GOSUB (go to a macro) and RETURN (from a macro) respectively. The linking macro for version 1A should look like Figure 1.13.

Each macro except \S would end in /XR~ instead of an /XG command. The /XR~ commands would increase the portability of each named range since it would no longer be necessary to specify the exact return point. Only the PROC label would be required.

Writing macros can be a forbidding experience at first. As you can see, structure is essential in creating useful, understandable, and efficient macros. But once you become more confident in using macros, you can write one for a function that *1-2-3* doesn't provide, no matter how complicated it may be, and use the macro in any *1-2-3* worksheet. You can create self-formatting worksheets that take data from the keyboard or from other worksheet files. The possibilities are limited only by your imagination.

Eric Weiss is a senior information specialist for the Firestone Tire and Rubber Company, Akron, Ohio. He is currently involved in the development of a variety of advanced information and modeling systems and teaches a regular monthly seminar on advanced applications of 1-2-3. *This article was originally published in* PC World, *Volume 2, Number 3.*

```
  ||   A   ||   B   ||   C   ||   D   ||   E   ||   F   ||   G
1 PROC       '/xcsetup~          Format worksheet
2            '/xcds~             Define storage
3            '/xc\i~             Accept inputs
4            '/xcpaycomp~        Compute payment
5            '/xcbuild~          Create amortization schedule
```

Figure 1.13 *PROC macro for* 1-2-3 *version 1.A.*

Linking Worksheets with Multiplan

Andrew T. Williams

As its name suggests, a major feature of *Multiplan* is that it can link up to eight worksheets into one multiple plan. To use this feature, you name a group of cells on one worksheet and then use that name to link that information to another worksheet. Once the link is established, the dependent worksheet (the one receiving information) is automatically updated each time it is loaded into memory.

The linking function is ideal for consolidating information from several sources, as, for example, when several supporting worksheets are consolidated into a summary report. *Multiplan* makes it easy to create quarterly summaries based on monthly data or divisional reports that draw on regional subtotals.

The linking feature can also be used to create complicated models in which each section of the model is stored on a separate worksheet. This is helpful for people who find it easier to work with relatively small parts of a larger model. Using the linking technique in this way speeds up recalculation time, since only the part of the model you are working with at a particular time is recalculated with each change.

However, some problems can arise when you use "what if" analyses with linked worksheets, because changing the numbers on one worksheet may necessitate loading several worksheets before the effect of the change can be observed. The time required to load and store the worksheets can be frustratingly long.

Linking worksheets also presents the problem of how to keep the relationships between worksheets straight. *Multiplan* doesn't give you any information about the links until you load a worksheet. Given that you can link up to eight worksheets, you run the risk of creating a rat's nest of interdependencies. A dependent worksheet is updated with information from a supporting worksheet only when the dependent worksheet is loaded. However, the information in the supporting worksheet may be wrong if it depends on a third worksheet that has not yet been updated.

Therefore, to update a set of linked worksheets correctly, you must load each worksheet in the correct order, beginning with a worksheet that depends on no other worksheet and then working your way through the dependencies. A complicated model should be accompanied by a dependency diagram like the one shown in Figure 1.14. You should draw this diagram as you create a model; unraveling the interrelationships after the model has been created can be difficult.

To update the set of worksheets diagramed in Figure 1.14, you would begin by making changes on sheets A and B (the ones that don't depend on any other worksheets). Then you would load worksheets C and D, which depend on A and B. When loaded, C and D would be updated with information from A and B. After worksheets C and D had been updated, you would load E (which depends on C and D) and finally F. If you loaded the worksheets in any other order, the information could be in error.

A Linking Session

The technique of linking worksheets will become clear as you work your way through an example. Before you start, consider an overview of the linking process. The first step is to build the dependent and supporting worksheets. Then you name the cells or groups of cells on the supporting worksheet that contain values you want to copy. When you're done, the supporting worksheet must be stored and the dependent worksheet loaded. Finally, the eXternal Copy command is used to copy the desired cells from the supporting worksheet to the dependent worksheet. This establishes a permanent link between the two worksheets.

As you go through this process, write down the file name of each worksheet and the exact spelling of each range name that you assign to the cells or groups of cells you want to copy from the supporting worksheets. *Multiplan* provides no way to obtain this information short of reloading the worksheets.

Figures 1.15 and 1.16 show a dependent and a supporting worksheet. The name assigned to the supporting worksheet is SPENCOST because that worksheet contains information about costs for Spencer Ceramics Inc. The dependent worksheet is a profit statement named SPENCER. These worksheets can

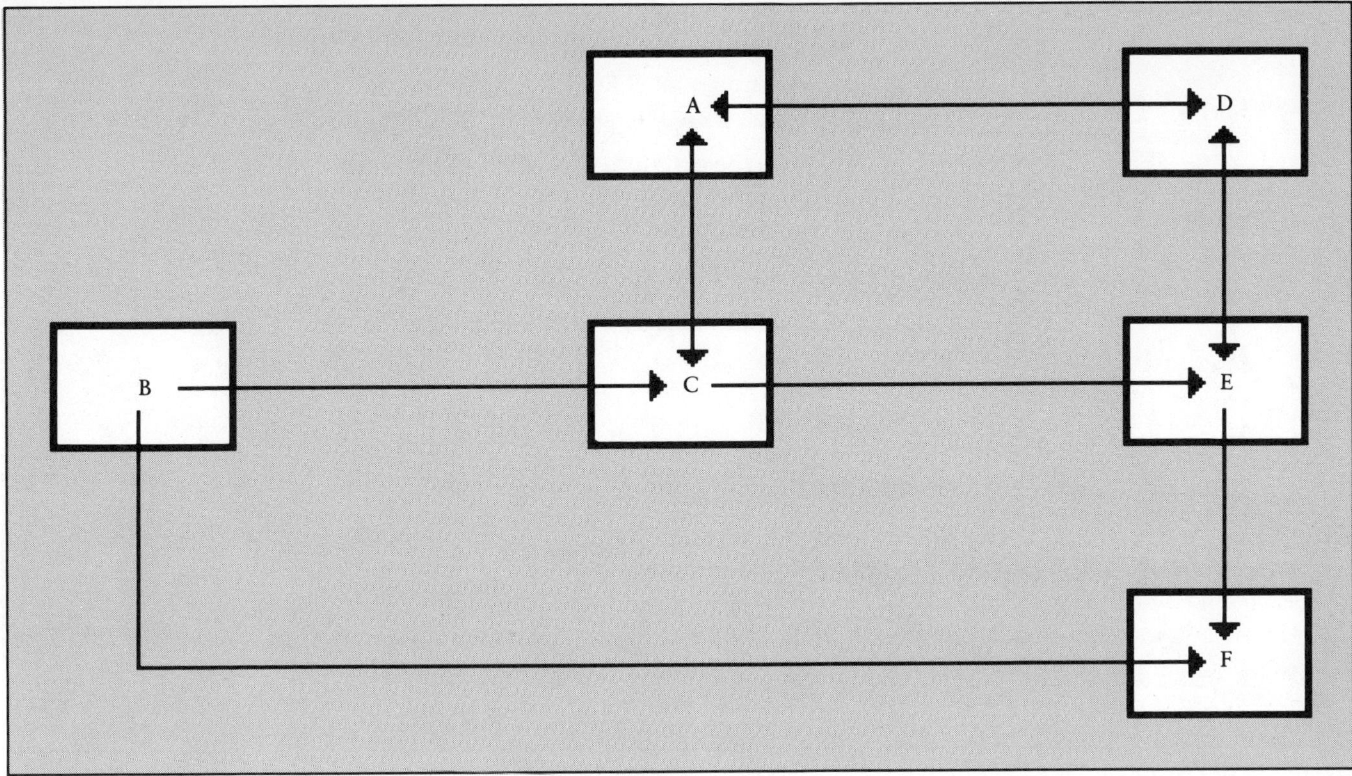

Figure 1.14 *A dependency diagram showing the linkage of* Multiplan *worksheets. If you don't create a dependency diagram before you link worksheets, updating becomes confusing and errors can occur.*

be found on the tutorial disk of the IBM version of *Multiplan*. The Microsoft version has no tutorial disk, but Microsoft's documentation gives instructions for constructing the worksheets.

The first step in establishing a link between these two worksheets is to name the groups of cells to be transferred from the supporting worksheet to the dependent worksheet. To do this, use the Transfer Load command to load the SPENCOST worksheet. Once the SPENCOST worksheet has been loaded, use *Multiplan*'s Name command to assign the name Material_Costs to the group of cells R9C2:13 and the name Overhead_Costs to the group of cells R17C2:13. (The cell-naming convention of *Multiplan* outlaws the use of blanks, so underlines are used in place of blanks.) When you have finished assigning the names and have written them down for future reference, use the Transfer Save command to save SPENCOST. Now load the SPENCER worksheet with the Transfer Load command.

Before you can establish a link between SPENCOST and SPENCER, you must blank the cells into which the information from the SPENCOST worksheet will be transferred. *Multiplan* will not allow you to transfer data into cells that already contain entries. The only exception is if the entries in the cells have been entered there via a previous transfer operation.

After you have blanked the appropriate cells in rows 6 and 8 of SPENCER, move the worksheet cursor to cell R6C2. This is the first cell of the group of cells into which you want to transfer the data named Material_Costs on the SPENCOST worksheet. Type **XC** (the Xternal Copy command). The command area will look like Figure 1.17.

This command has three fields. The first, where the edit line cursor is currently located, is labeled 'from sheet'. The prompt line tells you to 'Enter filename'. Do this by typing **SPENCOST**. Now move the edit line cursor to the next field, labeled 'name'. The command area will look like Figure 1.18.

Give the same name to row 6 on SPENCER that you used for the group of cells you want to have copied from SPENCOST. Type **Material_Costs**, the name you assigned to the line labeled Total Material Costs on the SPENCOST worksheet. The command area should look like Figure 1.19.

Now examine *Multiplan*'s proposed responses in the last two fields, 'to' and 'linked'. You want the copied material to begin in cell R6C2, the current active cell, so the proposed response for 'to' is correct. If you wanted the copied information to go somewhere other than the proposed response, you could use the cursor-movement keys to point to the correct position or you could type in the correct cell address.

Look at the 'linked' field; *Multiplan*'s proposed response (the item

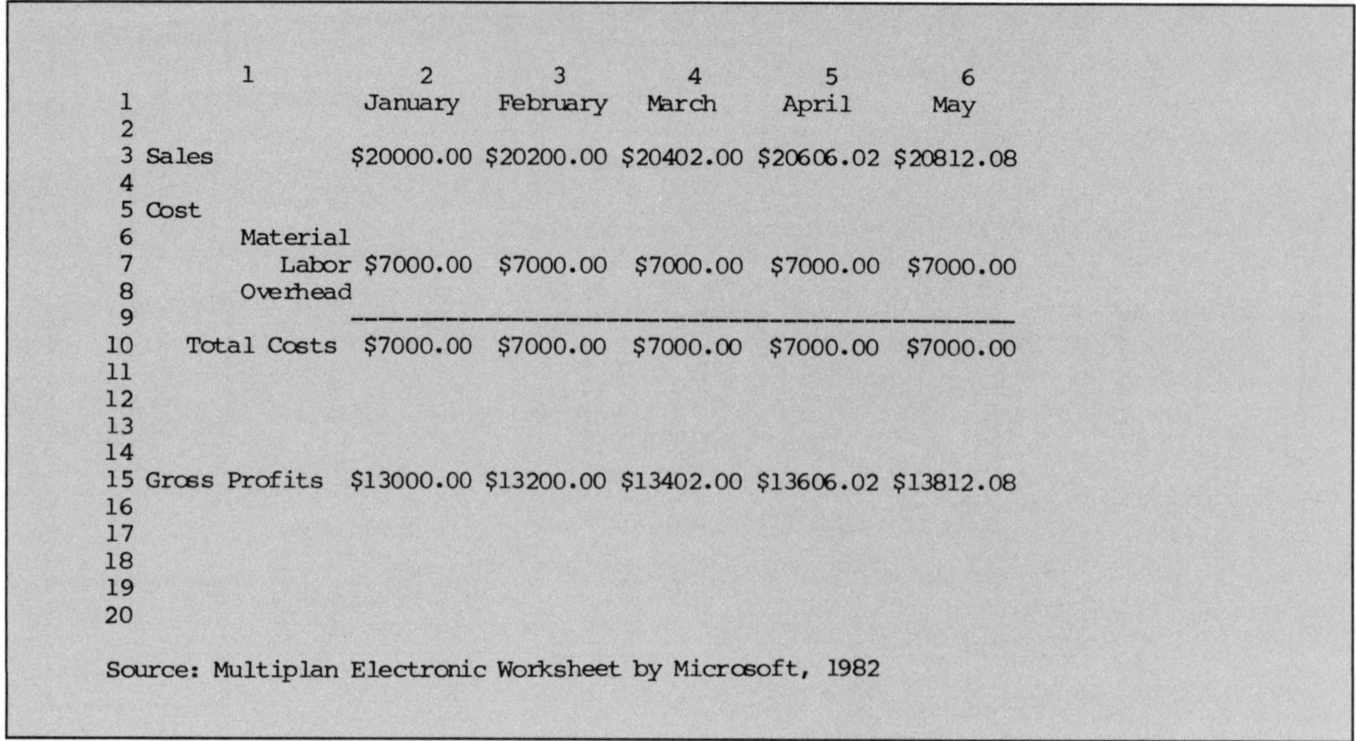

	1	2	3	4	5	6
1		January	February	March	April	May
2						
3	Sales	$20000.00	$20200.00	$20402.00	$20606.02	$20812.08
4						
5	Cost					
6	Material					
7	Labor	$7000.00	$7000.00	$7000.00	$7000.00	$7000.00
8	Overhead					
9		------------	------------	------------	------------	------------
10	Total Costs	$7000.00	$7000.00	$7000.00	$7000.00	$7000.00
11						
12						
13						
14						
15	Gross Profits	$13000.00	$13200.00	$13402.00	$13606.02	$13812.08
16						
17						
18						
19						
20						

Source: Multiplan Electronic Worksheet by Microsoft, 1982

Figure 1.15 *SPENCER, a dependent worksheet in* Multiplan, *ready for linking to the SPENCOST worksheet.*

	1	2	3	4	5
1		January	February	March	April
2	MATERIAL				
3	Clay	$2500.00	$2520.00	$2540.16	$2560.48
4	Glaze	$1500.00	$1512.00	$1524.10	$1536.29
5	Brushes	$500.00	$504.00	$508.03	$512.10
6	Sponges	$200.00	$201.60	$203.21	$204.84
7	Plaster	$300.00	$302.40	$304.82	$307.26
8	------------	------------	------------	------------	------------
9	Total Material Costs	$5000.00	$5040.00	$5080.32	$5120.96
10					
11	OVERHEAD				
12	Utilities	$1100.00	$1108.80	$1117.67	$1126.61
13	Rent	$2500.00	$2520.00	$2540.16	$2560.48
14	Telephone	$200.00	$201.60	$203.21	$204.84
15	Water	$200.00	$201.60	$203.21	$204.84
16	------------	------------	------------	------------	------------
17	Total Overhead Costs	$4000.00	$4032.00	$4064.26	$4096.77
18					
19					
20					

Source: Multiplan Electronic Worksheet by Microsoft, 1982

Figure 1.16 *SPENCOST, a supporting worksheet in* Multiplan. *Rows 9 and 17 are linked to SPENCER.*

enclosed in parentheses) is 'Yes'. Since you want to establish a permanent link between the two worksheets, this proposed response is also correct. If you wanted only to copy the information from SPENCOST to SPENCER and didn't want to establish a permanent link, you could tab over to the linked field and type **n** (for *no*).

Executing eXternal Copy

Once the copy procedure is properly set up, press <Enter> to execute the eXternal Copy command and to es-

7	8	9	10	11	12	13
June	July	August	September	October	November	December
$21020.20	$21230.40	$21442.71	$21657.13	$21873.71	$22092.44	$22313.37
$7000.00	$7000.00	$7000.00	$7000.00	$7000.00	$7000.00	$7000.00
$7000.00	$7000.00	$7000.00	$7000.00	$7000.00	$7000.00	$7000.00
$14020.20	$14230.40	$14442.71	$14657.13	$14873.71	$15092.44	$15313.37

Source: Multiplan Electronic Worksheet. Reprinted by permission of the copyright owner, Microsoft Corporation, 1982.

Figure 1.15 *(continued)*

6	7	8	9	10	11	12	13
May	June	July	August	September	October	November	December
$2580.97	$2601.61	$2622.43	$2643.41	$2664.55	$2685.87	$2707.36	$2729.01
$1548.58	$1560.97	$1573.46	$1586.04	$1598.73	$1611.52	$1624.41	$1637.41
$516.19	$520.32	$524.49	$528.68	$532.91	$537.17	$541.47	$545.80
$206.48	$208.13	$209.79	$211.47	$213.16	$214.87	$216.59	$218.32
$309.72	$312.19	$314.69	$317.21	$319.75	$322.30	$324.88	$327.48
$5161.93	$5203.23	$5244.85	$5286.81	$5329.10	$5371.74	$5414.71	$5458.03
$1135.62	$1144.71	$1153.87	$1163.10	$1172.40	$1181.78	$1191.24	$1200.77
$2580.97	$2601.61	$2622.43	$2643.41	$2664.55	$2685.87	$2707.36	$2729.01
$206.48	$208.13	$209.79	$211.47	$213.16	$214.87	$216.59	$218.32
$206.48	$208.13	$209.79	$211.47	$213.16	$214.87	$216.59	$218.32
$4129.54	$4162.58	$4195.88	$4229.45	$4263.28	$4297.39	$4331.77	$4366.42

Source: Multiplan Electronic Worksheet. Reprinted by permission of the copyright owner, Microsoft Corporation, 1982.

Figure 1.16 *(continued)*

tablish the link between SPENCOST and SPENCER. After you do this, *Multiplan* will load the specified information from SPENCOST into SPENCER and recalculate the SPENCER worksheet. At this stage you can name the area on SPENCER that has just received information from SPENCOST. Without moving the cursor, type **n** (for *name*). The command area will look like Figure 1.20.

```
EXTERNAL COPY from sheet:                    name:
                    to: R6C2                 linked (Yes)No
Enter filename
R6C2                                         94% Free   Multiplan: SPENCER
```

Figure 1.17 *The* Multiplan *command area after using the eXternal Copy command.*

```
EXTERNAL COPY from sheet: SPENCOST   name:
                    to: R6C2         linked (Yes)No
Enter name on external sheet
R6C2                                 94% Free   Multiplan: SPENCER
```

Figure 1.18 *The* Multiplan *command area after the file name is entered and the cursor is moved to the 'name' field.*

```
EXTERNAL COPY from sheet: SPENCOST   name: MATERIAL_COSTS
                    to: R6C2         linked (Yes)No
Enter filename
R6C2                                 94% Free   Multiplan: SPENCER
```

Figure 1.19 *The* Multiplan *command area after the name Material Costs has been assigned to row 6.*

```
NAME: define name: SPENCOST.MATERIAL_COST   to refer to: R6C2: 13

Enter name
R6C2   [SPENCOST.MATERIAL_COST]   93% Free   Multiplan: SPENCER
```

Figure 1.20 *The* Multiplan *command area after the information has been linked and the linked area on SPENCER has been named.*

The proposed response for the name of the group of cells receiving information from SPENCOST is the combination of the file name of the supporting worksheet and the name assigned to the linked cells. This default name tells you explicitly where the information comes from and identifies the cells R6C2:13 as dependent. You can choose the default by pressing <Enter>.

To complete this exercise, establish the link between Overhead_Costs on the supporting worksheet and the group of cells R8C2:12, labeled Overhead on the SPENCER worksheet. Once this has been done, the SPENCER worksheet will be updated with information from the SPENCOST worksheet each time the SPENCER worksheet is loaded. Try it out; make a change in SPENCOST and then reload SPENCER. The numbers will change on this dependent worksheet as well.

The *Multiplan* eXternal Copy command is easy to use, and you get plenty of help from the proposed responses along the way. Be sure to draw a dependency diagram illustrating how one worksheet depends on another. Write down all the names used in the linking process, including file names and the names assigned to cells and groups of cells.

The eXternal Copy command is only one of several eXternal subcommands. You can also use the eXternal command to list the file names of the worksheets on which the current worksheet depends and the file names of worksheets that depend on the current worksheet. You can use the eXternal Copy command to dissolve links between worksheets and to make one-time copies of named information from one worksheet to another without establishing a permanent link.

Andrew T. Williams is a Contributing Editor for PC World. *This material is reprinted from his book* WHAT IF? A User's Guide to Spreadsheets on the IBM PC *(New York, John Wiley & Sons, 1984) with permission from the publisher. This article was originally published in* PC World, *Volume 2, Number 10.*

```
A>COPY CON: LOTUS.BAT
ECHO OFF
COPY %1.CNF 123.CNF >NUL
LOTUSX
COPY 123X.CNF 123.CNF >NUL
<F6>
```

Figure 1.21 *LOTUS.BAT*

.

Star-Dot-Star

One product that has dominated both its software class and the *.* columns is Lotus's *1-2-3*. "Automatic 1-2-3 Subdirectories" describes a file-locating procedure that creates order from the potential chaos of so many subdirectories and too little time. "Worksheet Printer Controls" explains how to produce more attractive worksheets through the use of printer control commands and *WordStar* dot commands. "Legendary Graphs" shows how to put floating legends anywhere in a worksheet file, and "1-2-3 As a Calculator" explains how to make calculations without disturbing the worksheet. Finally, "1-2-3 Break" tells how to quickly and safely stop a worksheet printout.

Automatic 1-2-3 Subdirectories

As an avid *1-2-3* user, I like the fact that I can tailor the default settings to my needs. A problem arises, however, because I use a hard disk with worksheet files located in a number of different subdirectories. It's inconvenient to issue commands to change the default directory each time I use the program, so I have developed a batch file to do it for me.

Suppose that *1-2-3* is stored in the subdirectory \LOTUS and that I have worksheet files in the subdirectories \WP, \WP\BUDGET, and \PRODUCT\FORECAST. First copy the file 123.CNF to 123X.CNF and then run *1-2-3*. Issue the command /Worksheet Global Default Directory, type in the name of a subdirectory in which you have worksheet files, and then issue the Update command. Exit *1-2-3* and copy the file 123.CNF to a file whose name reflects the subdirectory name you just entered but ends with .CNF, such as BUDGET.CNF. Repeat these steps for each subdirectory as needed.

Rename the file LOTUS.COM as LOTUSX.COM. Then create a batch file as shown in LOTUS.BAT (Figure 1.21). To use the batch file, type LOTUS followed by the name you assigned to the .CNF file that corresponds to the subdirectory you desire, such as **LOTUS BUDGET**. If you don't specify a subdirectory, the original default directory stored in 123X.CNF will be used.

Joel Borden
Cupertino, California

Worksheet Printer Controls

I once wished for an easy way to put print attributes into *1-2-3* worksheets. The only method I knew for creating boldface print or underlining parts of a worksheet was to repeatedly use the Range and Setup string commands, but I would not call that easy. Recently I developed a technique that I have been using quite successfully: placing printer codes directly in worksheets.

To do this I first create some files that contain the control codes required by the printer to activate the various print enhancements. Each file contains the characters needed to activate one enhancement, and the files' names all end with the .PRN extension. I keep these .PRN files on my *1-2-3* system disk to allow selection of italic fonts, boldface, underlining, form feeds, and condensed print.

The trick is to read the desired file into a worksheet cell using *1-2-3*'s /File Import Text command. You will generally see some funny-looking characters on the screen, but you can ignore them; they are the IBM extended character-set representations for the print enhancement codes contained in the cell. If required, additional text can then be added to the cell using *1-2-3*'s edit mode. When *1-2-3* prints the cell, the printer switches to the desired mode until another printer control code is received.

You can use BASIC or the EDLIN program on the DOS disk to create .PRN files with the proper codes for your printer. (You can also use DEBUG, if you know how.) Just make sure that you do not accidentally put a carriage return and linefeed into the files when you create them, or you will have extra lines on your printouts.

Check your printer manual for the proper control codes to activate the various print enhancements and fonts your printer is capable of producing. You may also need codes to turn them off. If you have a keyboard enhancer such as *ProKey,* you can make the process of importing the enhancements into your worksheets completely painless.

Another way I enhance the printing of a *1-2-3* worksheet is by putting the printer control codes used by *WordStar,* my word processing program, into the worksheet, printing the worksheet to disk as a .PRN file, and then using the word processing program to send the .PRN file to the printer. For added power I set the worksheet's left margin at zero and put *WordStar* dot commands in the first column. For example, using a *WordStar* dot command, I can control page breaks, something that is not easy to do using the print facilities of *1-2-3*. Most popular word processing programs can be used to take advantage of these techniques.
Bill Castner
Bethesda, Maryland

Legendary Graphs

Here is an easy way to put floating legends virtually anywhere on a *1-2-3* graph. The trick is to create them as labels for an "invisible" data range—one that will not appear on the screen.

First set up a data range composed of blank cells. Enter the vertical coordinates of your text in the appropriate cell and leave the other cells blank. Choose a second blank range and enter the desired legend text in the corresponding cell.

For example, if a graph has 12 numbers in its X range, and you want to place text over the third number (at vertical coordinate 600), create a range of 12 cells, all blank except for '600' in the third cell. Create another range of 12 blank cells with the text of the legend in the third cell. Assign the two ranges at Data and Data Labels, respectively, and use the /Format Neither command to suppress the data range so that only the text will appear.

This technique is very flexible because there is no restriction on the length of the text (except for the size of the graph itself), and any number of leading spaces can be used to refine its position.
Everette Gardner, Jr.
Boiling Springs, Pennsylvania

1-2-3 As a Calculator

If you want to balance your checkbook in the middle of analyzing your stock portfolio, you can use *1-2-3* as a calculator without affecting the contents of your spreadsheet. You can also calculate with *1-2-3* and put the results of a calculation into a cell.

Information you enter appears on the second line of the display; the top line shows the cell contents and does not change. To get a total or subtotal, press <F9>, the Calc key. The second line changes to the result of the calculation. Don't use the < = > key.

If you want the results of a calculation to go into a cell, make sure that the cursor is at that cell, and press <Enter> after you press <F9>. The contents of the current cell will be replaced by the result of the calculation. If you don't want to change the contents of the current cell, never press <Enter>. As long as you don't press <Enter>, you won't change the values in the spreadsheet.

For example, while in the Ready mode type **25*4/(3+2)** <**F9**>, and 20 will appear on the second line. This value can be used as a subtotal by just continuing to enter data. For example, if you then type **^2-@SQRT(900)** <**F9**>, the result 370 appears. When you reach a total or want another calculation, press <Esc>. The second line will clear, allowing you to start anew.

When you have finished doing calculations and want to get back to the spreadsheet without changing anything, press <Esc> twice. The first time clears the second line, and the second time returns you to Ready mode.
Bill Weil
San Francisco, California

1-2-3 Break

Andrew Fluegelman's sidebar "If Wishes Were Horses" ["The *1-2-3* Checkbook Ledger," *PC World,* Vol. 1, No. 6] states that one of the shortcomings of *1-2-3* is that after giving the Go command, you may notice an error and want to stop the printout but that *1-2-3* does not allow you to do this. However, I have used *1-2-3* extensively to print graphs and worksheets and found that <Ctrl>-<Break> will stop a worksheet printout and return you to the menu. I hope that this information helps any *1-2-3* users who have had the same wish list as Mr. Fluegelman.

Kathy Lombardo
Melville, New York

2

Word Processing

Hands On

Today anybody who's serious about writing is at least thinking about getting a computer for word processing. A word processor can increase both your creativity and productivity, because the ability to revise your writing before you print it not only eliminates the drudgery of retyping final drafts, it can also ease the pain of committing words to paper. A word processor opens up several new possibilities: you can use word processing software to edit text captured by modem from mainframe computers and information services; if you're insecure about your spelling, you can proofread your electronic text with spelling-checker programs; and, when time is crucial, having your letters, articles, or reports on disk lets you transmit them instantly over phone lines.

Many who buy a computer for writing are soon surprised to find themselves becoming fascinated with their machine's possibilities. Others never go far beyond learning the basics of putting in a disk, writing, editing, and printing. If you feel that you want your PC to be more than a fancy typewriter, the articles in this chapter will introduce you to some advanced word processing techniques you can master with just a little tinkering.

The first two articles are about *WordStar,* the most popular PC word processing program. "WordStar Made To Order" shows you how to change *WordStar*'s default settings and customize everything from the function keys to how the program prints text and displays it on screen. "First-Class MailMerge" teaches you how to use *WordStar* and *MailMerge* to combine a mailing list with text and produce mass mailings with a personal touch.

"Enhancing the Personal Editor" gives you a series of macros that add word processing features to the IBM *Personal Editor.* With these routines you can transform the *Personal Editor* into a truly useful three-in-one program that can be used for program editing, simple word processing, and graphics.

The last article, "Getting the Word," introduces some of the unique capabilities of *MicroSoft Word,* a program many people criticize for being too complicated, but which has its passionate adherents among those who have taken the time to learn its unusual structure and commands. One particularly useful feature of *Word* is its ability to save "style sheets" containing your print formats—including indents, headers, footers, and titles— for various types of documents. The article demonstrates how to set up formats for a scientific paper, a screenplay, and a CRT display.

WordStar Made to Order

Emil Flock

The standard-issue *WordStar* is a powerful program. After three years of using it, I'm still discovering new features. The trouble is that after all this time the few complaints that linger seem to loom larger and larger.

As powerful as the program is, *WordStar* insists on "coming up" the way it wants to. When you put the disk in the drive and turn on the power, MicroPro's *WordStar* lays down the following commandments:

1) The Left Margin is Column 1.
2) The Right Margin is Column 65.
3) Variable Tabbing is ON.
4) Word Wrap is ON.
5) Justification is ON.
6) The Ruler Line display is ON.
7) The Page Break display is ON.
8) The Print Control display is ON.
9) Soft Hyphen entry is OFF.
10) Hyphen Help is ON.

Criticizing the program for these and other default values is difficult. The defaults were chosen to please most people most of the time. It would hardly do to force people to reconfigure *WordStar* each time they begin a session. But why did MicroPro neglect to provide IBM PC *WordStar* users with customization notes, the information they need to customize the program to their own needs? (Comparable notes for the CP/M-80 versions of *WordStar* are sold by MicroPro, and a sampling of these customization instructions is included in the user manual for CP/M-80 versions of the program.)

Patching WordStar

You don't have to be a programmer to customize, or patch, *WordStar.* The tool needed, called DEBUG.COM, is on the PC-DOS disk and is quite simple to use. DEBUG.COM alters the main *WordStar* command file, WS.COM. (All patches discussed here are made on the WS.COM file; no other *WordStar* command files need be changed.) The patches apply to *WordStar* versions 3.2, 3.2M, 3.21, 3.24, 3.3, and 3.31. If you are using version 3.02, you may obtain a free update by taking the original *WordStar* disk to your dealer. Before starting to patch, make a copy of the WS.COM file and then patch the copy only, saving the original for backup purposes.

Start by responding to the PC-DOS prompt like this:

A>**DEBUG WS.COM <Enter>**
–

Notice the minus sign that appears before the blinking cursor. This symbol is DEBUG's prompt, just as A> is the PC-DOS prompt and OK is the BASIC prompt. The prompt indicates that DEBUG has loaded WS.COM and is ready to accept commands. A complete explanation of DEBUG's commands is given in the PC-DOS manual. You use only three commands: F (Fill), W (Write), and Q (Quit). The F command does the actual patching on WS.COM, W writes the patched WS.COM to disk so that you can run it, and Q ends the DEBUG session.

We'll start out with a patch that changes the number of lines on the screen that can be used by your documents. Normally, it's impossible to use the 25th screen line to display part of your documents. Once you've changed the number of lines from 24 to 25, you'll be able to see an extra line of your documents on each screen.

The procedure for changing the default drive is

–F 248 L1 19 <Enter>

This procedure uses the F(Fill) command to place the value 19 in hexadecimal location 248 of the WS.COM file. 19 is the hexadecimal version of 25 decimal that replaces 18 (24 decimal), the old value for the number of screen lines. L1 refers to the length of the patch, in this case 1 byte.

When the fill command is finished, issue the W (Write) command:

–W <Enter>

DEBUG should respond with '–Writing 5000 bytes' (or '–Writing 5380 bytes' on some versions).

Early versions of DEBUG.COM (those that were supplied with DOS 1.0 and 1.05) do not return the message 'Writing 5000 bytes' when you issue a W command at the end of a

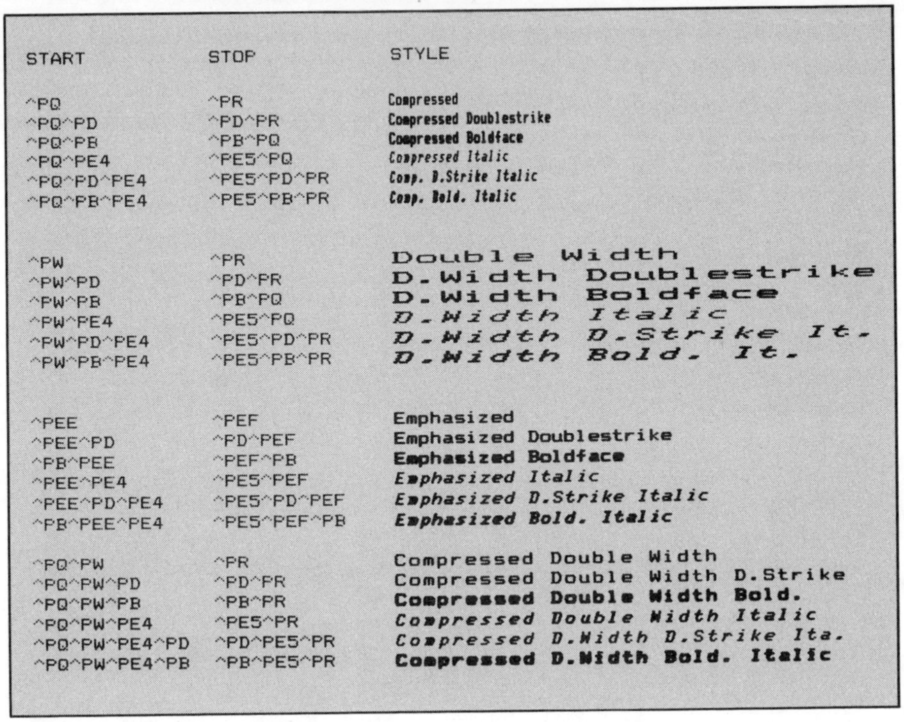

START	STOP	STYLE
^PQ	^PR	Compressed
^PQ^PD	^PD^PR	Compressed Doublestrike
^PQ^PB	^PB^PQ	Compressed Boldface
^PQ^PE4	^PE5^PQ	Compressed Italic
^PQ^PD^PE4	^PE5^PD^PR	Comp. D.Strike Italic
^PQ^PB^PE4	^PE5^PB^PR	Comp. Bold. Italic
^PW	^PR	Double Width
^PW^PD	^PD^PR	D.Width Doublestrike
^PW^PB	^PB^PQ	D.Width Boldface
^PW^PE4	^PE5^PQ	D.Width Italic
^PW^PD^PE4	^PE5^PD^PR	D.Width D.Strike It.
^PW^PB^PE4	^PE5^PB^PR	D.Width Bold. It.
^PEE	^PEF	Emphasized
^PEE^PD	^PD^PEF	Emphasized Doublestrike
^PB^PEE	^PEF^PB	Emphasized Boldface
^PEE^PE4	^PE5^PEF	Emphasized Italic
^PEE^PD^PE4	^PE5^PD^PEF	Emphasized D.Strike Italic
^PB^PEE^PE4	^PE5^PEF^PB	Emphasized Bold. Italic
^PQ^PW	^PR	Compressed Double Width
^PQ^PW^PD	^PD^PR	Compressed Double Width D.Strike
^PQ^PW^PB	^PB^PR	Compressed Double Width Bold.
^PQ^PW^PE4	^PE5^PR	Compressed Double Width Italic
^PQ^PW^PE4^PD	^PD^PE5^PR	Compressed D.Width D.Strike Ita.
^PQ^PW^PE4^PB	^PB^PE5^PR	Compressed D.Width Bold. Italic

Figure 2.1 *Advanced print enhancements.*

session. The bytes are, however, written. When you receive this message, you are ready to issue the Q (Quit) command to end the DEBUG session:

–Q <**Enter**>
A>

"WordStar Patches" is a list of 77 patches for *WordStar*. The patches have been separated into five categories: screen display, printing, advanced print enhancements, function keys, and others. Examples of the advanced print enhancements and the control codes required to produce them are shown in Figure 2.1.

Within the five categories are two types of patches: those that can be accessed from within *WordStar* (while the program is running) and those that must be patched before the program is run.

An Epson dot matrix printer was used to test the patches. Patches for daisy wheel printers were not tested. I've chosen values for the patches that might be typical. You can substitute different values (within limits) for the patches to suit your needs.

Each patch listing in "WordStar Patches" contains the information you need to make the patch. NAME gives the name of the patch; FUNCTION explains what the patch does; ADDRESS gives the patch's WS.COM location in hexadecimal notation; CHANGE gives the original value and suggests a new value; DEBUG is the command line you must enter to make each patch; and RESULT gives the effect of the patch on the workings of *WordStar*. ACCESS FROM WS tells how to access the patch while *WordStar* is running. ("No" indicates that the patch cannot be accessed while the program is running.)

Function Keys

Actually, each function key can be defined to supply up to six characters of your choosing. To change the definition for a key, first select the key's address from the following table:

Key	Address
F1	670
F2	679
F3	682
F4	68b
F5	694
F6	69d
F7	6a6
F8	6af
F9	6b8
F10	6c1

Next, determine which characters you want the key to supply. You may select no more than six characters per key, but they can be any letters, numbers, or control characters you wish. Obtain the numeric value of each character from Appendix G of the BASIC manual. The numbers on that list are in decimal (base 10), but you will need the hexadecimal (base 16) equivalents.

The conversion from decimal to hexadecimal can be done most easily by loading BASIC and typing **?HEX$** (*value*), replacing *value* with each number from the appendix. The HEX$ function will print the hexadecimal equivalent of the decimal value, and you should keep a record of the values. Remember, you will need one value for each character you want a key to supply.

To change a function key definition, execute DEBUG, wait for the hyphen prompt, and then type **F** *address* **L7** and a space—but do not press <Enter>. Instead, type the number of characters you will have the key produce, a space, and the list of hexadecimal values recorded earlier, separating each value from the others by a space. Press <**Enter**> when you have typed all the values for the key.

Name	Result	Address
Short Delay	0	2CP
Medium-Short Delay	0	2D0
Medium-Long Delay	0	2D1
Long Delay	4	2D2
Redisplay Delay	0	2DC
Enable Default Drive I	C:	2DC
Enable Default Drive II	C:	1E04
Enable Default Drive III	C:	1E05
Help Level	2	360
Help Message	ON	361
Insert	OFF	362
Right Margin	39	380
Justification	OFF	386
Hyphen Help	OFF	389
Page Numbers	Omit	3D3
Printer CR w/o LF		746
Quadstrike Boldface		747
Enable ESCape		789
		78A
Compressed	ON	77F
		780
Double Width	ON	784
		785
Comp. & D. Width	OFF	78E
		78F
		790

Table 2.1 *Customized version of* WordStar *for writing.*

The same technique can be used for the key definitions for ten of the cursor control keys on the right side of the keyboard. You may wish to change the effect of some of the keys such as <Home>, <End>, or <Del>. Make the changes using the above instructions for function key changes, using the key's address from the following table:

Key	**Address**
Home	6ca
Up	6d3
PgUp	6dc
Left	6e5
Right	6ee
End	6f7
Down	700
PgDn	709
Ins	712
Del	71b

Customized Program

Depending on your needs, you may want to customize several versions of *WordStar* for different applications. Versions can be designed for business letters, forms processing, or for providing output compatible with a spreadsheet or relational data base program.

I constructed two versions of *WordStar* for my own use. One is for writing, the other is for programming. My writing *WordStar* comes up in the configuration shown in Table 2.1. (For an explanation of delays, disk reset, and default drive, see Appendix C in the pre-Version 3.3 *WordStar Reference Manual*.) My programming *WordStar* comes up in the form shown in Table 2.2. With this configuration you can directly enter Non-Document mode by calling up the program with C>**ws** *filename*. (The table on page 4-5 of the *WordStar Reference Manual* gives the defaults for other parameters in Document and Non-Document modes.)

Name	Result	Address
Short Delay	0	2CF
Medium-Short Delay	0	2D0
Medium-Long Delay	0	2D1
Long Delay	4	2D2
Redisplay Delay	0	2D3
Enable Default Drive I	C:	2DC
Enable Default Drive II	C:	1E04
Enable Default Drive III	C:	1E05
Help Level	2	360
Page Numbers	Omit	3D3
Non-Document		392

Table 2.2 *Customized version of* WordStar *for programming.*

These patches (Figure 2.2) are only the beginning. If you take a few minutes to customize *WordStar*, in the long run you'll save time, use fewer keystrokes, and avoid errors. You don't have to accept *WordStar*'s defaults. You're in control.

Emil Flock is a computer hand-holder living in San Francisco and specializes in customizing WordStar. *His program, the* Customizer for WordStar, *automates some of these patches for the faint of heart (available at 1800 Market St. #91, San Francisco, CA 94102). The material in this piece was originally published in two separate articles in* PC World *Volume 1, Numbers 2 and 3.*

WordStar Patches

Screen Display

Short Delay
Function: Controls length of time that messages remain on screen
Address: 2cf
Change: From 1 to 0
Debug: -F 2cf L1 0
Result: Quicker messages
WS Access: No

Medium-Short Delay
Function: Controls length of time that messages remain on screen
Address: 2d0
Change: From 4 to 0
Debug: -F 2d0 L1 0
Result: Quicker messages
WS Access: No

Medium-Long Delay
Function: Controls length of time that messages remain on screen
Address: 2d1
Change: From 8 to 0
Debug: -F 2d1 L1 0
Result: Quicker messages
WS Access: No

Long Delay
Function: Controls length of time that messages remain on screen
Address: 2d2
Change: From 10 to 4
Debug: -F 2d2 L1 4
Result: Quicker messages
WS Access: No

Redisplay Delay
Function: Controls length of time that messages remain on screen
Address: 2d3
Change: From 9 to 0
Debug: -F 2d3 L1 0
Result: Quicker messages
WS Access: No

Help Level
Function: Determines initial appearance of on-screen help messages
Address: 360
Change: From 3 to 2
Debug: -F 360 L1 2
Result: Level 2
WS Access: Ctrl-JH2

Figure 2.2 WordStar *patches.*

Help Flag
Function: Produces initial help-level message
Address: 361
Change: From ff to 0
Debug: -F 361 L1 0
Result: Initial help message
WS Access: No

Insert
Function: Determines initial insert setting (ON or OFF)
Address: 362
Change: From ff to 0
Debug: -F 362 L1 0
Result: Off
WS Access: Ctrl-V

Directory
Function: Determines initial file directory setting (ON or OFF)
Address: 363
Change: From ff to 0
Debug: -F 363 L1 0
Result: Off
WS Access: F

Left Margin
Function: Determines initial left margin setting
Address: 37f
Change: From 0 to 11
Debug: -F 37f L1 11
Result: Margin 10(valid from 0 to Right Margin-3)
WS Access: Ctrl-OL

Right Margin
Function: Determines initial right margin setting
Address: 380
Change: From 40 to 27
Debug: -F 380 L1 27
Result: Margin 39(valid from 2 to Screen Width-4)
WS Access: Ctrl-OR

Word Wrap
Function: Determines initial word wrap setting (ON or OFF)
Address: 385
Change: From ff to 0
Debug: -F 385 L1 0
Result: Off
WS Access: Ctrl-OW

Justification
Function: Determines initial justification setting (ON or OFF)
Address: 386
Change: From ff to 0
Debug: -F 386 L1 0
Result: Ragged right
WS Access: Ctrl-OJ

Variable Tab
Function: Determines initial variable tabs setting (ON or OFF)
Address: 387
Change: From ff to 0
Debug: -F 387 L1 0
Result: Off
WS Access: Ctrl-OV

Soft Hyphen
Function: Determines initial soft hyphen setting (ON or OFF)
Address: 388
Change: From 0 to ff
Debug: -F 388 L1 ff
Result: Soft
WS Access: Ctrl-OE

Hyphen Help
Function: Determines initial hyphen help setting (ON or OFF)
Address: 389
Change: From ff to 0
Debug: -F 389 L1 0
Result: Off
WS Access: Ctrl-OH

Print Control Display
Function: Determines initial print-control display setting (ON or OFF)
Address: 38a
Change: From ff to 0
Debug: -F 38a L1 0
Result: Off
WS Access: Ctrl-OD

Ruler Line
Function: Determines initial ruler line setting (ON or OFF)
Address: 38b
Change: From ff to 0
Debug: -F 38b L1 0
Result: Off
WS Access: Ctrl-OT

Figure 2.2 *(continued)*

Page Break Display
Function: Determines initial page break display (dotted line) setting (ON or OFF).
Address: 38c
Change: From ff to 0
Debug: -F 38c L1 0
Result: Off
WS Access: Ctrl-OP

Page Break Suppress
Function: Determines initial page break setting (ON or OFF)
Address: 38d
Change: From ff to 0
Debug: -F 38d L1 0
Result: Off
WS Access: Ctrl-OP

Line Spacing
Function: Sets initial line spacing (from 1 to 9)
Address: 38e
Change: From 1 to 2
Debug: -F 38e L1 2
Result: Double space
WS Access: Ctrl-OS

Column Move Mode
Function: Determines initial column-move mode setting (ON or OFF)
Address: 38f
Change: From 0 to ff
Debug: -F 38f L1 ff
Result: Enable column
WS Access: Ctrl-KN

Change Decimal Point Tab Character
Function: Allows substitution of alternate character (e.g.',')for decimal point
Address: 393
Change: From 2e to 2c
Debug: -F 393 L1 2c
Result: Comma replaces decimal point
WS Access: No

Change Dot Command Character
Function: Allows substitution of an alternate character for period in dot commands
Address: 395
Change: From 2e to 25
Debug: -F 395 L1 25
Result: Percent sign replaces decimal point
WS Access: No

Change Nonbreak Space Character
Function: Allows substitution of alternate character for nonbreak space
Address: 396
Change: From f to 26
Debug: -F 396 L1 26
Result: Ampersand replaces Ctrl-O
WS Access: No

Hyphen Criterion
Function: Determines number of columns short of right margin that hyphen help is activated
Address: 39a
Change: From 4 to a
Debug: -F 39a L1 a
Result: 10 Columns
WS Access: No

Printing

Default for Print Options
Function: Sets default print query response to Yes
Address: 3ca
Change: From 0 to ff
Debug: -F 3ca L1 ff
Result: Disk file output: Yes
WS Access: P

Default for Print Options
Function: Sets default print query response to Yes
Address: 3cb
Change: From 0 to ff
Debug: -F 3cb L1 ff
Result: Use form feed: Yes
WS Access: P

Default for Print Options
Function: Sets default print query response to Yes
Address: 3cc
Change: From 0 to ff
Debug: -F 3cc L1 ff
Result: Suppress page format: Yes
WS Access: P

Default for Print Options
Function: Sets default print query response to Yes
Address: 3cd
Change: From 0 to ff
Debug: -F 3cd L1 ff
Result: Pause between pages: Yes
WS Access: P

Figure 2.2 *(continued)*

Omit Page Numbers
Function: Causes omission of page numbers
Address: 3d3
Change: From 0 to ff
Debug: -F 3d3 L1 ff
Result: No page numbers printed
WS Access: .OP

Microjustification
Function: Determines initial microjustification setting (ON or OFF)
Address: 3d4
Change: From ff to 0
Debug: -F 3d4 L1 0
Result: Off
WS Access: .UJ

Bidirectional Print
Function: Controls print-head movement during printing
Address: 3d5
Change: From ff to 0
Debug: -F 3d5 L1 0
Result: Off
WS Access: .BP

Paper Length I (Paper Length I, II, and III must be used together)
Function: Sets paper length
Address: 367
Change: From 42 to 3c
Debug: -F 367 L1 3c
Result: 60 lines
WS Access: .PL

Paper Length II
Function: Sets paper length
Address: 368
Change: From 10 to e0 (lsb in 1/48 inch format)
Debug: -F 368 L1 e0 (lsb in 1/48 inch format)
Result: 60 lines
WS Access: .PL

Paper Length III
Function: Sets paper length
Address: 369
Change: From 2 to 1 (msb in 1/48 inch format)
Debug: -F 369 L1 1 (msb in 1/48 inch format)
Result: 60 lines
WS Access: .PL

Top Margin I (Top Margin I, II, and III must be used together)
Function: Sets top margin
Address: 36b
Change: From 3 to 28
Debug: -F 36b L1 28
Result: 40 lines
WS Access: .MT

Top Margin II
Function: Sets top margin
Address: 36c
Change: From 18 to 40 (lsb in 1/48 inch format)
Debug: -F 36c L1 40 (lsb in 1/48 inch format)
Result: 40 lines
WS Access: .MT

Top Margin III
Function: Sets top margin
Address: 36d
Change: From 0 to 1 (msb in 1/48 inch format)
Debug: -F 36d L1 1 (msb in 1/48 inch format)
Result: 40 lines
WS Access: .MT

Bottom Margin I (Bottom Margin I, II, and III must be used together)
Function: Sets bottom margin
Address: 373
Change: From 8 to 24
Debug: -F 373 L1 24
Result: 36 lines
WS Access: .MB

Bottom Margin II
Function: Sets bottom margin
Address: 374
Change: From 40 to 20 (lsb in 1/48 inch format)
Debug: -F 374 L1 20 (lsb in 1/48 inch format)
Result: 36 lines
WS Access: .MB

Bottom Margin III
Function: Sets bottom margin
Address: 375
Change: From 0 to 1 (msb in 1/48 inch format)
Debug: -F 375 L1 1 (msb in 1/48 inch format)
Result: 36 lines
WS Access: .MB

Figure 2.2 *(continued)*

Standard Character Pitch
Function: Sets standard character pitch
Address: 37b
Change: From ff to 0
Debug: -F 37b L1 0
Result: Sets alternate pitch as default
WS Access: Ctrl-PA

Set Default Character Pitch
Function: Sets default character pitch
Address: 37c
Change: From 0c to 8
Debug: -F 37c L1 8
Result: 8 characters per inch (1/120-inch format)
WS Access: Ctrl-PA

Set Alternate Character Pitch
Function: Sets alternate character pitch
Address: 37d
Change: From 0a to 10
Debug: -F 37d L1 10
Result: 16 characters per inch (1/120-inch format)
WS Access: Ctrl-PA

Page Offset
Function: Sets page offset for form feeders
Address: 37e
Change: From 8 to 32
Debug: -F 37e L1 32
Result: 50 replaces 8 (for sheet feeders)
WS Access: .PO

Advanced Print Enhancements

Printer CR without LF
Function: Allows carriage return without line feed (may not apply to all printers)
Address: 746
Change: From 0 to ff
Debug: -F 746 L1 ff
Result: Allows CR without LF
WS Access: No

Quadstrike Boldface
Function: Allows quadruple-strike boldface
Address: 747
Change: From 2 to 4
Debug: -F 747 L1 4
Result: Quadstrike boldface
WS Access: No

Enable ESCape I (**Enable ESCape I and II must be used together**)
Function: Allows sending of escape (ASCII CHR$(27)) to printer
Address: 789
Change: From 0 to 1
Debug: -F 789 L1 1
Result: Send escape sequences
WS Access: Ctrl-PEx after installation

Enable ESCape II
Function: Allows sending of escape (ASCII CHR$(27)) to printer
Address: 78a
Change: From 0 to 1b
Debug: -F 78a L1 1b
Result: Send escape sequences
WS Access: Ctrl-PEx after installation

Compressed I (**The Compressed and Double Width patches should be used together**)
Function: Assigns codes for turning on compressed print to User Patch Q
Address: 77f
Change: From 0 to 1
Debug: -F 77f L1 1
Result: On
WS Access: Ctrl-PQ after installation

Compressed II
Function: Assigns codes for turning on compressed print to User Patch Q
Address: 780
Change: From 0 to f
Debug: -F 780 L1 f
Result: On
WS Access: Ctrl-PQ after installation

Double Width I
Function: Assigns codes for turning on double-width print to User Patch W
Address: 784
Change: From 0 to 1
Debug: -F 784 L1 1
Result: On
WS Access: Ctrl-PW after installation

Double Width II
Function: Assigns codes for turning on double-width print to User Patch W
Address: 785
Change: From 0 to e
Debug: -F 785 L1 e
Result: On
WS Access: Ctrl-PW after installation

Figure 2.2 *(continued)*

Compressed/Double Width I
Function: Assigns codes for turning off compressed and double-width print to User Patch R
Address: 78e
Change: From 0 to 2
Debug: -F 78e L1 2
Result: Off
WS Access: Ctrl-PR after installation

Compressed/Double Width II
Function: Assigns codes for turning off compressed and double-width print to User Patch R
Address: 78f
Change: From 0 to 12
Debug: -F 78f L1 12
Result: Off
WS Access: Ctrl-PR after installation

Compressed/Double Width III
Function: Assigns codes for turning off compressed and double-width print to User Patch R
Address: 790
Change: From 0 to 14
Debug: -F 790 L1 14
Result: Off
WS Access: Ctrl-PR after installation

Function Keys*

F1 Function Key I (F1 Function Key I and II must be used together)
Function: Sets F1 to Save—done edit
Address: 671
Change: From 0a to 0b
Debug: -F 671 L1 Ob
Result: Ctrl-KD
WS Access: No

F1 Function Key II
Function: Sets F1 to Save—done edit
Address: 672
Change: From 48 to 44
Debug: -F 672 L1 44
Result: Ctrl-KD
WS Access: No

F2 Function Key I (F2 Function Key I and II must be used together)
Function: Sets F2 to Abandon edit
Address: 67a
Change: From 0f to 0b
Debug: -F 67a L1 0b
Result: Ctrl-KQ
WS Access: No

F2 Function Key II
Function: Sets F2 to Abandon edit
Address: 67b
Change: From 47 to 51
Debug: -F 67b L1 51
Result: Ctrl-KQ
WS Access: No

F3 Function Key I (F3 Function Key I and II must be used together)
Function: Sets F3 to Reform paragraph
Address: 682
Change: From 3 to 1
Debug: -F 682 L1 1
Result: Ctrl-B
WS Access: No

F3 Function Key II
Function: Sets F3 to Reform paragraph
Address: 683
Change: From 0f to 2
Debug: -F 683 L1 2
Result: Ctrl-B
WS Access: No

F4 Function Key I (F4 Function Key I and II must be used together)
Function: Sets F4 to Delete word right
Address: 68b
Change: From 3 to 1
Debug: -F 68b L1 1
Result: Ctrl-T
WS Access: No

F4 Function Key II
Function: Sets F4 to Delete word right
Address: 68c
Change: From 0f to 14
Debug: -F 68c L1 14
Result: Ctrl-T
WS Access: No

Figure 2.2 *(continued)*

F5 Function Key

Function: Sets F5 to Left side screen
Address: 695
Change: From 10 to 11
Debug: -F 695 L1 11
Result: Ctrl-QS
WS Access: No

F6 Function Key I (F6 Function Key I and II must be used together)

Function: Sets F6 to Right end line
Address: 69e
Change: From 10 to 11
Debug: -F 69e L1 11
Result: Ctrl-QD
WS Access: No

F6 Function Key II

Function: Sets F6 to Right end line
Address: 69f
Change: From 42 to 44
Debug: -F 69f L1 44
Result: Ctrl-QD
WS Access: No

F7 Function Key I (F7 Function Key I and II must be used together)

Function: Sets F7 to Delete line
Address: 6a6
Change: From 02 to 01
Debug: -F 6a6 L1 01
Result: Ctrl-Y
WS Access: No

F7 Function Key II

Function: Sets F7 to Delete line
Address: 6a7
Change: From 0b to 19
Debug: -F 6a7 L1 19
Result: Ctrl-Y
WS Access: No

F8 Function Key I (F8 Function Key I and II must be used together)

Function: Sets F8 to Delete character
Address: 6af
Change: From 02 to 01
Debug: -F 6af L1 01
Result: Ctrl-G
WS Access: No

F8 Function Key II

Function: Sets F8 to Delete character
Address: 6b0
Change: From 11 to 01
Debug: -F 6b0 L1 01
Result: Ctrl-G
WS Access: No

F9 Function Key

Function: Sets F9 to Beginning of file
Address: 6ba
Change: From 43 to 52
Debug: -F 6ba L1 52
Result: Ctrl-QR
WS Access: No

F10 Function Key

Function: Sets F10 to End of file
Address: 6c3
Change: From 52 to 43
Debug: -F 6c3 L1 43
Result: Ctrl-QC
WS Access: No

*Michael Lacefield located the function key patch areas and provided the information.

Other

Disk Reset

Function: Prohibits disk reset
Address: 2db
Change: From 0 to ff
Debug: -F 2db L1 ff
Result: Reset never issued
WS Access: No

Enable Default Drive I (Enable Default Drive I, II, and III must be used together)

Function: Sets drive that program looks to for command files
Address: 2dc
Change: From 1 to 3
Debug: -F 2dc L1 3
Result: Drive C
WS Access: No

Figure 2.2 *(continued)*

Enable Default Drive II

Function:	Sets drive that program looks to for command files
Address:	1e04
Change:	From b1 to 90
Debug:	-F 1e04 L1 90
Result:	Enables Default Drive change
WS Access:	No

Enable Default Drive III

Function:	Sets drive that program looks to for command files
Address:	1e05
Change:	From 01 to 90
Debug:	-F 1e05 L1 90
Result:	Enables Default Drive change
WS Access:	No

Non-document Mode

Function:	Allows program to boot up in non-document mode
Address:	392
Change:	From 0 to ff
Debug:	-F 392 L1 ff
Result:	Non-document mode
WS Access:	N

Number of Screen Lines*

Function:	Change number of lines on screen
Address:	248
Change:	From 18 to 19
Debug:	-F 248 L1 19
Result:	25 lines WS
Access:	No

*C. Michael Barnett discovered the Number of Screen Lines patch.

Figure 2.2 *(continued)*

First-Class MailMerge

Bobbie Ray Leach

Most businesses still communicate by letter, whether sent via electronic mail or the post office. If you're like most PC users, you probably use *WordStar* to write the letters you send to customers, dealers, or potential clients. But what if you want to distribute essentially the same letter to 400 prospective clients? What they receive must look like it came straight from the typewriter. After all, people who may contribute to your prosperity appreciate—and expect—personal treatment. With *WordStar* and a letter quality printer, a letter can look like it sprang whole from a Selectric II.

But creating 400 personal letters is not so easy. You could copy the letter minus name and address in a file over and over with *WordStar*'s <Ctrl>-K C command, scroll to each copy of the letter, type in each client's name, company, and address, and eventually print the file. Heaven help you if, in an effort to be even more personal, the letter talks about a client's product; you'll have to insert the appropriate reference into every letter. And if you want to send the same people a different letter later on, this laborious process would have to be repeated.

For *WordStar* users, *MailMerge*—a best-selling companion to *WordStar* from MicroPro—can help automate the task of creating and printing a multitude of personalized letters. As its name suggests, *MailMerge* combines files. This article will show you how to deftly meld a mailing list with a form letter to produce personalized letters that can be printed out or stored on disk. To get the most out of the article, a working knowledge of *WordStar* is necessary; you should be able to open a file, create a document, save it, and print it. Familiarity with dot commands is also helpful.

Basic Dot Commands

MailMerge performs its magic with a few files and dot commands. The document file holds the form letter or other document; the data file holds the information to be inserted into the form letter; and a command file brings the two together. Dot commands in the document file direct the process, fetching files and controlling how a document is displayed and printed. Some dot commands are shared by *WordStar* and *MailMerge* (such as .pa, which inserts a page break into a document), while others are specific to one program. A dot command is a period followed by two letters; sometimes the command is followed by a number or text. When a dot command is typed into a document, a character appears on the far right of the screen. A *MailMerge* dot command is identified with an 'M'; an incorrect command is flagged with a question mark.

Many dot commands are available with *MailMerge*, but only a handful are needed for most applications (see "Defining Dot Commands"). A few rules must be followed, of course. Dot commands can be used in any *MailMerge* or *WordStar* document, but they must always be placed at the beginning of a line. In some cases one dot command must come before another. For example, .df identifies the data file to be merged, and .rv discloses to *MailMerge* what information is in that data file. Logic—and *MailMerge*—dictates that .df precede .rv. Some dot commands, such as .pl, which sets a document's page length, must be put at the beginning of a document.

The Document File

In *WordStar* a document file is created by typing **D**. The file contains the text of the form letter, the dot commands, and the data fields (such as date, name, and company) that will be filled in when the document file is merged with the data file holding the mailing list. Open a file in *WordStar* and type in the form letter CLIENT.LTR as shown in Figure 2.3. Note that every data field is bracketed by ampersands.

But what happens if a data field—such as company—is not "filled in" during a merge? By placing /O (the letter O) at the end of the data field, you can suppress the blank space that is left by the empty field and justify the text surrounding the field.

Three dot commands—.df, .rv, and .pa—are required in every document. The first command, .df, identifies the data file, such as CLIENT.DTA in Figure 2.4, to be merged with the letter; .rv specifies the fields in the data file; and .pa inserts a page break and directs the program to merge the next record in the data file with the form letter. The

```
.op
.df client.dta
.rv firstname,lastname,company,street,city,state,zip,item

&date&

&firstname& &lastname&
&company/O&
&street&
&city& &state& &zip&


Dear &firstname&:

I enjoyed our telephone conversation the other day and I think &item& has
real potential. We definitely would like to make a presentation to your firm
about marketing the product.

Please find enclosed our prospectus. I look forward to hearing from you
soon.

Warmest regards,

Alvin "Buzz" Feltzer
Senior Marketing Director

ABF/rl

.pa
```

Figure 2.3 *The form letter CLIENT.LTR as it appears in a* MailMerge *document file.*

```
John,Myers,The Fixtures,222 S. Rampart,Wattman,TX,65891,Fix-It-All
Bob,Smith,,1498 Exitor,St. Minna,NJ,07778,The Statue Maker
Elaine,Swisher,,98 Groton,Hickory,SC,01783,Elaine's Paste-Away
```

Figure 2.4 *CLIENT.DTA, a* MailMerge *data file.*

optional .op command prevents *MailMerge* from printing page numbers on the resulting letters.

The Data File

The data file (see Figure 2.4) supplies the information—in this case the names, addresses, and other information that make up the mailing list—to be inserted into the data fields in the form letter. Unlike a document file or a command file, the data file is created in *WordStar*'s nondocument mode (the 'N' menu option). The word wrap feature is thus turned off, and a record can be up to 240 characters long. A record is confined to one line and must be marked at the end with a carriage return (by pressing <Enter>). Fields in each record must match the type and sequence of the .rv line in the form letter. Data fields are separated by a comma, and a space cannot lie next to a comma.

If a record is missing information, such as a company name, its counterpart in the document file must be acknowledged in the data file with a comma. For example, as you type in the second record in CLIENT.DTA (see Figure 2.4), you will notice that 'Smith' is followed by two commas. Even if you do not supply information for a data field, you must type a comma to signal the program to move to the next data field. The two commas following 'Smith' tell the program to move ahead two data fields. If a comma is embedded in a field, the field must be surrounded by quotes. Once a data file is created, it can be used again with other form letters you write.

The Command File

A command file isn't required by *MailMerge,* but it does make the process easier. A command file is created in *WordStar*'s document mode and contains only dot commands. In some ways it resembles a batch file. Type in the command file COMMAND.MRG in Figure 2.5. When you finally run *MailMerge,* you will see how the dot commands in the file are executed in sequence. In COMMAND.MRG, '.cs' clears the screen, '.dm' displays a message, '.av' prompts the user for the date, while '.fi' calls in document file CLIENT.LTR, which in turn calls the data file for information.

```
.cs
.dm Printing the client form letter
.av Date
.fi CLIENT.LTR
```

Figure 2.5 *The command file* COMMAND.MRG. *This is the file name you give* MailMerge *in response to the program's 'Request for file to MailMerge' prompt.*

Making the Merge

Now that you have created the document, data, and command files, you can merge full speed ahead. Turn on the printer and select **M** from the *WordStar* menu. (Don't forget that the MAILMRGE.OVR file must be on the *WordStar* system disk.) You are asked to name the file to be merged, which in this case is COMMAND.MRG; type in the file name and press <Enter>. The next prompt asks if the merged result should be sent to a disk file. If you answer **Y**, type in a new file name, and answer *MailMerge*'s few questions; the merged result will be stored on disk. The advantage of merging to a disk file is that you can check your handiwork for errors before you print out hundreds of letters. If you answer **N**, *MailMerge* presents print options. Once an option is specified, the printer will start churning out letters.

Of course, *MailMerge* does more than create personalized form letters. With a properly crafted command file, *MailMerge* can quickly assemble large documents—such as contracts or updated manuals—that rely on many lengthy, standard clauses. *MailMerge*'s power can even be used to consolidate floppy disk files onto a hard disk drive. Though *MailMerge* can be fussy— particularly about the content of data files—you may find it a tool that's hard to put down once you've used it.

Bobbie Ray Leach is a former data processing manager and RPG programmer living in San Francisco. This article was originally published in PC World *Volume 2, Number 10.*

Defining Dot Commands

Dot commands work like simple programming commands. They can be used to clear the screen, create and display prompts, or format the printed result of merged files. Following are some commonly used MailMerge *dot commands.*

.dm *Display message. Text following this command is displayed on the screen. This command is usually placed in a* MailMerge *command file.*

.cs *Clear screen. This command removes any previously displayed image (such as a* WordStar *menu), making it easier to read* MailMerge *prompts that follow.*

.pa *Process the next record/insert a page break. This tells* MailMerge *to merge the next record with the document and advance the paper in the printer one page.*

.op *Turn off page numbering.* WordStar *automatically numbers pages when a document is printed. The .op command disables this feature when it is unwanted, as when letters are being printed out.*

.df *Define data file name. This specifies which data file will be used in a* MailMerge *operation. In this article the data file is* CLIENT.DTA.

.rv *Read variable. Specifies what data fields are in the document file. The sequence of these fields (in* CLIENT.DTA, *for instance, firstname, lastname, company, and so on) must correspond to the sequence of data in the data file (John,Myers,The Fixtures).*

.av *Ask for variable. This command is for those data fields, such as date, that change and thus should not be stored in a data file. The text following the .av command must match the field name in the document file. In* COMMAND.MRG *the .av command is tied to the date field in the form letter. 'Date?' appears as a prompt when the files are first merged; the user's response is automatically inserted into the date field of every letter printed during the cycle.*

.fi *Define file name. This command tells* MailMerge *which document file should be merged with a data file. This dot command is usually placed in a command file; if this command is encountered in a document file,* MailMerge *must insert the specified file into the document before continuing to the next field. The command is useful when you want to create a document by combining other documents.*

Enhancing the IBM Personal Editor

Steven J. Lagreca

Are you interested in a package that offers powerful text editing, reasonable word processing, and block graphics capabilities for $100? With a little effort IBM's *Personal Editor* can become just that. By adding macro functions (short commands that incorporate and implement a series of commands) to the *Personal Editor,* you can efficiently process text projects ranging from rough drafts, memos, organization charts, flow diagrams, and overhead projector foils to source code.

Chances are you are using a word processor for text and another editor for programming, each with its own long list of commands to memorize. For graphics, you're probably making do with lines composed of hyphens, equal signs, and asterisks.

Aside from the burden of memorizing an assortment of editing commands, using separate programs causes problems when you attempt to transfer data or documents between them. Word processors don't handle graphics, program editors generally have marginal printing capabilities, and special programs that generate overhead foils have little or no format flexibility. Completing a project requires a juggling act to apply the editing, word processing, and formatting functions of various products to the appropriate portions of the text.

In a world of specialized editing products the *Personal Editor*'s forte is versatility. Effort spent enhancing the basic package translates into more utility for your software dollar and less time spent learning (and relearning) additional programs to fill your needs.

Before and After

The *Personal Editor* scores high marks in several areas, a major asset being the capability of creating or revising several files concurrently (see "The Tailor-Made Editor," *PC World,* Vol. 1, No. 4). You can, for example, review program output from *VisiCalc* or *1-2-3* in one work space (file) while composing an accompanying report in another. It's also possible to move blocks of text between two sections of the same file. Using the *Personal Editor,* programmers can review combinations of source code, program output, and debugging information.

Another asset is the ease with which text can be moved, copied, shifted, or overlayed within a document on a character, line, or block basis. The search and replace function is also exemplary. On the other hand, the *Personal Editor* has been criticized for its lack of word processing capabilities, including the inability to reformat a paragraph easily after inserting text, the inability to print only a portion of a document, and the general lack of printer formatting capabilities.

Each of these limitations can be overcome by taking advantage of the program's macro definition function. This article demonstrates how this powerful facility can also be used to implement additional useful functions. You can use all the fonts available on your IBM or Epson printer to vary style and highlight text without memorizing printer control codes. You can automatically skip over the perforations on continuous-form paper without locating and manually resetting the internal printer switches. Printers with friction feed can be switched between continuous and single-sheet paper. Wide-carriage printers can be switched between 8½- and 13½-inch paper to ensure that text exceeding 80 columns won't print on the platen.

Another improvement you can implement with macros is the ability to switch between two monitors to increase productivity. This allows you to compose a document on one while placing help screens or other pertinent data on the other. Additional word processing functions include deleting a word, a line, or all words remaining on a line. A scale line is available to assist in report or screen design. Line spacing options allow white space for marking rough drafts or compressing text to cut paper costs.

Macros to the Rescue

The macro definition facility gives you the ability to create features not supplied with the original product. Defining a macro involves combining a series of simple functions, which when executed as a group produce a new, more sophisticated function. A macro is invoked by typing a function key or a two-key combination.

The *Personal Editor* provides 63 functions and 17 commands that are the building blocks used to create macro functions. The distinction between a command and a function is that a command can be executed either by typing it on the command line or from within a macro definition, whereas a function can be invoked from within a macro only. The word *macro* is used here to connote any combination of functions and/or commands used to produce additional features.

The enhanced macro functions described in this article fall into three broad categories: editing and word processing, printer control, and block graphics. Every attempt was made to assign (or reassign) functions to keys logically. Mnemonic assignments were used wherever possible. For instance, splitting a line is assigned to <Alt>-S. Similar functions were placed on adjacent keys. If the function came with the original product, the former key assignment is provided. In all, 34 significant functions have been added.

Editing and Word Processing

The majority of the macros in this article have been created to enhance editing and word processing. The most important macros have been assigned to the function keys (see Table 2.3). The first new function (<F2>) is set up to toggle between a text editing and a word processing environment. This is accomplished by using the macro command to load a word processing profile from the file WP.PRO or the default editing profile, PE.PRO, from the disk. (A profile is a library of macro definitions.)

Separate profiles are needed for two reasons. Certain functions such as text insertion, margin settings, and tab stops are performed differently depending on whether you are word processing documents or editing the text of a program. Also, the number of desirable functions has exceeded the available key assignments, forcing the line-spacing options into the word processing profile.

The macros to delete a line (<F6>), delete a word (<F7>), and delete to the end of a line (<F8>) are grouped together on the keyboard. Their logical counterparts, erase a line (<Alt>-<F6>), erase a word (<Alt>-<F7>), and erase to the end of a line (<Alt>- <F8>) are located on the same function keys for consistency. The delete functions cause remaining text to be shifted left and/or up, whereas the erase functions fill the erased area with blanks. Erase to the end of a line can be used to clear the command line of unwanted text. The vertical center command (<F10>) centers the current line in the middle of the screen, and the <F9> key switches the display between two files edited concurrently. The <Alt>-<F9> key switches to a monochrome screen and switching to a color screen is done with <Alt>-<F10>. Don't forget to use this feature with the switch files (<F9>) option for additional versatility.

The next group uses the <Alt> key plus the alpha keys, A through Z. The first new key assignment (<Alt>-G) changes all text in a designated area to lowercase. Although this key assignment is not mnemonic, the function is located immediately below the change-text-to-uppercase function (<Alt>-T). <Alt>-K produces a highlighted scale line. It can be moved once with <Alt>-M or deleted with <Alt>-D. <Alt>-N appends the word *notabs* to a File or Save command. This saves your work space without applying the usual compression algorithm.

The last five enhancements are stored in the Unnamed file, which can be accessed with the <Alt>-Q key. Simply mark the text you wish to restore and switch back to the previous work space using <F9>. The remaining group includes a few key assignments that implement functions differently, depending on whether you're in the editing or word processing environment.

One of the more vociferous criticisms of the original product concerned its inability to wrap text back into a newly inserted line only partially filled with text. Using the <Ins> key in the word processing environment now accomplishes this task in just one keystroke. To be sure that this feature will work properly, always leave a blank line at the bottom of the work space. The original function of the key (shifting text to the right as characters are inserted) has been preserved in the editing environment.

In the editing profile the <Enter> key simply moves the cursor to the beginning of the next line. In the word processing profile the

Function	Key Assignment	
	Enhanced Macro	Original Macro
Editing Environment:		
Help	<F1>	<F1>
Switch to editing or word processing profile	<F2>	-
File (save and quit) current work space	<F3>	<F3>
Quit without saving current work space	<F4>	<F4>
Insert line of text	<F5>	<F9>
Delete line of text	<F6>	-
Delete word	<F7>	*
Delete all characters to end of line	<F8>	-
Switch between work spaces	<F9>	<F8>
Vertically center current line	<F10>	*
Shift marked area left	<Alt>-<F1>	<Shift>-<F7>
Shift marked area right	<Alt>-<F2>	<Shift>-<F8>
Erase line	<Alt>-<F6>	<F5>
Erase word	<Alt>-<F7>	-
Erase all characters to end of line	<Alt>-<F8>	<F6>
Switch to monochrome screen	<Alt>-<F9>	-
Switch to color screen	<Alt>-<F10>	-
Undo changes to current line	<Alt>-A	<Shift>-<F4>
Mark block of text	<Alt>-B	<Alt>-B
Mark character	<Alt>-C	<Alt>-C
Delete marked area	<Alt>-D	<Alt>-D
Move cursor to end of marked area	<Alt>-E	<Alt>-E
Fill marked area with blanks	<Alt>-F	-
Make all characters in marked area lowercase	<Alt>-G	*
Join two adjacent lines	<Alt>-J	<Alt>-J
Display column line	<Alt>-K	-
Mark line	<Alt>-L	<Alt>-L
Move marked area to another area	<Alt>-M	<Alt>-M
Save or file with the no-tabs option	<Alt>-N	-
Overlay an area of text with marked area	<Alt>-O	<Alt>-O
Reformat paragraph	<Alt>-P	<Shift>-<F3>
Switch to unnamed file to salvage text	<Alt>-Q	-
Redraw screen after DOS message displayed	<Alt>-R	<Alt>-R
Split current line of text at cursor	<Alt>-S	<Alt>-S
Make all characters in marked area uppercase	<Alt>-T	*
Unmark marked area	<Alt>-U	<Alt>-U
Move cursor to beginning of marked area	<Alt>-W	<Alt>-Y
Save current work space	<Alt>-Y	<F3>
Copy marked area to another area	<Alt>-Z	<Alt>-Z
Move to next line	<Enter>	<Enter>
Insert text	<Ins>	<Ins>
Word Processing Environment:		
Single-spacing, 8 lines per inch	<Alt>-1	-
Single-spacing, 6 lines per inch	<Alt>-2	-
1½-spacing	<Alt>-3	-
Double-spacing	<Alt>-4	-
Triple-spacing	<Alt>-5	-
New paragraph	<Enter>	*
Reformat paragraph	<Ins>	-
Display next paragraph	<Alt>-P	-

*This function is mentioned in the Personal Editor manual but is not provided in the default profile.

Table 2.3 *Editing and word processing functions provided by macros. Enhanced custom macros (left) provide greater control over word processing and program editing than those provided by the* Personal Editor *(right).*

Function	Immediate (I) Embedded (E)	Enhanced Macro Key Assignments*
Print entire work space	I	<Alt>-<F3>
Print screen	I	<Alt>-<F4>
Print marked area of text	I	<Alt>-<F5>
Skip to next page	I	<Shift>-<F1>
Skip to next line	I	<Ctrl>-<F1>
Skip over perforations	I	<Shift>-<F2>
Reset all printer defaults	I	<Ctrl>-<F2>
Page width 80 columns	I	<Shift>-<F3>
Page width 132 columns	I	<Ctrl>-<F3>
Continuous paper	I	<Shift>-<F4>
Single-sheet paper	I	<Ctrl>-<F4>
Compressed printing font ON	E	<Shift>-<F5>
Compressed printing font OFF	E	<Ctrl>-<F5>
Double-strike printing ON	E	<Shift>-<F6>
Double-strike printing OFF	E	<Ctrl>-<F6>
Double-wide printing ON	E	<Shift>-<F7>
Double-wide printing OFF	E	<Ctrl>-<F7>
Emphasized printing ON	E	<Shift>-<F8>
Emphasized printing OFF	E	<Ctrl>-<F8>
Italics printing ON	E	<Shift>-<F9>
Italics printing OFF	E	<Ctrl>-<F9>
Page break	E	<Shift>-<F10>

* Equivalent function does not exist in the original macro functions.

Table 2.4 *Printer control functions.*

same key prepares a new paragraph by inserting a new line and then indenting.

The confirm change function combination (<Ctrl>-<Backspace>) has been relocated so that it is immediately above the ignore change function macro (<Ctrl>-<Enter>). In addition, either choice will now automatically reexecute the change command until the entire work space has been searched.

Instead of moving forward a page at a time, a macro in the word processing environment allows you to move paragraph by paragraph with <Alt>-P. The same key combination is used in the editing profile to reformat text.

Left and right margins are set to columns 1 and 254 in the editing profile and 5 and 70 in the word processing profile. Tabs advance the cursor a word at a time in the word processing profile and ten spaces at a time in the editing profile.

Printer Controls

Printer and block graphics functions can be used only in conjunction with the IBM Graphics printer or the Epson MX/FX series with Graftrax. Even though these two brands are closely related, subtle differences affect the implementation of some macros. These are noted where appropriate.

Three common printer functions have been located in one function key group (see Table 2.4). You can print a work space using <Alt>-<F3> and print a screen using <Alt>-<F4>. Any marked area can be printed using print mark (<Alt>-<F5>).

The two remaining function key groups, <Shift>-<F1> through <Shift>-<F10> and <Ctrl>-<F1> through <Ctrl>-<F10>, are used to control printer options. These options are of two types: those that take effect immediately and those that embed characters in the text and are interpreted by the printer as the document is printed.

The macros to skip to the top of the next page (<Shift>-<F1>), advance one line at a time (<Ctrl>-<F1>), and reset the printer (<Ctrl>-<F2>) take effect immediately and eliminate the need to adjust the printer manually. The reset function is available only for the Epson MX/FX series. The function that causes the printer to skip over perforations (<Shift>-<F2>) will remain in effect until the printer is turned off or reset. Column length can be automatically adjusted to accommodate wide paper with <Ctrl>-<F3> or to prevent text from spilling over the edge of narrow paper with <Shift>-<F3>. The single-sheet option (<Ctrl>-<F4>) allows the entire page to be printed; otherwise, the printer's paper-out sensor prematurely aborts the printing.

Function	Enhanced Macro Key Assignments*
Draw a horizontal line	<Alt>-H
Draw a vertical line	<Alt>-V
Vertical backspace	<Alt>-O
Change graphics fonts	<Alt>-I
Graphics character	
Upper left corner	<Alt>-1
Upper right corner	<Alt>-2
Lower right corner	<Alt>-3
Lower left corner	<Alt>-4
Four-way intersection	<Alt>-5
Left intersection	<Alt>-6
Right intersection	<Alt>-7
Up intersection	<Alt>-8
Down intersection	<Alt>-9

* Equivalent function does not exist in the original macro functions.

Table 2.5 *Block graphics functions and fonts.*

The remaining printer options control font styles. A particular font is enabled (turned on) with <Shift>-F*x* (where *x* is the number of the key assignment) and disabled (turned off) with <Ctrl>-F*x*. This arrangement has been consistently implemented and should therefore be easy to remember. As printer control characters are inserted, the text is automatically shifted to the right on the screen, but the document will be properly aligned when printed. The name of the font style invoked is also displayed on the command line as a helpful reminder. The italics font is available only on Epson printers with Graftrax. Page break (<Shift>-<F10>) is the embedded equivalent of the skip-to-next-page macro, which is useful for starting new sections, chapters, or exhibits.

Block Graphics and Fonts

The macros for block graphics can add dimension to documents, reports, and screens through the visual representation of ideas (see Table 2.5). Three basic fonts composed of single lines, double lines, and solid lines have been created. The single-line font is in effect when the *Personal Editor* is started. Fonts can be changed with <Alt>-I. Horizontal lines in the current font are drawn with <Alt>-H and vertical lines with <Alt>-V. Each line is one inch long. <Backspace> is used to shorten horizontal line length. Vertical lines can be quickly trimmed to any desired length with a new vertical backspace feature, <Alt>-0. The four corners used to form boxes and rectangles are located on <Alt>-1 through <Alt>-4. (See the side bar "Building a Box" for an easy way to draw a four-sided figure.) Printing these fonts requires an IBM Graphics printer.

Although the disk must be accessed to load each new font, the small size of the graphics profiles keeps this lag to a minimum. Reducing the waiting time is also the reason that font #1 is duplicated in both the default profile, PE.PRO, and GRAPHIC1.PRO.

Creating the Macros

Since each new macro is given a unique key assignment, the macros are easy to install as a permanent part of the *Personal Editor.* As a precautionary measure, I strongly advise making a duplicate copy of the original profile file, PE.PRO. This can be done using the DOS command **COPY PE.PRO PE.BAK**. Next, issue the command **PE PE.PRO**; this loads the *Personal Editor* and starts a work space with the name of the default profile.

Carefully type in the new definitions from those in Figure 2.6. Each macro begins with *def,* followed by the key assignment, an equal sign, and a compendium of functions and commands. To ensure success, any characters not enclosed in quotation marks must be lowercase. Each macro begins in column one, and the entire macro must reside on one line.

The editing macros require only straightforward typing. However, the printer control and block graphics macros are more complex and involve using the *Personal Editor*'s extended ASCII function. The printer control macros each require sending a one-, two-, or three-con-

```
set margins 1 254 1
set tabs 5 10 20 30 40 50 60 70 80 90 100 110 120 130 140 150 160 170
         180 190
def up =        [up]
def down =      [down]
def left =      [left]
def c-left =    [left40]
def right =     [right]
def c-right =   [right40]
def pgup =      [page up] [top edge] [up] [up]
def c-pgup =    [top edge]
def pgdn =      [page down] [bottom edge] [down] [down]
def c-pgdn =    [bottom edge]
def home =      [begin line]
def c-home =    [top] [begin line]
def end =       [end line]
def c-end =     [bottom] [end line]
def ins =       [insert toggle]
def del =       [delete char]
def enter =     [begin line] [down] [indent]
def c-enter =   [execute]
def backspace =     [rubout]
def c-backspace = [confirm change] [cursor command] [execute]
def esc =       [command toggle]
def tab =       [tab]
def s-tab =     [backtab]
def f1=      [cursor command][begin line][erase end line] 'E PE.HLP'
             [execute]
def f2 =     [cursor command] [begin line] [erase end line] 'Macro WP.PRO'
             [execute]
def f3 =     [cursor command] [begin line] [erase end line] 'File' [execute]
def f4 =     [cursor command] [begin line] [erase end line] 'Quit' [execute]
def f5 =     [insert line]
def f6 =     [delete line]
def f7 =     [unmark] [mark char] [tab word] [left] [mark char] [begin mark]
             [delete mark]
def f8 =     [unmark] [mark char] [end line] [mark char] [begin mark] [delete
             mark]
def f9 =     [cursor command] [begin line] [erase end line] 'E' [execute]
             [cursor data]
def f10 =    [center line]
def a-f1 =   [shift left]
def a-f2 =   [shift right]
def a-f3 =   [cursor command] [begin line] [erase end line] 'Print'[execute]
def a-f4 =   [unmark] [top edge] [mark line] [bottom edge] [mark line]
             [cursor command] [begin line] [erase end line] 'E Prntpage'
             [execute] [cursor data] [copy mark] [cursor command] [begin line]
             [erase end line] 'Print' [execute] [unmark] 'Q' [execute] 'Y'
def a-f5 =   [cursor command] [begin line] [erase end line] 'E Prntmark'
             [execute] [cursor data] [copy mark] [cursor command] [begin
             line] [erase end line] 'Print' [execute] 'Q' [execute] 'Y'
def a-f6 =   [erase end line]
```

Figure 2.6 *Editing macros—file PE.PRO.*

trol-character sequence to the printer to enable or disable the desired function.

The printer control codes are assigned to <Alt>-<F5>, <Shift>-<F1> through <Shift>-<F10>, and <Ctrl>-<F1> through <Ctrl>-<F10>. All printer control codes are located within single quotation marks and entered by following these steps: press and hold the <Alt> key, then type the letter X. When the 'type a character' message appears at the bottom line, use the keyboard's ten-key numeric pad to type in the ASCII number that represents the control code. Now release the <Alt> key; the character that appears will cause the printer to perform the enhanced function.

Figure 2.6 contains ASCII numbers rather than the actual control

```
def a-f7 = [unmark] [mark char] [tab word] [left] [mark char] [begin mark]
           [fill mark] [execute] ' ' [unmark]
def a-f8 = [erase end line]
def a-f9 = [cursor command] [begin line] [erase end line] 'Set Display Mono'
           [execute]
def a-f10 = [cursor command] [begin line] [erase end line] 'Set Display
            Color 80' [execute]
def s-f1 = [cursor command] [begin line] [erase end line] 'E SkipTOF'
           [execute] [cursor data] 'X12' [cursor command] [begin line]
           [erase end line] 'Print' [execute] 'Q' [execute] 'Y'
def s-f2 = [cursor command] [begin line] [erase end line] 'E SkipPERF'
           [execute] [cursor data] 'X27X78' [cursor command] [begin line]
           [erase end line] 'Print' [execute] 'Q' [execute] 'Y'
def s-f3 = [cursor command] [begin line] [erase end line] 'E Width80'
           [execute] [cursor data] 'X27X81X80' [cursor command] [begin
           line] [erase end line] 'Print' [execute] 'Q' [execute] 'Y'
def s-f4 = [cursor command] [begin line] [erase end line] 'E Contin'
           [execute] [cursor data] 'X27X57' [cursor command] [begin line]
           [erase end line] 'Print' [execute] 'Q' [execute] 'Y'
def s-f5 = [insert mode] 'X15'   [replace mode] [cursor command] [begin
           line] [erase end line] 'Compressed ON' [cursor data]
def s-f6 = [insert mode] 'X27X71'  [replace mode] [cursor command] [begin
           line] [erase end line] 'Double Strike ON' [cursor data]
def s-f7 = [insert mode] 'X14' [replace mode] [cursor command] [begin line]
           [erase end line] 'Double Wide ON for Current Line' [cursor data]
def s-f8 = [insert mode] 'X27X69'  [replace mode] [cursor command] [begin
           line] [erase end line] 'Emphasized ON' [cursor data]
def s-f9 = [insert mode] 'X27X52'  [replace mode] [cursor command] [begin
           line] [erase end line] 'Italics ON' [cursor data]
def s-f10 = [insert mode] 'X12'  [replace mode] [cursor command] [begin
            line] [erase end line] 'Skip to Next Page' [cursor data]
def c-f1 = [cursor command] [begin line] [erase end line] 'E SkipLINE'
           [execute] [cursor data] 'X32 ' [cursor command] [begin line]
           [erase end line] 'Print' [execute] 'Q' [execute] 'Y'
def c-f2 = [cursor command] [begin line] [erase end line] 'E Reset'
           [execute] [cursor data] 'X27X64' [cursor command] [begin line]
           [erase end line] 'Print' [execute] 'Q' [execute] 'Y'
def c-f3 = [cursor command] [begin line] [erase end line] 'E Width132'
           [execute] [cursor data] 'X27X81X132' [cursor command] [begin
           line] [erase end line] 'Print' [execute] 'Q' [execute] 'Y'
def c-f4 = [cursor command] [begin line] [erase end line] 'E Single'
           [execute] [cursor data] 'X27X56' [cursor command] [begin line]
           [erase end line] 'Print' [execute] 'Q' [execute] 'Y'
def c-f5 = [insert mode] 'X18'  [replace mode] [cursor command] [begin
           line] [erase end line] 'Compressed OFF' [cursor data]
def c-f6 = [insert mode] 'X27X72' [replace mode] [cursor command] [begin
           line] [erase end line] 'Double Strike OFF' [cursor data]
def c-f7 = [insert mode] 'X20' [replace mode]  [cursor command] [begin
           line] [erase end line] 'Double Wide OFF' [cursor data]
def c-f8 = [insert mode] 'X27X70' [replace mode] [cursor command] [begin
           line] [erase end line] 'Emphasized OFF' [cursor data]
def c-f9 = [insert mode] 'X27X53'  [replace mode] [cursor command] [begin
           line] [erase end line] 'Italics OFF' [cursor data]
```

Figure 2.6 *(continued)*

characters that are generated. This eliminates the need for translating the graphics control codes into ASCII equivalents, a tedious process that requires a journey into the more esoteric appendices of the Guide to Operations and your printer manual. Each control character (remember, there can be up to three) is preceded by an X. For instance, the double-strike print option (<Shift>-<F6>) contains the sequence X27X71, which corresponds to the ASCII numeric values 27 and 71. Accordingly, the correct control characters are generated by pressing <Alt>-X, typing 27 on the numeric keypad, pressing <Alt>-X again, then typing 71 on the pad.

```
def c-f10 =
def a-1 = 'X218' [left] [mark block] [right]
def a-2 = 'X191' [down] [left]
def a-3 = 'X217' [begin mark] [unmark] [down]
def a-4 = 'X192'
def a-5 = 'X197'
def a-6 = 'X180'
def a-7 = 'X195'
def a-8 = 'X193' [down] [left]
def a-9 = 'X194'
def a-0 = [up] ' ' [left]
def a-a = [undo]
def a-b = [mark block]
def a-c = [mark char]
def a-d = [delete mark]
def a-e = [end mark]
def a-f = [fill mark] ' ' [unmark]
def a-g = [lowercase]
def a-h = 'X196X196X196X196X196X196X196X196X196X196'
def a-i = [cursor command] [begin line] [erase end line] 'M Graphic2.pro'
          [execute]
def a-j = [join]
def a-k = [insert line] [begin line] '....5...10...15...20...25...30...35...
          40...45...50...55...60...65...70...75...80' [mark line] [begin
          line] [down]
def a-l = [mark line]
def a-m = [move mark]
def a-n = 'Notabs' [execute]
def a-o = [overlay block]
def a-p = [cursor data] [unmark] [mark line] [find blank line] [up] [mark
          line] [reflow] [end mark] [down] [down] [unmark]
def a-q = [cursor command] [begin line] [erase end line] 'E .Unnamed'
          [execute]
def a-r = [redraw]
def a-s = [split]
def a-t = [uppercase]
def a-u = [unmark]
def a-v = 'X179' [down] [left] 'X179' [down] [left] 'X179' [down] [left]
          'X179' [down] [left]
def a-w = [begin mark]
def a-x = [escape]
def a-y = [cursor command] [begin line] [erase end line] 'Save' [execute]
def a-z = [copy mark]
```

Figure 2.6 *(continued)*

Block graphics have been assigned to the keys from <Alt>-1 through <Alt>-9. For reference, the three fonts and their ASCII numeric equivalents can be found in Appendix G of the IBM BASIC manual. The same X notation scheme discussed above has been followed to make it easier to create the graphics fonts.

The final step is to save the work space containing the new macro definitions back to the disk using the File command. From now on each time the *Personal Editor* is used, the new profile containing the enhanced macros will be loaded and available for use.

Block graphics font #1 (Figure 2.7), font #2 (Figure 2.8), and font #3 (Figure 2.9) each use key assignments <Alt>-1 through <Alt>-9 for consistency in drawing objects. To reuse these key assignments each font must be stored in a separate profile. These files have been named GRAPHIC1.PRO, GRAPHIC2.PRO, and GRAPHIC3.PRO, respectively. Each file relies on the extended ASCII function to generate the graphics characters, and the now-familiar X notation is used again to reduce installation time.

The remaining profile, WP.PRO, is used to redefine selected key assignments and to add the additional line-spacing options (see Figure 2.10). Follow the same edit procedure to enter the macros, and save the work space to the disk file. This completes the installation process. Now you can enjoy the power and versatility afforded by the enhanced macros.

```
def a-1 = 'X218' [left] [mark block] [right]
def a-2 = 'X191' [down] [left]
def a-3 = 'X217' [begin mark] [unmark] [down]
def a-4 = 'X192'
def a-5 = 'X197'
def a-6 = 'X180'
def a-7 = 'X195'
def a-8 = 'X193' [down] [left]
def a-9 = 'X194'
def a-0 = [up] ' ' [left]
def a-h = 'X196X196X196X196X196X196X196X196X196X196'
def a-v = 'X179' [down] [left] 'X179' [down] [left] 'X179' [down] [left]
          'X179' [down] [left]
def a-i = [cursor command] [begin line] [erase end line] 'M Graphic2.pro'
          [execute]
```

Figure 2.7 *Single-line block graphics font—file GRAPHIC1.PRO.*

```
def a-1 = 'X201' [left] [mark block] [right]
def a-2 = 'X187' [down] [left]
def a-3 = 'X188' [begin mark] [unmark] [down]
def a-4 = 'X200'
def a-5 = 'X206'
def a-6 = 'X185'
def a-7 = 'X204'
def a-8 = 'X202' [down] [left]
def a-9 = 'X203'
def a-0 = [up] ' ' [left]
def a-h = 'X205X205X205X205X205X205X205X205X205X205'
def a-v = 'X186' [down] [left] 'X186' [down] [left] 'X186' [down] [left]
          'X186' [down] [left]
def a-i = [cursor command] [begin line] [erase end line] 'M Graphic3.pro'
          [execute]
```

Figure 2.8 *Double-line block graphics font—file GRAPHIC2.PRO.*

```
def a-1 = 'X219' [left] [mark block] [right]
def a-2 = 'X219' [down] [left]
def a-3 = 'X219' [begin mark] [unmark] [down]
def a-4 = 'X219'
def a-5 = 'X176'
def a-6 = 'X221'
def a-7 = 'X222'
def a-8 = 'X223'
def a-9 = 'X220' [down] [left]
def a-0 = [up] ' ' [left]
def a-h = 'X219X219X219X219X219X219X219X219X219X219'
def a-v = 'X219' [down] [left] 'X219' [down] [left] 'X219' [down] [left]
          'X219' [down] [left]
def a-i = [cursor command] [begin line] [erase end line] 'M Graphic1.pro'
          [execute]
```

Figure 2.9 *Solid-line block graphics font—file GRAPHIC3.PRO.*

```
set margins 5 70 5
def home = [begin line] [down] [tab word]
def ins =  [insert toggle] [unmark] [mark line] [find blank line] [up]
           [mark line] [reflow] [begin mark] [unmark]
def tab =   [tab word]
def s-tab = [backtab word]
def enter = [unmark] [split] [insert line] [down] [mark line] [find blank
            line] [up] [mark line] [reflow] [begin mark] [unmark] [tab]
            [replace mode]
def f2 =  [cursor command] [begin line] [erase end line] 'Macro PE.PRO'
          [execute]
def a-p = [down] [find blank line] [begin line] [down] [mark char] [find
          blank line] [begin mark] [unmark] [tab word]
def a-1 = [cursor command] [begin line] [erase end line] 'E Spacing'
          [execute] [cursor data] 'X27X65X10' [cursor command] [begin
          line] [erase end line] 'print' [execute] 'Q' [execute] 'Y'
def a-2 = [cursor command] [begin line] [erase end line] 'E Spacing'
          [execute] [cursor data] 'X27X65X12' [cursor command] [begin
          line] [erase end line] 'print' [execute] 'Q' [execute] 'Y'
def a-3 = [cursor command] [begin line] [erase end line] 'E Spacing'
          [execute] [cursor data] 'X27X65X18' [cursor command] [begin
          line] [erase end line] 'print' [execute] 'Q' [execute] 'Y'
def a-4 = [cursor command] [begin line] [erase end line] 'E Spacing'
          [execute] [cursor data] 'X27X65X24' [cursor command] [begin
          line] [erase end line] 'print' [execute] 'Q' [execute] 'Y'
def a-5 = [cursor command] [begin line] [erase end line] 'E Spacing'
          [execute] [cursor data] 'X27X65X32' [cursor command] [begin
          line] [erase end line] 'print' [execute] 'Q' [execute] 'Y'
def a-6 =
def a-7 =
def a-8 =
def a-9 =
def a-0 =
```

Figure 2.10 *Word processing macros—file WP.PRO.*

Steven J. Lagreca is a systems engineer at IBM's National Accounts Division, specializing in work station and office automation communications. The author wishes to acknowledge Chapin Day for providing portions of the original macros used within this article. This article was published in PC World *Volume 2, Number 11. It was originally published in* Update on IBM Software for the IBM Personal Computer Family©, *an IBM publication.*

Building a Box

Follow these steps to draw a box around text using block graphics on the IBM Graphics printer:

1) Position the cursor at the upper left corner of the text to be boxed. Create the first corner by pressing <Alt>-1.

2) Create a horizontal line by pressing <Alt>-H. Use the <Backspace> key, if necessary, to shorten the line.

3) Create the upper right corner by pressing <Alt>-2.

4) Create a vertical line by pressing <Alt>-V. Use the vertical backspace (<Alt>-0), if necessary, to shorten the line.

5) Create the lower right corner by pressing <Alt>-3. The cursor will automatically be repositioned to the upper left corner.

6) Create a second vertical line opposite the first.

7) Create the lower left corner by pressing <Alt>-4.

8) Finish the enclosure with a second horizontal line.

Getting the Word

Burton L. Alperson

Microsoft Word provides an embarrassment of riches. While other microcomputer word processors offer some of the features available in *Word,* none has combined features such as screen orientation, different format styles, and stored vocabularies in a single package. These advanced capabilities have been interwoven with outstanding human engineering.

However, no major advance in technology can be achieved without penalty. To use *Word* to best advantage, one must master some new concepts. While they are not particularly difficult to understand and use, they are unfamiliar to people who have been using other word processors. Microsoft's cryptic documentation makes these concepts unnecessarily obscure.

Word's Hierarchy

Before discussing the advanced features of *Word,* one must address the way the program structures a document. Three concepts are particularly important: divisions, paragraphs, and characters. It is most useful to view these concepts as members of a hierarchy: characters exist within paragraphs; paragraphs exist within divisions. In general, a division is any portion of a document that maintains a consistent page layout. For some documents it may be necessary to define only a single division. A term paper, a letter, a memo, and the chapters of a book are examples of documents that probably would require just one division. If the document includes such items as a table of contents, an appendix, a specially formatted title page, or tabular material with special formatting requirements, other divisions become necessary. The definition of a division depends on consistent formatting rather than length.

Formatting a division involves deciding whether you want page numbers and defining the physical parameters of the paper and margins, the placement of page numbers, the type of automatic page numbering (Arabic, uppercase or lowercase Roman, uppercase or lowercase alphabetic), the starting page number, and the locations of footnotes and running heads. You can define or change these parameters only by telling *Word* to format a division; they cannot be selected from any other menu.

A "paragraph" is any block of text that ends with <Enter>. This is a common definition used in most word processors. Formatting at the paragraph level enables you to set the alignment of paragraphs (flush left, centered, flush right, justified), the amount and type of indentation for first lines of paragraphs (a negative number produces a "hanging indent," a positive number produces a normal indent, and 0 produces a block paragraph), the amount of indentation for lines other than the first line (e.g., for extended quotations), line-spacing within and between paragraphs, and whether a paragraph can be broken between two pages.

The lowest level of the *Word* hierarchy is the character. In character formatting you decide how you want any set of characters to look in the document. Many of the parameters under your control at this level are called print enhancements in other word processors. Character formatting controls boldfacing, italics, underlining, small caps, cases, double underlining, subscripting, superscripting, overstriking, print fonts, and font sizes.

Galleries and Glossaries

To use *Word* in the simplest possible way, you need learn little more than the keyboard conventions and the concepts of divisions, paragraphs, and characters. The worst that can happen is that you won't have much more power at your disposal than you'd have using *WordStar.* However, using *Word* in this way is like driving a Porsche at 55 miles per hour; it does the job, but it seems like a waste.

A few additional concepts will enable you to take advantage of the full power of *Word.* All the parameters under your control for divisions, paragraphs, and characters may be saved in a special file called a style sheet. If you have created a document with a previously saved style sheet, this style will be applied automatically to the document. Each time you return to the document it will be loaded into memory with all its margins, tabs, and other formatting information intact.

Moreover, you can alter formats by attaching different style sheets to a document. It's useful to have a draft and a final sheet for each style you wish to define. The only difference between the two sheets might be that the draft style is single-spaced and the final style is double-spaced. This practice enables you to have more text on the screen for editing and composing and yet to retain the ability to print a double-spaced final version quickly.

Such a strategy is not practical in other word processors, which require you to reformat manually, paragraph by paragraph. In *Word,* only a few keystrokes are necessary to attach any style to an entire document. Typing <Esc> F S S *style* tells the program to engage the menu (<Esc>), format (F), style (S), and sheet (S) and type the name of the style or point to it in a list of styles (*style*).

You can keep a collection of style sheets on file in a menu called a "Gallery" (*Word*'s term to describe a library of styles). Your gallery might contain separate styles for articles, letters, memos, documents to be telecommunicated, documents formatted for CRT representation, etc. Each of these styles might exist in draft and final forms.

Style attributes are easy to invoke. If you have defined the way you wish a normal paragraph to look and named this attribute "NP," you need only type <Alt>-N P to begin typing normal paragraphs. This attribute will remain in force until you change it by engaging another attribute.

The "Glossary" is another way of saving and retrieving information relevant to a document or document type. If you repeatedly use certain words, phrases, paragraphs, or pages, you may assign an abbreviation to the string in one or more glossaries. Inserting the item in your document requires nothing more than typing the abbreviation and striking <F3>. You can use any glossary with any document, just as you can use style sheets.

Glossaries may contain limited formatting information as well as words and phrases. You can include information about hard page breaks with the text. If a glossary item has been saved in centered format, it will be inserted in centered format if the style of the document permits it.

Creating Style Sheets

Each style attribute you define has a specific purpose. It might exist to format a division, a paragraph, or characters. *Word* suggests several alternative labels for each of these purposes. These labels are called "usages."

When you define the styles for divisions, for example, you can employ the usages Normal, Front Matter, Appendix, Index, Contents, and Other. The names are meant to be suggestions; you don't have to use Appendix as a usage for an appendix. But you must choose one of these labels.

If you call a division Normal, you are telling *Word* that you wish this attribute to be the default for the style sheet. If you name a style sheet Normal, it will load automatically with the program and remain in force until you override it.

The suggested usages for paragraphs are Normal Paragraph, Nested, Footnote, Quotation, Table, Heading, List, Title, Author, Affiliation, Copyright, Running Head, and Other Paragraph. Usages available for characters are Normal Character, Emphasis, Index Term, Figure Reference, Sequence Number, Folio (page number), Superscript, Subscript, and Other Character.

These predefined usages may not supply enough options to meet all your needs. For example, you might need several kinds of headings, such as centered uppercase, centered lowercase, and flush left underlined. Here the concept of a "variant" becomes useful. You can label the most common heading variant 1, the next heading variant 2, and so on. (The latest version of *Word,* Version 2.0, simplifies this process considerably by providing only three usages: Character, Paragraph, Division, and simply numbering variants.)

Scientific Style

When I write a journal article I am required to use a format prescribed by the American Psychological Association (APA). The format is detailed and rigid and has been adopted by many scientific disciplines. Consequently, the APA style serves as a useful model for the construction of style sheets for articles.

Interpersonal Phenomenology in Dyads

1

Interpersonal Phenomenology as a Function of Sexual

Orientation, Gender, Sentiment, and Sex Roles

in Long Term Dyadic Relationships

Studies of marital relationships have demonstrated the importance of factors such as perceived similarity between the person (p) and other (o) (Burgess, Locke, & Thomes, 1971; Dymond, 1954, Murstein & Beck, 1972), p's validation of o's self concept (Laing, Phillipson, & Lee, 1966; Lucky, 1960), p's expectations that o agrees with p (Hawkins & Johnson, 1969; Ort, 1950), p's feelings of being understood by o (Laing, et al., 1966; Navran, 1967), understanding, or the accuracy with which p expects agreement or disagreement (Christensen & Wallace, 1976; Corsini, 1956; Dymond, 1954; Laing, et al., 1966; Murstein & Beck, 1972; Newmark, Woody, & Ziff, 1977; Tiggle, Peters, Kelley & Vincent, 1979) and realization or the accuracy with which p feels understood and misunderstood by o (Laing, et al., 1966). These variables have been shown to be related to enduring and satisfying heterosexual marriages.

Figure 2.11 *Sample manuscript paragraph in APA format.*

Figure 2.11 shows part of a typical manuscript page in APA format. Figure 2.12 shows *Word*'s representation of the style sheet responsible for formatting the manuscript. I have saved the style sheet under the name APAPS.STY to indicate that it produces final copy in APA format with proportional spacing. The style sheet in Figure 2.12 was printed by using the Print command in *Word*'s Gallery menu.

I have rearranged the Items in Figure 2.12 from the order in which they were written so that I can use the screen display of the sheet for fast reference. Items that I seldom need are placed toward the end of the document. Rearranging style attributes is easy, since style sheets can be edited in much the same way as other documents.

The first attribute created was for the basic APA division setup (Item 23). The first line of this item reveals that the key code is ND, which informs you that you can invoke the attribute at any time by typing <Alt>-N D. The usage is Normal Division, variant *a.* Variant *a* combined with the word Normal means that this attribute will be the default value. The second line of the attribute shows the paper size (8½ by 11 inches) and indicates that the page numbers (Folios) will be in Arabic numerals.

The rest of the information tells you that margins will be 1½ inches all around, with top and bottom running heads at ¾ inch and ½ inch from the top and bottom of the page, respectively. The last notation indicates that notes will be placed at the end of the article.

To create a style attribute, engage the Gallery menu (<Esc> G) and then invoke the Insert function (I). Now you can name the attribute, which entails defining the key code, usage, and variant and supplying any remarks.

Having named the attribute, you

```
1       Emphasis a                                    NORMAL CHARACTER
          BoldPS (roman a) 12.
2   U   Emphasis d                                    UNDERLINE
          BoldPS (roman a) 12 Underlined.
3   B   Emphasis b                                    BOLDFACE
          BoldPS (roman a) 12 Bold.
4   C   Other paragraph a                             CENTER TEXT
          BoldPS (roman a) 12/24. Centered.
5   -   Subscript 1                                   SUBSCRIPT
          BoldPS (roman a) 12 Subscript.
6   +   Superscript 1                                 SUPERSCRIPT
          BoldPS (roman a) 12 Superscript.
7   TI  Title a                                       APA TITLE PG: TITLE, AU, AFF
          BoldPS (roman a) 12/24. Centered.
8   RH  Running head 1                                APA RUNNING HEAD FORMAT
          BoldPS (roman a) 12/24. Flush right, right indent 15 p10.
9       Folio a                                       BOLDPS PAGE NUMBERS
          BoldPS (roman a) 12.
10  H1  Heading 1                                     HEAD-    5 LEVELS
          BoldPS (roman a) 12/24 Uppercase. Centered (keep in one column).
11  H2  Heading 2                                     HEAD-12345 LEVELS
          BoldPS (roman a) 12/24. Centered (keep in one column).
12  H3  Heading 3                                     HEAD-   45 LEVELS
          BoldPS (roman a) 12/24 Underlined. Centered (keep in one column).
13  H4  Heading 4                                     HEAD- 2345 LEVELS
          BoldPS (roman a) 12/24 Underlined. Flush left (keep in one column).
14  H5  Emphasis c                                    HEAD-  345 LEVELS (+TAB & .)
          BoldPS (roman a) 12 Underlined.
15  OP  Other paragraph d                             BLOCK PARAGRAPH
          BoldPS (roman a) 12/24. Justified.
16  NP  Normal paragraph                              APA PARAGRAPH
          BoldPS (roman a) 12/24. Justified (first line indent 5 p10).
17  EQ  Other paragraph b                             CASE STUDY OR EXTEND. QUOTE
          BoldPS (roman a) 12/24. Justified, Left indent 5 p10 (first line
          indent 10 p10).
18  O1  List 1                                        OUTLINE LEVEL 1
          BoldPS (roman a) 12/24. Justified, Left indent 4.2 p10 (first line
          indent -5 p10) (keep in one column).
19  O2  List 2                                        OUTLINE LEVEL 2
          BoldPS (roman a) 12/24. Justified, Left indent 9.2 p10 (first line
          indent -5 p10) (keep in one column).
20  O3  List 3                                        OUTLINE LEVEL 3
          BoldPS (roman a) 12/24. Justified, Left indent 14.2 p10 (first line
          indent -5 p10) (keep in one column).
21  O4  List 4                                        OUTLINE LEVEL 4
          BoldPS (roman a) 12/24. Justified, Left indent 19.2 p10 (first line
          indent -5 p10) (keep in one column).
22  RF  List a                                        APA REFERENCE FORMAT
          BoldPS (roman a) 12/24. Justified, Left indent 3 p10 (first line
          indent -5 p10) (keep in one column).
23  ND  Normal division a                             APA STANDARD SETUP
          Page break. Page length 110 p10; width 85 p10. Folios Arabic. Top
          margin 15 p10; bottom 15 p10; left 15 p10; right 15 p10. Top running
          head at 7.5 p10. Bottom running head at 5 p10. Footnotes at end.
```

(continues)

Figure 2.12 *Style sheet for APA format.*

```
24 TD Other division a                                    APA TABLE SETUP
       Page break. Page length 110 p10; width 85 p10. Folios Arabic at 10
       p10 from top 67.5 p10, from left. Top margin 15 p10; bottom 15 p10;
       left 0.79 p10; right 0.79 p10. Top running head at 7.5 p10. Bottom
       running head at 5 p10. Footnotes on same page.
25 TT Heading 6                                           APA TABLE TITLE FORMAT
       BoldPS (roman a) 12/24 Underlined. Flush left (keep in one column).
26 TH Table a                                             APA TABLE HEADERS
       BoldPS (roman a) 12/24. Flush left (keep in one column). Tabs at: 10
       p10 (right flush), 15.83 p10 (right flush), 21.66 p10 (right flush),
       27.5 p10 (right flush), 33.33 p10 (right flush), 39.16 p10 (right
       flush), 45 p10 (right flush), 50.83 p10 (right flush), 56.66 p10
       (right flush), 62.5 p10 (right flush), 68.33 p10 (right flush),
       74.16 p10 (right flush), 80 p10 (right flush).
27 TB Table b                                             APA TABLE BODY FORMAT
       BoldPS (roman a) 12/24. Flush left (keep in one column). Tabs at:
       7.5 p10 (dec. aligned), 13.33 p10 (dec. aligned), 19.16 p10 (dec.
       aligned), 25 p10 (dec. aligned), 30.83 p10 (dec. aligned), 36.66 p10
       (dec. aligned), 42.5 p10 (dec. aligned), 48.33 p10 (dec. aligned),
       54.16 p10 (dec. aligned), 60 p10 (dec. aligned), 65.83 p10 (dec.
       aligned), 71.66 p10 (dec. aligned), 77.5 p10 (dec. aligned).
28    Footnote reference a                                FOOTNOTE REFERENCE
       BoldPS (roman a) 12 Superscript.
```

Figure 2.12 *(continued)*

may define all aspects of the format. Since the usage has been named Normal Division, you may define only division attributes here. Defining a style format is identical to defining a direct format; you simply choose menu items and make appropriate entries. No aspect of this attribute is fixed in concrete. You may return at any time to modify the name or format.

The next attribute I defined was the default paragraph style (Item 16). The technique for creating this attribute is almost identical to the sequence described above. The only difference is that since the usage has been defined as a Normal Paragraph, you can access Character, Paragraph, and Tab formatting. The item shows that these paragraphs differ from *Word*'s own defaults in the print font, the justification, and the amount of the first line indent. The notation 12/24 means that the print size is 12 points (10 pitch) and the line spacing is 24 points (double-spaced).

Items 1 through 6 reinstate *Word*'s default key codes. If you didn't reinstate these codes you would still have access to the functions, but you would have to precede your commands with an X. For example, you would have to type <Alt>-X C instead of <Alt>-C to center text. Microsoft's choice of defaults is so natural and easy to remember that I prefer to keep them in their original form.

The choice between character and paragraph usage in Items 1 through 6 is governed by what I wish to accomplish. Subscript, Superscript, and the different Emphasis variants are character usages, which means that I can control the style or vertical location of individual characters in a line. The Other Paragraph usage gives me access to centering and line spacing.

Item 7 controls almost all aspects of an APA title page: title, author, and affiliation. The only element that remains to be indicated is the running head, which must appear toward the bottom of the title page.

This aspect is controlled by Item 15, Block Paragraph style.

Item 9 (Folio *a*) is supposed to enable you to define the print font of the page numbers. At this writing, the program has a bug and the item does not work. Consequently, I am forced to respond to a prompt to change the print thimble for each page number when I attempt to print on my letter quality printer. Another alternative, using Draft mode for printing, doesn't work with this style sheet because Draft mode produces strange effects on *Word*'s proportional spacing algorithms.

Microsoft has corrected the inability to define print fonts for folios in all versions later than version 1.0. If you have version 1.0 there is a way around the problem: enter the Running Head menu, select the page command, and press <Alt>-<Space> <Space>. The program will recognize the style sheet attribute and behave properly.

APA reference style requires the first line in each reference to be flush with the left margin and the remaining lines to be indented by three characters. This is a "hanging indent" in *Word*'s language, and it is accomplished with Item 22.

Headings in APA style must conform to a complicated set of rules. The automatic formatting of all levels of headings in Items 10 through 14 saves a lot of time. The headings are arranged from the highest to the lowest levels. Remarks attached to these items remind me that if I need five levels, I should use the order of subordination H1, H2, H3, H4, and H5. For four levels I should use H2, H3, H4, and H5; three levels require H2, H4, and H5; two levels require H2 and H4; and one level requires H2.

Items 24 through 27 are concerned with tabular material. The techniques described in those items would not work for all APA authors; however, since most of my publications deal with data of a single order of magnitude, shown with two-decimal accuracy, it is helpful to have a consistent table format on file.

Item 24 creates a new division for tables with redefined margins. Items 25 and 26 set up the title and the column headers. Item 26 sets up a series of decimal tabs in the appropriate locations for most of my tabular work. The decimal tabs in Item 27 (Table Body) are coordinated with the flush-right tabs of Item 26 (Table Headers), making it easy to lay out columns with the appropriate headers. I have only to type <Alt>-T D (for Table Division, Item 24) to engage the table format. I can return to standard APA text format at any time by typing <Alt>-N D (for Normal Division, Item 23).

Items 18 through 21 are not part of APA format, but they are so useful that I include them in all style sheets for articles. These items set up any of four hierarchical levels of indentation for outlining. Even if I don't intend to include an outline as part of the text, I can use these items to keep track of the organization of an article. After I've created an outline, I can store it in a file or in the glossary; this technique allows me to refer to the outline rapidly. Another option is to keep the outline constantly in view in one window while working on the text of the article in another window.

Two formatting features in this style sheet, running heads and footnotes, remain to be discussed. *Word* can set up multiple-line running heads with or without page numbers. Item 8 automatically places running heads in APA format (flush right). Creating a running head is a two-step process: definition followed by location formatting.

If you want a flush-right running head consisting of "Getting the Word" on the first line and automatic flush-right page numbering on the next line, first enter the running head area of the document with **<Esc> J R** (engage menu, jump to running head). Then type **Getting the Word<Enter>page<F3>**.

Entering 'page <F3>' invokes a special predefined *Word* glossary function that generates automatic page numbering in the indicated location. Since the flush-right format has been defined already as a default in Item 8 of the style sheet, no further action is required for alignment.

However, *Word* still does not know how you want your running head placed on the page. The next step is location formatting. You select the text of the running head, which is still visible on the screen, and engage running head formatting (<Esc>-F R, meaning engage menu, format running head). This option enables you to tell the program where to locate the running head (odd pages, even pages, top or bottom of page) and whether to omit the head on the first page.

Incidentally, one undocumented characteristic of the program can produce problems. You cannot call for page numbering in a division command and also have a running head if the head and the page number are to appear on the same half of the page. The easiest way to solve this problem is to turn off division page numbering and let the running head control page numbering.

Word has an elegant system for automatic footnoting. You move the cursor to the appropriate location for the footnote reference number and engage the Format Footnote mode in the menu (<Esc> F F <Enter>). This action automatically inserts a correctly numbered footnote reference at the cursor location and moves the cursor to the footnote storage area so that you can immediately type the text of the footnote. You can toggle back and forth between the footnote text and the reference location with a Jump command. The footnote reference is appropriately superscripted, since it takes on the default format specified in Item 28 of the style sheet.

Inserting a new footnote reference automatically renumbers footnotes that follow it. Deleting a footnote reference removes the footnote text and renumbers the remaining footnotes appropriately.

CONTINUED:

She tries to get up but cannot. Stuart comes back, a bit annoyed.

MOIRA
I'm too tired.

STUART
No, you're not, you're just talking yourself into it.

He grabs her arm and begins to pull her up.

MOIRA
Please...

STUART
You have to...you have to do it. There's nothing wrong with you.

Moira begins to cry.

MOIRA
Stu, there is...

Looking at her, Stuart's whole demeanor collapses. He plops down next to her and holds her.

STUART
(forcing optimism)
We had to give it a shot, didn't we?

(pause)
We'll come back here again when you're all better. King and queen of the mountain.

Moira looks into his eyes, looks down again, forces a smile. Stuart gently takes her face in his hands and kisses her.

53 ANOTHER ANGLE

From below, CAMERA looks up at Moira and Stuart, including the expansive view behind them.

54 INT. BROWNING BEDROOM - DAY

Moira is standing in front of a full length mirror, as if practicing. She is quite distraught.

CONTINUED:

Figure 2.13 *Sample screenplay format.*

Writing in APA format is not normally one of my favorite activities. But I am looking forward to my next journal article so that I can give this style sheet a workout. It is working very well as I write this article.

Script Style

Screenwriters have it tough. In addition to the usual problems that confront all writers, they are faced with complicated and inflexible formatting requirements. Major studios will not even look at an improperly formatted script. *Word* makes producing this format seem like child's play.

Figure 2.13 is a typical page from a script that has been formatted in the style required by a major studio.

```
1  C  Heading a                                    CHARACTER
         BoldPS (roman a) 12 Uppercase. Centered.
2  D  Other paragraph a                            DIALOGUE
         BoldPS (roman a) 12. Justified, Left indent 1.5", right indent 1.5",
         space after 1 li (keep in one column).
3  N  Normal paragraph                             NARRATIVE (ACTION DESC.)
         BoldPS (roman a) 12. Justified, Left indent 0.75", right indent
         0.75", space after 1 li (keep in one column).
4  P  Heading c                                    PARENTHETICAL
         BoldPS (roman a) 12. Flush right, right indent 3.17".
5  S  Heading b                                    SHOT # & DESCRIPTION
         BoldPS (roman a) 12 Uppercase. Flush left, space after 1 li. Tabs
         at: 0.67" (left flush), 6.75" (right flush).
6     Normal division a
         Page break. Page length 11"; width 8.5". Folios Arabic. Top margin
         1"; bottom 1"; left 1"; right 1". Top running head at 0.5". Bottom
         running head at 0.5". Footnotes on same page.
```

Figure 2.14 *Style sheet for screenplays.*

Figure 2.14 shows the style sheet that formatted this script. A separate format is required for each of five aspects of the script. Character references (name of the person speaking) must be uppercase and centered, with no space after the line (Item 1). Dialogue must be in block paragraph style, centered, and indented, with an extra space after each paragraph (Item 2). Narratives or action descriptions must be centered block paragraphs with an extra line after each paragraph (Item 3). The right margin of parentheticals (cues to the actors on interpreting dialogue) must be in the center of the page, and there must be no extra space between the parenthetical and the next line (Item 4). Shot numbers must extend beyond the left and right margins of narratives; shot descriptions (Item 5) must be uppercase.

A script is an interesting application because it demonstrates the usefulness of glossaries. Notice that the word CONTINUED followed by a colon appears in the upper left and lower right corners of the page; studios require this when a given script aspect is continued from one page to the next. The word must appear in the lower right corner preceding the page break and in the upper left corner of the next page. This whole sequence was stored in the glossary under the reference "CP" (a mnemonic for continuation page). After storing it, I had only to type C P-<F3>, and the word and appropriate page break would appear immediately.

The cast of characters was also stored in the glossary. The first time I typed the character name "Moira," I invoked the Character function from the style sheet with <Alt>-C. This centered the name and displayed it in uppercase. Then I saved this text in the glossary (<Esc> C M, for engage menu, copy to glossary under the abbreviation M). From that point on, I merely had to type M <F3> to make Moira's name appear in character format. All other characters were treated in the same way. I saved the glossary so that I could use it in future sessions without having to redefine the text.

CRT Layout Style

Many microcomputer users frequently need to format documents like the one shown in Figure 2.15 for display on CRTs (cathode ray tubes). This CRT style is helpful in preparing notices to be posted on bulletin boards or communications services like The Source or CompuServe. One of my few disappointments with *Word* is that the program provides no direct way to accomplish this task. However, a roundabout technique can be employed.

Figure 2.16 shows a style sheet for CRT formatting. Notice that measurements are specified not in inches but in 10-pitch characters; since the sheet refers to a CRT it is much easier to work in character measurement. *Word* gives you the luxury of specifying parameters in inches, centimeters, 10- or 12-pitch characters, or points. The program automatically handles all necessary conversions.

Items 1 through 3 contain nothing new. They allow for centering, block paragraphs of 74 characters with an extra following line, and indented paragraphs. Item 4 defines the page length to be equivalent to about one screen (23 lines). All margins are set to 0 so that there is no horizontal or vertical offset on the screen.

Word has no direct facility for saving formatted ASCII files. Consequently, after creating your document you must deal with it differently from the way you handle a document for normal printing. The program enables you to save a file in a special form so that you can send it to your printer with all printer con-

```
                         CRT LAYOUT EXAMPLE #1
     This is an example of a CRT layout style.  The paragraph format is an
indented first line with no extra lines between paragraphs.
     You might use a style sheet like this to post a notice on a service
like the one provided by the Source Telecommunicating company called the
SOURCE  or  the  one  provided  by  Compuserve  Information  Service  called
COMPUSERVE.
     Microsoft's WORD  program makes this operation a bit clumsy since it
provides no utility to send formatted ASCII text directly to a file.
```

Figure 2.15 *Sample CRT layout in indented paragraph style.*

```
1  C  Other paragraph b                          CENTER LINE
        Pica (modern a) 12. Centered, right indent 4 p10.
2  NP Normal paragraph                           INDENTED PARAGRAPHS
        Pica (modern a) 12. Justified (first line indent 5 p10), right
        indent 4 p10.
3  BP Other paragraph a                          BLOCK PARAGRAPHS
        Pica (modern a) 12. Justified, right indent 4 p10, space after 1 li.
4     Normal division a                          CRT LAYOUT FOR TELECOM.
        Page break. Page length 39 p10; width 78 p10. Folios Arabic. Top
        margin 0 p10; bottom 0 p10; left 0 p10; right 0 p10. Top running
        head at 5 p10. Bottom running head at 5 p10. Footnotes on same page.
```

Figure 2.16 *Style sheet for CRT layout.*

trol codes intact by using a DOS COPY or TYPE command. Type <**Esc**> **P** *filename* (for engage menu, print, *filename*).

To produce a correctly formatted ASCII file, you must trick the program into thinking it is dealing with a crude teletype printer. You can do so by specifying that your printer is a TTY in the Print Options menu (versions of *Word* later than 1.0 contain a printer driver called "Plain" for this purpose). The technique is not particularly elegant, but it works. It would be helpful if Microsoft would add a direct routine for this purpose in a revision of the program.

WordStar to Word and Back

The existence of *Word* puts me in a bind. After a few weeks of using this program, I find it painful to return to *WordStar.* The step from *WordStar* to *Word* feels almost as great as the step from a typewriter to *WordStar.*

The "house program" currently used by many magazines and journals, including *PC World,* is *WordStar.* Copy telecommunicated or submitted on disk to these periodicals must be in *WordStar* format. Microsoft supplies a *WordStar*-to-*Word* conversion utility with *Word* that converts *WordStar* data files so that they are usable with *Word.* Predictably, they do not supply a utility that works in the opposite direction.

A partial solution to the problem is that *Word* will save unformatted files containing nothing but raw text, including spaces and carriage returns. These files can be read successfully by *WordStar.*

Of course, you must still reformat your document paragraph by paragraph once it is sent to *WordStar.* But at least you end up with a document in a format acceptable to many publications. As clumsy as this procedure is, it is worth the effort to be able to compose and edit text with *Word. WordStar* has an established base of users that is unlikely to disappear in the immediate future. There is a real need for a conversion utility that works in both directions.

Word is by no means a perfect program. Some rough edges and bugs should be worked out. Some of the print routines are problematic, and some of the screen scrolling techniques are disconcerting. In spite of these drawbacks, I would rather use this word processor than any other I have tried. In terms of elegance, power, and potential, it is the *1-2-3* of word processors.

Burton L. Alperson, Ph.D, is a professor of psychology at California State University at Los Angeles. He is also a Contributing Editor to PC World *and Director of Training and Development for Regent Data Systems in Los Angeles. This article was originally published in* PC World *Volume 2, Number 4.*

✲•✲ Star-Dot-Star

WordStar's pervasive presence in the word processing arena is reflected by the overwhelming number of submissions received about the program each year. *WordStar* tips in this roundup begin with "DOS to WordStar to DOS," which shows how to strip the high-bit characters from *WordStar* files as well as converting ASCII files to *WordStar* format. "Strip Ease" is a second program that filters *WordStar* to DOS format. Next, "Faster Searches" vastly accelerates *WordStar* search and replace operations. Then "The WordStar WIP File" shows a keyboard macro that reduces the work needed to transfer volatile RAM data onto floppies. Non-*WordStar* tips explain how to squeeze DOS onto *pfs:write* system disks ("pfs:write with DOS 2.00"), use the DOS PATH command with *PeachText* ("More PATH and PeachText"), and increase *Volkswriter*'s running speed ("VW in Overdrive").

DOS to WordStar to DOS

If you receive a text file via telecommunications, it will probably come to you in standard DOS format; that is, with each line terminated by a carriage return/linefeed sequence. If you try to edit that file using the *WordStar* word processing program, you'll discover that it's exceedingly difficult to reformat paragraphs after making revisions.

The problem arises because *WordStar* uses an end-of-line convention for its document files that is different from DOS files. Lines in a standard DOS file, such as a file created by the DOS 'COPY CON:' command, terminate with two characters. The first of these characters is commonly called a carriage return. The ASCII value for this character is 13 in decimal (0D in hexadecimal). The second end-of-line character is commonly called a line feed. It has an ASCII value of 10 decimal, which is 0A in hexadecimal. If you use the DOS DEBUG.COM utility to examine one of your text files, you'll regularly see the two characters, '0D 0A', which signify the end of each line.

WordStar uses a different convention for its text files. Each line terminates with the ASCII characters 141 and 10. (All ASCII codes will subsequently be referred to in decimal notation.) The ASCII 141 represents the same character as the ASCII 13 carriage return, but with a one instead of a zero, as the most significant bit of 8 binary digits that make up the character. MicroPro calls this a high-bit character. The ASCII decimal value of a high-bit character is 128 greater than its low-bit version.

When *WordStar* sees one of these high-bit carriage returns and a linefeed (141 10) at the end of a line, it knows that it can reform that line to accommodate revisions or different margins. If *WordStar* sees a line ending with a regular carriage return and linefeed (13 10), it treats that line as the end of a paragraph and won't reform past it. That is why *WordStar* can't reform a text file that is in standard DOS format.

You could write a program that merely converts all the regular carriage returns, but then *WordStar* would treat the converted file as one big paragraph. Upon invocation of the reform command, the text would collapse into a solid block. What is needed is a program that decides where paragraph endings should be preserved.

A more complicated problem arises if you want to use a *WordStar*-created document as a standard DOS file. *WordStar* encodes the last character of each word as the high-bit version of that character; for example, a lowercase *e* (ASCII 101) at the end of a word is encoded as ASCII 229. If you view a *WordStar* document file with the DOS TYPE command, you'll see strange characters throughout the file. Once again, the solution is not as simple as converting all the high-bit characters to their low-bit equivalents. *WordStar* document files may contain various print enhancement characters such as <Ctrl>-S (ASCII 19) for underlining and <Ctrl>-B (ASCII 2) for boldface. Some lines may contain "dot" commands used for print formatting.

Furthermore, *WordStar* encodes "soft" hyphens as ASCII 31 characters. These must be stripped if they occur in the middle of a line but should appear as regular hyphens if they reside at the end of a line.

The program in Figure 2.17 handles all these problems. It will convert a DOS text file into *WordStar* text format and convert a *WordStar* document file into a standard DOS

```
2 ' WS-DOS.BAS
4 ' by Andrew Fluegelman
6 ' Copyright 1983, The Headlands Press, Inc.
8 '
10 DEFINT A-Z:ON ERROR GOTO 9000
15 A=0:A$="":L$="":p=0 'optimize key variables
20 CRLF$=CHR$(13)+CHR$(10):HBLF$=CHR$(141)+CHR$(10)'hard & soft CR/LF
25 SP$=CHR$(32):TB$=CHR$(9)'space & tab
30 SH$=CHR$(31):PB$=CHR$(20)'soft hyphen & placebo
35 DT=19:DIM D$(19):FOR P=1 TO DT:READ D$(P):NEXT'read dot commands
40 EN=4:DIM EN(4),ENO$(4),ENC$(4),MRK(4)'dim & read enhancement symbols
45 FOR P=1 TO EN:READ EN(P),ENO$(P),ENC$(P):MRK(P)=0:NEXT
100 KEY OFF:CLS
105 PRINT"            ==== CONVERT ====
110 PRINT
115 PRINT"               1 - DOS to WS
120 PRINT"               2 - WS to DOS
900 PRINT"               x - exit
905 PRINT
910 LOCATE ,10:PRINT"Choose:";
915 INPUT"",Q$:IF Q$="X" OR Q$="x" THEN SYSTEM
920 ON VAL(Q$) GOTO 1000,2000
925 BEEP:GOTO 100
930 '
1000 CLS
1005 PRINT"              === DOS-to-WORDSTAR CONVERTER ==="
1010 PRINT
1015 PRINT"This routine will convert a standard DOS file into the format
1020 PRINT"  required by WordStar for paragraph reforming by converting
1025 PRINT"  'hard' carriage returns (ASCII 13) into 'soft' CRs (ASCII 141).
1030 PRINT"If the file contains blank lines between paragraphs or indented
1035 PRINT"   paragraphs, hard returns will preserved at each paragraph end.
1040 PRINT
1045 GOSUB 8000:IF FL$="" THEN 100
1050 PRINT:PRINT"Conversion in progress...";
1055 IF EOF(1) THEN 8045 ELSE LINE INPUT #1,L$
1060 IF EOF(1) THEN PRINT #2,L$+CRLF$;:GOTO 8045
1065 LINE INPUT #1,A$
1070 IF A$="" THEN 1090 'test for blank line
1075 IF LEFT$(A$,2)=SP$+SP$ THEN 1090 'test for indent
1080 IF LEFT$(A$,1)=TB$ THEN 1090 'also test for tab
1085 PRINT #2,L$+HBLF$;:L$=A$:GOTO 1060 'write line with soft CR
1090 PRINT #2,L$+CRLF$;:L$=A$:PRINT PB$;:GOTO 1060 'write line and hard CR
1095 '
2000 CLS
2005 PRINT"              === WORDSTAR-to-DOS CONVERTER ==="
2010 PRINT
2015 PRINT"This routine converts a WordStar 'document' file
2020 PRINT"  into standard DOS format.  All 'high-bit' characters
2025 PRINT"  are converted to their 'low-bit' equivalents.
2030 PRINT"All 'soft' hyphens are stripped, except that any hyphens
2035 PRINT"  at the ends of lines are retained.
2040 PRINT
2045 PRINT"You can either strip or retain lines that contain dot commands.
2050 PRINT"As another option, you can either strip all print enhancements
2055 PRINT"  or replace certain enhancement codes as follows:
2060 PRINT
2065 PRINT"    underline (^S) becomes  << ... >>
2070 PRINT"     boldface (^B) becomes <<< ... >>>
2075 PRINT"  superscript (^T) becomes  <^ ... ^>
2080 PRINT"    subscript (^V) becomes  <_ ... _>
2085 PRINT
2090 PRINT:INPUT"Strip or Retain dot commands (s/r):",Q$
2095 IF Q$="S" OR Q$="s" THEN STRIPDOT=-1 ELSE STRIPDOT=0
2100 INPUT"Strip or Replace print enhancements (s/r):",Q$
2105 IF Q$="R" OR Q$="r" THEN ENHANCE=-1 ELSE ENHANCE=0
2110 GOSUB 8000:IF FL$="" THEN 100
2115 PRINT:PRINT"Conversion in progress...";
2120 L$=""
2125 IF EOF(1) THEN 8045 ELSE A$=INPUT$(1,#1):A=ASC(A$):IF A>30 AND A<128 THEN
     L$=L$+A$:GOTO 2125 'soft hyphen or normal ASCII, proceed
2130 IF A>127 THEN A=A-128:A$=CHR$(A) 'convert to low-bit character
2135 IF A>31 THEN L$=L$+A$:GOTO 2125 'now if normal ASCII, proceed
2140 IF A=13 THEN GOSUB 2170:A$=INPUT$(1,#1):GOTO 2120'eol, process & remove LF
2145 IF NOT ENHANCE THEN 2125
2150 ' deal with enhancements
2155 FOR P=1 TO EN:IF A<>EN(P) THEN 2165 'find special characters
2160 IF MRK(P) THEN L$=L$+ENC$(P):MRK(P)=0 ELSE L$=L$+ENO$(P):MRK(P)=-1'convert
2165 NEXT:GOTO 2125
```

Figure 2.17 *WS-DOS.BAS*

file. I've found it very useful in both receiving and sending text files over the phone lines. Copy the program carefully (especially the semicolons) and run it; it should get the job done.

Most of the program features are documented in the option prompts. If you enter a question mark in response to a file specification prompt, you'll see the files on the default drive. You can follow the question mark with any of the DOS filespec conventions. (Inputting **?b:*.BAS** will list all the .BAS files on drive B.) If you want to terminate when asked for a file specification, just press <Enter>.

The performance of the program improves considerably if the two files are on different disk drives. For optimum performance, put both files on an electronic drive. Incidentally, the program compiles very nicely using the '/e' option of the BASIC Compiler.

Andrew Fluegelman
Tiburon, California

Strip Ease

Some word processing programs (notably *WordStar*) create text files with the high-order bit of some characters set, thus adding 128 to the character's value. Such modified characters are not part of the standard character set and cause problems for some peripherals and programs.

The CP/M operating system provides a method to "strip" the high bit (set it to zero), but DOS provides no such utility. DOS does allow redirection of standard input and out-

```
2170 ' subroutine to strip soft hyphens and dot commands
2175 P=INSTR(L$,SH$):IF P=0 OR P>=LEN(L$)-1 THEN 2180 ELSE L$=LEFT$(L$,P-
     1)+RIGHT$(L$,LEN(L$)-P):GOTO 2175 'strip soft hyphens...
2180 IF RIGHT$(L$,1)=SH$ THEN MID$(L$,LEN(L$),1)="-" 'except at eol
2185 '
2190 IF STRIPDOT AND (LEFT$(L$,1)=".") THEN 2200 'possible dot command?
2195 PRINT #2,L$:PRINT PB$;:RETURN 'write line to disk
2200 B$=MID$(L$,2,1):A=ASC(B$):IF A>64 AND A<91 THEN A=A+32:B$=CHR$(A)
2205 C$=MID$(L$,3,1):A=ASC(C$):IF A>64 AND A<91 THEN A=A+32:C$=CHR$(A)
2210 DUMP=0:FOR P=1 TO DT:IF B$+C$=D$(P) THEN DUMP=-1 'search for dot cmds.
2215 NEXT:IF DUMP THEN RETURN ELSE GOTO 2195 'dump line if dot command
2220 '
8000 ' File specs
8005 INPUT"File to convert:",FL$:IF FL$="" THEN RETURN
8010 IF LEFT$(FL$,1)="?" THEN GOSUB 8035:GOTO 8005
8015 OPEN FL$ FOR INPUT AS #1
8020 INPUT"Convert to file:",FL$:IF FL$="" THEN 8005
8025 IF LEFT$(FL$,1)="?" THEN GOSUB 8035:GOTO 8020
8030 OPEN FL$ FOR OUTPUT AS #2:RETURN
8035 IF LEN(FL$)>1 THEN FL$=RIGHT$(FL$,LEN(FL$)-1) ELSE FL$="*.*"
8040 PRINT:FILES FL$:PRINT:RETURN
8045 CLOSE:BEEP:PRINT:PRINT"Done!":GOTO 105
8050 '
9000 ' Error Trapping
9005 IF ERL=8015 THEN CLOSE:BEEP:PRINT"===Filespec Error===":RESUME 8005
9010 IF ERL=8030 THEN CLOSE 2:BEEP:PRINT"===Filespec Error===":RESUME 8020
9015 IF ERL=8040 THEN CLOSE:BEEP:PRINT"===File(s) Not Found===":RESUME 8005
9020 ON ERROR GOTO 0
9025 '
10000 DATA bp,uj,po,cw,ig,cp,fo,fm,he,hm,lh,mb,mt,pa,op,pn,pc,sr,pl
10005 DATA 19,"<<",">>"
10010 DATA 2,"<<<",">>>"
10015 DATA 22,"<_","_>"
10020 DATA 20,"<^","^>"
```

Figure 2.17 *(continued)*

put and thus makes it possible to create a filter to strip high-order bits.

A filter is a program that reads from an input file, performs some operation on the data, and writes the result to an output file. IBM includes two filters on the DOS disk, SORT and MORE, and it is easy to create your own. All you have to do is write a program that reads input data from the keyboard and writes output data to the display. The redirection feature of DOS will take care of all the complex disk accessing functions.

The lines shown in STRIP can be used to create a DOS filter that strips the high-order bits from input data. The program uses DOS function calls to read and write characters and stops processing when it reads a '^Z' (the end-of-file mark). DOS function number 7 is used to read characters because it does not echo them to the screen, and function 6 is used to output characters without tab expansion or other interpretation. Note that a simple filter to expand tabs can be made by reading characters with function 7 and writing them with function 2.

To use STRIP, enter a command such as:

A>**STRIP**>*IN*>*OUT*,

where *IN* and *OUT* are the names of the input and output files, respectively. If you omit either file name (and its redirection prefix), STRIP will default to the keyboard or the screen.

Robert Showalter
San Bernadino, California

Editor's note: To create the stripping program, STRIP.COM, load BASIC, then type in the lines in X-MAKER.BAS (see Chapter 8) followed by the lines shown in Figure 2.18, STRIP. When everything is typed in, RUN the program and STRIP.COM will be written to the disk in the default drive. You may then use STRIP.COM as described. Thanks to Roland Hutchinson of Stanford, California for his revised version of STRIP which is listed here.

Faster Searches

I would like to share a little trick with other *WordStar* users. When you request a time-consuming task like "Find & Replace Without Asking," a considerable amount of time is used to display the requested string. When such a display is unnecessary (because the GN option has been selected), you can save time by entering a new command just after starting the execution of the first one. The new command might be either another Find and Replace (for instance, when you are formatting tables that have been output from a BASIC program) or a simple command like "Top of File" (<Ctrl>-QR).

For the incredulous reader, the simple test of replacing all instances of the letter *e* by *ee* in this submission to *.* took 1 minute, 32 seconds when the display was allowed to change, but only 7 seconds without the display. When you are editing long texts in which a frequent word or group of words has been replaced by a special character (~for instance) or formatting tables, this little trick can save a lot of time. Of course, the savings in time occurs for most other commands too.

P. Jeanty
New Haven, Connecticut

The *WordStar* WIP File

You can greatly improve the performance of *WordStar* by writing your text file on an emulated disk drive. If you are working on a long document and making use of extensive searches, block moves, and reformatting, the annoying delays caused by

```
1000 DATA "strip.com"
1010 DATA 1,BB,00,00,B9,01,00,BA,24,01,B4,3F,CD,21,3D,00,00,-1,17
1020 DATA 2,74,10,8A,16,24,01,80,E2,7F,B4,06,CD,21,80,FA,1A,-1,3F
1030 DATA 3,75,E4,CD,20,00,-1,EB,-1
```

Figure 2.18 *STRIP: A revised version of a program to remove special codings from* WordStar *document files.*

floppy disk access can be reduced to less than a second.

The problem, of course, is that you're in big trouble if there's a power glitch. Even if you have assiduously saved to disk with <Ctrl>-KS, your saved file is no more permanent than your power supply. The following command sequence can be assigned to a key macro with a utility such as *ProKey.* Giving this macro command will save your working file to a file on drive B called WIP (for *work in progress*) and return you to your present cursor position in the RAM disk text file:

^K1^QR^KB^QC^KK^KWb:
wip<Enter>Y^KH^Q1^K1

Some comments on the macro: ^K1 sets a place marker, ^QR moves to the beginning of the file, and ^KB marks the beginning of a block. ^QC moves to the end of the file and ^KK marks the end of a block. At this point the entire text file has been marked as one block: '^KWb:wip<Enter>' writes the block to the file WIP on drive B. The letter *Y* is necessary because, once the file B:WIP has been created, *WordStar* will ask you whether you want to overwrite it. The remaining commands hide the marked block, return to the place marker, and hide the place marker.

If you have assigned this macro command to a keystroke, such as <Alt>-S, it is executed very quickly with a disk emulator. You'll find this macro a convenient way to back up without breaking your work flow. Since the backup file is always called B:WIP, you do have to remember to save the file on disk under another name when your writing or editing session is completed.

Andrew Fluegelman
Tiburon, California

pfs:write with DOS 2.00

As a user of *pfs:write* I was quite disappointed to see that the manual warned against placing DOS 2.00 on the *pfs:write* system disk. The program works with DOS 2.00; it's just that you can't put DOS 2.00 on the disk to start the program automatically. The people at Software Publishing Corporation told me that the problem is due to insufficient disk space. As purchased, the *pfs:write* disk has 31,583 bytes free, and DOS 2.00 requires about 39,700 bytes.

I reviewed the disk directory and found a file named LOGO.EXE, which does nothing more than display a very nice *pfs* logo on the screen. By erasing the LOGO.EXE file I was able to create room for DOS 2.00. I also removed the reference to LOGO.EXE from the AUTOEXEC.BAT file so that the *pfs:write* program starts immediately.

Daniel Domzalski
Buffalo Grove, Illinois

Editor's note: It's a good idea to copy the LOGO.EXE program onto another disk before you delete it.

More PATH and *PeachText*

In *PC World,* Volume 2, Number 3, you published a *.* item by Larry Axsom that described a method for circumventing *PeachText*'s inability to recognize path names. Because of the number of steps involved in this procedure, I suspect it would be faster to simply copy the file(s) you want to work with into the directory containing *PeachText,* edit them, and then copy them back to their original subdirectory.

For users of the IBM version of *PeachText,* there is a much simpler way to access files in other directories. If you use the IBM version (not the Peachtree version, *PeachText 5000*), you can rename EDIT.PSI as

EDIT.EXE and rename PRINT.PSE as PRINT.EXE. If you're really lazy like me, you can use the names E.EXE and P.EXE and save a few more keystrokes. This allows you to bypass the *PeachText* main menu entirely. If you want to edit a file called FILENAME.DOC, simply type **EDIT FILENAME.** To print the file, type **PRINT FILENAME** (you can omit the extension because *PeachText* assumes the extension .DOC unless you type something else).

Assuming that you have EDIT.EXE in a subdirectory called WORDPROC, and you would like to edit documents in other subdirectories, you can simply use the command **PATH \WORDPROC** to establish a path to the WORDPROC subdirectory. Then, get into the subdirectory containing your file and type **EDIT FILENAME**. The PATH command will show DOS where to find the EDIT program.

I pass this along not only because it is a neat solution to the path name problem, but because I think that many *PeachText* users will appreciate the ability to bypass the menu for other reasons. Experienced users who no longer need to be prompted for commands and who don't use the onscreen help facility (including us oldtimers who loved *Magic Wand,* from which *PeachText* was derived, for its speed and simplicity) will appreciate being able to invoke EDIT and PRINT directly.

If you use *PeachText* as a program editor as well as a word processor, you only need EDIT.EXE on your disk and can save the space otherwise occupied by the menu and PRINT.EXE. The only sacrifice you make is that the REPRINT command, which allows you to reprint a file from the beginning, will not work unless you have called PRINT through the menu.

By the way, if anyone knows how to modify the PeachTree version of the *PeachText 5000* system so that EDIT and PRINT can be used without the menu, I would be eternally grateful for the information.
Miriam Liskin
Berkeley, California

VW in Overdrive

I use Camilo Wilson's *Volkswriter* frequently, and I'd like to share two ways I've found to speed up its operation.

The first speed-up is for PCs that have more than 128K, using the 128K version of *Volkswriter. Volkswriter* does a lot of disk access during operation. By putting a few key files in a disk emulator, the program can be accelerated dramatically, even if you don't have enough room to put the whole package in RAM.

Set up a disk emulator as drive C. Although the disk can be as big as your memory is capable of handling, to hold the key files you need only 17K. Now, copy these files from your *Volkswriter* disk onto drive C:

VWO.EXE
PRINTER*n*TBL
PWPWPWPW.PWP

Make drive C the default drive by typing **C:<Enter>**. Finally, start up *Volkswriter* by typing **A:VW<Enter>**. The speed enhancement is incredible. I put the above commands into an AUTOEXEC.BAT file on my *Volkswriter* disk so that everything is done automatically when I boot the disk.

The second speed-up is a little patch to *Volkswriter* itself. After using *Volkswriter* a few times, I got tired of sitting through the opening pyrotechnics. The following DEBUG session eliminates *Volkswriter*'s flashy title page and gets you down to business quicker.

Note that this patch applies only to the 128K version of *Volkswriter,* although I'm sure that something similar could be done for the 64K version. As with any program patch, the following steps should be attempted on a backup copy of *Volkswriter*—leave your master copy unaltered.

First, so that DEBUG doesn't perform relocation, change the .EXE extension on the *Volkswriter* program file with the command **RENAME VW.EXE VW.BUG<Enter>**. Now, get into DEBUG by typing **DEBUG VW.BUG<Enter>**. Activate DEBUG'S Enter command by typing **E 1DD3<Enter>**. Type in the following two-digit hexadecimal values, separating each pair with a space: **EB 03 90 90 90.** Ignore the values that DEBUG prints each time you press the space bar. After the last pair, press the <Enter> key.

Write the modified program back to disk by typing **W<Enter>**, and quit DEBUG by typing **Q<Enter>**. The last step is to restore the program file's proper name by typing **RENAME VW.BUG VW.EXE<Enter>**. Test the program. You should be able to go directly to the main menu without killing time while *Volkswriter* plays games with the screen.
David Whitman
Hanover, New Hampshire

3

Data Base Management

Hands On

Computers can store huge amounts of information in an efficient, compact form; in today's office a shelf of floppy disks can replace an entire wall of file cabinets. But no matter how impressive your storehouse of facts, files, and figures may be, it's useless unless you have some easy way to get at it. Data base management software lets you create record-keeping systems for quick retrieval of whatever information you may need. Data base programs search through files according to your specifications, perform calculations for you on the information they find, and format the results into clear reports. Data base management systems (DBMSs) are applicable to a wide variety of jobs, simplifying almost any task that involves keeping track of information.

The first two articles in this chapter use *dBASE II or III,* the most popular and one of the most powerful DBMSs for the PC. "Tracking Your Expenses with dBASE II" is a good place for data base beginners to start. The article defines basic terms and gives tips about how a data base should be structured by leading you through the steps of creating a record-keeping system that produces detailed expense reports for tax statements. "The dBASE REPORT," while still within the capabilities of novices, is a tutorial on one of *dBASE II*'s most useful yet more esoteric options, the REPORT FORM command. Mastering this command will help you produce more readable reports than those that can be produced with dBASE's LIST command. REPORT FORM enables you to format the information you've retrieved and to add headings, page numbers, and totaled columns of numbers. You can also save report forms you like and use them again.

The last two articles demonstrate the data management functions of Lotus Development's *1-2-3*. "The Little Black Book" constructs a record-keeping system for names, addresses, telephone numbers, and birthdays. The system uses macros to create a routine that simplifies the process of entering data, and shows how to create loops, input statements, and other programming functions with *1-2-3*'s /X macro commands. "The Little Black Book II" is an enhancement to the original application. This last article adds the ability to print mailing labels from the name and address file and shows you how to create menus that make the system easier to operate. You can use "The Little Black Book" with or without the enhancements in part II.

Tracking Your Expenses with dBASE II or dBASE III

Lawrence J. Magid

(Note: This article was originally written about dBASE II. *Subsequently Ashton Tate has released a new program called* dBASE III. *Both programs are currently being sold.* dBASE III *uses most of the same commands as* dBASE II *plus several more and is generally more powerful and easier to use than* dBASE II. *As it turns out, the procedures described in the original article, for the most part, apply to either program.)*

Because it's so powerful, many people think that the *dBASE II* data base management system is complicated and difficult to learn. That's because *dBASE II*'s extensive set of commands makes it function like another computer language. You can write dBASE programs just as you write in BASIC or other languages. Although learning to program in dBASE can be time consuming, you don't have to become a programmer to use dBASE. You can set up and use a *dBASE II* file in a very short time by learning only a few of its many commands.

This tutorial shows how to use dBASE to set up an expense record-keeping system. This model is not a tax preparation program, but a way to record and report your tax-deductible expenses. Even if you don't plan to use *dBASE II* for this purpose, the techniques demonstrated here can be applied to other data management tasks.

Data Base Terms

The following terms apply to most data base programs, including *dBASE II.*

A *data base* is the entire set of information with which you are working. An example of a data base is your address and phone directory.

A *record* (sometimes called a *case*) is one entry in a data base. While your entire phone directory is a data base, a listing for any one person is a record. A person or company's name, address, and phone number constitute one record.

A *field* is one item in a record. In an address book the person's name is a field, the phone number is a field, and the address is another field.

Planning the Data Base Structure

The first step in planning a data base structure is deciding what information you need. Since entering information takes time and storing information requires disk space, you should create a structure that provides room for everything you need without cluttering your disk with unnecessary information.

Another good practice is minimizing the number of fields in your data base. Each field must be filled in or left blank, which takes time and adds data to your disk.

To save space and avoid complexity, I have kept my expense-record data base structure simple, short, and general. It is so general that you can probably use it, even if you have a different tax scenario.

The data base is built around the following fields:

ITEM: The name of the item you are entering.
DATE: The date of expenditure.
AMOUNT: The amount of the expenditure.
MILEAGE: To be used only if you expense your car by the mile and used your car in conjunction with this expenditure.
CATEGORY: Any logical category used to sort your financial data.
VENDOR: The company or person from whom the item (or service) was purchased.
COMMENT: Anything else you care to enter that may help in the event of an audit.

Record Structure

For each field in your data base, *dBASE II* requires a record structure. You must define the field's name, type, width, and, in the case of numeric fields, decimal places. This is done as soon as you begin to build your data base, using the Create command. Of course, deciding the specifications for each field in advance is helpful—that's part of the planning process.

Name: The first category you must decide on is the name for each field. It may be anything you want, so long as it begins with a letter or number (no symbols), is no more than 10 characters, and contains no blank spaces.

Type: The next category to decide is the type of each field. *dBASE II* has three types of fields. Constant (C) is used for an alphabetic or numeric field that does not require any mathematical function. In this example the fields called Item, Date, Category, Vendor, and Comment contain alphanumeric data and are constant (C) fields. The fields called Amount and Mileage are numeric (N) fields. *dBASE II* also has a logical (L) field, but it isn't used in this example. (*dBASE III* also has a date field and memo field. The date field automatically assigns the appropriate number of characters. The memo field works much like a word processing program allowing you to add long comments to your records.)

Width: You must also decide the width of each field. The width determines the maximum number of spaces that will be allotted for each entry. Once you establish a width, data can be entered with fewer spaces than you have assigned, but you cannot enter data with more. *dBASE II* allocates as many bytes as the specified width for each item you enter, so you don't want to be overly generous with your width.

I chose 50 spaces for the width of the field called Item. This is more than enough to describe any item I might want to purchase. For Date, I selected 8; that's enough space for the longest possible date code, such as 12-14-83. For Amount I chose 8 digits with 2 decimal places (the decimal point counts in determining the width). Eight spaces allow for an expense of up to $99999.99 (commas aren't used in *dBASE II*).

For Category I allotted 4 digits, figuring I'd have to abbreviate the name of each type of expense and that 4 letters would suffice. For Mileage I selected 4 digits, enough for any trip under 10,000 miles. I allotted 15 digits for Vendor and 60 digits for Comment.

Decimal places are used for numeric fields only. If you are using whole numbers only, you can leave decimal places blank.

Creating a New File

Once you've planned the structure of your data base, enter *dBASE II* to create a file. Here's how it's done.

From the DOS prompt, type **DBASE**. You will see a sign-on message and a period, or dot, under the message at the left side of the screen. The dot is the program's prompt. All your commands are entered from this prompt.

You are now ready to create a file. This is done by typing **CREATE**. *dBASE II* responds with 'Enter Filename:'.

Let's call the file Taxes. Type **TAXES** and press <**Enter**>. *dBASE II* responds with the display shown in Figure 3.1.

It's time to specify what the first field will look like. Define the field in the order that appears on the second line of Figure 3.1 ('Field Name, Type, Width, Decimal Places'). The field number, 001, is entered automatically by the program.

To begin creating the data base described earlier, type:

ITEM,C,50 <Enter>

```
ENTER RECORD STRUCTURE AS
FOLLOWS:
FIELD     NAME, TYPE, WIDTH DECI-
          MAL PLACES
001
```

Figure 3.1 *Initial screen for defining record structure.*

Correcting Errors

If you make an error before pressing <Enter>, you can correct it by using the <Backspace> key and typing over the error. If you make a mistake after pressing <Enter>, you can use the editing features (see the *dBASE II* manual for more information on editing).

After you press <Enter> the screen will display '002', indicating that you are ready to go through the same process for the next field (Date). If you don't enter anything for a field, *dBASE II* assumes that you are finished creating your structure. Therefore, do not leave a field blank until you have finished. Remember, you can always go back and correct your errors.

Go through the same process for Amount, Mileage, Category, Vendor, and Comment. When you are done, your screen should look like Figure 3.2. Don't worry if your screen doesn't look that way; you will have a chance to make corrections later.

This data base has 7 fields, so when it asks for field 008, press <**Enter**>. That will terminate the Create phase. *dBASE II* will then ask you if you want to enter data. Type **N** for no.

```
ENTER RECORD STRUCTURE AS
FOLLOWS:
FIELD     NAME, TYPE, WIDTH, DECI-
          MAL PLACES
001       ITEM,C,50
002       DATE,C,8
003       AMOUNT,N,8,2
004       MILEAGE,N,4
005       CATEGORY,C,4
006       VENDOR,C,15
007       COMMENT,C,60
008
```

Figure 3.2 *Record structure for seven fields in file named Taxes.*

```
STRUCTURE FOR FILE:     TAXES.DBF
NUMBER OF RECORDS:      00000
DATE OF LAST UPDATE:    00/00/00
PRIMARY USE DATABASE
FLD     NAME      TYP  WIDTH  DEC
001     ITEM       C    050
002     DATE       C    008
003    AMOUNT      N    008    002
004    MILEAGE     N    004
005   CATEGORY     C    004
006    VENDOR      C    015
007   COMMENT      C    060
**TOTAL**               00150
```

Figure 3.3 *Example of the screen's contents when the Display Structure command is entered.*

Modifying the Structure

dBASE II provides a feature for modifying the structure of a data base. This can be used now or after you have entered the data, should you later decide to make a change. Be cautious about using this feature, however; modifying the structure erases any data in the data base. *dBASE II* provides a simple method for copying data to a scratch file before making modifications, so all the data can be retained. Be sure to consult the *dBASE II* manual if you decide to modify a structure after you have entered data. (With *dBASE III,* it is possible to modify a structure without erasing the data.)

Since you haven't entered data, it's safe to modify the structure without copying the file. But before you can do that, you have to tell *dBASE II* that you are using a file called Taxes. This is done from the '.' prompt by typing **USE TAXES** and pressing <**Enter**>, which loads the file into memory.

To display the structure, type **DISPLAY STRUCTURE** and press <**Enter**> (Figure 3.3 shows how the program responds). If you need to make a correction, type **MODIFY STRUCTURE.** *dBASE II* will warn you that modifying erases all data in the data base.

To modify the structure use the cursor movement keys to position the cursor where you want to make a change. Don't press <Enter>; just use the arrow keys (you can also use the same cursor controls used by *WordStar*—<Ctrl>-E, up; <Ctrl>-X, down; <Ctrl>-S, left; <Ctrl>-D, right). <Ctrl>-G deletes a character and <Ctrl>-V inserts a character. Once you are satisfied with the structure, you can type <Ctrl>-W (the W stands for "write") to save the modifications.

Quitting and Reentering

Before you enter any data, it's useful to know how to quit *dBASE II* and reenter the program. To quit, type **QUIT** from the '.' prompt and you will be returned to DOS. To reenter *dBASE II* type **DBASE.** You'll soon see the sign-on message and the familiar dot.

To access your Taxes data base (from the '.' prompt) type **USE TAXES.** You will see the familiar '.' prompt, but the next command you type, such as **APPEND** to add data, will present you with the first record. You are now ready to add data.

Adding Data

Several commands are used for adding data to a file, but the simplest is Append, which appends data to the end of the data base. Since you are starting with an empty data base, you will automatically begin with record number 00001 (Figure 3.4).

Enter information for each field and press <Enter> when you are done with that field. If you want to leave a field blank, press <Enter> to skip that field. The only exception to this procedure is the first field: the program assumes that you are finished appending data if you don't enter information in the first field. If for some reason you want to leave the first field ('Item' in Figure 3.4) blank, enter a space before you press the <Enter> key.

When you have entered data or skipped all the fields, *dBASE II* will

RECORD # 00001
ITEM
DATE
AMOUNT
MILEAGE
CATEGORY
VENDOR
COMMENT

Figure 3.4 *A sample record without data.*

clear the screen and take you to the next record.

Correcting Errors

dBASE II has several procedures for correcting errors. The simplest is when you discover them before pressing <Enter>. Use the <Backspace> key to move the cursor to where you made the error and either type over the error and insert a correction or delete unwanted material. You can delete characters one at a time with <Ctrl>-G; you get into insert mode with <Ctrl>-V. If you discover an error in a field after you have pressed <Enter> (but before you have left the record for which you are entering data), you can get back to that field using the cursor control keys.

Once you are satisfied that the record is correct, move to the last field in that record and press <Enter> to go to the next record. If you do not want to make further changes in the data base, leave the first field of that record blank (press <Enter> when it asks for 'Item'). That will write your data to the disk and take you out of Append mode. If you wish to add more data, you can reenter Append mode by typing **APPEND** from the '.' prompt. You can also correct errors after you have written data to a disk by using the Edit mode. (With *dBASE III* it is possible to correct errors in any field without exiting the Append command.)

Retrieving Information

Surely I haven't brought you this far just to leave you with a giant data base and no way to get the information out. There are many ways to get summary data or complete reports from *dBASE II*. Again, this article covers just a few; check the manual for more information.

Display Records

You can display the entire data base by typing:

DISPLAY ALL

from the '.' prompt. If you want to display everything except the record number, type:

DISPLAY OFF ALL

You can also display selected fields. Type:

DISP OFF ALL ITEM,AMOUNT

and you will get only the item and amount.

Summing Data

Now comes the fun part. Let's find out how much money you've spent. All your expenditures are in a field called Amount. To find out the total of all these expenditures, type:

SUM AMOUNT.

You can also find out how much you've spent for a particular category. If you have a category called Post for postage, type:

SUM AMOUNT FOR CATEGORY=
"POST"

to determine your total postage expenses. To find out how much you spent in November, type:

SUM AMOUNT FOR DATE="11"

You can sum for any field you wish. To find out how many miles you can write off, type:

SUM MILEAGE

To find out how many miles you drove to and from the post office, type:

SUM MILEAGE FOR CATEGORY=
"POST"

The possibilities are almost unlimited.

Sorting Data

dBASE II has a built-in report generator that makes it easy to create attractive and informative reports. In this example you are going to create a report based on categories. Before doing so, you must sort the data by category. This is done by sorting the entire file to another file. To do such a sort type:

SORT ON CATEGORY TO TAXCAT

The disk will spin for a while, and

```
ENTER REPORT FORM NAME: TAXREP
ENTER OPTIONS, M=LEFT MARGIN, L=LINES/PAGE, W=PAGE WIDTH
                                          M=1,L=55,W=70
PAGE HEADING? (Y/N) Y
ENTER PAGE HEADING: 1982 TAX REPORT
DOUBLE SPACE REPORT (Y/N) N
ARE TOTALS REQUIRED (Y/N) Y
SUBTOTALS IN REPORT? (Y/N) Y
ENTER SUBTOTALS FIELD: CATEGORY
SUMMARY REPORT ONLY? (Y/N) N
EJECT PAGE AFTER SUBTOTALS (Y/N) N
ENTER SUBTOTAL HEADING: CATEGORY

COL              WIDTH,CONTENTS
001              50,ITEM
ENTER HEADING: ITEM
002              8,DATE
ENTER HEADING: DATE
003              8,CATEGORY
ENTER HEADING: CATEGORY
004              8,AMOUNT
ENTER HEADING: AMOUNT
ARE TOTALS REQUIRED (Y/N) Y
005              4,MILEAGE
ENTER HEADING: MILES
ARE TOTALS REQUIRED (Y/N) Y
006              ENTER
```

Figure 3.5 *On-screen format for data base report; words in italics indicate items from data you've entered.*

the program will display a message when the sorting is complete. You have just created another data base, which is identical to Taxes except that it is sorted by category. You have the option of switching to the new data base or deleting the old one (called Taxes) and renaming the new one Taxes so that your data base always has the same name. If you want to rename it, you must type the following series of commands:

USE TAXCAT <Enter>
DELETE FILE TAXES <Enter>
RENAME TAXCAT TO TAXES <Enter>
USE TAXES <Enter>

You now have a "new" data base with the same name and you're ready to create your report format.

Alternatively, you can use the INDEX command in both *dBASE II* and *dBASE III*. This command doesn't actually sort the file, but creates a sorted index so that any reports from the file are in the desired order. It is faster than sorting and has the added advantage of not requiring you to create a new file.

To index by category, once you have entered the data, you would type:

INDEX ON CATEGORY TO CATIND

Then when you USE the file you would type:

USE TAXES INDEX CATIND

Now when you list or display the file, the data is displayed in order by category.

Creating the Report

Type **REPORT** from the '.' prompt. *dBASE II* will ask you a series of questions, prompting you to design your custom report. Answer them as shown in Figure 3.5. (With *dBASE III*, you type: **create report**. The prompt questions differ from those of dBASE II but are equally clear.)

When you have created the report format, press <Enter> and the program will immediately display the report (Figure 3.6). Look at the display as it scrolls by to see if it's what you want. Don't worry that it's scrolling faster than you can read; you can reproduce the display whenever you want and route it to a printer or to a disk file so that it can be used with most word processing programs.

You can display the report by typing:

REPORT FORM TAXREP

To print the report, type <Ctrl>-P followed by:

REPORT FORM TAXREP

Routing the Report to a Disk File

You can route your report to a disk file so that it can be edited and printed with a word processing program. This procedure uses *dBASE II*'s Alternate command sequence as follows:

PAGE NO. 00001
01/31/83

1982 Tax Report by Category

ITEM	DATE	CATEGORY	AMOUNT	MILES
* CATEGORY Car				
Meeting in San Rafael	02-04	Car	0.00	120
Meeting in San Jose	06-30	Car	0.00	50
Meeting in Santa Cruz	07-24	Car	0.00	90
** SUBTOTAL **				
			0.00	260
* CATEGORY Empl				
Secretarial Help	05-20	Empl	125.00	0
Secretarial Help	01-25	Empl	85.00	0
Secretarial Help	09-23	Empl	115.00	0
** SUBTOTAL **				
			325.00	0
* CATEGORY Ent				
Dinner with Sam Smith	02-21	Ent	24.95	55
Lunch with Harry Carlos	03-15	Ent	17.50	8
** SUBTOTAL **				
			42.45	63
* CATEGORY Soft				
dBASE II	12-08	Soft	675.00	0
VisiCalc	01-12	Soft	250.00	0
** SUBTOTAL **				
			925.00	0
* CATEGORY Subs				
Subscription to PC World	11-30	Subs	24.00	0
** SUBTOTAL **				
			24.00	0
* CATEGORY Sup				
Computer Paper	03-22	Sup	26.75	0
Office Supplies	02-21	Sup	45.86	10
Pencils	08-03	Sup	12.55	8
** SUBTOTAL **				
			85.16	18
* CATEGORY Trav				
Airfare to NY	02-15	Trav	438.00	60
** SUBTOTAL **				
			438.00	60

Figure 3.6 *Expense report produced by* dBASE II.

SET ALTERNATE TO FILENAME <**Enter**>
SET ALTERNATE ON <**Enter**>
REPORT FORM TAXREP <**Enter**>
[Report will scroll on screen]
SET ALTERNATE OFF <**Enter**>

The report is now written to a file called TAXREP.TXT. To view the report use your word processing program and enter the file. It can be incorporated into other documents if your word processing program allows you to insert or merge files.

Custom Reports

dBASE II provides a number of ways to customize reports. These ways are covered in the *dBASE II* manual. With a little practice you might even create a report that will impress the IRS.

Other Applications

The principles established in this article can be used for many other applications. *dBASE II* can be used to keep income records and household expenses, to do billing, and to handle a multitude of other tasks. Although the model described here is simple, the opportunities for advanced programming are enormous.

The most important thing to remember about *dBASE II* is that it's not as difficult to use as it would at first seem. Because the program lacks a menu, using it is not obvious at first, but a little practice will pay off very quickly.

Lawrence J. Magid is Executive Vice President of Know-How, a San Francisco-based microcomputer education company. He is a syndicated computer columnist for the Los Angeles Times *and a Contributing Editor to* PC World *magazine. This article was originally published in* PC World *Volume 1, Number 2.*

The dBASE.report

David Jenkins

Data management programs can be intimidating, and while *dBASE II* is friendlier than most (particularly for data retrieval), the thought of creating a formatted report is enough to make even a fairly experienced user feel a little jittery. If you own and use *dBASE II,* chances are you have used only the LIST command to generate reports. Although the LIST command enables you to display the contents of a file on the screen or print them on paper, it is not very discriminating. The REPORT FORM command, on the other hand, is sufficiently sophisticated to produce complex, formatted reports—and is still well within the capabilities of the *dBASE II* novice.

The LIST command allows you to extract specific records or fields from a file. For example, you can type **list all for lastname="Smith"** to obtain only the records that include the last name Smith, or you can type **LIST firstname,lastname for lastname ="Sm"** to select the records that include last names beginning with Sm. The LIST command supplies instant information, but the resulting reports will not be formatted and cannot include headings, page numbers, totaled columns of numbers, and other desirable features. You might look at a LIST report several days later and be unable to recall when it was produced or what the data refers to.

If you know the LIST command and are familiar with the use of field names in a file, you should be able to apply many of the REPORT FORM features to your data files. The REPORT FORM command can automatically create formatted reports for a number of situations. You can also save a format that you create with the REPORT FORM command and use it as a template for other data files—a time-saver once you've found a format you like.

A Simple Report

To practice with the REPORT FORM generator, you will need a copy of *dBASE II* and a sample data file. If you are a novice, you might want to recreate the Reptdemo data file as shown in Figure 3.7. After entering *dBASE II* from DOS, type **create reptdemo <Enter>**. (When using *dBASE II,* notice that it automatically inserts a space after the prompt. In copying the figure, do not insert an additional space.) *dBASE II's* queries (capitalized in the figures) ask you to specify all the fields you want to include in the file. Pressing <Enter> after an empty field (in this case 008) will immediately display the first record form. Key in the data following 00001 in Figure 3.7 using the APPEND command. You can later add records of your own using APPEND.

To produce a simple formatted report using a few basic features such as page headings and column definitions, enter the responses for the Vanilla report shown in Figure 3.8. With the Reptdemo data file in use, you initiate the REPORT FORM command by typing **report form vanilla.** *dBASE II* will look to the disk, find that there is no report named Vanilla, and ask a series of formatting questions. In this example, no changes have been made to the default options, which set the left margin of the report at column 8, the number of lines per page at 57, and the page width at 80 characters.

After specifying the page heading and answering a few more questions, you come to the column definitions. Each column is defined by its width (the number of one-character-wide columns across the page), the contents of the field, and the column heading. *dBASE II* automatically assembles the report when no further columns are defined. This report format is now saved in a file called vanilla.frm. If you want to display a report with this format, type:

use reptdemo <Enter>
report form vanilla <Enter>

Printing a Report

To print a report, you can either add TO PRINT to the REPORT FORM command line or use <Ctrl>-<PrtSc>. With the former, you would type **report form vanilla to print.** (When TO PRINT is used, it is always the last clause of a REPORT FORM command.) For example, if you introduced an additional clause or command, such as FOR, you would type **report form vanilla for age<20 to print.**

You can also print out a report by typing:

report form vanilla <Ctrl>-<PrtSc>
<Enter>

```
. CREATE reptdemo
ENTER RECORD STRUCTURE AS FOLLOWS:
 FIELD   NAME,TYPE,WIDTH,DECIMAL PLACES
 001     firstname,c,15
 002     lastname,c,20
 003     address,c,20
 004     city,c,20
 005     state,c,2
 006     zip,c,5
 007     age,n,5,2
 008

INPUT DATA NOW? y

 00001  Rachel           Johnson          111 Green St.      Berkeley
        CA 94703    6.50
 00002  Sally Elizabeth  Johnson          20 Filbert St.     Berkeley
        CA 94703    1.50
 00003  Alice            Stern            4000 10th Ave.     Syracuse
        NY 01234   30.00
 00004  Elizabeth        Frisby           4096 3rd Ave.      New York
        NY 01234   37.00
```

Figure 3.7 *Creating the sample data file.*

```
. USE reptdemo
. REPORT FORM vanilla
ENTER OPTIONS, M=LEFT MARGIN, L=LINES/PAGE, W=PAGE WIDTH
PAGE HEADING? (Y/N) y
ENTER PAGE HEADING: report demo, simple test
DOUBLE SPACE REPORT? (Y/N) n
ARE TOTALS REQUIRED? (Y/N) n
COL     WIDTH,CONTENTS
001     15,firstname
ENTER HEADING: first name
002     20,lastname
ENTER HEADING: last name
003     5,age
ENTER HEADING: age
004

        PAGE NO. 00001
        01/01/80

                          report demo, simple test

          first name      last name        age

        Rachel           Johnson          6.50
        Sally Elizabeth  Johnson          1.50
        Alice            Stern           30.00
        Elizabeth        Frisby          37.00
```

Figure 3.8 dBASE II *queries and Vanilla report.*

```
. USE reptdemo
. REPORT FORM format
ENTER OPTIONS, M=LEFT MARGIN, L=LINES/PAGE, W=PAGE WIDTH m=0,1=60,w=70
PAGE HEADING? (Y/N) y
ENTER PAGE HEADING: report demo; formatting capabilities
DOUBLE SPACE REPORT? (Y/N) y
ARE TOTALS REQUIRED? (Y/N) n
COL     WIDTH,CONTENTS
001     20,lastname+firstname
ENTER HEADING: <name;----
002     20,address+trim(city)+"   "+state+"   "+zip
ENTER HEADING: <address;-------
003     10,age
ENTER HEADING: >age;yrs
004     10,int (age*365)
ENTER HEADING:>age;in days
005


PAGE NO. 00001
01/01/80

                         report demo
                   formatting capabilities

name                address                     age          age
----                -------                     yrs      in days

Johnson             111 Green St.              6.50         2372
Rachel              Berkeley CA 94703

Johnson             20 Filbert St.             1.50          547
Sally Elizabeth     Berkeley CA 94703

Stern               4000 10th Ave.            30.00        10950
Alice               Syracuse NY 01234

Frisby              4096 3rd Ave.             37.00        13505
Elizabeth           New York NY 01234
```

Figure 3.9 *Print formatting with the REPORT FORM command.*

<Ctrl>-<PrtSc> acts as a printer toggle, turning the printer on if it is off, and vice versa. You can use this feature to get a printout as you define a report's format. (You will get *dBASE II*'s queries as well as your responses. Subsequent printouts of the report's format will provide you with only your responses—not *dBASE II*'s queries.) Such a printout is helpful if you later need to revise the report.

Formatting

Using the REPORT FORM command's features, you can generate another kind of report from the Reptdemo file. You can format a page and its headings, and put a number of items in a column. Figure 3.9 illustrates the REPORT FORM command's queries, the entered responses, and the resulting report.

Set the left margin at 0 (instead of the default 8), the lines per page at 60, and the page width at 70 columns. You can print a two-line page heading by separating the first line ('report demo') and the second line ('formatting capabilities') by a semicolon, which tells *dBASE II* to start a new line. Unless another position is specified *dBASE II* will center page and column headings over the data. You can move column headings flush left or flush right by using the respective less-than or greater- than symbol when you type the column heading. For example, in Figure 3.9 the < places the 'address' column heading at the left side of the column. Lining up a column heading with the data, particularly when there are large and small fields in a column, improves the look of a report.

Other column formatting features are available with the REPORT FORM command. You can underline a column heading by creating a two-line heading, with the second line defined as hyphens. Note too that column 001 prints out two fields from the file. The plus sign is the equivalent of "then print"; it tells *dBASE II* to print the last name and then the first name. Because the column width is set at 20 (the width of each single field), *dBASE II* will wrap the text around to the next line, and the first name will appear directly under the last name. This feature is useful when you want several data fields to line up, or when you have one long field that must be divided in two.

In the second column (address), more complicated *dBASE II* features are used. Although the city field was earlier defined as 20 characters long, not all entries will be this large. The trim function removes blanks to the right of the entry. The city field is thus printed next to the state and zip code field. You can also type the expression in the following form: address + city + state + " " + zip. The four fields would then occupy three lines, with the address, city, and state/zip each taking one line.

Notice that in Figure 3.9 a space surrounded by double quotes separates the city, state, and zip code fields. The quotes identify a literal—something that will be printed or displayed exactly as it is typed. In this case, since there is a space between the quotes, *dBASE II* places a space between fields. Without it, the printed result would be 'BerkeleyCA94703'.

The column width need not match the data field size. For example, the age column is 10 characters wide, even though an age field never exceeds five characters. Using the appropriate column width, you will avoid having to abbreviate or hyphenate a heading. A computation is also included in the example shown in Figure 3.9, where the age in years is multiplied by 365 and converted into an integer. Data that makes up the fourth column, age in days, is a result of the computation performed on the number in column three—a demonstration that the *dBASE II* report generator lets you manipulate the printed output, but leaves the contents of a file unchanged. You cannot change the data in your file during a report.

Totals

Subtotaling and totaling allow you to add any numeric expressions in a column. *dBASE II* will calculate the total amount for that column, adding only those records that are selected. The total is printed at the end of the report.

Subtotaling is useful only when data is organized in some order. In Figure 3.10 the four records are indexed by state. To produce subtotals, you must specify a subtotal field (ENTER SUBTOTALS FIELD: state), which triggers a subtotal whenever a break occurs in the data. When there are no more CA records, the command that adds up the accumulated numbers is triggered, and the California subtotals are printed. The new value in the subtotal field (NY) starts the process all over again. If you had answered yes to 'SUMMARY REPORT ONLY?', the report would include only the subtotal headings and the subtotals. For large files that are properly indexed, summary reports can be a quick way to distill information.

Variations on a Theme

The REPORT FORM command creates a template rather than an absolute definition of a report. Although *dBASE II* anticipates and provides most of the formatting features that a user might need, other formatting features can be specified each time a report is printed. The following is a list of some of these formatting features:

Temporary report headings: When you have a file that undergoes constant revision, you may want to change the report's heading to reflect each version. Typing **set heading to This is Draft 3** will print 'This is Draft 3' on the report until you change the heading with another SET HEADING TO command or exit *dBASE II.*

Date: Typing **set date to 08/02/85** will print that date below the page number on all reports.

Record selection: You can decide which records to print by specifying the report name (such as Vanilla or Format) and the indexed field after the REPORT FORM command. For

```
. USE reptdemo
. index on state to state
00004 RECORDS INDEXED
. set index to state
. report form totaling
ENTER OPTIONS, M=LEFT MARGIN, L=LINES/PAGE, W=PAGE WIDTH
PAGE HEADING? (Y/N) y
ENTER PAGE HEADING: report demo;subtotaling
DOUBLE SPACE REPORT? (Y/N) n
ARE TOTALS REQUIRED? (Y/N) y
SUBTOTALS IN REPORT? (Y/N) y
ENTER SUBTOTALS FIELD: state
SUMMARY REPORT ONLY? (Y/N) n
EJECT PAGE AFTER SUBTOTALS? (Y/N) n
ENTER SUBTOTAL HEADING: report for state =
COL    WIDTH,CONTENTS
001    20,lastname
ENTER HEADING: last name
002    20,firstname
ENTER HEADING: first name
003    10,age
ENTER HEADING: >age
ARE TOTALS REQUIRED? (Y/N) y
004    10,int (age*365)
ENTER HEADING: >age (days)
ARE TOTALS REQUIRED? (Y/N) y
005

    PAGE NO. 00001
    01/01/80

                         report demo
                         subtotaling

      last name           first name               age     age (days)

    * report for state =CA
    Johnson             Rachel                    6.50          2372
    Johnson             Sally Elizabeth           1.50           547
    ** SUBTOTAL **
                                                  8.00          2919

    * report for state =NY
    Stern               Alice                    30.00         10950
    Frisby              Elizabeth                37.00         13505
    ** SUBTOTAL **
                                                 67.00         24455

    ** TOTAL **                                  75.00         27374
```

Figure 3.10 *Totaling and subtotaling in a report.*

example, typing **report form vanilla for state="CA"** will select only those records containing CA in the state field.

Order: You can print the records in a file in a different order but use the same report format by setting the index to one of the originally defined fields. To display the same information in two different orders, type:

```
use reptdemo
set heading to This Report Is in Order
    Records Were Entered
report form Format
index on lastname to last
set index to last
set heading to This Report Is in
    Alphabetical Order by Last Names
report form Format
```

Moving formats: One report format can serve several data files, as long as all the file structures include the same field names. You could load a different file with USE, then call in a previously used report format.

Passing files: A *dBASE II* report can be converted into a standard ASCII file and later incorporated into a word processing document. You would type:

```
use reptdemo
set alternate to vanilla
set alternate on
report form vanilla
set alternate off
```

This command sequence will send a copy of the Vanilla report to a file named vanilla.txt, which can then be edited by a word processing program.

Changing a Report

Until you have more experience with *dBASE II,* you should create a new report format when you need one instead of changing an established one. Once a report format is defined, it is difficult to modify, since you must change the report definitions. Unfortunately, a format file does not store *dBASE II*'s queries but only your responses. Editing a format file (.frm) can be a "gruesome experience" in the words of one *dBASE II* programmer. If you wish to create a report using the name of an existing report, the first report must be deleted. For example, type **delete file vanilla.frm.**

Beyond the Report Generator

Interest in *dBASE II*'s report capabilities seems to be growing. SoftwareBanc has published a book called *Report Writing in dBASE II.* Ashton-Tate, the creator of *dBASE II,* is also issuing the *Advanced Programmer's Guide to dBASE II,* which devotes one section to report writing. The book includes a command file listing of FORMGEN, which simulates the REPORT FORM function with a *dBASE II* command file. FORMGEN could save a considerable amount of time when you need customized reports. And saving time is what data management is all about.

David Jenkins is a computer consultant based in Berkeley, California, who specializes in dBASE III *applications. He is currently writing a book on* dBASE III. *This article was originally published in* PC World *Volume 2, Number 5.*

The Little Black Book

Paul McDermott

The Little Black Book enables you to keep track of names, addresses, telephone numbers, and birthdays. It is a simple data management template that uses version 1A of Lotus Development Corporation's *1-2-3* to quickly file, retrieve, sort, and extract statistical information about employees, friends, and relatives.

The template is divided into two parts: the data input section, where the information is entered and stored, and the data query section, where the criteria by which the information will be extracted can be specified. The template uses many of *1-2-3*'s data management functions, and this article can serve as a tutorial on their use.

The Little Black Book makes use of *1-2-3*'s keyboard macro capabilities. The article shows how to use macros to create a routine for entering data and how to use the /X macro commands to create loops, input statements, and other programming functions usually found only in programming languages such as BASIC.

This article assumes familiarity with the overall *1-2-3* command structure and with basic movement around a *1-2-3* worksheet. The terms printed in *italics* are *1-2-3* commands. They can be entered either by typing the first letter of each command word or by using the cursor control and <Enter> keys to select the appropriate command.

Text and values to be entered into cells or in response to prompts are listed in **monofont** type. All cell references are given as capital letters followed by numbers; they can be entered either as direct references or by pointing.

Designing the Template

The first step in creating the template is designing the data input section. Start with a clean worksheet by giving the command */Worksheet Erase Yes*. Enter a title for the worksheet by moving to cell B2 and entering a label consisting of 21 asterisks: **'*********************.** Since an asterisk can be read as a mathematical operator, be sure to start the label with a single quotation mark (') to specify that the contents of the cell is a label and not a value to be calculated. Copy cell B2 to cell B4 with the command */Copy***B2** <**Enter**> **B4** <**Enter**>. Move to cell B3 and type **THE LITTLE BLACK BOOK.** Go to cell B7 and type **^First.** (The ^ character, a caret or shifted 6, will center the label in the cell.) Enter the rest of the headings in row 7 as follows:

C7: **^Last**
D7: **^Address**
E7: **^City**
F7: **St**
G7: **^Zip**
H7: **^Phone**
I7: **^D.O.B**
J7: **^Age**
K7: **^B.D.**
L7: **Code**
Skip column M
N7: **"Yr**
O7: **"Mn**
P7: **"Dy**

Move the cursor to N6 and type **Date of Birth.**

Before you go any further, you may want to switch *1-2-3* to manual recalculation mode by giving the command */Worksheet Global Recalculation Manual.* That command will prevent *1-2- 3* from recalculating the entire worksheet after each entry and thus will allow you to move from cell to cell more quickly.

Now set the width of column A to 3 characters by moving to any cell in that column and giving the command */Worksheet Column Set* **3** <**Enter**>. (Column A won't be used for data in this template; the empty column will leave a few spaces between the text and the worksheet border, making the data easier to read.) Using the same command, set the other columns as shown in Table 3.1.

Column	Characters	Hyphens in Row 6
A	3	0
B	10	9
C	15	14
D	20	19
E	13	12
F	4	3
G	7	6
H	14	13
I	11	10
J	5	4
K	8	7
L	5	4
N	5	
O	4	
P	5	

Table 3.1 *Column widths for The Little Black Book.*

The last step in setting up the data input section is to place hyphens above and below the row of labels. Go to cell B6 and enter 9 hyphens, beginning with a single quote ('). Move to C6 and enter a line of 14 hyphens. Continue the same procedure in cells D6 through L6, entering the number of hyphens shown in the last column of Table 3.1. Each line of hyphens is 1 character shorter than the width of the cell. The resulting space will help distinguish where one column ends and the next begins. Now copy the contents of row 6 to row 8 by moving to cell B6 and giving the command */Copy* **B6..L6** <**Enter**> **B8** <**Enter**>.

To accommodate *1-2-3*'s data management operations, you must assign names to various parts of the data input section before you begin entering any information. You can specify a name for the input area with the Range Name command. Go to cell B7 and issue the command */Range Name Create* **INPUT** <**Enter**> **B7..P11** <**Enter**>. Although the specified input range is small (4 rows), the program will expand the range with each new entry; there is no need to worry about accidentally entering data outside the input range.

The column headings should also be given range names. With the cursor at B7, give the command */Range Name Label Down* **B7..L7** <**Enter**>. This command assigns the name "First" to cell B8, the name "Last" to cell C8, the name "Address" to cell D8, and so on. These range names will be important later for data query functions. Before you begin entering data, save the worksheet to disk with the command */File Save* **BLACKBK** <**Enter**>.

Data Entry

You're now ready to enter your first record. To begin, go to cell B9. Press the <CapsLock> key and type in **JOHN.** Then move to cell C9 and enter **BROWN.** On the same row, under the Address heading (column D), enter **'123 ANYWHERE ST.** (Remember to start the entry with a single quotation mark to indicate that it is a label and not a value.) At cell E9 enter **ANYTOWN.** Move to F9 and enter **PA.** At cell G9 enter **'19040.** Go to cell H9 and type in **'215-555-8923.** Then move to L9 (the "Code" column) and enter **E.** This column will be used to distinguish between employees (E), relatives (R), friends (F), and so on. Finally, enter **58** in N9, **12** in O9, and **10** in P9.

Using Date Functions

Now that you have entered the first row of data, you are ready to create some of the formulas that make The Little Black Book work. One of *1-2-3*'s most advanced features is its ability to handle date arithmetic, and The Little Black Book takes advantage of that ability.

Go to cell I9 and enter the formula **@DATE(N9,O9,P9).** The result will be 21529. *1-2-3* calculates dates by determining the number of days since the beginning of the century. This number is the number of days between December 31, 1899, and the date of birth entered in cells N9, O9, and P9. The number doesn't help much until it is formatted in a way that is more easily understood. With the cursor still at cell I9, give the command */Range Format Date* <**Enter**> <**Enter**>. The Range Format Date command has three options for displaying dates. Since you just selected the first option, cell I9 should now read 10-Dec-58. To edit the data in column I, the date of birth (D.O.B.) column, you must make the necessary changes in columns N, O, and P and press the <F9> (Calc) key to see the effect.

Having the date of birth is handy, but to keep a list of current ages you must use another of *1-2-3*'s date arithmetic functions. At cell J9 enter the formula **@INT((@TODAY-I9)/365).** A person's current age will be found by calculating the difference between the current date (found by the date function @TODAY, which returns the date entered when you start the computer) and the date of birth (found in cell I9). The function @INT will display only the integer portion of the result of the calculation. Dividing by 365 expresses the result in years.

Column K, headed B.D. (for Birthday Data), uses date arithmetic to calculate and store the birthday for the current year. This data will be useful for data query operations such as birthday reminders. Before you set the formula, go to cell N4 and type **Cur't Yr:.** In cell P4 enter **84.** Move to N5 and type **\-** <**Enter**> */ Copy* <**Enter**> **O5..P5** <**Enter**>. Go to K9 and type in the formula **@DATE(P4,O9,P9).** The $ symbols in the P4 cell address indicate an abso-

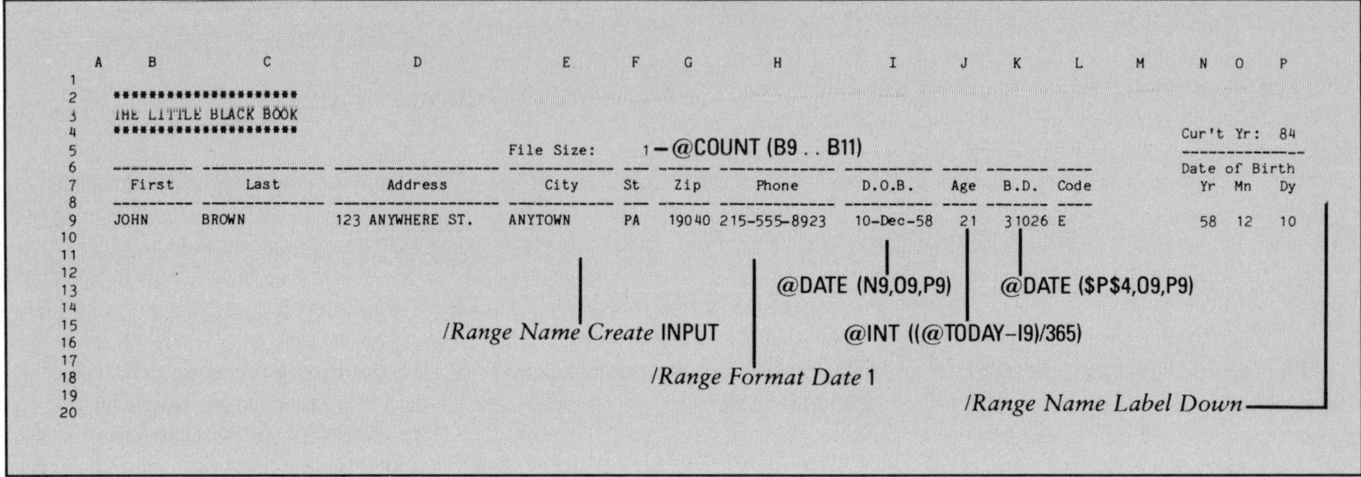

Figure 3.11 *The Little Black Book's data input section.*

lute cell reference, which won't change when the formula is copied later. The value in cell K9 represents the number of days that have elapsed since the beginning of the century (31026). You can leave this cell unformatted, since it will only be used for data query operations.

The last formula in the data input section is used to count the number of records (or rows). Go to cell E5 and type **"File Size:**. Move to cell F5 and enter the formula **@COUNT(B9..B11)**.

Figure 3.11 is a pictorial diagram of the worksheet to this point, showing the range names and formulas assigned to different cells, the format of the worksheet, and the first entry. You are now ready to start entering the rest of the data. Before you do, again save the worksheet template to a disk file using the command */File Save* <**Enter**> *Replace.*

Keyboard Macros

You could begin entering data at cell B10 and simply move the cursor right to the next column as you complete each field. When you finished one complete record (or row of data), the cursor would be at cell P10. Then you would return to column B to enter the next record. This is one way of entering information, but it's certainly not the quickest or easiest. Data entry can be made much easier by writing some simple *1-2-3* keyboard macros to prompt the user for an entry and to automatically copy the entry into the appropriate data cell.

A *1-2-3* keyboard macro is a specially named cell or range of cells that contains a series of keystrokes and commands that can be activated by simply pressing two keys. You can create a macro by simply typing the desired keystrokes in a cell and naming the cell or range with a 2-character range name. Macro range names consist of a backslash as the first character and any letter as the second character. Once the range is named, you can execute the macro by pressing the <Alt> key and the letter used in the range name.

Macros use a few special characters: The tilde (~) character is used to represent the <Enter> key; {right} is the equivalent of pressing the <CursorRight> key; and so on.

1-2-3 also has a number of special commands that can be used only in macros. The /X commands, which cannot be issued from the keyboard, create "program loops" or issue "GOTO" statements that let macros jump from section to section of instructions. The Little Black Book will use several of these commands to create a program for entering data.

Macros for Data Entry

To begin setting up a macro you need to find an area of the worksheet that won't be affected by sorting adjacent data. Move the cursor to cell C46 and type **MACRO FOR DATA ENTRY**. Then place a line of hyphens in cell C47 beneath that label; don't forget to begin with a single quotation mark.

Two types of macro input statements may be used to prompt for data entry. The first, /XL*message~range~*, displays a message (up to 39 characters) in the control panel and waits for data input. When the data is entered, *1-2-3* stores the data as a label in the specified range, which can be either a cell address or a named range. The other input command, /XN*message~range~*, works the same way, but it stores the data as a numeric entry.

Go to cell B52 and type **'/XLFirst name? ~B10**~. When this macro is executed, the message 'First name?' will appear in the control panel. When you type in the response, it will be copied into cell B10. (Notice that all this was accomplished without moving the cursor.)

Type the rest of the macro input statements into column B as follows:

B53: **'/XLLast name? ~C10~**
B54: **'/XLAddress? (# Street) ~D10~**
B55: **'/XLCity? ~E10~**
B56: **'/XLState? (xx) ~F10~**
B57: **'/XLZip code? (xxxxx) ~G10~**
B58: **'/XLPhone number? (xxx-xxx-xxxx) ~H10~**
B59: **'/XLCode? E=employee, R=relative, F=friend, ~L10~**

The first eight statements create label entries. The next three create numeric entries:

B60: **'/XNMonth born? (xx) ~O10~ (be sure to enter oh-one-zero, not zero-one-zero)**
B61: **'/XNDay born? (xx) ~P10~**
B62: **'/XNYear born? (xx) ~N10~**

These macros let you enter all the necessary data on line 10 without having to move the cursor to 11 different cells. Once the data is entered, the worksheet will need to use the date formulas from cells I9 through K9. To create the macro to access these cells, go to cell B63 and type {**GOTO**}**I9**~. Move down to cell B64 and type **'/C**{**RIGHT**}{**RIGHT**}~{**DOWN**}~. In cell B65 type {**HOME**} and in B66 enter {**CALC**}. These four macro cells will move the cursor to the cells containing the formulas, copy them to the input line (row 10), move the cursor back to the home position, and recalculate the worksheet.

Creating Loops

Once all the data entry macros are in place, you could process the data by executing the macro once for each record (or line of information). That means if you had 50 records to input, you would have to execute the macro 50 times. But an easier way is to use a "loop" and an "if . . . then . . . else" macro. Go to cell B49 and type in **'/XNWant to enter data? (Yes=1, No=0) ~ANSWER~**. Move to cell B70 and issue the command */Range Name Create* **ANSWER** <**Enter**> <**Enter**>. Then move up to cell B50 and type in **'/XIanswer=0~**{**HOME**} **/XQ~**. Move down to B51 and enter {**GOTO**}**A10~/WIR~**{**HOME**}.

The macro in cell B49 asks if you want to enter data and stores the response in a cell with the range name ANSWER. The macro in cell B50 determines if the value of ANSWER is equal to zero. If it is equal to zero, then the macro moves the cursor to the home position and stops executing the macro (/XQ means Quit Execution). If the value of ANSWER is not equal to zero, then *1-2-3* stops reading cell B50 and looks to cell B51 for its next macro command. The /XI command is *1-2-3*'s version of an "if . . . then . . . else" statement: if the condition is true, then continue to read the keystrokes in the same cell; if the condition is false, then stop reading this cell and look in the cell immediately below for further keystrokes.

The macro in cell B51 will insert a line (/Worksheet Insert Row) at row 10 and then return the cursor to cell A1 (home). Since all new data will be entered along row 10, it is important that this macro cell precede the data entry macros.

Just two more steps are needed to create a loop that will finish the data entry macro program. First go back to cell B49 and give the command */Range Name Create* **LOOP1** <**Enter**> <**Enter**>. Then move to cell B67 and type in **'/XGloop1~**. When executed, this cell causes *1-2-3* to "loop" back to cell B49; the prompt 'Want to enter data? (Yes=1, No=0)' will appear again. The /XG command is a macro GOTO statement that tells *1-2-3* where to look for its next macro keystroke. (This should not be confused with the <F5> function key (GOTO) that moves the cursor to a specified cell.)

Once you have finished creating the text of the macros, you are ready to name the cells that contain them. Go to cell B49 and issue the command */Range Name Create*\ **D** <**Enter**> <**Enter**>. You may have realized that cell B49 already had a range name. The name \D is used to execute the macro, while the name LOOP1 is used to refer to B49 from cell B67 ('/XGloop1~). The name LOOP1 was assigned to make the macro easier to understand. Before you go any further, save the worksheet with the command */File Save* <**Enter**> *Replace.*

Return the cursor to cell A1. You can now begin to enter the sample data given in Figure 3.12. To reduce the chance of later data query errors, turn on the <CapsLock> key so that the information will be consistently uppercase. Then activate the data entry macros by typing **D** while you hold down the <Alt> key. Enter all the data as it is shown; these examples will be used in this article and in its sequel, "Little Black Book II."

If errors occur during execution of the macro, first check the text of the macro for completeness. A common mistake is to omit the tilde (~) character. Also check the spelling of

JENNY	OSBORNE	21 MAPLE AVE.	HARRISBURG	PA	19045	215-555-4978	E	04/10/67
RICH	CARBO	221 WELLINGTON DR.	CINNAMINSON	NJ	08077	609-555-8253	R	09/03/56
DONNY	SMITH	259 TENBY RD.	DELRAN	NJ	08077	609-555-8211	F	12/02/58
DAN	HERBERT	179 MADISON AVE.	NORRISTOWN	PA	19457	215-555-1018	R	10/05/59
MEL	GRIES	351 TANNER AVE.	WARMINSTER	MD	21974	301-555-8187	R	05/21/57
JOAN	MOYER	118 MEREDITH AVE.	DOYLESTOWN	PA	19010	215-555-1697	E	05/29/59
JOHN	LANG	256 CLEARFIELD CT.	NEW BRITAIN	MD	21456	301-555-3096	F	06/12/57
FRAN	MC GLYNN	206 MOHEGAN ST.	BRISTOL	NJ	08901	609-555-9128	E	09/22/54
LORI	LIVEZEY	215 SANDY KNOLL DR.	HATBORO	PA	19901	215-555-6904	R	06/19/59
ROBERT	HITCHNER	206 MOHEGAN ST.	WARMINSTER	MD	21974	301-555-8947	F	02/14/60
PATTY	WALK	235 COTTMAN AVE.	MT. LAUREL	NJ	08054	609-555-0103	F	07/02/60
TIM	BOYLE	4237 PASSMORE ST.	PHILADELPHIA	PA	19135	215-555-1982	E	03/16/57
ED	SOTTALANA	295 BUCKMAN DR.	WILDWOOD	NJ	08054	609-555-0791	R	05/01/53
BRIAN	WYNNE	111 CATBRIER WAY	ROSEMENT	PA	18078	215-555-1331	F	12/31/58
VINCENT	RITTS	1105 PRIMROSE CT.	ANNAPOLIS	MD	21403	301-555-4131	R	04/15/52
MARY	TROUT	197 CHEW AVE.	PENNSAUKEN	NJ	08110	609-555-8190	R	02/05/54
JOHN	SWELTZ	527 SHERWOOD LA.	UPPER DARBY	PA	19835	215-555-1940	E	08/22/53
PAUL	BUNYAN	3109 WOODHAVEN DR.	PENNSAUKEN	NJ	08110	215-555-8253	F	09/18/56
ELAINE	HOUSTON	2083 PARKDALE AVE.	HORSHAM	PA	19154	215-555-8534	E	05/02/50

Figure 3.12 *Sample entries in The Little Black Book.*

the range names. If problems persist, execute the macro in the "step" mode. While in the step mode, the macros will be read one at a time with a pause between each keystroke. To enter the step mode press the <Alt> and <F1> keys before executing the macro. Type any key to continue to "step" through the macro until an error message appears. Note where the problem occurs and press <Alt>-<F1> again to exit the step mode. You can abort a macro any time by pressing <Ctrl>-<Break>.

Data Query

Setting up the data query section will complete the template. The data query section consists of the criterion range and the output area.

In the criterion range you can specify the criteria by which records will be selected for find or extract operations. The results of the data query operation are written in the output range.

Go to cell R30 and type **THE LITTLE BLACK BOOK.** Go to cell R31 and type **\ =**<**Enter**> */Copy* <**Enter**> **S31** <**Enter**> to place a row of equal signs beneath that label. Move to cell R34 and type **CRITERION.** In cell S34, type **Press** <**Alt**>**-X to extract.** Go to cell B90 and type **'/DQEQ{CALC}**. This macro will issue the Data Query Extract command, quit the data menu, and recalculate the worksheet. Then give the command */Range Name Create* **\X**<**Enter**><**Enter**>. Enter a label of nine hyphens in cell R35. Now copy the headings from the data input section to the data query section by giving the command */Copy* **B7..L7** <**Enter**> **R36** <**Enter**>.

To facilitate some reports from the data query section, you should swap the B.D. and Code column headings in the criterion section by issuing the following set of commands:

/Move **AA36** <**Enter**> **AA35** <**Enter**>
/Move **AB36** <**Enter**> **AA36** <**Enter**>
/Move **AA35** <**Enter**> **AB36** <**Enter**>

When this is done go to cell R41 and type **OUTPUT**. Then place a label of six hyphens in cell R42. Copy the headings from the criterion section to the output section by giving the command */Copy* **R36..AB36** <**Enter**> **R43** <**Enter**>. Reset the column widths as you did in the data input section. Move the cursor to column R and give the command */Worksheet Column Set* **10** <**Enter**>. Similarly, set column S to 15 characters, column T to 30 characters, column U to 13 characters, and column V to 4 characters. Also change column W to 8 characters, column X to 14 characters, column Y to 11 characters, columns Z and AA to 5 characters, and column AB to 7 characters.

The data query section uses only one formula, which simply keeps count of the number of output records. Release the <CapsLock> key, go to cell U38, and type **"Output Size:**. Then move to cell V38 and enter the formula **@COUNT(R44..R94).**

The range size in this formula will not expand with each new entry. Therefore if the value in cell F5 (which represents the total number of records) is greater than 50, the range in cell V38 should be increased. Go to cell R39 and create a repeating label of vertical lines by typing \|. Copy this cell across the row with the command */Copy* **R39** <**Enter**> **S39..AB39** <**Enter**>.

You should now create a few more range names, defining the criterion and output areas. Give

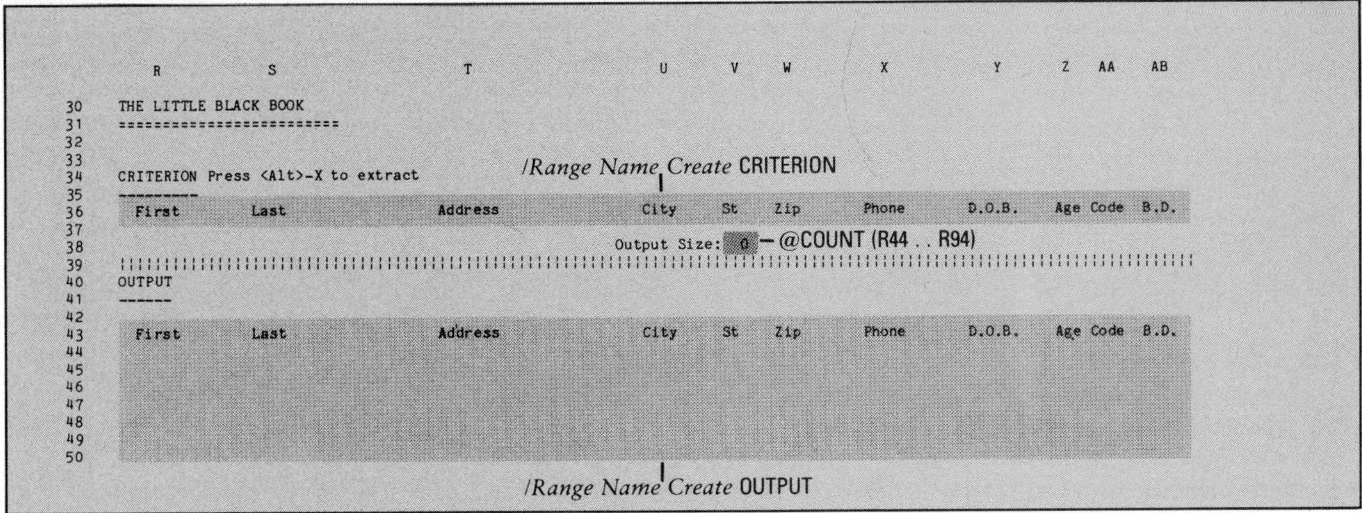

Figure 3.13 *The Little Black Book's data query section.*

the command */Range Name Create* **CRITERION** <**Enter**> **R36..AB37** <**Enter**>. Then issue the command to name the output section: */Range Name Create* **OUTPUT** <**Enter**> **R43..AB93** <**Enter**>. Again, if the data input section becomes larger than 50 records, the output range should be expanded.

If you have constructed the data query section correctly, it should look like Figure 3.13, except that the figure also shows the range names. This would be a good time to save the worksheet. Give the command */File Save* <**Enter**> *Replace.*

Extracting the Data

The Little Black Book uses the data query extract function to develop reports from the name and address data base. But before you can use any of the data query operations, the data input, data output, and criterion ranges must be defined. This will be easy since you previously named these areas with the Range Name command. You can define all three ranges at once with the following command: */Data Query Input* **INPUT** <**Enter**> *Criterion* **CRITERION** <**Enter**> *Output* **OUTPUT** <**Enter**> *Quit.*

Go to cell R37 and type **JOHN** and press <**Alt**>**-X** to execute the Data Query Extract macro. *1-2-3* will first look at the line or lines defined as the criterion range. Next it compares the criterion with the data in the input section. Any record that contains an item that matches the criterion will be copied to the output section. You should now have a list of everybody with the first name John.

Erase cell R37 with the command */Range Erase* **R37..R37** <**Enter**>. Then enter **NJ** in cell V37 and press <**Alt**>**-X** again. In a few seconds you will have a list of all New Jersey residents.

With NJ still in cell V37, move to U37, enter **PENNSAUKEN**, and press <**Alt**>**-X** again. Press <F7>, then <F9>. Notice that the size of the previous output list was reduced when you added another criterion.

Formulas are also permitted in the criterion range. For example, you can extract a list of all the people on your list who are over 30 years old. To begin, erase all entries in the criterion line with the command */Range Erase* **R37..AB37** <**Enter**>. Since we are dealing with age, we will use the Age column for the criterion, although an equivalent formula can be created in the date of birth (D.O.B.) column. Move to cell Z37 and enter the formula **+AGE>30**. The plus sign before the word AGE will tell *1-2-3* to treat this as a value and not as a label. Press <**Alt**>**-X** once again. Almost immediately the output section contains a list of people over 30 years old.

Complex Criteria

To make a birthday list truly useful, you'll want to get a report of birthdays that are coming up soon. For example, if you want to get a list of birthdays that are coming up this July, clear the criterion line and then go to the B.D. column. At cell AB37 type in the following formula:

+B.D.>=@DATE(84,7,1)#AND#B.D.
<=@DATE(84,7,31)

This somewhat complex formula can be broken down into easily understood segments. Simply stated, *1-2-3* will look for values in the B.D. column that are greater than or equal to the numerical value of @DATE(84,7,1) and less than or equal to the numerical value of @DATE(84,7,31). In other words, *1-2-3* will search and extract everybody with a birthday in July. Once you've entered the formula, press

<**Alt**>**-X** to perform the extract.

The data query function also has the capability to use wild-card characters for matching labels. The * character (asterisk) instructs *1-2-3* to accept any characters that follow it. For example, if you enter **S*** in the "Last" column of the criterion section and press <**Alt**>**-X**, you get a report containing records for Smith, Sottalana, and Sweltz. The ? character (question mark) tells *1-2-3* to accept any character it finds in that position. So specifying **JO?N** in the "First" column would return records for JOHN and JOAN. The last wild-card character is the ~ (tilde), which indicates "not this." If you were to place this character before a label, *1-2-3* would extract all items except those containing that character. Therefore, entering ~**E** in the code column would yield a list of all persons meeting the criterion except employees (E = employees).

Editing the Book

The data base template you have created in this tutorial is very flexible. It is easy to change the template to suit your needs. For example, you could add a column for titles or substitute some other calendar calculation for the date-of-birth column. Changes like these can turn The Little Black Book into an excellent marketing tool, for instance. With a little more effort and creativity, you could use the principles described in this article to devise a simple accounts receivable or accounts payable report system.

In the following article you'll learn how to extend The Little Black Book to print mailing labels, and you'll create your own menus so that The Little Black Book can be operated by even a *1-2-3* novice. Before you erase the sample data and start entering your own, save a copy of the worksheet under a new file name. That way you'll be sure the cell references in "Little Black Book II" (see the next article) will agree with the ones on your worksheet.

Paul McDermott is a senior microcomputer consultant for Mediq Information Systems in Pennsauken, New Jersey. He specializes in developing microcomputer applications for hospital budget forecasting, feasibility studies, and other financial projects related to the health care industry. Mr. McDermott also conducts in-house training seminars on 1-2-3. *This article was originally published in* PC World *Volume 2, Number 6.*

The Little Black Book II

Paul McDermott

The Little Black Book is a name and address file template to be used with version 1A only of Lotus Development Corporation's *1- 2-3*. The template enables you to quickly store and retrieve names, addresses, phone numbers, and birthdays of friends, employees, and relatives. In "The Little Black Book" I described how to set up the Data Input and Data Query areas of the template. In this article you will learn how to expand the template to incorporate features that print mailing labels from the name and address file and how to create your own menu to simplify the operation of the template.

Label Printing

Begin by loading *1-2-3* and recalling the file that contains The Little Black Book (blackbk). Erase any entries in the criterion line and go to cell V37. Type **PA** and press <**Alt**>- **X.** When the extract procedure is finished, you will have a list of names, addresses, and other data on all Pennsylvania residents. If you needed this information for mailing correspondence, you could make a hard copy with the / Print command and then type the names and addresses on envelopes. But this seems like a waste of time since the information is already typed. Ideally you would want *1-2-3* to print the data on mailing labels that could be affixed to the envelopes. The problem is that the address information in the output section is shown in a horizontal format, while the name, street address, and city, state, and zip code on a mailing label must be printed on separate lines.

To print one label using the /Print command, you would have to specify three print ranges: one for the first and last names, one for the address, and one for the city, state, and zip code. You would have to use about 30 keystrokes to print just one mailing label. That on top of trying to remember the proper spacing and other print options makes this method impractical. But you can create a macro program to do all that typing for you.

Before you start to create the label printing macro you should note a few assumptions. The labels used in this tutorial are assumed to be standard 3 ½- by 15/16-inch, single width (1-up Avery). We will be using only three out of the five lines available on each label; after seeing how the macros are set up, you can add a fourth or fifth line of text. Finally, the tutorial assumes that you are using an Epson printer. Other printers may or may not execute the correct spacing between labels.

The label printing macros consist of several parts. The first part moves the cursor to an instruction screen and gives the user the option of stopping there or continuing. If you choose to continue, a "counter" will be created, and the standard print options will be set. The next part prints a set of two labels. The last part causes the program to loop back to see if all records in the output section have been printed.

The Instruction Screen

To begin creating the macros, go to cell C92 and enter **MACROS FOR PRINTING LABELS.** Move to C93 and enter a line of 26 hyphens there. (Remember to start the hyphens with a single quotation mark (') to indicate a label.) Go to cell B95 and enter **{GOTO}label info** ~. Move the cursor down to cell A130 and give the command */Range Name Create***LABEL INFO** <**Enter**> <**Enter**>. The screen you now see is where the macro will pause before label printing starts. You will place a few instructions on this screen so that other users can understand the printing procedures.

Go to cell B132 and enter **INSTRUCTIONS FOR PRINTING LABELS.** Release the <CapsLock> key and enter the following instructions in cells B135 through B144:

B135: **Load labels in the printer.**
B137: **If labels are found to be misaligned after printing**
B138: <**Space**> <**Space**> **has begun, press** <**Ctrl**>-<**Break**> **and adjust.**
B140: **Press** <**Alt**>**-L to start printing again.**
B142: **Enter number for desired choice:**
B144: **BEGIN PRINTING = 1**
DO NOT PRINT = 0

Return the cursor to cell B96 and enter **'/XNEnter desired choice:~CHOICE~**. Go to cell B113 and give the command */Range Name Create***CHOICE** <**Enter**> <**Enter**>. Move to B97 and enter **'/XIchoice=0~{HOME}/XQ~**.

The macro in cell B95 will move the cursor to display a screen of instructions. The macro in cell B96 will prompt for input from the user and place that input into a cell called CHOICE (cell B113). The macro in cell B97 will evaluate the "choice" to determine whether to stop or continue executing the macro.

In cell B98 you will set up a "counter" that will keep track of the number of labels printed. With the cursor at B98 enter **{GOTO}counter~ + counter +1~**. Move to cell C98 and give the command */Range Name Create***COUNTER** **<Enter>** **<Enter>**. The formula in cell B98 will increase the value of cell C98 by 1 each time the worksheet is recalculated.

As long as you are giving out range names, you might as well create one more. Give the command */Range Name Create***COUNT** **<Enter>** **V38** **<Enter>**. Cell V38, as you may remember from "The Little Black Book" part I, is the cell that contains the formula to keep count of the records in the output section.

The macro in cell B98 causes the cursor to move away from the Data Query section, so you will want to return it to view the printing process. In cell B99 enter **{GOTO} criterion~**. From there you want the cursor to move down to the first line of data to be printed. Go to cell B100 and type **{GOTO}output~ {DOWN}{CALC}**. The print options will be set in cell B101. Move to B101 and enter **'/PPOMLO~S{ESC}\018~OUQQ.** This macro sets the left margin to zero, ensures the normal-size print mode will be selected on an Epson/IBM printer, and suppresses page breaks.

Cell B102 will contain an IF... THEN... ELSE statement. Move to cell B102 and enter **'/XIcounter >= count ~/REcounter~{CALC}{GOTO} criterion~/XQ~**.

Simply stated, if the counter (which keeps track of the number of labels printed) is greater than or equal to the count (the total number of labels to be printed), the macro will erase the counter, move the cursor to the top of the Data Query section (the criterion area), and stop executing. If the counter is less than the count, the macro will continue. The next part of the macro is for printing of the data.

The Printing Macros

The second part of the label printing macro will begin by printing two sets of labels and then moving the cursor down two lines. Next it will increase the counter before looping to the IF... THEN... ELSE statement. To have *1-2-3* perform this procedure, type the following macros in cells B103 through B109:

```
B103: '/PPR{BS}.{RIGHT}~LG
B104: 'R{BS}{RIGHT} {RIGHT}~G
B105: 'R{BS}{RIGHT}{RIGHT}
   {RIGHT}.{RIGHT}{RIGHT}~GLL
B106: 'R{BS}{DOWN}.{RIGHT}~LG
B107: 'R{BS}{DOWN}
   {RIGHT}{RIGHT}~G
B108: 'R{BS}{DOWN}{RIGHT}
   {RIGHT}{RIGHT}.{RIGHT}
   {RIGHT}~GLLQ
B109: '{DOWN}{DOWN}{CALC}{CALC}
```

Cells B103 through B105 print the first mailing label. Cells B106 through B109 print the second label, move the cursor to the next group, and increase the counter twice.

Adding a loop will complete the macro program. Go to cell B110 and enter **'/XGloop~2.** Next give the command */Range Name Create* **LOOP2** **<ENTER>** **B102** **<ENTER>**. This macro causes *1-2-3* to loop back to the IF ... THEN... ELSE statement in cell B102 to verify that all records have been printed. Finally, give the macro its name with the command */Range Name Create***\L** **<Enter>** **B95** **<Enter>**.

A list of Pennsylvania residents should be in the output section from the last Data Query Extract operation. Before you start executing the label printing macro, save the worksheet with the command */File Save* **<Enter>** *Replace.*

To test this macro it is not necessary to load labels in the printer. You can execute the macro by pressing **<Alt>-L**. Your output should look like Figure 3.14. While the macros are running, watch the control panel; notice how fast *1-2-3* executes the keystrokes and think how long it would have taken you to type the same commands.

If errors occur during execution of the macro, first check the text of the macro for completeness. A common mistake is to omit one or more tilde (~) characters. Also check the spelling of the range names. If problems persist, execute the macro in the "step" mode. In the step mode the macros are read one at a time with a pause between each key-

```
JOHN          BROWN
123 ANYWHERE ST.
ANYTOWN          PA   19040


ELAINE       HOUSTON
2083 PARKDALE AVE.
HORSHAM          PA   19154


JOHN          SWELTZ
527 SHERWOOD LA.
UPPER DARBY   PA   19835


BRIAN         WYNNE
111 CATBRIER WAY
ROSEMENT         PA   18078


TIM           BOYLE
4237 PASSMORE ST.
PHILADELPHIA PA   19135


LORI          LIVEZEY
215 SANDY KNOLL DR.
HATBORO          PA   19901


JOAN          MOYER
118 MEREDITH AVE.
DOYLESTOWN     PA   19010


DAN           HERBERT
179 MADISON AVE.
NORRISTOWN     PA   19457
```

Figure 3.14 *Printed mailing labels.*

stroke. To enter the step mode, press the <Alt> and <F1> keys before executing the macro. Type any key to continue to "step" through the macro until an error message appears. Note where the problem occurs and press <Alt>-<F1> again to exit the step mode. You can abort a macro anytime by pressing <Ctrl>-<Break>.

Create Your Own Menu

The last step in this tutorial is to organize the various sections in the worksheet to make the system easier to use. This can be accomplished by creating your own *1-2-3* menu with macros and the /XMlocation command.

With the /XMlocation command you can define your own menu, up to eight fields wide and two rows deep, similar to *1-2-3*'s menu. The first row contains the menu options. The second row may contain explanations for each of those options. The macros are stored below the second row.

When the menu macro is executed the menu will appear in the control panel. As with other *1-2-3* menus, you can select an option by typing the first letter of that option or by pointing with the cursor. When an option is selected *1-2-3* looks at the cell directly below the one containing that option for its first macro command.

The Little Black Book's menu will include options to execute the data entry macro, move the cursor to the Data Query section, execute the label-printing program, print the Data Query output section, and save the worksheet.

The /XMlocation Command

To begin go to cell C116 and enter **MACROS FOR THE MENU.** Place a line of 19 hyphens in C117 (starting the cell entry with a single quotation mark). Move to cell B119 and type **'/XMmenu~**. Create the two necessary range names with the following commands: */Range Name Create* **\M** <**Enter**> **B119** <**Enter**> and */Range Name Create* **menu** <**Enter**> **B121** <**Enter**>.

The first command assigns the macro its name, and the second names the location at which the menu can be found. The macro will therefore look for the first menu option at cell B121. Move the cursor to B121 and type **Input.** Go to cell B122 and type **Start to enter data.** In cell B123 type {**HOME**} and in B124 enter **/XG\d~**. These two macro cells will move the cursor to the home position (cell A1) and then begin executing the data entry macros. The range name \d used in cell B124 refers to the cells in which the data entry macros are located.

For the second menu option go to cell C121 and type **Data Query.** In cell C122 enter the description **Go to the Data Query section.** Move to C123 and enter {**GOTO**}**data query~**. Create the necessary range name with the command */Range Name Create* **DATA QUERY** <**Enter**> **R30..AA84** <**Enter**>. When you select Data Query from the menu, the cursor will quickly move to that section, allowing you to perform the extract function.

Go to cell D121 and enter **Print Queries.** In D122 enter the description **Print the Data Query section.** Move to cell D123 and enter **'/PPRdata query~**. Enter the remaining print commands in the following cells:

D124: **OML11~MR132~**
D125: **S{ESC}\015~OFQ**
D126: **AGPQ**

Whenever you use this menu item you should verify that the data in the output section does not extend beyond row 84. If it does, the range named DATA QUERY should be expanded accordingly.

The next column in the menu will contain the option for label printing. Go to cell E121 and enter **Labels.** Move down to E122 and enter **Print mailing labels from output section.** In cell E123 enter **'/XG**\L~. This macro cell, which is similar to the macro in cell B124, tells *1-2-3* where to read its next macro. In this case it will go to the label printing macros and begin executing them.

Move to cell F121 and enter **Save.** Type the description **Save the worksheet** in F122. Go to cell F123 and enter {**HOME**}**/FS**~**R.**

Finally, go to cell G121 and enter **Quit.** Move to G122 and enter the label **Leave the menu and return cursor to Home position.** In cell G123 enter {**HOME**}**/XQ**~. This last option provides an easy way to exit the menu. The other way would be to press the <Esc> or <Ctrl>-<Break> keys.

Once the macros for each of the menu options work properly, you should go back and make a few changes so that the menu will reappear after each menu option is executed. For the Input option go to cell B69 and change the contents from '/XI ANSWER=0~{HOME}/XQ~' to **'/XI ANSWER=0**~{**HOME**}**/XG \M**~.

For the Data Query option go to cell S34, press <**F2**> (the Edit key), and add ...**Press** <**Alt**>**-M to stop.** To alter the Print Queries option, go to cell D126 and change 'AGPQ' to **AGPQ/XG\M**~. For the Labels option go to cell B97 and change'/XI

A1:
Input Data Query Print Queries Labels Save Quit
Start to enter data

A1:
Input Data Query Print Queries Labels Save Quit
Go to the Data Query section

A1:
Input Data Query Print Queries Labels Save Quit
Print the Data Query section

A1:
Input Data Query Print Queries Labels Save Quit
Print mailing labels from Output section

A1:
Input Data Query Print Queries Labels Save Quit
Save the worksheet

A1:
Input Data Query Print Queries Labels Save Quit
Leave the menu and return the cursor to the home position

Figure 3.15 *Menus for The Little Black Book with different options selected.*

choice=0~{HOME}/XQ~' to **'/XI choice<=0**~{**HOME**}**/XG\M**~. And finally, to change the Save option, move the cursor to cell F123 and change '{HOME}/FS~R' to {**HOME**} **/FS**~**R/XG\M**~.

Auto-Start

You can put the finishing touch on The Little Black Book by using a macro feature called automatic macro execution. This technique causes a macro to execute automatically when the worksheet is loaded. Assign a special macro range name, \0, to the macro that you want to execute automatically as soon as the file containing The Little Black Book (blackbk) is retrieved. Give the command */Range Name Create* **\0** <**Enter**> **\M** <**Enter**>. Then give the command */File Save* <**Enter**> *Replace.*

When the worksheet is loaded the control panel should look like the first example in Figure 3.15. The other examples in the figure show what the control panel would look like with other options selected. With this menu, the prompts in the data entry macros, and the other on-screen instructions you have embedded in the spreadsheet, The Little Black Book can be used by a *1-2-3* novice.

Other Program Hints

Before you print labels with the macros, make sure a Setup code has already been entered. This can be done (if you are using an Epson printer) by typing the command */Print Printer Option Setup* **\018** or **\015** *Quit Quit.* If the Setup is blank and the macro executes {ESC}, *1-2-3* will leave the Setup option before it can enter the code.

Also, the macros can be documented while you create them or after they are created. The best way to document them is to enter a brief description of each macro in a column to the right of the macro. Since column C also contains some important macro data (the counter for example), you should use column D for the documentation in this case.

Once you have set up The Little Black Book, you will find many more possibilities for using the *1-2-3* features that you've learned. The Data Sort command is an excellent means of grouping or rearranging the data in the Output section. Columns can be sorted in either ascending or descending order with primary and secondary keys available. Refer to the *1-2-3* manual for more details.

The system for entering dates that is used in The Little Black Book is probably the easiest way to get around the limitations of *1-2-3*'s date arithmetic system. It allows you to enter the dates in a familiar format and still perform date calculations.

The label printing macro can be adapted to produce printed reports in almost any format. It selects and changes the range to be printed as it is executed and uses the printer controls on *1-2-3*'s print menu to adjust the paper in the printer as required.

The menu macro automates the procedures required to use the system on a day-to-day basis and allows a sophisticated system to be operated by a novice.

Paul McDermott is a senior microcomputer consultant for Mediq Information Systems in Pennsauken, New Jersey. He specializes in developing microcomputer applications for hospital budget forecasting, feasibility studies, and other financial projects related to the health care industry. Mr. McDermott also conducts in-house training seminars on 1-2-3. *This article was originally published in* PC World *Volume 2, Number 7.*

•
Star-Dot-Star

Following the pattern of the last two chapters, this selection is devoted to yet another software heavyweight: this time the program is the data management leader, *dBASE II.* "dBASE II SORT Magic" shows a quick way to sort while "dBOXES" provides a program that makes on-screen boxes with the PC's extended character set. The last two items help you control *dBASE II's* video output: "dBASE Displays" offers advice on the use of the SET COLOR command, while "dBASE Video" shows how you can reset the screen display attributes from within *dBASE II.*

dBASE II SORT Magic

When using *dBASE II* you may prefer the SORT command over the INDEX command because the former performs a physical rewrite of the data file, while the latter merely sorts an index file that contains pointers to the records in the data file. Unfortunately, the SORT command allows only one key field to be specified, whereas the INDEX command allows up to seven key fields.

What we would like to do is the following:

```
USE <oldfile>
SORT ON <field_1 + field_2 + ... +
   field_n> TO <newfile>
USE <newfile>
```

However, this form of SORT is not legal in *dBASE II.* The *dBASE II* manual suggests that sorting on several key fields be accomplished by cascading sorts. The most minor key is sorted first, then the next most minor key, and so on through the major key. This is an awkward and time-consuming solution at best.

The following sequence of commands performs the desired task in a much more straightforward manner:

```
USE <oldfile>
INDEX ON <field_1 + field_2 + ... +
   field_n> TO <tempfile>
COPY TO <newfile>
USE <newfile>
DELETE FILE <tempfile.ndx>
```

The only limitation to using the Index command is that descending sorts are not supported as they are with the Sort command.

Gary Kinsman
Chatsworth, California

dBoxes

Figure 3.16, MAKEBOX, is a *dBASE II* program that draws boxes using the horizontal, vertical, and corner characters of the IBM PC character set. The input to the program must be set to indicate the starting row and column position for the box and

```
**********************
*       MAKEBOX      *
**********************

* A = Upper Right Corner
* B = Horizontal Bar
* C = Upper Left Corner
* D = Lower Right Corner
* E = Lower Left Corner
* F = Vertical Bar

STORE CHR(201) TO A
STORE CHR(205) TO B
STORE CHR(187) TO C
STORE CHR(188) TO D
STORE CHR(200) TO E
STORE CHR(186) TO F

STORE RR TO ROW
STORE CC TO COL

@ ROW,COL SAY A
@ ROW+RI,COL SAY E
@ ROW,COL+CI SAY C
@ ROW+RI,COL+CI SAY D

DO WHILE COL<CI+CC-1
   STORE COL+1 TO COL
   @ ROW,COL SAY B
   @ ROW+RI,COL SAY B
ENDDO
STORE CC TO COL
DO WHILE ROW<RI+RR-1
   STORE ROW+1 TO ROW
   @ ROW,COL SAY F
   @ ROW,COL+CI SAY F
ENDDO
RETURN
```

Figure 3.16 *MAKEBOX: A* dBASE II *subroutine for drawing squares and rectangles.*

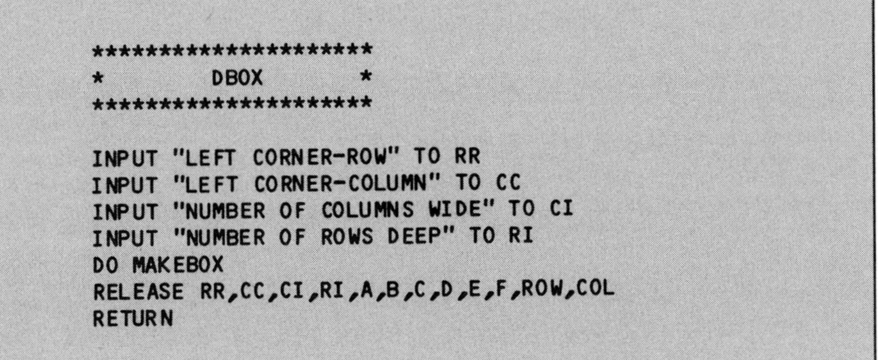

```
*********************
*       DBOX        *
*********************

INPUT "LEFT CORNER-ROW" TO RR
INPUT "LEFT CORNER-COLUMN" TO CC
INPUT "NUMBER OF COLUMNS WIDE" TO CI
INPUT "NUMBER OF ROWS DEEP" TO RI
DO MAKEBOX
RELEASE RR,CC,CI,RI,A,B,C,D,E,F,ROW,COL
RETURN
```

Figure 3.17 *DBOX: A* dBASE II *program that demonstrates MAKEBOX subroutine.*

the number of rows and columns for its height and width. The statements shown in DBOX (Figure 3.17) demonstrate the MAKEBOX program.
Raymond Sarnowski
Pittsburgh, Pennsylvania

dBASE Displays

The *dBASE II* SET COLOR command allows a user to set separate video attributes for data displayed by the program and data typed by the user. The format of the command is SET COLOR TO *get, say,* where *get* is the attribute assigned to GET statements (data typed by the user) and *say* is the value assigned to SAY statements (data displayed by the program).

I have found that DBVIDEO (Table 3.2) is a very useful tool for determining values for *get* and *say.* It works for *dBASE II*, version 2.4, and probably later versions as well.
Michael Gilbert
San Francisco, California

Intensity	**Flashing**	**Underlined**	**Reverse**	**Value**
Blank				0
Low				7
High				15
Low		xxx		1
High		xxx		9
Low	xxx			135
High	xxx			143
Low			xxx	112
High			xxx	120
Low	xxx	xxx		129
High	xxx	xxx		137
Low	xxx		xxx	240
High	xxx		xxx	248

Table 3.2 *Values for the* dBASE II *SET COLOR statement.*

dBASE Video

dBASE II displays data being edited in reverse video. A few hours of data entry in this black-on-white mode and you're assured "monitor eyes." Many users avoid the eyestrain by using the SET INTENSITY OFF command. However, there are times when you want some screen enhancement.

Figure 3.18 is a short program that allows you to reset the PC's display attributes while in *dBASE II.* The byte that specifies the way your monitor displays fields and GET phrases is at location 417 hexadecimal (1047 decimal). By resetting this byte you can use the IBM monochrome monitor's dual intensity,

```
***************************************************************
* PROGRAM NAME: DISPLAY.PRG                                   *
***************************************************************
* THIS PROGRAM ALLOWS THE USER TO RESET THE IBM PC'S VIDEO    *
* ATTRIBUTES.                                                 *
***************************************************************
ERASE
@ 5,5 SAY "THIS PROGRAM ALLOWS YOU TO RESET THE WAY YOUR IBM PC"
@ 6,5 SAY "DISPLAYS DATA FIELDS, GET PHRASES, ETC.
@ 8,5 SAY "JUST PRESS <ENTER> TO LEAVE DISPLAY ATTRIBUTE AS IT IS."
@ 10,10 SAY "1> REVERSE VIDEO"
@ 12,10 SAY "2> HIGH INTENSITY"
@ 14,10 SAY "3> UNDERLINED"
@ 16,10 SAY "4> HIGH INTENSITY UNDERLINED"
@ 18,10 SAY "5> BLINKING"
@ 20,10 SAY "6> NO ENHANCEMENT"
STORE "   " TO CHOICE
@ 23,5 SAY "PLEASE ENTER YOUR CHOICE"
@ 23,30 GET CHOICE
READ
DO CASE
   CASE CHOICE="1"
   POKE 1047,112
   CASE CHOICE="2"
   POKE 1047,15
   CASE CHOICE="3"
   POKE 1047,01
   CASE CHOICE="4"
   POKE 1047,09
   CASE CHOICE="5"
   POKE 1047,135
   CASE CHOICE "6"
   POKE 1047,07
ENDCASE
RETURN
```

Figure 3.18 *DISPLAY.PRG*

blinking, and underlining capabilities. The POKE command used in the program is not in the *dBASE II* manual, but it works.
Rick Bernauer
Kansas City, Missouri

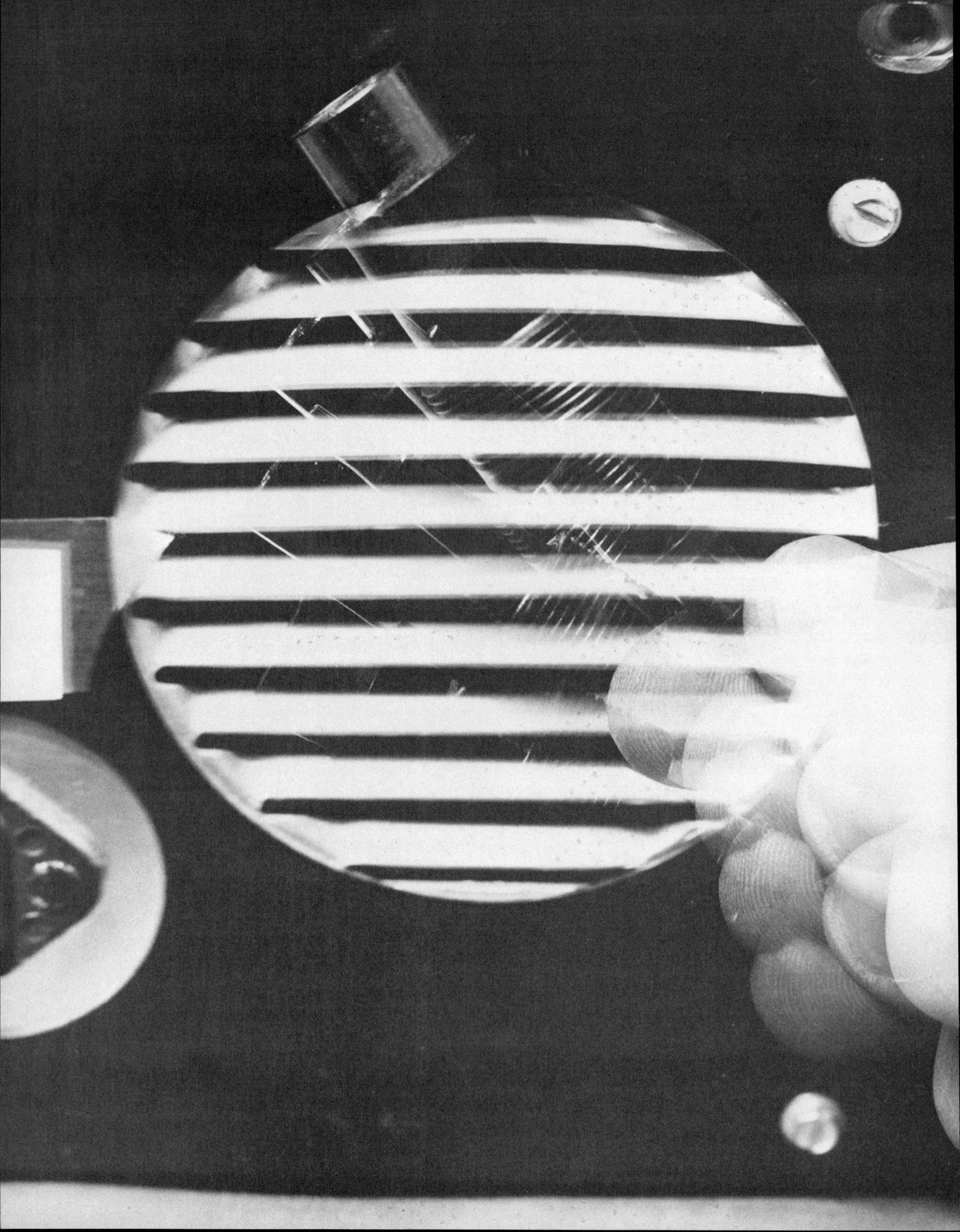

4

Graphics

Hands On

Computer graphics can mean anything from scrawls on a digitizing pad to the latest video game fantasy to architectural drawings produced by CAD/CAM software. Just like noncomputer graphics, computer graphics are used for art, for entertainment, and for communication. Besides being pleasing to the eye, computer graphics—whether they're produced by spreadsheet software or an educational program—can communicate complicated ideas and relationships quickly and effectively because humans remember visual images better than they do sounds or abstract ideas. The articles in this chapter sample only a small part of the spectrum of computer graphics applications, but they provide some useful utilities and give you a sense of what it's like to use programming to produce pictures.

The first two articles are well within the reach of the graphics novice. "A World for Your PC" not only gives you a clever Advanced BASIC (BASICA) program that draws a perspective image of a globe, rotated to any orientation you choose, but it has sentimental value for the editors of this book because the program created the globe pictured on the cover of *PC World*'s first issue. "1-2-3 Graphics Made Easy" takes you through the process of generating and printing a bar chart with Lotus *1-2-3.* Once you've completed this tutorial you will know the commands in the Lotus graphics package well enough to produce whatever type of graph or chart that you need.

The next two articles further explore the capabilities of BASICA and are more advanced. "Pixel to Printer" gives you GRUMP, a graphics screen dump program that enables you to print hard copy of pictures you make on your screen. The detailed, bits-and-bytes-level explanations of the GRUMP listings also make this article a good tutorial on BASIC programming techniques and commands. "Character Construction" gives you an assembly language program and a BASIC program that provide an easy means of designing custom characters or entire character sets that can be used with your word processing program and an Epson FX-80 printer. With a little programming, you can modify these programs to work with other printers that accept character fonts downloaded from the computer, such as the Texas Instruments 855.

The final article, "Screen Shots," offers detailed advice on how to take sharp, distortion-free photographs of your PC graphics without using special equipment. "Screen Shots" also provides a program that ensures you'll get the correct exposure every time, whether you're shooting a dazzling display or a single line of text.

A World for Your PC

Karl Koessel

This project began when the Art Director at *PC WORLD* asked me if I could help him create the cover of the magazine's premier issue. He wanted an image of the globe (see Figure 4.1) on the graphics monitor of the IBM PC. Although producing continental outlines would be an arduous task, the globular image suggested by the intersection of meridians and parallels, spaced every 15 degrees and drawn in perspective, seemed feasible. As he sketched an example of the globe, he told me he wasn't sure what size, portion, tilt, or screen position would be needed. This ruled out the possibility of drawing a single etch-a-sketch-type image, and I realized that what he needed was a program that would allow him to designate any orientation and then draw the appropriate image. With this type of program he could create and observe any number of different images and use whichever he preferred. A day and a half later I finished the program. I was amazed at how short and simple it turned out (see Figure 4.3 at the end of this article).

Load BASICA and type in the program. As always, reproduce the listing exactly. Many of the lines are very similar; take care.

Where In the World Are You?

The program contains sample data (see Figure 4.2) so that you can see one of the possible orientations without having to enter workable values (no checks are provided for improper entries). Run the sample by answering 'Want to see a sample run (Y/N)?' with 'yes', and study the queries and their sample responses.

The 'screen location of center of globe' values position the image on the screen. For the sample run, 160 and 100, the values for the program's variables XC and YC place the center of the image at the center of the screen. Smaller values for XC move the image to the left, and larger values to the right. Smaller values for YC move the image up, and larger values down.

The 'relative coordinates of observer' position the point of observation relative to the center of the image of the globe. This positioning is analogous to your seat number, floor, and row at a symphony concert: the first value, for the variable XOBS, is your position to the right of center when positive (or left of center when negative); the second, for YOBS, is your position above the stage when positive (or below when negative); and the third, for ZOBS, is your position away from the stage. ZOBS must be larger than the sphere's radius, which is entered later (you can't see the orchestra if you're sitting inside it). In other words, you may use any values for XOBS and YOBS, but ZOBS must be positive and larger than the radius.

The 'parallel, meridian, & image's tilt' values position the globe to a specified orientation. The first and second parameters (for the variables XROT and YROT) of this input determine the parallel (positive values are north, negative values are south) and meridian (positive values are east, negative values are west) that will cross at the image's center (assuming XOBS = 0 and YOBS = 0). The third parameter (for ZROT) is the number of degrees counterclockwise that the image will be turned around the specified parallel and meridian.

The 'sphere's radius' may be any positive value, but remember that ZOBS (observer's distance away from the screen) must be larger than the radius. All of the values for distance are entered in terms of the 320 horizontal and 200 vertical pixels of the PC's medium-resolution graphics mode.

The background color on the PC is chosen by a number from 0 to 15. Zero (black), one (blue), eight (gray), and nine (light blue) are the best choices; other values may match the color of some of the longitude and latitude lines, rendering them invisible.

The screen's aspect ratio (see the "Remarks" for the CIRCLE statement in the IBM BASIC manual) is the actual length of a number of vertical pixels divided by the actual length of the same number of horizontal pixels. The value you input must be a single number, not a ratio (for example, 1.21875, not 19.5/16).

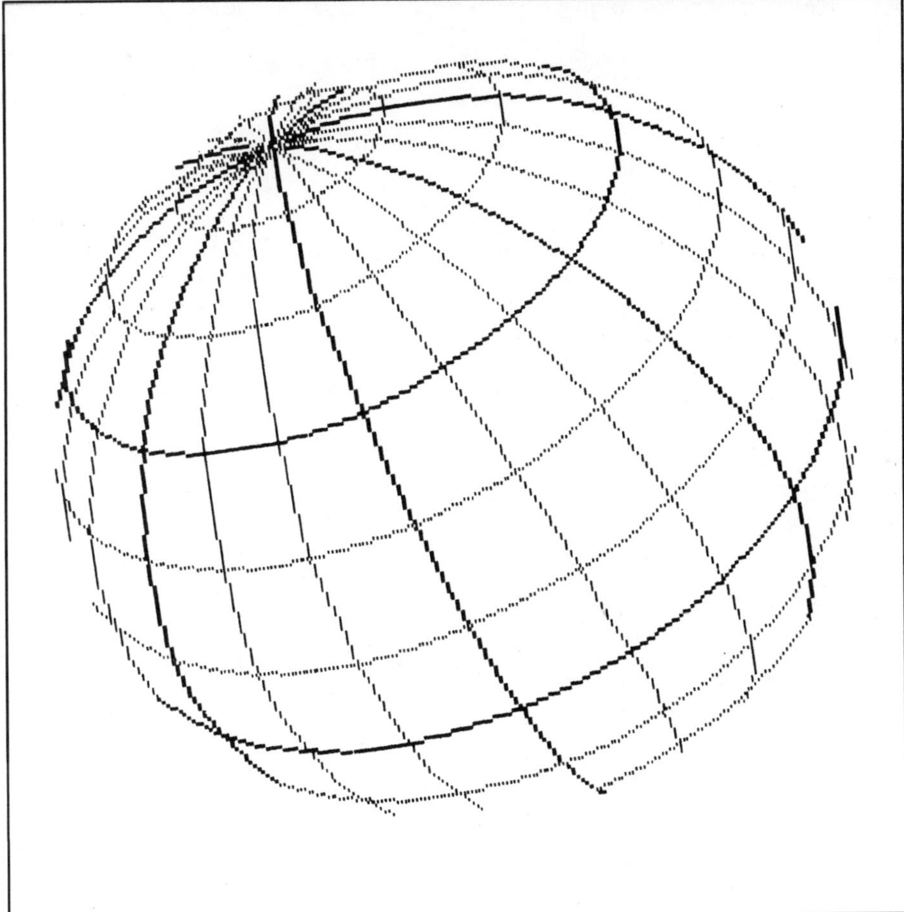

Figure 4.1 PC World *globe.*

```
Perspective Image of Rotated Globe

Want to see a sample run (Y/N)
? yes

Enter screen location of center of
globe (e.g. 160,100) ? 160 , 100

Enter relative coordinates of
  observer:
points left(−) / right(+) of X,
below(−) / above(+) Y,
and distance from the screen
(e.g. −9,0,456) ? − 9 , 0 , 456

Enter parallel, meridian, & image's
  tile
(e.g. 37,−123,23) ? 37 , − 123 , 23

Enter sphere's radius
(e.g. 100) ? 100

Enter background color and palette
(e.g. 1,1) ? 1 , 1

Enter this screen's aspect ratio
(e.g. 1.21875) ? 1.21875

Hit Any Key To Continue
```

Figure 4.2 *Screen dump of the program's queries as answered by the sample run.*

Different graphics monitors have different aspect ratios. The sample run uses the value 1.21875, but you should normally enter the correct value for your display. If you do not know your monitor's aspect ratio, stop the program (press <Ctrl>-<ScrollLock>), and type in this direct command: **CLS:DRAW "BM20,0R199D199L199U199"** then press <Enter>. Get a ruler and measure the lines on the display, and then calculate: aspect ratio = vertical length/horizontal length. Write it down, type **CONT**, and press <Enter>. Enter the screen's calculated aspect ratio, get up, and stretch. Approximately 4½ minutes are required to draw the globe.

Global Notes

If you choose values that keep the globe's image within the screen boundaries, you can cut the program's execution time about 6 to 7 percent by placing an apostrophe in front of 'Q=' on line 820 and in front of 'LX=' on line 840.

If you want the globe drawn in only one color, add the following line: **855 C$="3"**. You may use a 1 or a 2 instead of the 3 between the double-quotes. See the IBM BASIC manual for a list of actual colors drawn for different combinations of color values and palette values.

If you want to see the back side of the globe drawn as well as the front (as if you could see through the globe), place an apostrophe in front of 'IF' on line 810.

I hope this brief example has helped to demonstrate that with a little bit of programming, your PC world is what you make it.

Karl Koessel is PC World's *Technical Editor. This article was originally published in* PC World *Volume 1, Number 1.*

```
 10 SCREEN 1                          'PC WORLD
 20 CLS:KEY OFF                       'karl koessel
 30 PRINT "   Perspective Image of Rotated Globe"
 40 DEFINT L,R,X-Z
 50 CX=CY:CZ=SX:SY=SZ:I=J:R=A:B=C:A1=B2:C1=C2     'Order variables to optimize
 60 A3=B3:X=Y:XC=YC:LX=LY:B$=C$:RC=PI:LZ=ZS:Q=DR        'speed, aprox 3% faster
 70 DIM RC(11)
 80 FOR X=1 TO 11                                 'Prepare an array holding the
 90       RC(X)=(X-1) MOD 3+1                     'colors of parallels; pattern
 100      IF X>6 THEN RC(X)=(5-RC(X)) MOD 3+1     'reverses after equator which
 110  NEXT                                       'is brown or white (palette 0 or 1)
 120  PI=3.14159265#
 130  CF=PI/180#
 140  PRINT
 150  INPUT "Want to see a sample run (Y/N) ";S$
 160  S$=LEFT$(S$,1)
 170  IF S$="y" OR S$="Y" THEN GOSUB 900:GOTO 380
 180  PRINT
 190  PRINT "Enter screen location of center of globe";
 200  INPUT "      (e.g. 160,100)    ";XC,YC
 210  PRINT
 220  PRINT "Enter relative co-ordinates of observer:";
 230  PRINT " points left(-)/right(+) of X, below(-)/";
 240  PRINT "above(+) Y, and distance from the screen";
 250  INPUT "      (e.g. -9,0,456)   ";XOBS,YOBS,ZOBS
 260  PRINT
 270  PRINT "Enter parallel, meridian, & image's tilt";
 280  INPUT "      (e.g. 37,-123,23)";XROT,YROT,ZROT
 290  PRINT
 300  PRINT "Enter sphere's radius"
 310  INPUT "      (e.g. 100)        ";R
 320  PRINT
 330  PRINT "Enter background color and palette"
 340  INPUT "      (e.g. 1,1)        ";BCK,PAL
 350  PRINT
 360  PRINT "Enter this screen's aspect ratio"
 370  INPUT "      (e.g. 1.21875)    ";ASP
 380  CX=COS(CF*XROT+ATN(YOBS/ZOBS)):SX=SIN(CF*XROT+ATN(YOBS/ZOBS))
 390  CY=COS(CF*YROT+ATN(XOBS/ZOBS)):SY=SIN(CF*YROT+ATN(XOBS/ZOBS))
 400  CZ=COS(CF*ZROT):SZ=SIN(CF*ZROT)
 410  ZOBS=SQR(XOBS^2+YOBS^2+ZOBS^2)       'Observer's distance from globe's center
 420  ZS=R^2/ZOBS                          'Can't see if point's Z coordinate < ZS
 430  CLS:COLOR BCK,PAL
 440  FOR I=0 TO 3 STEP PI/12              '24 lines of longitude around poles
 450       RC=(I*12/PI+2) MOD 3+1          'Prime meridian color = equator color
 460       C$=STR$(RC)
 470       FOR J=0 TO 2.0001*PI STEP PI/24 'Step along the meridian circle
 480              A=R*SIN(I)*SIN(J)
 490              B=R*COS(J)
 500              C=R*COS(I)*SIN(J)
 510              GOSUB 730
 520              GOSUB 830
 530       NEXT J
 540  NEXT I
 550  FOR I=PI/12 TO 11*PI/12 STEP PI/12   '11 lines of latitude between poles
 560       RC=RC(I*12/PI)                  'From array of parallels' colors
 570       C$=STR$(RC)
 580       FOR J=0 TO 2.0001*PI STEP PI/24 'Step along the parallel circle
 590              A=R*SIN(I)*SIN(J)
 600              B=R*COS(I)
 610              C=R*SIN(I)*COS(J)
 620              GOSUB 730
```

Figure 4.3 *BASIC program listing for the globe graphic.*

```
630              GOSUB 830
640      NEXT J
650 NEXT I
660 OC=ASP*ZOBS*R/SQR(ZOBS^2-R^2)
670 CIRCLE(XC,YC),OC,3
680 LOCATE 1,1:PRINT "PC WORLD"
690 LINE (32,1)-(38,1),0:LINE (32,2)-(38,2),3
700 LINE (32,3)-(38,3),0:LINE (32,4)-(38,4),3
710 LINE (32,5)-(38,5),0
720 GOSUB 1180:GOTO 1200
730 A1=A*CY-C*SY                'Turn requested meridian to observer at 0,0,0
740 C1=A*SY+C*CY                '(B1=B, so B is used below for B1)
750 B2=B*CX-C1*SX               'Turn requested parallel to observer at 0,0,0
760 C2=B*SX+C1*CX               '(A2=A1, so A1 is used below for A2)
770 A3=A1*CZ-B2*SZ              'Turn image on axis perpendicular to screen
780 B3=A1*SZ+B2*CZ              '(C3=C2, so C2 is used below for C3)
790 DR=C2/(ZOBS-C2)+1           'Distance ratio for computing perspective
800 X=INT(A3*DR*ASP+XC)         'Screen's x (with perspective & aspect ratios)
810 Y=INT(B3*-DR+YC)            'Screen's y (with perspective, direction ratio)
820 RETURN                      '(Z=C3=C2, so C2 is used below for Z)
830 IF C2<ZS OR LZ<ZS THEN B$="BC":GOTO 860   'Insert ' before IF to draw back
840 Q=(X<0)+(X>319)+(Y<0)+(Y>199)+(LX<0)+(LX>319)+(LY<0)+(LY>199) 'Off screen?
850 IF Q+(J=0) THEN B$="BC" ELSE B$="C" 'Draw clear if Q or J=0 (new circle)
860 LX=X:LY=Y                   'LX,LY,LZ are X,Y,Z of last referenced point
870 LZ=C2
880 DRAW B$+C$+"M"+STR$(X)+","+STR$(Y)
890 RETURN
900 XC=160:YC=100                           'Data for sample run
910 XOBS=-9:YOBS=0:ZOBS=456
920 XROT=37:YROT=-123:ZROT=23
930 R=100
940 BCK=1:PAL=1
950 ASP=1.21875
960 LOCATE 5,1                              'Screen for sample run
970 PRINT "Enter screen location of center of globe";
980 PRINT "     (e.g. 160,100)   ?";XC","YC
990 PRINT
1000 PRINT "Enter relative co-ordinates of observer:";
1010 PRINT " points left(-)/right(+) of X, below(-)/";
1020 PRINT "above(+) Y, and distance from the screen";
1030 PRINT "     (e.g. -9,0,456)  ?";XOBS","YOBS","ZOBS
1040 PRINT
1050 PRINT "Enter parallel, meridian, & image's tilt";
1060 PRINT "     (e.g. 37,-123,23)?";XROT","YROT","ZROT
1070 PRINT
1080 PRINT "Enter sphere's radius"
1090 PRINT "     (e.g. 100)       ?";R
1100 PRINT
1110 PRINT "Enter background color and palette"
1120 PRINT "     (e.g. 1,1)       ?";BCK","PAL
1130 PRINT
1140 PRINT "Enter this screen's aspect ratio"
1150 PRINT "     (e.g. 1.21875)   ?";ASP
1160 LOCATE 25,1
1170 PRINT "HIT ANY KEY TO CONTINUE";
1180 IF INKEY$="" THEN 1180
1190 RETURN
1200 SCREEN 0,0,0,0:KEY ON
1210 END
```

Figure 4.3 *(continued)*

1-2-3 Graphics Made Easy

Joseph P. Celentano

Lotus Development's *1-2-3* is prized as an easy-to-use and powerful spreadsheet. The spreadsheet's partner in this integrated package—the graphics component—is often overlooked and underused. *1-2-3*'s graphics take data a step beyond the spreadsheet, presenting the information in ways that can be grasped quickly. And the graphics portion of the program follows the same easy command structure as does the spreadsheet.

This tutorial will take you through the steps needed to create, view, and print a simple bar chart—one of several types of graphs *1-2-3* is capable of producing. (*1-2-3* can also create stacked bar, line, *x-y,* and pie graphs.) The graph you will create is based on sales figures for a fictitious company called Systems Design Consultants (SDC). This exercise should acquaint you with enough of *1-2-3*'s graph functions to enable you to create graphs on your own.

The tutorial assumes that you are familiar with the overall *1-2-3* command structure. The terms listed in *italics* represent *1-2-3* commands that you perform. You can enter the commands by typing the first letter of each command word, or you can use the pointer and the <Enter> key to select the appropriate commands. Text in **monofont** represents text and values to be typed into cells or in response to prompts. To use *1-2-3*'s graph function as described in this article, you must have version 1A of *1-2-3,* and your PC must be equipped with a graphics board, 192K of RAM, and a graphics printer.

Building the Worksheet

1-2-3 constructs graphs based on data in a worksheet. To create a graph based on the SDC sales data, you must create the worksheet shown in Figure 4.4. Start with a clean worksheet (if necessary, give the command */Worksheet Erase Yes*). In cell C2 enter the label **^SDC CORPORATION SALES RECORD**. In cell C3 enter the label **^JAN 1, 1983 - JUN 30, 1983**. (The caret is added before a label to center it.) Enter the column headings shown in the figure into columns A through F of row 5, again using the caret to center the headings in the cells. To underscore the headings and to mark the boundaries of the columns, enter a single quotation mark followed by eight hyphens in cell A6. The single quotation mark indicates to *1-2-3* that the entry is a label and not a mathematical operator. Use the command */Copy* **<Enter> B6..F6 <Enter>** to copy the row of hyphens into each column in the row.

Enter the sample data shown in Figure 4.4 into columns A through F. In column G enter the month labels for each row, centering them with carets. Once the worksheet is complete, save the file to disk under the name SALESREC by giving the command */File Save* **SALESREC <Enter>**. You are now ready to graph this information.

Creating and Viewing the Graph

The worksheet that you created will remain on the screen after you save it. To access the functions that graph the data in the worksheet, give the command */Graph*. The Graph main menu is displayed in the control panel. From this menu you can design the graph by choosing attributes, or "settings." After each setting is made, this menu will be displayed again.

To tell *1-2-3* that you want to create a bar graph, give the command *Type Bar.* The next item in the Graph main menu, X, allows you to specify labels for the *x*-axis (horizontal axis) of the graph. For the SDC graph we'll use the month names in column G of the worksheet as lables. To specify this range of information, give the command *X* **G7..G12**. (An alternative method of specifying ranges in *1-2-3* is to position the pointer at the first cell in the range that you want to specify, press the period key to anchor the location, and move the pointer to the last cell in the range. When the area you want to specify is entirely highlighted, press <Enter>.) After you specify the range, the Graph main menu will be displayed again.

1-2-3 can graph up to six sets of data at once; you need only specify the range in the worksheet that contains each set of data, or the "data range." In this graph the sales figures for each city will be a separate data range. Items A through F in the Graph main menu allow you to specify the information that will be used for data ranges A through F. To specify the data ranges give the commands:

A **A7..A12**
B **B7..B12**
C **C7..C12**

A1: READY

	A	B	C	D	E	F	G	H
1								
2			SDC CORPORATION SALES RECORD					
3			JAN 1, 1983 - JUN 30, 1983					
4								
5	NY	SF	BOSTON	LA	PHIL	ATL		
6	--------	--------	--------	--------	--------	--------		
7	10000	14000	7000	18000	6000	11000	JAN	
8	11000	13000	9000	14000	9000	8000	FEB	
9	16000	11000	12000	13000	10000	9000	MAR	
10	17000	12000	13000	10000	13000	11000	APR	
11	18000	14000	12000	7000	13000	12000	MAY	
12	21000	16000	16000	11000	12000	15000	JUN	
13								
14								
15								
16								
17								
18								
19								
20								

Figure 4.4 *The SDC worksheet. This contains hypothetical sales figures on which the graph will be based.*

D **D7..D12**
E **E7..E12**
F **F7..F12**

The last setting you must specify determines whether the graph will be drawn in color or in black and white; to specify this choice, use the Options command in the Graph main menu. If you have a composite or black-and-white graphics monitor, select *Options B&W Quit*; for a color graphics monitor give the command *Options Color Quit*. The Quit command returns you to the Graph main menu.

Now that you have defined the attributes of the graph, you can view the results. From the Graph main menu select *View* to display the results (in the Ready mode you can press <F10>). A graph like the one in Figure 4.5 should be displayed.

Legends and Titles

The bar graph you have just created describes the data by month and sales volume, but a viewer would not know what information the graph depicts or what each bar represents. With the Options menu you can flesh out the graph with legends, titles, and other descriptions. Press any key to return to the Graph main menu.

To tell the viewer what the graph is about, you can add titles. *1-2-3* permits four levels of titles. The first title is positioned at the top of the page above the graph's borders. The second is inserted just below the first. The *x*-axis and *y*-axis titles appear next to the appropriate axes.

From the Graph main menu give the command *Options Titles First* **Systems Design Consultants <Enter>**. Add the other titles with the following commands:

Titles Second **Six-Month Sales History <Enter>**
Titles X-Axis **Month <Enter>**
Titles Y-Axis **Dollars <Enter>**

Then select *Quit* to return to the Graph main menu and *View* to display the graph again, with the titles you just added.

Now you can add a legend describing the city each bar represents. Press any key in order to return to the Graph main menu. Then give the command *Options Legend* A. A prompt appears in the control panel asking for the legend of the first data range (range A). Type **NY**. Identify each data range with its label on the worksheet (the name of the city for which it depicts sales) using the following commands:

Legend B **SF <Enter>**
Legend C **BOSTON <Enter>**
Legend D **LA <Enter>**
Legend E **PHIL <Enter>**
Legend F **ATL <Enter>**

The Legend command must be given each time, since *1-2-3* returns you to the Graph main menu after each command is given. Select *Quit View* to display the graph with the added legends, which appear beneath the graph border.

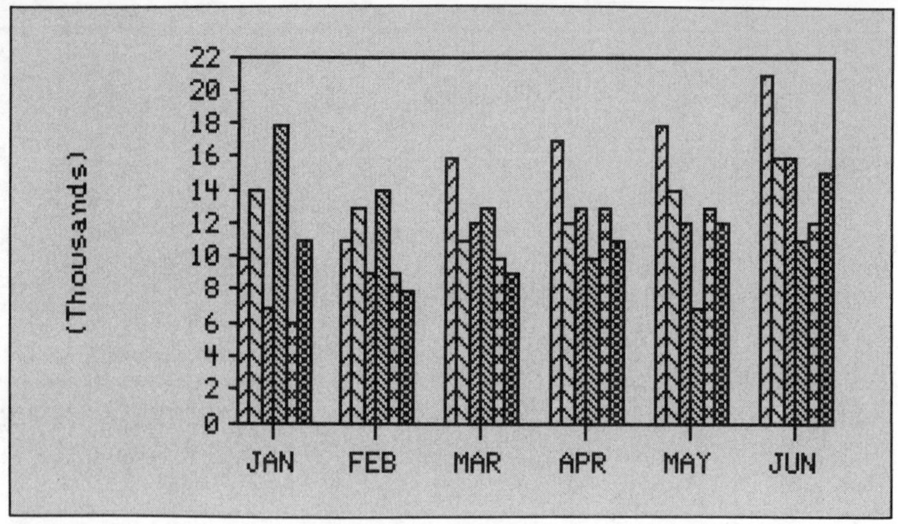

Figure 4.5 *The SDC graph with preliminary settings assigned. This basic configuration can be viewed after only a few commands are given.*

Scale Formats

For most graph types you can choose the scale in which the graph should be drawn. *1-2-3* will automatically choose a graph scale appropriate for the data. (We've used automatic scaling for the SDC graph in Figure 4.5.) But for special effects you can choose your own scale. For instance, to impress upon an audience of salespeople how much room there is for growth, you could set a much larger scale for the *y*-axis, leaving the sales bars cowering near the bottom of the graph.

For bar graphs, only the *y*-axis is numeric, so you will need to choose a scale for only that axis. The command *Options Scale* displays a menu with Y-Scale, X-Scale, and Skip options. (The Skip command tells *1-2-3* to graph every other data entry, such as A1, A3, A5, and A7.) To set the scale for the *y*-axis, give the command *Y-Scale Manual Upper* **60000** <**Enter**>. *1-2-3* will use 0 for the scale's lower limit unless another number is specified.

1-2-3 also allows you to choose from several formats for the data displayed in each axis of the graph. You can choose from Fixed Scientific, Currency, General, +/−, Percent, Date, and Text. The graph data is in sales dollars, so the format of the *y*-axis scale should be set to show currency($). Since you've just set the scale for the *y*-axis, the control panel still displays the options for the Y-Scale. Select *Format Currency*. A prompt appears requesting the number of decimal places to display. (The default is 2.) Type **0** <**Enter**>. Then select *Quit Quit* to return to the Graph main menu.

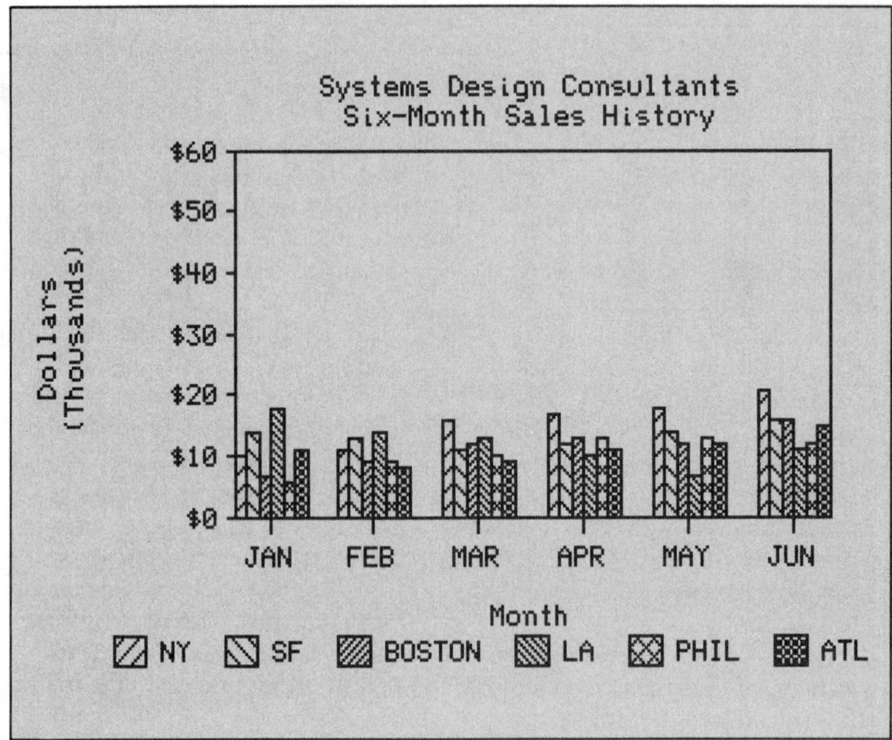

Figure 4.6 *The finished graph. Added titles and legends make the graph suitable for presentations.*

Use the *View* command to look at the completed graph with the bars scaled small enough to inspire the sales force. The displayed graph should be similar to the one in Figure 4.6. Then press any key to return to the Graph main menu.

Saving the Graph

To save the settings you have chosen, you must give the graph a name; in this case we'll use "SDC." To name the graph, give the command *Name Create* **SDC** <**Enter**> from the Graph main menu. The graph is saved as part of the worksheet file (SALESREC.WKS). Anytime you want to view the graph, you can call up the worksheet file and press <F10>. You can save several different graphs based on the same data in the worksheet file by giving each graph a different name. For instance, you could also store a pie chart based on the sales figures you've typed in the worksheet.

The creation of the graph is now complete. Since the graph is named, it will remain in the worksheet file. To manipulate or view the graph at any time after you have named it with the Name Create command, you must give the Name Use command from the Graph main menu. This makes the graph "current." Once the graph is current, you can change the graph type, the data ranges, the legends, and the other settings.

Before you go any further, you should save the worksheet file that contains the graph. To do this, return to the main menu (with the command *Quit*) and then use the command */File Save* **SALESREC** <**Enter**> *Replace.*

Printing the Graph

Although a graph can be viewed and manipulated in a worksheet file, it cannot be printed. To print it you must save it in a graph file (to which *1-2-3* automatically assigns the file extension .PIC). Since the graph was just saved with the worksheet, you must recall it again, or make it current. To do this from the Graph main menu, give the command *Name Use* **SDC** <**Enter**>. After you give the command, the Graph main menu will be displayed again.

To save the graph in a "picture" file, give the command *Save* **SDC** <**Enter**> from the Graph main menu; this creates the graph file SDC.PIC on the disk. To print the graph, you will access this new file. Leave *1-2-3* by giving the command *Quit Quit Yes.* The screen displays the Lotus Access System. If you are working with floppy disk drives, you must insert the PrintGraph disk in drive A: before you continue. Then select *PrintGraph* from the menu to load the program. The PrintGraph menu that appears lets you control several attributes of the graph, including the font style and the position and size of the graph on the page.

You can use two different fonts in a graph; the first is used for the first graph title, and the second is used for the rest of the graph. (If you do not choose a second font, the first font you select will be used for the entire graph.) Specify the first font by using the command *Options Font 1.* The screen displays a list of type styles available for the graph. The names of the fonts are followed by a 1 or a 2. A 1 following the font name means that the font is the regular (light) face of that type style; a 2 means the boldface version of the font. Select the font you want by using the <Space> bar or the cursor control keys to highlight your choice; then press <Enter>. To select the second font, give the command *Font* **2** and select from the menu in the same way.

After you select the fonts, the control panel returns to the Options menu. (Notice that the status screen, below the Options menu, is updated to show your new selections.) From the Options menu select the graph size with the command *Size Full.* This tells the program to size the graph for a full sheet of 8½- by 11-inch paper. Selecting *Half* prints the graph on half of an 8½- by 11-inch page. The *Manual* command allows you to choose your own values for the length and width of the graph, the size of the graph's margins, and the rotation of the graph on the page. After you specify graph size, return to the PrintGraph main menu by giving the command *Quit Quit.*

Ready to Print

Unless your hardware conforms to the default specifications in PrintGraph, you will need to set the drive, device, interface, and page size options with the Configure command. PrintGraph assumes that you are using an Epson FX-80/1 printer, that the picture file is in drive B:, that the Font file (on the PrintGraph disk) is in drive A:, and that you want to print on 8½- by 11-inch paper (the Epson's default).

If the graph file is not in drive B:, you must specify its drive location by using the *Configure Files Pictures* command. When you are prompted to do so, enter the name of the drive that contains the picture file. Then give the *Quit* command. These commands tell the program that the picture file (graph) is in the disk drive you specify, and then they return you to the Configure menu.

To tell the program what kind of printer you are using, give the *Device* command. A list of printers and plotters that the program supports is displayed. Use the <Space> bar or cursor control keys to move the pointer to the desired printer and press <Enter>. Back at the Configure menu, select *Interface* and indicate the computer port to which the printer is attached. After you have selected the interface, the program returns to the Configure menu.

The other two items in the menu, Save and Reset, are used later to change and save new configurations. Return to the PrintGraph main menu using *Quit*. Then give the *Select* command. A menu displays the name of the graph and gives directions for selecting that graph for printing. With the graph name (SDC.PIC) highlighted, press <Enter>. You will be returned to the PrintGraph menu.

You are now ready to print the graph. Turn on your printer and select *Go* from the PrintGraph menu; printing will start.

Variations

This article gives only one example of *1-2-3*'s graphics capabilities, but once you learn the basic process of defining settings for graphs and choosing PrintGraph options, you should be able to use *1-2-3*'s other graphics features. To make a pie chart or a stacked bar graph, you use many of the same commands that you used to create this sample bar chart.

Once you have created and named a graph, you can visually explore the ramifications of changes in the underlying data. After you revise the worksheet, the <F10> Graph command will quickly display the graph based on the new data, using the settings you've already chosen. You can also experiment with different ways of presenting the same data—to determine, for instance, whether a pie chart gives a clearer picture than a stacked bar graph or whether an effect you want can be achieved by lengthening a scale or using different data ranges. Your reports will never be the same.

Joseph P. Celentano is a 1-2-3 *instructor and applications specialist for Bechtel Power Corporation in San Francisco. This article was originally published in* PC World *Volume 2, Number 9.*

Pixel to Printer

Peter Baenziger

Almost everyone knows you can print a text screen with a single keystroke—<Shift>-<PrtSc>. This combination works well with most dot matrix printers, but it is limited to text mode. Pressing <Shift>-<PrtSc> with a graphics screen full of your beautiful designs will print gibberish unless you have both DOS 2.00 (or later version) and an Epson graphics or IBM dot matrix printer.

If you don't have an Epson graphics printer and you want to print out graphics, you'll need a special graphics screen dump program. Commercially available programs are fast and flexible, but they can cost as much as $50 each. And if you own an unusual dot matrix printer (one not commonly used with the PC), the program may not work.

Writing your own program can be a frustrating chore. Graphics screen dump programs written in BASIC are incredibly slow. They are full of DEF SEGs, PEEKs, POKEs, loops within loops, and memory addresses by the thousands—certainly not the kind of program you whip out in a couple of hours. But don't dismiss BASIC altogether, in particular BASICA. An effective, relatively small graphics dump routine, GRUMP, can be written with only one DEF SEG and PEEK, and it prints in less than three minutes.

What do you need to make GRUMP work? The answer: an IBM PC with an IBM Color/Graphics Adapter, a monitor, one disk drive, and Advanced BASIC (BASICA)—in other words, a standard PC configuration for graphics work. (Disk BASIC does not have the necessary graphics commands.) You will also need a dot matrix printer with bit graphics mode, which allows free form printing. Keep the printer manual on hand; you may need it to adapt GRUMP to your printer.

You don't have to be a programmer, but you should be familiar with BASIC's commonly used commands, statements, and functions.

Printer Primer

GRUMP performs two major tasks: it reads the screen and converts the graphic images into a form easily accessible to BASIC, and it converts data for the printer and prints it.

Most dot matrix printers with the exception of the original IBM PC printer have a bit graphics mode. What exactly does *bit graphics* mean? The printhead of a dot matrix printer has seven to nine needles that individually push out against an inked ribbon and print the miniature dots comprising a dot matrix character.

The printer normally prints a prestored pattern. When the PC tells the printer to print the letter *A*, it sends the printer a 1-byte number that identifies the letter *A*. The printer references the correct shape in its ROM and then prints it.

In bit graphics mode the printer does not use prestored patterns, and the PC tells the printer which individual needles to extend. Each byte sent by the PC prints only one column of tiny dots. (One regular line has between 480 and 1440 dots, depending on the printer.) Since the needles are user controlled, you can print any shape. To print the letter *A* in bit graphics mode the PC must know the shape of the letter and send the printer anywhere from 8 to 15 bytes describing where to print the dots that make up the letter. Thus, speed and simplicity are traded for greater freedom.

A Matter of Bits

How does the PC tell the printer which needles to extend? It all depends on bits and bytes. All data in a computer is represented by the numbers 0 and 1, which correspond to the absence or presence of electricity in a circuit. Each 0 (off) or 1 (on) is a bit. A byte consists of 8 bits, which can represent a letter, a number, or in this case a small piece of a graphic image on a screen. Since 0 and 1 are the only numbers used, all information is represented in binary, or base 2.

The first bit in a byte, 0, can have a maximum value of 1; it is called the low bit. The second bit, 1, can have a maximum value of 2. Each position doubles as you move up the byte (see Figure 4.7). The last or highest bit is number 7; its decimal value is 128. Every printer uses a slightly different approach, but a typical, "idealized" dot matrix printer has eight needles stacked on top of each other; thus eight dots can be printed at a time.

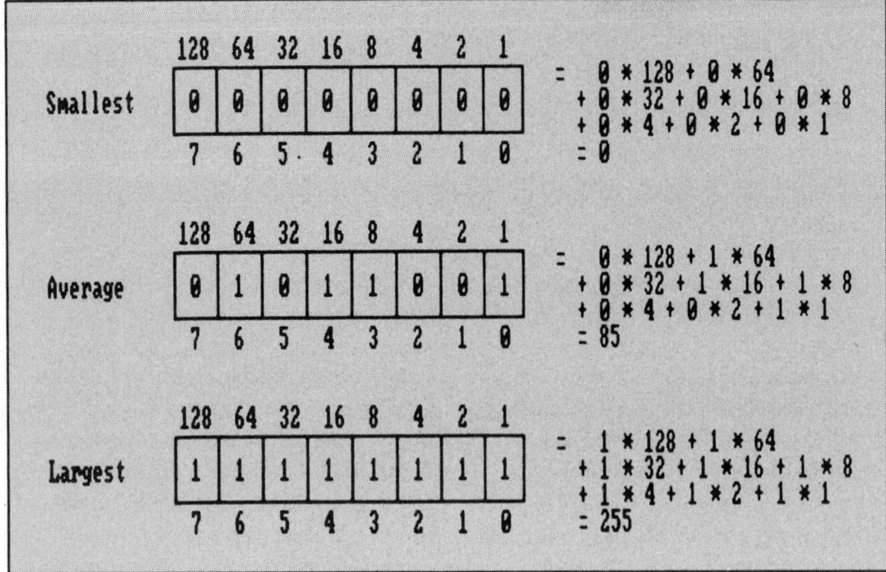

Figure 4.7 *Smallest, average, and largest bytes.*

When the PC sends a byte to our idealized printer, each bit of the byte is matched up with a needle (see Figure 4.8). If a bit is 1, one dot is printed; if a bit is 0, no dots are printed. The high bit (7) is matched with the top dot position; the low bit (0) is matched with the bottom dot position.

Thus, if LPRINT CHR$(89) is keyed in, the PC sends the byte with the value 89 to the printer, and the printer prints the pattern shown at the left in Figure 4.8. Sending any byte between 0 and 255 will print a dot pattern that exactly matches the bit pattern of the number.

But in the real world of printers, what you send is not always what you get. Some printers print the byte upside down, with the low bit up (see Figure 4.9). The number of dots printed also varies. Some printers print only 6 or 7 of the 8 bits. This information is important since GRUMP stores and refers to this number in a constant called NUMDOTS.

The Radio Shack LPVIII printer won't print the byte at all—CHR$(89) is not an acceptable graphic byte to this printer. It expects all graphic bytes to have the high bit set to 1. The high bit must be set to 1 before sending it the byte; it then prints the bottom 7 bits. Setting the high bit turns CHR$(89) into CHR$(217). However, if CHR$(217) is sent to another printer, that printer will balk since the high bit is expected to be 0. Obviously, this matter of bits is important to printers and GRUMP. The routine stores data that tells which bits need setting in the variables SETBITS and CLEARBITS.

Don't forget to check the printer's instruction manual. Table 4.1 summarizes characteristics common to most printers and the questions to which you should seek answers in your manual. Keep in mind that variations and changes in printers do occur, so use this table as a guide.

Finding some of this information in your manual may be difficult. Rather than telling you how many bits it prints or that bit 7 should be 1 or 0, it may tell you, for example, that valid graphic characters are those that have ASCII values of 64 to 127 decimal (or hexadecimal 40 to 7F). These values describe a printer that prints 6 dots. Since the numbers are smaller than 128, bit 7 must be 0, and because the numbers are 64 or greater, bit 6 must be 1. Another example is ASCII values 128 through 255. In this instance, the printer prints 7 dots, and because the numbers are greater than 128, bit 7 must be 1. Values from 0 to 255 indicate a printer that uses all 8 bits.

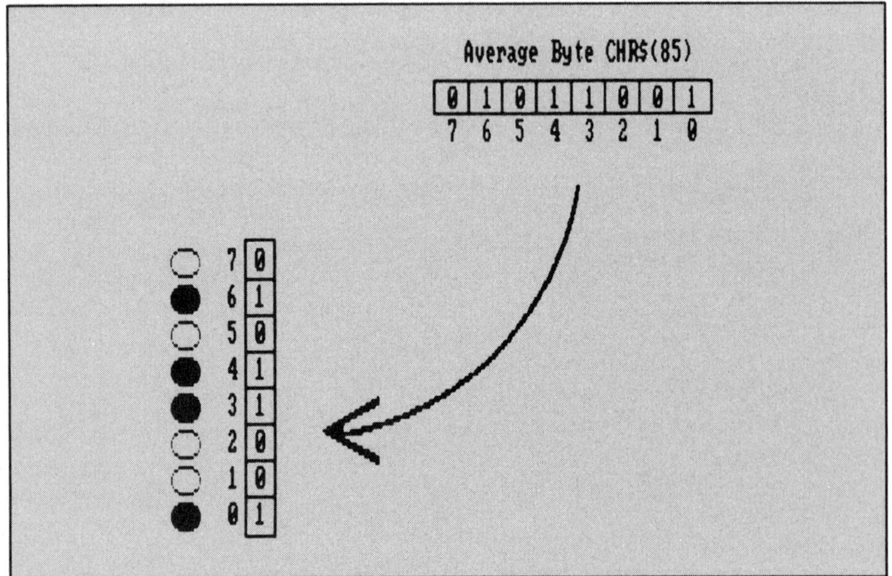

Figure 4.8 *Average byte being printed by idealized dot matrix printer.*

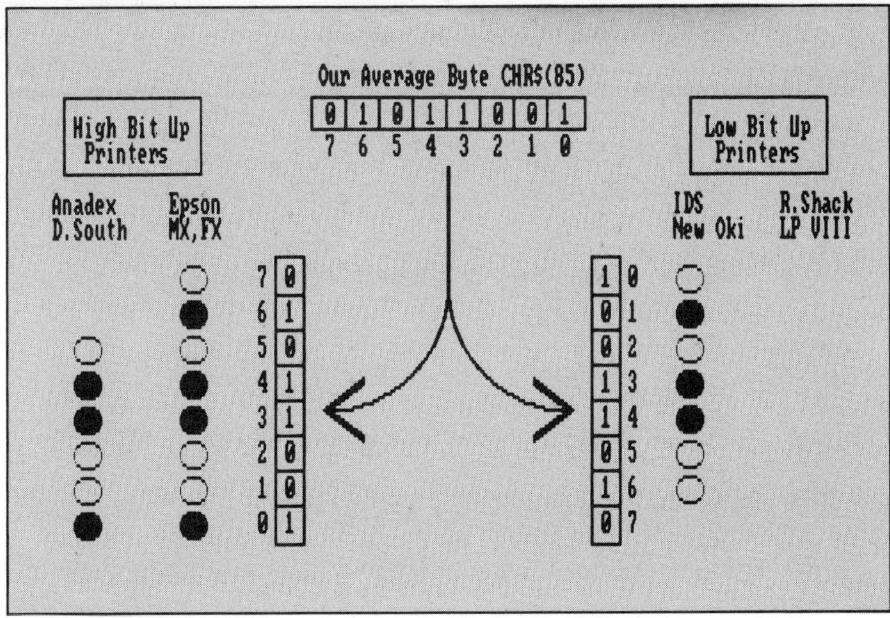

Figure 4.9 *How some printers print our average byte (or don't).*

Printer Commands

Four printer commands are needed to make GRUMP work: TOGRAPH$, SETCRLF$ and CRLF$, LMARGIN$, and TOREG$. TOGRAPH$ is a special command that switches printers to bit graphics mode. The command may be one character or a series of characters. Some printers stay in graphics mode until the mode is switched. Other printers need the TOGRAPH$ command repeated at the beginning of every line because they switch out of graphics mode automatically after printing a specified number of bytes.

With printers that switch at the end of every line, the TOGRAPH$ command often has to include the number of graphics bytes to be sent, usually 400 for GRUMP. But you can't send 400 because a byte's value cannot exceed 255. You must break the number into 2 bytes in a way that's easy for printers and computers to understand. You subtract 256 from 400 and send the difference (144) as the first byte. The second byte is 1, because you subtracted 256 only once. If you had to send 600 bytes, 256 would be subtracted twice. The first byte would be 88 and the second byte 2.

SETCRLF$ and CRLF$ commands can be used to override standard printer carriage returns. When a printer starts a new line, it advances the paper more than the height of the characters to allow some space between lines. In graphics printing, empty space is not desirable. The lines should butt seamlessly to make one continuous picture.

Some printers require special carriage return control characters. Others let you use the regular CRLF$ command, CHR$(13) CHR$(10), but you must preset the paper advance with a special SETCRLF$ command. A few printers will require either both or none.

Some printers allow you to preset a left margin (LMARGIN$), while others require that the left margin be specified after each line. How wide should the left margin be? That decision depends on the number of dots the printer lays down on a line, varying from 480 to 1440 dots for a regular 8-inch line. GRUMP can print a graphic image 400, 600, or even 800 dots wide. If, for example, a printer prints 480 dots across and GRUMP sends a picture 400 dots wide, the left margin would be 40 dots. Depending on the printer, you may be able to preset your margin to the 40-dot position, or you may have to send a positioning command at the beginning of each line. With printers that switch out of graphics mode at the end of each line, it may be easier to insert 6 or 7 spaces in regular character mode so the printhead is close to the 40-dot position.

The TOREG$ command resets a printer from bit graphics mode to regular mode. It may change only the printing mode, and the carriage return may need to be reset. You may also want to include a CHR$(12) command to advance to the next page.

One last point: some printers require that certain graphics character codes (SPECNUM) be sent twice because the code by itself has a special meaning. Some printers use CHR$(3) to switch to graphics printing. Thus, if you wanted to print the dot pattern corresponding to 3, you would send SPECNUM CHR$(3) twice—once to switch the printer to bit graphics mode and the second time to generate the pattern.

Getting off the Screen

The PC screen displays 200 rows of dots (see Figure 4.10). The rows are numbered from 0 at the top (SCRTOP) to 199 at the bottom (SCRBOT); each row is made up of points of light called pixels. In medium resolution, a row has 320 pixels; in high resolution, 640. The pixels are numbered from 0 on the left (SCRLEFT) to either 639 or 319 on the right (SCRRIGHT). BASICA

	IDS[1], New Okidata[2]	DataSouth, Anadex[3]	Radio Shack VIII
Byte orientation	Low up	High up	Low up
Dots printed	7	6	7
Requirements for bits not printed			
Bit 7 (the eighth bit)		Should be 0	Should be 1
Bit 6 (the seventh bit)		Should be 1	
Graphics mode command (TOGRAPH$)	CHR$(3)	CHR$(28)	CHR$(18)
Does printer stay in graphics mode?	Yes	Yes	Yes
Command for graphic line length			
Carriage return command (CRLF$)	CHR$(3) CHR$(14)	"6"	CHR$(13) CHR$(10)
Can you preset paper advance distance?	Optional	No	No
Preset command (SETCRLF$)	CHR$(27) "C 4$"		
Can you preset the left margin?	Yes	No	No
How do you set/preset left margin? (LMARGIN$) (8-inch paper width)	CHR$(27) "J 120 960$"	";100"	CHR$(27) CHR$(16) CHR$(0) CHR$(40)
Regular print mode command (TOREG$)	CHR$(3) CHR$(2)	CHR$(29)	CHR$(30)

[1] Applies to all Integral Data Systems models.
[2] Older (pre-1983) Okidata printers use different codes.
[3] Some Anadex models used different codes.

Table 4.1 *Printer characteristics.*

2.0 (or a later version) allows you to use different numbering systems, but this system works for all versions.

A row is always represented by 80 bytes in memory. In high resolution (SCREEN 2) each bit in a byte stands for 1 pixel. Thus, 8 pixels are in a byte; 80 bytes for 640 pixels. A bit value of 1 corresponds to a visible pixel.

In medium resolution (SCREEN 1) 2 bits in each byte represent 1 pixel. Each byte stands for 4 pixels and 80 bytes for 320. Two bits can have four combinations: 00, 01, 10, or 11. The combination 00 stands for no dot, and the other three stand for the three colors allowed in medium resolution. Since most printers can't print color, 11 is printed as black, 01 and 10 as grey stripes, and 00 as white.

Because the screen is shaped like a piece of paper held sideways, printing from the screen is simplified by dumping graphics onto paper in the same orientation—sideways. The top of the screen doesn't correspond to the top of the paper, but to the right or the left edge, depending on the printer. With a low-bit-up printer the right side of the screen becomes the top of the paper; with a high-bit-up printer the left side becomes the top.

If you are using BASICA's GET statement, a column of graphics bytes can be taken off the screen very quickly—200 columns in about 5 seconds. Screen memory addresses, or how the screen is arranged in memory, are handled by

Figure 4.10 *High- and medium-resolution screens.*

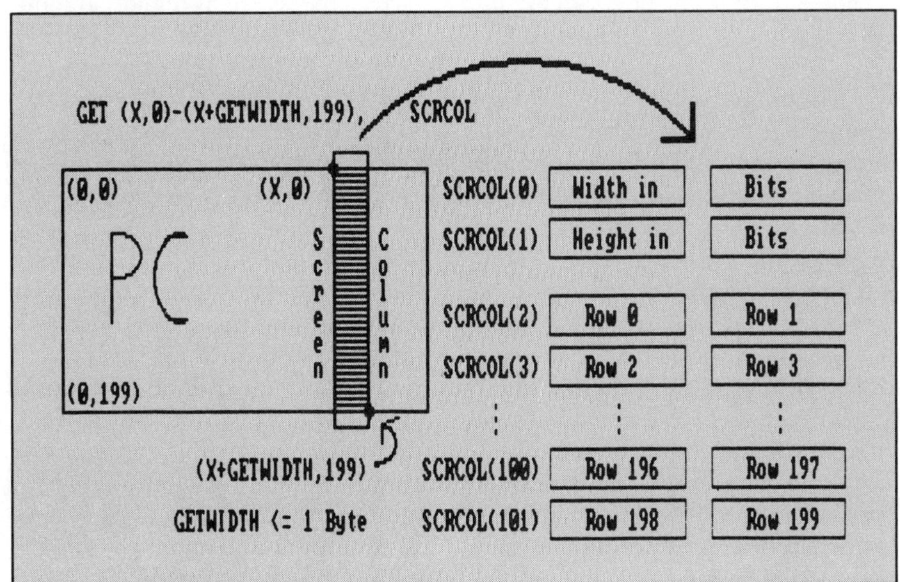

Figure 4.11 *How screen bytes are stored in array SCRCOL.*

BASICA. You specify the coordinates of two diagonally opposite corners of a column (it doesn't matter which) and tell BASIC where to put the bytes. In high resolution, GET (0,0)-(7,199),SCRCOL takes the left-most column of bytes off the screen and stores them in an array called SCRCOL. In medium resolution, in which 4 pixels are represented in 1 byte, GET (0,0)-(3,199),SCRCOL produces the same effect.

SCRCOL is a numerical array big enough to hold all the bytes taken off the screen. It doesn't matter what kind of numerical array you use (string arrays won't work) as long as there is sufficient space. The IBM BASIC manual gives the formula for determining how large the array should be.

Once you move bytes off the screen and store them in SCRCOL (see Figure 4.11), how do you send them to the printer? You can't LPRINT CHR$(SCRCOL(N)). BASIC interprets the 2 bytes as one number rather than two separate numbers. And this number could exceed the maximum byte value of 255.

Luckily, BASIC has a function called MKI$() (make integer string) that lets you deal with each byte individually. MKI$() doesn't change the bytes—only the way BASIC looks at them.

But there are additional complications. LPRINT MKI$(SCRCOL(N)) does not produce desirable results. First, if one of the bytes is a 13 (normally a carriage return), LPRINT automatically adds another byte (a 10) which is normally a linefeed. On most printers the result looks like chicken tracks because the printer is in bit graphics mode and here 13 is a pattern of dots. You can avoid this problem by using PRINT #1 wherever LPRINT is required. Thus, the command would be:

```
OPEN "LPT1:" AS #1: WIDTH #1, 225:
    PRINT #1, MKI$(SCRCOL(N))
```

The picture you finally get after all this will resemble what was on the screen—and that is another problem. The printed image will look as if there aren't enough dots in the vertical axis of the picture. Consider that a typical 12- by 9-inch monitor has a width-to-side ratio of 4 to 3. Corresponding to the 12 inches across are 640 pixels, versus 200 pixels for 9 inches, for a ratio of 4 to 1.25. The PC makes up for this unevenness by displaying pixels taller than they are wide.

A printer dot is usually "squarer" than a screen dot, and thus does not match a pixel on the screen, so two and sometimes even three dots are necessary. The number of dots used will depend on the printer. The solution is to pull the 2 bytes in each element of SCRCOL and double or triple them using the LEFT$( ) and RIGHT$( ) functions and REPS, which set how many times a byte is repeated.

Using the Listings

Before using any of the listings accompanying this article, review your printer manual. In particular, be aware of low- and high-bit placement, setting the printer for graphics mode, and setting left margins. All the listings run under BASIC 1.1 (or a later version) and work with the major printer types. GRUMP2ID is for Okidata and Integral Data Systems' P-Series printers (formerly IDS Prism), specifically model 80 (see Figure 4.12).

GRUMP2RS is for the Radio Shack Line Printer VIII and newer DMP printers (see Figure 4.13). GRUMP2AD works on most Anadex and DataSouth printers (see Figure 4.14). (Don't forget that on DataSouth printers function 49 must be set to print any graphics.)

All versions of GRUMP start turning variables by default into integer variables. Integer variables are stored in memory as 2 bytes. This makes the program run slightly faster and sets up the proper format for SCRCOL, the array at which the graphics bytes from the screen are stored.

The subroutine called by GOSUB 4000 determines whether the screen has high or medium resolution; the value is stored in the variable SCREENSTAT. After returning from the subroutine, the program checks to see if the value is between 4 and 6. A SCREENSTAT value of 6 means a high-resolution screen (SCREEN 2); 4 or 5 means medium resolution (SCREEN 1). If the value is not 4, 5, or 6, the program jumps to a short error message routine at line 5000.

The program then loads the machine language printing subroutine. There are several ways to integrate a machine language subroutine into a BASIC program. The best and easiest method is to reserve space for the routine within the BASIC work space (line 4500). DIM PR(48) creates an integer array having 49 elements of 2 bytes each. BASIC sets each byte to zero and then leaves this memory space alone unless you assign a value to one of the elements. In lines 4520 to 4540, values are assigned to PR(7) through PR(48) with DATA statements.

Lines 1000 to 1250 declare all constants and most variables. Screen constants come first and are the same for all versions of GRUMP. SCRCOL(SCRCOLSIZE) is the holding array for the bytes you GET off the screen. SCRLEFT, SCRRIGHT, SCRTOP, and SCRBOT are the four extremes of the PC graphics screen.

Lines 1070 through 1240 declare the printer-dependent variables. REPS indicates how many times a byte from the screen is repeated for printing. REPS will be 2 for most printers. SETBITS holds the value of the bit(s) that you want to set to 1. CLEARBITS sets a bit to 0. You subtract the value of the bit you want to clear from 255. For example, **CLEARBITS = 255-128** clears bit 7 because it has a value of 128.

NUMDOTS (line 1110) is the number of dots a printer prints, be it 6, 7, or 8. Closely related is STEPSIZE (line 1120), which sets the size of the "step" the computer takes across the screen as it takes graphics bytes. You should set a STEPSIZE to take the NUMDOTS value previously specified. (If your printer prints 6 dots, a step should be 6. This means that a column 6 pixels across and 200 lines high is taken.)

Remember that STEPSIZE for medium-resolution graphics is half that for high-resolution graphics because each pixel is 2 bits. With 7-dot printers, STEPSIZE is always the same since you can't take 3½ pixels. The sign of STEPSIZE is positive if the printer is a high-bit-up type and negative if it is a low-bit-up type.

GETWIDTH (line 1130) is the width of the column taken off the screen measured in pixels. Because GET takes both "edges" of a screen column, the value of GETWIDTH must be 1 pixel less. For an 8-dot printer GETWIDTH is 7 in high resolution and 3 in medium resolution; for 6-bit printers GETWIDTH is 5 in high resolution and 2 in medium resolution.

REMAINDER (line 1140) is the number of pixels left over after you've stepped through the screen—for 6- and 7-dot printers (8- dot printers don't have a remainder). In high resolution, for example, 639 pixels divided by 7 (for a 7-dot printer) leaves a REMAINDER of 2;

```
10 ' *****************************************************
20 ' *****        GRUMP for P-Series Printers        *****
30 ' *****    High and Medium Resolution Screens     *****
40 ' *****        Machine Language Subroutine        *****
50 ' *****************************************************
60 ' This program prints IBM PC high and medium resolution
70 ' graphic screens (SCREEN 1, SCREEN 2) on a P-Series printer
80 ' using a machine language routine. It works with
90 ' BASICA 1.1 and BASICA 2.0.
100 'Peter Baenziger, 1215 Lane Blvd., Kalamazoo, MI 49001
110 '
120 '
130 '
140 DEFINT A-Z
150 GOSUB 4000 ' Determine what screen we're on
160 IF SCREENSTAT>6 OR SCREENSTAT <4 THEN ERRMSG$="Screen not in graphics
    mode":GOTO 5000
170 '
180 GOSUB 4500 ' Load machine language subroutine
190 IF CROSSCHECK<>CHECK THEN ERRMSG$="One or more of the numbers in the
    DATA is wrong":GOTO 5000
970 '
980 ' Screen related variables
990 ' -----------------------
1000 SCRCOLSIZE=101
1010 DIM SCRCOL(SCRCOLSIZE) ' Holding array for data "gotten" from screen
1020 SCRLEFT=0:IF SCREENSTAT=6 THEN SCRRIGHT=639 ELSE SCRRIGHT=319 ' Screen
     column numbers
1030 SCRTOP=0:SCRBOT=199 ' Screen row numbers
1040 '
1050 ' Printer dependent variables
1060 ' --------------------------
1070 REPS=2 ' How many times a byte should be repeated in printing
1080 SETBITS=0 ' 0 means no bits need setting.  To set a bit, set SETBITS
     to the value of the bit you want to set
1090 CLEARBITS=255-128 ' 255 means no bits need clearing.  To clear a bit,
     subtract its value from 255.
1100 SPECNUM=3 ' Any special number for your printer that needs printing
     twice, such as 3 for P-Series printers.  SPECNUM=0 means no special number
1110 NUMDOTS=7 ' How many dots the printer prints in one pass
1120 STEPSIZE=-NUMDOTS ' How we step through the screen
1130 IF SCREENSTAT=6 THEN GETWIDTH=6 ELSE GETWIDTH=3 ' GETWIDTH+1 dots are
     taken off the screen in one pass
1140 REMAINDER=SCRRIGHT MOD NUMDOTS ' Screen column number of last printer
     line (HiRes) or last two lines (MedRes)
1150 SHIFT=1 ' Number of bit positions to shift to right. 0 means no shift.
1160 PRINTROW=0 ' This variable will hold the address of the printing
     routine
1190 '
1200 TOGRAPH$=CHR$(3) ' Switch to graphics
1210 TOREG$=CHR$(3)+CHR$(2)+CHR$(12) ' Switch back & advance to next page
1220 SETCRLF$=CHR$(27)+"C 4 $ " ' Set linefeed advance distance
1230 CRLF$=CHR$(3)+CHR$(14) ' Actual graphic carriage return/linefeed
1240 LMARGIN$= CHR$(27)+ "J 150 960 $ " ' Left paper margin to center image
1970 '
1980 ' Setting up the printer
1990 ' ---------------------
2000 ON ERROR GOTO 5000:ERRMSG$="Printer is not responding"
2010 OPEN "LPT1:" AS #1 ' Printing in random mode
2020 WIDTH #1, 255 ' Keep BASIC from adding carriage returns every 80 bytes
2030 PRINT #1, SETCRLF$ LMARGIN$; ' Set advance and left margin
2040 PRINT #1, TOGRAPH$; ' Switch graphics mode on
2050 PRINT #1, CRLF$;
2060 '
2070 IF SCREENSTAT<>6 THEN 2500 ' MedRes printing
2080 '
```

(continues)

Figure 4.12 *GRUMP2ID for Integral Data Systems P-Series printer.*

```
2090 ' High Resolution Printing
2100 ' ------------------------
2110 FOR COL=SCRRIGHT TO REMAINDER+1 STEP STEPSIZE
2120 GET (COL,SCRTOP)-(COL-GETWIDTH,SCRBOT),SCRCOL
2130 GOSUB 3000 ' Printing routine
2140 NEXT
2150 '
2160 GET (REMAINDER,SCRTOP)-(SCRLEFT,SCRBOT),SCRCOL ' Last line, which is
     smaller
2170 SHIFT=8-(REMAINDER+1)
2180 GOSUB 3000 ' Printing routine
2190 GOTO 2640 ' To end
2470 '
2480 ' Medium Resolution Printing
2490 ' --------------------------
2500 FOR COL=SCRRIGHT TO REMAINDER+1 STEP STEPSIZE
2510 GET (COL,SCRTOP)-(COL-GETWIDTH,SCRBOT),SCRCOL
2520 SHIFT=0:GOSUB 3000 'Printing
2530 GET (COL-GETWIDTH,SCRTOP)-(COL-2*GETWIDTH,SCRBOT),SCRCOL
2540 SHIFT=1:GOSUB 3000 'Printing
2550 NEXT
2560 '
2570 GET (REMAINDER,SCRTOP)-(REMAINDER-GETWIDTH,SCRBOT),SCRCOL '
     Second to last line
2580 SHIFT=0:GOSUB 3000 ' Printing
2590 GET (REMAINDER-GETWIDTH,SCRTOP)-(SCRLEFT,SCRBOT),SCRCOL ' Last line
2600 SHIFT=5:GOSUB 3000 ' Printing
2610 '
2620 ' Switch printer back to regular mode
2630 ' -----------------------------------
2640 PRINT #1, TOREG$;
2650 END
2970 '
2980 ' Machine language printing subroutine
2990 ' ------------------------------------
3000 PR(0)=REPS:PR(1)=SPECNUM:PR(2)=CLEARBITS:PR(3)=SETBITS:PR(4)=SHIFT '
     Transfer parameters so PRINTROW can get to them
3010 PR(5)=VARPTR(SCRCOL(2)) ' Transfer starting address of SCRCOL
3020 PR(6)=0 ' Clear error flag
3030 '
3040 '
3050 PRINTROW=VARPTR(PR(7)) ' Address of machine language routine
```

Figure 4.12 *(continued)*

639 divided by 6 (for a 6-dot printer) leaves 3. The MOD function computes the REMAINDER.

As mentioned before, when the program GETs a graphics byte from the screen, it stores it in SCRCOL. However, when BASIC GETs fewer than 8 bits at a time (such as 7 bits for a 7-bit printer), it left justifies bits into the 8 bit positions of a byte starting from the highest bit.

But printers prefer the bits to be right justified. So you must undo what BASIC has done and SHIFT the bits back to the right. For a 7-bit column you have to SHIFT 1 position. For a REMAINDER of 3 the SHIFT is 3.

The beginning of the main routine (line 2000) starts with an error trap in case the printer malfunctions or you forget to turn it on. RESUME does not follow because there is no point in printing a graphics image with an error message printed over it. It's best not to insert this line in your own GRUMP version until it is fully debugged, because any error (not just printer errors) will send the program to the error message routine.

The printer is set to "infinite" width with the WIDTH #1, 255 statement (line 2020), which keeps BASIC from inserting unwanted carriage returns and paper advances at the end of every line.

Next the printer is set for graphics printing. CRLF$ (line 2050) at the end of the initialization clears the printer's buffers by printing it out. The exact procedure varies from printer to printer, but the pattern is essentially the same.

Finally, the system is ready to start getting bytes off the screen and begin printing. The actual print sub-

```
3060 CALL PRINTROW(PR(0))
3070 IF PR(6) THEN ERROR 24 ' Error 24 is Device Timeout, traps to 5000
3080 PRINT #1, CRLF$;
3090 RETURN
3970 '
3980 ' Find out what screen we're on
3990 ' ----------------------------
4000 DEF SEG = 0:SCREENSTAT=PEEK(1024+73):DEF SEG
4010 RETURN
4470 '
4480 ' Load machine language printing routine
4490 ' ---------------------------------------------
4500 DIM PR(48) ' Array to hold machine language subroutine
4510 CHECK=0 ' Check-value, to catch typos in entering the &H'numbers
4520 FOR N=7 TO 48 ' PR(0) to PR(6) hold data, so start with 6
4530 READ PR(N):CHECK=CHECK XOR PR(N)
4540 NEXT
4550 READ CROSSCHECK ' CHECK and CROSSCHECK should be the same
4560 RETURN
4570 '
4580 ' Data for machine language routine
4590 ' ---------------------------------
4600 ' Data on following line is for printer that prints LOW BIT UP.  For
     printers that print HIGH BIT UP, change to &HBAFD
4610 DATA &HBAFC
4620 ' Data on following line is for LPT1:.  For LPT2: change it to &H0001,
     for LPT3: to &H0002
4630 DATA &H0000
4640 ' Data on following 5 lines is the same for all versions
4650 DATA &H8B55,&H8BEC,&H065E,&H778B,&H8A0A,&H084F,&HC8BF,&HAC00,&HE8D2
4660 DATA &H4722,&H0A04,&H0647,&H22E8,&H0A00,&H75E4,&HF617,&H0247,&H74FF
4670 DATA &H3A0C,&H0247,&H0775,&H10E8,&H0A00,&H75E4,&H4F05,&HDB75,&HC033
4680 DATA &H4789,&H5D0C,&H02CA,&H8A00,&H322F,&HCDE4,&HF617,&H01C4,&H0B75
4690 DATA &HCDFE,&HF375,&HE432,&H00C3
4700 ' Next line is a CROSSCHECK for LOW BIT UP printers and LPT1:. For
     HIGH BIT UP printers and LPT1: change to &H3452
4710 DATA &H3453
4970 '
4980 ' Error messages
4990 ' --------------
5000 BEEP:PRINT ERRMSG$:END
```

Figure 4.12 *(continued)*

routines start at line 3000.

Because machine language is so fast, PRINTROW always performs operations such as shifting, setting, and clearing bits and checking for special numbers even if the printer doesn't need it. Thus, PRINTROW works for all printers. The five familiar BASIC variables—REPS, SPECNUM, CLEARBITS, SETBITS, and SHIFT— determine what the routine does. By changing two DATA statements (lines 4610 and 4630), you can customize the routine for low- or high-bit-up printers.

If your printer doesn't need a particular function, you can set SPECNUM, SETBITS, and SHIFT to 0, or CLEARBITS to 255 to keep them from having any effect. The actual printing bypasses BASIC and DOS; PRINTROW uses a printing routine that's built into the BIOS ROM chip of the PC.

First, the variables needed by PRINTROW are assigned to PR(0) through PR(4). Then the beginning address of SCRCOL is transferred through PR(5). For low-bit-up printers the beginning address is that of SCRCOL(2). For high-bit-up printers, the beginning is at the other end, one more than the address of SCRCOL(SCRCOLSIZE).

PR(6) is used as an error flag, and it is cleared before calling PRINTROW. If something goes wrong in the printing, PRINTROW sets PR(6) to a value other than 0 and generates a Device Timeout Error. The ON ERROR GOTO 5000 statement from line 2000 goes into effect, and an error message is sent.

On printers that require it, con-

```
10 ' *******************************************************
20 ' *****        GRUMP for the Radio Shack LP VIII      *****
30 ' *****      High and Medium Resolution Screens       *****
40 ' *****         Machine Language Subroutine           *****
50 ' *******************************************************
60 ' This program prints IBM PC high and medium resolution
70 ' graphic screens (SCREEN 1, SCREEN 2) on an RS LP VIII
80 ' printer using a machine language routine. It works with
90 ' BASICA 1.1 and BASICA 2.0.
100'

100-1060 same as in Listing 1

1070 REPS=2 ' How many times a byte should be repeated in printing
1080 SETBITS=128 ' 0 means no bits need setting.  To set a bit, set SETBITS
     to the value of the bit you want to set
1090 CLEARBITS=255 '255 means no bits need clearing.  To clear a bit,
     subtract its value from 255.
1100 SPECNUM=0 ' Any special numbers for your printer that need printing
     twice, such as 3 for P-Series printers.  SPECNUM=0 means no special number
1110 NUMDOTS=7 ' How many dots the printer prints in one pass
1120 STEPSIZE=-NUMDOTS 'How we step through the screen
1130 IF SCREENSTAT=6 THEN GETWIDTH=6 ELSE GETWIDTH=3 ' GETWIDTH+1 dots are
     taken off the screen in one pass
1140 REMAINDER=SCRRIGHT MOD NUMDOTS ' Screen column number of last printer
     line (HiRes) or last two lines (MedRes)
1150 SHIFT=1 ' Number of bit positions to shift to right. 0 means no shift.
1160 PRINTROW=0 ' This variable will hold the address of the printing routine
1190 '
1200 TOGRAPH$=CHR$(18) ' Switch to graphics
1210 TOREG$=CHR$(30)+STRING$(8,10)+CHR$(13) ' Switch back to regular
1220 ' SETCRLF$, not needed for this printer
1230 CRLF$=CHR$(13)+CHR$(10) ' Actual graphic carriage return/linefeed
1240 LMARGIN$= CHR$(27)+ CHR$(16)+CHR$(0)+CHR$(40) ' Not preset
1970 '
1980 ' Setting up the printer
1990 ' ----------------------
2000 ON ERROR GOTO 5000:ERRMSG$="Printer is not responding"
2010 OPEN "LPT2:" AS #1 ' Printing in random mode
2020 WIDTH #1, 255 ' Keep BASIC from adding carriage returns every 80 bytes
2030 PRINT #1, TOGRAPH$; ' Switch graphics mode on
2040 PRINT #1, CRLF$;
2050 '
2060 IF SCREENSTAT<>6 THEN 2500 ' MedRes printing
2070 '
2080 ' High Resolution Printing
2090 ' ------------------------
2100 FOR COL=SCRRIGHT TO REMAINDER+1 STEP STEPSIZE
2110 GET (COL,SCRTOP)-(COL-GETWIDTH,SCRBOT),SCRCOL
2120 GOSUB 3000 ' Printing routine
2130 NEXT
2140 '
2150 GET (REMAINDER,SCRTOP)-(SCRLEFT,SCRBOT),SCRCOL ' Last line, which is
     smaller
2160 SHIFT=8-(REMAINDER+1)
2170 GOSUB 3000 ' Printing routine
2180 GOTO 2640 ' To end
2470 '
2480 ' Medium Resolution Printing
2490 ' --------------------------
2500 FOR COL=SCRRIGHT TO REMAINDER+1 STEP STEPSIZE
2510 GET (COL,SCRTOP)-(COL-GETWIDTH,SCRBOT),SCRCOL
2520 SHIFT=0:GOSUB 3000 'Printing
2530 GET (COL-GETWIDTH,SCRTOP)-(COL-2*GETWIDTH,SCRBOT),SCRCOL
```

Figure 4.13 *GRUMP2RS for Radio Shack Line Printer VIII.*

```
2540 SHIFT=1:GOSUB 3000 'Printing
2550 NEXT
2560 '
2570 GET (REMAINDER,SCRTOP)-(REMAINDER-GETWIDTH,SCRBOT),SCRCOL '
     Second to last line
2580 SHIFT=0:GOSUB 3000 ' Printing
2590 GET (REMAINDER-GETWIDTH,SCRTOP)-(SCRLEFT,SCRBOT),SCRCOL ' Last line
2600 SHIFT=5:GOSUB 3000 ' Printing
2610 '
2620 ' Switch printer back to regular mode
2630 ' ----------------------------------
2640 PRINT #1, TOREG$;
2650 END
2970 '
2980 ' Machine language printing subroutine
2990 ' -----------------------------------
3000 PR(0)=REPS:PR(1)=SPECNUM:PR(2)=CLEARBITS:PR(3)=SETBITS:PR(4)=SHIFT '
     Transfer parameters so PRINTROW can get to them
3010 PR(5)=VARPTR(SCRCOL(2)) ' Transfer starting address of SCRCOL
3020 PR(6)=0 ' Clear error flag
3030 '
3040 PRINT #1, LMARGIN$;
3050 PRINTROW=VARPTR(PR(7)) ' Address of machine language routine
3060 CALL PRINTROW(PR(0))
3070 IF PR(6) THEN ERROR 24 ' Error 24 is Device Timeout, traps to 5000
3080 PRINT #1, CRLF$;
3090 RETURN
3970 '
3980 ' Find out what screen we're on
3990 ' ----------------------------
4000 DEF SEG = 0:SCREENSTAT=PEEK(1024+73):DEF SEG
4010 RETURN
4470 '
4480 ' Load machine language printing routine
4490 ' ---------------------------------------------
4500 DIM PR(48) ' Array to hold machine language subroutine
4510 CHECK=0 ' Check-value, to catch typos in entering the &H'numbers
4520 FOR N=7 TO 48 ' PR(0) to PR(6) hold data, so start with 6
4530 READ PR(N):CHECK=CHECK XOR PR(N)
4540 NEXT
4550 READ CROSSCHECK ' CHECK and CROSSCHECK should be the same
4560 RETURN
4570 '
4580 ' Data for machine language routine
4590 ' --------------------------------
4600 ' Data on following line is for printer that prints LOW BIT UP.
     For printers that print HIGH BIT UP, change to &HBAFD
4610 DATA &HBAFC
4620 ' Data on following line is for LPT2:.  For LPT1: change it to &H0000,
     for LPT3: to &H0002
4630 DATA &H0001
4640 ' Data on following 5 lines is the same for all versions
4650 DATA &H8B55,&H8BEC,&H065E,&H778B,&H8A0A,&H084F,&HC8BF,&HAC00,&HE8D2
4660 DATA &H4722,&H0A04,&H0647,&H22E8,&H0A00,&H75E4,&HF617,&H0247,&H74FF
4670 DATA &H3A0C,&H0247,&H0775,&H10E8,&H0A00,&H75E4,&H4F05,&HDB75,&HC033
4680 DATA &H4789,&H5D0C,&H02CA,&H8A00,&H322F,&HCDE4,&HF617,&H01C4,&H0B75
4690 DATA &HCDFE,&HF375,&HE432,&H00C3
4700 ' Next line is a CROSSCHECK for LOW BIT UP printers and LPT2:. For
     HIGH BIT UP printers and LPT2: change to &H3453
4710 DATA &H3452
4970 '
4980 ' Error messages
4990 ' --------------
5000 BEEP:PRINT ERRMSG$:END
```

Figure 4.13 *(continued)*

```
10 ' *****************************************************
20 ' *****    GRUMP for Anadex & DataSouth Printers    *****
30 ' *****     High and Medium Resolution Screens      *****
40 ' *****        Machine Language Subroutine          *****
50 ' *****************************************************
60 ' This program prints IBM PC high and medium resolution
70 ' graphic screens (SCREEN 1, SCREEN 2) on many Anadex &
80 ' DataSouth printers using a machine language routine.
90 ' Compatible with BASICA 1.1 and BASICA 2.0.
100'

100-1060 same as in Listing 1

1070 REPS=2 ' How many times a byte should be repeated in printing
1080 SETBITS=64 ' 0 means no bits need setting.  To set a bit, set SETBITS
     to the value of the bit you want to set. 64 means set bit 6.
1090 CLEARBITS=255-128 ' 255 means no bits need clearing.  To clear a bit,
     subtract its value from 255. 255-128 means clear the high bit.
1100 SPECNUM=0 ' Any special number for your printer that needs printing
     twice, such as 3 for P-Series printers.  SPECNUM=0 means no special number
1110 NUMDOTS=6 ' How many dots the printer prints in one pass
1120 IF SCREENSTAT=6 THEN STEPSIZE=NUMDOTS ELSE STEPSIZE=NUMDOTS\2 ' MedRes
     dots are 2 bits, so we step only half the number of dots
1130 IF SCREENSTAT=6 THEN GETWIDTH=5 ELSE GETWIDTH=2 ' GETWIDTH +1 dots are
     taken off the screen in one pass
1140 REMAINDER=SCRRIGHT MOD STEPSIZE ' Screen column number of first
     narrower printer line
1150 IF SCREENSTAT=6 THEN SHIFT=8-(REMAINDER+1) ELSE SHIFT=
     8-((REMAINDER+1)*2) 'Number of bits to shift for the first remainder
     column
1160 PRINTROW=0 ' Variable will hold the address of the printing routine
1190 '
1200 TOGRAPH$=CHR$(28) ' Switch to graphics
1210 TOREG$=CHR$(29)+CHR$(12) ' Switch back & advance to next page
1220 ' SETCRLF$, not needed for this printer
1230 CRLF$="6" ' Actual graphic carriage return/linefeed
1240 LMARGIN$= ";100" ' Left paper margin to center image, not preset
1970 '
1980 ' Setting up the printer
1990 ' ----------------------
2000 ON ERROR GOTO 5000:ERRMSG$="Printer is not responding"
2010 OPEN "LPT1:" AS #1 ' Printing in random mode
2020 WIDTH #1, 255 ' Keep BASIC from adding carriage returns every 80 bytes
2030 PRINT #1, TOGRAPH$; ' Switch graphics mode on
2040 PRINT #1, CRLF$;
2050 '
2060 ' High and Medium Resolution Printing
2070 ' -----------------------------------
2080 GET (SCRLEFT,SCRTOP)-(REMAINDER,SCRBOT),SCRCOL ' First line, which is
     smaller
2090 GOSUB 3000 ' Printing routine
2100 '
2110 SHIFT=2
2120 FOR COL=REMAINDER+1 TO SCRRIGHT STEP STEPSIZE
2130 GET (COL,SCRTOP)-(COL+GETWIDTH,SCRBOT),SCRCOL
2140 GOSUB 3000 ' Printing routine
2150 NEXT
```

Figure 4.14 *GRUMP2AD for Anadex and Datasouth printers.*

trol strings are sent just before printing a graphics line. PRINTROW is called, a line is printed, and control returns to the main routine.

And that's how GRUMP works.

Even if the printer you have isn't listed here, you should be able to modify a GRUMP program without major problems. If I'm wrong, please don't call me at 2 a.m.; I'm quite grumpy when awakened.

Peter Baenziger is a freelance programmer and sometime writer who, however, mainly works as manager of photographic and audiovisual services for the Upjohn Company. This article was originally published in PC World *Volume 1, Number 10.*

```
2160 '
2170 ' Switch printer back to regular mode
2180 ' ----------------------------------
2190 PRINT #1, TOREG$;
2200 END
2970 '
2980 ' Machine language printing subroutine
2990 ' ------------------------------------
3000 PR(0)=REPS:PR(1)=SPECNUM:PR(2)=CLEARBITS:PR(3)=SETBITS:PR(4)=SHIFT '
     Transfer parameters so PRINTROW can get to them
3010 PR(5)=VARPTR(SCRCOL(SCRCOLSIZE))+1 ' Transfer starting address of SCRCOL
3020 PR(6)=0 ' Clear error flag
3030 '
3040 PRINT #1, LMARGIN$;
3050 PRINTROW=VARPTR(PR(7)) ' Address of machine language routine
3060 CALL PRINTROW(PR(0))
3070 IF PR(6) THEN ERROR 24 ' Error 24 is Device Timeout, traps to 5000
3080 PRINT #1, CRLF$;
3090 RETURN
3970 '
3980 ' Find out what screen we're on
3990 ' ----------------------------
4000 DEF SEG = 0:SCREENSTAT=PEEK(1024+73):DEF SEG
4010 RETURN
4470 '
4480 ' Load machine language printing routine
4490 ' ----------------------------------------------
4500 DIM PR(48) ' Array to hold machine language subroutine
4510 CHECK=0 ' Check-value, to catch typos in entering the &H'numbers
4520 FOR N=7 TO 48 ' PR(0) to PR(6) hold data, so start with 6
4530 READ PR(N):CHECK=CHECK XOR PR(N)
4540 NEXT
4550 READ CROSSCHECK ' CHECK and CROSSCHECK should be the same
4560 RETURN
4570 '
4580 ' Data for machine language routine
4590 ' --------------------------------
4600 ' Data on following line is for printer that prints HIGH BIT UP. For
     printers that print LOW BIT UP, change to &HBAFC
4610 DATA &HBAFD
4620 ' Data on following line is for LPT1:.  For LPT2: change it to &H0001,
     for LPT3: to &H0002
4630 DATA &H0000
4640 ' Data on following 5 lines is the same for all versions
4650 DATA &H8B55,&H8BEC,&H065E,&H778B,&H8A0A,&H084F,&HC8BF,&HAC00,&HE8D2
4660 DATA &H4722,&H0A04,&H0647,&H22E8,&H0A00,&H75E4,&HF617,&H0247,&H74FF
4670 DATA &H3A0C,&H0247,&H0775,&H10E8,&H0A00,&H75E4,&H4F05,&HDB75,&HC033
4680 DATA &H4789,&H5D0C,&H02CA,&H8A00,&H322F,&HCDE4,&HF617,&H29C4,&H0B75
4690 DATA &HCDFE,&HF375,&HE432,&H00C3
4700 ' Next line is a CROSSCHECK for HIGH BIT UP printers and LPT1:. For
     LOW BIT UP printers and LPT1: change to &H3453
4710 DATA &H3452
4970 '
4980 ' Error messages
4990 ' --------------
5000 BEEP:PRINT ERRMSG$:END
```

Figure 4.14 *(continued)*

Character Construction

J. G. Vaughan

Let's face it. The character sets of printers that work with the IBM PC, or any computer for that matter, are rather limited. Even with its extended character set, the PC still can't display or print many of the special characters used frequently in word processing applications. Scientists, engineers, and foreign language writers have been forced to buy expensive letter quality printers and specialized print wheels to print the characters and symbols they need. These print wheels are often difficult to find.

For those who have graphics dot matrix printers, creating special characters is possible but extremely difficult. The process requires extensive tampering with the word processing program and frequent switching back and forth between text and graphics modes. Each pin of the dot matrix printhead must be individually instructed, and only one character can be sent to the printer at a time. In some cases this process can be simplified somewhat with add-on ROM chips and specialized word processing programs that can send extended fonts. But even those systems are limited to certain character fonts that only run on certain printers.

Several of the newer dot matrix printers such as the Epson FX-80 and the TI 855 accept character fonts that are downloaded from the computer. This feature allows you to send entire fonts to the printer without having to switch back and forth between graphics and text modes.

The main drawback to downloading any dot matrix character or graphics font is that you must first construct a dot pattern from the printhead's allowable dot matrix and transfer it to the printer. This process can be tedious when done by hand. After drawing the pattern on paper, you have to transfer the value of each dot individually to the printer. With the help of the programs described in this article and the IBM PC, however, the process of creating and downloading a font is greatly simplified.

After an alternate character font has been downloaded, any word processing program with the ability to send control codes to the printer can switch back and forth between the normal character set and the alternate font you've created. Most word processing programs, including *WordStar,* have this capability.

Figures 4.17 and 4.18 (program listings at the end of this article) show two programs that download an alternate character font to the Epson FX-80 printer. These programs could easily be modified to work on the TI 855 or any other printer that allows downloading of fonts. The first program, DEFINE, is written in BASIC and requires BASICA, a color graphics board, and a graphics monitor. This program lets you construct a symbol or special character, download it to the printer, print it, save it for future downloading, and list and view any characters saved earlier. The assembly language program DOWNLOAD.ASM (Figure 4.18) contains data for a sample alternate character set and downloads much faster than the BASIC program DEFINE.

DEFINE presents a menu showing seven functions: you can construct a character using the 11- by 8-dot pattern allowed on the Epson FX-80, download this character or an entire file of characters to the printer, list all characters defined in a given file, print one or all characters downloaded to the printer, save a constructed character to a file, view the dot pattern of the currently defined character or of a character previously saved to a file, or end the program.

Constructing a Character

Building characters is the most time-consuming step in the process of creating and downloading a font. Before getting too involved in forming special characters, look in the appendix of the Epson printer manual to see how standard characters are formed.

Selecting option C from DEFINE's main menu clears the screen and displays a printhead pattern 11 dots wide by 8 dots high (see Figure 4.15). Use the arrow keys to move around the grid. The <Ins> key turns a white dot red, indicating a print position. (In the illustration in this book, the white dots are grey and the red dots are black.) To delete a print dot, move the cursor to the appropriate position and press the <Del> key.

If you try to define two horizontally adjacent print dots, an error message is displayed. The Epson FX-80 uses adjacent dots for emphasized print mode only, so it will not

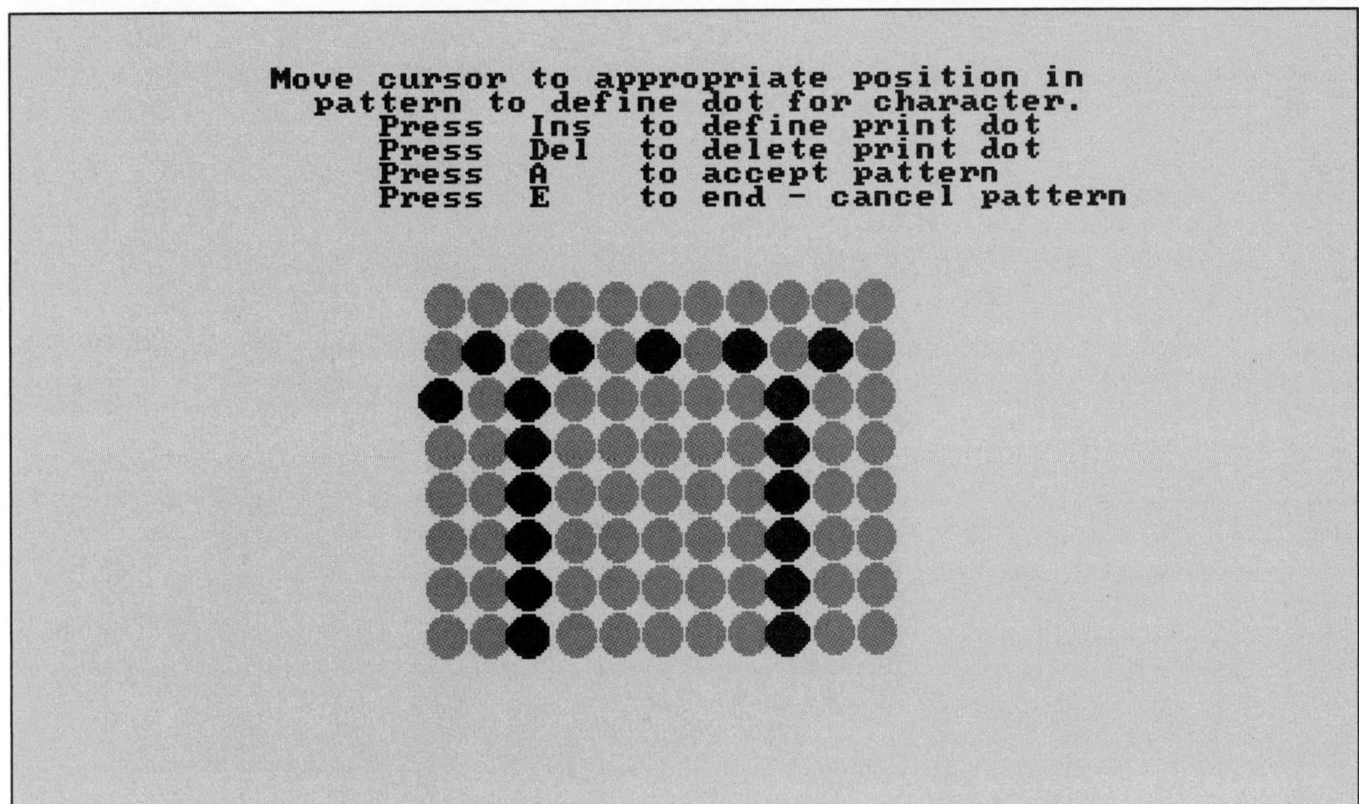

Figure 4.15 *Constructing π with DEFINE.*

allow adjacent dots in a nonemphasized font. If you try to move the cursor outside the pattern, a warning message appears.

After the screen display pattern is complete, press the A key to accept the pattern. An E cancels the pattern you have defined and allows you to start over. If you press A, the program asks if you want to continue the definition process. Responding with N allows you to change the pattern, while Y causes the program to accept the pattern, clear the screen, and request a name for the character. You can't use that name for downloading, but it's handy for quickly determining a special symbol's meaning when you review all the stored characters.

DEFINE next asks for the ASCII code the character represents. Allowable answers range from 32 through 255. However, to access the upper 128 characters, you must use the standard Epson escape calls for the upper character set. For example, it would be reasonable to use the ASCII code for a lowercase *a* (97) to define the Greek symbol alpha α. Once the ASCII code has been entered, the program requests spacing information. DEFINE automatically sets horizontal spacing at 11 dots. If you want proportional spacing (in which spacing between letters is varied for a typeset look), you must first supply the starting and ending column of the character pattern. Finally, the program asks if you would like your character to have descender attributes (as in the letters *y*, *j*, and *p*). When this question has been answered the definition process is complete, and the program returns to the main menu.

Within the program the proportional and descender information is stored in a print-attribute byte. The lower 4 bits of the attribute byte contain the starting print position of the defined character. The next 3 bits give the ending print position, and the high-order bit, if zero, indicates descender printing. The dots that form the character are defined by placing a one in the corresponding positions within the 11- by 8-dot table. The character pattern is then coverted from the binary code of TABLE(11,8) into a decimal code and stored in array DOTPAT(11). This is accomplished by multiplying each of the eight rows in a given column of the table by increasing powers of two, thereby converting them to decimal numbers.

Downloading the Character

After the character definition is complete, it's ready to send to the printer. First, check the DIP switches on the FX-80 to make sure switch 1-4 is off. This disables the FX-80's input buffer and makes downloading fonts possible. Then try downloading the character to the printer and printing it to see how it looks.

If you are not satisfied, select option V to view the character's dot pattern and correct it. It should be noted that a character defined from the construction option is held in volatile memory until you select the construction menu option again. At that time the character is overwritten with the new construction pattern. If you are satisfied with the print appearance, press the S key to save the character definition to a disk file with a name of your choosing. You can create a permanent definition only by saving the definition to a disk file.

Selections other than the construction options are menu prompted, so they won't be discussed in detail here. Limited error-trapping within the program catches problems such as failing to turn on the printer or requesting a nonexistent file. These error traps return you to the menu option that will enable you to correct the indicated problem. If an error occurs for which a trap does not exist, the program will halt and display the untrapped error. In such a case you will have to look up the meaning of the error code in the BASIC manual.

Faster in Assembler

Once all the characters and symbols have been constructed and defined, you can load them from the file into the Epson's download character font by using DEFINE's option D. In a word processing environment, however, the assembler program DOWNLOAD.ASM will make this step much easier and faster. For example, you could create the batch file WSALTCHR.BAT containing the commands:

```
DOWNLOAD
WS %1
```

which would first download the alternate character set to your printer and then call *WordStar.*

In DOWNLOAD.ASM the download character data is given in INITSTR and BITVAL of the BYTABLE data segment. The data in INITSTR begins with an ESC @ sequence, which initializes the printer and sets the top-of-form to the current paper position. The 7 in the next line beeps the printer to indicate the start of the download definition sequence.

The rest of the INITSTR code defines the sequence ESC, &, 0, 32, 127. This sequence tells the printer to prepare to receive alternate definitions for ASCII characters 32 through 127. BITVAL defines 12 bytes per character in hexadecimal form. These 12 bytes are the print attribute and 11 columns of character definition—the download information the Epson printer is looking for. The data in BITVAL could just as well be in decimal, taken directly from the BASIC construction file. To change back to decimal, eliminate the .RADIX16 statement before BITVAL.

The code segment DOWN sends the data in INITSTR and BITVAL to the printer. LOOP_INITSTR sends the 8 bytes of INITSTR, using the CX register as the loop counter. LOOP_BITVAL sends the 96 characters in BITVAL, with LOOP_COLUMNS picking up the 12 bytes for each of the 96 characters. The data is sent to the printer through SEND using the INT 21H command, with register AH containing the required value of 05H and register DL containing the data to be sent.

Finally, a beep is sent to the printer to indicate the end of the download procedure, and control is returned to DOS.

DOWNLOAD.ASM takes about 1 second to run. The resulting character set is my version of a character-to-character map of the General Scientific 10 Diablo 630 print wheel. Figure 4.16 shows this special character set mapped to the IBM PC keyboard.

To modify DOWNLOAD.ASM for use with data produced by the BASIC program DEFINE, only a few statements must be changed. First the ASCII codes 32 and 127 in lines 6 and 7 of BYTABLE should be changed to cover the range of code numbers you wish to define. Also, register CX should be loaded with the number of characters to be defined—in this case, 32 through 127, inclusive, is 96 characters and CX is set to that value by the statement MOV CX, 96.

If you wish to make DOWNLOAD.ASM slightly more flexible for use with data generated from DEFINE, send a modified INITSTR consisting of ESC, &, 0 before every

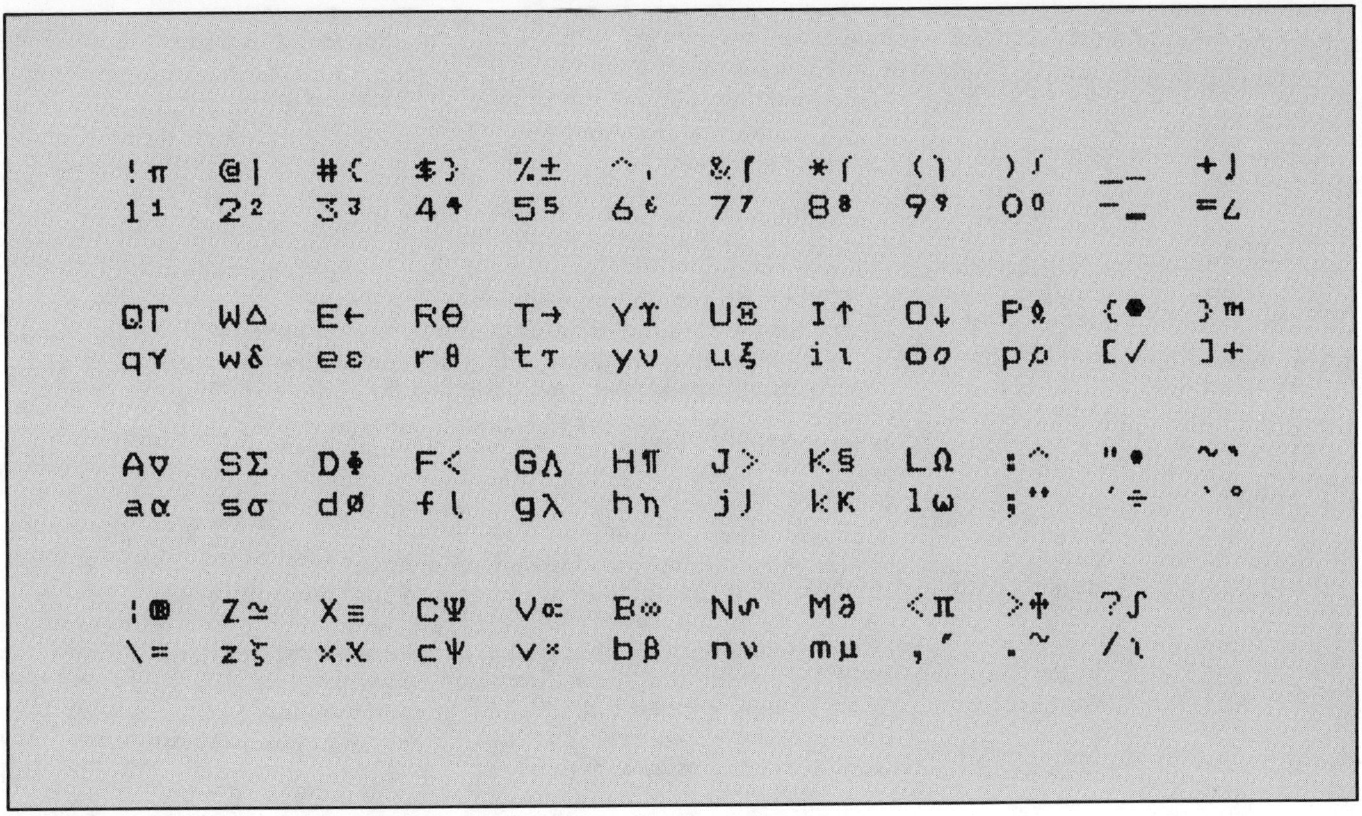

Figure 4.16 *Character map of ASCII character codes for the special character and symbol font.*

code sequence of BITVAL. However, BITVAL would then have to consist of 14 bytes of information: the ASCII character code represented (sent twice), the print attribute giving proportional and descender information, and the data for the 11 columns of the printhead. That sequence is the same as the data sequence generated by the BASIC construction program, with the exception that the optional character name at the end should be separated from the remaining data by a semicolon. In this way the character definition data for DOWNLOAD.ASM can be copied directly from the saved disk file created by DEFINE. This technique is a little less efficient than the code of DOWNLOAD.ASM, but it is acceptable.

The programs discussed here provide an easy method of constructing custom character fonts and downloading them to an Epson FX-80 printer. The process is time-consuming, but once the characters are defined they can be easily accessed by any word processor or program capable of sending the appropriate download access and ending sequences.

J. G. Vaughan is an assistant professor of mechanical engineering at the University of Mississippi. He is actively involved in materials science research and uses computers in data acquisition, data reduction and analysis, and report writing. This article was originally published in PC World *Volume 2, Number 4.*

```
100 REM   Program: DEFINE -- Download Character Definition for Epson FX Printer
110 REM
120 REM   Written by:    James G. Vaughan       University of Mississippi
130 REM
140 REM   Copyrighted by James G. Vaughan  1983        Not to be copied for sale
150 REM
160 REM   Requirements:    BASICA and color-graphics monitor/board
170 REM
180 REM   Major Variable Defintions:
190 REM        FILE$          : File name for download character storage
200 REM        TABLE(11,8)    : Table containing binary dot pattern representation
210 REM        DOTPAT(11)     : Array containing decimal dot pattern representation
220 REM        DOTA(11)       : Dummy input array for dot pattern
230 REM        A$             : Answer for menu questions
240 REM        B              : Graphics representation of red circle, radius 8
250 REM        C              : Graphics representation of white circle, radius 7
260 REM        D              : Graphics representation of blue cusor, radius 4
270 REM        N$             : Optional name of defined character
280 REM        CHAR           : ASCII code number of defined character
290 REM        ATTR           : Attribute of defined character giving proportional
300 REM                             spacing and descender information
310 REM        DFLAG          : If = 1 then retain white dot at present cusor
320 REM        EFLAG          : If = 1 then erase error/warning message
330 REM        PFLAG          : If = 1 then retain red dot at present cusor
340 REM        VFLAG          : If = 1 then character defined from previous pattern
350 REM        DEFFLAG        : If = 1 then character presently defined in memory
360 REM
370 REM ======================================================================
1000 REM
1010 REM--Initialize program and Define menu options
1020 CLEAR ,,4000 : CLS : KEY OFF : WIDTH 40 : SCREEN 1
1030 DEFINT I,J,L,X,Y
1040 DIM TABLE(11,8), DOTPAT(11), DOTA(11), B(80), C(80), D(80)
1050 FILE$="-none-"
1060 ON ERROR GOTO 8110
1070 '  Define red circle
1080 CIRCLE (160,100),8,2 : PAINT (160,100),2,2 : GET (152,92)-(168,108),B
1090 '  Define white circle
1100 CIRCLE (160,80),7,3,,,1 : PAINT(160,80),3,3 : GET (152,72)-(168,88),C
1110 '  Define blue cusor
1120 CIRCLE (160,60),4,1 : PAINT(160,60),1,1 : GET (156,56)-(164,64),D
1130 CLS : SCREEN 0 : LOCATE 1,1,1
1140 PRINT "   Download Character Definition for"
1150 PRINT "              Epson FX Printer" : PRINT
1160 PRINT : PRINT "Main Selection Menu" : PRINT
1170 PRINT : PRINT "  C  Construct character from pattern"
1180 PRINT : PRINT "  D  Download character(s) to printer"
1190 PRINT : PRINT "  L  List characters defined in file"
1200 PRINT : PRINT "  P  Print download character(s)"
1210 PRINT : PRINT "  S  Save constructed character to file"
1220 PRINT : PRINT "  V  View dot pattern of previous char."
1230 PRINT : PRINT "  E  End program"
1240 PRINT : PRINT "Make your selection ?";
1250 A$=INKEY$
1260 IF A$="c" OR A$="C" GOTO 2010
1270 IF A$="d" OR A$="D" GOTO 3010
1280 IF A$="l" OR A$="L" GOTO 4010
1290 IF A$="p" OR A$="P" GOTO 5010
```

Figure 4.17 *DEFINE*

```
1300 IF A$="s" OR A$="S" GOTO 6010
1310 IF A$="v" OR A$="V" GOTO 7010
1320 IF A$="e" OR A$="E" GOTO 8010
1330 GOTO 1250
1340 '
1350 ' ======================================================================
1360 '
2000 REM--Construct and Define character from dot pattern
2010 CLS : SCREEN 1,1 : COLOR 0,1
2020 DEFFLAG=0
2030 PRINT "Move cusor to appropriate position in"
2040 PRINT "  pattern to define dot for character"
2050 PRINT "      Press  Ins  to define print dot"
2060 PRINT "      Press  Del  to delete print dot"
2070 PRINT "      Press  A    to accept pattern"
2080 PRINT "      Press  E    to end - cancel pattern"
2090 YC=48
2100 FOR J = 1 TO 8
2110   XC=48 : YC=YC+16
2120   IF VFLAG<>1
        THEN DOTPAT(J)=0
2130   FOR I = 1 TO 11
2140     XC=XC+16 : PUT(XC,YC),C
2150     IF VFLAG<>1
          THEN TABLE(I,J)=0
          ELSE IF TABLE(I,J)=1 THEN PUT(XC,YC),B,PSET
2160   NEXT I
2170 NEXT J
2180 DFLAG=0 : OFLAG=0 : PFLAG=0 : EFLAG=0
2190 X=144 : Y=128 : PUT (X+4,Y+4),D,AND
2200 A$=INKEY$ : IF A$="" THEN 2200
2210 ALEN=LEN(A$) : X1=X : XX=(X-48)/16 : Y1=Y : YY=(Y-48)/16
2220 IF DFLAG=1 THEN PUT(X1,Y1),C,OR : DFLAG=0
2230 IF EFLAG=1 THEN LINE(0,48)-(320,56),0,BF : EFLAG=0
2240 IF PFLAG=1 THEN PUT(X1,Y1),B,PSET : PFLAG=0
2250 IF ALEN=2 AND RIGHT$(A$,1)="H" THEN Y=Y-16 : GOTO 2360
2260 IF ALEN=2 AND RIGHT$(A$,1)="M" THEN X=X+16 : GOTO 2360
2270 IF ALEN=2 AND RIGHT$(A$,1)="P" THEN Y=Y+16 : GOTO 2360
2280 IF ALEN=2 AND RIGHT$(A$,1)="K" THEN X=X-16 : GOTO 2360
2290 IF ALEN=2 AND RIGHT$(A$,1)="R" THEN 2420
2300 IF ALEN=2 AND RIGHT$(A$,1)="S" THEN 2520
2310 IF A$="a" OR A$="A" THEN 2570
2320 IF A$="e" OR A$="E" THEN VFLAG=0: GOTO 1130
2330 GOTO 2200
2340 '   ==========
2350 '   Move cusor while retaining preset pattern
2360 IF X<64 OR X>224 OR Y<64 OR Y>176
      THEN LOCATE 7,1 : BEEP : PRINT "WARNING Can't move cusor out of pattern"
      : X=X1 : Y=Y1 : EFLAG=1 : GOTO 2200
2370 IF TABLE(XX,YY)=1
      THEN PUT(X1,Y1),B,PSET
      ELSE PUT(X1,Y1),C,PSET
2380 PUT (X+4,Y+4),D,AND
2390 GOTO 2200
2400 '   ==========
2410 '   Define red print dot on screen and in TABLE
2420 PFLAG=1 : PUT(X,Y),B,PSET
```

Figure 4.17 *(continued)*

```
2430 TABLE(XX,YY)=1
2440 XCONM=XX-1 : XCONP=XX+1
2450 IF XCONM>0
      THEN IF TABLE(XCONM,YY)=1 THEN 2470
                                ELSE 2460
2460 IF XCONP<12
      THEN IF TABLE(XCONP,YY)=1 THEN 2470
                                ELSE 2200 ELSE 2200
2470 LOCATE 7,1 : BEEP : PRINT "ERROR : Can't have two consective dots"
2480 PFLAG=0 : EFLAG=1 : TABLE(XX,YY)=0 : PUT(X,Y),C,PSET
2490 GOTO 2200
2500 '   ==========
2510 '   Erase red dot and replace with white dot on screen and in TABLE
2520 DFLAG=1 : PUT(X,Y),C,PSET
2530 TABLE(XX,YY)=0
2540 GOTO 2200
2550 '   ==========
2560 '   Accept dot pattern and define character parameters
2570 LOCATE 7,1
2580 PRINT "Is pattern okay - press ( Y or N )"
2590 X$=INKEY$
2600 IF X$="n" OR X$="N" THEN LINE(1,48)-(320,56),0,BF
      : IF TABLE(XX,YY)=1 THEN PUT(X,Y),B,PSET : GOTO 2190
                          ELSE PUT(X,Y),C,PSET : GOTO 2190
2610 IF X$="y" OR X$="Y"
      THEN WIDTH 80
      ELSE 2590
2620 PRINT "Input data below to finish the character definition"
     : PRINT "*******************************************************" : PRINT
2630 IF VFLAG<>1 THEN 2670
2640 PRINT "Do you wish to keep the previously defined name,"
2650 INPUT "ASCII code, proportional and descender information ( Y OR N )";A$
2660 PRINT : IF A$="y" OR A$="Y" THEN 2820
2670 PRINT "What name will you identify this pattern with (optional)"
2680 LINE INPUT "?";N$
2690 PRINT
2700 INPUT "What ASCII character code number does this pattern represent";CHAR
2710 IF CHAR>255 OR CHAR<32
      THEN PRINT "  Unacceptable number" : GOTO 2690
2720 STARTCOL=0 : ENDCOL=11
2730 PRINT
2740 INPUT "Is this character to have proportional spacing ( Y or N )";P$
2750 IF P$="y" OR P$="Y"
      THEN INPUT "   starting column position ";STARTCOL
      : INPUT "   ending column position   ";ENDCOL : GOTO 2770
2760 IF P$="n" OR P$="N"
      THEN 2770
      ELSE 2730
2770 PRINT : INPUT"Is character to have descender properties ( Y or N ) ";D$
2780 IF D$="y" OR D$="Y"
      THEN DES=0 : GOTO 2800
2790 IF D$="n" OR D$="N"
      THEN DES=1
      ELSE 2770
2800 PRINT
2810 ATTR=ENDCOL+(STARTCOL*16)+(DES*128)
```

Figure 4.17 *(continued)*

```
2820 FOR J = 1 TO 11
2830   DOTPAT(J)=0  : I=1
2840   FOR L = 8 TO 1 STEP -1
2850     DOTPAT(J)=(TABLE(J,L)*I)+DOTPAT(J)
2860     I=I*2
2870   NEXT L
2880 NEXT J
2890 DEFFLAG=1 : VFLAG=0
2900 PRINT : PRINT "*******************" : PRINT "Definition complete"
     : PRINT "*******************" : PRINT : GOSUB 9110
2910 WIDTH 40 : GOTO 1130
2920 '
2930 ' ======================================================================
2940 '
3000 REM--Download Character to Printer
3010 CLS : PRINT "Download Character to Printer" : PRINT
3020 PRINT "Selection Menu"
3030 PRINT : PRINT "   F   File characters downloaded"
3040 IF DEFFLAG<>1 THEN 3070
3050 PRINT : PRINT "   C   Character in present definition"
3060         PRINT "       downloaded"
3070 PRINT : PRINT "   E   End download selection"
3080 PRINT : PRINT "Make your selection ?";
3090 A$=INKEY$
3100 IF A$="f" OR A$="F" THEN 3150
3110 IF A$="c" OR A$="C" AND DEFFLAG=1 THEN 3250
3120 IF A$="e" OR A$="E" THEN 1130 ELSE 3090
3130 '   ==========
3140 '   Select file and download all characters
3150 GOSUB 9010                          'Select and OPEN file
3160 LPRINT CHR$(7)
3170 IF EOF(1) THEN 3210
3180 GOSUB 9210                          'Input character definition from file
3190 GOSUB 9310                          'Send character definition to FX
3200 GOTO 3170
3210 CLOSE#1 : LPRINT CHR$(7) : CLS : PRINT " Download completed"
3220 PRINT "*******************" : PRINT : GOSUB 9110 : GOTO 3010
3230 '   ==========
3240 '   Download character in present definition
3250 CHARA=CHAR : ATTRA=ATTR
3260 FOR J = 1 TO 11
3270   DOTA(J)=DOTPAT(J)
3280 NEXT
3290 GOSUB 9310                          'Send character definition to FX
3300 GOTO 3210
3310 '
3320 ' ======================================================================
3330 '
4000 REM--List character(s) already defined in file
4010 CLS : PRINT "List of characters defined in file"
4020 GOSUB 9010                          'Select and OPEN file
4030 WIDTH 80
4040 CLS : PRINT "Character name","ASCII code number"
4050 I=0
4060 IF EOF(1) THEN GOSUB 9110 : GOTO 4110
4070 INPUT#1, CHARA,CHARA,ATTRA,X1,X2,X3,X4,X5,X6,X7,X8,X9,X10,X11,NN$
4080 PRINT NN$;TAB(35);CHARA : I=I+1 : IF I<23 THEN 4060
```

Figure 4.17 *(continued)*

```
4090 PRINT "Press any key to continue listing; <Esc> to quit"
4100 A$=INKEY$ : IF A$="" THEN 4100 ELSE IF A$<>CHR$(27) THEN 4040
4110 CLOSE #1
4120 WIDTH 40 : GOTO 1130
4130 '
4140 ' ========================================================================
4150 '
5000 REM--Print Download Character(s)
5010 CLS : PRINT "Print Download Characters" : PRINT
5020 PRINT "Selection menu"
5030 PRINT : PRINT "   F   Present FX download ":
           PRINT SPC(10); "characters printed"
5040 IF DEFFLAG<>1 THEN 5070
5050 PRINT : PRINT "   C   Character in present definition"
5060         PRINT "       printed"
5070 PRINT : PRINT "   E   End print selection"
5080 PRINT : PRINT "Make your selection ?";
5090 A$=INKEY$
5100 IF A$="f" OR A$="F" THEN 5150
5110 IF A$="c" OR A$="C" AND DEFFLAG=1 THEN 5260
5120 IF A$="e" OR A$="E" THEN 1130 ELSE 5090
5130 '   ==========
5140 '   Print all downloaded characters requested
5150 PRINT : PRINT "Input ASCII character code range to be   printed"
5160 INPUT "       Starting code number";STCH
5170 INPUT "       Ending code number  ";EDCH
5180 LPRINT CHR$(27);"%";CHR$(1);CHR$(0);     'Set FX to use download characters
5190 FOR I = STCH TO EDCH
5200   LPRINT CHR$(I);
5210 NEXT I
5220 LPRINT CHR$(27);"%";CHR$(0);CHR$(0)      'Set FX to use normal characters
5230 CLS : PRINT "Printing complete" : PRINT "*****************" : PRINT
     : GOSUB 9110 : GOTO 5010
5240 '   ==========
5250 '   Print single character in present definition
5260 STCH=CHAR : EDCH=CHAR : GOTO 5180
5270 '
5280 ' =========================================================================
5290 '
6000 REM--Save defined characters to file
6010 CLS : PRINT "Save defined character to file" : PRINT
6020 IF DEFFLAG<>1
      THEN PRINT : BEEP : PRINT "No character presently defined" : PRINT
      : GOSUB 9110 : GOTO 1130
6030 SAV=-1 : GOSUB 9010 : SAV=0
6040 IF EOF(1) AND RFLAG=0      THEN 6110
6050 IF EOF(1) AND RFLAG=1      THEN PRINT : GOTO 6080
6060 INPUT#1, CHARA,CHARA,ATTRA,X1,X2,X3,X4,X5,X6,X7,X8,X9,X10,X11,NN$
6070 IF CHARA=CHAR THEN RFLAG=1 : PRINT : PRINT : BEEP : PRINT
     "WARNING: Present character has already" : PRINT "  been defined as ("
     ;NN$;")" : PRINT "  code number  : ";CHARA : GOTO 6050 ELSE 6040
6080 PRINT "If you continue, only the present"
     : PRINT "  character definition will be accepted" : PRINT "  on printer"
     : PRINT
6090 PRINT "Press C to continue" : PRINT "Press E to end"
```

Figure 4.17 *(continued)*

```
6100 A$=INKEY$ : IF A$="c" OR A$="C" THEN 6110
                 ELSE IF A$="e" OR A$="E" THEN CLOSE #1 : GOTO 1130
                                              ELSE 6100
6110 CLOSE #1
6120 OPEN FILE$ FOR APPEND AS #1
6130 PRINT#1, CHAR;",";CHAR;",";ATTR;",";
6140 FOR J =1 TO 11
6150   PRINT#1, DOTPAT(J);",";
6160 NEXT J
6170 PRINT#1, CHR$(34);N$;CHR$(34)
6180 CLOSE #1
6190 PRINT : PRINT "Save completed" : PRINT : GOSUB 9110
6200 GOTO 1130
6210 '
6220 ' =====================================================================
6230 '
7000 REM--View dot pattern of previously defined charater
7010 CLS : PRINT "View dot pattern of previous character"
7020 PRINT : PRINT "Selection menu"
7030 PRINT : PRINT "   F   File defined character"
7040 IF DEFFLAG<>1 THEN 7060
7050 PRINT : PRINT "   C   Character in present definition"
7060 PRINT : PRINT "   E   End review of dot pattern"
7070 PRINT : PRINT "Make your selection ?";
7080 A$=INKEY$
7090 IF A$="f" OR A$="F" THEN 7140
7100 IF A$="c" OR A$="C" AND DEFFLAG=1 THEN 7330
7110 IF A$="e" OR A$="E" THEN 1130 ELSE 7080
7120 '   ==========
7130 '   Reconstruct dot pattern of character defined in file
7140 GOSUB 9010
7150 PRINT : PRINT "Input name of character pattern to be"
7160 PRINT "  viewed. For any name to be acceptable,  input a  *  character"
7170 INPUT AN$
7180 PRINT : INPUT "Input ASCII code of character";ACHAR
7190 GOSUB 9210
7200 IF ACHAR=CHARA AND AN$=NN$   OR     ACHAR=CHARA AND AN$="*"
      THEN CHAR=CHARA : ATTR=ATTRA : N$=NN$
      : FOR J = 1 TO 11 : DOTPAT(J)=DOTA(J) : NEXT J : VFLAG=1
7210 IF EOF(1) THEN CLOSE#1 ELSE 7190
7220 FOR I = 1 TO 11
7230   L=128
7240   FOR J = 1 TO 8
7250     IF INT(DOTPAT(I)/L) = 1
          THEN TABLE(I,J)=1 : DOTPAT(I)=DOTPAT(I)-L
          ELSE TABLE(I,J)=0
7260     L=L/2
7270   NEXT J
7280 NEXT I
7290 IF VFLAG=1         THEN 2010
7300 BEEP : PRINT "Can't find character ";ACHAR : PRINT "  named ";AN$
      : PRINT : GOSUB 9110 : GOTO 7150
7310 '   ==========
7320 '   Reconstruct dot pattern from present character
7330 VFLAG=1
7340 GOTO 2010
7350 '
```

Figure 4.17 *(continued)*

```
7360 ' =========================================================================
7370 '
8000 REM--Error trapping code and program termination
8010 WIDTH 80 : KEY ON : PRINT "Program Termination"
8020 END
8030 '   ==========
8100 '   Error trapping rountine
8110 BEEP
8120 IF (ERR=24) OR (ERR=27)
      THEN LOCATE ,1 : PRINT "ERROR : TURN PRINTER ON and then"
      : GOSUB 9110 : RESUME NEXT
8130 IF (ERR=5) AND (ERL=1080)
      THEN PRINT "This program requires the color/graphics adapter" : PRINT
8140 IF ERR=53 THEN PRINT "Can't find file ";FILE$;"  - try again" : PRINT
8150 IF ERR=64 THEN PRINT "Your file name ";FILE$;" is illegal" : PRINT
8160 IF ERR=71 THEN PRINT "Requested disk is not ready" : PRINT
8170 IF ERR=73 THEN PRINT "This program requires Advanced BASIC     (BASICA)"
      : PRINT
8180 IF ERL= 9070 THEN RESUME 9010
8190 PRINT "Error trapping unable to recover" : PRINT
8200 ON ERROR GOTO 0 : END
8210 '
8220 ' =========================================================================
8230 '
9000 REM--Subroutine to OPEN default or new file of download character
9010 LOCATE ,1
9020 PRINT "Input file name "; : IF SAV THEN PRINT "for saving": PRINT SPC(3);
9030 PRINT "of download characters"
9040 PRINT "Default file ";FILE$; : INPUT " ";FILEX$
9050 IF FILEX$="" THEN 9060
                 ELSE Y=CSRLIN : LOCATE Y-1,1 : FILE$=FILEX$
                 : PRINT "New default file name : ";FILE$; SPC(15) : PRINT
9060 IF SAV THEN RFLAG=0 : OPEN FILE$ FOR APPEND AS #1 : CLOSE #1
9070 OPEN FILE$ FOR INPUT AS #1
9080 RETURN
9090 '
9100 REM--Subroutine to pause until user hits key
9110 PRINT : PRINT "press any key to continue";: A$=INPUT$(1)
9120 RETURN
9130 '
9200 REM--Subroutine to input download character from file
9210 INPUT#1, CHARA,CHARA,ATTRA
9220 FOR J = 1 TO 11
9230   INPUT#1, DOTA(J)
9240 NEXT J
9250 INPUT#1, NN$
9260 RETURN
9270 '
9300 REM--Subroutine to send download character to FX printer
9310 LPRINT CHR$(27);"&";CHR$(0);       'Set FX to accept character definition
9320 LPRINT CHR$(CHARA);CHR$(CHARA);CHR$(ATTRA);
9330 FOR J = 1 TO 11
9340   LPRINT CHR$(DOTA(J));
9350 NEXT J
9360 LPRINT
9370 RETURN
```

Figure 4.17 *(continued)*

```
TITLE  'DOWNLOAD - CHARACTER GENERATION FOR THE EPSON FX  10/83'

;*****************************************************************
;       Character generation of Epson FX characters to produce
;       Diablo scientific compatible characters using a
;       download definition
;
;             By   J. G. Vaughan     University of Mississippi

;             Copyright by  J. G. Vaughan, 1983

;       Requires "MASM" macro assembler
;
;*****************************************************************


;***********************
;
;  Define a temporary stack.  Required for initialization
;  of program only.
;
;***********************

STACK SEGMENT PARA STACK
     DB   8  DUP('STACK   ')
STACK ENDS


BYTABLE SEGMENT PARA

INITSTR DB      27      ; Initialization of EPSON FX with "ESC @"
        DB     "@"      ;
        DB      7       ; BEEP the printer to indicate start of download
        DB      27      ; Define EPSON FX DOWNLOAD character generation
        DB     "&"      ; Sequence of ESC, "&", 0 with n-m
        DB      0       ;
        DB      32      ; n  is position of first character
        DB      127     ; m  is position of last character defined

;************************
;
; Define characters...12 bytes per character
;
;               as print attribute and 11 columns of print dot location
;               to form the complete character definition

;************************

        .RADIX 16       ; All values are in hexadecimal


BITVAL     DB   08BH,000,000,000,000,000,000,000,000,000,000,000   ; 32
           DB   08BH,000,010,000,03E,000,020,000,03E,000,020,000   ; 33
           DB   08BH,000,000,000,030,048,030,048,030,000,000,000   ; 34
```

Figure 4.18 *DOWNLOAD.ASM*

```
DB     08BH,000,000,000,010,000,06C,082,000,082,000,000    ; 35
DB     08BH,000,000,082,000,082,06C,000,010,000,000,000    ; 36
DB     08BH,000,022,000,022,000,0FA,000,022,000,022,000    ; 37
DB     08BH,000,000,000,000,000,07F,080,040,080,000,000    ; 38
DB     08BH,000,010,000,010,044,010,044,010,000,010,000    ; 39
DB     08BH,000,000,080,000,040,03F,000,000,000,000,000    ; 40
DB     08BH,000,000,000,004,000,078,000,080,000,000,000    ; 41
DB     08BH,000,000,000,000,000,03F,040,000,080,000,000    ; 42
DB     08BH,000,000,001,002,001,0FE,000,000,000,000,000    ; 43
DB     08BH,000,000,000,000,000,060,080,040,080,000,000    ; 44
DB     08BH,000,003,000,003,000,003,000,003,000,003,000    ; 45
DB     08BH,000,040,080,000,080,040,020,000,020,040,000    ; 46
DB     08BH,000,000,000,020,000,01E,000,001,000,000,000    ; 47
DB     08BH,000,000,000,070,088,000,088,070,000,000,000    ; 48
DB     08BH,000,000,000,048,000,0F8,000,008,000,000,000    ; 49
DB     08BH,000,000,000,048,090,008,0A0,048,000,000,000    ; 50
DB     08BH,000,000,000,090,008,080,028,0D0,000,000,000    ; 51
DB     08BH,000,000,000,020,040,0A0,000,0F8,000,020,000    ; 52
DB     08BH,000,000,000,0E8,000,0A8,000,0A8,010,000,000    ; 53
DB     08BH,000,000,000,000,030,048,020,088,010,000,000    ; 54
DB     08BH,000,000,000,088,010,0A0,040,080,000,000,000    ; 55
DB     08BH,000,000,000,050,0A8,000,0A8,050,000,000,000    ; 56
DB     08BH,000,000,000,040,0A0,008,0B0,040,000,000,000    ; 57
DB     08BH,000,020,000,040,000,080,000,040,000,020,000    ; 58
DB     08BH,000,040,0A0,040,000,000,000,040,0A0,040,000    ; 59
DB     08BH,000,042,000,07E,000,040,000,07E,000,042,000    ; 60
DB     08BH,000,003,004,009,010,021,000,003,000,000,000    ; 61
DB     08BH,000,010,028,010,080,07F,080,010,028,010,000    ; 62
DB     08BH,000,002,001,000,001,07E,080,000,080,040,000    ; 63
DB     08BH,000,000,000,000,000,0FF,000,000,000,000,000    ; 64
DB     08BH,000,040,030,048,004,042,004,048,030,040,000    ; 65
DB     08BH,000,018,000,024,000,018,000,024,000,018,000    ; 66
DB     08BH,000,0E0,010,00A,080,07E,080,00A,010,0E0,000    ; 67
DB     08BH,000,000,010,028,082,07C,082,028,010,000,000    ; 68
DB     08BH,000,010,028,054,000,010,000,010,000,010,000    ; 69
DB     08BH,000,010,000,028,000,044,000,082,000,000,000    ; 70
DB     08BH,000,003,004,019,060,080,060,019,004,003,000    ; 71
DB     08BH,000,000,060,080,07E,080,000,0FE,000,080,000    ; 72
DB     08BH,000,000,020,040,000,0FE,000,040,020,000,000    ; 73
DB     08BH,000,000,000,082,000,044,000,028,000,010,000    ; 74
DB     08BH,000,000,050,0AA,000,0AA,000,0AA,014,000,000    ; 75
DB     08BH,000,002,038,046,080,000,080,046,038,002,000    ; 76
DB     08BH,000,000,004,048,092,000,092,044,038,000,000    ; 77
DB     08BH,000,018,004,000,004,038,040,000,040,030,000    ; 78
DB     08BH,000,000,004,002,000,07F,000,002,004,000,000    ; 79
DB     08BH,000,000,000,032,048,084,048,032,004,000,000    ; 80
DB     08BH,000,080,000,0FF,000,080,000,080,000,0C0,000    ; 81
DB     08BH,000,038,044,092,000,092,000,092,044,038,000    ; 82
DB     08BH,000,082,000,0C6,028,092,000,082,000,0C6,000    ; 83
DB     08BH,000,010,000,010,000,010,000,054,028,010,000    ; 84
DB     08BH,000,044,082,038,082,010,082,038,082,044,000    ; 85
DB     08BH,000,018,024,000,024,018,000,024,000,024,000    ; 86
DB     08BH,000,00C,010,024,040,084,040,024,010,00C,000    ; 87
DB     08BH,000,000,02A,000,02A,000,02A,000,02A,000,000    ; 88
```

Figure 4.18 *(continued)*

```
            DB    08BH,000,040,000,082,040,03E,040,082,000,040,000    ; 89
            DB    08BH,000,024,040,004,040,024,010,004,010,024,000    ; 90
            DB    08BH,000,008,004,002,004,008,010,020,040,080,000    ; 91
            DB    08BH,000,000,028,000,028,000,028,000,028,000,000    ; 92
            DB    08BH,000,010,000,010,000,07C,000,010,000,010,000    ; 93
            DB    08BH,000,000,000,00DH,000,00E,000,000,000,000,000   ; 94
            DB    08BH,000,001,000,001,000,001,000,001,000,001,000    ; 95
            DB    08BH,000,000,000,000,040,0A0,000,0A0,040,000,000    ; 96
            DB    08BH,000,000,01C,022,000,022,010,00C,010,022,000    ; 97
            DB    08BH,000,000,001,07E,080,012,080,052,02C,000,000    ; 98
            DB    08BH,000,040,030,008,000,0FF,000,008,010,060,000    ; 99
            DB    08BH,000,000,03A,044,008,054,020,044,0B8,000,000    ; 100
            DB    08BH,000,000,014,02A,000,02A,000,022,014,000,000    ; 101
            DB    08BH,000,000,000,000,000,0FC,002,000,001,000,000    ; 102
            DB    08BH,000,041,002,044,028,010,008,004,002,001,000    ; 103
            DB    08BH,000,040,020,01E,020,000,020,010,00F,000,000    ; 104
            DB    08BH,000,000,000,020,000,03E,000,002,000,000,000    ; 105
            DB    08BH,000,000,001,000,002,0FC,000,000,000,000,000    ; 106
            DB    08BH,000,000,07E,000,010,028,040,004,042,000,000    ; 107
            DB    08BH,000,01C,022,000,006,008,006,000,022,01C,000    ; 108
            DB    08BH,000,000,001,03E,000,002,000,002,03C,002,000    ; 109
            DB    08BH,000,000,020,010,00C,002,004,020,018,000,000    ; 110
            DB    08BH,000,000,00C,010,022,000,022,004,038,000,000    ; 111
            DB    08BH,000,001,002,00C,010,022,000,022,000,01C,000    ; 112
            DB    08BH,000,020,000,020,010,00E,010,020,040,000,000    ; 113
            DB    08BH,000,000,000,07C,082,010,082,07C,000,000,000    ; 114
            DB    08BH,000,00C,012,020,002,020,012,02C,000,020,000    ; 115
            DB    08BH,000,010,020,000,022,01C,020,000,020,000,000    ; 116
            DB    08BH,000,000,004,088,034,0C1,014,081,006,000,000    ; 117
            DB    08BH,000,000,000,028,000,010,000,028,000,000,000    ; 118
            DB    08BH,000,000,00C,052,0A2,012,088,044,000,000,000    ; 119
            DB    08BH,000,042,000,064,010,008,014,022,040,002,000    ; 120
            DB    08BH,000,020,018,004,002,000,002,004,038,000,000    ; 121
            DB    08BH,000,000,080,058,005,060,005,042,000,040,000    ; 122
            DB    08BH,000,020,050,088,070,088,050,088,050,020,000    ; 123
            DB    08BH,000,078,084,000,0FC,000,0D4,028,084,078,000    ; 124
            DB    08BH,000,040,038,040,000,078,000,020,000,078,000    ; 125
            DB    08BH,000,000,000,080,040,080,060,000,000,000,000    ; 126
            DB    08BH,000,000,000,000,000,000,000,000,000,000,000    ; 127


BYTABLE ENDS


DOWN SEGMENT PARA

ASSUME  CS:DOWN,DS:BYTABLE,SS:STACK,ES:NOTHING

        ORG     100H
```

Figure 4.18 *(continued)*

```
START PROC FAR
        PUSH    DS                ; Save address of segment register
        MOV     AX,0
        PUSH    AX                ; Save zero return address
        MOV     AX,BYTABLE
        MOV     DS,AX             ; Data resides in BYTABLE data segment
        MOV     AX,STACK
        MOV     SS,AX             ; Stack segment initialized
        MOV     SI,0              ; Initialize address index to 0
        MOV     CX,8              ; Will loop for the 8 chars of INITSTR
LOOP_INITSTR:
        MOV     DL,INITSTR[SI]    ; Set up DL to contents of INITSTR
        CALL    SEND              ; Call print routine
        INC     SI                ; Update to next address of INITSTR
        LOOP    LOOP_INITSTR      ; Loop until done
        MOV     SI,0              ; Initialize address index to 0
        MOV     CX,96             ; Will loop for 96 chars of BITVAL
LOOP_BITVAL:
        CALL    SEND_TWELVE       ; Print 12 chars in BITVAL
        LOOP    LOOP_BITVAL       ; Loop until done
        MOV     DL,7              ; BEEP the printer to indicate finish
        CALL    SEND

        RET
START ENDP


SEND PROC NEAR
        MOV     AH,05H            ; Set function call for printer output
        INT     21H               ; Print contents of DL
        RET
SEND ENDP


SEND_TWELVE PROC NEAR
        PUSH    CX
        MOV     CX,12             ; Will loop for the 12 columns of BITVAL
LOOP_COLUMNS:
        MOV     DL,BITVAL[SI]     ; Set up DL to contents of BITVAL - column one
        CALL    SEND              ; Call print routine
        INC     SI                ; Move to next column of BITVAL
        LOOP    LOOP_COLUMNS      ; Loop until done
        POP     CX
        RET

SEND_TWELVE ENDP


DOWN ENDS

        END     START
```

Figure 4.18 *(continued)*

Screen Shots

Alan. J. Fridlund

It's often desirable to photograph images on the PC screen. You may want to make slides for a business talk or school presentation, or prints for documentation or publication. You don't need to be a professional photographer to make picture-perfect prints or slides in color or in black and white; this article will tell you about a way that's nearly error free.

You will need a few common pieces of photo equipment: a 35 mm camera that allows manual control of both lens aperture and shutter speed, a lens with a focal length of at least 100 mm, and a tripod (either tabletop or floor mounting).

Setting Up

Secure the camera on the tripod facing the monitor. Try to make the optical axis exactly perpendicular to the faceplate of the monitor. This will ensure that the screen corners are equidistant from the lens so that perspective distortion will be minimized and focus will be sharp across the screen.

A long lens (100 mm or more) is necessary. To get a full-frame image with a standard 50 mm lens you would have to place it very close to the screen, which would result in an image with barrel distortion. Barrel distortion means that straight lines at the screen edge look bowed out (see Figure 4.19).

A long lens eliminates barrel distortion (see Figure 4.20). The camera should be set at the distance necessary to focus on the image to be photographed (either a full-screen or partial-screen display). The longer the focal length of the lens, the farther the camera will have to be from the screen. With a 100 mm lens you will need to have the camera 3 to 5 feet from the monitor's faceplate. Focus the lens to get a sharp image of the display.

Some long lenses cannot be focused when the monitor is placed close enough to fill the entire frame. If your lens is too long, you have two options. You can obtain a +1 or +2 diopter close-up lens, which can be purchased for under $20 at a photography store. When screwed on the front of your long lens, the diopter lens allows the display to be brought into focus. Your second option is to buy a 2X converter, typically available for $30 to $40. This extender mounts between a 50 mm lens and the camera body, converting the 50 mm lens into one with a 100 mm effective focal length. A supplementary close-up lens can be used with the 2X and 50 mm lens combination if extra-close shots of portions of the screen are desired.

Short of buying a special screen graphics camera, you'll get the best results with a 100 mm macro lens designed for flat-field, distortion-free images.

After you get the image in approximate focus, you can move the tripod closer to or farther away from the monitor to crop the image within the camera's field of view.

Getting the Right Exposure

Setting the exposure can be tricky, but the PC allows a simple, nearly error-free method. The PC doesn't make the display image all at once. Like a standard TV, the image is scanned across the screen at least 30 times per second. Because of this, you can't use short exposure times for your photos; these may capture only a partially scanned image.

A simple rule of thumb is to use exposure times (shutter speeds) no shorter than 1/10 second. Ranges from 1/5 to 5 or even 10 seconds are better. For all of these extended exposure times, be sure to use a shutter cable release or the camera's timer to trip the shutter. This will avoid jarring the camera and blurring the image on the film.

Now for a neat trick. Most exposure meters are averaging meters. This means the meter assumes that the scene it is measuring includes an average mixture of dark and light tones. If you were to set the exposure using a screen on which all pixels were illuminated, any shot of a typical display would look dark. On the other hand, setting exposure time based on a nearly dark screen might overexpose the film on a typical display. So, our task is to take a reading of the PC screen while it displays an image that approximates the average image the metering system assumes.

This process is simpler than you might think; we can easily paint the screen to achieve a calibration standard. The BASIC program CALSCR.BAS in Figure 4.21 will accomplish this. The effect of this program is to paint the screen with

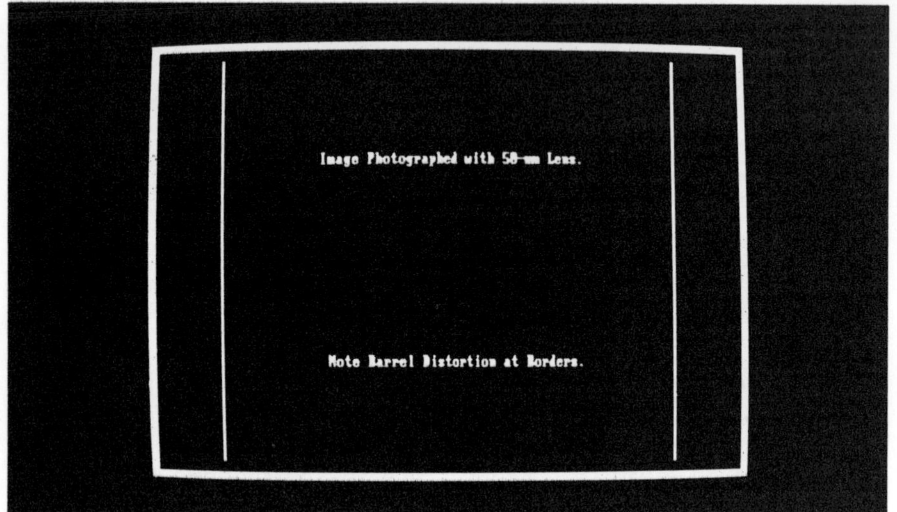

Figure 4.19 *Photograph of IBM Monochrome Display taken with 50 mm lens showing barrel distortion (exposure: 4 seconds at f5.6, lens 18 inches from display).*

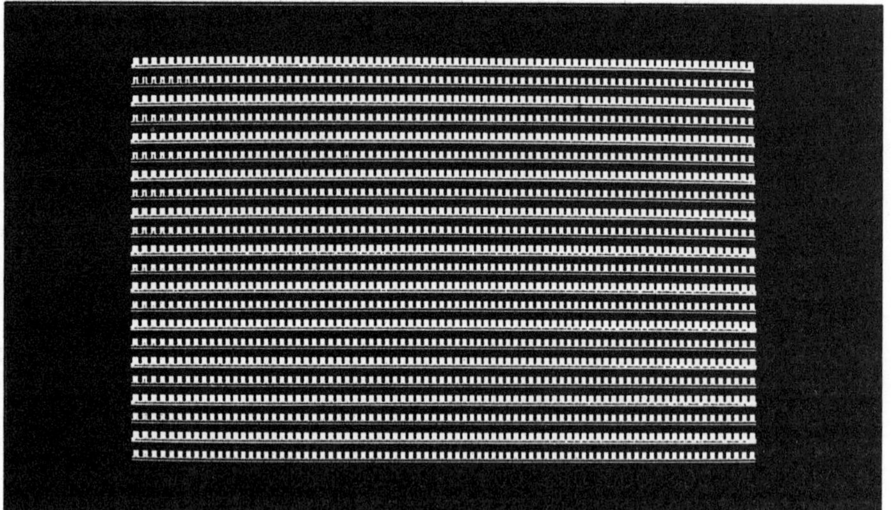

Figure 4.20 *IBM Monochrome Display photographed with 100 mm lens showing correction of barrel distortion (exposure: 8 seconds at f3.5, lens approximately 4 feet from display).*

the ASCII character whose code is 202—a display that happens to occupy about the right area of screen space. The IBM Monochrome Display version should look like Figure 4.22. Notice that alternate rows are set for normal and high-intensity characters. This allows for displays that may be composed of a wide range of intensities and saturations. Color screens should be set using CALSCR.BAS to show alternating rows of normal and high-intensity white characters. Calibration of the camera should then hold for the palette of color and intensity options.

Shooting

Load the program in Figure 4.21 and adjust the PC display for a bright, clear image (avoid excessive brightness and consequent blooming of the image). If your camera has an automatic exposure mode, be sure it is turned off and that you are in the manual mode. Set an approximate shutter speed in the range specified previously and with the room lights out set the lens aperture to the setting indicated by your light meter. The camera will then be set accurately for any display. You may want to bracket the shooting of each image by also shooting the display at one f-stop above and one f-stop below the correct setting, just to be sure. All shooting should be performed with room lights out.

One complication might be that your camera indicates an exposure with a lens aperture wider than your lens permits. If this happens you have three alternatives. You can increase the display's brightness within its usable bloom-free range. You can increase exposure time (again, times up to 10 seconds are quite acceptable; remember to reset your camera's aperture using CALSCR.BAS). Or you can use a faster film. (Note all photos were taken with Ektachrome 64 slide film.)

Following these procedures should enable you to obtain good-quality prints or slides with a minimum of effort. The technique described here works well with either color or monochrome (green, amber, or black and white) displays.

Users of the IBM Monochrome Display will note a softness in the images recorded on film. This is a result of the display's "high- persistence" phosphors, which eliminate

```
10 REM Program CALSCR.BAS - to establish calibration screen.
20 REM Alan J. Fridlund, 1983.
30 REM Clear screen and set width to 80 columns.
40 KEY OFF: CLS
50 WIDTH 80
60 REM Paint screen.
70 FOR ROW=2 to 23
80 REM Alternate normal- and high-intensity rows.
90 IF ROW MOD 2=0 THEN COLOR 7,0 ELSE COLOR 15,0
100 LOCATE ROW
110 FOR COLUMN = 1 TO 80
120 PRINT CHR$(202);
130 NEXT COLUMN
140 NEXT ROW
150 REM Depress space bar to re-establish cursor.
160 A$=INKEY$: IF A$ = " " THEN END ELSE GOTO 160
```

Figure 4.21 *CALSCR.BAS*

flicker but are prone to blooming (see Figures 4.19, 4.20, and 4.22). The best pictures of the IBM Monochrome Display are obtained when the display is set at its minimum usable intensity. Other monochrome monitors or RGB color monitors produce sharper images. If you feel particularly adventurous, you can experiment with color filters, gratings, and other accessories to enhance your display shots.

Several companies have entered the market with software specifically designed to produce camera-ready titles and displays in several colors and print fonts. This type of program can reduce the time and money needed to produce handsome lettered graphics for professional publication and presentation.

Figure 4.22 *Photograph of screen created by program CALSCR.BAS (see Figure 4.21), used for calibrating camera exposure parameters (exposure: 100 mm lens, 8 seconds at f3.5, lens approximately 4 feet from display).*

Alan. J. Fridlund, Ph.D., is a clinical psychologist and psychophysiologist and an Assistant Professor of Psychology at the University of Pennsylvania. He studies emotion and brain-behavior relationships and uses photography extensively in his work. This article was originally published in PC World *Volume 1, Number 5.*

. Star-Dot-Star

Tips large and small in scope make up this section, beginning with instructions on using the OUT command to display high-resolution graphics ("Colorful Tip"). A chart of the IBM graphics characters comes in handy ("ASCII Graphics Chart"), and users with video cassette recorders will learn how to use them to connect the PC to a television set ("VCR as RF Modulator"). "PC Cartography" draws an outline of the United States, and every graphics user will appreciate "Secret Graphics Mode," which enables the PC to display 16 colors in a special low-resolution mode.

Colorful Tip

If you want to display a high-resolution graphics image in color, use the command **OUT 985**, *colornum*, where *colornum* is the number of the desired color. For example, the command **SCREEN 2:OUT 985, 14** changes everything on the screen to yellow, as yellow is color number 14.

Note that this changes the foreground color; the background remains black. The command does not require DEF SEG, because no PEEKing or POKEing is involved. The OUT command can be used to change colors as often as needed.
Eric Hedstrom
Pleasanton, California

ASCII Graphics Chart

Rich Schinnell passed along a chart that finally makes sense of IBM'S haphazard ASCII numbering of the PC's graphics characters (the chart is reproduced in Figure 4.23, "ASCII Graphics"). Paste the chart inside the cover of your BASIC manual and you'll never again have to wade through Appendix I just to draw a box.

VCR as RF Modulator

The color graphics board on the IBM PC and on the Compaq has a small, round RCA connector for composite video monitors, but it cannot be connected to an ordinary television set without the aid of an RF modulator. If you own a video

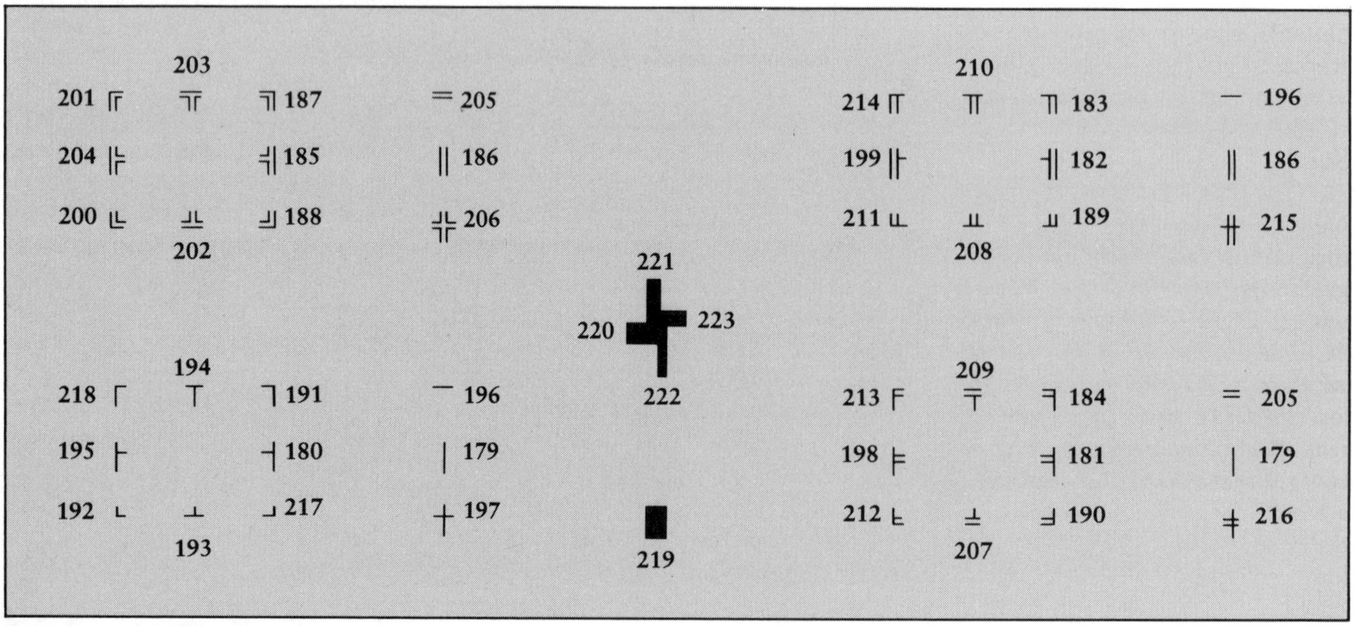

Figure 4.23 *ASCII graphics.*

tape recorder, you can use it in place of an RF modulator. Connect an inexpensive dubbing cable with the computer's composite video output and the VCR "camera" input and flip the switch on the VCR from "tuner" to "camera."
Phil Howitt
Los Angeles, California

Editor's note: You can also use the VCR to record computer output. In my experiments the signals from the color graphics board were not strong enough for the recorder, and while the result was very clear, the recording played back in black and white.

PC Cartography

The program in Figure 4.24 will draw a respectable outline of the United States. Many of your readers may find this interesting.
David T. Kjellquist
Richardson, Texas

Secret Graphics Mode

I read in IBM's technical reference manual that, with some special programming, a low-resolution mode with 16 colors is possible on the IBM PC. The manual fails to mention what must be done to obtain this low-resolution mode, but with some reading and research I finally discovered the secret. LOWRES.BAS is a BASIC program that demonstrates the IBM Color/Graphics Adapter's low-resolution mode, in which the screen is divided into 16,000 blocks (160 horizontal by 100 vertical), each of which can be any of 16 colors (see Figure 4.25).

To plot a point, set the variable PIXCOL equal to a color number from 0 to 15, set variables *X* and *Y* to the desired pixel coordinates, and then issue a GOSUB to the pixel-plotting routine. For demonstration purposes, LOWRES.BAS contains a subroutine that draws a picture on the screen using this mode and all of the 16 possible colors.

The program works by setting the registers of the Color/Graphics Adapter's 6845 CRT controller chip so that it produces a screen 80 characters wide by 100 characters long. Each character cell is a small rectangle twice as wide as it is tall. The program then sets each character byte of the display to 222 decimal. This value specifies a character that fills the left half of the character cell with the background color and the right half with the foreground color. Next, the program sets the character attribute bytes to 0. This makes both the foreground and background colors, and thus the entire screen, black. The attribute bytes can now be used to control the foreground and background colors of a character cell; the foreground is displayed as the left half of the cell and the background as the right half. Being able to control the left and right halves of each "character" yields 160 blocks per line.

Clearing the screen takes a few seconds, but an assembly language routine could be written to control the character and attribute bytes at a dramatically faster rate.

It's a shame that IBM didn't include this mode in BASIC, but one hopes they will in the future. The graphics that can be produced are well worth the loss of resolution.
Bernie Lawrence
Garland, Texas

Editor's note: This program generates a great deal of video "snow" when accessing the screen, another situation that assembly language programming can correct.

```
10 'DRAW OUTLINE OF UNITED STATES
20 'BY DAVID T KJELLQUIST
30 INPUT "INPUT SCALE 4 TO 20 ";SCALE
40 'DEFINE STRING TO DRAW MAP
50 A$="D4G1D7F2D3F5R2F2R4E1R2F3R2F3D1F1R2U1E4R2F1R4H1U1R5F1E1F1D2F3R
   2U4H2U4E3U1E1U1H2U1F1E1U3E3H1U2E3L2H2L2D3G2L2G1D1G1L2D1G2L2E1U1H1
   D1L2U3L2G1D3G1L2U4E1R2U1L5E1L2G1L2E2L5H1L19D1L2H1"
60 SCREEN 1    'SET GRAPHICS MODE
70 KEY OFF     'TURN FUNCTION KEYS OFF
80 CLS
90 DRAW "BM20,40"        'INITIAL POINT UPPER LEFT CORNER OF MAP
100 DRAW "S=SCALE;XA$;"        'DRAW MAP
```

Figure 4.24 *PC Cartography.*

```
10 SCREEN 0
20 DEFINT A-Z
30 '
40 'Color/Graphics Adapter definitions
50 '
60 MODEREG=&H3D8:COLORREG=&H3D9          'control registers
70 MODESAVE=&H465:COLORSAVE=&H466        'BIOS saves the regs here
80 CRTREG = &H3D4:CRTDATA = &H3D5        '6845 CRT controller regs
90 HIRES=1: GRAPH=2: BW=4: VIDEO=8       'Mode register bits
100 G640=16: BLINK=32
110 '
120 '
130 'set up Color/Graphics Adapter for 160- by 100-block graphics
140 '
150 DEF SEG=0
160 MODE=0
170 POKE MODESAVE,MODE : OUT MODEREG,MODE
180 POKE COLORSAVE,0 : OUT COLORREG,0
190 '
200 'Load new parameters into 6845 CRT controller
210 FOR REGISTER= 0 TO 11
220     READ REGDATA
230     OUT CRTREG,REGISTER:OUT CRTDATA,REGDATA
240 NEXT
```

Figure 4.25 *LOWRES.BAS: A low-resolution, 16-color graphics demonstration program.*

```
250 '
260 'set mode for 80 column color and enable
270 MODE=HIRES+VIDEO
280 POKE MODESAVE,MODE: OUT MODEREG,MODE
290 '
300 'clear screen:  Character = &hDE, Attributes=0
310 DEF SEG=&HB800
320 FOR CHAR=0 TO 15998 STEP 2: POKE CHAR,&HDE : NEXT
330 FOR ATTR=1 TO 16000 STEP 2: POKE ATTR,0    :NEXT
340 '
350 '
360 'initial data for 6845 (80 x 100 characters)
370 '
380 DATA 113    :'register 0    horizontal total
390 DATA  80    :'register 1    horizontal displayed
400 DATA  90    :'register 2    horizontal sync position
410 DATA  10    :'register 3    horizontal sync width
420 DATA 127    :'register 4    vertical total
430 DATA   6    :'register 5    vertical adjust
440 DATA 100    :'register 6    vertical displayed
450 DATA 112    :'register 7    vertical sync position
460 DATA   2    :'register 8    interlace mode (non-interlace)
470 DATA   1    :'register 9    maximum scan line address
480 DATA  32    :'register 10   cursor start (disables cursor display)
490 DATA   0    :'register 11   cursor end
500 '
510 '
520 'draw screen
530 PIXCOL=0:Y=0
540 FOR T=1 TO 39
550     Y=Y+1
560     IF T MOD 5 = 0 THEN PIXCOL=PIXCOL+1 MOD 15
570     FOR X=1 TO T
580             GOSUB 720                  'plot pixel at x,y
590     NEXT
600 NEXT
610 X=1:PIXCOL=8
620 FOR T=1 TO 39
630     X=X+1
640     IF T MOD 5=0 THEN PIXCOL=PIXCOL+1 MOD 15
```

Figure 4.25 *(continued)*

```
650 '
660     FOR Y=1 TO T
670             GOSUB 720                    'plot pixel at x,y
680     NEXT
690 NEXT
700 WHILE INKEY$="":WEND
710 SCREEN 2 : END
720 '=======================================================
730 'plot PIXCOL at (X,Y)
740 '
750 PIXEL=X+(Y*160):PIXELADDR=(PIXEL AND &HFFFE)+1
760 NIBBLE=PIXEL MOD 2
770 IF NIBBLE=0 THEN POKE PIXELADDR,(PEEK(PIXELADDR) AND &HF)
    +PIXCOL*&H10
780 IF NIBBLE=1 THEN POKE PIXELADDR,(PEEK(PIXELADDR) AND &HF0)
     + PIXCOL
790 RETURN
```

Figure 4.25 *(continued)*

IBM

5

Entertainment

Hands On

IBM PC proponents are always pointing out that that their machine was the first really *serious* personal computer, but the same power that enables the PC to be such a workhorse makes it extremely suitable for more imaginative purposes as well. The introduction of the PC almost immediately inspired programmers to write innovative new applications, such as Microsoft's *Flight Simulator.* Certainly the fact that *Flight Simulator* ranks among the best-selling personal computer programs nationwide— right up there with the spreadsheets, word processors, and other *serious* programs—gives the lie to the PC's "strictly business" image.

None of the three games in this chapter represents a dramatic video game breakthrough: "Video Game Graphics" demonstrates *Blockbuster,* a pong-style game; "Snake in the Glass" presents an old reflex and strategy favorite adapted for the PC; and "Digital Deduction" offers a number-guessing game. But the games are fun, and the explanations of the game listings will introduce you to the commands and strategies used in video game programming.

Music is the other form of entertainment this chapter offers. Because it can play only one note at a time the PC is no virtuoso instrument, but its ability to pipe out a preprogrammed tune on command makes it perfect for the performance-shy among us. If you've ever been curious about computer music, "Programming Sound in BASIC" introduces you to the full range of the PC's sound-producing options and gives you listings for two Bach minuets.

With the selections in this chapter, you will not only create programs to enjoy during break times, but you will come away with the confidence (if you have never programmed before) and the ability to produce totally original games or sound effects. So roll up your sleeves and go to work; then sit back and . . . enjoy.

Video Game Graphics

Dan Illowsky and Michael Abrash

The graphics commands used to construct this game, which we've named *Blockbuster,* vary in complexity: some are simple to understand and execute, while others are more difficult. If you are unfamiliar with some of these commands, refer to the IBM BASIC manual as you follow the information given here. Thanks to the graphics capabilities of Advanced BASIC, you'll find *Blockbuster* surprisingly compact and easy to implement. Besides Advanced BASIC, you'll need a PC with a color graphics adapter.

Game Design

The most important part of producing a game is creating a good design. The first step in this process is outlining how the program will accomplish each element of the game. Before writing a single line in BASIC, figure out the complete specifications for the playfield and moving objects, and decide how you'll handle the interactions among all components of the game. Once these decisions are made, you can easily write the program from your specifications without worrying about overall program logic.

Improper game design results in frustrating bugs in the program, especially in more complex programs. The "top-down" design we use ensures that each section of the program works well with the others. A good design creates a logically composed program, which makes later additions and changes much easier. The game designed here, *Blockbuster,* is a pong-type game in which a ball directed by a player-controlled paddle bounces around a playfield and into a wall of bricks (see Figure 5.1). Each time the ball hits a brick the brick vanishes. The game ends when the player clears the field of bricks or runs out of balls.

There are five sections of the program—the playfield, the bricks, the paddle, the ball, and housekeeping—that must be designed before you can produce the game.

The Playfield

The playfield is closed on three sides and open on the fourth. The paddle is located on the open side, which is at the bottom of the screen. Putting the open side on the bottom replicates a sense of gravity, with the ball falling toward the bottom, where the player will be waiting with the paddle. The playfield is nearly square at 166 rows by 162 columns (all coordinates are measured in pixels). The exact dimensions are changeable, so experiment with them. The playfield is black, as that is the easiest background color on which to follow the action. The area surrounding the playfield is a solid color, the selection of which is always a dilemma when you are programming color graphics on the IBM PC.

In medium-resolution graphics

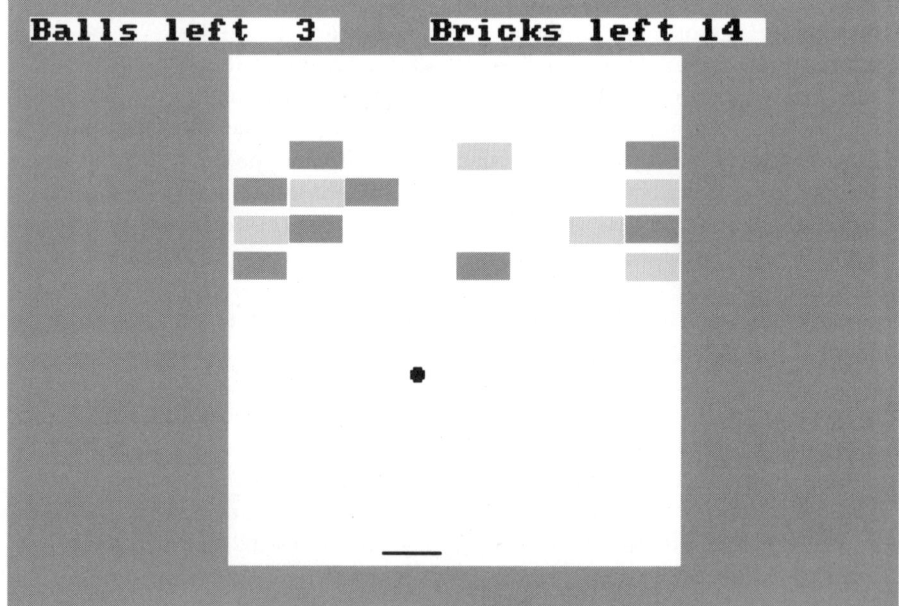

Figure 5.1 Blockbuster *in action.*

there is a choice of two palettes. Palette 0, with red, green, and brown is vivid on a high-quality monitor, but all three colors look brownish on a TV screen. Palette 1 has magenta, white, and cyan, which are less striking but look better on a TV. For *Blockbuster* we will use palette 1, but feel free to alter the program to use whichever palette and background you prefer. The area surrounding the playfield is supposed to be magenta, but it appears as anything from pink to deep red on the various displays.

The Bricks

Once the playfield is set, the bricks can be placed on it. There are four rows of eight bricks each, arrayed about two-thirds of the way to the top of the playfield. Each brick is 9 rows by 19 columns. There are no rules regarding placement and sizing of objects. The usual approach is to use graph paper, a pencil, and a large eraser to experiment. The upper edge of the top row of bricks begins at row 42, measured from the top of the screen. Each brick is 4 rows below the brick above and 2 columns from each brick to the side. The bricks are alternately magenta and cyan.

The Paddle

The paddle is a horizontal white line 21 columns wide in row 181 of the screen. The paddle's range of movement is the full width of the playfield, from column 80 to 241.

Although a joystick is an ideal paddle controller, not all PC owners have joysticks. Therefore, *Blockbuster* uses the keyboard to control the paddle, even though keyboard control is not as easy as a joystick. One method of keyboard control involves moving the paddle one unit each time a certain key is pressed. Approximately 25 keystrokes are required to move the paddle across the screen. Since the PC keyboard doesn't immediately repeat a key command (i.e., continually send the same key command when that key is held down), this method would leave the player whacking repeatedly at the keyboard.

A better approach to keyboard-controlled movement is to start the paddle moving when a key is pressed and to allow that movement to stop only when another key is pressed or the paddle reaches the edge of the playfield. In *Blockbuster* the z key starts the paddle moving left, the x key stops it, and the c key starts it moving right. Of course, you may select other keys if these don't appeal to you.

The Ball

Handling the ball is the most complex portion of the program, since the ball interacts with all the elements previously discussed. Draw the ball as a white circle of radius 2. The ball starts on the left of the playfield, below the bricks.

To create the impression that the ball is moving, the program erases the ball at its current location, adds the ball's coordinates an increment in each of the x and y directions, and then redraws the ball in the new location. The x and y increments fully describe the movement that the ball makes and can be either positive or negative for motion in all directions.

To determine if the ball has hit any of the edges of the playfield, simply compare coordinates. If the ball is at row 80, for example, and tries to move to the left, it has hit the left edge; you must reverse the x increment of its direction.

Similarly, compare coordinates to check if the ball has hit the paddle or gone off the bottom of the screen. If the ball reaches the paddle row, it either hits the paddle or misses the paddle and is lost. If the ball hits the paddle, the y increment is set to move the ball up, and the x increment is set according to how close to the center of the paddle the ball hit.

There is always the temptation to let the computer carry out the same movement every time, in this case to bounce the ball off the paddle at the same angle every time. Varying the path of the ball as it bounces off the paddle makes the game more interesting and creates the impression that the ball and paddle are real objects. In reality, balls bounce with spin, so we must create the illusion that this is happening in our game as well. Small touches like this make the game feel right to players, even though they may not know why they have that feeling.

If the ball misses the paddle, restart it the same way you did at the beginning of the game. The remaining number of balls will be handled in the program's housekeeping section.

Use the POINT function to check whether the ball has hit a brick. If the ball hasn't hit any of the playfield's edges or the paddle, and if the point where the center of the ball is about to move is not black, then a brick must have been hit. Disposing of the brick is simple; PAINT it out, starting at the point you just checked with POINT.

In understanding the ball's motion and the collision checks, it's important to understand the nature of program execution. While you, the game designer, are trying to create the impression of continuous action, you're actually dealing with discrete, sequential events. Hence, in *Blockbuster* you know that any point not black is a brick because you have already eliminated the possibility that the point is the edge of the playfield or the paddle. If the order of the checks is reversed, the program won't work. Again, you must PAINT over the brick after the ball is taken off screen at the old location and before the ball is drawn at the new location, or you may PAINT the ball off as well.

The discrete nature of video game programming is one reason for doing extensive game design before programming; the events must be sequenced so that they interact properly and without interference. It's impossible to replicate real-world action perfectly, so use good design to produce good illusion. Fortunately, fast action and the impressionable eye often cover for a good deal of imprecision.

Housekeeping

A game must have a beginning, an end, and a scoring method. In *Blockbuster* the score is the number of bricks hit, and the end comes when three balls are lost or when all the bricks are gone. You must keep track of the number of bricks and balls.

The beginning of the game consists of initializing and drawing the playfield, bricks, paddle, and ball. Initializing the paddle and ball by starting the ball aimed right at the paddle makes the game easier to play. If a player is confused or unprepared, for example, the ball won't be lost immediately. Also, the ball bouncing off the paddle makes the basic idea of the game more readily apparent to the novice.

Programming the Game

Now that *Blockbuster* is designed, you can program it in BASIC. You could just sit down with your specifications and start writing, but it's more productive to program a game in modules (i.e., to write each section in turn, thoroughly testing and debugging it before proceeding to the next section). Modular programming, especially important with large programs, is easier to do with compiled languages or in assembly language, but it can be applied in interpretive BASIC.

This game is programmed in five steps, with a pause after each step to test your progress to that stage. These five steps correspond to the five sections of the program: playfield, bricks, paddle, ball, and housekeeping. Before starting, note that the program listings shown seem to have gaps in the line numbering. For example, the line numbers run 100, 130, 140, skipping 110 and 120. The missing numbers are reserved for lines dealing with later steps, such as housekeeping. Also note that there are many statements on each line, which can make the program difficult to read. As an interpreted language, BASIC is not as fast as some other languages, but it can run statements faster if they're on the same line. *Blockbuster* uses multistatement lines for greater speed. Similarly, there are no comments in the listings because BASIC wastes a surprising amount of time when it encounters REM statements and single-quote comments. In general, however, commenting is a very desirable programming practice.

Programming the Playfield

The program in Figure 5.2 sets up the playfield. Line 100 clears the screen and selects medium-resolution color mode and palette 1 on a black background. Notice that the DEFINT statement makes all variables integers. This is important in programming games because BASIC works with integers much more quickly than with real numbers, particularly for arithmetic operations. The first LINE statement on line 130 colors the entire screen magenta, while the second LINE statement makes the playfield area black. Run

```
100 DEFINT A-Z:CLS:SCREEN 1,0:COLOR 0,1
130 LINE(0,0)-(319,199),2,BF:LINE(80,20)-(241,185),0,BF
```

Figure 5.2 *Drawing the playfield for* Blockbuster.

```
100 DEFINT A-Z:CLS:SCREEN 1,0:COLOR 0,1
130 LINE(0,0)-(319,199),2,BF:LINE(80,20)-(241,185),0,BF
140 FOR I=0 TO 7:FOR J=0 TO 3:LINE(82+20*I,48+J*12)-STEP(18,8),
    ((I+J) MOD 2)+1,BF:NEXT J:NEXT I
```

Figure 5.3 *Drawing the bricks.*

```
100 DEFINT A-Z:CLS:SCREEN 1,0:COLOR 0,1
130 LINE(0,0)-(319,199),2,BF:LINE(80,20)-(241,185),0,BF
140 FOR I=0 TO 7:FOR J=0 TO 3:LINE(82+20*I,48+J*12)-STEP(18,8),
    ((I+J) MOD 2)+1,BF:NEXT J:NEXT I
160 PX=150:PXINC=0
190 A$=INKEY$:IF A$="c" THEN PXINC=5 ELSE IF A$="z" THEN PXINC=-5
    ELSE IF A$="x" THEN PXINC=0
200 OLDPX=PX:PX=PX+PXINC:IF PX<80 OR PX>221 THEN PX=OLDPX
210 LINE(OLDPX,181)-(OLDPX+20,181),0:LINE (PX,181)-(PX+20,181),3:OLDPX=PX
270 GOTO 190
```

Figure 5.4 *Moving the paddle.*

the program to see the constructed playfield.

Programming the Bricks

Figure 5.3 draws the playfield and sets up the bricks. In line 140 the FOR . . . NEXT loop with the I variable runs through the eight columns of bricks, and the FOR . . . NEXT loop with the J variable runs through the four rows of bricks. The heart of line 140 is the LINE statement: the coordinates for the upper-left corner of each brick are calculated based on the upper-left brick, which is at coordinates 82,48. Each column is 20 dots wide, so the x coordinate of any brick is 82 + I* 20, where I is the column number of that brick. Similarly, each row is 12 dots high, so the y coordinate is 48 + J* 12, where J is the column number of the brick.

For each brick the rectangle drawn with the LINE statement is 19 columns by 9 rows and is created with the STEP command relative to the upper-left corner of the brick. The rectangle is filled in with alternating blocks of magenta and cyan using the MOD operator. The MOD function finds the necessary values for the LINE statement's color parameter to color in the bricks. If the formula (I + J) produces an even number, then the MOD 2 function, for example, returns the value 0; if the formula (I + J) produces an odd number, then MOD 2 returns the value 1. Cyan and magenta, however, are given the values 1 and 2, respectively. To make the MOD values 0 and 1 correspond to the color values 1 and 2, the value 1 is added to the MOD value. In this case the MOD 2 value of 0 indicates the color cyan (color 1) and the MOD 2 value of 1 indicates magenta (color 2).

Run the program in Figure 5.3. Notice that it simply adds line 140 to the program in Figure 5.2.

Programming the Paddle

Now comes the action. The program in Figure 5.4 initializes the paddle and lets you move it back and forth. The program also sets up the playfield and the bricks.

Line 160 initializes the paddle's x coordinate, the variable PX. The paddle's y coordinate never changes, so a constant is used. To move the paddle you need a loop that repeatedly executes the paddle movement commands. If line 160 were inside this loop, the paddle would constantly be returned to its initial position. Lines 190, 200, and 210 are the

```
100 DEFINT A-Z:CLS:SCREEN 1,0:COLOR 0,1
110 CIRCLE(3,3),2,3:PAINT STEP(0,0),3
120 DIM BALL(10):GET(0,0)-(5,5),BALL
130 LINE(0,0)-(319,199),2,BF:LINE(80,20)-(241,185),0,BF
140 FOR I=0 TO 7:FOR J=0 TO 3:LINE(82+20*I,48+J*12)-STEP(18,8),
    ((I+J) MOD 2)+1,BF:NEXT J:NEXT I
160 PX=150:PXINC=0
170 REM *placekeeping line*
180 BX=80:BY=100:BXINC=4:BYINC=4:PUT(BX,BY),BALL
190 A$=INKEY$:IF A$="c" THEN PXINC=5 ELSE IF A$="z" THEN PXINC=-5
    ELSE IF A$="x" THEN PXINC=0
200 OLDPX=PX:PX=PX+PXINC:IF PX<80 OR PX>221 THEN PX=OLDPX
210 LINE(OLDPX,181)-(OLDPX+20,181),0:LINE (PX,181)-(PX+20,181),3:OLDPX=PX
220 OLDBX=BX:BX=BX+BXINC:IF BX<80 OR BX>234 THEN BXINC=-BXINC:BX=BX+2*BXINC
230 OLDBY=BY:BY=BY+BYINC:IF BY<24 THEN BYINC=-BYINC:BY=BY+2*BYINC
240 IF BY>175 THEN IF BX<PX-5 OR BX>PX+20 THEN 280 ELSE BYINC=-BYINC:
    BY=BY+2*BYINC:BXINC=(BX-PX)\2-4
250 PUT(OLDBX,OLDBY),BALL:IF POINT(BX+2,BY+2)=0 THEN GOTO 260 ELSE
    PAINT(BX+2,BY+2),0:BYINC=-BYINC:BY=BY+2*BYINC
260 PUT(BX,BY),BALL
270 GOTO 190
280 REM *placekeeping line*
290 PUT (OLDBX,OLDBY),BALL:GOTO 170
```

Figure 5.5 *Moving the ball.*

paddle movement commands. Line 190 uses the INKEY$ command to get keyboard input, if any, without disturbing the screen. (Keystrokes obtained with INKEY$ are not shown on the screen.) If there is no input, INKEY$ returns an empty string. If the input is one of the three movement keys—z, x, or c (the keys must be lowercase)—then action is taken. The action is to set the variable PXINC (the increment by which the paddle moves) to -5 to move left, 0 to stop, or 5 to move right. Moving the paddle at fewer than five dots at a time produces slower motion, while moving it at more than five dots produces jerky motion that's difficult to control.

Line 200 guards against the paddle moving off the edge of the screen by saving the current location in OLDPX and then performing a trial move of the paddle by adding the paddle movement increment PXINC to the current *x* coordinate. If the new location is off either edge, it is set back to the old location and no move takes place.

Line 210 moves the paddle. (If PX equals OLDPX, either because PXINC is 0 or because the edge has been reached, then no move occurs. Instead, the paddle is erased and drawn again in precisely the same spot.) The first LINE statement uses OLDPX to erase the paddle at its old location, and the second LINE statement uses PX to draw the paddle at its new location.

Line 270 loops back to perform the paddle movement commands again. The initialization in line 160 is not reexecuted.

Run the program in Figure 5.4. Notice that the paddle moves very rapidly. This is to be expected, because the lines dealing with the ball's movement are not being executed yet. These lines slow the action down considerably. Also remember that this program is an endless loop, so use <Ctrl>-<Break> to stop it.

Programming the Ball

The program in Figure 5.5 adds the ball to what you've already created. To program the ball, draw and initialize it, check for collisions with the edges, paddle, and bricks, and then move and redraw the ball.

The ball must first be drawn so that it can be saved for future use. Line 110 creates a white circle of radius 2, and line 120 uses the graphics GET command to save the form of the ball into the array variable BALL.

Line 180 sets the ball's coordinates (BX and BY) and motion (BXINC and BYINC). BX and BY are set to start the ball on the left side below the bricks. BXINC and BYINC are set initially to move the ball down and to the right to intersect the paddle's starting position. The PUT graphics statement at the end of the line draws the ball on the screen at its starting spot. Remember that the PUT statement is a rapid way to draw an image previously saved with the GET statement.

Line 220 moves the ball horizontally and checks for collision with the sides. The current location is saved in OLDBX for later reference. BXINC (the horizontal motion) is then added to the current *x* coordinate. If this new location is off either edge, the horizontal motion variable BXINC is negated (that is, multiplied by -1) and twice the new motion is added to the *x* coordinate. This cancels the move made at the beginning of line 220 and moves the ball one normal distance. After this line executes, the ball's *x* coordinate is moved by BXINC. When checks are made for collisions, remember that BX and BY are the coordinates of the upper-left corner of the ball. Since the ball is five dots wide, its right edge is at BX+4. The same is true for the paddle, the right edge of which is at PX+20.

Line 230 is similar to line 220, except that it handles vertical motion. Only the top edge is checked for in this line. If the ball has reached the top, BYINC (the vertical motion) is negated.

Line 240 checks whether the ball hits the paddle. If the ball hasn't reached the paddle row, no check is necessary. If the ball has reached the paddle row, the ball has either hit the paddle and bounced or hasn't hit the paddle and has gone off the screen. If the ball hits the paddle, the ball's vertical motion is reversed just as when the ball hits the top edge of the playfield. The horizontal motion varies, depending on how close to the center the ball hits, thereby creating the impression of spin. The last statement on line 240 sets this variable horizontal motion.

If the ball misses the paddle, it must be taken off the screen and restarted. This is done in line 290. Note that line 170 (where the ball is restarted) is a REM statement. This line, like line 280, is used in the housekeeping section, so the REM statement is merely a placekeeper for now.

If the ball hasn't gone off the bottom edge of the screen, it must be erased so it can be moved. Line 250 erases the ball from its old location by exclusive ORing it out of the screen. Line 250 uses the POINT function to see if there is anything on the screen where the ball's center is to go. Since the ball is not allowed to hit the boundary or the paddle, if any color but black is there, the ball must be hitting a brick. Because the brick is surrounded by black, it is PAINTED off the screen, and the ball reverses direction as if it hit the top edge of the screen.

With line 260 the ball is redrawn in its new location. The program loops to line 190 to execute the whole sequence of ball and paddle movements.

When you run the program in Figure 5.5, remember to terminate it with <Ctrl>-<Break>.

Programming the Housekeeping

Only a few details remain to make *Blockbuster* a working game. The program must check to see if any bricks remain and count the balls as they're lost. Line 150 sets the initial number of balls and bricks. Line 280 reduces the number of balls after each ball is lost and then loops to line 170, which indicates on the screen how many balls remain and terminates the game with the message 'YOU LOST!!!!!' if no balls remain.

In line 250 the number of bricks is reduced each time a brick is hit. If there are no bricks left, the game is terminated with the message 'YOU WON!!!!'. Line 250 also indicates on the screen how many bricks remain.

The program in Figure 5.6 is *Blockbuster* in its entirety. Review the listing and relate each line to its function as you play. You might also find it worthwhile to follow the program through a few loops by printing variables such as BXINC and BYINC on an unused portion of the screen or on your printer as the game is playing.

You Win!

That's all there is to programming a video game. *Blockbuster* isn't as polished as it might be; we left some rough edges for you to smooth out. The best way to acquire game-making skills is to experiment with the program and redesign the game. You also might want to review the commented version of the program in Figure 5.7; it may be of use to you in working with the program.

If you graduate to programming games in assembly language, you'll find that the basic principles of game design and implementation are the

```
100 DEFINT A-Z:CLS:SCREEN 1,0:COLOR 0,1
110 CIRCLE(3,3),2,3:PAINT STEP(0,0),3
120 DIM BALL(10):GET(0,0)-(5,5),BALL
130 LINE(0,0)-(319,199),2,BF:LINE(80,20)-(241,185),0,BF
140 FOR I=0 TO 7:FOR J=0 TO 3:LINE(82+20*I,48+J*12)-STEP(18,8),
    ((I+J) MOD 2)+1,BF:NEXT J:NEXT I
150 NBALLS=3:NBRKS=32
160 PX=150:PXINC=0
170 LOCATE 2,2:PRINT "Balls left ";NBALLS:IF NBALLS=0 THEN LOCATE 15,13:
    PRINT "YOU LOST!!!!!":END
180 BX=80:BY=100:BXINC=4:BYINC=4:PUT(BX,BY),BALL
190 A$=INKEY$:IF A$="c" THEN PXINC=5 ELSE IF A$="z" THEN PXINC=-5
    ELSE IF A$="x" THEN PXINC=0
200 OLDPX=PX:PX=PX+PXINC:IF PX<80 OR PX>221 THEN PX=OLDPX
210 LINE(OLDPX,181)-(OLDPX+20,181),0:LINE (PX,181)-(PX+20,181),3:OLDPX=PX
220 OLDBX=BX:BX=BX+BXINC:IF BX<80 OR BX>234 THEN BXINC=-BXINC:BX=BX+2*BXINC
230 OLDBY=BY:BY=BY+BYINC:IF BY<24 THEN BYINC=-BYINC:BY=BY+2*BYINC
240 IF BY>175 THEN IF BX<PX-5 OR BX>PX+20 THEN 280 ELSE BYINC=-BYINC:
    BY=BY+2*BYINC:BXINC=(BX-PX)\2-4
250 PUT(OLDBX,OLDBY),BALL:IF POINT(BX+2,BY+2)=0 THEN GOTO 260 ELSE
    PAINT(BX+2,BY+2),0:BYINC=-BYINC:BY=BY+2*BYINC:LOCATE 2,20:
    NBRKS=NBRKS-1:PRINT "Bricks left";NBRKS:IF NBRKS=0 THEN LOCATE 15,13:
    PRINT "YOU WON!!!!":END
260 PUT(BX,BY),BALL
270 GOTO 190
280 NBALLS=NBALLS-1
290 PUT (OLDBX,OLDBY),BALL:GOTO 170
```

Figure 5.6 *Housekeeping (finished program).*

same. So fool around with *Blockbuster,* or better yet, write your own video game. Using the graphics commands you've learned here, you may be amazed at what you can make your PC do.

Dan Illowsky and Michael Abrash are the authors of several popular video games, including Snack Attack *and* Cosmic Crusaders. *They are also founders of MIDA Corporation, a consulting firm located in Audubon, Pennsylvania. This article was originally published in* PC World *Volume 1, Number 5 and is an excerpt from the book* Graphics for the IBM PC *published by Howard W. Sams and Company, Inc., 1984.*

```
95  rem Block Buster-- A pong-type video game
100 DEFINT A-Z:CLS:SCREEN 1,0:COLOR 0,1
105 rem draw the ball and fill it in
110 CIRCLE(3,3),2,3:PAINT STEP(0,0),3
115 rem save the ball in array called BALL
120 DIM BALL(10):GET(0,0)-(5,5),BALL
125 rem draw the playfield
130 LINE(0,0)-(319,199),2,BF:LINE(80,20)-(241,185),0,BF
135 rem draw the bricks in the playfield
140 FOR I=0 TO 7:FOR J=0 TO 3:LINE(82+20*I,48+J*12)-STEP(18,8),
    ((I+J) MOD 2)+1,BF:NEXT J:NEXT I
145 rem initialize the number of balls and number of bricks
150 NBALLS=3:NBRKS=32
155 rem set initial paddle position and movement
160 PX=150:PXINC=0
165 rem keep track of number of balls left, if none then end game
170 LOCATE 2,2:PRINT "Balls left ";NBALLS:IF NBALLS=0 THEN LOCATE 15,13:
    PRINT "YOU LOST!!!!!":END
175 rem start new ball and direction
180 BX=80:BY=100:BXINC=4:BYINC=4:PUT(BX,BY),BALL
185 rem set paddle direction according to what key is pressed
190 A$=INKEY$:IF A$="c" THEN PXINC=5 ELSE IF A$="z" THEN PXINC=-5
    ELSE IF A$="x" THEN PXINC=0
195 rem find new paddle location--do not let it go off playing field
200 OLDPX=PX:PX=PX+PXINC:IF PX<80 OR PX>221 THEN PX=OLDPX
202 rem draw the paddle at its new location which then becomes the
204 rem   old location
210 LINE(OLDPX,181)-(OLDPX+20,181),0:LINE (PX,181)-(PX+20,181),3:OLDPX=PX
215 rem find new horizontal ball location-- if it would hit a wall then
    go in other direction
220 OLDBX=BX:BX=BX+BXINC:IF BX<80 OR BX>234 THEN BXINC=-BXINC:BX=BX+2*BXINC
225 rem find new vertical ball location-- if it hits the top then go down
230 OLDBY=BY:BY=BY+BYINC:IF BY<24 THEN BYINC=-BYINC:BY=BY+2*BYINC
232 rem if ball is at paddle row and missed the paddle then goto line 280
234 rem if ball is at paddle line and hit the paddle then set ball to go up
236 rem   and set the horizontal movement according to where the paddle was
238 rem   hit
240 IF BY>175 THEN IF BX<PX-5 OR BX>PX+20 THEN 280 ELSE BYINC=-BYINC:
    BY=BY+2*BYINC:BXINC=(BX-PX)\2-4
242 rem erase the ball, restoring the background. if the dot at the center
244 rem   of where the ball is to be put next is black then go to 260. if
246 rem   not, then a brick has been hit, so erase the brick by PAINTing it
248 rem   the background color, then reverse the direction of the ball and
249 rem   reduce the brick count by one. if no bricks left, you won!!!
250 PUT(OLDBX,OLDBY),BALL:IF POINT(BX+2,BY+2)=0 THEN GOTO 260 ELSE
    PAINT(BX+2,BY+2),0:BYINC=-BYINC:BY=BY+2*BYINC:LOCATE 2,20:
    NBRKS=NBRKS-1:PRINT "Bricks left";NBRKS:IF NBRKS=0 THEN LOCATE 15,13:
    PRINT "YOU WON!!!!":END
252 rem draw the ball at its new location
260 PUT(BX,BY),BALL
265 rem loop back and do it all again
270 GOTO 190
275 rem the ball went past the paddle, so there is one less ball
280 NBALLS=NBALLS-1
285 rem erase the old ball and goto where a new ball will be started
290 PUT (OLDBX,OLDBY),BALL:GOTO 170
```

Figure 5.7 *Complete* Blockbuster *game with comments.*

Snake in the Glass

Peter Quinn

Snake is a simple computer game that dates back to the time when medium-resolution graphics became common. I first played it in 1979 on the original Commodore Pet, and I am told that early Datapoint Systems had a similar game. The Atari VCS game console version, which has many variations, is called *Surround.* A portion of the arcade game *Tron* is similar also. The Apple has a best-selling machine language game, *Snake Byte,* based on the same theme.

Snake is primarily a reaction-time game, but some strategy is involved. In this game two "snakes" grow longer in an enclosed area. One is controlled by the computer, the other by the player. Both snakes grow at a constant rate, and control consists of changing the direction of growth. The game ends when one snake runs into the playing area boundary, the other snake, or itself. The object of the game is to avoid running into anything until the other snake does; this is accomplished by "walling off" the other snake in a small area while retaining a larger area in which to maneuver.

I have implemented this standard version with a few embellishments for the IBM PC. The program occupies less than 1.5K of memory but uses Advanced BASIC features. Scoring is based on the length of the game (it's more difficult to win a long game than a short one). By varying the speed at which the snake grows, the game has unlimited variation in levels of difficulty. Adding to the difficulty of the game, the computer snake never runs into a wall

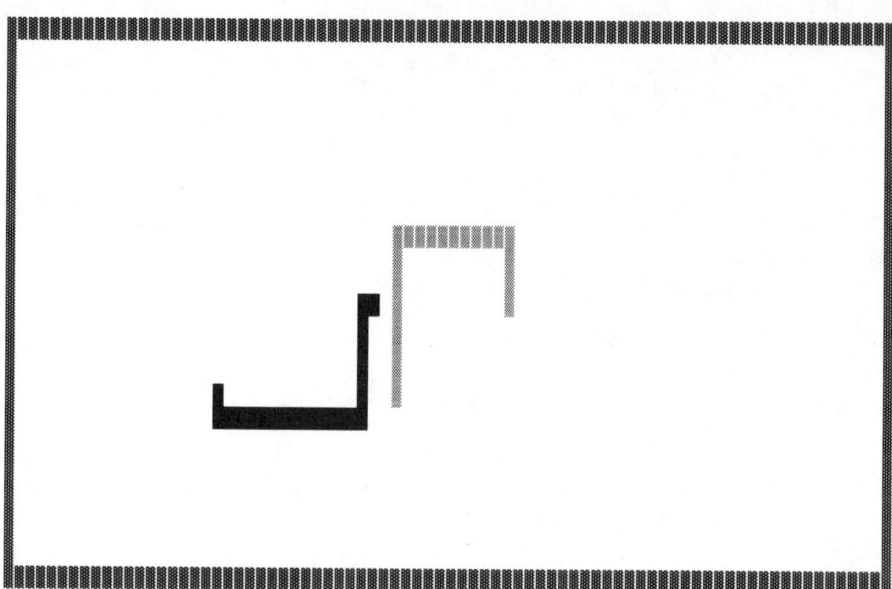

Figure 5.8 *Game after 21 moves.*

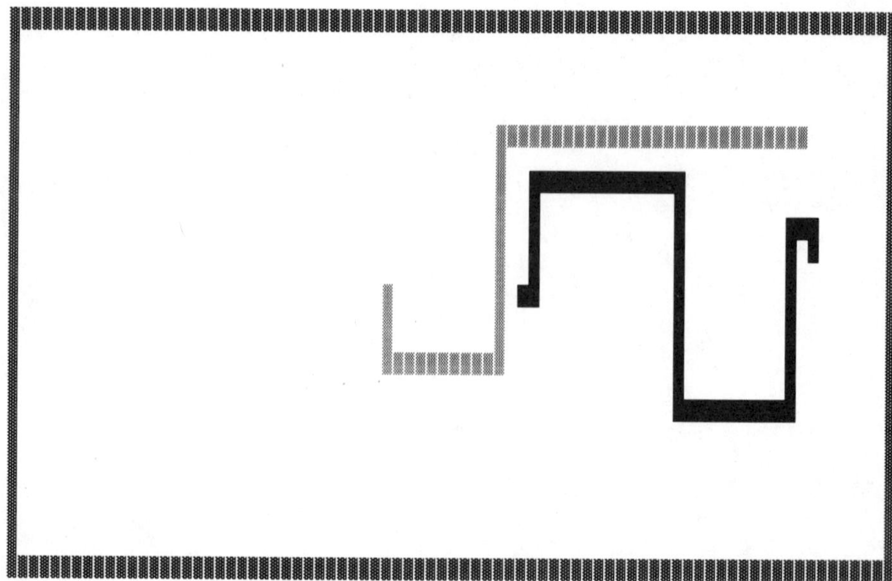

Figure 5.9 *Game after 51 moves.*

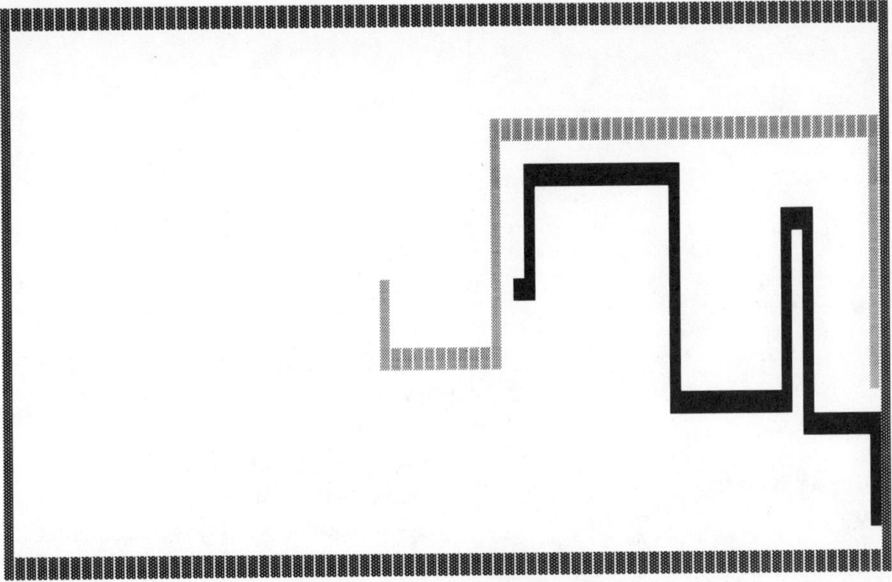

Figure 5.10 *Player gets in position to cut off computer snake.*

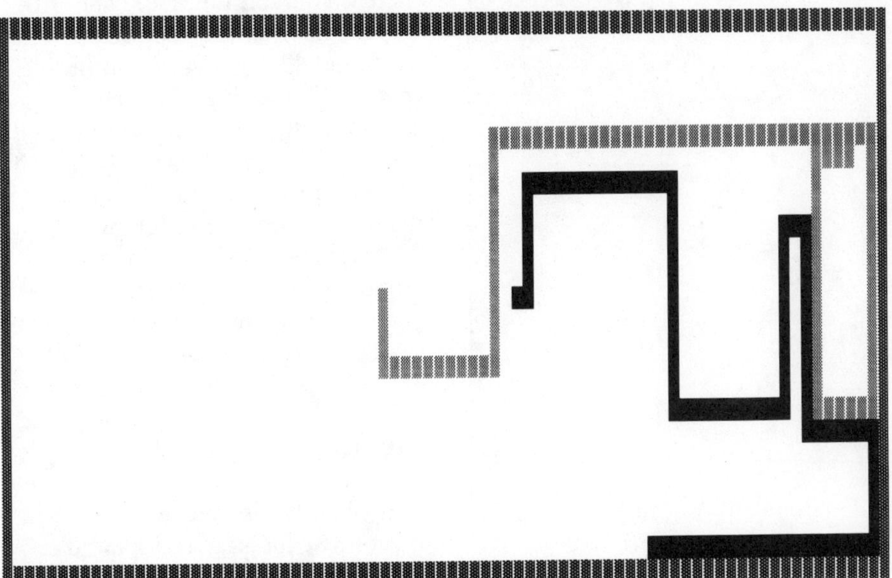

Figure 5.11 *Computer snake boxes itself in.*

unless trapped and occasionally changes direction for no particular reason. To the player's advantage, however, the computer snake also has very little strategy. I experimented with giving the snake smarter strategy, but because its reflexes are so much better than mine, a more sophisticated snake is almost unbeatable at high speeds.

The progress of a game of *Snake* is shown in Figures 5.8 to 5.11. The player's snake is solid; the computer snake is dotted. Figure 5.8 shows the situation after 21 moves. The computer started down and has made two random turns. The player is getting into position to box the computer snake in whichever direction the computer moves. Some 30 moves later, the computer snake has moved up and to the right and the player moves to box it in, turning downward to get into position to cut the computer off in case it doubles back (Figure 5.9). The next frame shows that the computer has turned down and is blocked by the player (Figure 5.10). In Figure 5.11 the computer has boxed itself in and must lose unless the player is suicidal. If the computer turned left instead of right, it would have had a possible escape route. Note that in a high-speed game the action to this point would have taken about 15 seconds.

The Program

The first lines of the program are an initialization routine (see Figure 5.12). These lines define all variables to be integers (line 30), reset the random number generator (lines 40 and 50), dimension two arrays (line 70), and set the screen attributes (line 80) and the memory segment to the Color/Graphics Adapter (line 90). If you are using the Monochrome Adapter, change 'DEF SEG = &HB800' to 'DEF SEG = &HB000'.

You can vary the speed of the program by entering a number when the message 'Enter value for delay' shows up on the screen. This value is used to determine the number of times a delay is executed for each move of the snakes (lines 100 to 130). Try starting at 50.

Next, several variables are initialized that control the initial position and direction of both snakes and how often the computer snake makes random turns. The next section of the program draws the border barrier around the edge of the screen (lines 200 to 270).

Player input is accepted by lines 280 to 340. When one of the cursor control keys is pressed, the program determines your snake's travel direction (lines 450 to 480). Your snake turns in the direction of the arrow

```
10 REM                 Snake - a traditional computer game
20 REM                 (c) 1982 Peter Quinn
30 DEFINT A-Z
40 TI=VAL(RIGHT$(TIME$,2))
50 RANDOMIZE TI
60 OPTION BASE 1
70 DIM P(2),D(2)
80 KEY OFF:CLS:SCREEN 0,0,0:WIDTH 80
90 DEF SEG=&H40
92 IF (PEEK(&H10) AND &H30)=&H30 THEN DEF SEG=&HB000 ELSE DEF SEG=&HB800
95 PRINT">>>>>>>>>>>>>>>>SNAKE>>>>>>>>>>>>>>>
100 INPUT "Enter value for delay ('Q' for QUIT, 'RETURN' for same value)";Z1$
105 CLS:C=C+1
110 IF Z1$="Q" OR Z1$="q" THEN GOTO 650
120 IF Z1$="" THEN GOTO 140
130 Z=VAL(Z1$)
140 A=219:B=177
150 P(1)=2010
160 D(1)=2
170 P(2)=1990
180 D(2)=-2
190 R!=.8
200 FOR I=0 TO 160 STEP 2
210 POKE I,178
220 POKE I+(4000-160),178
230 NEXT I
240 FOR I=0 TO 4000 STEP 160
250 POKE I,178
260 POKE I+158,178
270 NEXT
280 FOR I=11 TO 14
290 KEY (I) ON
300 NEXT
310 ON KEY(11) GOSUB 450
320 ON KEY(12) GOSUB 460
330 ON KEY(13) GOSUB 470
340 ON KEY(14) GOSUB 480
350 P(1)=P(1)+D(1)
360 P(2)=P(2)+D(2)
370 R!=R!+(1-R!)/20:N=N+1
380 IF PEEK(P(1))<>32 THEN GOTO 490
390 IF PEEK(P(2))<>32 THEN GOTO 500
400 POKE P(1),A
410 POKE P(2),B
420 GOSUB 510
430 FOR Q=1 TO Z:NEXT Q
440 GOTO 350
450 D(1)=-160:RETURN
460 D(1)=-2:RETURN
470 D(1)=2:RETURN
480 D(1)=160:RETURN
490 GOSUB 700:PRINT CHR$(11);"YOU LOSE   ";:N=N/10:GOTO 600
500 GOSUB 710:PRINT CHR$(11);"YOU WIN    ";:GOTO 600
510 IF PEEK(P(2)+D(2))=32 AND RND<R! THEN RETURN
520 IF ABS(D(2))=2 THEN D(2)=160:GOTO 560
530 IF ABS(D(2))=160 THEN D(2)=2
540 IF P(2)<2000 AND D(2)=160 THEN D(2)=-D(2)
550 GOTO 580
560 DI=P(2)/160
570 IF DI>12 THEN D(2)=-D(2):GOTO 580
580 IF PEEK(D(2)+P(2))<>32 THEN D(2)=-D(2)
590 RETURN
600 FOR I=1 TO 1000:NEXT
610 IF N>HIGH THEN HIGH=N
620 PT=PT+N:PRINT"SCORE:";N;" AVERAGE SCORE:";INT(PT/C);"HIGH SCORE:"HIGH
630 N=0
640 GOTO 100
650 PRINT"AVERAGE SCORE:";INT(PT/C);"HIGH SCORE:"HIGH
660 PRINT"THANKS FOR PLAYING"
670 END
700 FOR I=100 TO 50 STEP -5:SOUND I,1:NEXT                        'loser sound
705 FOR I=1 TO 8:SOUND 37,1:SOUND 39,1:NEXT:RETURN
710 FOR I=200 TO 300 STEP 20:SOUND I,1:NEXT:SOUND 32767,2  'winner sound
715 FOR I=1 TO 2:SOUND 400,3:SOUND 600,4:SOUND 32767,1:NEXT:RETURN
```

Figure 5.12 Snake.

on the key. If you press the arrow pointing in the opposite direction of current movement, your snake reverses direction, runs into itself, and you lose. Pressing the arrow pointing in the same direction as current movement has no effect.

The next section (350 to 440) is the main body of the program. The first two lines move each snake one unit. Variables P(1) and P(2) store the position of the player's snake and the computer's snake respectively, and D(1) and D(2) store the directions. Line 370 increments a variable (R!) to make it less likely that the computer snake will turn randomly. Also, your score (N) is incremented.

Lines 380 and 390 test for wall contact by either of the snakes and branch to the win/lose routine if there is contact. Lines 400 and 410 add the next unit to each snake. The next line (420) goes to a subroutine that determines if the snake is going to hit a wall in its next movement; if so, it should make a random turn. If not, you return to line 430 in the main section of the program. Line 430 provides a delay by looping the number of times you specified when you responded to the 'Delay' input.

The next group of lines (450 to 480) changes the direction of movement of your snake when one of the direction keys is pressed.

When the game ends, one of the next two lines is executed, and the win or lose message is displayed at the top of the screen. The scores are calculated by incrementing a variable (N). If you win the game, you receive all the points in that variable. If you lose, you gain 10 percent of those points. This is to encourage aggressive winning rather than having the game last a long time and losing. Also, to get a high score you need to take risks; immediately killing off your opponent will yield fewer points than playing the game for awhile and then killing it off.

Lines 600 to 640 compute and display your current score, average score, and high score. If you want to play another game, the program returns to line 100. If not, lines 650 to 670 display your high and average scores when the program ends.

Variations

After you have become proficient at *Snake,* you'll probably want to add some variations. One involves eliminating the border around the playing area, allowing the snakes to run off one side and come back on the other. This horizontal wraparound is automatic when the borders on each side are removed. For vertical wraparound, other changes are required. One way to program for vertical wraparound is to insert the following lines of code:

```
365 IF P(1) >= 3840 THEN P(1)=(P(1)
    MOD 160):GOTO 367
366 IF P(1) <= 0 THEN P(1)=(P(1) MOD
    160) +3840
367 IF P(2) >= 3840 THEN P(2)=(P(2)
    MOD 160):GOTO 370
368 IF P(2) <= 0 THEN P(2)=(P(2) MOD
    160) + 3840
```

Other variations include putting in barriers of various shapes and locations to restrict each snake's area of movement. This can be done at setup time with BASIC's LOCATE and PRINT instructions. Using them during the game slows things down too much.

If you're interested in doing games or other programs featuring graphics that change fairly rapidly, the *IBM PC Technical Reference Manual* may be useful. Otherwise, just enjoy *Snake* for what it is: an opportunity to challenge your computer in a game of quick reactions and clever strategies.

Peter Quinn is a chemical engineering major at the University of California at Berkeley. He has a strong interest in programming, especially writing games. He has consulted on applications software, operating systems, and regression testing. This article was originally published in PC World *Volume 1, Number 2.*

Digital Deduction

Karl Koessel

Digital Deduction is written in BASIC and will run on any IBM PC system. It is short enough to be keyed in during your lunch break and still leave you plenty of time to play (see Figure 5.13).

If your lunch break is short, you may want to skip keying in the REMarks. The REMarks in this program all begin with apostrophes. You do not have to key in the apostrophe or any characters to its right, with the exception of line 160, which contains an apostrophe that is part of a PRINT statement, not the beginning of a REMark.

In this game you try to guess the computer's secret number. The game has three levels. Trying to guess a number that is two digits long is the easiest level, and guessing three digits correctly is easier than guessing four.

After you tell the computer how many digits you want in the secret number, it builds a number with a different nonzero digit in each place. You are then prompted to enter a guess. Line 50 sets the NumLock status on so that the numeric keypad on the right side of the keyboard may be used to enter your guess.

The digits you enter are printed as black characters inside a "window" of white on the left side of the display screen. You may use the <Backspace> key to erase a digit should you wish to change its value—unless it is the last digit of your guess. The last digit of your guess fills the window and signals the computer to compare your guess to the secret number.

The computer responds by clearing the line with the window, its prompt, and your guess. Then the headings of the clue table are printed, under which is printed your guess (in column 1) and two clues. The first clue (in column 2) tells you how many digits in the guess have the right value and are in the right place.

If the secret number were 42 and you guessed 49, column 2 would show a 1 because one of the digits (the 4) in the guess has the same value and is in the same place as one of the digits in the secret number.

The second clue (column 3) tells you how many digits in your guess have the right value but are in the wrong place. If the secret number were 42 and you guessed 23, column 3 would show a 1 because one of the digits (the 2) in the guess has the same value as one of the digits in the secret number but is in the wrong place.

If your guess is not the secret number, the computer beeps, and on the line below your last guess a new guess window appears with its prompt asking you to enter another guess. Each new guess is added to the table. Using the clues provided after each guess, you should eventually be able to deduce what digit belongs in what place.

If you guess the secret number, you are congratulated and given a score based on how many guesses you needed. For a two-digit secret number, you are allowed 8 guesses. You have 12 guesses for a three-digit number and 15 for a four-digit number. If you do not guess the secret number before you reach the maximum number of guesses allowed, the secret number is revealed.

Whether you win or lose, you are asked if you wish to quit or play again by a prompt printed in inverse characters (black on white) on the bottom line of the screen. The first word of the prompt is printed in blinking characters for emphasis.

If the <Esc> key is pressed, the program resets the NumLock status to the state that was in effect before the program was run, clears the screen, and ends. If any other key is pressed, the program will begin again, asking how many digits you want in the new secret number. If the "any other key" you press is a 2, 3, or 4, the value of the key pressed will determine the number of digits in the new secret number, and the program will skip the "how many digits" question.

Take care to key in the program character-for-character; don't miss any blanks or semicolons. If you don't enter it correctly, the program won't work and you will have to perform an entirely different sort of digital deduction.

Karl Koessel is PC World*'s Technical Editor. This article was originally published in* PC World *Volume 1, Number 2.*

```
1 '                                Digital Deduction!
2 '                                    PC WORLD
3 '                                  karl koessel
10 DEFINT A-Z                                    'Integer numeric variables
20 GUESS(2)=8                                    'Set constants. Number of...
30 GUESS(3)=12                                   '...digits determines number...
40 GUESS(4)=15                                   '...of guesses allowed
50 DEF SEG=65:KBS=PEEK(7):POKE 7,(KBS AND -33)+32  'Save NumLock status, set ON
60 SCREEN 0,0,0,0                                'Set text mode screen
70 WIDTH 80                                      '80 characters per screen line
80 COLOR 7,0                                     'White characters, black field
90 KEY OFF                                       'Turn off soft keys' display
100 CLS                                          'Clear the screen
110 COLOR 0,7                                    'Inverse characters
120 LOCATE ,30:PRINT " Digital Deduction! "      'Center title on top line
130 COLOR 7,0                                    'Standard characters
140 GOTO 230                                     'Check if length already chosen
150 LOCATE 3,1                                   'Choose secret number's length
160 PRINT "In this game, you try to guess the computer's secret number."
170 PRINT "Would you like a 2, 3, or 4 digit secret number? ";
180 COLOR 0,7:PRINT " ";                         'Print an inverse space (white)
190 LOCATE 4,POS(0)-1,1                          'Cursor on (flashing) in space
200 COLOR 7,0                                    'Standard characters
210 DIGITS=VAL(INPUT$(1))                        'Length = value of single input
220 LOCATE 4,1:PRINT SPACE$(80)                  'Clear line 4 of all characters
230 IF DIGITS<2 OR DIGITS>4 THEN 150             'Invalid secret number length?
240 RANDOMIZE(VAL(RIGHT$(TIME$,2)))              'Reseed RaNDom number generator
250 NUMBER=0:GUESS=0                             'Initialize variables
260 FOR I=1 TO DIGITS                            'Construct secret number
270      D(I)=RND*9 MOD 9+1                      'Pick a RaNDom digit (1 thru 9)
280      USED=0                                  'Reset USED flag
290      FOR J=1 TO I-1                          'Check previously picked digits
300              IF D(I)=D(J) THEN USED=-1       'Has digit already been USED?
310      NEXT
320      IF USED THEN 270                        'Don't use same digit twice
330      NUMBER=NUMBER*10+D(I)                   'Value of secret number
340 NEXT
350 LOCATE 3,1:PRINT "Ok, the computer has chosen a";            'Instructions
360 PRINT DIGITS"digit number. Zero is not one of the digits."
370 PRINT "You may use the numeric keypad on the right side of the keyboard."
380 LOCATE 5+GUESS,4+DIGITS                      'Locate next to window
390 PRINT "<--- Enter your guess"                'Print prompt
400 COLOR 0,7                                    'Inverse characters
410 LOCATE 5+GUESS,3:PRINT SPC(DIGITS);          'Make `window'
420 IF INKEY$>"" THEN 420                        'Clear Keyboard buffer
430 FOR I=1 TO DIGITS                            'Fill window with guess
440      LOCATE 5+GUESS,2+I,1                    'Locate in window, cursor on
450      G$(I)=INPUT$(1)                         'Get single character input
460      IF G$(I)=CHR$(27) THEN 1070             'Quitting?
470      IF G$(I)=CHR$(8) THEN GOSUB 750:GOTO 440'Backspace?
480      IF G$(I)<"1" OR G$(I)>"9" THEN 440      'Invalid input?
490      PRINT G$(I);                            'Print digit in window
500 NEXT                                         'Window is full
510 COLOR 7,0                                    'Standard characters
520 LOCATE 5+GUESS,1:PRINT SPACE$(80)            'Erase line with window, prompt
530 GUESS=GUESS+1                                'Keep track of # of guesses
540 IF GUESS=1 THEN GOSUB 790                    'Time to print table headings?
550 RP=0:WP=0                                    'Initialize variables RP and WP
560 FOR I=1 TO DIGITS                            'Compare guess to secret number
570      IF D(I)=VAL(G$(I)) THEN RP=RP+1:GOTO 620'Right digit in right place?
580      FOR J=1 TO DIGITS                 'Check for right digit in wrong place
590              IF I=J THEN 610           'If same place, skip wrong place check
600              IF D(I)=VAL(G$(J)) THEN WP=WP+1:J=DIGITS'Digit in wrong place?
610      NEXT
620 NEXT
630 LOCATE 4+GUESS,3                               'Indent each guess on new line
640 FOR I=1 TO DIGITS
650      PRINT G$(I);                              'Print each digit of guess
660 NEXT
670 LOCATE ,25                                     'Print # of correct digits...
680 PRINT RP;                                      '...in the right place
690 LOCATE ,54                                     'Print # of correct digits...
700 PRINT WP                                       '...in the wrong place
710 IF DIGITS=RP THEN 890                  'Do all places have the correct digits?
720 IF GUESS=GUESS(DIGITS) THEN 930        'Reached maximum # of guesses allowed?
730 BEEP                                           'Guess isn't secret number,...
740 GOTO 380                                       '...GOTO guess again!
750 IF I=1 THEN RETURN                     'Subroutine to backspace digit of guess
760 LOCATE ,POS(0)-1:PRINT " ";                    'A destructive backspace erases
770 I=I-1                                          'Decrement guess digit index
780 RETURN
790 LOCATE 3,1                             'Subroutine to print table headings
800 PRINT SPACE$(160)                              'Clear lines for table headings
810 LOCATE 3,1:PRINT "Number"SPC(10)               'Print top line, space columns
820 PRINT "# of correct digits"SPC(10)"# of correct digits"   'Finish top line
830 IF (PEEK(0) AND 48)=48 THEN COLOR 1,0          'If monochrome monitor, then...
840 PRINT "Guessed";                               '...underline characters of...
850 LOCATE ,17:PRINT " in the right place";        '...the bottom lines of the...
860 LOCATE ,46:PRINT " in the wrong place"         '...table headings
870 COLOR 7,0                                      'Standard characters
880 RETURN
890 SOUND 440,5:SOUND 880,15                       'Guess is secret number!!!!!!!!
900 PRINT "You guessed the number!  ";             'Print congratulant
910 PRINT USING "Your score is ##_.";GUESS;        'Print score
920 GOTO 990                                       'GOTO `play again?' routine
930 SOUND 100,20                          'Number not found and all guesses used!
940 PRINT "You have had"GUESS"tries. The number is ";   'Print number of tries
950 COLOR 0,7                                      'Inverse characters
960 PRINT USING STRING$(DIGITS,"#");NUMBER;        'Reveal secret number
970 COLOR 7,0                                      'Standard characters
980 PRINT ".";                                     'Punctuate revealed secret #
990 COLOR 16,7             'Play AGAIN? routine-----Inverse, blinking characters
1000 LOCATE 25,16,0:PRINT " Press ";               'Cursor off, begin prompt
1010 COLOR 0,7                                     'Inverse characters
1020 PRINT "ESC to quit; any other key to play again. ";
1030 COLOR 7,0                                     'Standard characters
1040 IF INKEY$>"" THEN 1040                        'Clear keyboard buffer
1050 AGAIN$=INPUT$(1)                              'Get `play AGAIN?' input
1060 IF AGAIN$<>CHR$(27) THEN DIGITS=VAL(AGAIN$):GOTO 100       'Play again?
1070 COLOR 7,0:CLS                                 'Not playing again
1080 POKE 7,KBS                                    'Reset NumLock status
1090 END
```

Figure 5.13 Digital Deduction.

Programming Sound in BASIC

Lon Poole

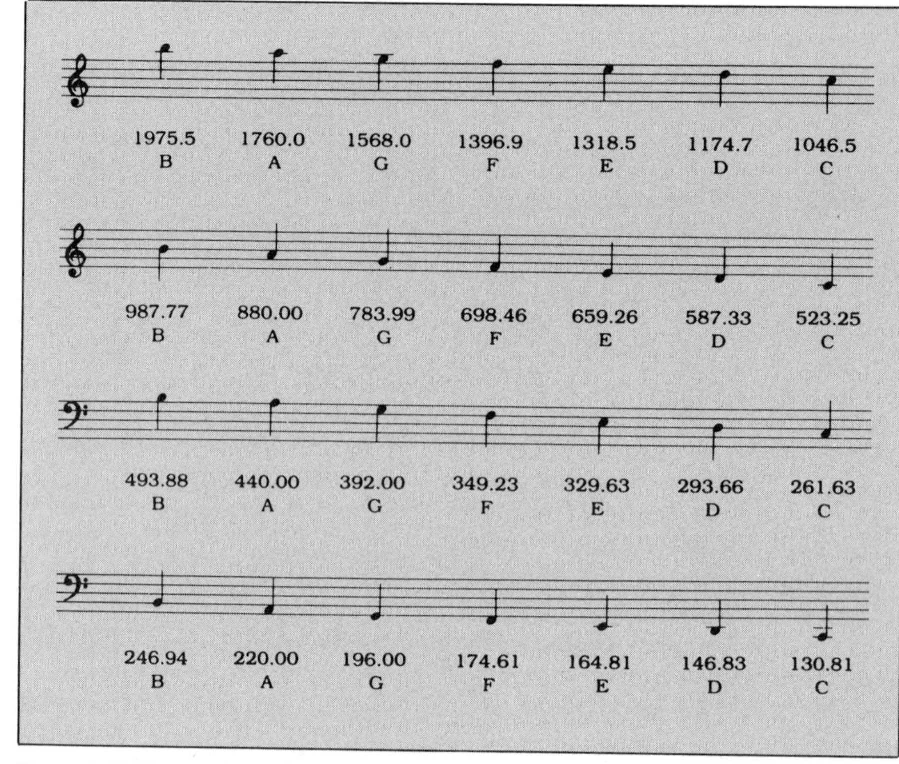

Figure 5.14 *Frequencies in hertz of the musical notes in the four octaves surrounding middle C.*

The PC can generate sounds and music through its built-in speaker using either of two BASIC statements, SOUND or PLAY. Both statements give you control over the frequency and duration of a tone, but neither statement can control loudness. Tones produced are always pure; there is no direct way to distort them for sound effects.

Generating Tones

The SOUND statement generates a tone of any frequency between 37 and 32,767 hertz (cycles per second), lasting for any duration from a split second to a half hour. Here is an example:

```
SOUND 523.25, 18.2
```

This example generates a tone that has a frequency of 523.25 hertz, which is the note middle C. Figure 5.14 illustrates the frequencies of the natural notes spanning two octaves above and below middle C.

The second number in a SOUND statement determines the duration of the tone. Duration is measured in *clock ticks,* and there are 18.2 ticks per second. Figure 5.15 compares selected clock-tick values with typical music tempos and their equivalent number of beats per minute.

PC BASIC does not wait for a SOUND statement to finish before going on to the next statement. The following example demonstrates:

```
10 CLS:WIDTH 40
20 SOUND 440, 27.3
30 FOR K=1 TO 40
40 LOCATE RND(1)*23+1,RND(1)*39+1
50 PRINT CHR$(14);
60 NEXT K
70 LOCATE 24,1
```

After clearing the screen, the program above generates the note A below middle C for a second and a half. While it holds the note, PC BASIC executes the rest of the program, which displays musical note characters at random locations on the screen. In fact, the program finishes before the note stops.

PC BASIC will not overlap execution of two SOUND statements, however. If a second SOUND statement occurs before the end of a tone from a prior SOUND statement, the PC waits until the first tone finishes. For example, if the following line were added to the previous example, the note it generates (D above middle C) would not occur until after the earlier note lasted its 1½ seconds:

```
80 SOUND 587.33, 9.1
```

You can turn sound off at any time by executing a SOUND statement with a duration of zero, like this:

Clock ticks	Tempo	Beats per minute
↑	Larghissimo	↑
27.30		40
↕	Largo	↕
18.20		60
↕	Larghetto Grave Lento	↕
16.55		66
↕	Adagio Adagietto	↕
14.37		76
↕	Andante Andantino	↕
10.11		108
↕	Moderato Allegretto	↕
9.10		120
↕	Allegro Vivace	↕
6.50		168
↕	Presto	↕
5.25		208
↓	Prestissimo	↓

Figure 5.15 *Musical tempos.*

```
SOUND 1760,32767
Ok
SOUND 100,0
Ok
```

Tones above 25,000 hertz are inaudible; in fact most people cannot hear tones above 15,000 hertz. Therefore, a SOUND statement that specifies a high frequency will generate periods of silence.

Sound Effects You can use the SOUND statement to create some acceptable sound effects. Unfortunately, there are no rules or guidelines that apply; all you can do is experiment. Figure 5.16 shows some program lines that you can use as a starting point.

Music

While it is possible to play music using the SOUND statement, the requisite translation of notes to multidigit numbers is awkward at best. In Advanced BASIC (BASICA), you can use the PLAY statement instead. It has a special music language that makes it easy to program tunes. The music language consists of 19 subcommands, which are listed in Figure 5.17. To play a tune, you make up a string value that contains the appropriate sequence of subcommands, as explained in the following paragraphs.

Naming Notes There are two ways to specify notes in a PLAY statement subcommand string. You can name the note by letter, like this:

```
100 PLAY " C D E F G A B "
```

This example plays a seven-note scale, starting with the C above middle C.

For sharp notes, suffix the name of the note with a pound sign (#) or a plus sign (+). For flat notes use a minus sign (-) as a suffix. Sharps and flats that have no corresponding black key on a piano are not allowed, namely B-sharp, E-sharp, C-flat, and F- flat.

To change octaves, use the O subcommand. The PLAY command has seven octaves, three below middle C numbered 0 through 2 and four above it numbered 3 to 6. The following example plays all the notes, including half steps, in the octave starting with middle C:

```
110 PLAY " O3 C C# D D# E F F# G G# A
    A# B "
```

Altogether there are 84 notes in the seven available octaves (see Figure 5.18). Instead of designating them by octave and name, you can designate them by number, using the N subcommand. The following example generates the same scale as the last example:

```
PLAY " N37 N38 N39 N40 N41 N42 N43
    N44 N45 N46 N47 N48 "
```

Note Length Notes in the examples so far have had the length of a quarter note. To change the length of a note, suffix it with a number, like this:

```
PLAY " O3 C1 C2 C4 C8 C16 C32 C64 "
```

The length of the note is equal to one divided by the number that follows the note. Thus a suffix of 1 designates a whole note, a 2 designates a half note, and so on. The example above plays seven middle C notes: first a whole note, next a half note, then a quarter note, a sixteenth note, a thirty-second note, and last a sixty-fourth note (see Figure 5.19).

You can use the L subcommand to establish a default note length. Just suffix it with a number as described in the preceding paragraph. The following example plays a descending scale of eighth notes:

PLAY " O2 L8 C B A G F E D "

To play a dotted note, suffix it with a period. You can use more than one period after a note; each period increases the note's length by 50 percent. Here is an example of a dotted half note and a dotted eighth note:

PLAY " C2. G8. "

Pauses (Rests) The P subcommand establishes pauses (rests), with

```
10 REM '--Random noise----------------
20 SOUND RND(1)*300+440,RND(1)*RND(1)
30 GOTO 20

10 '--Bouncing------------------------
20 FOR K=60 TO 1 STEP -2
30 SOUND 246.94-K/2,K/20
40 SOUND 32767,K/15
50 NEXT K

10 '--Falling-------------------------
20 FOR K=2000 TO 550 STEP -10
30 SOUND K,K/4000
40 NEXT K

10 '--Siren---------------------------
20 FOR L=650 TO -650 STEP -4
30 SOUND 780-ABS(L),.3
40 L=L-2/650
50 NEXT L
60 GOTO 20

10 '--Hi-lo alarm---------------------
20 SOUND 987.7,5
30 SOUND 329.63,5
40 GOTO 20

10 '--Motor---------------------------
20 FOR L=50 TO 60 STEP 10
30 SOUND L,.002
40 NEXT L
50 GOTO 20
```

Figure 5.16 *Sample sound effects programs.*

Subcommand	Interpretation
note	Play a named note (C, D, E, F, G, A, or B) in the current octave, either sharp (suffix + or #), flat (suffix -), or natural (letter alone)
O*oct*	Set octave number, 0 to 6 (middle C is octave 3)
N*nbr*	Play a note by number, 0 to 84 (0 means rest)
L*len*	Set the length of all later notes, from a whole note (*len* = 1) to a 64th note (*len* = 64); Optionally, *len* alone may suffix a single note to only affect that note
P*len*	Pause (rest): *len* as described for the L subcommand
dots	Each period that suffixes a note or pause subcommand holds the note or pause 1½ times normal
T*beat*	Set the tempo in beats per minute, 32 to 255
MF	Music foreground, program waits
MB	Music background, program continues
MN	Music normal, not legato or staccato
ML	Music legato
MS	Music staccato
X*s$*:	Execute subcommands from another string

Figure 5.17 *PLAY statement subcommands.*

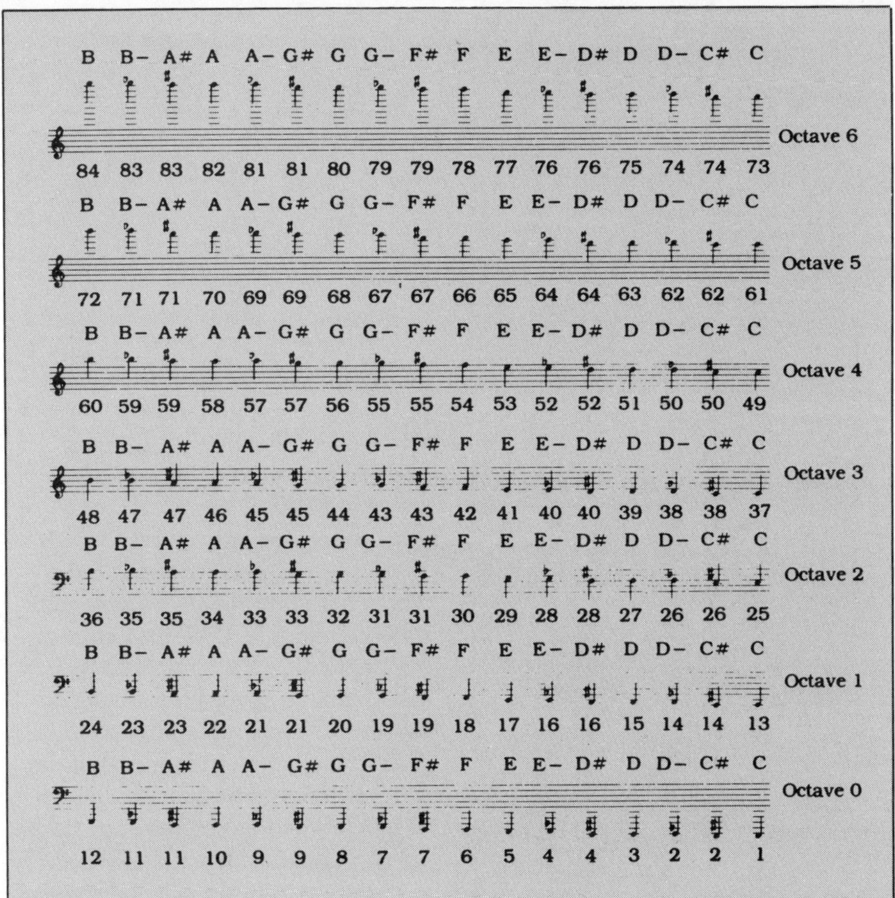

Figure 5.18 *Notes available in the PLAY statement. (Numbers shown below notes are for the N subcommand.)*

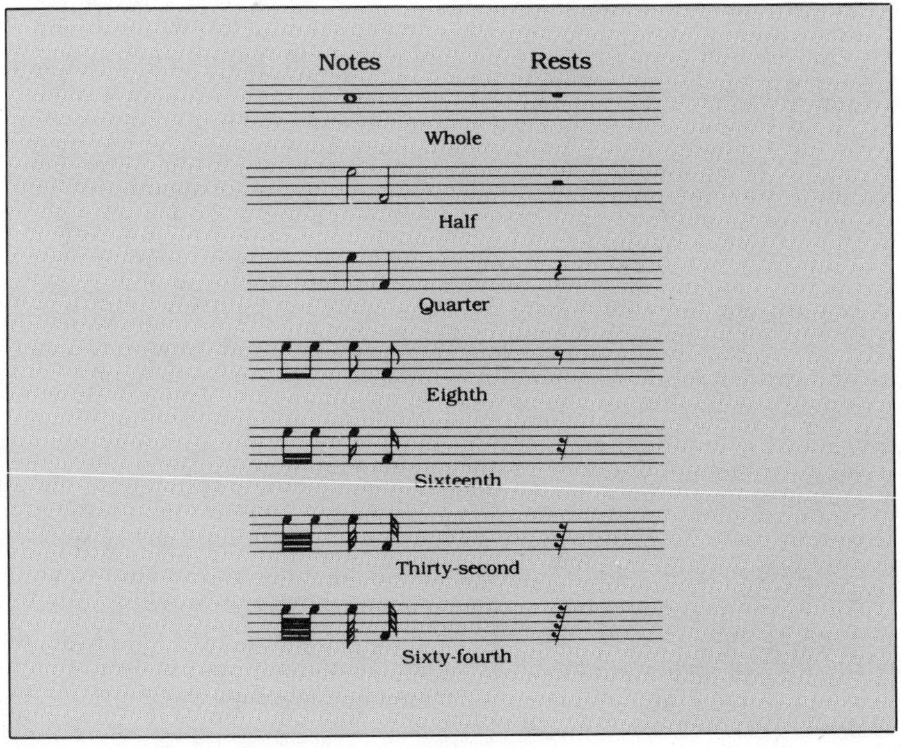

Figure 5.19 *Note and rest lengths.*

the length determined by a number the same as for the L subcommand (see Figure 5.19). Here is an example:

```
PLAY " O3 C P1 C P2 C P4 C P8 C P16 C "
```

Tempo The tempo of a musical composition (the rate of speed at which it is played) is indicated by notations like *allegro* and *andante,* and so forth or by metronome timing. The T subcommand sets the tempo using metronome timing. Figure 5.15 compares tempo notations like *allegro* and *andante* with metronome timing.

Music Foreground or Background Normally, Advanced BASIC will not proceed to the next note in a tune until the current note finishes playing. That is called *music foreground* mode. The MB subcommand tells Advanced BASIC to process up to 32 notes and store them in a memory buffer and to play music from the buffer while it goes ahead with program execution. That is called *music background* mode. So for short tunes with up to 32 notes and rests, it is possible to have the computer do two things at once: play a tune and keep executing the remainder of the program.

Style: Staccato, Legato, Normal The PLAY statement can play notes staccato, with distinct breaks between them; it can play notes legato, with no breaks between them; or it can play notes normally, with just enough pause between them to make them distinct. The MS

Figure 5.20 *"Minuet" from Anna Magdalena Notebook, by J. S. Bach.*

subcommand produces a staccato performance by holding each note for ¾ of its nominal length and resting for the remaining ¼ beat. The ML subcommand creates a legato performance by holding each note for its full length, so that succeeding notes seem to run together. Subcommand MN produces a normal performance by playing notes ⅞ of their nominal lengths, resting for the remaining ⅛ beat.

Playing Music The PLAY statement does a credible job performing simple tunes, especially those written for keyboard instruments like the piano or the organ. It is limited, however, to playing just one part. Two suitable compositions by Johann Sebastian Bach, the Minuet and the Minuet in D minor from his *Anna Magdalena Notebook,* are shown in Figures 5.20 and 5.21. Programs that play them are listed in Figures 5.22 and 5.23. To make comparing the programs with the music easier, the name of each note is printed underneath it on the musical score. The following paragraphs briefly analyze how the programs work and how the musical scores were translated into subcommands.

Both programs work the same way. They store the PLAY statement subcommands in DATA statements starting at line 1010 and read the subcommand strings into string array TUNES one measure at a time. Then, playing the tune stored in the array is simply a matter of using an X subcommand to incorporate each array element in turn.

The score for the Minuet specifies a tempo of *moderato* (see Figure 5.20), which Figure 5.15 says equals 108 to 120 beats per minute. The subcommand in the first measure (see Figure 5.22, line 1010) sets the tempo at 110. The next subcommand establishes the default note length as an eighth note. The dot over the first note in the first measure means it is to be played staccato, so the MS subcommand designates that. The note itself is a D in octave 4 (the default octave), and it is a quarter note, so the subcommand D4 plays it. The next subcommand, MN, sets normal performance style, since the remainder of the notes in the measure are not marked staccato. The next note is in octave 3, and the O3 subcommand stipulates that. The G, A, and B subcommands play the appropriate eighth notes. The last note in the measure is C in octave 4, played by subcommands O4 and C. Each of the other 31 measures in the composition is similarly translated to a single DATA statement (lines 1020 to 1320).

Figure 5.21 *"Minuet in D minor" from Anna Magdalena Notebook, by J. S. Bach.*

The tempo in the second composition (Figure 5.21) is *andante.* The first subcommand (see Figure 5.23, line 1010) sets the tempo at 90 beats per minute, which is within the range indicated by Figure 5.15. The ML subcommand then establishes a legato performance, as directed by the musical score. The rest of the DATA statements translate the composition into subcommands in a straightforward way. (Note: Figures 5.22 and 5.23 may be found on the following pages.)

Lon Poole lives in Oakland, California, and has been writing about personal computers since 1976. He is the author of such books as MacWork MacPlay *and* Apple II Users Guide. *This article was excerpted from* Using Your IBM Personal Computer *published by Howard W. Sams & Co., Indianapolis (copyright 1983, Lon Poole). It is reprinted with permission of the publisher.*

Speak Up

Alan Fridlund

The tinny 2 ½-inch speaker that IBM uses in the PC provides only a small voice for the PC's sound capabilities. In noisy environments the PC sounds are almost inaudible. While external speakers can be added, there is an easier remedy: the speaker can be replaced with a 3-inch variety (Radio Shack Catalog Number 40-248) placed inside the cabinet. Just follow these steps:

1) Remove the system unit cover, unscrew the speaker retaining bracket, and unplug the speaker from the connector on the system board.

2) Unsnap the PC speaker from the retaining bracket fingers and unsolder the wires from the speaker.

3) Bend out the metal fingers on the retaining bracket. Place the new speaker in the basket of the retaining bracket until the speaker magnet rests against the back of the bracket. Solder the speaker wires to the new speaker. Then use fast-curing epoxy to cement the 3-inch speaker frame to the bracket fingers.

4) Remount the bracket containing the new speaker and reconnect the speaker plug to the system board.

The difference in tone quality (especially on tones below 200 hertz) will be very noticeable, as will increased volume on all tones.

Alan J. Fridlund is a clinical psychologist and psychophysiologist who studies emotion and brain-behavior relationships. He is Assistant Professor of Psychology at the University of Pennsylvania.

```
10 DIM TUNE$(4)
20 CLS:WIDTH 40:KEY OFF
30 LOCATE 11,17:PRINT "Minuet"
40 LOCATE 12,15:PRINT "J.S. Bach"
90 REM '--Read music from data-----------------------------------------
100 FOR MEASURE=1 TO 32
110 READ NOTES$
120 TUNE$(MEASURE\8)=TUNE$(MEASURE\8)+NOTES$
130 NEXT MEASURE
190 '--Play the tune-----------------------------------------------
200 PLAY "xTUNE$(0); xTUNE$(1); xTUNE$(2); xTUNE$(3); xTUNE$(4);"
1000 '--Music, measure by measure-----------------------------------
1010 DATA T110 L8 MS D4 MN O3 G A B O4 C
1020 DATA D4 O3 MS G4 MN G4
1030 DATA O4 MS E4 MN C D E F#
1040 DATA G4 O3 MS G4 MN G4
1050 DATA MS O4 C4 MN D C O3 B A
1060 DATA MS B4 MN O4 C O3 B A G
1070 DATA MS F#4 MN G A B G
1080 DATA B4 A2
1090 DATA O4 MS D4 MN O3 G A B O4 C
1100 DATA D4 O3 MS G4 G4
1110 DATA O4 E4 MN C D E F#
1120 DATA G4 O3 MS G4 G4
1130 DATA O4 C4 MN D C O3 B A
1140 DATA B4 O4 C O3 B A G
1150 DATA A4 B A G F#
1160 DATA G2.
1170 DATA O4 B4 G A B G
1180 DATA A4 D E F# D
1190 DATA G4 E F# G D
1200 DATA C#4 O3 B O4 C# O3 A4
1210 DATA A B O4 C# D E F#
1220 DATA MS G4 MN F#4 E4
1230 DATA MS F#4 O3 A4 O4 C#4
1240 DATA MN D2.
1250 DATA D4 O3 G F# G4
1260 DATA O4 E4 O3 G F# G4
1270 DATA O4 D4 C4 O3 B4
1280 DATA A G F# G A4
1290 DATA D E F# G A B
1300 DATA O4 C4 O3 B4 A4
1310 DATA B O4 D O3 G4 F#4
1320 DATA G2.
```

Figure 5.22 *Program to play Bach Minuet (see Figure 5.20).*

```
 0 DIM TUNE$(4)
20 CLS:WIDTH 40:KEY OFF
30 LOCATE 11,12:PRINT "Minuet in D minor"
40 LOCATE 12,17:PRINT "J.S. Bach"
90 REM '--Read music from data-----------------------------------
100 FOR MEASURE=1 TO 32
110 READ NOTES$
120 TUNE$(MEASURE\8)=TUNE$(MEASURE\8)+NOTES$
130 NEXT MEASURE
190 '--Play the tune-----------------------------------------------
200 PLAY "xTUNE$(0); xTUNE$(1); xTUNE$(2); xTUNE$(3); xTUNE$(4);"
1000 '--Music, measure by measure--------------------------------
1010 DATA T90 ML L8 O3 A4 O4 F E D C#
1020 DATA D4 O3 A4 B-4
1030 DATA O3 C# E G B- A G
1040 DATA F4 E F D4
1050 DATA F4 B- A O4 D C
1060 DATA F4 E D C O3 B-
1070 DATA A B-16 O4 C16 O3 F4 E4
1080 DATA F2.
1090 DATA A4 O4 F E D C#
1100 DATA D4 O3 A4 B-4
1110 DATA C# E G B- A G
1120 DATA F4 E F D4
1130 DATA F4 B- A O4 D C
1140 DATA F4 E D C O3 B-
1150 DATA A B-16 O4 C16 O3 F4 E4
1160 DATA F2.
1170 DATA MS O4 A4 O3 F ML O4 A G F
1180 DATA E16 F16 G C2
1190 DATA MS F4 O3 D ML O4 F E D
1200 DATA C#16 D16 E O3 A2
1210 DATA A B O4 C# D E F
1220 DATA G E C# B- A G
1230 DATA F16 E16 D E4 C#4
1240 DATA D2.
1250 DATA MS A4 O3 F ML O4 A G F
1260 DATA E16 F16 G C2
1270 DATA MS F4 O3 D ML O4 F E D
1280 DATA C#16 D16 E O3 A2
1290 DATA A B O4 C# D E F
1300 DATA G E C# B- A G
1310 DATA F16 E16 D E4 C#4
1320 DATA D2.
```

Figure 5.23 *Program to play Bach Minuet in D minor (see Figure 5.21).*

. Star-Dot-Star

Everyone needs a painless diversion from their arduous tasks, be they data entry, spreadsheet analysis, or programming. For digit-weary workers everywhere, our entertainment offering is a homemade derivative of *Space Invaders* called "Mine Field."

Mine Field

The program reproduced in Figure 5.24, "MINE.BAS," is for all the readers who plow through mountains of technical information and need the relief of a short game that can be typed into the computer in a few minutes. Here it is.

Name: Mine Field

Object: To proceed as far as possible through the mine field. Your score, which is equal to the number of the mines passed, is kept on the lower-left corner of the screen.

Instructions: You are represented by a down arrow on the screen. Its movement is controlled manually by using the <CursorLeft> and <CursorRight> keys on the numeric keypad. <CursorLeft> moves you one space to the left every time the key is pressed, and <CursorRight> moves you one space to the right.

The mines are represented by stars. The game ends when you collide with a mine. Good luck.

Jean Pickett
Trenton, New Jersey

Editor's Note: To start the game, choose the mine field density on a scale from 1 to 10. The game slows down as the density increases, but you'll need all the help you can get.

```
10 DEFINT A-Z:WIDTH 40:KEY OFF:M=1
20 S=20:T=-18:CLS
30 LOCATE 2,1:INPUT "Minefield density (1-10):",M$
40 IF VAL(M$)<>0 THEN M=VAL(M$)
50 COLOR 3,0:LOCATE 23,1:PRINT "|";:LOCATE 23,39:PRINT "|"
60 COLOR 6,0:FOR I=1 TO M:X=RND*36+2:LOCATE 23,X:PRINT CHR$(15);:NEXT
70 T=T+1:LOCATE 25,1:PRINT T:I$=INKEY$
80 IF I$=CHR$(0)+CHR$(77) THEN S=S+1:SOUND 1000,.5 ELSE IF
     I$=CHR$(0)+CHR$(75) THEN S=S-1:SOUND 1000,.5
90 P=SCREEN(5,S):IF P<>32 AND P<>0 THEN 110
100 COLOR 4,0:LOCATE 5,S:SOUND 200,.5:PRINT CHR$(25):GOTO 50
110 IF S>5 THEN S=S-5
120 COLOR 5,0:LOCATE 5,S:PRINT "<<< ZAP! >>>";
130 FOR X=1000 TO 1900 STEP 100:SOUND X,.5:NEXT
140 FOR X=1 TO 10:SOUND 500,.5:SOUND 1000,.5
150 FOR DV=1 TO 100:NEXT DV:NEXT X
160 LOCATE 25,1:COLOR 0,7:PRINT "SCORE:";T;:COLOR 7,0
170 LOCATE 24,1:WHILE INKEY$<>"":WEND
180 PRINT"Press 'P' to play again...";
190 Q$=INKEY$:IF Q$="" THEN 190
200 IF Q$="P" OR Q$="p" THEN 20 ELSE END
```

Figure 5.24 *MINE.BAS*

6

Communications

Hands On

When the PC made its debut *telecommunications* was a term associated with the remote, almost unthinkably technical operations of institutions like the phone company or defense department. But a year later a *PC World* survey revealed that nearly half the magazine's readers owned modems, the devices that convert digital computer data into the analog form required for telephone transmission and that reconvert received analog data into digital form.

Use of the PC's communications capabilities will continue to expand, not only because modems continue to become smaller, cheaper, faster, and smarter, but because their applications will continue to increase and make telecommunicating even more attractive. Already, anyone who has instantly transmitted a letter or report across country or searched through a vast data base in a matter of minutes doesn't need to be convinced of the usefulness of computer communications. But such developments as the spread of electronic banking and stock trading facilities, the increasing use of remote PCs to access mainframe computers, and the appearance of videotex networks with high-quality graphics and a vast range of services promise to change the way we communicate and do business as significantly as did the invention of the telephone itself.

The first two articles in this chapter provide programs to be used with a Hayes Smartmodem. The Smartmodem was one of the first "intelligent" modems on the market, and it remains by far the most popular. Intellegent modems have their own memory and processor chips, enabling them to be programmed to perform a variety of functions.

"Smartmodem 450" shows how to use BASIC's OUT command to make the PC trick the Hayes Smartmodem 300 into running at the nonstandard rate of 450 bits per second (bps). While still not fast enough for extensive file transfer, this 50 percent increase in speed can save you time and maybe the need to upgrade to a faster modem. The article includes modifications to *PC Talk III,* the user-supported communications program authored by *PC World*'s own Andrew Fluegelman.

"Smartmodem Gets Smarter" isn't really about *communications* as it's usually understood in computer circles. Instead of using the modem to transmit or receive computer data, the BASIC program in this article turns your modem into a telephone-dialing machine. The program handles SPRINT or MCI codes and, among its other capabilities, will redial any of up to 40 phone numbers for as long as you want. So instead of wasting your time trying to put calls through, your PC can make your connections for you.

Finally, for those on the go, "PC CTTY" explains the use of the DOS 2.00 CTTY command, which enables you to control your PC from a remote terminal.

Smartmodem 450

Larry Jordan

Although Hayes Microcomputer Products does not advertise it and IBM BASIC does not directly support it, the Hayes Smartmodem 300 (or a Smartmodem 1200 running in the 300 bps mode) can operate at 450 bps. Most people cannot read a terminal display much faster than 450 bps (450 words per minute) anyway. The only real advantage of 1200 bps over 300 bps is for file transfers. If most of your communications is with local bulletin boards or directly with other PC owners, this 50 percent increase in data throughput might be enough to keep you from upgrading from a 300 bps to a 1200 bps modem.

The standard data transfer rates used with serial communications are discrete values: 110, 150, 300, 600, and 1200 bps. The 450 bps is not one of those standard discrete values and is not one of the "valid speeds" specified in the IBM BASIC manual for the OPEN "COM command. This nonstandard rate of 450 can be easily achieved, however, through use of the mysterious BASIC OUT command. The Hayes Smartmodem 300 will respond at that speed, just as it does at 300 bps.

How It's Done

A Hayes Smartmodem 300 is capable of receiving commands at any data rate up to 1200 bps. The Smartmodem's microprocessor senses the speed (bps) used with commands and automatically switches speed to match. The modem will respond to commands at 300, 450, 600, or 1200 bps, or any other speed between 50 and 1200 bps. The Smartmodem 300 will also attempt to transmit data at the same rate it receives commands when instructed to go into the on-line data mode.

The Smartmodem 300's limit for reasonably accurate data transfer, however, is 450 bps. At 450 the data transfer error rate is acceptable for conversation-mode interaction with another computer, but above 450 bps the error rate is unacceptable. Files can be transferred at 450 bps, but an error-checking protocol such as Xmodem must be used to correct data transfer errors. Files transferred with the Smartmodem and the Xmodem protocol should be as error free at 450 bps as they are at 300 bps.

Once the communications software and the Smartmodem 300 are operating at 450 bps, the next hurdle is to get the two to "talk" to each other at 450 bps through the serial communications adapter. IBM and most other vendors use the INS8250 LSI chip to control serial communications. This chip is capable of running at any speed from 1 to 19,200 bps (IBM says 50 to 9600 bps, but they are keeping secrets).

The 8250 contains a Baud Rate Generator capable of taking the IBM PC clock input (1.8432 MHz) and dividing it by some number (the divisor) to get any speed (bps) rate you want (refer to the *IBM Personal Computer Technical Reference* manual for more specific details). To select 450 bps you must determine the correct divisor, then place that divisor into a 2-byte register in the 8250 chip. This is done using the OUT command in BASIC or assembly language. The OUT command allows data to be sent to the 8250 I/O ports used to set the bps rate, control the modem, and send and receive data from the modem.

To reset the 8250 chip, you first have to enable the chip's divisor registers, and then, after changing the speed (bps), you have to disable the divisor registers to lock in the new rate. After interpolating a divisor value of 100 (hex) from the table in the *IBM Technical Reference* manual and identifying the COM1: divisor registers as 3F8 and 3F9, you are ready to start "talking" to the 8250 chip. You start by telling the 8250 Line Control register, address 3FB, that you are about to load a new divisor. To do this you change bit 7 in this register from a 0 to a 1. You then load the low- and high-order divisor registers. To lock in the new bps rate and begin communications at that rate, you then change bit 7 of the Line Control register back to a 0. The BASIC commands that achieve this sequence are shown in Figure 6.1.

Fast Talking

A merge file for *PC-Talk III* is included as Figure 6.2 to illustrate the implementation of 450 bps with the IBM PC. This merge file, developed by Dorn Stickle of Amarillo, Texas, places a 450 bps option in the *PC-Talk III* parameters list (accessed

```
OUT &H3FB,(INP(&H3FB) OR &H80) 'Enable divisor registers.
OUT &H3F8,0 'Low order byte of X'0100'
OUT &H3F9,1 'High order byte of X'0100'
OUT &H3FB,(INP(&H3FB) AND &H7F) 'Disable divisor registers.
```

Figure 6.1 *BASIC code for resetting the 8250 chip.*

```
200  'PC-TALK.III 450 Baud merge file by Dorn W. Stickle of
     Amarillo,TX
425 CLOSE #1:OPEN COMM$ AS #1:PRINT #1,MODMINIT$;:IF BAU450 THEN
    GOSUB 11000
5026 PRINT"    5 -   450,E,7,1   (text)       6 -   450,N,8,1
     (binary)
5055 IF Q$="F" THEN PRINT Q$:GOSUB 5815:PRINT:PRINT"Parameters
     reset to:";:DORN=0:GOSUB 5100:GOTO 5095
5060 DORN=0:Q=VAL(Q$):IF Q<1 OR Q>6 THEN BEEP:GOTO 5045 ELSE
     PRINT Q
5081 IF Q=6 THEN PAR$="N":DTA$="8
5086 IF Q=5 OR Q=6 THEN GOSUB 11000
5090 PRINT:PRINT"New parameters are: ";:GOSUB 5100
5095 PRINT GO$:GOSUB 2800:GOTO 515
5100 COLOR BG,FG:IF DORN=1 THEN 5101 ELSE PRINT
     MID$(COMM$,6,10);:COLOR FG,BG:PRINT:PRINT:GOTO 5105
5101 PRINT "450,"+PAR$+","+DTA$+","+STP$;:COLOR FG,BG:PRINT:PRIN'
11000 OUT &H3FB,(INP(&H3FB) OR &H80):OUT &H3F8,0:OUT &H3F9,1:OUT
      &H3FB,(INP(&H3FB) AND &H7F):DORN=1:RETURN
```

Figure 6.2 *PC-Talk 450 bps merge file.*

with the <Alt>-P command).

After merging the 450 "patch" into the interpreted version of *PC-Talk,* the program can be recompiled using the instructions in the *PC-Talk III* manual. With the 450 bps option, you can access local RBBS-PC bulletin boards at 300 bps and then switch the data transfer rate to 450 bps by selecting the New Baud option on the bulletin board's main menu. When calling a system that allows you to switch from 300 to 450 bps, one caution should be followed: be sure that the Smartmodem switch 1 is in the down position (the Smartmodem ignores Data Terminal Ready, or DTR, status) before initiating the call. If switch 1 is up (Smartmodem monitors DTR status) when the IBM PC changes communications parameters, the telephone connection with the host will be lost. The DTR signal is momentarily dropped while the modem divisor registers are being changed, and with switch 1 up, the Smartmodem drops the carrier signal as the DTR signal drops.

Larry Jordan is Director of Computer Applications for NUS Corporation. He coauthored the book Communications and Networking for the IBM PC, *published by The Brady Company. This article was originally published in* PC World *Volume 1, Number 8.*

Smartmodem Gets Smarter

Burton L. Alperson

The popular Hayes Smartmodem has capabilities beyond those necessary for communication with other computers. To take advantage of some of these, I wrote PHONE.BAS (see Figure 6.3), a program that turns the modem into an automatic telephone dialing instrument. The program stores up to 40 names and phone numbers, and the latter may be stored with any necessary long-distance access codes such as those for SPRINT or MCI. To dial a stored number you need only enter the number's one- or two-digit code and press <Enter>; other telephone numbers may be dialed by entering the number and pressing <Enter>. PHONE.BAS also features one-key entry of SPRINT or MCI codes, one-key redial of the last number dialed, and automatic repeated redialing of the last number dialed.

Program Operation

Instructions for operating PHONE.BAS appear on the program's screen display (see Figure 6.4). Dial telephone numbers by typing the appropriate code or the number itself and then pressing <Enter>. If you make a mistake, simply type an asterisk, press <Enter>, and then reenter the code or the number. (Because of programming considerations that I'll explain later, you cannot use <Backspace> to correct errors.)

If you want to use an MCI or SPRINT access code, press <F1> and type in the area code and number you want to dial. You redial a number by pressing the R key. Automatic redialing is invoked by pressing the A key, and this routine is terminated while in progress when you strike any key. The automatic redialing routine makes up to 200 attempts to complete a call, but you can easily change this parameter to several million attempts (over six months of continuous dialing.) Pressing the E key terminates the program, resets the modem to default status, and returns you to DOS.

The structure of PHONE.BAS is shown in the Warnier-Orr diagram (see Figure 6.5) accompanying "More on Warnier-Orrs." The program's most basic structure is simply initialize, get data, print screen, and operate. PHONE.BAS is written in BASIC, but the Warnier-Orr diagram is language independent, so implementing the diagram in most other high-level languages would be easy.

PHONE.BAS has been widely tested in Los Angeles. Telephone service in some areas of the country may be subject to local conditions such as slow dialing speed, so some adjustments may be necessary to make the program work satisfactorily in your area.

Customizing PHONE.BAS

The initialization routine (lines 1000 to 1050) contains some options for tailoring the program to your hardware configuration and local phone conditions. If your modem is attached to your second serial port, the reference in line 1010 should be changed to COM2:.

The statement S11 = 51 in line 1020 controls touch-tone dialing speed. The number 51 generates extremely fast dialing—51 milliseconds (msec) for both tones and intertone intervals. If you find that the program dials too fast for your telephone system, try eliminating the speed statement entirely; the Hayes modem will default to S11 = 70. If you still can't dial successfully, try parameters up to 255 msec.

You may also want to change the statement S7 = 10 in line 1020. If you like to dial while the telephone is in its cradle, this parameter gives you only 10 seconds to pick up the phone before the modem hangs up (picking up the phone overrides the modem's attempt to hang up). You can allow as much as 255 seconds for this parameter if you wish, but I recommend trying the program for a while before you change the value of the S7 register.

The statement S0 = 0 in line 1020 should not be changed. This parameter guarantees that the modem will not enter the auto-answer mode. If the modem is in auto-answer while PHONE.BAS is running, anyone calling your number will be greeted by the squeal of the carrier tone.

PHONE.BAS assumes that you have touch-tone dialing in your area. If this is not the case, change the statement AT M0 DT in line 540 to AT M0 D, and change the statement AT M1 DT in lines 600 and 760 to AT M1 D.

The setting of the modem speaker reflects my personal preferences. The speaker is off on the first attempt to dial any number (M0 in

```
1 ' Telephone dialing program for 300 or 1200 baud Hayes Smartmodem.
2 ' Written by Burton L. Alperson

10 GOSUB 1000
20 GOSUB 3000
30 GOSUB 2000

100 ACTION%=0
110 ENTRY$=INKEY$:LOCATE 24,65,0:PRINT"TIME: "+TIME$;
    :LOCATE 1,1:PRINT"CALL:";
120 IF ENTRY$="" THEN 110

200 IF ENTRY$="E" OR ENTRY$="e" THEN ACTION%=1
210 IF ENTRY$="H" OR ENTRY$="h" THEN ACTION%=2
220 IF ENTRY$="R" OR ENTRY$="r" THEN ACTION%=3
230 IF ENTRY$="A" OR ENTRY$="a" THEN ACTION%=4
240 IF ACTION%=0 THEN 500
250 ON ACTION% GOTO 300,400,600,700

300 PRINT #1, "AT Z":CLOSE:COLOR 7,0:CLS:SYSTEM

400 PRINT #1,"AT H,":LOCATE 1,1:PRINT STRING$(79,32):GOTO 100

500 LOCATE 1,7:PRINT ENTRY$;:LINE INPUT DUMMY$:DUMMY$=ENTRY$+DUMMY$
510 IF RIGHT$(DUMMY$,1)="*" THEN LOCATE 1,1:PRINT STRING$(79,32):GOTO 100
520 IF LEN(DUMMY$)<3 THEN DIAL$=NUMBER$(VAL(DUMMY$)):LASTNUM$=DIAL$
530 IF LEN(DUMMY$)>2 THEN DIAL$=DUMMY$:LASTNUM$=DIAL$
540 PRINT #1, "AT M0 DT"+DIAL$
550 LOCATE 1,1: PRINT STRING$(79,32)
560 LOCATE 1,65-LEN(DIAL$):PRINT "NUMBER DIALED: ";DIAL$;: GOTO 100

600 PRINT #1, "AT M1 DT"+LASTNUM$
610 LOCATE 1,1:  PRINT STRING$(79,32)
620 LOCATE 1,69-LEN(LASTNUM$):  PRINT "REDIALING: ";LASTNUM$;:  GOTO 100

700 FOR I=1 TO 200
710 COLOR 18,0:LOCATE 24,65:PRINT"ATTEMPT NO ";
720 COLOR 15,0:PRINT USING"###";I;
730 COLOR 18,0:LOCATE 1,1:PRINT STRING$(79,32);
740 LOCATE 1,1:PRINT  "AUTO REDIAL FOR ";:COLOR 15,0:PRINT LASTNUM$;
750 LOCATE 1,45:COLOR 15,0:PRINT "STRIKE ANY KEY TO ABORT AUTO REDIAL"
760 PRINT #1, "AT M1 DT"+LASTNUM$
770 FOR J=1 TO 2000
780 R$=INKEY$
790 IF R$<>"" THEN LOCATE 1,1:PRINT #1,"ATH":PRINT STRING$(79,32);:GOTO 100
800 NEXT J
810 PRINT #1, "ATH"
820 FOR Y=1 TO 833:NEXT Y
830 NEXT I
840 LOCATE 1,1:PRINT STRING$(79,32);:GOTO 100
1000 KEY OFF
1010 OPEN "COM1:,,,,CS,DS" AS #1
1020 PRINT #1, "AT S11=51 S0=0 S7=10"
1030 DIM NUMBER$(40),PARTY$(40)
1040 CLS
1050 RETURN
```

(continues)

Figure 6.3 *PHONE.BAS*

```
2000 CR$=CHR$(17)+CHR$(196)+CHR$(217)
2010 LOCATE 2,1:COLOR 0,7:PRINT "E: Exit     R: Redial";
2020 PRINT "     A: AutoRedial     H: Hang Up       *"+CR$+"
     To Correct Errors";
2030 LOCATE 25,1:PRINT " MCI: F1 + Area Code + Number.  ";
2040 PRINT "UNLISTED NUMBERS: Type number instead of code.";:COLOR 7,0
2050 COLOR 9,0:LOCATE 3,1: PRINT "CODE  NAME";STRING$(30,32);"CODE  NAME";
2060 PRINT STRING$(29,32);:COLOR 7,0
2070 FOR I=1 TO 20
2080 LOCATE I+3,1:PRINT USING "####";I;:PRINT "  ";:PRINT PARTY$(I);
2090 LOCATE I+3,41:PRINT USING "####";I+20;:PRINT "  ";:PRINT PARTY$(I+20);
2100 NEXT I
2110 COLOR 15,0
2120 RETURN

3000 KEY 1,"INSERT MCI OR SPRINT CODES HERE"
3005 FOR I=1 TO 40:READ PARTY$(I),NUMBER$(I):NEXT I
3010 DATA "INSERT NAME OF PARTY #1","INSERT PHONE NUMBER OF PARTY #1"
3020 DATA "INSERT NAME OF PARTY #2","INSERT PHONE NUMBER OF PARTY #2"
3030 DATA "",""
3040 DATA "",""
3050 DATA "",""
          .
          .
          .
[NOTE:  There  must  be  40 lines of data statements to make the  program
run properly.   If  you do not have 40 entries for your phone directory,
use  the format shown in lines 3030-3050 and 3380-3400 for blank data
statements.]
          .
          .
          .
3380 DATA "",""
3390 DATA "",""
3400 DATA "",""
3410 RETURN
```

Figure 6.3 *PHONE.BAS*

line 540) to prevent the possibility of acoustic feedback between speaker and telephone. During redial and auto-redial operations, the speaker is turned on (M1 in lines 600 and 740). This arrangement enables you to move around the room and do other work while listening to the progress of your phone call. Use M1 to turn the speaker on and M0 to turn it off if your preferences are different from mine.

The Hayes modem was not designed to be used as a telephone dialer. Consequently the device does not recognize an answering party picking up the phone; it recognizes only a carrier tone generated by another modem. Because of the problems introduced by the lack of this capacity, I had to make some compromises in the auto-redial routine of PHONE.BAS.

One such compromise is that the frequency of attempts to redial a number must be controlled with fixed timing parameters rather than with a busy signal or an answering party. The timing parameters involved are J=1 TO 2000 in line 770 (test for auto-redial termination for about 13.5 seconds), S7=10 in line 1020 (allow 10 seconds after dialing before hanging up), and S6=2 (wait 2 seconds for a dial tone before dialing). The S6 parameter is not explicitly stated in the program since it is the Hayes modem default. To change the S6 parameter to a 3-second wait, for example, insert the statement S6=3 into the string in line 1020. Do not change line 820, since the modem requires at least a 1-second delay to reset before redialing.

Entering Your Directory

You can store names and telephone numbers in the data statements in lines 3010-3410. This method is less elegant than storing data in external data files, as it eliminates the option

```
CALL:

E: Exit        R: Redial        A: AutoRedial        H: Hang Up        *To Correct Errors

CODE NAME                                        CODE NAME
--------------------------------------------------------------------------------
  1 AAA Auto Service                              21 Plumber—Major Kramer
  2 ABC Premiums                                  22 Restaurant—Anna Maria
  3 Adray—Wilshire                                23 Restaurant—Any Restaurant
  4 Allstate Insurance—Greg Ray                   24 Restaurant—Paul Bhalla's
  5 American Home Security                        25 Restaurant—The Egg and the Eye
  6 Ametron                                       26 Restaurant—Green Jade
  7 Amica Insurance                               27 Restaurant—Mon Grenier
  8 Audio Mart—John Romero                        28 Restaurant—Sea Food Bay
  9 Computer—Bob Rice                             29 Restaurant—Sorrentino's
 10 Computer—ComputerLand Glendale                30 Restaurant—Supreme Pizza
 11 Computer—ComputerLand Pasadena                31 Restaurant—Sushi Fune
 12 Computer—IBM Product Center—BH                32 Restaurant—Tokyo Kaikan
 13 CSU Bookstore                                 33 Shiatsu—Jean
 14 CSU Library—Reference                         34 Sparkletts Water
 15 Dentist—UCLA Clinic                           35 Taxes
 16 IBM Selectric Service (Zone 0931)             36 Zen Carpentry—Bill Jordan
 17 INMAC—Mark Brown                              37
 18 Mazda Service (Savage)                        38
 19 MD—Hamm                                       39
 20 PC World—Kearney Rietmann                     40
                                                                 TIME: 12:26:11
MCI: F1 + Area Code + Number. UNLISTED NUMBERS: Type number instead of code.
```

Figure 6.4 *PHONE.BAS screen display.*

of using built-in editing and appending routines. On the other hand, using data statements is appreciably faster than using external files. This is particularly true if the program is on a floppy disk rather than a hard or RAM disk. Since I typically want to load and run PHONE.BAS as quickly as possible, data statements were the appropriate choice; using your computer to dial your telephone doesn't make sense if you can do it faster by hand.

An MCI or SPRINT code may be inserted in line 3000. MCI, for example, requires that you dial a telephone access number, wait for a dial tone, then dial an account code before you can dial your number. If your access number were 555-5555 and your account number were 12345, line 3000 would be:

```
3000 KEY 1,"5555555,,,12345"
```

Each comma causes the modem to pause for 2 seconds to wait for a dial tone before entering the account number. The hyphen is not included in the access number because BASIC imposes a 15-character limit on strings assigned to function keys.

If your access code requires more than 15 characters (including commas for timing), you might get around the problem by using the S8 register of the Hayes modem. This register controls the duration of the delay generated by a comma. For example, if line 1020 were written as:

```
1020 PRINT #1, "AT S11=51 S0=0
          S7=10 S8=6"
```

then line 3000 could be written as:

```
3000 KEY 1, "5555555,12345"
```

If you have several long-distance codes, they can be assigned to function keys 2 through 10 in similar fashion, and appropriate references can be added to the prompt in line 2030.

You can make directory entries for local, long-distance, and long-distance SPRINT or MCI numbers. The following entries are all acceptable:

```
3010 DATA "PHILISTINE, A.","999-9999"
3020 DATA "REAGAN, R.","1 (202)
          999-9999"
3030 DATA "HUN, A.","555-5555,,,12345
          (999) 999-9999"
```

Keyboard Entry Routine

Most of the code in PHONE.BAS is straightforward and requires little explanation. However, the keyboard entry routine uses some strategies and BASIC operations that may be unfamiliar to many programmers

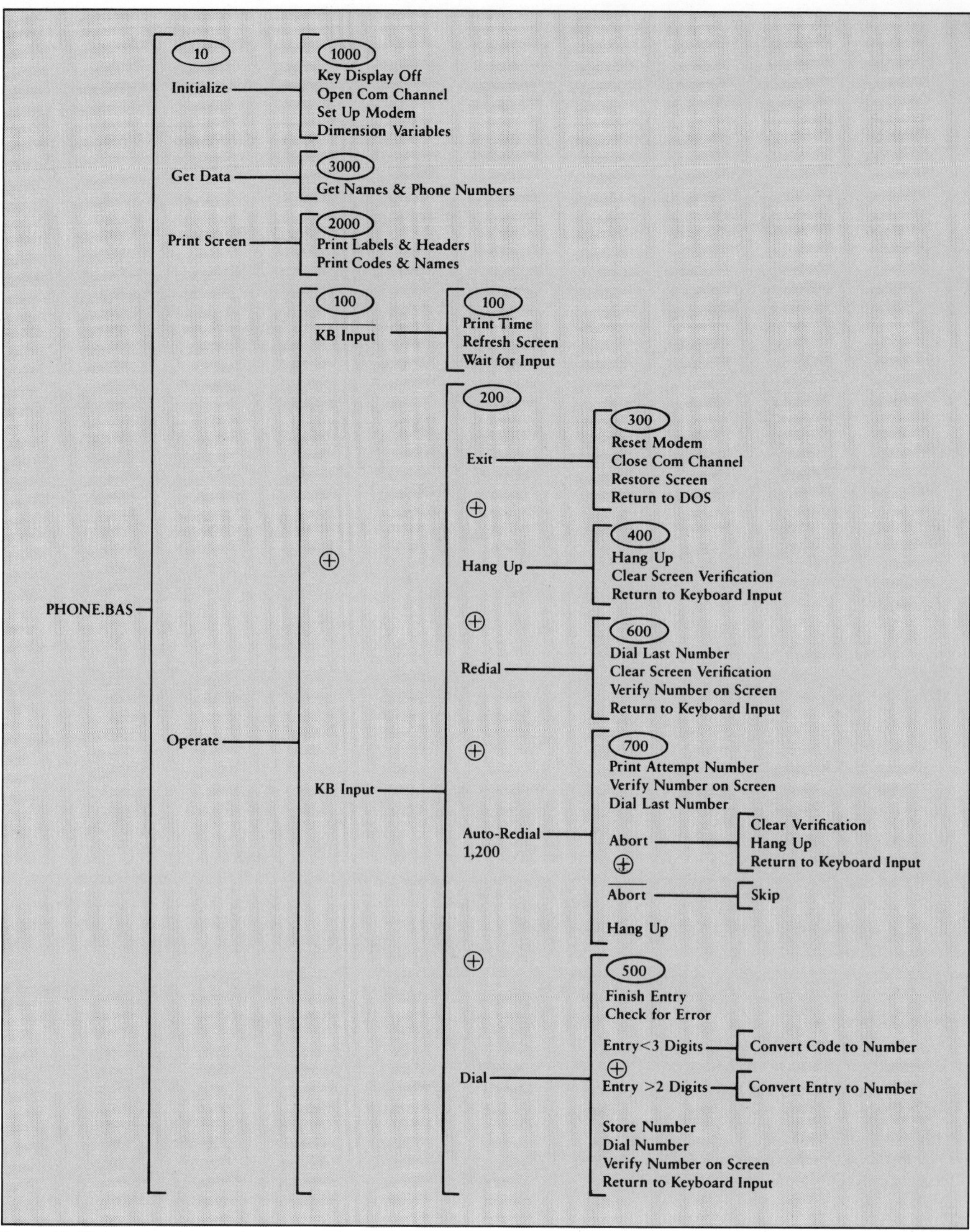

Figure 6.5 *Warnier-Orr diagram for PHONE.BAS.*

(i.e., dummy variables, case structures, INKEY$, RIGHT$, LEN, LINE INPUT, VAL, and ON . . . GOTO). I used these techniques to minimize the number of keystrokes required for data entry. The keyboard entry routine has to recognize whether the input is a single-character command that begins an operation, an asterisk indicating a correction, the first digit of a code representing a number to be dialed, or the first character of an actual telephone number. If the entry is the first digit of a code, the rest of the code must be appended to it and the code must be converted to a telephone number. If the entry is the first digit of a telephone number, the rest of the number must be appended to it.

Line 110 traps the first keystroke and defines it as the string constant ENTRY$. If ENTRY$ is any of the single-character commands, the program takes immediate action (lines 200 to 230). If ENTRY$ fails all the tests of lines 200 to 230, it must be a code, a telephone number, or an instruction to correct an entry. Once this has been determined, the rest of the keyboard input is appended to ENTRY$ and the concatenated string is defined as DUMMY$ (line 500). DUMMY$ is then tested for an error-correction instruction (line 510). If DUMMY$ does not have an error-correction symbol as its rightmost character, the program tests the string's length. If DUMMY$ is less than 3 characters long, it must be a code; the number the code represents is retrieved and defined as the number to be dialed (line 520). If DUMMY$ is more than 2 characters long, it must be a telephone number; it is defined as the number to be dialed (line 530).

This routine works well, but using <Backspace> to correct errors disrupts the logic and produces unpredictable results. Instead, you have to use the asterisk to signal correction of input errors.

A Final Word

Like most programs, PHONE.BAS will only be of use to you if it fits your needs and is well integrated into your system. The major considerations for a program like PHONE.BAS are that it be quick and convenient. One way to speed up access to PHONE.BAS is to use a keyboard macro program like *ProKey* or *Keynote* to assign command sequences to a single key. In my own system, for example, three versions of PHONE.BAS can be called up quickly by pressing <F5>, <Alt>-<F5>, or <Shift>-<F5>; the commands assigned to these keys are BASICA PHONE-P, BASICA PHONE-B, and BASICA PHONE-E. PHONE-P and PHONE-E are two programs that have personal directories, and PHONE-B contains a directory of numbers that I need for business.

While the usefulness of this dialing program is currently limited to times when your computer isn't otherwise occupied, multitasking and concurrent operation on the PC aren't very far away. When you can press a key and instantly switch operations, and then press another key and resume where you left off, the issue of tying up the computer or interrupting a process will no longer be of concern.

If you use floppy disks, the location of PHONE.BAS on the disk is a critical factor in determining how fast the program can be invoked. If loading speed is important to you, BASICA.COM and PHONE.BAS should be among the first programs you copy onto a newly formatted disk.

Paying attention to system considerations increases the usefulness of many programs. The kind of system integration described above has made PHONE.BAS one of the most frequently used programs in my library.

Burton L. Alperson, Ph.D., is a professor of psychology at California State University at Los Angeles. He is also a Contributing Editor to PC World *magazine and Director of Training and Development at Regents Data Systems in Los Angeles. This article was originally published in* PC World *Volume 1, Number 7.*

More on Warnier-Orrs

Warnier-Orr diagrams were first developed by the French computer scientist and logician Jean Dominique Warnier as a part of his efforts to develop a completely automatic procedure for designing computer programs based on mathematical set theory. The techniques Warnier developed are very useful for business applications such as data base management and financial programs. They are less useful for scientific applications, although the procedure can still save time and effort by eliminating superfluous programming.

Warnier's techniques were improved and refined by Ken Orr of the United States. In addition to several conventions that he added to Warnier's diagrams, Orr developed a design technique called Structured Systems Design that is one of the most powerful and elegant methods in the so-called top-down structured programming revolution.

*Warnier-Orr diagrams deliver an enormous amount of information in a compact format. Labels are descriptive titles for operations to be performed (such as initialize and print screen). A line over a label means that an event has not taken place or an operation is not to be performed. A plus sign is an inclusive "or" (print to the screen, to the printer, or to both). A circled plus sign is an exclusive "or" (abort the routine or don't abort the routine). Repetition is indicated by 1,*n *where* n *is the maximum number of repetitions. Orr developed additional conventions (e.g., for representing mathematical operations), but the set described above serves our purposes.*

The beauty of this procedure is that a single diagram can immediately tell you the what, when, why, and how of a complete program. Reading the label informs you what function each operation performs. Reading the diagram from top to bottom tells you when operations are performed; reading the diagram from right to left tells you the purpose of each step; and reading the diagram from left to right tells you how to do things.

In the Warnier-Orr diagram of PHONE.BAS, for example, the sequence of events is initialize, get data, print screen, and finally operate. Reading from left to right, you can see that to initialize you must turn the key display off, open a communications channel, set up the modem, and then dimension your variables. If you need to know why you are printing the time, refreshing the screen, and waiting for input, by reading from right to left you can see it's because there has been no keyboard input.

Notice that up to this point nothing has been said about BASIC or any other programming language. Warnier-Orr diagrams are language independent. They show the structure of a program and can be implemented in any language.

Strictly speaking, the numbers in the ovals in this diagram are not part of a Warnier-Orr diagram; they are part of what Orr calls the physical implementation of the diagram. These are the line numbers of PHONE.BAS. The initialization routine, for example, begins in line 1000 of Figure 6.3, the auto-redial routine begins in line 700, and control of the basic structure of PHONE.BAS begins in line 10.

A few experiences with Warnier-Orr programming can produce something akin to a religious conversion. I wrote PHONE.BAS before I knew of this approach to programming, so I decided to revise the program for publication by using Warnier-Orr techniques. Although I was sure I had originally written tight, nonredundant code, application of the Warnier-Orr techniques produced a 23 percent reduction in active program size. The program now runs better and faster than before.

Many introductory programming texts solemnly inform you that programming should begin with flow charts. Few experienced programmers bother with them, however; they are most frequently used only as expedient devices to impress management. Unlike flow charts, Warnier-Orr diagrams are genuine design tools that can dramatically reduce programming time and effort and improve programs.

PC CTTY

Richard Steck

It was the hacker in me that contributed to my initial resistance to PC-DOS. Early DOS simply did not have the complexity and flexibility of CP/M. DOS seemed to be a watered-down version of what had become the de facto S-100 operating system standard. Five months passed after IBM's announcement of the PC before I could get myself to take the plunge. DOS 1.10 offered some improvements over 1.00, but DOS 2.00 permited me to forget my excitement over CP/M. It should take me many months to discover and test all the features in DOS 2.00. What follows is one such encounter.

While thumbing through the advanced features section of my PC-DOS 2.00 manual, I came upon a command named CTTY (change console). According to the manual, CTTY "changes the standard input and output console to an auxiliary console, or restores the keyboard and screen as the standard input and output devices." The sparseness of this description prompted my curiosity to find out more.

CTTY immediately reminded me of the CP/M command STAT, which can assign the normal console to a user-defined port. This enables you to control a system through an external terminal, modem, or another system. The CP/M command is

```
STAT UC1: = CON
```

This feature is one of the pleasures of CP/M because it permits the user to take full remote control of a system even to the extent of running most spreadsheets and word processing programs without any special communications software. My first question was: is the DOS CTTY command as powerful as the CP/M STAT command?

Taking Control

Before proceeding further you will need, as a minimum, the following: (1) an asynchronous communications adapter, also called a communications card or board; (2) a dumb terminal such as those made by Lear Siegler, Hazeltine, ADDS, or Televideo, or a second personal computer such as another PC, an Apple, or a TRS-80 to function as a remote terminal; (3) a modem eliminator cable; and (4) communications software for the remote terminal (if you use a personal computer).

Connect the remote terminal to the PC COM1: or COM2: port using the modem eliminator cable. Set the baud rate, parity, and other bit characteristics of the terminal. The defaults for the DOS MODE command (9600 baud, even parity, 7 data bits, and 1 stop bit) work just fine.

In the discussion that follows, COM1: and COM2: will be referred to as COMn:. Replace *n* with the number that corresponds to the communications port you decide to use. Type the DOS MODE command at the PC as follows:

```
MODE COMn:9600
```

If all is working well, you should be able to issue a CTTY command at the PC as follows:

```
CTTY COMn
```

Once this command is given, the remote terminal should begin to function as the PC's terminal. The command usually works, but sometimes the RTS and DTR signals of the COMn: are not supplied with the voltages required by some modems and terminals.

A BASIC program can activate the RTS and DTR signals by issuing a command such as:

```
OPEN "COM1:baudrate,parity,
    databits,stopbits" AS #1
```

An example of the command is:

```
OPEN "COM1:9600,E,7,1" AS #1
```

This activates the COM1: port and permits you to read and write data to it. When the program ends either normally or abruptly, however, the active COMn: files are closed and the communications ports are deactivated. In other words, there is no simple way to open a COMn: port and hold it open with BASIC. A similar problem occurs when you try to use the DOS 2.00 PRINT command and route output to the COM1: port; the port cannot be held open.

After some experimenting, I created the program shown in Figure 6.6. to open the COMn: ports and hold them open for use with the

```
10 '     This program fixes COM1:  by turning on RTS, DTR
20 '
30 OUT &H3F9,&HB
40 OUT &H3FB,&H1A
50 OUT &H3FC,&HB
60 OUT &H3FE,&HF0
70 SYSTEM


10 '     This program fixes COM2:  by turning on RTS, DTR
20 '
30 OUT &H2F9,&HB
40 OUT &H2FB,&H1A
50 OUT &H2FC,&HB
60 OUT &H2FE,&HF0
70 SYSTEM
```

Figure 6.6 *Listing for opening the COM ports for CTTY and PRINT.*

CTTY and PRINT commands. The program pokes the appropriate addresses given in the *IBM Personal Computer Technical Reference* manual.

Once the COMn: port is active, you can issue the CTTY command at the PC:

CTTY COMn:

At this point the PC keyboard and screen become inactive and a DOS prompt appears on the remote terminal. You can issue some simple commands such as DIR or CHKDSK to get the idea of how this works. You can also issue the following command to return control of the console back to the PC:

CTTY CON

After CTTY transfers control to a remote terminal, nearly all DOS, EDLIN, and DEBUG commands can be used from the remote terminal. Some commands do not function properly, however. For example, the familiar command:

COPY CON: *filename*

(frequently used to create short text files directly from the keyboard) does not operate remotely. Instead, you must type:

COPY COMn: *filename*

to get the same effect. But even this command has problems. For some reason, when used remotely, the COPY command does not accept carriage returns. All remotely entered text enters the file in a continuous line. To add to the confusion, linefeeds (Ctrl-J) are accepted. Two carriage returns in succession cause the destination file to be closed. The reverse process:

COPY *filename* **COMn:**

works as you would expect, as does the TYPE command.

A Few Quirks

I encountered another problem in using BASIC through a remote terminal. Even when executed from a remote terminal, BASIC programs continue to display output on the PC screen. Programs can be written to route output to the remote terminal by OPENing the COMn: port and sending output directly to the port, but as soon as the program ends, COMn: is CLOSED and the terminal is disconnected. You can run noninteractive BASIC programs through a remote terminal as long as the last statement in each program is a SYSTEM command.

Many other problems are involved in using BASIC from a remote terminal. If you need full access to your PC through a remote terminal, consider using a program such as *Remote Access* from Custom Software.

A few other minor quirks should be mentioned about using a remote terminal. To stop scrolling use <Ctrl>-S or you will lose data. True BREAK is not recognized, but <Ctrl>-C seems to have the same effect in a BASIC program. The type-ahead buffer works erratically, which is equivalent to saying that it does not work.

Control Via Modem

If you want to control your system remotely through a modem, you will need an auto-answer modem. The

```
10 ' Sets Up Hayes Smartmodem For Autoanswer
20 '
30 OPEN "COM1:300,E,7,1" AS #1
40 PRINT #1, "AT SO=1"
50 FOR I = 1 TO 2000 : NEXT I        'DELAY WINDOW
60 PRINT #1, "AT H"
70 SYSTEM
```

Figure 6.7 *Auto-answer listing for Hayes Smartmodem.*

Hayes Smartmodem (300 and 1200 baud) works well. To put the Smartmodem into an auto-answer state, you can set its internal switches or run the program shown in Figure 6.7. After the AA indicator lights up, type **CTTY COMn**: and dial from a remote modem. When the DOS > prompt appears, you're in business. You can make repeat calls as long as you don't lose control of the CTTY command or lock up the system. Accessing DOS in this manner is still very primitive compared to the results achieved with the *Remote Access* program. *Remote Access* gives nearly total remote control, while CTTY gives limited control.

Of what use is the DOS CTTY command? If you need to operate your PC through a remote terminal or a modem, CTTY can help you. CTTY gives you reliable access to a limited number of DOS functions from a remote hard-wired terminal, a computer, or a modem. You can use it to extract text files from the PC, to initiate batch jobs, and to access EDLIN or DEBUG. You can also attach an auto-answer modem and take control of your system via telephone.

Uses for CTTY are limited only by your imagination and a few quirks that accompany the command. The command does not match the performance of a program specifically designed for accessing the PC through a remote terminal.

Richard Steck is an investment professional, microcomputing enthusiast, and author. His most recent effort is a book, Apple to IBM PC Conversion Guide, *published by Scott, Foresman. This article was originally published under the title "Trouble in PC CTTY" in* PC World *Volume 1, Number 6.*

Star-Dot-Star

Communications software may be less error-prone than other applications, or perhaps it is just too intimidating for users to tangle with, because we don't receive the amount of mail concerning it as we do for the other genres. We have, however, included a tip to improve communications between *PC-Talk III* and the mainframe world ("PC-Beep III"), a compatibility correction for the mating of Microcom's modem to *PC-Talk III* ("PC-Talk III & Microcom Marriage"), and an assembly language version of the CTTYFIX program ("Built-In Assembler").

PC-Beep III

If you use *PC-Talk III* to communicate with a mainframe that gives a relatively slow response, try adding the four lines shown in Figure 6.8, PCBEEP. They cause the PC to beep when a character is received if the user of the mainframe has not transmitted anything for at least 15 seconds. The beep summons you back if you have walked away from the PC or if your thoughts have wandered while you were waiting for a response.

This is for the interpreted version of *PC-Talk;* for the compiled version, the number 1000 in line 607 should be much larger.

Michael A. Covington
San Gabriel, California

```
522 XXMACXX=0
560 IF EOF (1) THEN XXMACXX=XXMACXX+1:GOTO 515 ELSE 605
607 IF XXMACXX>1000 THEN BEEP
608 XXMACXX=0
```

Figure 6.8 *PCBEEP, a patch for using* PC-Talk III *with a slow-responding mainframe.*

PC-Talk III and Microcom Marriage

I have written a few BASIC lines, shown in Figure 6.9, PCS-TALK.PAT, that can be merged with the communications program *PC-Talk III* allowing the use of the Microcom PCS 2000 modem.

The modem initialization string for the PCS is 45, but simply using this string in the program default menu will not work because the initialization sequence for the PCS requires a 4, a pause, and then a 5. A subroutine to perform this sequence is shown in lines 821 to 829. It sends a 4 to the communications port, pauses for 1 second, and then sends a 5. Use of the modem initialization string from the default parameter list is eliminated.

You'll need to initialize the PCS modem at the start of the program (line 430) when you specify new communications parameters (line 5095), change program defaults (line 5290), or dial a number from the *PC-Talk* dialing directory (line 6250). This modification works with either the interpreted or compiled versions of *PC-Talk*.

The 1-second delay in lines 825 through 827 is taken from a contribution to this column by Graham Pearson, "Making 'Em Pause" (*PC World,* Vol. 2, No. 1, and in Chapter 8's **.**). This forces the delay interval to be the same whether Interpreted or Compiled BASIC is used.

Of course, typing 45 to manually initialize the PCS each time the communications file is reopened is perfectly functional, but these modifications simplify interaction with this fine modem.

Robert D. Thomsen
Springfield, Oregon

Built-In Assembler

I found Richard Steck's article "Trouble in PC CTTY" (*PC World,* Vol. 1, No. 6; reprinted in this chapter as "PC CTTY") quite useful, but it seemed like a lot of overhead to use the BASIC interpreter just to output a few bytes to control the RTS and DTR signals. Until recently that was the only method available to PC owners who didn't have an assembler. But since the release of DOS 2.00, the DEBUG program accepts assembly language statements and

```
425 CLOSE#1:OPEN COMM$ AS #1
430 ROW=1:COL=1:GOSUB 2820:LOCATE 1,1,1:PRINT GO$:GOSUB 821

821 '
822 '-Initialize MICROCOM PCS modem
823 '
824 PRINT #1,"4";
825 PAUSE%=1     ' PAUSE 1 SECOND
826 SEC%=VAL(RIGHT$(TIME$,2)) :ENOUGH%=(SEC%+PAUSE%) MOD 60
827 WHILE SEC%<>ENOUGH%  :SEC%=VAL(RIGHT$(TIME$,2))  :WEND
828 PRINT #1,"5";
829 RETURN

5095 PRINT GO$:GOSUB 821:GOSUB 2800:GOTO 515

5290 COLOR FG,BG,BG:PRINT GO$:GOSUB 821:GOSUB 2800:GOTO 515

6260 CLS:LOCATE 1,1,1:GOSUB 821:PRINT "===DIALING ";N$
```

Figure 6.9 *PCS-TALK.PAT*

assembles them directly into memory. The process sounds more complicated than it actually is, and I encourage readers to experiment with this facility if they are curious about assembly language programming.

The statements shown in CTTYFIX (see Figure 6.10) illustrate the steps needed to create a program called CTTYFIX.COM to replace Mr. Steck's program

```
A>DEBUG <Enter>
-A 100 <Enter>
3A35:0100 MOV AL,0B <Enter>
3A35:0102 MOV DX,03F9 <Enter>        ;use 2F9 for COM2:
3A35:0105 OUT DX,AL  <Enter>
3A35:0106 MOV AL,1A  <Enter>
3A35:0108 MOV DX,03FB <Enter>        ;use 2FB for COM2:
3A35:010B OUT DX,AL  <Enter>
3A35:010C MOV AL,0B  <Enter>
3A35:010E MOV DX,03FC <Enter>        ;use 2FC for COM2:
3A35:0111 OUT DX,AL  <Enter>
3A35:0112 MOV AL,F0  <Enter>
3A35:0114 MOV DX,03FE <Enter>        ;use 2FE for COM2:
3A35:0117 OUT DX,AL  <Enter>
3A35:0118 INT 20 <Enter>
3A35:011A <Enter>
-R BX <Enter>
BX 0000
:0 <Enter>
-R CX <Enter>
CX 0000
:1A <Enter>
-N A:CTTYFIX.COM <Enter>
-W <Enter>
Writing 001A bytes
-Q <Enter>
A>
```

Figure 6.10 *CTTYFIX*

CTTYFIX.BAS. Place a disk containing a copy of the DOS 2.00 version of DEBUG.COM into drive A and type **DEBUG**; the DEBUG program will display a hyphen as its prompt. Type the command **A 100** to indicate that you want to assemble statements into memory beginning at hexadecimal address 100, the address where all .COM programs must begin.

DEBUG will respond to the Assemble command (A) by printing the address of the active segment followed by a colon and the current offset (100); it will then wait for you to enter an assembly language statement. (The segment number will vary depending on the configuration of your PC.) DEBUG automatically increments the offset as it assembles each line and then waits for another statement. When you are finished, press <Enter> without typing anything else, and DEBUG will return to its command mode.

After the statements have been entered, you can save them on disk. First use DEBUG's Register command to set the CX and BX registers to reflect the number of bytes to be written to disk. The BX register must be set to zero for any program less than 64K long. Set the CX register to 100 (hex) less than the last offset value (the one displayed on the line when you pressed only <Enter>). In this example the last offset was 011A, so the program length is 1A bytes.

To set the BX register to zero, type **R BX** and then press <Enter>. DEBUG will display a colon and allow you to enter a new value for the BX register. Type a zero and then press <Enter>. Use the same procedure to set the value of the CX register: type **R CX**, press <Enter>, and then type **1A** <**Enter**> after the colon.

If you have any doubts about the length of a program, you can use DEBUG's hex calculator by typing the letter **H** at the hyphen prompt, followed by the last offset value, followed by **100**. DEBUG responds with two values that are, respectively, the sum and the difference of the two values you typed after the letter **H**. The difference value is the length of your program.

Use DEBUG's Name command to assign a file name to the program. After the hyphen prompt, type the letter **N** followed by the file name—for example, **N A:CTTYFIX.COM**. Once a file name has been assigned, you must use the Write command to store the program on a disk. Simply type the letter **W** and press <Enter>. In this example, DEBUG will respond with the message 'Writing 001A bytes'; when it has finished, it will return to its command mode. To exit DEBUG, type the letter **Q** and press <Enter>.

I find that using DEBUG to create small programs is actually easier and faster than using the IBM Macro Assembler, and anyone who has DOS 2.00 can use this technique to "hand compile" BASIC programs that simply POKE values into memory. The commonly used statements translate as follows: 'DEF SEG = &H*xxxx*' becomes 'MOV DS,*xxxx*'; 'POKE &H*xxxx*,&H*yy*'; 'SYSTEM' becomes 'INT 20'.

Roland Hutchinson
Stanford, California

7

Enhancing the Operating System

Hands On

Writers often try to explain the somewhat abstract notion of an operating system by personifying it—common choices include a traffic cop, a conductor, and a translator. An operating system works like a cop or a conductor in that it directs the operation and interaction of the various parts of the computer system (the hardware, the applications program, and the programs stored in ROM), invoking a routine or turning on a piece of equipment as a task requires. Like a translator, the operating system acts as an interface between the different parts of the computer and its user. In this way, the operating system enables the user or an applications program to "talk" to the hardware without having to use the machine language statements—composed solely of zeros and ones—that the hardware understands. The operating system makes programming a lot easier because it provides a standardized way of performing such chores as storing data on disk or moving data between internal memory and devices such as printers or monitors.

Because the operating system remains transparent during the functioning of most applications programs, many PC users work with their machines for years without ever learning more about this vital system than how to use it to format a disk or copy a file. While using the power of the operating system may not be absolutely required for successful computing, learning to do so will help you cope with situations that are out of the ordinary and will give you more flexibility and control.

The most common operating system on the IBM PC is DOS, the Disk Operating System; the following articles are designed to be used with DOS 2.00. Additions such as its hard disk management features, extended batch file facilities, heirarchical filing system, and new filter commands (SORT, MORE, and FIND) make DOS 2.00 a significant improvement over earlier versions, and these articles help you take advantage of many of these enhancements. "Menus Made Easy" shows you how to use the extended batch facility and the tree-structured directory to create a menu-driven system that helps organize message and phone number list processing. Both "Changing Keys" and "Macro Mastery" use macros to assign new functions to the PC keys. "Changing Keys" shows you how to use DOS 2.00's own capabilities to redefine any of the keys on the PC keyboard, while "Macro Mastery" uses the powerful macro program *ProKey* to create a menu-driven front end that makes using DOS 2.00 easier. With the system described in the article, or one you create using the principles and commands illustrated in the article, you can invoke applications programs, DOS commands, or batch files from two menus with only a few keystrokes.

Menus Made Easy

Tom Sheldon

One of the most useful features of DOS 2.00 is the extended batch file facility. The procedure outlined in this article shows how the batch facility can be combined with DOS 2.00's tree-structured directory to create a menu-driven system that will help organize messages and phone number lists. DOS 2.00 is generally oriented toward a hard disk system like the IBM Personal Computer XT. The procedures described here, however, assume a system with dual floppy drives, since that is still the most common arrangement.

In general, the tree-structured directory system that is part of DOS 2.00 will be less useful to the person who uses a dual floppy system. This type of system is excellent for hard disk users, however, because it provides a means to group files stored on a disk. A root directory is the starting point from which several subdirectories are created. If several people are using the system, each user may store files in his or her own subdirectory. Applications programs and related data files could also be kept in separate directories.

The usefulness of the tree structure on a floppy-based system is limited. It's easier to keep track of different types of data and programs by simply using a different floppy disk for each application. A floppy disk may, however, be divided into several subdirectories if necessary. In creating the menu system described here, you will use one directory for programs and another for data files. All programs and data will be stored on the default drive (A).

If you've ever been confused or unimpressed by the simple system prompt (A>) that appears when you start your system, you'll appreciate the value of the following menu system. It is designed to make it easier to use the operating system. The objective is to create the screen shown in Figure 7.1. The menu system leaves enough room on the disk for one or more applications programs of your choice.

Create the Menu Display

The first step in setting up the menu system is to "draw" the menu on the screen as you want it to appear and save the image as a text file. Figure 7.2 shows a chart of the graphics characters that can be used to create the menu. Also shown are the ASCII character codes used to represent the graphic characters.

You can use any text editor (e.g., IBM's *Personal Editor* or the EDLIN line editor that comes with DOS) to create the text file. Figure 7.1 contains the text file for the menu screen. Using EDLIN, the top line can be formed by using an Alt-201 character for the left corner bracket,

```
IBM PERSONAL COMPUTER MAIN MENU
DOS 2.0 OPERATING SYSTEM

 1. DISK STATUS [d:]
 2. SORT DIRECTORY ALPHABETICALLY [d:]
 3. SORT DIRECTORY BY DATE [d:]
 4. SORT DIRECTORY FOR GIVEN DATE [d: mm-dd-yy]
 5. LIST MAIL FILES
 6. READ MAIL [filename]
 7. WRITE MAIL
 8. DELETE MAIL [filename]
 9. FIND PHONE NUMBER [NAME]
10. ADD PHONE NUMBER
11. Available for applications program
12. EXIT MENU/RETURN CONTROL TO DOS
```

Figure 7.1 *Screen image of main menu.*

ASCII Character Value			
179	│	199	╟
180	┤	200	╚
181	╡	201	╔
182	╢	202	╩
183	╖	203	╦
184	╕	204	╠
185	╣	205	═
186	║	206	╬
187	╗	207	╧
188	╝	208	╨
189	╜	209	╤
190	╛	210	╥
191	┐	211	╙
192	└	212	╘
193	┴	213	╒
194	┬	214	╓
195	├	215	╫
196	─	216	╪
197	┼	217	┘
198	╞	218	┌

Figure 7.2 *Extended ASCII graphics characters.*

the Alt-205 character for the double horizontal line, and the Alt-187 character for the upper-right corner. The double vertical lines are created by the Alt-186 characters. Alt-204 is the left end of the fifth line, and Alt-185 is the right end. Alt-200 is the bottom-left corner, and the Alt-188 is the bottom-right corner. To create an Alt-combination character, depress and hold the <Alt> key, then type the three numbers using the ten-key numeric pad on the right side of the keyboard. Release the <Alt> key after typing all three numbers and the character will appear on the screen.

A Batchwork Quilt

Format a new system disk and copy the following DOS 2.00 files onto it: CHKDSK.COM, EDLIN.COM, MORE.COM, TREE.COM, FIND.EXE, and SORT.EXE.

If you are using a hard disk system such as the XT, make a directory called MENU by typing **MD MENU**. MD means make directory. After creating MENU, move into the new directory by typing **CD MENU**. You may type in all of the following batch files as they are shown here, but you must substitute the command CD\MENU for CD\ wherever it occurs. Be sure you are in the MENU directory before proceeding.

Copy the MENU.SCR screen file from the scratch disk to your new DOS disk and create a subdirectory called MAIL. Type **MD MAIL** at the system prompt. The first batch file you should create is AUTOEXEC.BAT. This is the file that the system looks for and executes each time it starts up. Type in the commands as shown in Figure 7.3. Make sure you press <F6> and <Enter> at the end of the file. Do not type in the comments shown in parentheses.

This file needs some explanation. The command CD\MAIL moves to the directory called MAIL, which holds all the mail files as they are created. You can write notes to yourself or anyone else who uses the system by selecting number 7 from the menu. The line that reads 'if not exist *.mal' looks in the mail subdirectory to see if any mail files are present. If there is mail, processing continues with the next line, and the 'You have mail' message is displayed. If no mail files are found, processing jumps to the label :A which goes back to the directory that contains the menu and changes the prompt.

The last line of the AUTOEXEC.BAT file contains the prompt command included in DOS 2.00. PROMPT allows you to change the system prompt (normally A>) to anything you want. In this example, the prompt is a comment. Special "metastrings" can be embedded in the prompt command in the form *$c* where *c* is one of the strings listed in Figure 7.4.

To try the AUTOEXEC.BAT file, reboot the system and watch it go through its paces. The menu is displayed on the screen, and the new prompt appears at the bottom. The prompt can be changed back to A> (showing the default disk drive) by typing **PROMPT** and pressing <Enter>. At this point you can create the batch file for selection 12 on the menu by typing the following commands. Then you can use it to stay out of trouble as you create the rest of the menu system.

```
copy con:autoexec.bat

echo off
date
cls
type menu.scr
cd\mail
if not exist *.mal goto a
echo        YOU HAVE MAIL
:a
echo off
cd\
prompt ENTER SELECTION NUMBER [and criteria if required] $g
<F6>
```

Figure 7.3 *AUTOEXEC.BAT listing.*

```
copy con:12.bat
echo off
prompt
cls
<F6>
```

Now any strange prompts you create may be immediately returned to normal by typing 12. This batch file returns control to DOS and doesn't display a menu. You may want to see the menu again later, so you should create a batch file called MENU.BAT (see Figure 7.5) that will clear the screen and display the menu at any time.

Selection 1 on the menu will require two batch files. File 1.BAT will explain the use of the STAT.BAT batch file. The STAT.BAT file will run the CHKDSK (check disk) program on the designated drive, display the TREE structure, if any, and then display files with the specified extension. Figure 7.6 contains the commands that will create these two batch files.

The VOL command simply displays the volume label of the disk, if any. TREE will display the tree structures of any subdirectories on the disk.

Run the file by typing **STAT A BAT**. The screen display should indicate that the disk contains a directory called MAIL and batch files called AUTOEXEC, 1, 12, and STAT.

Metastring Command	Produces This Prompt
prompt $g	>
prompt $$	$
prompt $t (time)	3:51:47.29
prompt $d (date)	Tue 30183
prompt $p (current directory)	A:\MAIL
prompt ng (default drive & >)	A>
prompt tg (time & >)	3:55:23.58>
prompt d_tg (two line prompt)	Tue 3011983 3:58:34.30>
prompt WAITING$g	WAITING>

Figure 7.4 *Metastrings in Prompt command.*

Type the following commands to create the file for selection 2:

```
copy con:2.bat
echo off
prompt
cls
echo PLEASE WAIT
dir %1: | sort>sort.dir
more < sort.dir
pause
echo off
cls
type menu.scr
prompt ENTER SELECTION NUMBER [and
    criteria if required] $g
<F6>
```

File 2.BAT uses a set of commands:

```
dir | sort>sort.dir
```

that sorts the directory and pipes the result into the file SORT.DIR. The MORE command then gets its data from SORT.DIR. MORE is a DOS 2.00 command that displays one full screen of information and waits until any key is pressed to display more. The MORE command is similar to TYPE, except that MORE causes the screen display to pause.

Note that you may choose either drive A or B. Typing B would execute the command for drive B. A space must be included after the B, but a trailing colon is not required. The selection 2 file can be edited to create files for selection 3 and selection 4. Simply copy the file A:2.BAT to A:3.BAT using the copy command. Then use EDLIN to go in and change line number 5. Add **/+25** after the SORT command (as shown

```
copy con:menu.bat

echo off
prompt ENTER SELECTION NUMBER [and criteria if required] $g
cls
type menu.scr
<F6>
```

Figure 7.5 *MENU.BAT listing.*

```
copy con:1.bat

echo off
cls
echo USING THE STAT COMMAND
echo ----------------------
echo REQUIRED:  You MUST specify a drive; a colon is not required.
echo OPTIONAL:  Enter a file extension in CAPS to display particular files.
echo EXAMPLE:   stat a BAT would display the status of all batch files on A:

copy con:stat.bat

echo off
prompt $n$g
cls
echo STATUS OF DISK IN DRIVE %1
echo -------------------------
vol %1:
chkdsk %1:
pause
cls
echo TREE STRUCTURE FOR DISK IN DRIVE %1
echo ---------------------------------
echo NOTE: <Ctrl><NumLock> will stop scroll during this listing.
tree %1:
pause
cls
echo DIRECTORY LISTING FOR DISK IN DRIVE %1 WITH EXTENSION OF %2
echo -----------------------------------------------------------
dir %1:*.%2/P
pause
echo off
cls
type menu.scr
prompt ENTER SELECTION NUMBER [and criteria if required] $g
<F6>
```

Figure 7.6 *1.BAT and STAT.BAT listings.*

in the following set of commands) so that the sort will be based on the date column, which starts with the 25th character.

The following commands and computer responses will be displayed on the screen as you create the 3.BAT file.

copy 2.bat 3.bat
1 File(s) copied
edlin 3.bat
End of input file * 5
5:*dir %1: | sort > sort.dir
5:*dir %1: | sort /+25 > sort.dir
***e**

The selection 4 batch file is exactly like 2 and 3 except for line 5. Copy file 3.BAT to file 4.BAT and use EDLIN to change line 5 to:

dir %1: ¦ find "%2" ¦ sort > sort.dir.

The syntax for using this batch file command is '4 d:3-01-83'. Any

```
copy con:5.bat

echo off
prompt $p$g
cls
cd\mail
path \
echo        CURRENT MAIL ON THIS DISK
for %%a in (*.mal) do find "SUBJECT" %%a
echo --------------END OF LIST--------------
echo To return to main menu:
pause
echo off
cls
cd\
type menu.scr
prompt ENTER SELECTION NUMBER [and criteria if required] $g
<F6>
```

Figure 7.7 *5.BAT listing.*

```
copy con:6.bat

echo off
cls
prompt $p$g
cd\mail
dir %1.mal
more < %1.mal
pause
echo off
cls
cd\
type menu.scr
prompt ENTER SELECTION NUMBER [and criteria if required] $g
<F6>
```

Figure 7.8 *6.BAT listing.*

drive or date may be specified.

Selection 5 is the first file in the MAIL section of the system. 5.BAT will move into the MAIL subdirectory and search for all files with the extension of MAL. It will search for a line of text containing the word SUBJECT in each file and display that line once it's found. When writing a mail file (selection 7), the user is prompted to type the word SUBJECT in uppercase letters on the first line of the file. This insures a proper match when the batch file searches for the word. The SUBJECT line will provide a brief summary of each file. Figure 7.7 details the contents of the batch file for selection 5 (List Mail Files).

To let the user read mail in the mail files, file 6.BAT (see Figure 7.8) changes the prompt to display the current directory, then changes directories to mail, displays the directory entry for the specified mail file, and sends the file to the screen by way of the MORE command, one screenful at a time.

The file 7.BAT (Figure 7.9) contains the instructions for WRITE.BAT, the mail-writing routine. WRITE.BAT moves to the mail directory and opens a file with the specified name using the COPY command. It then returns to the main directory and displays the menu.

Figure 7.10 is the 8.BAT file that provides a facility for deleting mail files once they've been read. It simply moves into the mail directory, deletes the specified file, and returns to the main directory and the menu system.

```
copy con:7.bat

echo off
prompt $n$g
cls
echo WRITE MAIL
echo ----------
echo REQUIRED:  The first line of every mail file must start with the
echo            word SUBJECT.  SUBJECT must be in all caps, and may
echo            be followed by a description of the file.
echo
echo TYPE:  "write filename" to begin.
<F6>


copy con:write.bat

echo off
cls
cd\mail
echo off
echo -----Press <F6> then <Enter> to end and save the file.-----
echo --------------------CURRENTLY WRITING FILE--------------------
COPY CON:%1.MAL
echo FILE WRITTEN TO DISK
cd\
echo off
cls
type menu.scr
prompt ENTER SELECTION NUMBER [and criteria if required] $g
<F6>
```

Figure 7.9 *7.BAT listing.*

```
copy con:8.bat

echo off
cls
cd\mail
erase %1.mal
echo FILE DELETED
cd\
echo off
cls
type menu.scr
prompt ENTER SELECTION NUMBER [and criteria if required] $g
<F6>
```

Figure 7.10 *8.BAT listing.*

A Handy Phone Directory

Selections 9 and 10 combine to make up a simple phone list system. Names (in uppercase) and phone numbers may be entered in the phone list file in no particular order. When you need a number, the FIND command searches for the name and displays the number (see Figure 7.11).

The 10.BAT file (Figure 7.12) lets you append names and phone numbers to the phone list by opening the PHONE.LST file under the EDLIN line editor. You start adding names by giving the command **insert text** on the line just past the last entry in the file. The file then displays a message to confirm that the phone numbers

```
copy con:9.bat

echo off
cls
echo LOOKING IN PHONE LIST FOR: %1
find "%1" phone.lst
pause
echo off
cls
type menu.scr
prompt ENTER SELECTION NUMBER [and criteria if required] $g
<F6>
```

Figure 7.11 *9.BAT listing.*

```
copy con:10.bat

echo off
cls
echo APPEND PHONE NUMBERS
echo --------------------
echo **PRESS THE CAPS LOCK KEY!**
echo off
echo INSTRUCTIONS: Type "L" to list the file.  Add 1 to the last line number
echo               and type the resulting number and "I" (for insert).
echo               Add all the names and numbers you want. Then press
echo               <Ctrl><Break> and "E" to end and save the file.
edlin phone.lst
echo PHONE NUMBER(S) APPENDED
echo off
cls
type menu.scr
prompt ENTER SELECTION NUMBER [and criteria if required] $g
<F6>
```

Figure 7.12 *10.BAT listing.*

have been added and returns to the menu.

10.BAT is the last of the files in the menu system. The system should now be ready to go if everything has been typed in correctly. You may add one or more applications programs, depending on available disk space. The batch files you've just created and the utility programs they require take up about 64K of disk space.

The menu system will be of varying usefulness depending on how you use your computer, but the simple principles and sophisticated new DOS facilities described here can provide the basis for other customized menu systems you might want to create. Use an editor to create a menu display. Include some graphic symbols to make the display more attractive. Then develop batch files using the extended batch facility of DOS 2.00 to carry out the commands listed on the menu. Experiment and enjoy.

Tom Sheldon is a technical writer and consultant. He is the author of the book Introducing PC DOS, A Guide for Beginning and Advanced Techniques *published by McGraw-Hill. This article was originally published under the title "One from Column A, One from Column B" in* PC World *Volume 1, Number 5.*

Changing Keys

Brian Mann

One reason the PC is so versatile is that you can define not only its function keys but also its standard keys. The definition process is somewhat complicated, particularly when the escape code (ASCII character 27) is required. This character is interpreted as an "erase line" command, and care must be taken when including it not to inadvertently destroy code or text.

Another problem is reassigning keys back to their original DOS definitions It is often necessary to reassign key values so that other programs, such as the IBM *Personal Editor,* can define keys for their own purposes. By studying Chapter 13 in the DOS 2.00 manual, "Using Extended Screen and Keyboard Control," and using the DOS batch file in this article, the problems attendant with assigning and reassigning keys can be avoided.

Before the assigned key definitions, including those for the function keys, can be changed, the ANSI driver must be resident in the PC. First, a CONFIG.SYS file containing the statement DEVICE = ANSI.SYS must be created on the boot disk. The CONFIG.SYS file will, among other things, install a program that is not "native" to DOS—in this case, the ANSI driver. The ANSI.SYS file, which is included on the DOS 2.00 disk, must also be on the boot disk. To create this CONFIG.SYS file, first place the boot disk in drive A. At the DOS A> prompt, type **COPY CON: CONFIG.SYS** and then press <**Enter**>. Type **DEVICE = ANSI.SYS** and press <**Enter**>. Finally, press <**F6**> (or <**Ctrl**>-**Z**) and press <**Enter**>.

The CONFIG.SYS file is read automatically when the PC is turned on or restarted with the <Ctrl>-<Alt>-<Del> sequence. The PC must be started using a disk containing CONFIG.SYS before any keyboard reassignment program can be run.

Using an editor such as EDLIN, enter the batch program KEYS.BAT (see Figure 7.13) onto a disk in drive A. If you have an emulated disk drive, operation will be faster if you first copy KEYS.BAT there. If you type **KEYS ON** from DOS, the program will execute and define the keys you specify. If you type **KEYS OFF**, the keys will return to their original DOS definitions.

How It Works

The first line in KEYS.BAT illustrates the undocumented fact that DOS treats a statement beginning with a period as a comment. The second line turns ECHO off so DOS won't display the KEYS.BAT statements as they execute. The "%1" used in the next four statements is equal to the parameter entered after the file name. In other words, when **keys on** is entered, KEYS.BAT is loaded and "%1" is set equal to "on." The statements determine what "%1" is equal to ("ON," "on," "OFF," or "off") and jump to the proper label, either ":ON" or ":OFF," or to ":END" if no value is set equal to "%1". Next, ECHO is turned back on. ECHO must be on so that the following key assignments accomplished via the DOS command PROMPT will work.

Defining Keys

The PROMPT command is often used to change the standard DOS prompt. For example, PROMPT WHAT NEXT? would cause DOS to display WHAT NEXT? as a DOS prompt instead of A>. In KEYS.BAT the PROMPT command issues an escape code (ASCII character 27) with the symbol "$e"; this code is necessary when ANSI.SYS is used to define the keys.

Keys are defined in the first section of the batch file following the ":ON" label. If an automatic return is desired, the definition should be followed by ";13p"; if no return is desired, a "p" should be used. It must be in lowercase.

Almost any key's value may be redefined. In order to change a key, the ASCII code representing that key must be sent to the ANSI driver via a special escape sequence. The ASCII codes of standard keys such as the A or backslash keys are only one character long, and a sequence would look like:

prompt $e[50;"definition "p

The PC has an extended set of ASCII codes to represent the special keys on the keyboard. The special keys

```
.Keyboard Key Reassignment batch program by Brian D. Mann, 08/18/83
echo off
if %1 == ON goto ON
if %1 == on goto ON
if %1 == OFF goto OFF
if %1 == off goto OFF
goto END
:ON
echo on
prompt $e[0;59;"DIR "p
prompt $e[0;60;"TYPE "p
prompt $e[0;61;"COPY "p
prompt $e[0;62;"ERASE "p
prompt $e[0;63;"A: "p
prompt $e[0;64;0;64p
prompt $e[0;65;"B: "p
prompt $e[0;66;"C: "p
prompt $e[0;67;"D: "p
prompt $e[0;68;"A:BASICA ";13p
prompt $e[0;120;"A:KEYS ON";13p
prompt $e[0;129;"A:KEYS OFF";13p
.The Function Keys have been Defined
goto END
:OFF
echo on
prompt $e[0;59;0;59p
prompt $e[0;60;0;60p
prompt $e[0;61;0;61p
prompt $e[0;62;0;62p
prompt $e[0;63;0;63p
prompt $e[0;64;0;64p
prompt $e[0;65;0;65p
prompt $e[0;66;0;66p
prompt $e[0;67;0;67p
prompt $e[0;68;0;68p
.The Function Keys have been Disabled
:END
prompt
```

Figure 7.13 *KEYS.BAT*

(mostly function keys and keys shifted using <Alt> or <Ctrl>) are two characters long and are prefaced by a zero and a semicolon. A sequence would look like:

prompt $e[0;59;"DIR "p

Getting ANSI

But how are original DOS definitions restored? To understand the process, the role of the ANSI driver must be considered.

The ASCII code of the letter is not sent to the computer, but rather a scan code determined by the location of the key is sent. The ANSI driver, which can be imagined as a box between the keyboard and the PC, intercepts the ASCII code sent by the keyboard and compares it against a reassignment list. If the key has not been reassigned, the ANSI driver passes the ASCII value to the PC. If the key has been reassigned, the ANSI driver sends out the character string that was given to the key.

Restoring a key to its original DOS value involves writing over the last key definition. For example, the first prompt statement in Figure 7.13 following the ":ON" label (prompt $e[0;59;"DIR "p) tells the ANSI driver to send out DIR when it intercepts the ASCII code. The first prompt line after the ":OFF" label (prompt $e[0;59;0;59p) tells the ANSI driver to send out 0;59 when it intercepts the ASCII code. The computer is not aware that the ASCII code was ever intercepted and applies the original DOS definition (0;59) to the key. In reassigning the original definitions, it is not necessary to include an automatic return.

```
echo off
date
time
echo on
prompt $e[0;59;"DIR "p
prompt $e[0;60;"TYPE "p
prompt $e[0;61;"COPY "p
prompt $e[0;62;"ERASE "p
prompt $e[0;63;"A: "p
prompt $e[0;64;0;64p
prompt $e[0;65;"B: "p
prompt $e[0;66;"C: "p
prompt $e[0;67;"D: "p
prompt $e[0;68;"A:BASICA ";13p
prompt $e[0;120;"A:KEYS ON";13p
prompt $e[0;129;"A:KEYS OFF";13p
.The Function Keys have been Defined
prompt
echo off
mode 80
verify on
graphics
cls
ver
vol a:
```

Figure 7.14 *Example AUTOEXEC.BAT file.*

Off and On

In Figure 7.13 the <Alt>-1 combination (ASCII code 0;120) issues the command A:KEYS ON, and the <Alt>-0 combination (ASCII code 0;129) issues the command A:KEYS OFF. These definitions are not changed by the KEYS OFF command, since the above ASCII codes do not appear below the ":OFF" label. Once KEYS ON is executed, pressing <Alt>-0 returns the keyboard to the original DOS definitions; <Alt>-1 reassigns the keyboard.

After the reassignments or original assignments are made, KEYS.BAT jumps to the ":END" label, which sets the prompt back to A>. If execution is aborted by <Ctrl>-<Break>, the prompt will not appear, and **prompt** must be entered to return the prompt to the screen.

Keys may be defined as desired, but there is a catch. If you exceed 190 characters of ANSI driver definitions, a portion of DOS kept in memory is likely to be overwritten. The computer will freeze up, and you will be forced to turn it off and start all over.

Using the PROMPT command will sometimes produce an 'Out of environment space' error message. This will not freeze up the computer, but it will prevent key redefinition. The environment, as defined by DOS 2.00, is a place where the operating system puts information so other programs can access it. (This is not the same as the ANSI definition space discussed above.) Issuing the command SET from DOS will display the environment, for example:

COMSPEC=A:\COMMAND.COM
PATH=A: B: C:
PROMPT=ng

When the PC is started, 127 bytes are allocated to the environment. If more space is needed, DOS will attempt to acquire more space. If a resident program such as MODE, PRINT, or GRAPHICS has been executed, space is not available and the 'Out of environment space' error message will show up. In the case of KEYS.BAT, the error message occurs when a large PROMPT statement is put into the environment after a resident program has been run.

There are two solutions to the problem. You can include key definitions in an AUTOEXEC.BAT file before any resident programs are run (see Figure 7.14). The second method is more complicated but may be superior. If you have an editor that permits use of the escape code (ASCII character 27), read the KEYS.BAT file into the editor, remove the "prompt" statement after the ":END" label, and replace all occurrences of "prompt $e" to ECHO followed by your editor's code for Escape. The ECHO statement prints the key definition text; this circumvents the prompt statement and the alteration of the environment altogether.

Brian Mann works as a nuclear engineer. He is a charter member of the Central Virginia IBM PC Users Group and chairman of the club's software exchange. This article was originally published in PC World *Volume 2, Number 3.*

Macro Mastery

Burton L. Alperson

Imagine that you have a task that you perform frequently on a computer. Each time you perform it you have to enter a sequence of 20 commands. Each command might require several keystrokes, and there may be minor variations each time you run the sequence. It would be helpful to have the ability to assign the whole sequence to a single key so that all you have to do is strike the key to initiate it. It would be even more helpful if you could make the sequence pause to wait for you to enter any variations.

Imagine that you have purchased an expensive applications program only to find that its syntax is clumsy or inconsistent with all the other programs you use. It might be a word processing program that forces you to delete the character to the left with <Del> and the character at the current cursor location with <Ctrl>-G, or a financial program that requires you to enter the same information repeatedly to process a single series of checks. It would be helpful to be able to reassign the keys so that the program is consistent with the rest of your programs, or to be able to enter information once and reenter it with a single keystroke whenever necessary.

Imagine that you want to develop a turnkey system so that a person who has minimal computer experience can perform a task that requires the integration of several programs from various authors. It would be helpful to be able to load and run the sequence of programs automatically. It would be even more helpful if you could replace the syntax of the program with menus phrased in the language of the application rather than the computerese of the individual programs.

Imagine that you could accomplish all of the above without knowing anything about BASIC, Pascal, C, assembly, or any other programming language.

The operations described above are not items in a wish list for a future super program. They are all straightforward applications of a class of existing programs called macro processors. Macros are simply abbreviations for longer strings of characters or commands.

For a number of months now I have been using *ProKey,* a powerful keyboard customizer that can accomplish every task just described and more. *ProKey* is easy to use, carefully written, and well documented. In all the time I have used this program I have yet to come up with a single serious criticism.

With *ProKey,* assigning a character string to a key is a simple operation. If you want to assign CHKDSK to the <F1> key, you type:

<Alt>-= <F1> CHKDSK
<Alt>-<hyphen>

<Alt>-= informs *ProKey* that you are beginning a definition; <Alt>-<hyphen> (the <Alt> key pressed in conjunction with the <hyphen> key informs *ProKey* that you have finished the definition. The first keystroke after <Alt>-= is the key to which you are assigning the string. Anything you type at that point until you type <Alt>-<hyphen> becomes the string that will be produced by the key you have specified. Up to 137 keys or key combinations may be defined, and up to 1000 keystrokes can be stored in each key assignment. (Version 3.0 of *ProKey* allows you to define almost 300 keys or key combinations.)

A set of key assignments may be saved in a file and reused at any time. *ProKey* is unique in that key assignments can be stored as standard ASCII files. This means that you can easily alter a set of definitions by editing the file with any text editor.

The *ProKey* command syntax consists of:

PROKEY *FILESPEC*/**COMMAND**

where COMMAND represents any of six operations. The commands are R (read in a file of definitions), M (merge a file of definitions into the current set), W (save the current definitions in a file), C (clear the current set of definitions from memory), I (install *ProKey* without using definitions in a file), and Q (quit *ProKey*).

If you make a mistake while defining a macro, you can correct it with the <Backspace> key. If you wish to abort the definition or the operation of a macro, press <Ctrl>-<Esc>.

One of the most powerful aspects of *ProKey* and a feature that

```
MAIN MENU

UTILITIES:
    CHANGE DIRECTORY                F1
    PROFESSIONAL EDITOR             Alt-F1
    EDLIN                           Ctl-F1
    DIRECTORY                       Sft-F1

    COPY                            F3
    CHKDSK                          Alt-F3
    MOVE FILE TO NEW DIRECT         Ctl-F3
    BACK UP HARD DISK               Sft-F3

    BURT'S PHONE                    F5
    BUSINESS PHONE                  Alt-F5
    ERMA'S PHONE                    Sft-F5

PRINTER & DISPLAY SELECTION:
    DISPLAY: MONOCHROME             F6
    DISPLAY: COLOR 80               Alt-F6
    DISPLAY: COLOR 40               Ctl-F6

    PRINTER: NEC/EPSON SWITCH       Alt-F2

OPERATIONS:
    MENUS & KEY ASSIGNMENTS:
        APPLICATIONS MENU           F2
        MAIN MENU                   F8
        CLEAR PROKEY                Alt-F8

    CUSTOMIZED BASICA               F7

    COMPILE A .BAS PROGRAM          Alt-F7

    PRINTING: FORM FEED             F4
    PRINTING: QUE A FILE            Sft-F8

DRIVE IDENTIFIERS:
    A:    F9          B:    F10
    C: Alt-F9         D: Alt-F10

EPSON PRINTER OPTIONS:
    ELITE TYPE                      Alt-F4
    CONDENSED TYPE                  Ctl-F4
    PICA TYPE                       Sft-F4
```

Figure 7.15 *Main Menu (STD.DOC).*

sets it apart from other macro processors is its ability to pause during macro execution and wait for keyboard input. Two kinds of input are allowed: fixed and variable fields. Fixed field input means that as soon as a predefined number of characters is received from the keyboard, macro execution will continue. Variable field input means than any number of characters may be entered, and macro execution continues as soon as you press <Enter>. Fixed field input is defined when you delimit the desired number of characters with <Ctrl>-]. Variable field input is defined by using <Ctrl>-<hyphen> as a delimiter.

Another unique and powerful feature of *ProKey* is its capacity for nesting definitions and calling them up as a reflexive operation. You can define a *ProKey* assignment, either from the keyboard or from a file, and instruct *ProKey* to call for that assignment later in the string or from another key assignment. Thus, you might enter information from the keyboard that *ProKey* assigns to the <Backtab> key. If you refer to the <Backtab> key later in a *ProKey* macro, the program will treat <Backtab> as an address and will retrieve the information that has been assigned to <Backtab>.

A Front End for DOS 2.00

DOS 2.00 is fertile ground for *ProKey* applications. Because the operating system is so rich and the syntax so lengthy and convoluted, a menu-driven front end is helpful. Figure 7.15 shows such a menu. The screen display is simply ASCII file, STD.DOC called by the AUTOEXEC.BAT file or the <F8> key. The menu is also displayed by batch files at the conclusion of most operations. (See "Menus Made Easy" in this chapter to create a menu using an extended graphics set.)

To make the front end easier to use, the menu is divided into activities that seem similar. These personal categories include various utilities, printer and display selection, operations, drive identifiers, and control of some Epson printer options.

The display in Figure 7.15 is one of two menus in the front end. The second, the Applications Menu, is called by the <F2> key (Figure 7.16). Like the Main Menu, the Applications Menu is divided into logical groupings: word processing, communications, spreadsheet/data base, graphics, money, and food. (The last category contains two mutually exclusive programs that allow me to plan meals and diets.) This menu is another ASCII file called PGMS.DOC.

The *ProKey* implementation of this front end is contained in a file called STD.PRO (Figure 7.17). Note that the line numbers in the listings are not part of STD.PRO; they are included only for reference purposes.

The <F1> key assignment for changing directories quickly is im-

APPLICATIONS MENU

WORD PROCESSING:	GRAPHICS:
Alt-A: WORDSTAR with Epson Printer	Alt-M: 1-2-3 GRAPH
Alt-B: WORDSTAR with NEC Printer	Alt-N: PC CRAYON
Alt-C: PROOFREADER	MONEY:
Alt-D: GRAMMATIK	Alt-O: FINANCIER PERSONAL
Alt-E: Convert Document to ASCII	Alt-P: FINANCIER TAX
Alt-F: Add to Address File	FOOD:
Alt-G: Enter Document from B:	Alt-Q: COMPUTER CHEF
Alt-H: Enter Document from User Area	Alt-R: DIET MONITOR
COMMUNICATIONS:	
Alt-I: Smartcom II	
Alt-J: PC-TALK III	
SPREADSHEET/DATABASE:	
Alt-K: 1-2-3	
Alt-L: DATA BASE MANAGER II	

PRESS F8 TO RETURN TO MAIN MENU

Figure 7.16 *Applications Menu (PGMS.DOC).*

plemented in lines 73-75 of Figure 7.17. The syntax begins with <Alt>-=, the initial delimiter for any *ProKey* assignment. This delimiter is followed by the name of the key to be assigned, <f1> in this case. The key name is then followed by a string, and the sequence is concluded with <alt->, the *ProKey* final delimiter. (In Version 3.0 of *ProKey,* "<Alt>-=" is represented as "<begdef>," and "<Alt>-<hyphen>" is represented as "<enddef>.")

The command itself is the DOS command to change directories (CD). *ProKey*'s ability to pause and wait for keyboard input during macro execution makes it possible to have the function wait for the name of the new directory. This is the purpose of <vfld> ... <vfld>, the variable field delimiters. Since directories can have names that differ in length, variable field input was chosen rather than fixed field input. After the name is entered, the function supplies a carriage return (<enter>) and instructs DOS to search for files in the root directory if they are not found in the new directory (PATH \<enter>).

The following are sample *ProKey* definitions I have assigned for my system (see Figure 7.17). Some may be applicable to your system and habits, especially if you have a hard disk running under DOS 2.00. Some assignments are straightforward and don't require explanations: the assignments to <F2> (lines 77-79) display the Applications Menu; <F8> (lines 96-98) displays the Main Menu; and <Alt>-<F8> (lines 160-161) clears current *ProKey* definitions.

The assignments to <F7> (lines 93-94) and <Alt>-<F7> (lines 151-158) both call batch files. <F7> invokes BASICA with my choice of key assignments rather than IBM's. <Alt>-<F7> calls the file GO.BAT that resides in my Compiler subdirectory and calls up the IBM BASIC Compiler in the configuration that I prefer.

Line 135 allows you to engage the IBM *Professional Editor* by pressing <Alt>-<F1>. PROFEDIT is a batch file consisting of:

```
PROKEY/C
EDIT %1
PROKEY STD.PRO/R
CLS
TYPE \STD.DOC
```

The first line of this file clears all previous *ProKey* assignments. The second brings in the *Professional Editor* with any input file that may have been specified. When activity with this program is completed, the remaining lines restore the standard *ProKey* assignments, clear the screen, and display the Main Menu, which is stored in the root directory.

The other text editor in the system, EDLIN, is engaged in a similar fashion. The only difference is that the second line is **EDLIN %1.** This assignment is made to <Ctrl>-<F1>, which calls a batch file named FILENAME (line 118).

The fast directory command, <Shift>-<F1>, saves several keystrokes. With a hard disk, most directories rapidly accumulate enough files to require more than a single screen display, making the '/P' parameter (which freezes the screen

```
<alt=><alta>BASICA ELITE<enter>
WS-EPSON<enter>
<alt->

<alt=><altb>WS-NEC<enter>
<alt->

<alt=><altc>CD \WP<enter>
PATH \<enter>
PROOF <vfld>...<vfld><enter>
<alt->

<alt=><altd>CD \WP<enter>
PATH \<enter>
GRAM <vfld>...<vfld><enter>
<alt->

<alt=><alte>ASCON<enter>
<alt->

<alt=><altf>BASICA ADDNAMES<enter>
<alt->

<alt=><altg>CLS<enter>
. ***=====>  When the cursor gets fat, type the name of the file to<enter>
.            transfer (do not use an extension).<enter>
COPY B:<vfld>...<vfld>.* \WP<enter>
<alt->

<alt=><alth>CLS<enter>
. ***=====>  When the cursor gets fat, enter your name.<enter>
. ***=====>  When the cursor gets fat again, enter the name of the file<enter>
.<tab><tab> to be transferred (do not use an extension), <enter>
.<tab><tab> then press [ENTER].<enter>
COPY \WP\<ffld>....<ffld>\<vfld>...<vfld>.* \WP<enter>
<alt->

<alt=><alti>SCOM<enter>
<alt->

<alt=><altj>PC-TALK<enter>
<alt->

<alt=><altk>123<enter>
<alt->

<alt=><altl>DBMII<enter>
<alt->

<alt=><altm>123GRAPH<enter>
<alt->

<alt=><altn>CD \GRAPH<enter>
PATH \<enter>
CRAYON<enter>
<alt->
```

(continues)

Figure 7.17 *STD.PRO*

```
58 <alt=><altq>CD \FOOD<enter>
59 CCHEF<enter>
60 <alt->
61
62 <alt=><altr>CD \FOOD<enter>
63 DIET<enter>
64 <alt->
65
66 <alt=><home>CLS<enter>
67 <alt->
68
69 <alt=><^pgup><alt->
70
71 <alt=><^pgdn>\<alt->
72
73 <alt=><f1>CD \<vfld>...<vfld><enter>
74 PATH \<enter>
75 <alt->
76
77 <alt=><f2>CLS<enter>
78 TYPE \PGMS.DOC<enter>
79 <alt->
80
81 <alt=><f3>COPY <alt->
82
83 <alt=><f4>BASICA FORMFEED<enter>
84 TYPE \STD.DOC<enter>
85 <alt->
86
87 <alt=><f5>PERS-TEL<enter>
88 <alt->
89
90 <alt=><f6>MODE MONO<enter>
91 <alt->
92
93 <alt=><f7>BAS<enter>
94 <alt->
95
96 <alt=><f8>CLS<enter>
97 TYPE \STD.DOC<enter>
98 <alt->
99
100 <alt=><f9>A:<alt->
101
102 <alt=><f10>B:<alt->
103
104 <alt=><capsf1>DIR /P \<vfld>...<vfld><enter>
105 <alt->
106
107 <alt=><capsf3>BACKUP C:\ A:/S/A/M<alt->
108
109 <alt=><capsf4>BASICA \PICA<enter>
110 <alt->
111
112 <alt=><capsf5>ERMA-TEL<enter>
```

Figure 7.17 *(continued)*

once it is full) a necessity. The *Pro-Key* assignment in line 104 supplies the parameter as well as the '\' subdirectory prefix. The function then waits for any additional specifications to be added.

The assignments to <F3> (COPY) and <Alt>-<F3> (CHKDSK) in lines 81 and 140 enter these DOS commands rapidly. I've recently made a slight but important change to the hard disk backup command assigned to <Shift>-<F3> in line 107. It originally contained an <enter> statement before

```
<alt->
<alt=><capsf8>PRINT <vfld>...<vfld><enter>
<alt->
<alt=><ctrlf1>FILENAME <alt->
<alt=><ctrlf3>cls<enter>
.Path and file name for source file: <alt=><^pgup><alt-><enter>
.Destination directory: <alt=><^pgdn>\<alt-><enter>
COPY <^pgup> <^pgdn><enter>
DEL <^pgup><enter>
cls<enter>
.        <^pgup> has been moved to <^pgdn>.<enter>
<alt->
<alt=><ctrlf4>BASICA \CONDENSE<enter>
<alt->
<alt=><ctrlf6>MODE CO40<enter>
<alt->
<alt=><altf1>PROFEDIT <alt->
<alt=><altf2>BASICA LPTSWTCH<enter>
<alt->
<alt=><altf3>CHKDSK <alt->
<alt=><altf4>BASICA \ELITE<enter>
<alt->
<alt=><altf5>BUSN-TEL<enter>
<alt->
<alt=><altf6>MODE CO80<enter>
<alt->
<alt=><altf7>CD \COMPILER<enter>
PATH \<enter>
CLS<enter>
.     Type filename (without extension) if no compiler switches are<enter>
.     required.  If switches are needed, press [ENTER] and include<enter>
.     them in response to the appropriate compiler prompts.<enter>
GO <vfld>...<vfld><enter>
<alt->
<alt=><altf8>PROKEY/C<enter>
<alt->
<alt=><altf9>C:<alt->
<alt=><altf10>D:<alt->
```

Figure 7.17 *(continued)*

<Alt>-<hyphen> to invoke the backup command immediately. After hitting <Shift>-<F3> accidentally several times, I decided that it would be safer to require a separate <Enter> keystroke to protect any floppy disk I might have left in drive A. Because the *ProKey* assignments are stored in an ASCII file, it was possible to delete the <enter> statement instead of retyping the entire string.

I frequently move files between subdirectories. After downloading a file while in my communications subdirectory, for example, I may want to edit it in the word processing subdirectory. The assignment to <Ctrl>-<F3> in lines 120-127 quickly accomplishes this transfer. It also illustrates *ProKey*'s reflexive capability.

The <Ctrl>-<F3> routine asks for the name and path of the file to be moved. It then assigns the name and path to <Ctrl>-<PgUp>. (This assignment is transparent in operation. <Ctrl>-<PgUp> simply serves as an address that contains the name of the file to be moved. The assignment of the destination subdirectory to <Ctrl>-<PgDn> serves a similar purpose.) The periods at the beginning of several of the lines take advantage of an undocumented DOS feature. Periods can be used in place of REM (remark) statements to print a message to the screen during the operation of a batch file. This method allows you to single-space between successive remarks. (Unfortunately, this undocumented feature has disappeared in DOS 3.00.)

In actual operation, <Ctrl>-<F3> clears the screen and prints 'Path and file name for source file:' (lines 120-121). The cursor freezes and waits for input from the keyboard. As soon as this input is received, 'Destination directory: \' is printed on the screen, and the routine waits for additional input (line 122). As soon as the destination directory is entered, the routine copies the file to the destination directory and erases it from the source directory (lines 123-124). The final step is verification that the operation has taken place (lines 125-126).

The <F5> key serves as a fast access key for PHONE.BAS, a program that uses a modem to dial and redial the telephone (see "Smartmodem Gets Smarter" in Chapter 6). The assignments to <F5>, <Alt>-<F5>, and <Shift>-<F5> are made in lines 87-88, 145-146, and 112-113 respectively. Each of these keys calls up a batch file similar to the following:

```
PROKEY/C
FLIP NUM ON
BASICA PHONE-B
PROKEY STD.PRO/R
FLIP NUM OFF
CLS
TYPE \STD.DOC
```

The commands in this file clear all *ProKey* assignments, invoke Tom Foth's *Flip Lock* assembly language program to make the numeric keypad indicate number values rather than cursor movements (see "Flip Lock," *.*, this chapter) and then run one of the telephone programs. When you exit from the telephone program, the remaining commands restore the *ProKey* assignments, turn the number keys off, clear the screen, and display the Main Menu.

Output Assignments

Since I have two monitors and two printers in my system, I often need to choose among output devices. The assignments to <F6> (line 90), <Alt>-<F6> (line 148), and <Ctrl>-<F6> (line 132) select monochrome, 80-column color, or 40-column color display, respectively.

Selecting a printer is a bit more difficult. Since both printers are configured for parallel output and DOS does not provide a way to switch between LPT1: and LPT2:, I use a BASIC program called *LPTSWTCH,* written by Bob Rice of Regent Data Systems, to select a printer. This program, invoked by the *ProKey* assignment to <Alt>-<F2> shown in lines 137-138, consists of:

```
10   DEF SEG = &H40
20   A = PEEK(&H8):B = PEEK(&H9)
30   C = PEEK(&HA):D = PEEK(&HB)
40   POKE &H8,C:POKE &H9,D
50   POKE &HA,A:POKE &HB,B
60   LPT$ = "NEC":IF A = &H78 THEN
        LPT$ = "EPSON"
70   PRINT "The " + LPT$ + " is now the
        active printer."
80   SYSTEM
```

The assignments to <F4> (lines 83-85), <Alt>-<F4> (lines 142-143), <Ctrl>-<F4> (lines 129-130), and <Shift>-<F4> (lines 109-110) all invoke short BASIC programs related to printer operations. <F4> invokes a one-line program called FORMFEED:

```
10   LPRINT CHR$(12):SYSTEM
```

This program produces a form feed on both the NEC/SELLUM and the Epson FX-80 printers. The *ProKey* assignment here concludes with a display of the Main Menu.

The assignments to

```
10 ON ERROR GOTO 20:LPRINT CHR$(27);"@";CHR$(27);"M";:SYSTEM
20 KEY OFF:COLOR 15,7:LOCATE 12,10:BEEP
30 PRINT "TURN THE PRINTER ON, DUMMY! Press <Enter> when ready.";
40 BEEP:LINE INPUT D$
50 COLOR 7,0:CLS:RESUME
```

Figure 7.18 *ELITE.BAS*

```
10 ON ERROR GOTO 20:LPRINT CHR$(27);"@";CHR$(27);CHR$(15);:SYSTEM
20 KEY OFF:COLOR 15,7:LOCATE 12,10:BEEP
30 PRINT "TURN THE PRINTER ON, DUMMY! Press <Enter> when ready.";
40 BEEP:LINE INPUT D$
50 COLOR 7,0:CLS:RESUME
```

Figure 7.19 *CONDENSE.BAS*

```
10 ON ERROR GOTO 20:LPRINT CHR$(27);"@";CHR$(27);"P";:SYSTEM
20 KEY OFF:COLOR 15,7:LOCATE 12,10:BEEP
30 PRINT "TURN THE PRINTER ON, DUMMY! Press <Enter> when ready.";
40 BEEP:LINE INPUT D$
50 COLOR 7,0:CLS:RESUME
```

Figure 7.20 *PICA.BAS*

<Alt>-<F4>, <Ctrl>-<F4>, and <Shift>-<F4> control the type style of the Epson FX-80. <Alt>-<F4> causes the Epson to produce elite type by calling the program ELITE.BAS (see Figure 7.18). Condensed type is produced by the CONDENSE.BAS program invoked by <Ctrl>-<F4> (see Figure 7.19). Pica type is produced by the PICA.BAS program called by <Shift>-<F4> (see Figure 7.20). With the exception of ELITE.BAS, these programs should also work for the Epson MX-80, MX-100, and the IBM dot matrix printers.

The remaining assignments in the Main Menu simply save typing effort. <Shift>-<F8> (lines 115-116 in Figure 7.17) invokes the DOS print queue program. <F9> (line 100), <F10> (line 102), <Alt>-<F9> (line 163), and <Alt>-<F10> (line 165) type the drive identifiers for two floppy disks (A and B) and two hard disks (C and D).

WordStar Simplified

All other assignments in the STD.PRO file (lines 1-67) deal with applications programs. Many of the word processing macros shown in Figure 7.16 are designed to compensate for *WordStar*'s deficiencies. It is necessary, for example, to keep two versions of *WordStar* on line, each configured to support a different printer, because there is no way to select a printer from within the program. Thus, <Alt>-A (lines 1-3 in Figure 7.17), after calling a BASIC program to force the Epson printer into elite mode, calls the batch file WS-EPSON.BAT. This batch program then calls a copy of WS.COM (the main *WordStar* program) that has been installed for an IBM Parallel Printer and renamed WS-EPSON.COM. The complete batch program consists of:

```
PROKEY WS.PRO/R
CD \WP
WS-EPSON
CD \
PROKEY STD.PRO/R
CLS
TYPE STD.DOC
```

The first command replaces the *ProKey* standard set with a special set of assignments designed to tame *WordStar*'s syntax. Since *WordStar* lacks the capacity to use DOS 2.00's tree-structured directories, the next command moves all operations to a word processing subdirectory (WP) that contains the *WordStar* command files, overlays, and text files. Calling WS-EPSON engages the properly configured command file for word processing operations. At the conclu-

```
10 INPUT "INPUT FILE NAME->";I$
20 INPUT "OUTPUT FILE NAME->";O$
30 OPEN "I",1,I$
40 OPEN "O",2,O$
50 A$=INPUT$(1,1):IF ASC(A$)>127 THEN A$=CHR$(ASC(A$)-128)
60 PRINT #2,A$;
70 IF EOF(1)=O THEN 50
80 CLOSE
90 PRINT "DONE...":BEEP
```

Figure 7.21 *ASCON*

sion of the *WordStar* session, the batch file moves all operations back to the root directory, restores the *ProKey* assignments, clears the screen, and displays the Main Menu. Thanks to *ProKey,* all this is accomplished with a single keystroke.

<Alt>-<B> (lines 5-6) calls the batch file WS-NEC.BAT. The only difference between this program and WS-EPSON.BAT is that it calls for a different copy of WS.COM that has been installed for an NEC 5510/5520 Spinwriter, and renamed WS-NEC.COM.

The assignments to <Alt>-<C> and <Alt>-<D> (lines 8-11 and 13-16) go to the word processing subdirectory and engage a spelling checker, *Proofreader,* and a grammar checker, *Grammatik.* Like *WordStar,* these programs cannot make use of tree-structured directories, so all spelling and grammar operations take place in the word processing subdirectory.

The assignment to <Alt>-E (lines 18-19 in Figure 7.17) resolves another *WordStar* problem. Although the documentation gives the impression that *WordStar* can produce a readable ASCII output file, that is simply not the case. Any attempt to print a *WordStar* document to a file (unless the document was created in nondocument mode) produces character salad. The ASCON program invoked by <Alt>-E makes *WordStar* files readable (see Figure 7.21).

<Alt>-<F> (lines 21-22 in Figure 7.17) invokes a convenient BASIC program for adding names to the *MailMerge* data file ADDR.DAT. This program is called ADDNAMES.BAS (see Figure 7.22).

Although my system has hard disks, I use floppies to archive text files. Thus, I frequently want to load a set of files into the word processing subdirectory to modify them. <Alt>-G (lines 24-28 in Figure 7.17) invokes a simple utility to perform this transfer. The statement in line 25, "When the cursor gets fat . . . ," refers to a helpful *ProKey* feature. Whenever the program is waiting for keyboard input, the cursor automatically grows fat to indicate that nothing will happen until there is appropriate keyboard activity.

The final word processing utility, assigned to <Alt>-H (lines 30-36), brings files from personal user subdirectories into the word processing subdirectory. This routine exists to compensate, again, for *WordStar*'s inability to deal with tree-structured directories.

The routine illustrates another of *ProKey*'s features, the ability to wait for fixed field input from the keyboard. Since both users of my system have names that are four characters long, the *ProKey* macro was set up to continue immediately after receiving the fourth character of the user's name. This fixed field operation is generated by the <ffld> (fixed field) commands in line 35.

When a *ProKey* macro is entered dynamically from the keyboard, <Ctrl>-] produces <ffld> in the string. Line 35 was generated by typing:

COPY \WP\ <Ctrl>-] Space Space Space Space <Ctrl>-]\ <Ctrl>-<hyphen> <Ctrl>-<hyphen>.* \WP <Enter>

The use of <Ctrl>-] and <Ctrl>-<hyphen> generated the fixed and variable field delimiters in the string.

This use of fixed fields is a relatively trivial application of a powerful function. Other applications include the ability to have one-key responses to menu items (similar to the INKEY$ function in BASIC), multiple-key responses to menu items without the need for a carriage return, and routines that transfer files from electronic to physical disk while in a word processing program.

The assignments in lines 38-64 for <Alt>-I through <Alt>-R call batch files for various applications programs that I use frequently. The assignments to <Alt>-O and <Alt>-T for the personal finance programs have not yet been implemented because their copy-protection schemes prevent using them with a hard disk. They will be updated if and when the programs are revised. The final assignment

```
1000 KEY OFF
1010 OPEN "ADDR.DAT" FOR APPEND AS 1
1020 CLS:PRINT "ENTER '***' TO EXIT PROGRAM AFTER LAST ENTRY."
1030 FOR I=1 TO 5
1040 LOCATE 4+I,1
1050 PRINT "ADDRESS LINE";I;"- ";
1060 LINE INPUT A$(I):IF LEFT$(A$(I),3)="***" THEN 1110
1070 NEXT
1080 LINE INPUT "SALUTATION (Include , or :) - ";A$(6)
1090 WRITE #1,A$(1),A$(2),A$(3),A$(4),A$(5),A$(6)
1100 GOTO 1020
1110 CLOSE
1120 CLS:SYSTEM
```

Figure 7.22 *ADDNAMES.BAS*

(lines 66-67) allows me to clear the screen in DOS by striking the <Home> key.

Looking at the Main Menu and the Applications Menu in Figures 7.15 and 7.16, it becomes apparent that *ProKey* has integrated close to 50 commands and programs into a single, coherent system. It makes no difference that the software comes from many authors and sources. The *ProKey* front end combined with various batch files simply calls on the programs as needed. There is no need for reference cards and documentation to remember how to engage a program.

The front end described here represents my personal taste. Although bits and pieces of it may be helpful to others, few will want to adopt the complete front end without modification. The beauty of a program like *ProKey* is that you don't have to adopt my system as a whole. You can choose any aspect that you like and then embellish it with your own creations. In addition, the program can work from within many applications programs, allowing you to make and reuse macro definitions at will. *ProKey* helps you turn the PC into a very personal computer.

Burton L. Alperson, Ph.D., is a professor in the psychology department at California State University at Los Angeles. He is also a Contributing Editor to PC World *magazine and Director of Training and Development at Regent Data Systems in Los Angeles. This article was originally published in* PC World *Volume 2, Number 1.*

. Star-Dot-Star

Although your operating system translates your typed English instructions into electronic machine code, operating system commands can be cumbersome and confusing. The following tips can improve your resident translator's usefulness. For example, if you've searched through a hard disk full of subdirectories without finding your file, try "File Finder" for quick relief. "Hard Disk Organization" provides menu access to application files through batch file programming. "Defensive Disk Driving" and "Greasing the Pipe" are steps you can take to lessen disk drive wear and provide faster "pipe" activity, respectively. "Build a Better Blanker" offers a useful program that will automatically darken your PC's display when it's not in use, and "Say What You Mean" will prevent you from accidentally formatting your data-packed hard disk. Then "Key Reassignments with Debug" shows how you can create powerful command files to redefine the keyboard in as many ways as you desire. Finally, "Flip Lock" gives you a BASIC program that enables you to change the status of the <NumLock> and <CapsLock> keys and to switch between color and monochrome monitors.

File Finder

With over 500 files in 21 subdirectories on my hard disk, I frequently forget where any particular file is located. I use the command **CHKDSK/V ¦ FIND** *filename.ext* to track them down. When CHKDSK is invoked with the /V option, it lists all the files with their directory names in uppercase letters. By piping the output to the DOS filter FIND instead of to the screen, I can search for any file (by placing the file name and the extension in uppercase letters between the double quotation marks) or group of files (by placing just an extension in uppercase letters between the double quotation marks), or list portions of the directory tree (by placing the name of the directory in uppercase letters between the double marks). And the output can be redirected to the printer by appending the characters >**PRN**.

Jim Weisz
Lombard, Illinois

Editor's note: CHKDSK.COM and FIND.EXE must be in the current directory of the default drive or in a directory available via PATH. Also, you can save yourself a few keystrokes by creating the following one-line batch file (called LOCATE.BAT):

```
CHKDSK /V ¦ FIND "%1"
```

Now you can just type **LOCATE** string, *where* string *is the file(s), extension, or directory you want to find. You must still enter* string *in uppercase letters but without the double quotation marks.*

Hard Disk Organization

Over the last two years I've helped numerous friends and business acquaintances install software on hard disks and networks. In doing so I developed a simple method of creating menus using batch files so that these people could access numerous pieces of software without having to remember the startup commands for each one. Because I used standard PC-DOS batch commands, these people are able to modify their own menus with EDLIN or a standard word processor, eliminating the need for any maintenance on my part.

As an example, let's assume that we have an IBM XT (with the hard disk as drive C), *WordStar, 1-2-3, dBASE II,* and DOS. We also have an AST Combo-Plus board with clock software. First, using the CHANGE DIRECTORY command we make sure the current directory is the root directory:

```
C>CD \
```

Using the MAKE DIRECTORY command, we make subdirectories for each of the packages:

```
C>MD WS
C>MD LOTUS
C>MD DBASE
C>MD DOS
```

We copy all the files from the disks of each package to the appropriate subdirectory on the IBM XT:

```
C>COPY A:*.* C:\WS
C>COPY A:*.* C:\LOTUS
C>COPY A:*.* C:\DBASE
C>COPY A:*.* C:\DOS
```

We also need, in the root directory, the utility to set the system date and time:

```
C>COPY A:ASTCLOCK.COM C:\
```

Now we create the following AUTOEXEC batch file. It will set the system date and time and put us in the DOS subdirectory, which I consider "home base."

```
C>COPY CON: AUTOEXEC.BAT
ECHO OFF
CLS
ASTCLOCK
CD \DOS
MENU
<F6>
```

Note that the line with the command MENU calls a batch file that displays the menu. This batch file resides in the DOS subdirectory, as do all of our menu choices. Now we create MENU.BAT:

```
C>CD \DOS
C>COPY CON: MENU.BAT
ECHO OFF
CLS
TYPE MENU.TXT
<F6>
```

MENU.TXT is a text file containing a list of the software available on the system. By creating a separate file for the actual display of choices, we don't need to use messy REM statements and we never have to modify MENU.BAT. The text file can also contain Christmas messages, shutdown notices, and so on. The text file should look like this:

```
C>COPY CON: MENU.TXT
XYZ SYSTEM
TYPE 1 For WordStar
     2 For 1-2-3
     3 For dBASE II
     4 For DOS CHKDSK
<F6>
```

If we boot the XT now, the screen will clear and the text file above will be printed on the screen. We still must create the actual batch files to do the work:

```
C>COPY CON:1.BAT

ECHO OFF
CD \WS
WS
CD \DOS
MENU
<F6>

C>COPY CON: 2.BAT
ECHO OFF
CD \LOTUS
LOTUS
CD \DOS
MENU
<F6>

C>COPY CON: 3.BAT
ECHO OFF
CD \DBASE
DBASE
CD \DOS
MENU
<F6>

C>COPY CON: 4.BAT
ECHO OFF
CHKDSK
MENU
<F6>
```

Those batch files complete the task. Whenever you turn on the XT, the system displays the menu. When you type 1, the system changes directories to WS and loads *WordStar.* After you exit *WordStar,* the batch is still active and you are taken back to the DOS subdirectory, where the menu is displayed again. To add another item to the menu, just edit MENU.TXT and add a file called 5.BAT.

Mike Falkner
Orangevale, California

Editor's note: Further organization may be achieved by placing the batch files and MENU.TXT in another subdirectory (e.g., \BATCH) instead of keeping these files in the \DOS subdirectory. If this is done, two other changes to Mr. Falkner's routines are needed. The AUTOEXEC.BAT file needs to contain the command 'PATH \DOS; \BATCH' after the 'CLS', so that DOS will search these subdirectories as well as the current directory for subsequent commands. The command 'TYPE MENU.TXT' in the file MENU.BAT must be changed to 'TYPE \BATCH\MENU.TXT.'

In addition, as suggested in "More PATH and PeachText" by Ms. Liskin (Chapter 2), if the PATH command also included the path \WS; the menu choices and their associated batch files could be arranged to change to some subdirectory (e.g., \MEMOS or \LETTERS) and then call WordStar *without needing to*

```
echo off
ramdisk c: >nul
copy continue.bat c: >nul
c:continue
```

Figure 7.23 *RAMBATCH.BAT*

change to the WS subdirectory. This practice not only keeps your documents in a directory other than the one holding your word processor, it also allows different kinds of documents to be kept in different directories.

Defensive Disk Driving

I find that I put lots of commands into my AUTOEXEC.BAT files. Between asking the clock what time it is and setting up the serial port, print spooler, and disk emulator, most of the batch files are 10 to 15 lines long. The problem is that the long batch files result in a lot of disk drive head movement as DOS reads a line from the batch file, executes the command, and then goes back to read another line. I've adopted the following technique to help guard my disk drives from excessive wear.

As shown in Figure 7.23, RAMBATCH.BAT, my AUTOEXEC.BAT files create a disk emulator, copy a batch file containing the remainder of the start-up commands into the disk emulator, and then transfer execution to that file. The secondary batch file is read from the floppy disk in one large block rather than line by line; the results are less disk activity and faster operation.

Notice the characters '>nul' after each command in the batch file. They cause the screen output to be suppressed. I use them to prevent messages such as '1 file(s) copied' from appearing after an ECHO OFF command has been issued.

The I/O redirection feature of DOS 2.00 can also be used to provide a much more powerful form of batch processing. The commands shown in COMMANDS.BAT cause a secondary copy of the DOS command interpreter (COMMAND.COM) to take control and to receive its input from a disk file instead of from the keyboard.

Passing control in this way is especially useful because data is taken from the disk file in place of all keyboard input, including responses to the prompts of other programs. I use the extension .SPL for these files to distinguish them from batch files because some lines in .SPL files are commands, but other lines are the responses to program prompts.

The last line in the file must be the EXIT command. This is very important because the secondary copy of COMMAND.COM will take its input only from the disk file. Without the EXIT command there doesn't seem to be any way to regain control short of rebooting.
Jon Shemitz
Ben Lomond, California

Editor's note: Loading a secondary copy of COMMAND.COM consumes about 17K of RAM.

Greasing the Pipe

Pipes in DOS 2.00, such as SORT and MORE, are useful but slow because any intermediate output is written to the default disk drive. If you have an emulated disk on your PC, the COMMAND.COM patch described below will route intermediate output (%PIPE*x*.$$$) to your emulated (electronic) disk (drive C in the example), resulting in a great increase in speed. The patch replaces an ADD instruction used in computing the default drive with a MOV instruction that inserts the desired drive letter.

First, copy COMMAND.COM from a DOS 2.00 disk to another disk so you can patch the copy, not the original. Assuming that the disk to be patched is in drive B and DEBUG is on the disk in drive A, issue the following commands (your typed input is in boldface; remember to press <Enter> at the end of each line input):

```
A> DEBUG B:COMMAND.COM
-D 1869 L2
xxxx:1869 04 41
-F 1869 L2 B0 "C"
-W
Writing 4500 bytes
-Q
```

The 'C' above indicates drive C. You may, of course, designate a different emulated drive. Now, with the patched disk in drive A, reboot the system and "install" your emulated drive. For a comparison, try the following, using both the standard and patched version with a large disk directory: **DIR|SORT|MORE**

Larry Bradley
Orleans, Ontario

Editor's note: Be sure to set up your emulated disk drive before using the pipes SORT or MORE under the patched version of COMMAND.COM. Otherwise, the new COMMAND.COM tries to write the sorted directory to a nonexistent drive and then issues the 'Not ready reading drive C' prompt. At this point the system will not abort; a system reset is necessary.

Build a Better Blanker

Concerning the program BLANK.COM (*.*, *PC World,* Vol. 2, No. 4), it might interest you to know that some of the information provided by the author was, to say the least, incorrect.

The author said the program was incompatible with BASIC, and indeed it was, but that was not BASIC's fault. He also implies that the screen would switch to page 7 after 5 minutes of elapsed time. Well, the counter was set to 01F4H, which equals 500 decimal and corresponds to 27½ seconds.

The most important problem is that the interrupt routine does not restore the DS register. Therefore, at times the DS register is set to a value that causes the system's memory to be modified randomly. Correcting the program to preserve the DS register will cause it to work as it should, and under BASIC, too. However, an even more subtle problem stands out when the delay to blank the screen has been reduced to 27½ seconds.

Assume that you have a long job to run, one that takes more time than the delay time before the screen goes blank. The screen switches to page 7 (actually page 3 in 80-character mode) and sits there waiting for you to return from your coffee break and press a key. If the job has a few errors, however, they are displayed on the screen because page 7 is active. You come back, see the errors, and decide to fix them. As soon as you touch the keyboard (even the key to print the screen), page 7 goes away and the errors remain a mystery until the screen goes blank again. (It won't actually be blank, since the errors will be displayed.)

Therefore, the program should check to see not only if you type on the keyboard but also if a character is sent to the screen. Before a character is sent to the screen, the program should switch back to the original screen page.

Finally, one last problem. Sometimes when I type a character, say the first character of the command DIR, the screen shows nothing. Why? Because the keyboard is checked only 18.2 times per second. If a key is pressed at the beginning of that cycle, the keyboard routine sets a flag until the routine is over. In the meantime, the system has processed the *D* and sent it to screen page 7, but you won't see it because the screen page will be changed too quickly. The system still recognizes that *D* as part of your command, and although the line will read 'A>IR', the command will work. If you notice the missing *D* and backspace to correct the line, the internal command will be DDIR, which will not work. I fixed that problem by forcing an interrupt to restore the screen.

The result of my work is the program BLANK2.ASM. I used the standard DOS function calls to get and set interrupt vectors, and I used the series 60H vectors because the manual states that they are "reserved for user software interrupts," and I'm a user. I have a lot of memory in my PC, so I did not bother to optimize the memory requirements of my program. And since nobody is perfect, there may be errors in this program, too.

In conclusion, let me give ample credit to Christopher Wiley for his program, for I often thought about the wear on the screen, but the idea of his program did not occur to me. Leonardo da Vinci and the Wright brothers all deserve credit for their

```
;     ------------------------------------------------------------
;     Program BLANK2.COM to blank the screen after two minutes of
;     inactivity.  This program by Gerard Perreault is based on
;     the program BLANK.COM submitted by Christopher Wiley in
;     PC World Volume 2, Number 4.  Modified by Steve Cook 1-JUN-84.
;     ------------------------------------------------------------

; Define the code segment, and set things up for a .COM program

CSEG     segment para public 'CODE'
         assume cs:CSEG,ds:CSEG

; Programs which are to be put through EXE2BIN must start at address
; 100H, so...

         org     100H

START:   jmp     GO               ; jump around the data area

SWFLAG   db      0                ; video not switched off (1 if we did)
KEYFLAG  db      0                ; no key input nor display since video off
COUNT    dw      0                ; timer count

addr_6845        equ     63H      ; CRT control port base address
crt_mode_set     equ     65H      ; current state of CRT mode register

GO:
         mov     ah,35H           ; get address at 1C vector (timer 18.2
         mov     al,1CH           ; times per second frequency)
         int     21H
         push    es               ; move ES:BX to DS:DX
         push    bx
         pop     dx
         pop     ds
         mov     ah,25H           ; set into interrupt 60H as replacement
         mov     al,60H
         int     21H

         mov     ah,35H           ; Do same for keyboard interrupt
         mov     al,09H
         int     21H
         push    es
         push    bx
         pop     dx
         pop     ds
         mov     ah,25H
         mov     al,61H
         int     21H

         mov     ah,35H           ; Do same for video interrupt
         mov     al,10H
         int     21H
         push    es
```

Figure 7.24 *BLANK2.ASM*

work on flying machines. My advice is, come up with great ideas, and someone else will improve on them.
Gerard Perreault
Quebec, Canada

Editor's note: Indeed, Mr. Perreault's program has already been improved. As originally supplied, the program switched the display to screen page 7 after 2 minutes of inactivity. Unfortunately, only the color graphics board supports that screen page. Therefore, as published here, BLANK2.ASM (see Figure 7.24) has been modified to turn off the video enable bit of the CRT controller

```
        push    bx
        pop     dx
        pop     ds
        mov     ah,25H
        mov     al,62H
        int     21H

        push    cs                ; now set new values in the vectors
        pop     ds                ; 1CH, 09H, and 10H
        mov     dx,offset TICKER
        mov     ah,25H
        mov     al,1CH            ; ... as TICKER
        int     21H

        push    cs
        pop     ds
        mov     dx,offset KEY_IN
        mov     ah,25H
        mov     al,09H            ; ... as KEY_IN
        int     21H

        push    cs
        pop     ds
        mov     dx,offset VIDEO_OUT
        mov     ah,25H
        mov     al,10H            ; ... as VIDEO_OUT
        int     21H

        mov     dx,(offset END_PR)+100H ; Finished, leave resident and
        int     27H     ; add more room than needed to avoid INT 27H bug

; Process the 1CH interrupt which occurs 18.2 times per second
TICKER:
        sti                       ; restore interrupts
        push    ax                ; save some registers
        push    ds
        push    cs                ; set the DS register the same as CS
        pop     ds
        cmp     swflag,0          ; have we switched the video off?
        jne     t01               ; yes.
        inc     count             ; no, keep counting the clock pulses
        cmp     count,0888H       ; until we get to 2 minutes
        jnae    t02               ; by the way, did we hit the limit?
        mov     count,0           ; yes, reset the count and
        push    dx                ; save these registers, too
        push    es                ; Now to switch the video off...
        mov     ax,0040H          ; (base address of ROM data area)
        mov     es,ax
        mov     dx,es:addr_6845 ; Get base address of the video controller
        add     dx,4              ; point to controller's mode register
        mov     al,es:crt_mode_set ; Get current mode settings
```

(continues)

Figure 7.24 *(continued)*

chip, a technique that works with either type of display. Pressing the <Shift>, <Alt>, or <Ctrl> key will restore the screen without sending a character to the computer.

The data lines in Figure 7.25, BLANK2.DAT, can be MERGEd with XMAKER.BAS (see "XMAKER," Chapter 8) to create this new and improved version of BLANK.COM. Be aware that BLANK.COM should be run only once each time the PC has been turned on or rebooted. If you attempt to run the program a second time, the system will lock up and require that you turn the PC off and then on again. Also, this version of BLANK.COM does not work with Compiled BASIC programs.

```
        and     al,11110111B    ; Clear the video enable bit to
        out     dx,al           ; turn off the video.
        pop     es
        pop     dx
        mov     swflag,1        ; flag that we have switched off
        jmp     short t02       ; standard exit.
t01:
        cmp     keyflag,0       ; We have switched off.  Has a key been
                                ; pressed or attempt been made to display a
        je      t02             ; character since then?  No.
        push    dx              ; Yes.  Restore the video signal
        push    es
        mov     ax,0040H        ; First, point to the ROM data area
        mov     es,ax
        mov     dx,es:addr_6845 ; Get base address of video controller
        add     dx,4            ; and point to controller mode register
        mov     al,es:crt_mode_set ; Get the old mode settings and
        out     dx,al              ; restore them.
        pop     es
        pop     dx
        mov     keyflag,0       ; Reset the flags as: No key in/video
        mov     swflag,0        ; not switched
        mov     count,0         ; reset (again) count to 0
t02:
        pop     ds              ; standard exit.  Restore used registers
        pop     ax              ; and process whatever was
        int     60H             ; at int 1CH before this
        iret                    ; program came into action.

; The user has pressed a key...
KEY_IN:
        sti                     ; restore interrupts
        push    ax              ; save the registers which we will use
        push    ds
        push    cs              ; set DS to the same as CS
        pop     ds
        cmp     swflag,0        ; Are we already switched off?
        je      k01             ; No.
        mov     keyflag,1       ; Yes. Set the flag that we got a key
        int     1CH
k01:
        mov     count,0         ; reset count to 0
        pop     ds              ; restore the saved register and inform
        pop     ax              ; the system by causing the equivalent
        int     61H             ; of an int 09H in this program.
        iret
```

(continues)

Figure 7.24 *(continued)*

Say What You Mean

The patch FORMATFIX2 (see Figure 7.26) modifies FORMAT.COM so that it requires a drive specification. If you type the command **FORMAT** without specifying a drive, the program terminates with the message 'Invalid Drive Specification'.

James Morgan
Orlando, Florida

Editor's note: Remember, while this patch has been tested, we cannot guarantee that your version of FORMAT.COM is identical to ours. Please exercise caution if you elect

```
; The system wants to output to the screen...
VIDEO_OUT:
        sti                     ; restore interrupts
        push    ax              ; save registers
        push    ds
        push    cs              ; make DS the same as CS
        pop     ds
        cmp     swflag,0        ; Have we switched the video off?
        je      v01             ; No.
        mov     keyflag,1       ; Yes. Flag that we want video on
        int     1CH
v01:    mov     count,0         ; reset the count to 0
        pop     ds              ; restore registers
        pop     ax
        int     62H             ; process the video request
        iret

END_PR:                         ; used to determine length of program

CSEG    ends
        end     start
```

Figure 7.24 *(continued)*

```
1000 DATA "blank.com"
1010 DATA 1,EB,05,90,00,00,00,00,B4,35,B0,1C,CD,21,06,53,5A,-1,8E
1020 DATA 2,1F,B4,25,B0,60,CD,21,B4,35,B0,09,CD,21,06,53,5A,-1,09
1030 DATA 3,1F,B4,25,B0,61,CD,21,B4,35,B0,10,CD,21,06,53,5A,-1,DA
1040 DATA 4,1F,B4,25,B0,62,CD,21,0E,1F,BA,5D,01,B4,25,B0,1C,-1,71
1050 DATA 5,CD,21,0E,1F,BA,CC,01,B4,25,B0,09,CD,21,0E,1F,BA,-1,33
1060 DATA 6,EA,01,B4,25,B0,10,CD,21,BA,08,03,CD,27,FB,50,1E,-1,4B
1070 DATA 7,0E,1F,80,3E,03,01,00,75,31,FF,06,05,01,81,3E,05,-1,1B
1080 DATA 8,01,88,08,72,52,C7,06,05,01,00,00,52,06,B8,40,00,-1,8D
1090 DATA 9,8E,C0,26,8B,16,63,00,83,C2,04,26,A0,65,00,24,F7,-1,A6
1100 DATA 10,EE,07,5A,C6,06,03,01,01,EB,2D,80,3E,04,01,00,74,-1,FB
1110 DATA 11,26,52,06,B8,40,00,8E,C0,26,8B,16,63,00,83,C2,04,-1,B4
1120 DATA 12,26,A0,65,00,EE,07,5A,C6,06,04,01,00,C6,06,03,01,-1,E0
1130 DATA 13,00,C7,06,05,01,00,00,1F,58,CD,60,CF,FB,50,1E,0E,-1,7C
1140 DATA 14,1F,80,3E,03,01,00,74,07,C6,06,04,01,01,CD,1C,C7,-1,A8
1150 DATA 15,06,05,01,00,00,1F,58,CD,61,CF,FB,50,1E,0E,1F,80,-1,E0
1160 DATA 16,3E,03,01,00,74,07,C6,06,04,01,01,CD,1C,C7,06,05,-1,47
1170 DATA 17,01,00,00,1F,58,CD,62,CF,-1,02,-1
```

Figure 7.25 *BLANK2.DAT*

to use these modifications. Do not modify your only copy of FORMAT.COM; test the program after you have patched it to be sure that it works properly. If your computer has a hard disk, don't test anything until you have made a backup.

Key Reassignments Using DEBUG

Readers without the Macro Assembler can enjoy the benefits of Larry Axsom's key redefinition pro-

```
For DOS 2.00:

A> DATE 12/12/2012
A> DEBUG FORMAT.COM
- E169 EB F5 90 90
- W
Writing xxxx bytes
- Q
A>

For DOS 2.10:

A> DATE 12/12/2012
A> DEBUG FORMAT.COM
- E174 EB F5 90 90
- W
Writing xxxx bytes
- Q
A>

For DOS 3.00:

A> DATE 12/12/2012
A> DEBUG FORMAT.COM
- E648 EB D5 90 90
- W
Writing xxxx bytes
- Q
A>
```

Figure 7.26 *FORMATFIX2: A patch that modifies FORMAT.COM to require that the user specify which drive contains the disk to be formatted.*

gram ("ANSI.SYS Key Reassignment," *.*, *PC World,* Vol. 2, No. 6) by using the DOS 2.*xx* version of DEBUG to assemble the necessary statements.

KEYDEFS (Figure 7.27) shows the screen output as you use this technique to create the file MYKEYS.COM, which redefines the keys <F1> through <F10>, <Alt>-1, and <Alt>-0. You can create a file to implement your own set of key definitions by entering the four assembly statements followed by as many lines of characters as are needed for your function key definitions. After the definitions are entered, add the line **DB'$'**, which adds a dollar sign, used by DOS to mark the end of text to be output.

When you have typed this line, press the <Enter> key twice to get the hyphen prompt. Use the Unassemble and Dump commands to verify that you have entered the assembly language statements and key definitions correctly. After the lines have been entered correctly, use the Name command to assign a file name ending with the .COM extension.

Use the command **R CX** to display the contents of register CX and enter the length of the program in response to the colon prompt. The program's length is the offset value that appears on the line below the '$' entry, minus 100 hexadecimal. In KEYDEFS the value is 01D1, so MYKEYS.COM is 00D1 bytes long. The W command writes the newly entered program on the disk with the name you selected earlier, stating the number of bytes being written.

The Quit command returns control to DOS. You can use the Quit command any time you have the hyphen prompt, but everything you have entered will be lost unless you first use the Write command to store it on disk. The Quit command is a good way to stop everything and start over if you have made mistakes. The DOS manual explains more about how to use DEBUG.
Michael J. Grabel
Windsor, Connecticut

Editor's note: This is perhaps the fastest way to implement new key definitions. You may want to create several such .COM files to define various keys as needed.

Flip Lock

One of the most conspicuous failings of the PC keyboard is the lack of indicators regarding the status of the <CapsLock> and the <NumLock> keys. Why else would people keep trying to come up with the definitive way of correcting the problem? If you're willing to type 384 bytes worth of data statements, you can create a DOS.COM file to do the job.

Figure 7.28 is a BASIC program that creates a program file called FLIP.COM. Enter the program while in BASICA to make it run. After entering line 340, be sure that the DOS disk is in drive A and that the write-protect tab is removed. Then either press <F2> or type **RUN** <**Enter**>. If a message appears saying 'Checksum error; verify data statements', a mistake has been made entering the numbers in lines 260 through 286. Otherwise a new file will have been created on the DOS disk called FLIP.COM.

Now go back to DOS by typing **SYSTEM** and run the new program. It can be used by entering any of the following command lines:

FLIP CAP ON sets keyboard to uppercase letters.

```
A>DEBUG <Enter>
-A 100 <Enter>
xxxx:0100 MOV  AH,9 <Enter>
xxxx:0102 MOV  DX,109 <Enter>
xxxx:0105 INT  21 <Enter>
xxxx:0107 INT  20 <Enter>
xxxx:0109 DB 1B'[0;59;"DIR "p' <Enter>
xxxx:0117 DB 1B'[0;60;"DIR /W"p' <Enter>
xxxx:0127 DB 1B'[0;61;"*."p' <Enter>
xxxx:0133 DB 1B'[0;62;".* ";13p' <Enter>
xxxx:0143 DB 1B'[0;63;"COPY "p' <Enter>
xxxx:0152 DB 1B'[0;64;"ERASE "p' <Enter>
xxxx:0162 DB 1B'[0;65;"EAZE ";13p' <Enter>
xxxx:0174 DB 1B'[0;66;"BASIC ";13p' <Enter>
xxxx:0187 DB 1B'[0;67;"MORE <"p' <Enter>
xxxx:0197 DB 1B'[0;68;"EDIT "p' <Enter>
xxxx:01A6 DB 1B'[0;120;"MYKEYS ";13p' <Enter>
xxxx:01BB DB 1B'[0;129;"NOKEYS ";13p' <Enter>
xxxx:01D0 DB '$' <Enter>
xxxx:01D1 <Enter>
-U 100 108 <Enter>
xxxx:0100 B409          MOV     AH,09
xxxx:0102 BA0901        MOV     DX,0109
xxxx:0105 CD21          INT     21
xxxx:0107 CD20          INT     20
-D 109 1D0 <Enter>
xxxx:0109  1B 5B 30 3B 35 39 3B                                  .[0;59;
xxxx:0110  22 44 49 52 20 22 70 1B-5B 30 3B 36 30 3B 22 44   "DIR "p.[0;60;"D
xxxx:0120  49 52 20 2F 57 22 70 1B-5B 30 3B 36 31 3B 22 2A   IR /W"p.[0;61;"*
xxxx:0130  2E 22 70 1B 5B 30 3B 36-32 3B 22 2E 2A 20 22 3B   ."p.[0;62;".* ";
xxxx:0140  31 33 70 1B 5B 30 3B 36-33 3B 22 43 4F 50 59 20   13p.[0;63;*"COPY
xxxx:0150  22 70 1B 5B 30 3B 36 34-3B 22 45 52 41 53 45 20   "p.[0;64;"ERASE
xxxx:0160  22 70 1B 5B 30 3B 36 35-3B 22 45 41 5A 45 20 22   "p.[0;65;"EAZE "
xxxx:0170  3B 31 33 70 1B 5B 30 3B-36 36 3B 22 42 41 53 49   ;13p.[0;66;"BASI
xxxx:0180  43 20 22 3B 31 33 70 1B-5B 30 3B 36 37 3B 22 40   C ";13p.[0;67;"M
xxxx:0190  4F 52 45 20 3C 22 70 1B-5B 30 3B 36 38 3B 22 45   ORE <"p.[0;68;"E
xxxx:01A0  44 49 54 20 22 70 1B 5B-30 3B 31 32 30 3B 22 4D   DIT "p.[0;120;"M
xxxx:01B0  59 4B 45 59 53 20 22 3B-31 33 70 1B 5B 30 3B 31   YKEYS ";13p.[0;1
xxxx:01C0  32 39 3B 22 4E 4F 4B 45-59 53 20 22 3B 31 33 70   29;"NOKEYS ";13p
xxxx:01D0  24                                                $
-N MYKEYS.COM <Enter>
-R BX <Enter>
BX 0000
:0 <Enter>
-R CX <Enter>
CX 0000
:D1 <Enter>
-W <Enter>
Writing 00D1 bytes
-Q <Enter>
A>
```

Figure 7.27 *KEYDEFS*

```
10 REM
20 REM This program makes the DOS command FLIP ---
30 REM
40 REM Copyright (c) 1982 Thomas J. Foth
50 REM Permission granted to copy and distribute this source with
60 REM inclusion of this notice but not for profit
70 REM
80 REM Author makes no warranty, expressed or implied, as to
90 REM the correct nature and operation of this software.
100 REM
110 REM Command syntax
120 REM
130 REM FLIP ¦NUM ¦ ¦ON ¦        - Flip numeric pad on or off
140 REM      ¦CAP ¦ ¦OFF¦        - Flip caps lock on or off
150 REM or
160 REM FLIP ¦MONO ¦             - Flip to monochrome adapter
170 REM      ¦COLOR¦     ¦40¦    - Flip to color adapter in either 40 or
180 REM                  ¦80¦      80 column mode
181 REM
182 REM
190 FOR I = 1 TO 258 : READ N : C = C + N : NEXT
200 READ N : IF n <> C THEN 330
210 RESTORE : OPEN "R",#1,"FLIP.COM",1
220 FIELD #1,1 AS N$
230 FOR I = 1 TO 258: READ N:LSET N$=CHR$(N)
240 PUT 1:NEXT:CLOSE
250 END
260 DATA 184,64,0,142,216,179,64,190,93,0,191,203,1,185,3,0,252,243,46,166
262 DATA 131,249,0,116,19,179,32,190,93,0,191,206,1,185,3,0,243,46,166,131
264 DATA 249,0,117,44,190,109,0,46,161,198,1,38,59,4,116,26,190,109,0,191
266 DATA 200,1,185,3,0,243,46,166,131,249,0,117,44,128,243,255,32,30,23,0
268 DATA 205,32,8,30,23,0,205,32,190,93,0,191,209,1,185,4,0,243,46,166
270 DATA 131,249,0,117,25,128,14,16,0,48,184,7,0,205,16,205,32,186,222,1
272 DATA 140,200,142,216,180,9,205,33,205,32,190,93,0,191,213,1,185,5,0,243
274 DATA 46,166,131,249,0,117,226,190,109,0,46,161,218,1,38,59,4,117,8,177
276 DATA 32,187,2,0,235,15,144,46,161,220,1,38,59,4,117,197,177,16,187,0
278 DATA 0,176,207,34,6,16,0,10,193,162,16,0,139,195,205,16,205,32,79,78
280 DATA 79,70,70,67,65,80,78,85,77,77,79,78,79,67,79,76,79,82,56,48
282 DATA 52,48,10,13,70,76,73,80,32,105,103,110,111,114,101,100,58,32,73,110
284 DATA 118,97,108,105,100,32,112,97,114,97,109,101,116,101,114,10,13,36
286 DATA 24871
330 PRINT "Checksum Error: verify data statements"
340 END
```

Figure 7.28 *FLIP.COM file.*

```
800 `START NUMERIC SHIFT
900 DEF SEG=&H40:B%=PEEK(&H17)B%=B% OR &H20:POKE &H17,B%
905 `START UPPER CASE SHIFT
910 DEF SEG=&H40:B%=PEEK(&H17)B%=B% OR &H40:POKE &H17,B%
915 `RESTORE CURSOR MOVEMENT SHIFT
920 DEF SEG=&H40:B%=PEEK(&H17)B%=B% AND &HDF:POKE &H17,B%
925 `RESTORE LOWER CASE SHIFT
930 DEF SEG=&H40:B%=PEEK(&H17)B%=B% AND &HBF:POKE &H17,B%
935 `SWITCH TO 40 COLUMN COLOR
940 WIDTH 80:DEF SEG=0:A=PEEK(&H410):POKE &H410,(A AND &HCF) OR
    &H20:WIDTH 40:SCREEN 1:SCREEN 0:LOCATE,,1,6,7
945 `SWITCH TO MONOCHROME DISPLAY
950 WIDTH 40:DEF SEG=0:A=PEEK(&H410):POKE &H410,A OR &H30:WIDTH
    80:LOCATE ,,1,12,13
```

Figure 7.29 *FLIP.COM for BASIC.*

FLIP CAP OFF sets keyboard to lowercase letters.
FLIP NUM ON sets numeric keypad to numbers.
FLIP NUM OFF sets numeric keypad to cursor control characters.
FLIP MONO changes default monitor to the monochrome display.
FLIP COLOR 40 changes default monitor to a 40-column color graphics display.
FLIP COLOR 80 changes default monitor to an 80-column color graphics display.

Now you might say that it's easier to reach over and press the <CapsLock> or <NumLock> key than to type in this command. That may be true; however, you still have to remember to do that. By including these commands in an AUTOEXEC.BAT file, the computer will remember to do that procedure for you. The procedure to set up an AUTOEXEC.BAT file is covered in the DOS manual. Remember that this will work in DOS only. To do the same thing in BASICA you need to include the lines in Figure 7.29 in your BASIC programs (they may be included near the beginning of your program or as a GOSUB routine elsewhere in the program).

Tom Foth
Madison, Wisconsin

8

BASIC Programming

Hands On

Computer programming is often regarded as a mysterious art whose practice is limited to white-smocked technicians, half-crazed "nerds," and teenage geniuses. In reality computer programming is scarcely more difficult than giving concise instructions. Compared to human languages, computer languages have minute vocabularies and lack the ambiguities and double meanings that make foreign languages difficult to learn. Learning just 10 or 20 computer words will allow you to create your own custom programs for almost any task you would like your computer to perform. Unlike commercial software, your own programs can be enlarged and adapted to fit your needs.

The computer language BASIC (Beginners' All-purpose Symbolic Instruction Code) is built into the PC. Its popularity as a programming language is a direct result of its ease of use. In fact, BASIC was designed for teaching computer programming skills. The BASIC language supplied with the PC is an expanded and enhanced version of the original BASIC and offers capabilities that were not available to any computer user when BASIC was first introduced.

The articles in this chapter are useful for programmers and would-be programmers alike. If you have never written a computer program, "Building a BASIC Program" will take you through the paces as you create a useful tool for counting words in documents. "Disk Data Files" explains the ins and outs of that most important aspect of computer programming, and "Optimizing for BASCOM" provides tips for squeezing the most from programs written for digestion by the BASIC compiler. If you're looking for top-notch performance, "BASIC Block Moves" has the information you'll need for ultra-fast processing of screen displays and other large blocks of data.

Remember, you can't damage your computer by typing on the keyboard. With the information provided here, you'll not only be writing programs that are useful, you'll have the satisfaction of saying "I wrote it myself." You might even show some teenage genius a thing or two.

Building a BASIC Program

Donald B. Trivette

You've had your IBM PC for several months; you've learned to run *1-2-3* and *WordStar;* you've mastered DOS, at least as far as formatting disks and backing up files; now you're ready for the fun—writing your own programs. In preparation, you've skimmed a book on BASIC and read Chapters 2 and 3 of the IBM BASIC manual. (If you haven't read these chapters, do so now.) All well and good, but how to begin?

First you need a problem to solve, one that you can do by hand or in your head. If you don't know how to solve the problem manually, you can't possibly tell a machine how to come up with the answer.

This article shows you how to write a program to count the number of words in a disk file. If the file were a typewritten report, you would start in the upper left corner of each page and count each word in each line, top to bottom, page after page. When there are no more pages, you have the answer.

Now that you know how to do it manually, which admittedly would take a dunce about one second to deduce, you can think about how to actually get started programming.

Computer programs are built, not written. Even the most experienced programmer doesn't start at the beginning and work straight through to the end. Start with the core and work outward—add a statement here, move a statement there, test a section, add a few more statements, test again, try something different. Programming is not a sequential or exact process.

When you wrote a term paper in school, you made note cards, an outline, a draft, and then the final report. Didn't you? Books that teach computer programming recommend that you write a flow chart first (the outline), and then translate that into a computer language. A good idea, but in practice most flow charts, like most outlines, get written after the program. It's human nature.

You could begin by writing statements to read records from a disk file, but that's not much fun. Input/output statements are tedious, and I always need to get out the manual to check on formats, commas, device numbers and the like. A better plan is to get the program running first with a simple statement that will provide data to test the word-counting algorithm (*algorithm* is a fancy way of saying plan or method), and worry later about getting the data from disk.

Building the Program

The following will do as a first statement to test the counting program:

```
100  A$="The quick brown fox jumped
        over the lazy dog."
```

'A$' was selected as the variable name for no other reason than that it is short and easily typed. It could just as well have been 'SENTENCE$' OR 'MYDATA$'.

In fact, if you like self-documenting programs, it probably should be something more descriptive. If you're lazy, A$ is fine. The dollar sign after the A tells BASIC that the variable will store characters rather than numbers. Variables that store characters are called string variables.

Next you'll need a statement or statements to compute how many words are in A$. That's the algorithm. Suppose you count the number of blanks. That works as long as one word is separated from another by a blank. Thus the definition of a word will be a group of characters separated by blanks. This means you will be counting things like 5280', 280Z, and 5'-9" as words. Whether this is acceptable largely depends on why you're counting words in the first place. If you are a typist paid by the word, then it's acceptable to count "$ .10" as two words.

In order to count blanks your program must find blanks. The BASIC function INSTR (IN STRing) can do that.

```
100  A$="The quick brown fox jumped
        over the lazy dog."
120  I=INSTR(J,A$," ")
```

INSTR will start looking in A$ at position J for the first occurrence of " " (blank). It will assign the position of the first blank it finds to the variable I. This seems to be what we are after, but we must give J an initial value—a place to begin looking. This can be done with the following statements:

```
100  A$="The quick brown fox jumped
        over the lazy dog."
118  J=1
120  I=INSTR(J,A$," ")
```

Just to be sure you understand how INSTR works, put a temporary print statement after line 120 (e.g., **125 PRINT I**) and run the program. The value of I should be 4—the location of the first blank. Type **RUN** and press <Enter>; you should see:

```
100  A$="The quick brown fox jumped
         over the lazy dog."
118  J=1
120  I=INSTR(J,A$,"")
125  PRINT I
RUN 4
OK
```

This last step demonstrates the value of working with an interactive language like BASIC. Whenever you are unsure of how a section of a program works, you can put in print statements temporarily and run it.

Now that you have found the first blank, you have also found the first word. The next step is to add a statement to keep count of the words—something like **W=W+1.** Initial values should go at the top of the program, so you should add these lines to produce the following:

```
20   W=0
100  A$="The quick brown fox jumped
         over the lazy dog."
118  J=1
120  I=INSTR(J,A$," ")
125  W=W+1
```

The new line 125 replaces the PRINT statement added earlier.

We are now ready to loop—to go back to line 120 and look for the next blank. If you don't make changes, the program will look for the next blank starting in position 1, and it will find the blank in 4 again. this is an example of the famous, endless loop (few things are actually endless; after a while the value of W would get so large that the computer would report an error and stop). To avoid this, set J to the value of I+1. This causes the computer to resume looking one position after where it found the last blank.

```
20   W=0
100  A$="The quick brown fox jumped
         over the lazy dog."
118  J=1
120  I=INSTR(J,A$,"")
125  W=W+1
130  J=I+1
140  GOTO 120
```

Type **RUN** and press <Enter> to see what happens. If you don't know what the <Ctrl>-<Break> keys do, now is a good time to learn. The program is an endless loop again. To find out what's wrong, insert as a temporary statement 121 PRINT I and rerun the program.

```
20   W=0
100  A$="The quick brown fox jumped
         over the lazy dog."
118  J=1
120  I=INSTR(J,A$,"")
121  PRINT I
125  W=W+1
130  J=I+1
240  GOTO 120
```

The screen will rapidly fill with 4, 10, 16, 20, 27, 32, 36, 41, 0, 4, 10, 16. Those are locations of the blanks all right, but when the program gets to the end of the sentence, it goes back to the beginning, over and over. Why?

When the INSTR function doesn't find a blank, it returns a zero value. Zero plus 1 is 1, so J is reset to 1 and the program begins looking at the first character again. In short, you didn't tell it what to do when there were no more blanks. You need an IF statement and a statement to print the value of W. The program should look like this:

```
20   W=0
100  A$="The quick brown fox jumped
         over the lazy dog."
118  J=1
120  I=INSTR(J,A$,"")
122  IF I=0 THEN 150
125  W=W+1
130  J=I+1
140  GOTO 120
150  PRINT W
```

Just one problem: The program counts the number of words as eight (there are nine). This is the old fence post paradox—how many fence posts, spaced 10 feet apart, does it take to erect a 100-foot fence? One more than you first thought. There is one more word in your sentence than there are blanks. This calls attention to a flaw in the algorithm—it's counting blanks instead of words. What would happen if a typist put two blanks between some words? If you're in doubt, alter the text in line 100 and run the program.

The solution is to add statements to cause the program to skip over consecutive blanks without incrementing the word count. You can do this by saving the location of the last blank (we will call it OLDI), and comparing it with the position of the current blank. If the location of the current blank (I) is just one greater than the location of the old blank (OLDI), you do not want the word count to increase. Instead, OLDI should be set equal to I, and the program should look for the next blank. It's a little confusing at first, but this idea is used frequently in computer programming. Three statements are needed to modify the algorithm.

```
20   W=0
100  A$="The quick brown fox jumped
         over the lazy dog."
105  I=0
118  J=1
119  OLDI=I
120  I=INSTR(J,A$,"")
122  IF I=0 THEN 150
123  IF OLDI+1=I THEN 130
125  W=W+1
130  J=I+1
140  GOTO 119
150  PRINT W
```

Be sure to change line 140 to jump to line 119 instead of line 120.

We still have the problem of the last word not getting counted when there are no trailing blanks. One way to assure that a trailing blank will be there is to always add one. A statement like **104 A$=A$+" "** would accomplish this.

```
20   W=0
100  A$="The quick brown fox jumped
         over the lazy dog."
104  A$=A$+" "
105  I=0
118  J=1
119  OLDI=I
120  I=INSTR(J,A$," ")
122  IF I=0 THEN 150
123  IF OLDI+1=I THEN 130
125  W=W+1
130  J=I+1
140  GOTO 119
150  PRINT W
```

But does it really work? You can't be sure until you've tested every combination of data you can imagine. Here are some sample tests:

```
100  A$="The quick brown fox jumped
         the brown dog."
100  A$="The quick brown fox jumped
         over the lazy dog and the lazy
         dog jumped over the quick
         fox."
100  A$="The quick fox jumped the
         dog."
100  A$="The fox."
100  A$="The."
100  A$=" "
100  A$="  "
100  A$="The brown fox."
```

The last test points to a problem. The program counts four words in "The brown fox ."; the period is counted as a word because it is preceded by a space.

Is this a bug? The answer depends on how the program is to be used. If the purpose is to fire MX missiles based on a word count, then it is a serious bug indeed. Fortunately, this program will give only an idea of the length of a document.

Even after careful testing you can be sure someone, some day, will try to use your program for a purpose or with data you never intended. If the program gives the correct answer, the user will feel like a genius; if not, he or she will swear there's a bug in your program.

Reading a Disk File

The next step is to add statements to cause the program to read data from a disk file. BASIC supports two types of files: random and sequential. Random files store data in groups called records. When you are done with one record, you must specifically select the next record you want. In sequential files, all the data is stored as one large group. Text is usually stored in a sequential file, so this demonstration will use input statements that perform sequential input.

There are two such statements—INPUT # and LINE INPUT #. INPUT # reads a string of characters until it finds a comma and then terminates. Clearly this is not what you want. The LINE INPUT # statement reads all the characters in the input file until it encounters a carriage return. But the maximum length of a string is 255 characters, and since it is entirely possible that your data file will contain more than 255 characters in a row without a carriage return, the LINE INPUT # statement cannot be used. To get around this limitation, use a series of commands to read the file in 255-

character chunks. In place of the assignment statement in line 100, change the program as follows:

```
20   W=0
40   OPEN "WORDS.BAS" FOR INPUT AS
          #1
90   A$=" "
100  FOR X=1 TO 255
101  X$=INPUT$(1,#1)
102  IF X$=CHR$(13) THEN A$=A$+"
          ":GOTO 105
103  A$=A$+X$
104  NEXT
105  I=0
118  J=1
119  OLDI=I
120  I=INSTR(J,A$," ")
122  IF I=0 THEN 90
123  IF OLDI+1=I THEN 130
125  W=W+1
130  J=I+1
140  GOTO 119
145  CLOSE #1
150  PRINT W
```

This change reads up to 255 characters one at a time from the file to prevent lines from becoming longer than BASIC can handle. The IF statement in line 102 converts carriage return characters to spaces. Thus, the end of a line is treated as a blank so there is no need to add a blank to the end of each line.

The file number specification, #1, could have been #2 or even #9. Its purpose is to associate this input statement with a DOS file name. The file name and some other characteristics must be supplied prior to the input statement in an OPEN statement. Look up the OPEN statement in the BASIC manual and fill in the file name.

OPEN *"filename"* **FOR INPUT AS #1**

(Note the quotation marks around the file name.) You should close a gate that you've opened, and the same goes for files— this is done with a CLOSE statement.

If you don't have a test file on disk, you can make one now by using the ASCII option to save a BASIC program. In fact, if you name this program we're working on WORDS, you can save it; type:

```
SAVE "WORDS.BAS",A
```

and then have the program count the number of words in itself.

In addition to OPEN, CLOSE, and INPUT, you'll need to modify the program logic to loop back to line 90 so that once it has counted the words in one character string, it will go back for another. You can do this by modifying line 130. When you run the program in this form, you will see the error 'Input past end in line 101'. Also, the program won't print out the number of words in the file.

```
20   W=0
40   OPEN "WORDS.BAS" FOR INPUT AS
          #1
90   A$=" "
100  FOR X=1 TO 255
101  X$=INPUT(1,#1)
102  IF X$=CHR$(13) THEN A$=A$+
          " ":GOTO 105
103  A$=A$+X$
104  NEXT
105  I=0
118  J=1
119  OLDI=I
120  I=INSTR(J,A$," ")
122  IF I=0 THEN 90
123  IF OLDI+1=I THEN 130
125  W=W+1
130  J=I+1:IF J>255 THEN 90
140  GOTO 119
145  CLOSE #1
150  PRINT W
```

Line 150 prints the value of W, but the program doesn't have any way to get to line 150. Simple as this is, it's one of the most common errors in programming. If something doesn't work, at least half the time it's because the statements aren't getting executed.

The message about 'Input past end . . . ' probably won't make sense to the beginning programmer. When a BASIC program reads the last record in a disk file, it notices (and remembers) that it has reached the End of the File (EOF). If you try to read from that file again, BASIC displays the message 'Input past end . . . ' and stops the program. Check Appendix A of the BASIC manual for explanations of error messages.

If you thumb through the BASIC manual (maybe a lot of thumbing if you don't know what to look for), you'll find a built-in function called EOF. The value of EOF is false until the last data is read, and then it is true. You can use this to signal the program to jump to line 145 when it can't read any more records.

The placement of this statement is confusing. If you put it after the INPUT statement, the last data won't get processed. The EOF condition is set when the last record is read—not after—so we must check the condition before the next input, too. Modify line 103 by adding an end of file test. You should also modify line 122 to jump back to line 90, rather than jumping to line 150, and add a test at line 95.

```
20   W=0
40   OPEN "WORDS.BAS" FOR INPUT AS
        #1
90   A$=""
95   IF EOF(1) THEN 145
100  FOR X=1 TO 255
101  X$=INPUT (1,#1)
102  IF X$=CHR$(13) THEN A$=A$+
        " ":GOTO 105
103  A$=A$+X$:IF EOF(1) THEN 105
104  NEXT
105  I=0
118  J=1
119  OLDI=I
120  I=INSTR(J,A$," ")
122  IF I=0 THEN 90
123  IF OLDI+1=I THEN 130
125  W=W+1
130  J=I+1:IF J>255 THEN 90
140  GOTO 119
145  CLOSE #1
150  PRINT W
```

For a final test, run the program on itself. It counts 72 "words"—72 groups of characters separated by one or more blanks.

Clean-Up

The final two steps in writing a program are clean-up and documentation. In the clean-up phase you should look for ways to make the program more efficient—to eliminate unnecessary statements and

```
10 DEFINT A-Z
15 PRINT "This program counts the number of words in"
16 PRINT "a sequential ASCII file by counting the blanks"
17 PRINT "between groups of characters."
20 W=0  'word counter
35 PRINT:INPUT "ENTER FILENAME:";FILENAME$
40 OPEN FILENAME$ FOR INPUT AS #1
90 PRINT:PRINT "RUNNING TOTAL IS ";W;" WORDS":A$=""
95 IF EOF(1) THEN 145
100 FOR X=1 TO 255
101 X$=INPUT$(1,#1)
102 IF X$=CHR$(13) THEN A$=A$+" ":GOTO 105 'convert CR to a blank
103 A$=A$+X$:IF EOF(1) THEN 105
104 NEXT
105 I=0          'location of blank
106 PRINT A$
118 J=1          'start looking here
119 OLDI=I       'save location of last blank
120 I=INSTR(J,A$," ")   'find a blank
122 IF I=0 THEN 90      'get next line
123 IF OLDI+1=I THEN 130       '2 blanks together, don't add
125 W=W+1        'add one to count
130 J=I+1:IF J>255 THEN 90      'next location
140 GOTO 119     'keep looking
145 CLOSE #1
150 PRINT:PRINT FILENAME$;" CONTAINS ";W;" WORDS"
```

Figure 8.1 *BASIC listing after cleanup.*

perhaps combine others. You might realize that counting words is an integer task. BASIC makes more efficient use of storage if it knows that everything will be whole numbers. Statement 10 DEFines all variable starting with the characters A through Z to be INTegers.

Clean-up also involves making the input and output as friendly and easy to read as possible. For this example, your program will print a description of what the program is designed to do, ask the user for the file name, and tidy up the output. The friendly, documented, more efficient program is now what you see in Figure 8.1.

No program is ever finished; there's always some way to make it more efficient, easier to use, more useful, and better documented. In this program, statements 123 and 125 could be combined; the program could check to be sure the file name exists on the disk and report an error if it doesn't; you could produce a frequency count by . . . and then you could. . . .

Donald B. Trivette is the author of A BASIC Primer for the IBM Personal Computer: Programming Business Applications *published by Scott, Foresman & Co., and* Putting Junior to Work, *published by Compute! Publications. He writes a monthly column for* Compute! *magazine. This article was originally published in* PC World *Volume 1, Number 3.*

Disk Data Files

Lon Poole

When the amount of data a program handles gets large enough, it must be organized into files and stored outside the PC's dynamic memory, or RAM. Disks are the most efficient media for external data storage, and most PC systems have at least one disk drive. This article describes how a BASIC program can store and retrieve data on disk files. The statements and functions described here apply only to Disk BASIC and Advanced BASIC.

Data File Structure

Disk files can be likened to the file drawers in a filing cabinet but data file organization extends beyond that. Each file is further subdivided into one or more *records,* which are like the file folders in a file drawer. Each record usually contains several data values, just as file folders usually contain individual items. Each data value is called a *field.*

Typically, a file is organized so that every record has the same configuration. The number of fields, their sequence, and their lengths are all the same from one record to the next. The only things that vary are the values of the fields. Therefore two things define a file's layout: the configuration of its records and the number of records it has.

Thus a list of fields in one record will adequately describe the structure of a file. Programmers often list the fields on a preprinted form and call the result a *file layout* (Figure 8.2). The file layout usually shows

FILE NAME	RECORD SIZE	NO. OF RECORDS
ITEM. DAT	129	

DESCRIPTION: Personal inventory file—sequential

VARIABLE	FIELD DESCRIPTION	MAX. SIZE	COMMENTS
ITMNR$	Item number	3	
CTGRY$	Category	10	
DSCR$(1)	Description-line 1	20	
DSCR$(2)	Description-line 2	20	
DSCR$(3)	Description-line 3	20	
IDNBR$	Identification number	15	
LCN$	Location	15	
ACQRD$	Date acquired	8	
COST#	Cost	9	
VALU#	Value	9	

Figure 8.2 *File layout for a sample sequential-access personal inventory file.*

the file name, states the number of records it has, and lists its fields in order. For each field, the layout shows the description, the length, and the variable name that will be used to hold its value in a program.

A disk drive can only access a finite amount of data, so it's a good idea to calculate ahead of time whether enough space remains on a particular diskette for a new file you are planning. To calculate the disk space a file will require, add up the field lengths of one record and multiply the sum times the number of records in the file. Do that for every data file you plan to put on a disk and compare the total to the total disk capacity. (The DOS command CHKDSK reports disk capacity.) There must be enough room left over to accommodate the program files that you plan to put on the same disk.

Sometimes reducing the size of a field or two will make a too-large file fit. If not, you will have to divide it into several files and distribute the smaller files among several disks. You can split a file into several volumes, putting part of its records on one disk and part on another. Or you can split up each record, putting some of its fields into a file on one disk and other fields into a file on another disk.

Sequential and Random Access BASIC offers two ways of locating a desired record. The simplest is called *sequential access,* because the program must always start at the beginning of a file and examine each record in turn, until it finds the one it wants. The alternative method lets the program access records by number, in any order. It is called *random access.*

A file may be set up to use either sequential access or random access, but not both. Each method has its pros and cons. Sequential access is much simpler to program and tends to use less disk space, but it can be slow in finding a record near the end of a long file. Also, updating existing records is difficult with sequential-access files, and may be impossible. Random-access files require more programming and usually take more disk space, but they are very easy to update and all records can be found with equal speed.

Record length in a random-access file is constant, while in a sequential-access file it need not be. In a sequential-access file, the length of a record depends directly on the value of each field. Since field values are not the same in every record, record lengths will differ. Random-access record length is set when the file is created, and each field gets a fixed amount of space on the record. Values must fit in the space allocated. Long values are truncated and short values are padded with blank spaces. To minimize truncation, the size of each field is usually made large enough to accommodate its largest likely value.

Using Disk Data Files To get at a particular field in a record, a program must first open the file, then locate the proper record, next transfer the record from disk to RAM, and finally isolate the desired field as the value of a variable. Writing data to a file is similar, but this time the program transfers data values in the other direction, from RAM to the disk file.

To reduce the number of disk accesses, BASIC transfers data values to and from disk in blocks, not one value at a time. It sets aside part of dynamic memory for transfer areas, called *file buffers*. Each active file has its own file buffer.

Generally, BASIC manages the file buffers automatically, and you do not have to be concerned about them. But when a program finishes writing to a file, there will probably be some data left in the file buffer that BASIC has not written to the disk. Somehow the program must force BASIC to write out the final buffer contents. Closing a file will write out anything left over in the file buffer. At the same time, it updates the disk directory with changes to the file extents or other statistics kept there. Therefore, when a program finishes with a file, it must close the file or risk losing part of the file contents.

File Names and Numbers Data files are identified on disk by a standard file name that conforms to the DOS guidelines. Programs, though, refer to data files mainly by number. The OPEN statement correlates a file name with a file number. Here is an example:

```
1050 OPEN "B:ITEM.DAT" AS #1
```

The file name can be specified by a string constant, variable, or expression. A drive designation prefix is required unless the file is on the default drive.

The file number can be specified by a numeric constant, variable, or expression. Normally, only three different file numbers are allowed. Each file number can identify just one file

Access mode	Sample OPEN statement formats*
Write starting at the beginning of a new sequential-access file	1050 OPEN "B:ITEM.DAT" FOR OUTPUT AS #1
Write starting at the end of an existing sequential-access file	1835 OPEN "ADDRESS.DAT" FOR APPEND AS #3
Read starting at the beginning of an existing sequential-access file	2320 OPEN "A:ITEM.DAT" FOR INPUT AS #2
Write or read a random-access file	1040 OPEN "ITEM.DAT" AS #1 LEN=126

*The line numbers, file names, file numbers, and record length shown are all arbitrary and are for illustration only.

Table 8.1 *OPEN statement alternatives for data files.*

at a time, so a program can have at most three files open simultaneously. A way to raise that limit is described at the end of this article.

A program can have fewer data files open while it uses PRINT# or PRINT# USING statements with the printer or display screen, because it must use one file/device number for each open device or file. If two devices are open (say the printer and display screen), the program can only have one data file open at the same time. However, the regular PRINT, PRINT USING, LPRINT, and LPRINT USING statements do not use file/device numbers, so a program can use those statements freely, even with all three file/device numbers assigned to data files.

The CLOSE statement frees a file/device number for re-use in a subsequent OPEN statement. Here is an example:

```
1100 OPEN "LPT1:" AS #1
7510 CLOSE #1
7520 OPEN "A:TAXRATE.DAT" AS #1
```

A CLOSE statement that lists one number, like the one above (line 7510), closes just the specified file or device it is assigned to. To close more than one file with a single CLOSE statement, you can list several file numbers, separating them with commas, like this:

```
2140 CLOSE #1,#3
```

A plain CLOSE statement that lists no file numbers will close all open files and devices. Several other BASIC statements do the same thing, including END, CHAIN (but not CHAIN MERGE), LOAD, NEW, RUN, and SYSTEM. However, most programmers prefer the positive, precise effect of a CLOSE statement with explicit file numbers listed.

Sequential Disk Files

A BASIC program can create a new sequential-access data file and store data values there, or it can add values to the end of an existing file. It can also retrieve values from an existing file. Data on a sequential-access file must be read or written in consecutive order. In order to retrieve a value from the middle of the file, a program must read past all the values that come before it. Values can only be written at the end of a sequential-access file. That means there is no way to read a value from a sequential-access file, change the value, and rewrite it in the same place on that file.

Sequential-access files use file buffers in a simple-minded way. Data sent to a sequential-access file accumulates in the file buffer. When the file buffer gets full, BASIC writes the whole thing at once onto the disk file, clearing the buffer for subsequent outgoing data. Going the other direction, program requests for data retrieval are filled from the file buffer, not directly from the disk surface. When the program has retrieved all the data in the buffer, BASIC replenishes it all at once from the disk file.

Opening and Closing Sequential-Access Files In addition to assigning a file number to a named file, the OPEN statement determines the access mode that will be allowed with the file. For sequential-access files, a program may either write data starting at the beginning of a new file, write data starting at the end of an existing file, or read data. Table 8.1 lists the OPEN statement format that selects each access mode.

An OPEN statement with the FOR OUTPUT clause creates a new disk file with the specified file name. If a file already exists with that name, BASIC will automatically delete it and create a new file with the same name. An OPEN-FOR APPEND statement looks for an existing file to start at the end of, but if it finds none, it creates a new file with the specified name. An OPEN statement with the FOR INPUT clause must find the named data file or an error occurs.

It is possible to open a sequential-access file in append mode using one file number, and in input mode using another. But each file number uses a different file buffer, and there is no cross-communication between them. Therefore, in order to change access modes on a file, you need to close the file and reopen it. However, different files can be open simultaneously for unlike access modes.

Writing and Reading Sequential-Access Files The PRINT# and PRINT# USING statements will write values to a disk file. INPUT# or INPUT# LINE statements will read the values back in and assign them to variables. Here is a simple example:

```
List
10    OPEN "SAMPLE.DAT" FOR OUTPUT
         AS #1
20    PRINT#1, 123 'Write value to disk
         file #1
30    CLOSE #1
40    OPEN "SAMPLE.DAT" FOR INPUT
         AS #1
50    INPUT#1, A 'Read value from disk
         file #1
60    PRINT "First value on file: ";A
70    CLOSE #1
Ok
run
First value on file: 123
Ok
```

PRINT# statements format output in exactly the same manner no matter what the output device is. They always append an extra blank space to the end of each numeric value. Other than that, semicolons concatenate neighboring values and commas introduce extra blank spaces between them. The extra blank spaces needlessly use up disk space, so semicolons are preferable.

PRINT# USING statement template characters work the same with disk files as with the display screen or printer. Use caution with monetary prefixes ($$, **, and **$), because they put numeric values into nonnumeric formats. Numeric values prefixed with $ or * characters on a disk file cannot be read back in as numeric values. The following example illustrates:

```
List
10    OPEN "SAMPLE.DAT" FOR OUTPUT
         AS #2
20    PRINT#2, USING
         "$$###.##";99.50
30    CLOSE #2
40    OPEN "SAMPLE.DAT" FOR INPUT
         AS #2
50    INPUT#2, A
60    PRINT "First value on file: ";A
70    CLOSE #2
Ok
run
First value on file: 0
Ok
```

In the program above, the PRINT# USING statement (line 20) sends the characters "$99.50" (the quotation marks are not sent) to file SAMPLE.DAT. The INPUT# statement tries to read them as a numeric value, but the $ character makes the value nonnumeric, so its numeric value is zero.

The absence of a terminal semicolon in a PRINT# or PRINT# USING statement yields a carriage return character after the last value. A terminal semicolon suppresses the carriage return character.

Separating Values on Sequential-Access Files In order for the INPUT# statement to read values correctly from a disk file, the values must be separated from each other on the file. That means the PRINT# and PRINT# USING statements that write values to disk files must also write a character between each value to separate it from its neighbor. Without such a delimiting character, the INPUT# statement runs neighboring values together. The following example demonstrates what can happen:

```
List
10    OPEN "TEST.DAT" FOR OUTPUT AS
         #3
20    PRINT#3, "Silicon";14;28.0855
30    CLOSE #3
40    OPEN "TEST.DAT" FOR INPUT AS
         #3
50    FOR K%=1 TO 3:INPUT#3, A$
60    PRINT "Value no." ;K%;":";A$
70    NEXT K%:CLOSE #3
Ok
run
Value no. 1 : Silicon 14 28.0855
Input past end in 50
Ok
```

The PRINT# statement (line 20) writes three values, but the semicolons that separate them cause them to be run together on the file. When the INPUT# statement tries to read them (line 50), they all come back combined into one value. There is no second or third value on the file, so an error occurs when the program tries to read past the last value on file.

For string values, the delimiting character can be a comma or a carriage return. Those same characters or blank spaces will delimit numeric values. There are any number of ways to make sure a delimiting character occurs between values. One of the simplest is to assign a comma to a string variable and write that variable between every value in a PRINT# statement, like this:

```
5    D$ = ","
20   PRINT#3, "Silicon";D$;14;
         D$;28.0855
```

The INPUT# statement interprets every comma it encounters as the end of a value. The only exception is a comma that is enclosed in quotation marks on the file itself. In other words, quotation marks must be written to the disk file around any string value that might contain a comma. The INPUT# statement will eliminate the quotation marks from the value. Here is an example:

```
List
10   OPEN "TEST.DAT" FOR OUTPUT AS
         #1
20   PRINT#1, CHR$(34);"Managua,
         Nicaragua"; CHR$(34)
30   CLOSE #1
40   OPEN "TEST.DAT" FOR INPUT AS
         #1
50   INPUT#1, A$
60   PRINT "First value on file: ";A$
70   CLOSE #1
Ok
run
First value on file: Managua, Nicaragua
Ok
```

Ignoring Disk Field Delimiters A related problem arises with a PRINT# USING statement that has a comma included in a numeric template. A single numeric value written with such a template ends up being several values on the disk file. Here is an example:

```
List
10   OPEN "SAMPLE.DAT" FOR OUTPUT
         AS #2
20   PRINT#2, USING
         "#,##########";
         123456789
30   CLOSE #2
40   OPEN "SAMPLE.DAT" FOR INPUT
         AS #2
50   INPUT#2, A
60   PRINT "First value on file: " ;A
70   CLOSE #2
Ok
run
First value on file: 123
Ok
```

The LINE INPUT# statement, which reads a single string value, sidesteps the comma problem by only recognizing carriage returns as value separators. Commas and quotation marks are just the same as any other string character. Here is an example:

```
List
10   OPEN "SAMPLE.DAT" FOR OUTPUT
         AS #3
20   PRINT#3, "Stine, Frank N."
30   CLOSE #3
40   OPEN "SAMPLE.DAT" FOR INPUT
         AS #1
50   LINE INPUT#1, A$
60   PRINT "First value on file: " ;A$
70   CLOSE #1
Ok
run
First value on file: Stine, Frank N.
Ok
```

Recognizing the End of the File An INPUT# or INPUT# LINE statement that tries to read past the end of a sequential-access file causes an error. To avoid that error, the program must somehow recognize when it has read the last value from the file and stop reading at that point. An EOF function in a WHILE or IF-THEN statement provides the easiest way to do that. Here is an example:

```
1850 IF NOT EOF(1) THEN 1700 ELSE
         CLOSE #2
```

The numeric value in parentheses specifies the file number. The EOF function returns a value of false (numeric 0) as long as there are more values left, but it returns a value of true (numeric-1) after the last value has been read.

Using Sequential-Access Data Files

Sequential access will work for most data files, though it is certainly less convenient than random access for files that must be updated periodically. But it is adequate for files with static contents, or for files which only have new records added to them from time to time. For example, a simple program that keeps track of major personal possessions is unlikely to change frequently. Figure 8.2 presents a layout for such a file, and Figure 8.3 lists a program that stores personal inventory records on a sequential-access disk file. Figure 8.4 lists a program that reads back the records created by the program in Figure 8.3 and displays them one at a time on the screen.

```
990 '--Open file----------------------------------------------------------
1000 CLS:KEY OFF:WIDTH 40
1020 PRINT "Personal Inventory Program--Entry phase"
1030 PRINT "Erase existing file? (Y/N)"
1040 INPUT;"",NTRY$
1050 IF NTRY$="Y" OR NTRY$="y" THEN OPEN "ITEM.DAT" FOR OUTPUT AS #1
 ELSE OPEN "ITEM.DAT" FOR APPEND AS #1
1060 D$="," 'Delimiting comma for file output
1390 '--Enter all items in sequence-----------------------------------------
1400 CLS
1410 PRINT "Personal Inventory Program--Entry Phase"
1420 LOCATE 5,1
1430 INPUT "Item number";ITMNR$
1440 INPUT "Category";CTGRY$
1450 INPUT "Description-1";DSCR$(1)
1460 INPUT "Description-2";DSCR$(2)
1470 INPUT "Description-3";DSCR$(3)
1480 INPUT "ID number";IDNBR$
1490 INPUT "Location";LCN$
1500 INPUT "Date acquired";ACQRD$
1510 INPUT "Cost";COST#
1520 INPUT "value";VALU#
1790 '--Output one record to data file-------------------------------------
1800 PRINT#1,ITMNR$;D$;CTGRY$;D$;DSCR$(1);D$;DSCR$(2);D$;DSCR$(3);D$;
1810 PRINT#1,IDNBR$;D$;LCN$;D$;ACQRD$;D$;COST#;D$;VALU#
1890 '--Continue with entries?---------------------------------------------
1900 LOCATE 2,1
1910 PRINT "Enter another item? (Y/N)"
1920 INPUT;"",NTRY$
1930 IF NTRY$<>"N" OR NTRY$<>"n" THEN 1400
1940 CLOSE #1 'no more entries this time
1990 '--Review file contents?----------------------------------------------
2000 CLS
2010 PRINT "Personal Inventory Program-Review Phase"
2020 PRINT "Review file contents? (Y/N)"
2030 INPUT;"",NTRY$
2040 IF NTRY$="y" OR NTRY$="Y" THEN CHAIN "12-3",1000,DELETE 1000-7000
2090 '--End of program----------------------------------------------------
2100 CLS
2110 PRINT "Personal Inventory Program--Ended";TAB(39);
2120 PRINT TAB(5);TIME$;TAB(15);DATE$
2130 END
7000 REM End of CHAIN-DELETE range (see line 2040)
```

Figure 8.3 *Personal inventory creation program—sequential-access output.*

```
1000 CLS:KEY OFF:WIDTH 40
1010 PRINT "Personal Inventory Program-Review phase"
1030 OPEN "ITEM.DAT" FOR INPUT AS #1
1190 '--Input next record from file---------------------------------------
1200 WHILE NOT EOF(1)
1210 INPUT#1,ITMNR$,CTGRY$,DSCR$(1),DSCR$(2),DSCR$(3)
1220 INPUT#1,IDNBR$,LCN$,ACQRD$,COST#,VALU#
1290 '--Display review form-----------------------------------------------
1300 CLS
1310 PRINT "Personal Inventory Program-Review phase"
1320 RESTORE 7000
1330 FOR ROW%=5 TO 14
1340 READ COL%,LABEL$
1350 LOCATE ROW%,COL%:PRINT LABEL$;STRING$(13-LEN(LABEL$),".")
1360 NEXT
1390 '--Display all values------------------------------------------------
1400 LOCATE 5,18:PRINT ITMNR$
1410 LOCATE 6,18:PRINT CTGRY$
1420 LOCATE 7,18:PRINT DSCR$(1)
1430 LOCATE 8,18:PRINT DSCR$(2)
1440 LOCATE 9,18:PRINT DSCR$(3)
1450 LOCATE 10,18:PRINT IDNBR$
1460 LOCATE 11,18:PRINT LCN$
1470 LOCATE 12,18:PRINT ACQRD$
1480 LOCATE 13,18:PRINT USING "######.##";COST#
1490 LOCATE 14,18:PRINT USING "######.##";VALU#
1890 '--Continue with entries or end program?------------------------------
1900 LOCATE 2,1:PRINT "Review another item?  (Y/N)";TAB(40)
1910 LOCATE 3,1:PRINT TAB(40) 'Erase stale text
1920 LOCATE 3,1:INPUT;"",NTRY$
1930 IF NTRY$="N" OR NTRY$="n" THEN 2100
1940 WEND
2090 '--End of program----------------------------------------------------
2100 CLS
2110 PRINT "Personal Inventory Program--Ended"
2120 PRINT TAB(5);TIME$;TAB(15);DATE$
2130 CLOSE #1
2140 END
6980 '---locations and labels----------------------------------------------
6990 '   for entry form
7000 DATA 4,Item number,4,Category,4,Description-1,4,Description-2,4,
 Description-3,4,ID number,4,Location,4,Date acquired,4,Cost,4,Value
```

Figure 8.4 *Personal inventory review program—sequential-access input.*

Personal Inventory File Creation Program Analysis The personal inventory creation program (Figure 8.3) begins by asking the user whether he wishes to add records to the existing file, or start a new file (lines 1030 and 1040). Depending on the user's response, the program opens file ITEM.DAT using the FOR OUTPUT or FOR APPEND access mode (line 1050). Variable D$ contains a comma for delimiting values written to the disk file (line 1060). The program uses two PRINT# statements to write each record on the sequential-access disk file (lines 1800 and 1810). After the user finishes entering items, he has a choice of reviewing the whole file or ending the program altogether (lines 2000-2040).

To keep the program simple, the keyboard entry phase is crude (lines 1400 through 1520).

Personal Inventory File Review Program Analysis The personal inventory file review program (Figure 8.4) displays one record at a time on a display screen form. The program starts by opening file ITEM.DAT for input (line 1030). Then until it finds the end of the file (line 1200), it reads the values in the next record (lines 1210 and 1220). It displays the screen form (lines 1300-1360) and the values it just read (lines 1400-1490). After that, the program asks whether it should continue with the next item (lines 1900-1930). If so, it continues reading records; if not, it ends.

FILE NAME	RECORD SIZE	NO. OF RECORDS
ITEM. DAT	126	10

DESCRIPTION: Personal inventory file — random access

VARIABLE	FIELD DESCRIPTION	MAX. SIZE	COMMENTS
ITMNR$	Item number	2	ITMNR%
CTGRY$	Category	10	
DSCR$(1)	Description-line 1	20	
DSCR$(2)	Description-line 2	20	
DSCR$(3)	Description-line 3	20	
IDNBR$	Identification number	15	
LCN$	Location	15	
AC2RD$	Date acquired	8	
COST$	Cost	8	COST#
VALU$	Value	8	VALU#

Figure 8.5 *File layout for a sample random-access personal inventory file.*

Random-Access Files

BASIC has a special set of statements designed to read and write random-access files. The only familiar statements are OPEN and CLOSE. There are new statements to use instead of PRINT# for output and INPUT# for input. Another new statement declares which variables will identify field values, and there are even special statements and functions for assigning those variables new values.

Random-access files use file buffers to minimize the number of disk accesses. A file buffer is usually large enough to hold one record, sometimes more. When a program wants a certain record, BASIC first looks to see if that record is in the file buffer. If so, no disk access is necessary. If not, it transfers the desired record into the file buffer.

Opening Random-Access Files Opening a file for random access assigns it a file number and establishes the length of each record on the file. All records in a single file must have the same length. Here is an example:

```
1010 OPEN "ITEM.DAT" AS #1 LEN=128
```

A LEN= clause following the AS specification in an OPEN statement specifies a record length and means the file will be opened for random-access mode, which allows both reading and writing.

All records in a random-access file have the same fixed length. It is important to specify the record length correctly in order to avoid garbling the file contents. Normally, the maximum record length is 128 bytes, but there is a way to increase that, as explained at the end of this chapter.

To compute the length of a record, add up the lengths of the fields in it. Allow two characters for each integer value, four characters for each single-precision value, and eight characters for each double-precision value. For a string field, use the maximum number of characters you plan to allow it to have. Write these numbers on the file layout you prepare (Figure 8.5).

Declaring Record Structure After opening a random-access file, a program must declare the structure of the file's records. The FIELD statement does that. Here is an example:

```
1020 FIELD #2, 3 AS I$, 10 AS C$, 10 AS
        D$(1)
```

The field statement identifies the file it pertains to by number, as usual. Then it lists the fields in the order that they appear on the file. For each field, it states the length and names a variable that the program will use to identify the field. All fields for a single file must be listed in one FIELD statement, separated by commas.

The total length of all fields declared by a FIELD statement must not exceed the record length established by the corresponding OPEN statement. If it does, an error occurs.

All values are transferred to and from a random-access file via the variables listed in a FIELD statement. All variables listed in a FIELD statement must be string variables. The FIELD statement effectively defines fixed lengths for each of the variables listed in it. Numeric values have to be converted to string values using special functions, a process which will be described shortly.

Using FIELD Statement Variables Two special statements, LSET and RSET, are used to assign values to the variables defined in the field statement. Here are examples:

```
5340 RSET DAT$ = NTRY$
5550 LSET LCN$ = BLDG$ + ROOM$
```

Never use a variable listed in a FIELD statement in an INPUT statement of any kind. Never assign such a variable a value in a LET statement (with or without the command word LET present). Breaking either rule cancels the association that the FIELD statement established, so that the program can no longer use the variable to transfer a value to and from random-access file records.

The LSET and RSET statements guarantee that the variable's length will exactly match its FIELD statement definition. If the value assigned is too short, it is padded with blank spaces. The LSET statement aligns the value on the left, padding with extra blanks on the right, and the RSET statement does the opposite. If the value assigned is too long, both LSET and RSET drop characters from the right. The following example uses the RSET statement to illustrate:

```
List
10    OPEN "SAMPLE.DAT" AS #1
          LEN = 20
20    FIELD #1, 10 AS A$
30    RSET A$ = "DISK"
40    PRINT A$
      run
      DISK
Ok
```

Numeric Values on Disk Files In order to store numeric values on a random-access file, they need to be converted to numeric strings. BASIC has three functions ideally suited to the job.

The MKI$, MKS$, and MKD$ functions make numeric values into integer, single-precision, and double-precision string values, respectively. MKI$ always returns a two-character string, MKS$ a four-character string, and MKD$ an eight-character string. For large values, they achieve a considerable savings in string length over any other conversion functions.

The MKI$, MKS$, and MKD$ functions do not convert numeric values to their ASCII character equivalents, as the other conversion functions do. Instead, they pack the values into two, four, or eight characters using the same scheme the PC uses to represent numeric values in RAM memory. Therefore, you cannot print or display the results of an MKI$, MKS$, or MKD$ function with a PRINT statement.

The converted numeric values must still be assigned to file variables using the LSET or RSET statements, like this:

```
4700 LSET COST$ = MKD$(NTRY#)
```

Numeric string values generated by the MKI$, MKS$, and MKD$ functions can be converted back to numeric values by the CVI, CVS, and CVD functions, respectively.

Writing to Random-Access Files When a program is ready to write an entire record out to a random-access file, it must use a PUT# statement. Here is an example:

```
1550 PUT #1,ITMNR%
```

The first value in a PUT# statement specifies the file number and the second value specifies the record number. The record number is optional; if it is omitted, BASIC uses a record number one higher than the last record number used with the same file number.

Reading From a Random-Access File The GET# statement reads an entire random-access record. After that, the program can use the variables named in the FIELD statement to get at the field values. Here is an example:

```
4020 GET#1, ITMNR%
```

The first value in a GET# statement is the file number and the second value is the record number. If the record number is absent, BASIC uses a record number one higher than the last record number used with the same file number.

End of File Programs can read or write past the nominal end of a random-access file without a direct error. If a GET# statement specifies a record higher than any ever written by a PUT# statement to that file, BASIC assigns each character of every field variable a character code number of 0. (The CVI, CVS, and CVD functions all convert that to a numeric 0.) A PUT# statement that specifies a record number higher than any on the file increases the file size enough to accommodate the specified record. Any unused records between it and the former highest record will contain garbage. A GET# statement that retrieves one of those intermediate records will get garbage, which may cause errors elsewhere in the program. Therefore, programs should take steps to restrict the record numbers that will be accessed.

A random-access file has no length restrictions except the amount of disk space remaining. The LOF function tells you how much space the file is taking.

The LOC function identifies the current record number, that is, the record number last used in a GET# or PUT# statement to the specified file. Here is an example:

```
1650 IF LOC(1)=150 THEN CLOSE:END
```

The value in parentheses specifies the file number.

Trapping Errors

Using disk data files makes a program vulnerable to several errors that will stop it prematurely. For example, when a diskette fills up, the message "Disk full . . . " appears, files are closed automatically, and the program stops. Or suppose someone mistakenly puts a write-protect label on a diskette that the program needs to write on. In that case, the message "Disk Write Protected . . . " appears and the program stops.

A BASIC program can take control of more than 70 errors (not all of them disk-related, to be sure) that would otherwise disrupt program execution. The ON ERROR GOTO statement makes that possible. It stipulates a line number to which BASIC will branch should it detect an error later. Here is an example:

```
ON ERROR GOTO 30000
```

Most programmers place a statement like the one above in the first part of a program and put a special routine at the specified line number to handle the errors that occur. The action taken by the error-handling routine depends on the nature of the error. For a disk write-protect error, it might give the program user a choice of ending the program or fixing the problem and retrying the operation.

The error-handling routine can test the value of function ERR to determine what kind of error occurred. Errors are classified by number, and Appendix A of the IBM BASIC manual has a list of error numbers and interpretations. Sometimes the error number alone is not enough. For example, a program that opens more than one file risks a separate write-protect error at each OPEN statement, and it may need to handle each one differently. The ERL function divulges the line number where the last error occurred, so a program can use it to differentiate between errors that have the same code.

The error-handling routine must conclude with a RESUME statement. If the program executes a STOP, END, or RETURN statement first, an error occurs. The RESUME statement has three forms. The simplest is the solitary command word, and it terminates the error-handling routine by branching back to the very statement that caused the error. Another option is the RESUME NEXT statement, which branches back to the statement after the one that caused the error. The third alternative lets you specify a line number to branch to, like this:

```
RESUME 30100
```

You certainly will not want to write an error-handling routine that attends individually to each of the more than 70 error codes. Fortunately, BASIC will take over error recovery if the program executes an ON ERROR GOTO 0 statement during the error-handling routine. In that case, program execution halts and the standard message appears for the error that occurred.

BASIC can only cope with one error at a time. If an ON ERROR GOTO statement sends a program into an error-handling routine in which a second error occurs, the second error will not be trapped, but will cause an error message to appear and the program to halt.

```
20 GOTO 1000 'Jump to start of main program
190 '==General input subroutine================================================
200 LOCATE INROW%,INCOL%,1:PRINT STRING$(INLEN%,INTMPL$); ' Display template
210 LOCATE INROW%,INCOL%,1 'Set cursor for  entry
220 NTRY$="" ' Clear stale entry
230 K$=INKEY$:IF LEN(K$)=0 THEN 230 ELSE K%=ASC(K$) ' Wait for a keystroke
240 IF K%=13 THEN 300 ' <--' ends entry
250 IF K%=8 THEN 350 ' Backspace
260 IF LEN(NTRY$)=INLEN% THEN 230 'Entry full?
270 IF K%>31 OR (K%<28 AND K%>13) OR (K%<8 AND K%>0) THEN PRINT K$;
 :NTRY$=NTRY$+K$ ELSE BEEP 'If keystroke ok, echo it; otherwise ignore it
280 GOTO 230 ' Get another character
290 '--Done; check numeric range-------------
300 NTRY#=VAL(NTRY$) ' convert to numeric
310 IF NTRY#>INMAX# THEN ERM$="smaller":GOTO 400 ' too big
320 IF NTRY#<INMIN# THEN ERM$="larger":GOTO 400 ' too small
330 RETURN
340 '--Backspace 1 character-----------------
350 IF LEN(NTRY$)=0 THEN 230 ' Not if entry is empty
360 PRINT CHR$(29);LEFT$(INTMPL$,1);CHR$(29); 'Redisplay template
370 NTRY$=LEFT$(NTRY$,LEN(NTRY$)-1) ' Delete last character
380 GOTO 230 ' Get another character
390 '--Flash error message 3 times---------------
400 FOR X1%=1 TO 3
410 LOCATE INROW%,INCOL%,0:PRINT LEFT$(ERM$,INLEN%); 'Display message
420 BEEP
430 FOR X2%=1 TO 500:NEXT 'Pause
440 LOCATE INROW%,INCOL%,0:PRINT SPACE$(INLEN%); 'Erase message
450 FOR X2%=1 TO 500:NEXT 'Pause
460 NEXT X1%
470 GOTO 200 'Restart entry
890 '--Error handling routine--------------------
900 IF ERR=61 AND ERL=1120 THEN 950
910 ON ERROR GOTO 0 'Handle misc. errors
920 STOP: GOTO 910
940 '  Disk full; reopen file
950 OPEN "item.dat" AS #1 LEN=126
960 FILSIZ%=FIX(LOF(1)/126)
970 PUT #1,FILSIZ%
980 RESUME 1140
990 '++Start of main program++++++++++++++++++++++++++++++++++++++++++++++++
1000 CLS:KEY OFF:WIDTH 40
1010 PRINT "Personal Inventory Program--File changes"
1020 FILSIZ%=10 'Set max. no. or records for new file
1030 RETKEY$=CHR$(17)+CHR$(196)+CHR$(217) 'Facsimile of <--' key
1040 OPEN "ITEM.DAT" AS #1 LEN=126
1050 FIELD #1, 2 AS ITMNR$, 10 AS CTGRY$, 20 AS DSCR$(1), 20 AS DSCR$(2),
 20 AS DSCR$(3), 15 AS IDNBR$, 15 AS LCN$, 8 AS ACQRD$, 8 AS COST$, 8 AS VALU$
1060 IF LOF(1)>0 THEN 1200
1070 '--Initialize empty file-------------------------------------------
1080 PRINT "Please stand by for file initialization"
1090 ON ERROR GOTO 900 'Trap full disk error
1100 LSET ITMNR$=MKI$(-1) 'Initialize all records to item no. -1
1110 WHILE LOC(1)<FILSIZ%
1120 PUT #1
1130 LOCATE 5,10:PRINT "Item";LOC(1);"initialized";
1140 WEND
1150 '--Wait for user to read screen------------------------------------
1160 LOCATE 7,1:PRINT "That is the highest usable item number"
1170 LOCATE 9,6,1:PRINT "Press space bar to continue";
1180 K$=INKEY$:IF K$<>" " THEN 1180
1190 '--Input number of record to change or enter-----------------------
1200 CLS
1210 PRINT "Personal Inventory Program--File changes"
1220 LOCATE 2,1:PRINT "Enter item number (Type END to quit)."
1230 LOCATE 3,4:PRINT "  (Press ";RETKEY$;" alone for next item.)"
1240 INLEN%=3:INMAX#=FILSIZ%:INMIN#=0:INROW%=3:INCOL%=1:INTMPL$="*":GOSUB 200
1250 IF NTRY$="end" OR NTRY$="END" THEN 2100 'End program
1260 IF NTRY#>0 THEN ITMNR%=NTRY#:GOTO 1280
1270 IF NTRY#=0 AND LOC(1)<FILSIZ% THEN ITMNR%=LOC(1)+1 ELSE BEEP: GOTO 1240
1280 GET #1,ITMNR% 'Retrieve requested record
1290 '--Display entry form-----------------------------------------------
1300 RESTORE 7000
1310 FOR ROW%=5 TO 14
```

Figure 8.6 *Personal inventory program—random access.*

Using Random-Access Data Files

The two personal inventory programs described earlier in this chapter can be improved by using a random-access file. That allows immediate updating of volatile information like location and value. The file layout in Figure 8.5 describes the file structure, and the program in Figure 8.6 will create new records, review existing records, and allow changes to be made to existing records.

Improved Personal Inventory Program Analysis The improved personal inventory program (Figure 8.6) includes a general input subroutine that controls keyboard entry better than the crude method used in the sequential-access inventory program (lines 190-470).

The main program starts by setting up the display screen (lines 1000 and 1010) and assigning a couple of variables (lines 1020 and 1030). Variable FILSIZ% sets the maximum number of records in file ITEM.DAT. Variable RETKEY$ contains the characters needed to display a facsimile of the symbol printed atop the <Enter> key.

Next the program opens the file ITEM.DAT, the inventory file, for random access and defines the field variables (lines 1040 and 1050). If the file is empty, the program initializes every record by setting the item number to -1 (lines 1060 through 1140). If the disk should become full in the process, that error is trapped (line 1090). An error handling routine (lines 900 through 960) reopens the file and bypasses further initialization. After all records have been initialized, the program pauses to let the user read the highest usable item number off the screen (lines 1160 through 1180).

When the inventory file is ready, the program asks the user for the first item number (lines 1200 through 1240) and retrieves the corresponding inventory record (lines 1260 and 1280). If the user makes no entry other than pressing the <Enter> key, the program automatically retrieves the next record (lines 1270 and 1280). If the user enters the word "END" or "end," the program ends (line 1250).

```
1320 READ COL%,LABEL$
1330 LOCATE ROW%,COL%:PRINT LABEL$;STRING$(13-LEN(LABEL$),".")
1340 NEXT
1370 '--Enter values (new records) or display values (existing records)---
1380 IF CVI(ITMNR$)>0 THEN 1460 'Is record not blank?
1390 '--Enter all values in sequence----------------------------------
1400 LOCATE 5,22:PRINT "(New item)"
1410 FOR N%=1 TO 10
1420 GOSUB 4000
1430 NEXT
1440 GOTO 1600 'Skip redisplaying values
1450 '--Display existing values----------------------------------------
1460 LOCATE 5,18:PRINT CVI(ITMNR$)
1470 LOCATE 6,18:PRINT CTGRY$
1480 LOCATE 7,18:PRINT DSCR$(1)
1490 LOCATE 8,18:PRINT DSCR$(2)
1500 LOCATE 9,18:PRINT DSCR$(3)
1510 LOCATE 10,18:PRINT IDNBR$
1520 LOCATE 11,18:PRINT LCN$
1530 LOCATE 12,18:PRINT ACQRD$
1540 LOCATE 13,18:PRINT USING "######.##";CVD(COST$)
1550 LOCATE 14,18:PRINT USING "######.##";CVD(VALU$)
1590 '--Allow changes to entries----------------------------------------------
1600 N%=2 'Start pointer at item 2
1610 LOCATE 2,1:PRINT "To input entry pointed to, press ";CHR$(26);" key."
1620 PRINT CHR$(24);" and ";CHR$(25);" move pointer.  End key exits. "
1630 LOCATE N%+4,2,0:PRINT CHR$(16); 'Display pointer
1640 K$=INKEY$:IF LEN(K$)=0 THEN 1640 'Wait for keystroke
1650 PRINT CHR$(29);" "; 'Erase pointer
1660 '--Ignore meaningless keys
1670 IF LEN(K$)<>2 THEN BEEP:GOTO 1630 ELSE K%=ASC(RIGHT$(K$,1))
1680 IF K%=77 THEN GOSUB 4000:GOTO 1610 'right arrow
1690 IF K%=79 THEN 1800 'End key struck
1700 IF K%=72 AND N%>2 THEN N%=N%-1:GOTO 1630 'Up arrow
1710 IF K%=80 AND N%<10 THEN N%=N%+1:GOTO 1630 'Down arrow
1720 BEEP:GOTO 1630 'Meaningless key struck
1790 '--Output one record to data file------------------------------------
1800 PUT#1,ITMNR%
1810 GOTO 1200
2090 '--End program---------------------------------------------------------
2100 CLS
2110 PRINT "Personal Inventory Program--Ended";TAB(39);
2120 PRINT TAB(5);TIME$;TAB(15);DATE$
2130 CLOSE #1
2140 END
3990 '==Input entry number N%==================================================
4000 LOCATE 2,1,0:PRINT "Type over the template.";TAB(40)
4010 LOCATE 3,1:PRINT "Press ";RETKEY$;" to end entry.";TAB(40)
4020 INMAX#=1D+20:INMIN#=-INMAX#:INROW%=N%+4:INCOL%=18:INTMPL$="*"
4050 ON N% GOTO 4100,4200,4300,4300,4300,4400,4500,4600,4700,4800
4090 '--Item number--------------------------------------------------
4100 LOCATE INROW%,INCOL%:PRINT ITMNR%
4110 LSET ITMNR$=MKI$(ITMNR%):RETURN
4120 PRINT SPACE$(INLEN%-LEN(NTRY$));:RETURN
4190 '--Category-----------------------------------------------------
4200 INLEN%=10:GOSUB 200:LSET CTGRY$=NTRY$:GOTO 4120
4290 '--Description 1,2, & 3-----------------------------------------
4300 INLEN%=20:GOSUB 200:LSET DSCR$(N%-2)=NTRY$:GOTO 4120
4390 '--ID number----------------------------------------------------
4400 INLEN%=15:GOSUB 200:LSET IDNBR$=NTRY$:GOTO 4120
4490 '--Location-----------------------------------------------------
4500 INLEN%=15:GOSUB 200:LSET LCN$=NTRY$:GOTO 4120
4590 '--Date acquired------------------------------------------------
4600 INLEN%=8:GOSUB 200:LSET ACQRD$=NTRY$:GOTO 4120
4690 '--Cost---------------------------------------------------------
4700 INMAX#=999999.99#:INMIN#=0:INLEN%=9:GOSUB 200:LSET COST$=MKD$(NTRY#)
4710 '--Redisplay numeric entry--------------------------------------
4720 LOCATE INROW%,INCOL%:PRINT USING "######.##";NTRY#;:RETURN
4790 '--Value--------------------------------------------------------
4800 INMAX#=999999.99#:INMIN#=0:INLEN%=9:GOSUB 200:LSET VALU$=MKD$(NTRY#)
4810 GOTO 4720
6980 '---locations and labels-------------------------------------------------
6990 '   for entry form
7000 DATA 4,Item number,4,Category,4,Description-1,4,Description-2,4,
 Description-3,4,ID number,4,Location,4,Date acquired,4,Cost,4,Value
```

Figure 8.6 *(continued)*

If the record has never been used before, it will have an item number of -1 (thanks to the initialization of new files on lines 1060 through 1140). In that case, the program has the user enter all values before asking for changes (lines 1400 through 1440). Otherwise, it displays the values read from the disk file (lines 1460 through 1550).

With the record's current values on display, the program lets the user change any one except the item number (lines 1610 through 1720). Item number changes are prohibited to protect the integrity of the file. The user selects the entry to change with the cursor control keys. When the user finishes making changes, the program writes the record (line 1800) and branches back to get another item number.

Notice that the program never uses the field variables with INPUT statements, nor does it assign any of them values with LET statements.

Changing Disk File Limits

BASIC normally establishes a limit on the number of files and devices that can be open at the same time (three), and another limit on the maximum length of a random-access record (128 characters). These limits can be changed at the time DOS hands over control of the PC to either the Disk BASIC or Advanced BASIC interpreter.

To change the maximum number of concurrently open files and devices, suffix the DOS command BASIC or BASICA with the characters "/F:" and the number of files and devices you need to have open simultaneously. Here is an example:

```
A>basica /f:5
```

The command above would start Advanced BASIC with an allowance for five files and devices open at the same time. The absolute maximum number is 15.

The maximum length of random-access records equals the file buffer size. You can change the file buffer size by suffixing the DOS command BASIC or BASICA with a blank space, the characters "/S:" and the buffer size you want. For example:

```
B>a:basic /s:512
```

The command above would start Disk BASIC with a file buffer size of 512 bytes (characters). The maximum file buffer size is 32767. IBM recommends 512 for best results.

You may combine the effect of the two options described above by including both suffixes at the end of the BASIC or BASICA command, in either order. Here is one possibility:

```
A>basic /f:5 /s:512
```

Requisitioning additional file positions or larger file buffers has a price. Each file position appropriates dynamic memory in the amount of 190 bytes plus the size of the file buffer, which is 128 bytes unless changed as described above. Thus, increasing the number of files that can be open or increasing the file buffer size (or both) will decrease the amount of RAM available for program statements and variables.

Lon Poole lives in Oakland, California, and has been writing about personal computers since 1976. He is the author of such books as MacWork MacPlay *and* Apple II Users Guide. *This article was excerpted from the book* Using Your IBM Personal Computer *published by Howard W. Sams & Co., Indianapolis, copyright 1983, Lon Poole, and is reprinted with the permission of the publisher. It was published in* PC World *Volume 1, Number 2.*

Optimizing for BASCOM

Dan Rollins

BASCOM, Microsoft's BASIC Compiler for the IBM Personal Computer, is a tool every serious BASIC programmer needs. A BASIC program may be written and debugged using the BASIC interpreter and then compiled into speedy, 8088 machine code. In addition to the speed advantage of compiled programs, the source code is protected; coding secrets remain the property of the software author. Also, compiled programs can take advantage of the expanded memory available with the PC.

Programmers who wince at the thought of BASIC, preferring more structured languages such as Pascal or C, should take a good look at Compiled BASIC. Many of the disadvantages of Interpretive BASIC do not apply to the compiled version. For example, you can leave plenty of remarks and clarifying spaces in the source code without causing a slowdown at run time. Program lines need not start with line numbers except when needed as labels for GOTO or GOSUB statements. Program lines are not limited in length, so nested IF . . . THEN statements can be formatted nicely and made clearly readable.

There are certain drawbacks to using the compiler: the generated code is often much larger than its interpreted counterpart, certain BASIC commands work differently when compiled, and the debugging process can be painfully slow. In cases where the compiler's speed advantage is needed and the only alternative is writing in assembly language, these disadvantages lessen in importance.

Speed is the essence of compiler programming. A short program I wrote to delete remarks and extra spaces from BASIC programs (to make them run faster with the interpreter) was taking 20 minutes to do its job. The same program, once compiled, did the same job in under 3 minutes. The program used a lot of string memory and was spending time collecting string garbage. Also, the interpreter was so slow to process an input line that the disk would stop spinning before the line was ready to be output. This caused a delay for each input as the disk drive was started and brought up to speed. The compiled version had neither of these problems.

A graphics-oriented game program I wrote would have been ridiculously slow in Interpretive BASIC. By compiling the code and CALLing assembly language routines at critical points, I was able to make it fast enough to be usable.

In the case of the game program, I needed to squeeze as much speed as possible from the compiled code. There also came a point when the program would no longer fit in a 64K system, and I needed to do some size optimization to make it marketable. This article describes some of the techniques I used to accomplish these ends, but first a few of the differences between Interpretive and Compiled BASIC.

The BASIC Difference

Many BASIC programs can be saved in ASCII and compiled without change, but usually the file must be edited to conform to the restrictions described in the compiler manual. Notably, arrays must be explicitly dimensioned; nesting of FOR . . . NEXT and WHILE . . . WEND loops must be physical as well as logical; DEF FN and DEF type declarations must occur physically early in the source code, and the DRAW and PLAY statements must use VARPTR$ to locate any variable parts of their control strings. Also, the USR and CALL statements work differently in Compiled BASIC.

Certain BASIC commands are meaningless to the compiler. RENUM, LIST, SAVE, and NEW are examples. Some statements will only work when special compiler parameters are specified at compile time. For example, ON KEY(n) and STRIG(n) are only acceptable when the /V or /W parameters have been included in the BASCOM command line. ON ERROR GOTO will only work when a /E or /X parameter has been specified. The action of the CHAIN statement varies according to whether the /O parameter is used.

A careful eye is needed to convert the more subtle differences. One such difference is in the way Compiled BASIC handles numeric-precision conversions. Interpretive BASIC can make variable precision decisions on the fly, but the compiler must decide in advance which type of precision to use. This makes overflow errors possible. For example:

```
J% = -10000:K%=20000:L%=20000
A% = J% + K% + L%
```

will return an erroneous result. K% is added to L%, resulting in an overflow (an integer variable cannot exceed 32,767). Parentheses should be used whenever you expect that such an overflow might happen:

```
A% = (J% + K%) + L%
```

The compiler's line editor (used in INPUT and LINE INPUT statements) will only operate on one screen line at a time. Thus most of the cursor control keys don't work as expected. When an unacceptable key is pressed, the compiler makes an irritating beeping sound and ignores the key. Of course all the keys included in the extended ASCII character set may be read via the INKEY$ command and processed as desired. <Ctrl>-<Break>, for example, returns a key code of 03 and can be ignored to prevent the program from being stopped.

The PRINT function also works slightly differently. Compiled BASIC will ignore cursor control characters in a string. For example, Interpretive BASIC allows the printing of a multiline box:

```
CD$ = CHR$(31) :CL$ = STRING$(4,29)
   'cursor down, left by 4
PRINT"---";CD$;CL$;"I I";CD$;CL$;"---";
```

Compiled BASIC does not support this technique.

Some of the PEEKs and POKEs mentioned in the BASIC manual will not work with the compiler. For example:

```
DEF SEG :POKE &H4E,C
```

won't change the color of your medium-resolution character set and

```
DEF SEG :POKE &H6A, 0
```

won't flush the keyboard input buffer.

The compiler allows strings to be as long as 32,767 characters; this won't cause any problems in converting straight BASIC code, but it does affect the way a CALLed routine must handle string parameters. Also, string space is controlled differently with the compiler, making garbage collection much faster. This also means that any program that POKEs into string memory will likely confuse the system and cause a String Space Corrupt error.

A couple of major differences are not mentioned in the compiler manual. First, the storage area for J% is the same 2 bytes as the storage area for J%(0). Generally, any variable is the same as the 0th element of the array with the same name. I spent hours debugging because of this problem.

The compiler apparently recognizes GO and SUB separately. The graphics program I was writing included an array for storing the location and various attributes of a submarine. I tried to name the array SUB%(), but that resulted in a syntax error.

Writing Faster Code

The following discussion gives samples of techniques that force the compiler to generate more efficient and faster-running code. When I explain why one method is faster than another, I'll be using terms that are familiar only to experienced 8088 assembly language programmers, but you can use these techniques even if you have only a little knowledge of BASIC.

Some of the following examples are accompanied by proof of the speedup—either a timed benchmark or a listing that counts the clock cycles required to perform a function. You can prove the validity of any of these techniques by using the following batch file:

```
REM --- TEST.BAT ---
BASCOM CON:,NUL,CON: /N/O/A;
```

This invokes the compiler specifying the keyboard as the input file. After you have entered some BASIC program lines, press F6 or Ctrl-Z to signal the end of the file. The compiler will immediately begin processing and then display the 8088 mnemonics of the opcodes that it generates. Be ready to press <Ctrl>-<NumLock> to halt the listing for inspection. You might also want to press <Ctrl>-<PrtSc> to obtain a printed copy of the display.

The most obvious way to speed up a program is to use integer variables whenever possible, because integer arithmetic operations are done rapidly within the 8088 registers. The following techniques are based on the arithmetic optimizations that the compiler performs only with integer variables. A simple example will make the point. The BASIC line:

```
X!= Y! + Z!
```

compiles to:

```
MOV DI,OFFSET Z!    ;point to the operands
MOV SI,OFFSET Y!
CALL $FADA          ;invoke floating-point addition routine
MOV DI,OFFSET X!    ;point to the destination
CALL $FASC          ;move the result to the destination
```

The same operation performed using integer variables;

```
X% = Y% + Z%
```

produces these lines when compiled:

```
MOV AX,Z%           ;get the 16-bit Z% value into the accumulator
ADD AX,Y%           ;add the 16-bit Y% value
MOV X%,AX           ;place the sum into X% storage area
```

The first example, using single-precision (floating-point) addition, takes over three times longer to execute than the second, which uses integer addition. Because of this, most of the following examples assume that a DEFINT A-Z declaration has defined all variables as integers.

Similar time improvements are obtained when an integer constant is added to an integer variable. In certain cases the performance for integers is even better. For example, when 1, 2, 3, or 4 is added to an integer, the compiler uses the efficient INC opcode to perform the math. (Likewise, DEC is used for subtractions and additions of small, negative values.) On the other hand, adding *any* value to a single- or double-precision number requires time-consuming calls to the floating-point arithmetic routines.

Comparing two values in a program is much faster if they are integer numbers. Many programs that use the keyboard to control an object use the INKEY$ function for keyboard input of one character. The following lines are typically used in this respect:

```
K$ = INKEY$ :IF K$ = "" THEN RETURN
IF K$ = "U" THEN Y = Y-1
IF K$ = "D" THEN Y = Y+1
'..., etc.
```

This, however, forces multiple calls to $SCMA, the string compare routine. The following code is much more efficient:

```
K$ = INKEY$ :IF K$ = " " THEN
   RETURN
K = ASC(K$)
IF K = 85 THEN Y = Y-1 'test ASCII
   value of "U"
IF K = 68 THEN Y = Y+1 'test ASCII
   value of "D"
..., etc.
```

Doing some preprocessing in the CPU above your shoulders will save a great deal of processing at run time.

Constantly Slow

When writing in Interpretive BASIC, I like to avoid constants. Early in the program I define:

```
FALSE = 0 :TRUE = NOT FALSE
```

Then I can easily set or flip-flop the state of a flag variable while keeping the code from becoming too cryptic. Unfortunately, this technique slows down the operation when compiled. For example:

```
MATCH.FOUND = TRUE
```

generates the 28-clock-cycle sequence:

```
MOV AX,TRUE%
MOV MATCH.FOUND%,AX
```

The more efficient alternative method:

```
MATCH.FOUND = -1 'set it to true
```

generates the 20-clock-cycle opcode:

```
MOV MATCH.FOUND%,0FFFFH
```

Generally, you write more efficient (but possibly less readable) code when you use immediate, or constant, values wherever possible.

Faster Arithmetic

The 8088 microprocessor is blessed with hardware multiply and divide. Of course, the compiler uses this fact, and it shows up in speedy execution of all such arithmetic operations. Even so, an integer multiplication takes a minimum of 128 CPU clock cycles because the compiler always does 32-bit multiplication (two 16-bit operands). As experienced assembly language programmers know, certain multiplications and divisions can be accomplished in a fraction of that time. The speedy SHL and SAR instructions will respectively multiply and divide a number by a factor of 2 in only 2 clock cycles—a 600 percent increase in speed.

The programmers at Microsoft did not miss this point. The compiler takes advantage of shift instructions whenever possible. When it sees:

```
X = Y*4
```

it generates the opcodes:

```
MOV AX,Y%        ;retrieve the first
                 factor
SHL AX,1         ;multiply it
                 times 2
SHL AX,1         ;times 4
MOV X%,AX        ;save the product
```

This optimization can only take place when one of the factors is a power of 2, and that factor must be a constant in the program. For example, both **Z = 2 :X = Y*Z** and **X = Y*5** will use the slower IMUL opcode to perform the multiplication.

You can take advantage of this optimization in your own coding. Multiplication by 5 in the latter example can be replaced with:

```
TEMP = Y*4 :X = TEMP+Y
```

Even with the extra variable manipulation and the extra addition operation, this multiplication is almost twice as fast as one that uses the 8088 IMUL instruction.

Speeding Array Operations

Programs that use multidimension arrays can be dramatically speeded up using this next tip. All variables stored in any type of array can be considered as a single list of values. BASIC string arrays are lists of pointers to string-descriptor blocks. Integer arrays are lists of 2-byte words containing the values of each of the array variables. A two-dimensional array is just two one-dimensional arrays stored one right after the other.

First we'll look at how the compiler works with a one-dimensional array. You can think of this type of array as a list of values, each of which is held in a 2-byte word of memory. The 8088 has powerful tools for manipulating arrays, namely its index registers. To access the *Xth* element of a one-dimensional array, you calculate the offset from the start of the array by multiplying *X* by 2 (the number of bytes in an integer array element) and place this value in an index register. The 8088 can automatically "look up" the address by adding the index register to the address of the start of the array. The address thus formed can then be used as a memory operand and manipulated as if it were a register.

The statements:

```
DIM A%(20)
A%(X%)=Q%
```

generate these instructions when compiled:

```
MOV DI,X%        ;index register be-
                 comes element to
                 access
SAL DI,1         ;multiply by 2 to
                 point to address
                 of A(X)
MOV BX,Q%        ;set up register
                 with new value
MOV A%[DI],BX    ;transfer the data
                 into the array
                 memory
```

This sequence will take exactly 60 clock cycles.

Figure 8.7 illustrates the way that BASIC stores a two-dimensional array of integers. The A%() array has been allocated with the statement **DIM A%(2,5)**.

Therefore the computer has initialized a list of 18 locations to hold the array data (this includes the 0th elements of each dimension). Notice that the memory location for A%(1,0) is sequentially adjacent to the address of A%(0,5). Now consider the actions taken when you assign a value to an array element:

```
A(X,Y) = Q
```

1) Retrieve the value of *Y*

2) Multiply that by the number of rows of the array

3) Add the value of *X*

4) Use the sum as the index into the array

5) Move the value of Q into the address formed by adding the index pointer to the address of A(0,0)

In other words, move your pencil

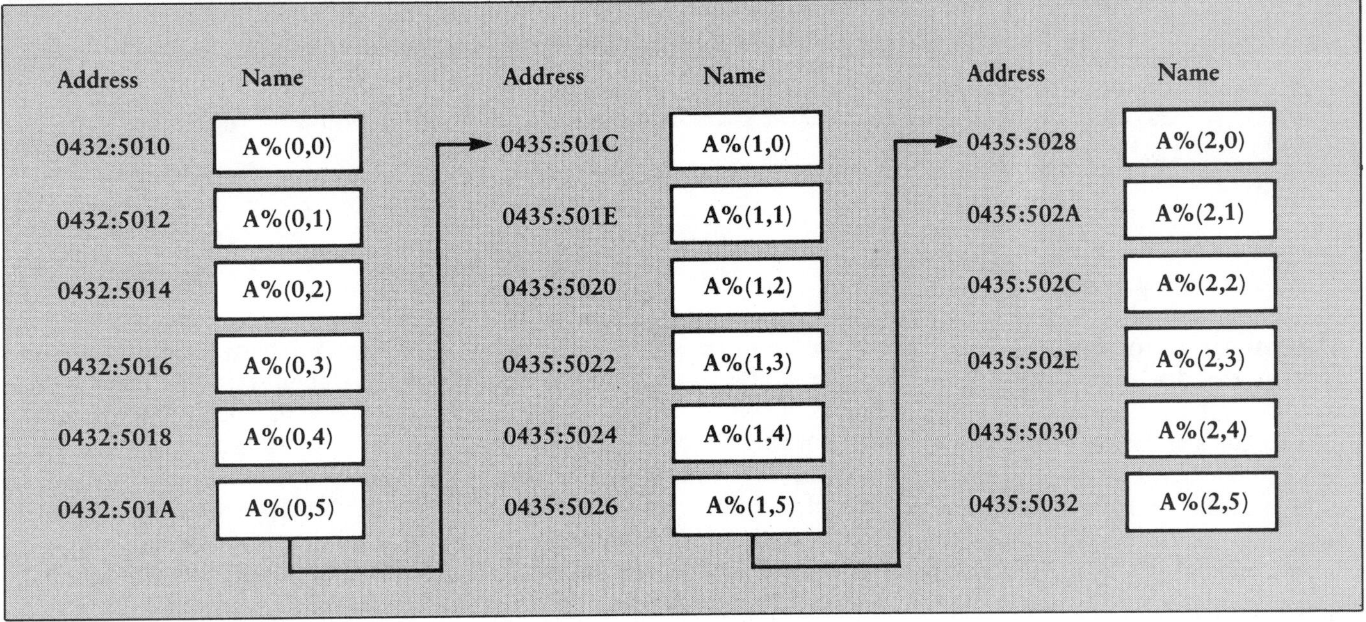

Figure 8.7 *Conceptual diagram of array storage in memory.*

down the list to the start of the row indicated by *Y*, adjust it *X* more to point to element (*X*,*Y*), and then write a new value in that address.

If you enter these lines into the compiler using TEST.BAT:

```
DEFINT A-Z :DIM A(2,5)
A(X,Y)=Q
^Z
```

these opcode mnemonics will be generated by the compiler:

```
MOV AX,0003H      ;get the number
                  of rows
IMUL Y%           ;calculate the start
                  of this row
XCHG AX,DI        ;set up index reg-
                  ister
ADD DI,X%         ;point to the ele-
                  ment on this row
SAL DI,1          ;multiply by 2
                  (bytes per ele-
                  ment)
MOV BX,Q%         ;get ready to store
                  the new value
MOV A%[DI],BX     ;store the new
                  value in the array
```

The above operation requires a minimum of 212 and a maximum of 238 clock cycles. The IMUL calculation is by far the slowest component of the calculations needed to form the address. It also accounts for the possible variation in times—IMUL timing varies according to the bit patterns of the operands.

The calculation to form the offset address of any element of a multidimensional array must be performed, but it needn't be done by the time-consuming IMUL opcode. Consider what happens when the array has been dimensioned thus:

```
DEFINT A-Z :DIM A(3,5)
A(X,Y)=Q
```

The compiler generates:

```
MOV DI,Y%         ;get the number
                  of rows
SAL DI,1
    SAL DI,1      ;calculate the start
                  of this row
ADD DI,X%         ;point to the ele-
                  ment in this row
SAL DI,1          ;multiply by 2 for
                  bytes per element
MOV BX,Q%         ;register must
                  temporarily hold
                  value
MOV A%[DI],BX     ;store the new
                  value
```

This sequence takes exactly 83 clock cycles. That is at least twice and possibly three times as fast! The difference is that IMUL has been avoided because the compiler knows that one of the offset factors will always be a power of 2. Therefore, even if your program uses only the first 3 columns of an array, i.e., (0,n), (1,n), and (2,n), it is wise to dimension the array with 4 columns, as in the latter example.

Generally, you should dimension arrays (string, integer, or floating point) so that the number of subscripts is a multiple of 2. Unless you use the OPTION BASE 1 statement, this means that the first subscript should be 1 less than a power of 2, i.e. $2^n - 1$. For three-dimensional arrays, declare the first two values using multiples of 2. For example, accessing elements of an array dimensioned **DIM A!(3,7,20)** is more than four times faster than if the array is declared **DIM A!(2,5,20)**. As you might expect, there is a trade-off for this gain in speed. The unused array elements will take up storage area. In this example, you would be wasting a total of 1360 bytes (340 unused elements times 4 bytes per single-precision value.)

Maximizing Compiler Optimization

IBM Pascal is an example of a two-pass compiler. After it has generated code, it checks back through the listing to find if it can generate more efficient code. BASCOM is a faster and smaller program, mainly because the folks at Microsoft chose to have it do everything in one pass. It therefore tends to create less efficient code.

BASCOM optimizes code, but only to a lesser degree. After it has generated the opcodes for a single source line, it checks back through that line to remove superfluous calculations. Among other things, it also tries to hold temporary values in registers, so as to avoid the more time-consuming storage and retrieval to RAM.

To get the most optimization, you should pack a lot of statements on one line.

```
100   Q=A(X,Y) :R=A(X,Y)+1
```

will generate more efficient code than:

```
100   Q=A(X,Y)
110   R=A(X,Y)+1
```

simply because the address of A(X,Y) will be computed twice in the second example.

If you are willing to give up the advantage of debugging with the interpreter, you can write code that is highly optimized by using the /N compiler directive and placing line numbers only where they are needed as labels. This technique allows large blocks of code to be optimized by the compiler.

This gives you the added advantage of producing very readable source code. In my programming I have developed a line numbering convention that has proven very useful. Figure 8.8, which I'll explain in a moment, uses this convention. Notice that each line number label is on a line by itself followed immediately by a colon. This allows me to find that line number easily by using my text editor's global search capability (the search for 1000: will never stop at GOTO 1000).

Use PUT not PRINT

One of the slowest operations of the PC is the PRINT command. When your BASIC program does a lot of printing to the screen, it is likely that compilation will not speed it up much. Word processing programs written in BASIC will be far too slow to be useful unless the author has coded a more efficient print routine in assembly language, but it is possible to print a string of characters in text mode at ten times the speed of even Compiled BASIC.

Graphics mode character printing is even faster than text mode printing, but coding a graphics print routine is more difficult and results in less time savings. In my graphics game I was updating the player's score (and the high score) at the end of every game cycle. This was slowing the game down to a crawl.

The first thing I did was skip the print when there had been no change in the score between cycles (an obvious step in retrospect). Later, I discovered a method of displaying the score without using PRINT at all. Figure 8.8 illustrates the method.

ASCII characters printed while in graphics mode are simply a collection of graphical dots arranged in specific shapes. Another way to display these shapes is to define a table of shape strings and use the DRAW command. A faster method is to use the graphics PUT command. The program in Figure 8.8 does a timing test of the normal printing of a 5-digit score compared against using a subroutine to display the same 5 digits by using the PUT command. Note that the program requires a color/graphics adapter and a suitable monitor.

The statements in Line 10 time an empty loop. The execution speed of the empty loop is saved and subtracted from the results of the following tests so that a valid percentage can be determined. Line 20 prints all five digits of scores ranging from 00000 to 10000 and displays the time it took.

Line 30 defines each of the 10 digits and GETS them each into an array. Then line 40 calls the subroutine to display each of the 10,001 values and displays the required time.

The subroutine at 2000: displays all five digits of any number less than 32,767 starting at the pixel coordinate specified by *CX* and *CY*.

The timed results prove that using PUT to display these digits in medium-resolution graphics is 37 percent faster than PRINTing the same characters. Another advantage

```
      '** compiled BASIC routine to time PRINT vs. PUT
      '** for 5-digit numbers
      '** Dan Rollins  3/12/83

defint a-z
dim c0(8),c1(8),c2(8),c3(8),c4(8),c5(8),c6(8),c7(8),c8(8),c9(8)

screen 1,0    'mid resolution graphics

      '** time an empty loop
10:
      print :print "timing the empty loop"
      t$=time$ :t1 = 60*val(mid$(t$,4,2))+val(right$(t$,2))
      '------
      for j=0 to 10000 :next
      '------
      t$=time$ :t2 = 60*val(mid$(t$,4,2))+val(right$(t$,2))
      empty.loop = t2-t1

      '** time the PRINT display
20:
      print :print "timing the PRINT function"
      t$=time$ :t1 = 60*val(mid$(t$,4,2))+val(right$(t$,2))
      '------
      for j=0 to 10000
            locate 1,1
            a$=str$(j) :a$=right$(a$,len(a$)-1)
            print right$("0000"+a$,5)            'add the leading zeros
      next
      '------
      t$=time$ :t2 = 60*val(mid$(t$,4,2))+val(right$(t$,2))
      prtime=t2-t1-empty.loop
      locate 5,1: print "using PRINT: ";prtime

      '** test the PUT display
30:
      print :print "timing the PUT function"
      gosub 1000     'define the digits
      t$=time$ :t1 = 60*val(mid$(t$,4,2))+val(right$(t$,2))
      '------
      for j=0 to 10000
            cx=0 :cy=0 :num=j
            gosub 2000            'display the number
      next
      '------
      t$=time$ :t2 = 60*val(mid$(t$,4,2))+val(right$(t$,2))
      putime=t2-t1-empty.loop
      locate 9,1 :print "using PUT:   ";putime

      print :print"PUT is";100-int((100*putime)/prtime);"% faster"

while inkey$="" :wend    '** examine the results
end

      '$page
      '** subroutine saves the digits in PUT arrays
      '**
```

Figure 8.8 *Compiled BASIC routine to time PRINT vs. PUT.*

```
1000:
      locate 1,1 :print"0"  :get (0,0)-(6,6),c0
      locate 1,1 :print"1"  :get (0,0)-(6,6),c1
      locate 1,1 :print"2"  :get (0,0)-(6,6),c2
      locate 1,1 :print"3"  :get (0,0)-(6,6),c3
      locate 1,1 :print"4"  :get (0,0)-(6,6),c4
      locate 1,1 :print"5"  :get (0,0)-(6,6),c5
      locate 1,1 :print"6"  :get (0,0)-(6,6),c6
      locate 1,1 :print"7"  :get (0,0)-(6,6),c7
      locate 1,1 :print"8"  :get (0,0)-(6,6),c8
      locate 1,1 :print"9"  :get (0,0)-(6,6),c9
return

      '** subroutine displays a 5-digit number NUM, at CX, CY

2000:
      n=num\10000              :gosub 3000 :tn=num-n*10000
      n=tn\1000     :cx=cx+8   :gosub 3000 :tn=tn-n*1000
      n=tn\100      :cx=cx+8   :gosub 3000 :tn=tn-n*100
      n=tn\10       :cx=cx+8   :gosub 3000 :tn=tn-n*10
      n=tn          :cx=cx+8

3000:
      if n=0 then put (cx,cy), c0, pset :return
      if n=1 then put (cx,cy), c1, pset :return
      if n=2 then put (cx,cy), c2, pset :return
      if n=3 then put (cx,cy), c3, pset :return
      if n=4 then put (cx,cy), c4, pset :return
      if n=5 then put (cx,cy), c5, pset :return
      if n=6 then put (cx,cy), c6, pset :return
      if n=7 then put (cx,cy), c7, pset :return
      if n=8 then put (cx,cy), c8, pset :return
      put (cx,cy), c9, pset :return
```

Figure 8.8 *(continued)*

is that the digits can be displayed at any part of the screen, while printing is limited to 998 locations (you can't PRINT to location 24,40 or 25,40 without causing the screen to scroll). Incidentally, the series of IF... THEN commands in Line 3000: turned out to be slightly faster than a corresponding ON... GOTO sequence.

Optimizing Program Size

So far, my suggestions have been centered around optimizing the speed of a Compiled BASIC program. There may come a time when your code will become too large to fit in a 64K machine. This problem can be very difficult to solve. If you are compiling with the /O directive, there is a minimum code overhead of about 18K, and there is nothing you can do about it until IBM changes its licensing policy. Therefore, you must look to your program to find ways to get the job done in fewer bytes.

Use subroutines as much as possible for any code that is repeated. This may mean that you will need to generalize some procedures to use variables instead of constants so that they don't rely on specific values.

If your program contains a lot of DATA lines defining numeric values, you are using a lot of extra space. Because the compiler cannot be sure where the values will eventually be stored (or even assume that the values are numeric), it must store the entire DATA line as written in the source code. The lines:

```
READ X%
DATA -12345
```

will require 6 bytes of static storage and 2 bytes for the variable X%. When you are reading an entire array of integers from DATA lines, you waste as much as 6 bytes per element.

One alternative is to read the array from a sequential disk file. A faster method is to write a short program to read in the array, and then BSAVE the values, starting at element 0 with a length of 2 bytes per element:

```
10    DIM A%(999)
20    FOR J = 0 TO 999 :READ A%(J)
          :NEXT
30    BSAVE "array.dat", VARPTR(A%(0)),
          2000
```

The VARPTR function returns the starting address of the array. There are 1000 2-byte elements, so the length of the array is 2000 bytes. The applications program that uses the array can now avoid the lengthy READ and store process by directly BLOADing the values starting at the address of the 0th element:

```
DEFINT A-Z :DIM MY.ARRAY(999)
BLOAD "array.dat",
   VARPTR(MY.ARRAY(0))
```

If possible, avoid using the more exotic BASIC commands. Using DRAW, for example, will add almost 900 bytes to your program. The RND function will superficially cost about 300 bytes. By coding my own assembly routine to return a random number between two values, I was able to save 200 bytes, plus all the time required for the floating-point multiplications needed with BASIC's RND function.

This illustrates perhaps your biggest resource in code compression—writing custom routines with the assembler to avoid the bulky, generalized BASIC commands. If your BASIC program is written in clear-cut modules, you should be able to rewrite entire subroutines in assembly language.

The CALL command allows you to pass as many as 60 variables to a machine language subroutine. For example:

```
MIN = 0 :MAX = 20
CALL MY_RND(RND.NUM, MAX, MIN)
```

will pass three addresses to the random number generator I wrote. It does this by PUSHing the addresses of the variables onto the stack one at a time. You can shorten this process by placing the values in an array and passing only one address—that of the array's 0th element:

```
RND.NUM(1)=0 :RND.NUM(2)=20
CALL MY_RND(RND.NUM(0)) 'or CALL
   MY_RND(RND.NUM)
```

The assembly language routine must assume that the address it receives points to 6 bytes of data and that the first 2 are for the return value, the next 2 are the minimum and the last 2 are the maximum value. This saves time and code in both the compiled program and your own routine.

The IBM BASIC Compiler has limitations, but it is a logical choice over writing applications in assembly language. By studying the code that the compiler generates and taking advantage of its optimization techniques, it is possible to make faster running, more efficient programs. By doing some mental and programmatic preprocessing and using some ingenuity, you can squeeze the most value from this programming tool.

Dan Rollins is a freelance writer and programmer who is currently the technical editor at Personal Computer Age. *His most recent book is* IBM PC: 8088 MACRO Assembler Programming *published by Macmillan. This article was originally published in* PC World *Volume 1, Number 4.*

BASIC Block Moves

Stuart Greenberg

In my day-to-day programming I draw from a library of several general subroutines when I "build" a program. Most are in BASIC, but some are in assembly language. I add a routine to this library whenever I feel that it would be of general use. One of these subroutines is written in assembly language and is called BMOVE.

Moving Blocks

BMOVE is short for block move and, as the name suggests, it will move a block of data from one location in memory to another. The block move instruction was introduced to the microcomputer world by the Z-80 microprocessor chip. This chip included two instructions, LDIR and LDDR, that would move data from an area pointed to by one register to an area pointed to by another register and automatically loop until a third register counted down to zero. The increase in speed achieved by using these instructions was dramatic, and it was immediately exploited. For example, many TRS-80 games and other programs use block move routines to move data quickly from memory to screen and vice versa.

Naturally, when 16-bit microprocessors were designed, the block move command was designed into them. Pointers to the source and destination areas and a count of bytes are simply loaded into registers (storage locations in the 8088), and the block move instruction (REP MOVSB) takes care of the rest. This coding was designed to be easy to implement, but the subroutine presented here is complicated slightly by passing variables from BASIC.

The sample programs presented later in the article show you how to use the BMOVE subroutine to fill an integer array with a value, move part of an integer array up or down, save screen images in memory, and flash stored screen images back to the screen. The application section of the article describes how the subroutine might be used.

How It's Done

Don't let the fact that BMOVE is in assembly language bother you. Knowledge of assembly language is not required for use of BMOVE, but even novices should try to follow the detailed explanation that follows.

BMOVE (see Figure 8.9) was written using a framework common to all of my assembly language subroutines. This framework is based on one that appeared in issue 1.7 of *Revolution,* the newsletter of the Autumn Revolution Users' Group, and it produces very clear and well-formatted code. Consider the framework line by line as you examine the actual details of the code.

Lines 1 through 3 specify the name of the routine and printing options to the assembler. Unfortunately, space will not permit a thorough tutorial on assembly language. NAME, PAGE, TITLE, and other specific items not described in detail here are described in the IBM *Macro Assembler* manual.

The comments on lines 10 through 21 list the BASIC variables and show the call statement necessary to invoke BMOVE from a BASIC program. Notice that the type of BASIC variable is shown by suffixing the variable name with the appropriate character; in this case a percent sign indicates an integer variable. Different types of BASIC variables require different amounts of storage space. The suffix is a reminder to use the proper assembly language instructions when you are accessing each variable, and it also helps you avoid using the wrong variable type in a BASIC program that calls the routine. It may not seem important when you first code the routine, but this documentation proves very handy when you need to write a program to call the routine a month or a year later.

The *Macro Assembler* allows programs to be divided into manageable parts, called segments. Each segment can be up to 64K in length and is pointed to by each of four segment registers. One such segment that BMOVE must define is an area in memory for temporary storage, called the stack segment. Pointers to the BASIC variables and a return vector to BASIC are in known locations (offsets) in the stack segment when BMOVE gets control. BMOVE can also use the PUSH and POP commands (described later) to save and restore the contents of the 8088's registers via the stack.

```
1                    NAME BMOVE
2                    PAGE 60,132
3                    TITLE   .     BMOVE - BASIC BLOCK MOVE ROUTINE
4
5            ; BMOVE - Basic Block Move Routine
6            ;      Written by Stuart Greenberg
7            ;         Copyright May,1983
8            ;          May not be copied for commercial use!
9
10           ; Called by Basic Program As Follows:
11
12           ; CALL BMOVE%(FROMSEG%,FROMOFF%,TOSEG%,TOOFF%,COUNT%,DIRECTION%)
13
14           ; Where:
15
16           ; FROMSEG%=source segment
17           ; FROMOFF%=source offset
18           ; TOSEG%=destination segment
19           ; TOOFF%=destination offset
20           ; COUNT%=number of bytes to move
21           ; DIRECTION%=direction of move (0=forward, all others=backward)
22
23   0000      STACK_AREA      SEGMENT STACK
24   0000      STACK_AREA      ENDS
25
26   0000      CODE_AREA       SEGMENT
27
28             ASSUME CS:CODE_AREA, SS:STACK_AREA
29   0000      BMOVE           PROC         FAR
30
31   = 0006    NUM_ARG     EQU       6
32             ;                            Offset of Pointer to:
33   = 0010    FROM_SEG    EQU       (NUM_ARG-1)*2+6  ;       FROMSEG%
34   = 000E    FROM_OFFSET EQU       (NUM_ARG-2)*2+6  ;       FROMOFF%
35   = 000C    TO_SEG      EQU       (NUM_ARG-3)*2+6  ;       TOSEG%
36   = 000A    TO_OFFSET   EQU       (NUM_ARG-4)*2+6  ;       TOOFF%
37   = 0008    COUNT       EQU       (NUM_ARG-5)*2+6  ;       COUNT%
38   = 0006    DIRECTION   EQU       (NUM_ARG-6)*2+6  ;       DIRECTION%
39
40   0000 55         PUSH     BP                      ; Save BP
```

Figure 8.9 *BMOVE*

Since BASIC defines and maintains a stack of sufficient size, all BMOVE has to do is name an area and tell the assembler that the Stack Segment (SS) register already points to it. The statements in lines 23 and 24 of Figure 8.9 take care of the former, and the SS:STACK_AREA specification in the ASSUME statement (line 28) accomplishes the latter. The ASSUME statement also tells the assembler that the Code Segment (CS) register will be pointing to the BMOVE code segment, which begins at line 26, when the subroutine is invoked from BASIC. The other two segments, data and extra, do not need to be defined since BMOVE will not access them directly. The Data Segment (DS) and Extra Segment (ES) registers will be pointing to BASIC's data segment when BMOVE is invoked from BASIC. BMOVE will find the passed variable values via the DS register and will alter the DS and ES registers later on to point to the source and destination memory blocks.

The PROC statement (line 29) indicates the beginning of a block of related code called a procedure (PROC for short). The FAR operand of the PROC statement is required for procedures called from BASIC programs. It tells the assembler that both the segment and offset addresses were used to invoke BMOVE. BASIC uses the DEF SEG= and CALL statements, respectively, to define these values. The

```
41   0001 8B EC       MOV      BP,SP                      ; Put SP in BP
42
43   0003 FC          CLD                         ; Set-up for Forward Direction
44   0004 8B 5E 06    MOV   BX,[BP]+DIRECTION     ; Get Pointer to DIRECTION%
45   0007 83 3F 00    CMP   WORD PTR [BX],0       ; Is Direction Forward?
46   000A 74 01       JE    SET_REGS              ; YES-Don't Change Direction Flag
47   000C FD          STD                         ; NO - Set-up for Backward
48                                                ; Direction
49   000D             SET_REGS:
50   000D 8B 5E 0E    MOV      BX,[BP]+FROM_OFFSET    ; Get Pointer to FROMOFF%
51   0010 8B 37       MOV      SI,[BX]                ; Store Value in SI
52   0012 8B 5E 0C    MOV      BX,[BP]+TO_SEG         ; Get Pointer to TOSEG%
53   0015 06          PUSH     ES                     ; Preserve ES Register
54   0016 8E 07       MOV      ES,[BX]                ; Store Value in ES
55   0018 8B 5E 0A    MOV      BX,[BP]+TO_OFFSET      ; Get Pointer to TOOFF%
56   001B 8B 3F       MOV      DI,[BX]                ; Store Value in DI
57   001D 8B 5E 08    MOV      BX,[BP]+COUNT          ; Get Pointer to COUNT%
58   0020 8B 0F       MOV      CX,[BX]                ; Store Value in CX
59   0022 8B 5E 10    MOV      BX,[BP]+FROM_SEG       ; Get Pointer to FROMSEG%
60   0025 1E          PUSH     DS                     ; Preserve DS Register
61   0026 8E 1F       MOV      DS,[BX]                ; Store Value in DS
62
63   0028 F3/ A4      REP      MOVSB                  ;Do Move: [DS:SI] -> [ES:DI]
64                                              ; CX <- CX - 1
65                                              ; DS:SI <- DS:SI +/- 1
66                                              ; ES:DI <- ES:DI +/- 1
67                                              ; Repeat Until CX = 0
68
69   002A 1F          POP      DS               ; Restore Segment
70   002B 07          POP      ES               ; Registers
71   002C 5D          POP      BP               ; Restore BP
72
73   002D CA 000C     RET      2*NUM_ARG        ; Return
74
75   0030             BMOVE    ENDP
76
77   0030             CODE_AREA        ENDS
78
79                    END      BMOVE
```

Figure 8.9 *(continued)*

Return (RET) statement in line 73 uses this information to generate the code needed to return to BASIC. A version of CALL and RET uses only the offset address (NEAR), but BASIC is not able to use that type of addressing for calling subroutines.

Lines 31 through 38 assign values to variable names that will be used within the code that follows that section. There are several reasons for doing this. If a value is used in many places throughout the code but may be changed in the future, assigning it a name enables you to change only the line defining the name and have the assembler automatically assign the new value wherever the name is used. A name might also be assigned if repeatedly using an expression to represent a value would require an excessive amount of typing or if the name would be easier to understand than the expression would be when you are reading the code. The result of each expression in lines 33 through 38 is the offset from a known location in the stack segment, stored in the Stack Pointer (SP) register, where a pointer to the actual passed data is stored. The derivation of this expression is described in Appendix C of the BASIC manual.

At last we come to some executable code! In lines 40 and 41 the original value of the Base Pointer (BP) register is saved on the stack (PUSHed) and given the value of the SP register. The SP register points to the position in the stack where our variable pointers were stored by BASIC; now BP points there too.

BMOVE can move a block of data either forward or backward through memory. The application section of this article discusses the importance of the direction of a block move. Lines 43 through 47 in Figure 8.9 set or reset an indicator in the 8088 called the direction flag. If the value for the BASIC variable DIRECTION% is zero, the direction flag will be cleared (indicating forward movement); otherwise it is set (indicating backward movement). The program first assumes a forward direction with the Clear Direction Flag (CLD) instruction in line 43. Line 44 loads the pointer to DIRECTION% into the BX register. Line 45 refers to the actual value of DIRECTION% as the two bytes (WORD) pointed to (PTR) by the Base register (BX). If DIRECTION% is equal to zero, the Jump If Equal (JE) instruction in line 46 will bypass the Set Direction Flag (STD) instruction in line 47; otherwise the STD instruction will be executed and a backward move will be indicated to the 8088.

The BASIC variables are loaded into the proper 8088 registers in lines 50 through 61. Line 50 loads the pointer to FROMOFF% into the BX register, as was done for DIRECTION% in line 44. Remember that the BX register is being used for temporary storage and, since it is no longer needed to point to DIRECTION%, it can now be reused. Using the BX register as a pointer to the actual data, line 51 loads the value of FROMOFF% into the Source Index (SI) register. The method used in these lines (loading the pointer to the data into BX, then using BX as a pointer to load the data into the desired register) is repeated for each register that needs loading (ES, DI, CX, and DS). The two PUSH instructions, one in line 53 and the other in line 60, preserve the ES and DS registers so that the values can be restored to the original values that were passed from BASIC. You may have noticed that with the exception of the DS register the registers were loaded in the same order as the associated variables in the BASIC CALL statement. The order is actually arbitrary except for the loading of the DS register. This register is used by the other MOV instructions to point to the data segment containing the BASIC variables. Changing the DS register too soon causes the 8088 to lose track of BASIC's data segment and load invalid data.

And now the moment you've been waiting for: the actual block move instruction. When line 63 is executed, COUNT% (CS register) number of bytes starting at the address pointed to by FROMSEG% and FROMOFF% (DS and SI registers) is moved to an area pointed to by TOSEG% and TOOFF% (ES and DI registers). If the direction chosen is forward, the addresses are incremented by one each time a byte is moved; otherwise the addresses are decremented by one. You can get a feel for the power of the REP MOVSB instruction by looking at all the instructions required to move the few bytes necessary to set up for the block move and knowing that as many as 64K bytes (the capacity of the CX register) can be moved with this one line of code.

Clean It Up

We're in the home stretch now. Before exiting back to BASIC, BMOVE has to comply with what I call Roddenberry's Rule of Order (also known as the Noninterference Directive), which states that a program will not interfere with the normal execution of another program. The BASIC manual dictates that if the contents of any of the segment or SP registers are altered during the execution of the subroutine, the original value or values must be restored before the subroutine is completed. The BMOVE routine also restores the BP register. This process isn't specifically required but doesn't hurt. The values in the affected registers were saved by the earlier PUSH instructions (lines 40, 53, and 60), which preserved the original values of the BP, ES, and DS registers. The original values are restored by the POP instructions in lines 69 through 71. Notice that the order of the POP instructions is opposite that of the PUSH instructions. The 8088 uses a last-in, first-out (LIFO) stack—the last register PUSHed must be the first register POPped.

At this point the only item remaining to be restored is the condition of the stack. Remember that the pointers to the variables were passed to BMOVE by PUSHing them onto the stack. BMOVE must remove the pointers to free up the space on the stack; otherwise the stack would

```
50000 ' Subroutine Name = BMOVE      Length = 48
50001 '
50002 ' Data Statements and Load Routine
50003 DATA &H55,&H8B,&HEC,&HFC,&H8B,&H5E,&H06,&H83,&H3F,&H00,&H74,&H01,&HFD
50004 DATA &H8B,&H5E,&H0E,&H8B,&H37,&H8B,&H5E,&H0C,&H06,&H8E,&H07,&H8B,&H5E
50005 DATA &H0A,&H8B,&H3F,&H8B,&H5E,&H08,&H8B,&H0F,&H8B,&H5E,&H10,&H1E,&H8E
50007 DATA &H1F,&HF3,&HA4,&H1F,&H07,&H5D,&HCA,&H0C,&H00
50008 RESTORE 50003
50009 BM.PGM$=STRING$(48,32)
50010 FOR X.X=1 TO 48
50011   READ X.A:MID$(BM.PGM$,X.X,1)=CHR$(X.A)
50012 NEXT X.X
50013 DEF SEG:BM.STRING=VARPTR(BM.PGM$)
50014 BM.ENTRY=PEEK(BM.STRING+1)+PEEK(BM.STRING+2)*256
50015 ' Initialize Parameters. . .
50016 BM.FROMSEG%=0:BM.FROMOFF%=0:BM.TOSEG%=0:BM.TOOFF%=0:BM.COUNT%=0:
      BM.DIRECTION%=0
50017 RETURN
50020 ' GOSUB 50020 to Execute CALL. . .
50021 DEF SEG:BM.STRING=VARPTR(BM.PGM$)
50022 BM.ENTRY=PEEK(BM.STRING+1)+PEEK(BM.STRING+2)*256
50023 DEF SEG:CALL BM.ENTRY(BM.FROMSEG%,BM.FROMOFF%,BM.TOSEG%,BM.TOOFF%,
50024 BM.COUNT%,BM.DIRECTION%)
      RETURN
```

Figure 8.10 *Subroutine for BMOVE.*

grow unnecessarily each time BMOVE is invoked. The 8088 makes the clean-up task easy by allowing a certain number of bytes on the stack to be discarded after accessing the return vector. Since the pointers take up 2 bytes each, the number of bytes to skip is equal to twice the number of arguments passed to the subroutine. The Return (RET) instruction in line 73 notifies the 8088 to discard the proper number of bytes (2*NUM_ARG) and returns control to BASIC.

The remaining lines are housekeeping. Line 75 indicates the end of the procedure, line 77 marks the end of the code segment, and finally, line 79 ends the assembly language code.

BMOVE Applications

As you will see, it isn't necessary to know what each and every byte of BMOVE does in order to make use of it. You may wish to treat BMOVE as a black box and simply learn how to set up the necessary variables and issue the CALL instruction in BASIC.

Figure 8.10 has two subroutines. The first one (starting at line 50000) uses a technique known as string packing to load BMOVE into memory as a BASIC string (BM.PGM$). String packing eliminates the need to reserve extra memory outside BASIC, which can be difficult if you have a limited amount of memory available. As you can see, several variables are set in this routine. Notice that the variables directly related to BMOVE all use the prefix BM. The prefix is used to avoid conflict with other variables in the main BASIC program, allowing BMOVE to be used in an existing program by simply inserting the code in Figure 8.10 without the fear of inserting problems along with it.

BASIC's VARPTR function is used to find the location of the string descriptor for BM.PGM$, and PEEKs are used to obtain the offset address of BM.PGM$ within BASIC's data segment. This value is assigned to BM.ENTRY% and is the entry address of BMOVE. The second subroutine (starting on line 50020) performs an actual CALL to BMOVE using a standard set of variables as parameters. To use BMOVE you must execute a GOSUB to line 50000 early in your main program, set up the parameter variables, and execute a GOSUB to 50020.

Type in the routines in Figure 8.10 and save them with the ASCII option (**SAVE"BMOVE.SUB",A**) so you can merge them back in later.

Figure 8.11 has three sample routines. They all operate on integer arrays and perform functions that you may have already written into BASIC programs. The first sample program involves initializing a 1001 element array (elements 0 through 1000) to a constant value. Both the traditional BASIC code and the BMOVE equivalent are demonstrated here to show the difference in execution speed. Figure 8.12 shows how an element may be propagated throughout an entire array by using BMOVE in a forward direction with overlapping data.

The second sample program allows an element to be inserted into an array at a specified point. The elements from this point to the bottom

```
1 ' MOVARRAY.DEM - Demonstration program for the BMOVE Subroutine
2 '
3 '                  Written by: Stuart Greenberg
4 '                  Copyright May, 1983 - May not be copied for commercial
5 '                  use
10 DEF SEG=0:BASIC.SEG%=PEEK(&H510)+PEEK(&H511)*256:BASIC.TOP%=BASIC.
   SEG%+&H1000
20 ' Set-up BMOVE Routine
30 GOSUB 50000
40 CLS:KEY OFF
100 ' The following three routines (1000, 2000, 3000) perform
110 ' demonstrations of the BMOVE subroutine. In each case
120 ' parameter variables are assigned appropriate values
130 ' and a GOSUB to 50020 is executed. The parameter
140 ' variables are:
150 '        FROMSEG% - The segment address of the source block
160 '        FROMOFF% - The offset address of the source block
170 '        TOSEG%   - The segment address of the destination block
180 '        TOOFF%   - The offset address of the destination block
185 '        COUNT%   - The number of bytes to move (1 integer=2 bytes)
190 '        DIRECTION% - 0=Forward, Any other value=Backward
200 '
210 '=================================================================
220 '
1000 ' DEMO #1 - This demo will load an integer array containing 1001
           elements using the FOR/NEXT method and then the BMOVE
1010 '     subroutine. The FOR/NEXT loop will load the array with
1020 '     zeroes and BMOVE will reassign each element the value
1030 '     1983. After hitting the space bar the array is
1040 '     displayed to show that all elements really and truly
1050 '     contain 1983.
1060 '
1065 PRINT "D E M O   # 1"
1070 DIM A%(1000)                                'Define array
1075 PRINT TAB(25);"--START-";TAB(40);"---END--"
1080 PRINT "FOR/NEXT loop: ";TAB(25);TIME$;
1090 FOR X%=0 TO 1000                            'FOR/NEXT loop
1100    A%(X%)=0                                 '  assigns 0 to
1110 NEXT                                        '  each element
1120 '
1130 PRINT TAB(40);TIME$:PRINT "BMOVE:";TAB(25);TIME$;
1140 A%(0)=1983                                  'First element=1983
1150 BM.FROMSEG%=BASIC.SEG%:BM.TOSEG%=BASIC.SEG% 'From & to segments
1155 '                                            are Basic's work area
1160 DEF SEG                                     'Set segment for VARPTR
1170 BM.FROMOFF%=VARPTR(A%(0))                   'Address of 1st element
1180 BM.TOOFF%=BM.FROMOFF%+2                     'Address of 2nd element
1190 BM.COUNT%=2000                              '2000 bytes to move
1200 BM.DIRECTION%=0                             'Forward direction
1210 GOSUB 50020                                 'Invoke BMOVE
1220 PRINT TAB(40);TIME$
1230 '
1240 GOSUB 45000
1255 LOCATE 25,1:PRINT SPACE$(79);:LOCATE 4,1
1257 PRINT:PRINT:PRINT "--ARRAY VERIFICATION--"          'Verify entire array
1260 FOR X%=0 TO 5
1270    PRINT USING "Element ####    = ####";X%,A%(X%)  'First 5 visually
1280 NEXT
```

(continues)

Figure 8.11 *Demonstration program for the BMOVE subroutine.*

```
1290 PRINT STRING$(22,249)
1300 FOR X%=6 TO 995
1310   LOCATE CSRLIN,1                                'Middle 990 visually
1320   IF A%(X%)<>1983 THEN STOP                      'and use IF
1330   PRINT USING "Element 6 - ### = ####";X%,A%(X%); 'statement since
1340 NEXT                                             'this goes by too
1350 PRINT:PRINT STRING$(22,249)                      'fast
1360 FOR X%=996 TO 1000
1370   PRINT USING "Element    #### = ####";X%,A%(X%)  'Last 5 visually
1380 NEXT
1390 ' E N D   O F   D E M O   # 1
1400 '
1410 '======================================================================
1420 '
2000 ' DEMO #2 - This demo will move the lower part of an array down to
2010 '     make room for a value to be inserted in the middle. Elements 31
2020 '     thru 99 will move to 32 thru 100 and a new value will be assigned
2030 '     to element 31. This method can be the basis of an insertion
2040 '     sort where each element is checked against a new value and
2050 '     inserted in its proper place.
2060 '
2062 GOSUB 45000
2065 CLS:PRINT "D E M O   # 2"
2067 PRINT "Before:"
2070 DIM B%(100)                                      'Define array
2080 FOR X%=0 TO 100                                  'Initialize to
2090   B%(X%)=X%                                      '  sequential values
2095   PRINT B%(X%),                                  '  AND PRINT THEM
2100 NEXT
2110 '
2120 BM.FROMSEG%=BASIC.SEG%:BM.TOSEG%=BASIC.SEG%      'From & to segments
2130 '                                                 are Basic's work area
2140 DEF SEG                                          'Set segment for VARPTR
2150 BM.FROMOFF%=VARPTR(B%(99))+1                     'Address of element 99
2160 BM.TOOFF%=BM.FROMOFF%+2                          'Address of element 100
2170 BM.COUNT%=138                                    'Byte count=2*elements
2180 BM.DIRECTION%=1                                  'Backward direction
2190 GOSUB 50020                                      'Invoke BMOVE
2200 B%(31)=1983                                      'Set element 31
2202 GOSUB 45000
2205 LOCATE 2,1:COLOR 15,0:PRINT "After: "
2210 FOR X%=0 TO 100                                  'Reprint array showing
2220   PRINT B%(X%),                                  '  new values
2230 NEXT
2240 ' E N D   O F   D E M O   # 2
2250 '
2260 '======================================================================
2270 '
3000 ' DEMO #3 - This demo will move the lower part of an array up to
3010 '     delete an element form the middle. Elements 32 thru 100 will
3020 '     move up to 31 thru 99 thus deleting element 31.
3060 '
3070 GOSUB 45000                                      'Wait to continue
3080 LOCATE 1,1:COLOR 7,0:PRINT "D E M O   # 3"
3090 PRINT "Before:"
3100 FOR X%=0 TO 100                                  'Reprint array showing
3110   PRINT B%(X%),                                  '  starting values
3115 NEXT
3120 BM.FROMSEG%=BASIC.SEG%:BM.TOSEG%=BASIC.SEG%      'From & to segments
```

Figure 8.11 *(continued)*

```
3130 '                                          are Basic's work area
3140 DEF SEG                                    'Set segment for VARPTR
3150 BM.FROMOFF%=VARPTR(B%(32))                 'Address of element 32
3160 BM.TOOFF%=BM.FROMOFF%-2                    'Address of element 31
3170 BM.COUNT%=138                              'Byte count=2*elements
3180 BM.DIRECTION%=0                            'Forward direction
3190 GOSUB 50020                                'Invoke BMOVE
3192 GOSUB 45000
3195 LOCATE 2,1:COLOR 15,0:PRINT "After: "
3210 FOR X%=0 TO 100                            'Reprint array showing
3220   PRINT B%(X%),                            '  new values
3230 NEXT
3240 COLOR 7,0
3250 '
3260 ' E N D   O F   D E M O   # 3
3270 '
3280 '=====================================================================
4000 GOSUB 45000                                'Wait to continue
4010 CLS:PRINT "E N D   O F   D E M O S"        'End of Demo routines
4020 END
45000 LOCATE 25,1:COLOR 23,0:PRINT TAB(28);"Hit Space Bar to Continue"
      ;:COLOR 7,0
45001 A$=INKEY$:IF A$<>" " THEN 45001
45002 LOCATE 25,1:PRINT SPACE$(79);:LOCATE 4,1:RETURN
50000 'Merge BMOVE routine here
```

Figure 8.11 *(continued)*

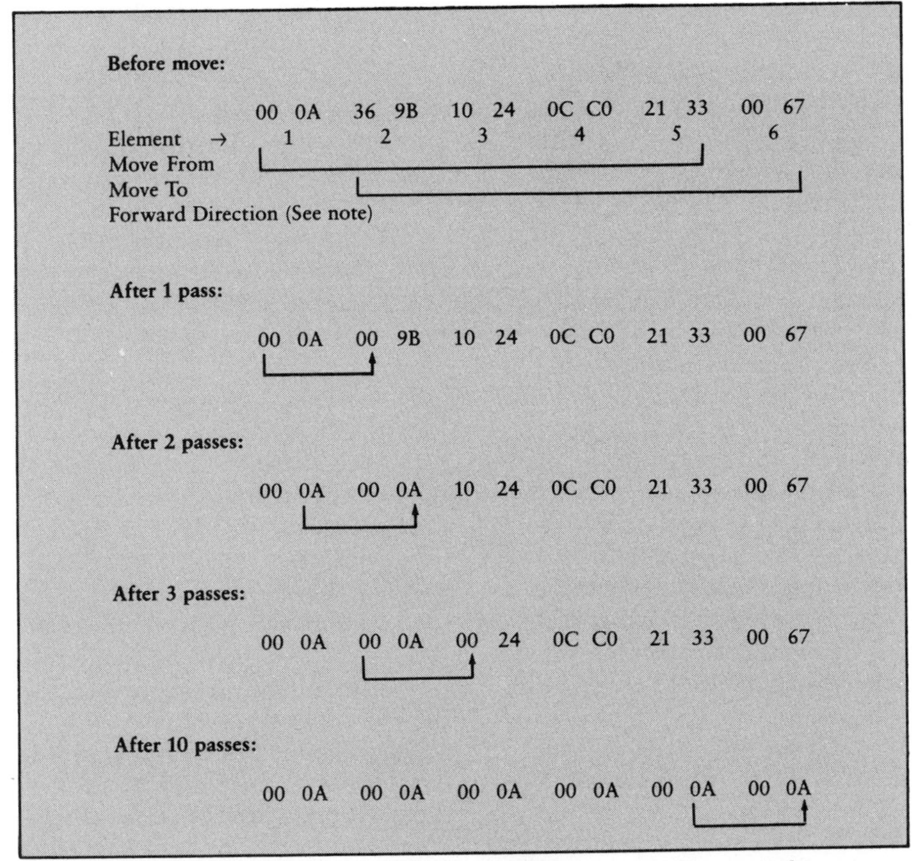

Figure 8.12 *The from address is less than the to address, forward direction. Element 1 is copied into 2 through 6.*

are moved down to make way for the newcomer, and the last element's value is discarded. Among the uses of this technique is the insertion sort in which each value is added to the array by moving down all elements containing a higher value and inserting the new value in its proper place.

The third sample program eliminates an element by moving all the following elements up and overlaying the departing element. After the elements are moved up, the last element will be duplicated into the next-to-last element. If this side-effect is a problem, a new value for the last element will have to be assigned manually. Figures 8.13 and 8.14 show how data-block overlap and movement direction are used to shift memory forward or backward as was done in these two sample programs.

One way to combine all these techniques is to use the technique in Demo #1 (see Figure 8.11) to ini-

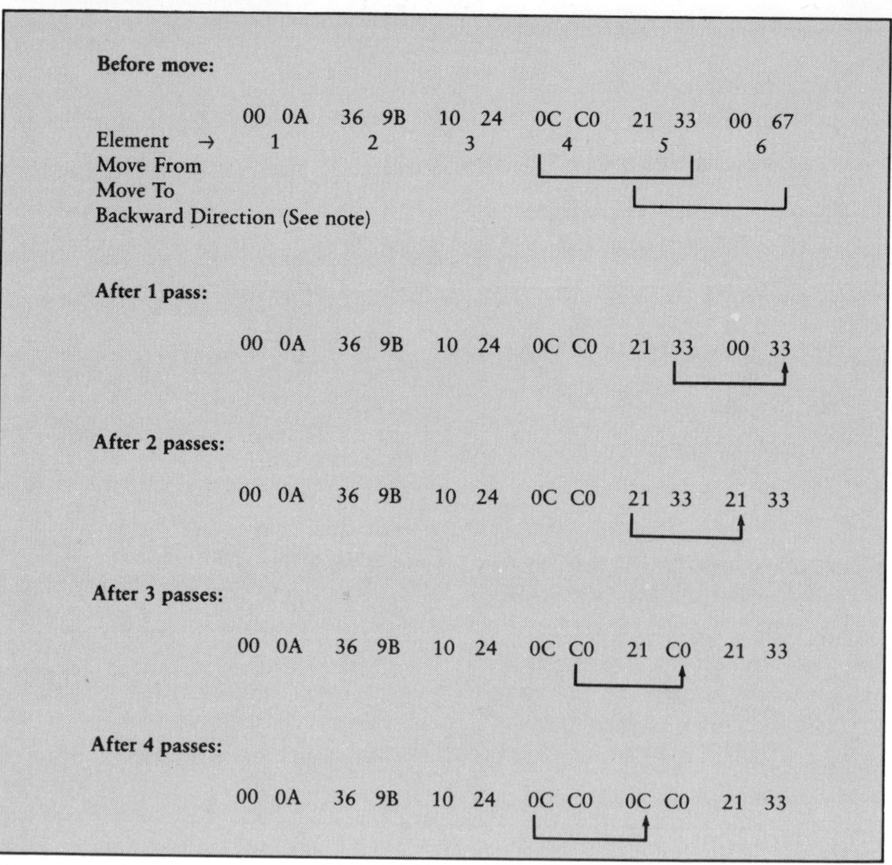

Figure 8.13 *The from address is less than the to address, backward direction. Elements 4 and 5 move down to 5 and 6.*

tialize an array to a special value and add values in ascending order using the technique in Demo #2. If you want to delete a value in the middle, you can use the technique in Demo #3 and set the last element equal to the special value to indicate that the array is not full. The existence of the special value in the last element assures you that the array has not filled up and that insertion of another value will not cause a loss of data. The array always contains the values in sorted order followed by elements set to the special value.

Before executing the sample routines in the program MOVARRAY.DEM, examine some of the code in Figure 8.11. Line 10 PEEKs locations 0510H and 0511H to obtain the segment address of the start of BASIC's work space (see the IBM *Personal Computer Technical Reference* manual, page 3-22), assigns the value to the variable BASIC.SEG%, adds 1000H to BASIC.SEG% to determine the top of BASIC's work space, and assigns this value to BASIC.TOP%. BASIC.SEG% is needed when an assembly language subroutine needs to access data within BASIC's work space. In Demo #1, for example, the array A%. BASIC.TOP% contains the next available segment above BASIC's 64K work space and can be used to indicate the start of a safe haven for code or data to be stored outside BASIC's influence. This assumes a full 64K BASIC work space. If you have less than 96K of memory or you have high memory reserved for a RAM disk or spooler, you will have to change this value manually. The steps required to make this manual setting are beyond the scope of this article but are described in the BASIC manual.

In the course of writing these sample routines, the desirability of a subroutine to halt execution and wait for an operator request to continue became obvious. The subroutine was added starting at line 45000. When invoked via a GOSUB 45000, it will display a flashing message, wait for the operator to hit the space bar, and continue processing. This subroutine saved a considerable amount of coding that would have been required had the routine been typed in each time it was needed.

Type in the code for the sample program MOVARRAY.DEM, and if it isn't already present, merge in the BMOVE subroutine you saved earlier. Save the entire program to disk with the command **SAVE"MOVARRAY.DEM"**, and when you type RUN the first demo will start. You will notice that the BMOVE routine runs significantly faster than the FOR . . . NEXT loop.

By the way, if you don't believe that all the elements have been set to 1983, just press the space bar. The entire array will be displayed on the screen and each element will be equal to 1983. Continue through the demonstration routines by pressing the space bar when requested, and note the effect on the array after Demos #2 and #3. They used a small array (101 elements) for easy viewing since the speed of BMOVE was already demonstrated in Demo #1. If you need to be convinced of the true speed advantage of the BMOVE routine, change the DIMensions and BMOVE parameters to use a larger array for each demo. A 5001 element array will

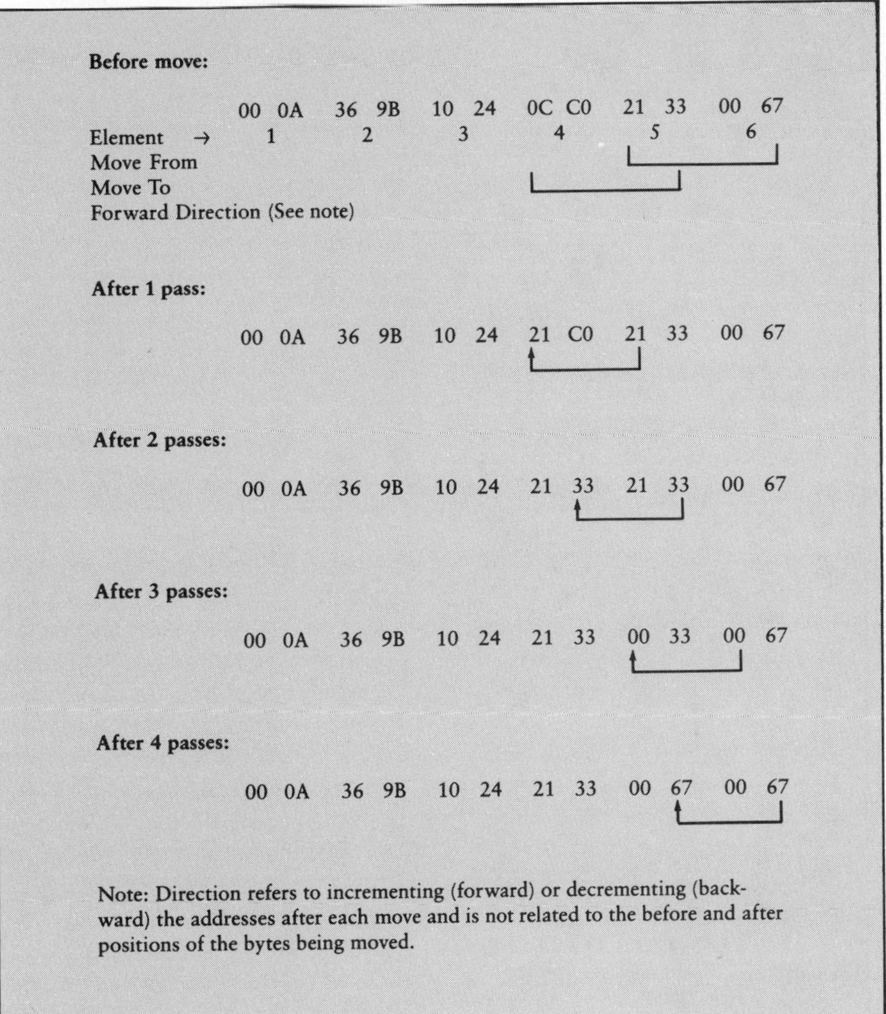

Figure 8.14 *The from address is greater than the to address, forward direction. Elements 5 and 6 move up to 4 and 5.*

take approximately 30 seconds to initialize using FOR . . . NEXT, but it will be instantaneous using BMOVE. You'll find BMOVE a valuable tool as you experiment with BMOVEing pieces of arrays.

Hold That Screen

Figure 8.15 is another subroutine called Screen Slinger. It allows you to create screens and store them in memory. When you want to display one of the screens, just give Screen Slinger the G command and the screen is BMOVEd from memory to the display in the blink of an eye. Screen Slinger can be used to display menus and the legends for fill-in-the-blank-type data screens. It can also be used for creating animated effects by saving the individual "snap shot" of screens and "slinging" them rapidly in succession.

When you are using Screen Slinger, the main consideration is the amount of memory available above BASIC (beyond BASIC.TOP%). Each monochrome display screen requires 4K, and each color graphics display screen requires 16K. The number of screens is limited only by the amount of available memory; of course, if you have no memory available, you can't use Screen Slinger at all. Each screen is stored contiguously in memory and is accessed by its assigned screen number. Screen Slinger can also save or load a block of screens to and from the disk so that you need only create the screen once and call it into memory from disk when the target program is run. Alternatively, you could load all the screens needed for an application when you start it. That way they will remain resident even when you chain to another program.

Screen Slinger is split into two sections, each having four functions. The split is necessary because the method used to save text screens is different from that used to save graphics screens. The text screen is simply a contiguous block of 4K bytes of memory, while the graphics screen consists of two 8K blocks. The variable SS.MODE$ contains T for text or G for graphics to allow Screen Slinger to choose the correct routine to perform the required function. The function itself is chosen by setting the variable SS.CMD$ to one of the following values:

G Gets a block of screens from disk
P Puts a block of screens to disk
S Stores a screen in memory
R Restores a screen to the display

The variable SS.SRNNUM% must contain the desired screen number for commands S and R. Since Screen Slinger uses BLOAD to get the screens from disk, it must load all the screens saved in a file at one time, but it can store any or all screens currently stored in memory. In either case, SS.SRNNUM% indicates the first screen number, and for

```
1 ' SCRNSLGR.DEM - Demonstration program for the SCRNSLGR subroutine
2 '
3 '                  Written by: Stuart Greenberg
4 '                  Copyright May, 1983 - May not be copied for
5 '                  commercial use!
10 DEF SEG=0:BASIC.SEG%=PEEK(&H510)+PEEK(&H511)*256:BASIC.TOP%=BASIC.
   SEG%+&H1000
20 DEF SEG=&H40:SCREENSEG%=&HB000-((PEEK(&H10) AND &H30)<>&H30)*&H800
30 KEY OFF:CLS
40 GOSUB 50000                                'Initialize BMOVE
50 '                                           Basic + 16 bytes
60 '                                           Mode of screen=text
70 SS.BASE%=BASIC.TOP%+1                      'Start of screen storage=Top of
80 '                                           Basic + 16 bytes
90 SS.MODE$="G"                               'Mode of screen=text
91 '
92 PRINT "Demonstration of Screen Slinger":PRINT
94 INPUT "Enter 1 to create screens or 2 to use saved screens: ",A
96 IF A=2 THEN INPUT "Enter filename: ",SS.NAME$:CLS:GOTO 540 ELSE CLS
98 '
100 A$=CHR$(249)+CHR$(250)+CHR$(250)
110 B$="BMOVE - The Block Move Subroutine by Stuart Greenberg"
    'Message to print
120 '
130 ' Create first screen:
140 '
150 Y=0                                       'Set border offset
160 GOSUB 1000                                'Display border
170 SS.CMD$="S":SS.SRNNUM%=1:GOSUB 49100      'Save screen 1
180 '
190 ' Create second screen:
200 '
210 Y=2                                       'Set border offset
220 LOCATE 13,15:COLOR 15,0:PRINT B$;:COLOR 7,0 'Display msg highlighted
230 GOSUB 1000                                'Display border
240 SS.CMD$="S":SS.SRNNUM%=2:GOSUB 49100      'Save screen 2
250 '
260 ' Create third screen:
270 '
280 Y=1                                       'Set border offset
290 LOCATE 13,15:PRINT B$;                    'Display msg normal
300 GOSUB 1000                                'Display border
310 SS.CMD$="S":SS.SRNNUM%=3:GOSUB 49100      'Save screen 3
320 '
330 ' Display each screen in turn - repeate indefinately
340 '
350 X=1
360 SS.CMD$="R"                               'RESTORE command
370 SS.SRNNUM%=X:GOSUB 49100                  'Each screen (X=1 to 3)
380 X=X+1:IF X>3 THEN X=1                     'Increment X
390 FOR Y=1 TO 50:NEXT Y                      'Display delay
400 IF INKEY$="" THEN 370 ELSE IF LOOP=1 THEN 630 'Check for keypress
410 '
420 ' When any key is pressed - continue:
430 '
440 COLOR 7,0                                 'Reset color
450 LOCATE 13,15:PRINT SPACE$(LEN(B$))        'Blank msg
460 LOCATE 13,15:INPUT "Enter filename for screen save: ",SS.NAME$
470 SS.SRNNUM%=1                              'First screen number=1
480 SS.SRNCNT%=3                              'Number of screens to save=3
```

(continues)

Figure 8.15 *SCRNSLGR.DEM*

```
490 SS.CMD$="P"                                        'PUT command
500 GOSUB 49100                                        'Save screens
510 '
520 ' Now to reload screens:
530 '
540 LOCATE 13,15:PRINT SPACE$(LEN(B$))                      'Blank msg
550 LOCATE 13,15:PRINT "Reloading screens from: ";SS.NAME$;
560 SS.SRNNUM%=1                                            'First screen number
570 SS.CMD$="G"                                             'GET command
580 GOSUB 49100                                             'Reload screens
590 LOOP=1
600 GOTO 350                                                'Redisplay screens
610 '
620 ' End of demo message
630 CLS:PRINT "End of demonstration":END                    'End of Demo routine
640 '
650 ' End of mainline code
1000 '
1010 ' Display boarder subroutine:
1020 '
1030 ' Top:
1040 '
1050 FOR X=1 TO 79
1060   Y=Y+1:IF Y>3 THEN Y=1
1070   IF Y=1 THEN COLOR 15,0 ELSE COLOR 7,0
1080   LOCATE 1,X:PRINT MID$(A$,Y,1);
1090 NEXT X
1100 '
1110 ' Right side:
1120 '
1130 FOR X=2 TO 24
1140   Y=Y+1:IF Y>3 THEN Y=1
1150   IF Y=1 THEN COLOR 15,0 ELSE COLOR 7,0
1160   LOCATE X,79:PRINT MID$(A$,Y,1);
1170 NEXT X
1180 '
1190 ' Bottom:
1200 '
1210 FOR X=79 TO 1 STEP -1
1220   Y=Y+1:IF Y>3 THEN Y=1
1230   IF Y=1 THEN COLOR 15,0 ELSE COLOR 7,0
1240   LOCATE 25,X:PRINT MID$(A$,Y,1);
1250 NEXT X
1260 '
1270 ' Left side:
1280 '
1290 FOR X=24 TO 2 STEP -1
1300   Y=Y+1:IF Y>3 THEN Y=1
1310   IF Y=1 THEN COLOR 15,0 ELSE COLOR 7,0
1320   LOCATE X,1:PRINT MID$(A$,Y,1);
1330 NEXT X
1340 '
1350 RETURN
50000 'Merge BMOVE routine here
```

Figure 8.15 *(continued)*

```
49101 IF SS.MODE$="G" THEN 49110
49102 'Text Display:
49103 ON INSTR("SRPG",SS.CMD$) GOTO 49104,49105,49106,49107:RETURN
49104 BM.FROMSEG%=SCREENSEG%:BM.FROMOFF%=0:BM.TOSEG%=SS.BASE%:BM.
      TOOFF%=4096*(SS.SRNNUM%-1):BM.COUNT%=4096:GOSUB 50020:RETURN
49105 BM.FROMSEG%=SS.BASE%:BM.FROMOFF%=4096*(SS.SRNNUM%-1):BM.
      TOSEG%=SCREENSEG%:BM.TOOFF%=0:BM.COUNT%=4096:GOSUB 50020:RETURN
49106 DEF SEG=SS.BASE%:BSAVE SS.NAME$,4096*(SS.SRNNUM%-1),4096*SS.
      SRNCNT%:RETURN
49107 DEF SEG=SS.BASE%:BLOAD SS.NAME$,4096*(SS.SRNNUM%-1):RETURN
49108 '
49109 'Graphics Display:
49110 ON INSTR("SRPG",SS.CMD$) GOTO 49111,49113,49115,49116:RETURN
49111 BM.FROMSEG%=SCREENSEG%:BM.FROMOFF%=0:BM.
      TOSEG%=SS.BASE%+(SS.SRNNUM%-1)*1000:BM.
      TOOFF%=0:BM.COUNT%=8000:GOSUB 50020
49112 BM.FROMSEG%=SCREENSEG%+&H200:BM.FROMOFF%=0:BM.
      TOSEG%=SS.BASE%+(SS.SRNNUM%-1)*1000:BM.TOOFF%=8000:BM.
      COUNT%=8000:GOSUB 50020:RETURN
49113 BM.FROMSEG%=SS.BASE%+(SS.SRNNUM%-1)*1000:BM.FROMOFF%=0:BM.
      TOSEG%=SCREENSEG%:BM.TOOFF%=0:BM.COUNT%=8000:GOSUB 50020
49114 BM.FROMSEG%=SS.BASE%+(SS.SRNNUM%-1)*1000:BM.FROMOFF%=8000:BM.
      TOSEG%=SCREENSEG%+&H200:BM.TOOFF%=0:BM.
      COUNT%=8000:GOSUB 50020:RETURN
49115 DEF SEG=SS.BASE%:BSAVE SS.NAME$,16000*(SS.SRNNUM%-1),16000*SS.
      SRNCNT:RETURN
49116 DEF SEG=SS.BASE%;BLOAD SS.NAME$,16000*(SS.SRNNUM%-1):RETURN
```

Figure 8.16 *Screen Slinger subroutine.*

the P command SS.COUNT% must contain the number of screens to put to disk. For commands G and P the variable SS.NAME$ must contain the name of a disk file. Finally, the variable SS.BASE% must be set to the beginning of the memory area used to store the screens.

Type in Figure 8.15 and save it in ASCII format using the command **SAVE"SCRNSLGR",A**. Now type in Figure 8.16. If necessary, merge the Screen Slinger subroutine back in with the command **MERGE"SCRNSLGR"** and save the complete program by typing **SAVE"SCRNSLGR.DEM"**. If you are using a color monitor, you will have to make a few changes to the demo program. The starting segment address for the screen memory will automatically be set by line 10 unless you have both color and monochrome display interfaces in your machine. If you do have both you can replace the code in line 20 to set the variable SCREENSEG% to either &HB000 for monochrome or &HB800 for color. Although the demo program is set up for text mode, you can save color graphics screens just as easily. Simply change the T in line 90 to a G and replace the screen creation code with appropriate code to create screens in either SCREEN 1 or SCREEN 2 mode. Screen Slinger will automatically manipulate the 16K graphics screen instead of the 4K text screen. Remember that the number of screens you can hold is limited to the amount of free memory above BASIC and that graphics screens take up four times as much space as text screens. You might also like to enter COLOR statements here and there to be fancy.

You can now run the Screen Slinger demo to create and flash a few screens around. When the program starts it will ask whether you want to create screens or restore them from a file. The first time you run the demo, choose option 1; three screens will appear. After each screen is created, it is saved in memory starting 16 bytes above the top of BASIC (BASIC.TOP% + 1). I add 16 bytes as a buffer (sometimes I'm overly cautious). Notice that the saves are virtually instantaneous. When all three screens are saved, they will be flashed on the screen in rapid succession, creating an animated effect. To stop the show, press the space bar and enter a file name. The three screens will now be saved to disk, reloaded, and redisplayed. Press the space bar again to exit the program. If you wish, you may re-run the program at any time, select option 2, and enter the file name entered in the previous run. The screens will be reloaded, and the animated display will reappear. After a short examination of the demo program, you will be able to create "slingable" screens for your own applications programs.

Stuart Greenberg is a programmer and coordinator of microcomputer services for a large corporation. He also does independent consulting for IBM PC users, is membership officer of the PC User Group of the Long Island Computer Association, and lives in Holtsville, New York. This article was originally published under the title "We Interrupt this Program" in PC World *Volume 1, Number 7.*

. Star-Dot-Star

Whether you have only recently learned the basics of BASIC or you're a "hacker" who would rather write programs than sleep, you'll probably find that the tips in this section can help smooth the road as you work the bugs out of your latest creation. For starters, "BASIC Cross Reference" offers a program to unravel the rat's nest of line numbers characteristic of the BASIC language. If your program is large, you'll be glad to have "BASIC Variable Reference" when it comes time to make some changes, and "Cross Reference Checker" gives a one-line command you can type to insure your programs are in order before they are put into use. "Making 'Em Pause" and "Save the Keys" are subroutines you'll want to add to many of your own programs: one measures specific durations of time and the other ends programs in an orderly manner. Finally, "XMAKER" and "DATAMKR" are a set of tools for converting machine language programs to and from an easy-to-type format that's used for several other *.* items in this book.

BASIC Cross-Reference

After seeing the *Program Squisher* in "BBS of the Month" (*BBS Watch, PC World,* Vol. 1, No. 10), I realized that within that program was a cross-reference program just dying to get out. The program XREF.BAS (see Figure 8.17) is the result of a few nights of work after this revelation.

The program assumes that you want to cross-reference a BASIC file and will append .BAS if it doesn't detect a period in the file name. (If the file doesn't have an extension, enter the file name followed immediately by a period, and .BAS will not be appended.)

The program keeps a running commentary (on screen) of the line number being scanned and the number of references found. The screen displays the number of references found and shows the current depth of the sort to give you an idea of how long the sort will take and how far the program is into the sort.

I substituted the Quicksort program for the simple bubble sort because it is only an "order n" sorting algorithm (bubble sorts are "order n-squared"). Sorting a large program with the bubble sort took about 35 minutes. With Quick-sort it took about 1.5 minutes. And if you can use the BASIC Compiler, it can do the sort in less than a minute.

XREF.BAS was "squished" to save space and increase speed, so type it in very carefully, exactly as shown.

Donald G. Johnston
Moose Jaw, Saskatchewan, Canada

BASIC Variable Reference

Many times while writing a long program I find that I would like to know all the locations (line numbers) of a certain variable or command. Rather than do a complete cross-reference of the program, which takes too much time, I use the program VARREF.BAS (see Figure 8.18). I save the program to be searched in ASCII under the name XREF.BAS and then run VARREF.BAS. VARREF.BAS quickly locates the proper lines for any entered string.

Kirk Brennan
York, Pennsylvania

Cross-Reference Checker

An easy way to check all the cross-references in a BASIC program is to renumber an imaginary line beyond the end of the program. For example, if your line numbers end at 4000, type the following in direct mode:

```
RENUM 9999,9999
```

BASIC checks all the line number references and issues any error messages without renumbering your program. If the only reply is 'Ok', then all your GOTOs and GOSUBs refer to existing line numbers.

Carl Wagner
Rochester, Minnesota

```
1 '*************************************************
2 '*                                               *
3 '*  BASIC CROSS-REFERENCE PROGRAM                *
4 '*  DEC 1983 . . . DONALD G. JOHNSTON            *
5 '*  SCANNING AS USED IN SQUISH FROM PC WORLD     *
6 '*  QUICKSORT WRITTEN BY JOHN W. ROSS            *
7 '*                                               *
8 '*************************************************
100 '
110  'INITIALIZE.  DETERMINE FILE AND OPEN IT.
120  '
130 SD=0:XR$="":T=0:T1=0:T2=0:V$="":X=0:ZC=0:DIM LO(50),HI(50),REF(1000),LN(1000):
SCREEN 0,0,0:WIDTH 80:COLOR 11,0:KEY OFF:CLS:LINE INPUT "Enter the name of the
 program to be cross-referenced: ";XR$:IF 0=INSTR(XR$,".") THEN XR$=XR$+".BAS"
140 PRINT:PRINT"Opening ";XR$:ON ERROR GOTO 1000:OPEN XR$ FOR INPUT AS #1:PRINT:
PRINT"Scanning ";XR$;" now ..... Line # = ":PRINT:PRINT"# of references = 0"
200 '
210 'SCAN LINES OF CODE FOR CROSS-REFERENCES.
220 '
230 IF EOF(1) THEN CLOSE #1:GOTO 430
240 LINE INPUT #1,A$:IF ASC(A$)>58 THEN COLOR 12,0:PRINT:PRINT"**** '";XR$"' is
 not an ASCII file ****":PRINT:COLOR 11,0:END
250 HH=INSTR(A$," "):LN=VAL(LEFT$(A$,HH)):LOCATE 5,29+LEN(XR$):PRINT LN:G1=1:G2=
1:G3=1:G4=1:G5=1:G6=1:G7=1
260 D=4:T=INSTR(G1,A$,"THEN"):IF T THEN G1=T+D:GOTO 340
270 T=INSTR(G2,A$,"GOTO"):IF T THEN G2=T+D:GOTO 340
280 T=INSTR(G3,A$,"ELSE"):IF T THEN G3=T+D:GOTO 340
290 T=INSTR(G4,A$,"GOSUB"):IF T THEN D=5:G4=T+D:GOTO 340
300 T=INSTR(G5,A$,"RESUME"):IF T THEN D=6:G5=T+D:GOTO 340
310 T=INSTR(G6,A$,"RUN"):IF T THEN D=3:G6=T+D:GOTO 340
320 T=INSTR(G7,A$,"RESTORE"):IF T THEN D=7:G7=T+D:GOTO 340
330 GOTO 230
340 A=VAL(MID$(A$,T+D)):IF A THEN R=R+1:REF(R)=A:LN(R)=LN:LOCATE 7,18:PRINT R
350 IF A>0 THEN T=T+D:D=1:T1=INSTR(T,A$,","):T2=INSTR(T,A$,":"):IF T1>0 AND (T2=
0 OR T1<T2) THEN T=T1:GOTO 340
360 GOTO 260
400 '
410 ' USE QUICKSORT TO ORDER THE REFERENCED LINES
420 '
430 CLOSE:LOCATE 9,1:PRINT"Sorting the cross references... (Depth of sort shown
 below.)":LO(1)=1:HI(1)=R:II=1
440 IF II<=0 THEN 630
450 IF LO(II)>=HI(II) THEN II=II-1:PRINT II;:GOTO 440
460 I=LO(II)-1:J=HI(II):IL=J
470 IF I>=J THEN 520
480 I=I+1:IF REF(I)<REF(IL) OR (REF(I)=REF(IL) AND LN(I)<LN(IL)) THEN 480
```

Figure 8.17 *XREF.BAS*

```
490 J=J-1:IF J>1 THEN IF REF(J)>REF(IL) OR (REF(J)=REF(IL) AND LN(J)>LN(IL))
 THEN 490
500 IF I<J THEN SWAP REF(I),REF(J):SWAP LN(I),LN(J)
510 GOTO 470
520 J=HI(II):SWAP REF(I),REF(J):SWAP LN(I),LN(J):IF I-LO(II)<HI(II)-1 THEN
 LO(II+1)=LO(II):HI(II+1)=I-1:LO(II)=I+1:GOTO 540
530 LO(II+1)=I+1:HI(II+1)=HI(II):HI(II)=I-1
540 II=II+1:PRINT II;:GOTO 440
600 '
610 'FORMAT THE OUTPUT LISTING
620 '
630 PRINT:PRINT"Ready to output the results now!"
640 PRINT"Do you want it to the screen (s) or printer (p)?":A$="":WHILE A$="":
A$=INKEY$:WEND:IF A$="s" OR A$="S" THEN CLS:A$="scrn:" ELSE IF A$="p" OR A$="P"
 THEN A$="lpt1:"ELSE PRINT:PRINT"s or p Please!":PRINT:GOTO 640
650 OPEN A$ FOR OUTPUT AS #1:PRINT #1,"Cross-references of line numbers for
 ";XR$:PRINT #1,STRING$(37+LEN(XR$),"-"):PRINT #1," "
660 PRINT #1,"Reference:","Line numbers":PRINT #1,STRING$(30,"-"):PRINT #1,
REF (1);":",LN(1);:FOR I=2 TO R:IF REF(I)=REF(I-1) THEN GOSUB 680 ELSE PRINT #1,
" ":PRINT #1,STRING$(30,"-"):PRINT #1,REF(I);":",LN(I);
670 NEXT:PRINT #1," ":END
680 IF A$="scrn:" THEN AX=POS(0) ELSE IF A$="lpt1:" THEN AX=LPOS(1) ELSE END
690 IF AX>73 THEN PRINT #1,"":PRINT #1,"",LN(I);ELSE PRINT #1,LN(I);
700 RETURN
1000 IF ERR=53 THEN RUN ELSE ON ERROR GOTO 0
```

Figure 8.17 *(continued)*

```
10 REM VARREF PROGRAM
60 OPEN "XREF.BAS" FOR INPUT AS #1
70 CLS:LINE INPUT "ENTER VARIABLE NAME ";B$
80 IF B$="" THEN END
90 LPRINT B$
120 IF EOF(1) THEN LPRINT "FINISHED":CLOSE:GOTO 10
130 LINE INPUT #1,A$
150 IF INSTR(A$,B$) > 0 THEN LPRINT LEFT$(A$,5)" ";
200 GOTO 120
```

Figure 8.18 *VARREF.BAS*

Making 'Em Pause

I have seen several published BASIC programs in which an empty FOR . . . NEXT loop has been used to produce a pause in the program. A typical piece of code looks like this: 'FOR I = 1 to 1500 : NEXT'.

If you know BASIC instruction times, you can calculate a value for the loop counter that produces an appropriate pause. Alternatively, you can plug in a number and time what happens. Either of these exercises is time consuming. They are also fruitless if you subsequently compile your BASIC program; watch your painfully programmed, user-friendly messages flash on the screen for a tenth of the time they did on the BASIC Interpreter version!

Below are six BASIC statements that produce a predictable pause, whether you use the BASIC Interpreter or Compiled BASIC. Forget about instruction speeds; the internal clock is the best pause calculator you have at your disposal. By changing the value of PAUSE% in the code below, the parent program will pause for as little as 1 second or as long as 59 seconds. The example code below produces a pause of 5 seconds.

```
9  REM  Lines 10-20 will store current function key definitions in K$()
10 DEF SEG
11 P=0
12 FOR X=1 TO 10
13   K$(X)=""
14   WHILE PEEK(P+1619)<>0
15     K$(X)=K$(X)+CHR$(PEEK(P+1619))
16     P=P+1
17   WEND
18   P=X*16
19   K$(X)=K$(X)+CHR$(0)
20 NEXT
29 REM  Lines 30-35 will restore function keys to definitions stored in K$()
30 DEF SEG
31 FOR X=1 TO 10
32   FOR Y=1 TO LEN(K$(X))
33     POKE 1618+(X-1)*16+Y,ASC(MID$(K$(X),Y))
34 NEXT Y,X
35 KEY OFF : KEY ON
```

Figure 8.19 *KEYDEFS.BAS*

```
10   PAUSE% = 5
20   SECS% = VAL(RIGHT%(TIME$,2))
30   ENOUGH% = (SECS% + PAUSE%)
        MOD 60
40   WHILE SECS% <> ENOUGH%
50   SECS% = VAL(RIGHT$(TIME$,2))
60   WEND
```

If for some reason you need the program to pause for longer than 59 seconds, put this code in a FOR ... NEXT loop.
Graham Pearson
Houston, Texas

Save the Keys

I have seen that many BASIC programs use the line 'FOR X=1 TO 10:KEY X,"":NEXT' to turn off the function keys. That is a good way to prevent unwanted input, but it makes it inconvenient to restore the original function key definitions when the program terminates. The statements shown in Figure 8.19, KEYDEFS.BAS, can be used to save the function key definitions in an array before they are changed so that they can be restored at a later time.

BASIC marks the end of a key definition with a CHR$(0), so line 19 places that code at the end of each K$() to prevent the inclusion of extraneous data when the definitions are restored. The 'KEY OFF' and 'KEY ON' statements in line 35 force BASIC to update the bottom line of the screen to display the newly restored key definitions.
Roger Host
Woodstock, Illinois

XMAKER

In the past we have published various BASIC programs to recreate binary files; some readers provide the program with their submissions, and sometimes we write them ourselves. We use the program shown in Figure 8.20, XMAKER.BAS, as the standard program for all such items. Once you have typed XMAKER.BAS and saved it on a disk, you will be able to use it to recreate the binary files we publish. Because XMAKER.BAS incorporates a more sophisticated error-checking routine than we have used in the past, it will notice any typing error that you might make, and it will identify the line that contains the error to help you make corrections quickly.
Editors of PC World

DATAMKR

The companion program for XMAKER.BAS is DATAMKR.BAS (Figure 8.21), which converts a binary file into a series of DATA statements that can be added to XMAKER.BAS to recreate the binary file. DATAMKR.BAS adds a data line number and checksum to each group of 16 bytes.
Editors of PC World

```
10 DEFINT A-Z:CLS:KEY OFF:DEF FNHEX(X$)=VAL("&h"+X$)
20 LOCATE 3,1:PRINT "X-Maker":READ F$
30 LOCATE 5,1,1:PRINT "Now testing for data errors...please wait";
40 SUM=0:READ LN:IF LN<0 THEN 80
50 READ H$:IF VAL(H$)<0 THEN 70
60 SUM=(SUM+FNHEX(H$))*2:SUM=(SUM\256)+(SUM MOD 256):GOTO 50
70 READ CKSUM$:IF SUM=FNHEX(CKSUM$) THEN 40 ELSE GOTO 170
80 RESTORE:CLS:LOCATE 3,1:PRINT "X-Maker":READ F$
90 LOCATE 5,1,1:PRINT "Press any key to create ";F$;": ";
100 A$=INPUT$(1):PRINT:IF A$=CHR$(27) THEN END
110 LOCATE 6,1:PRINT "Working...";
120 OPEN F$ AS #1 LEN=1:FIELD #1,1 AS BYTE$
130 READ LN:IF LN<0 THEN 160
140 READ H$:IF VAL(H$)<0 THEN READ CKSUM$:GOTO 130
150 LSET BYTE$=CHR$(FNHEX(H$)):PUT #1:GOTO 140
160 CLOSE:PRINT:PRINT F$;" has now been created.":END
170 PRINT:PRINT "Error in DATA line";STR$(LN);". ";
180 PRINT "Check your work.":BEEP:END
```

Figure 8.20 *XMAKER.BAS*

```
10 DEFINT A-Z:CLS:KEY OFF:LOCATE 5,1:PRINT "Data Maker"
20 DEF FNH$(X)=RIGHT$("0"+HEX$(X),2):CM$=CHR$(44)
30 '
40 PRINT:INPUT "Input filename--",N$:IF N$="" THEN END
50 OPEN N$ FOR INPUT AS #1
60 INPUT "Output filename--",F$
70 OPEN F$ FOR OUTPUT AS #2
80 '
90 LN=0:INPUT "Beginning DATA line number";BL           'start a new line
100 PRINT #2,STR$(BL);" DATA ";:WRITE #2,N$
110 SUM=0:LN=LN+1:LX=0
120 PRINT #2,BL+(LN*10);"DATA";:PRINT #2,STR$(LN);CM$;
130 '
140 IF EOF(1) THEN 210
150 X=ASC(INPUT$(1,1)):SUM=(SUM+X)*2:SUM=(SUM\256)+(SUM MOD 256) 'checksum
160 '
170 IF LX>0 THEN PRINT #2,CM$;                          'commas between items
180 PRINT #2,FNH$(X);:LX=LX+1:IF LX<16 THEN 140         'count bytes per line
190 PRINT #2,CM$;"-1";CM$;FNH$(SUM):SUM=0:GOTO 110      'terminate after 16
200 '
210 IF LX>1 THEN PRINT #2,CM$;"-1";CM$;FNH$(SUM);       'partial checksum
220 PRINT #2,CM$;"-1":PRINT "Complete.":CLOSE:GOTO 40
```

Figure 8.21 *DATAMKR.BAS*

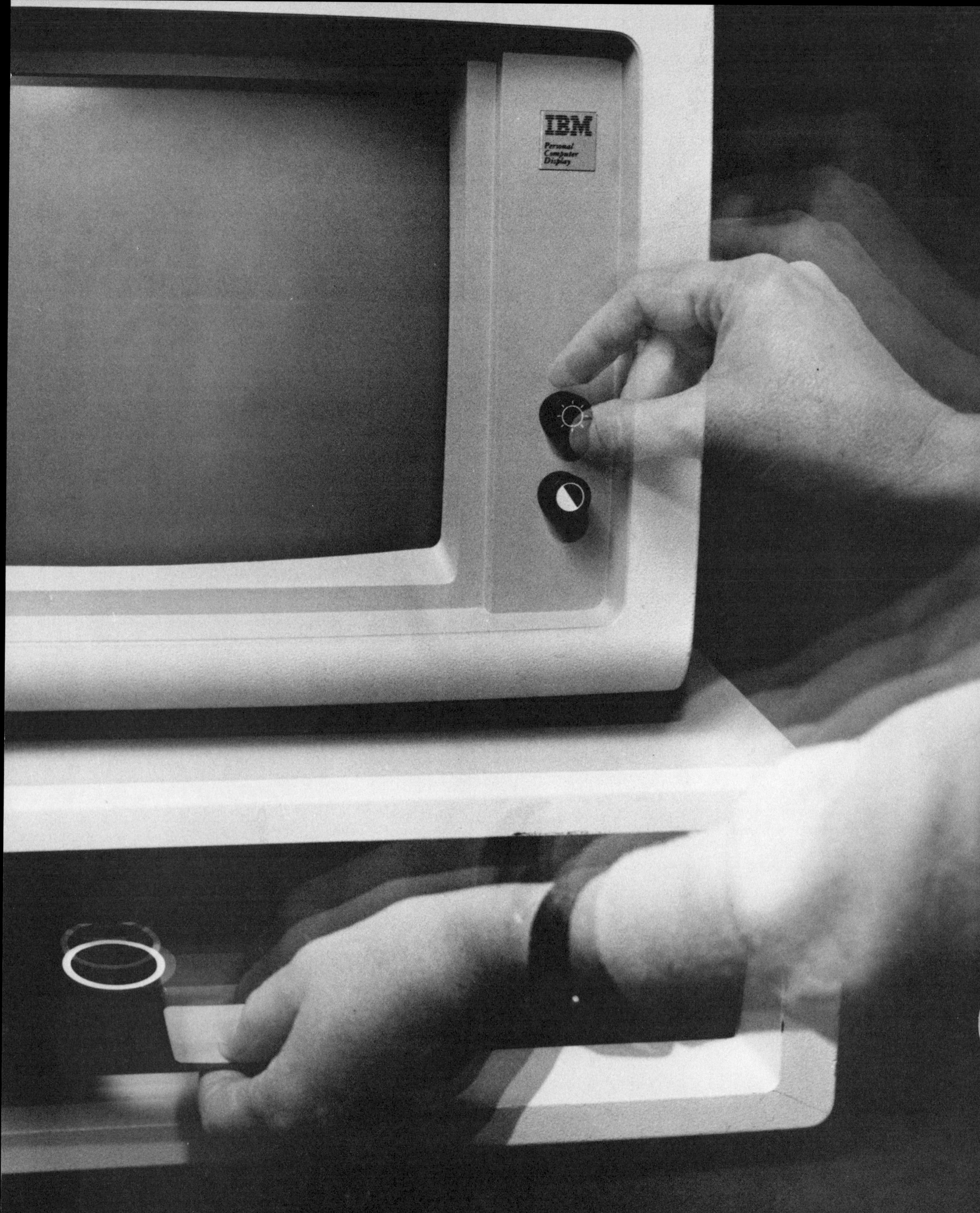
IBM
Personal
Computer
Display

9

Hardware

Hands On

Most of the chapters in this book give you ideas about what the PC can do, but how does the PC do what it does? If you've ever had trouble envisioning just how the computer remembers things or exactly what a chip does, or if you've wondered what all those beeps, clicks, and whirrs really mean, the articles in this chapter will encourage you to pull off the PC's lid and find out. Learning to negotiate your way around the motherboard will give you the same kind of good working relationship with your computer that doing your own tune-ups gives you with your car. It can also save you time and money when it comes time to add new equipment or troubleshoot a problem.

The first article, "How the PC Thinks," is an excellent introduction to the PC's nervous system. The article examines the PC brain—the 8088 microprocessor—and how it works with the computer's memory. You'll learn about such fundamentals as binary arithmetic, hexadecimal numbering, bits, bytes, and the ASCII character code.

For people who do a lot of number crunching, "Getting Started with an 8087" evaluates the strengths and limitations of this Numeric Data Processor that's designed to work as a coprocessor with the PC's 8088. The article tells how the 8087 works and what it's good for; looks at its accuracy, speed, and the range of numbers it handles; and explains how to install the chip on the PC motherboard.

"The Cassette Port Lives," shows how to put the little-used cassette port to work turning almost anything on and off. For example, the article provides programs for the PC to turn your house lights on and off, to generate Morse code, and to sound a burglar alarm.

How the PC Thinks

Peter Norton

Hardly an issue of the weekly newsmagazines appears that doesn't have an article on computers. The message is clear: computer literacy will be important in the coming years. If you understand how computers work, you will be better equipped to survive in the age of computers.

This article is intended to help you understand the insides of the IBM PC. We'll look at the basic workings of the Intel 8088 microprocessor, the brains of the PC, and we'll describe the PC's memory—how it is used to store values and how it is addressed. We'll also discuss the notorious hexadecimal number system and memory segments, as well as PC memory organization.

Memory

The computer, like the human brain, depends on memory to store information. Think of computers as electronic office workers: the microprocessor is the worker; disks are the filing cabinets where information is stored; operating systems, such as PC-DOS or CP/M, are like the worker's general education; and applications programs such as *VisiCalc* or *WordStar* are like specific job training.

A computer's memory is like a desk top for an office worker. In the same way that a desk top may have a telephone or a dictionary sitting on one corner, part of computer's memory is reserved for fixed uses such as holding part of an operating system. The largest part of the computer's memory is allocated for working storage for programs and data being used at the moment. The computer's memory is a temporary holding place for the work being done.

Computer memory is organized into many storage locations. Each location is like a post office box that can hold values such as numbers or letters of the alphabet. Storage locations are identified by their numerical addresses, just as post office boxes are identified by their numbers.

The size of the locations and the kind of values that can be stored in them vary from computer to computer. Some older computers have very large memory locations called *words*. The Cray super computers and Univac computers are word oriented.

The difficulty with a large word size is that the programs running on the computer often need to work with less than a full word of information, which can be clumsy on a word-oriented computer. Most modern computers, including personal computers, use a smaller storage location made up of 8 bits, called a *byte*.

A bit is the smallest unit of information a computer can handle. (*Bit* is a blend of the phrase *binary digit.*) Bits, binary entities, have two values: zero or one. A string of bits looks like this: 10110001010101. A byte is a handy unit of information because it is the right size to hold a single letter of the alphabet or character (the terms *byte* and *character* are sometimes used interchangeably).

Each storage location in the PC holds 1 byte, which can contain any value that can be expressed in eight bits. This allows for two to the eighth power of possible values, or 256 values. The way those values are interpreted depends upon the way they are used. A byte could be interpreted to hold the coding for an alphabetic character or a number. As a number, the 256 possible values could be taken as positive numbers ranging from 0 to 255 or as a signed range of numbers from -128 to +127. On the other hand, a single byte could be used as part of a larger amount of data such as a series of characters or as a 2-byte number.

To manipulate character data, a computer needs to have the characters translated into byte values in a well-organized code. Most computers, including the PC, use the American Standard Code for Information Interchange (ASCII). Most of IBM's large computers use another character coding scheme known as EBCDIC. ASCII and EBCDIC are organized differently, but translating from one to the other is not difficult.

ASCII assigns numeric values to all the conventionally used characters, such as letters of the alphabet (both uppercase and lowercase), numeric digits, and punctuation symbols. ASCII also reserves a small number of codes for control purposes such as indicating the end of a string of characters. The special control codes appear mostly in the first 32 ASCII characters, which are referred to in BASIC as CHR$(0) to CHR$(31).

ASCII is a 7-bit code with 128 possible code values. Since a byte has eight bits, ASCII uses only the first 128 of the 256 possible byte values, allowing other purposes to be assigned to the remaining 128 code values to make up an extended ASCII character set. No standards exist for what the extended codes should be used for, and different computer devices apply them differently. For the PC display, IBM uses the extended ASCII character set to represent mathematical symbols, characters used in languages other than English, and shapes used for graphics. The BASIC program given in Figure 9.1 displays the PC's special symbols.

The standard IBM dot matrix printer, a version of the Epson MX-80, translates the extended ASCII character codes into printed shapes different from the characters the PC display screen shows. If you run the demonstration program and then use the Print-Screen operation to print out the display with an Epson printer, you will be able to compare the display and printer versions of the same extended ASCII character codes.

You can find tables of ASCII character codes and the PC extended ASCII character codes in many places. One table is in the back of the IBM BASIC manual (Appendix G). A very useful form of the table is given in the *IBM Technical Reference* manual (Appendix C).

We have considered how the PC's memory may be used 1 byte at a time, but often several bytes are used to represent more complex values. When strings of characters are needed, the characters are stored 1 character per byte in adjacent memory locations. The first, or left-most, character of a string is stored in the lowest address location.

When integers larger than a single byte are needed, they are stored in several bytes in adjacent locations. The most common format uses 2 bytes, or 16 bits, a convenient size for a 16-bit microprocessor like the PC's 8088. In the terminology of the 8088, two bytes together are called a *word*. Many of the instructions in the 8088 are made for manipulating 16-bit numbers. Longer formats can be used (3, 4, or more bytes), but they are not as common as 2-byte numbers and require special programming.

When numbers of 2 bytes or more are stored in the 8088's memory, they are placed with the least significant byte first, which is the opposite of what many people are accustomed to. If you examine individual bytes of the PC's memory you should be aware of this storage convention.

Memory Addresses

Every memory location has an address. Address numbers begin with zero for the first location and extend to the highest location. Since addresses are numbers, the computer uses its arithmetic abilities to calculate and manipulate memory addresses.

Each computer design has its own limitations on how many locations it can address. The highest possible number for an address determines the size of the address space of the computer, which is to say, how much memory it can have. Computers often have less actual memory attached than their address spaces allow. A small address space can put a limit on the problem-solving capability of a computer. Ideally, address spaces are made as large as possible.

The PC makes use of the full address space of its microprocessor's design. In the 8088, addresses are 20 bits—the processor has an address space of 2 to the twentieth power, or a little over 1 million byte locations. In the common K notation for memory, in which each K is made of 1,024 bytes of storage, the PC has an address space of 1,024 K; the exact amount in decimal-based numbers is 1,048,576. For a personal computer, that's a lot of room.

Creating a PC with such a large address space enabled IBM to be liberal in its use of memory and to dedicate some portions of memory to special purposes. Before we go into that subject, we'll look at how a 16-bit computer is able to work with 20-bit addresses, and see how it places limits on your programs.

Internally, computers always work with binary digits, or bits. Looking at numbers in binary notation isn't very illuminating. With many bits, the numbers get long, and they aren't easy to comprehend, even for experienced users. Hexadecimal

Listing 1:

```
1000 REM                    Listing 1—A program to display all screen characters
1010 REM                    From the book "Inside the IBM Personal Computer"
1020 REM                    (C) Copyright 1982, Peter Norton
1030 REM
1040 GOSUB 2000 ' TITLE
1050 GOSUB 3000 ' GET WHICH DISPLAY TYPE, AND SET ADDRESS
1060 GOSUB 2000 ' SET THE TITLE AGAIN
1070 GOSUB 4000 ' BUILD THE SURROUNDING COMMENTS
1080 GOSUB 5000 ' BUILD THE DISPLAY ARRAY
1090 GOSUB 6000 ' FINISH UP AND RETURN TO DOS

2000 REM  Title subroutine
2010 KEY OFF : CLS : WIDTH 80
2020 REM
2030 PRINT "                Programs for INSIDE THE IBM PERSONAL COMPUTER"
2040 PRINT "                (C) Copyright 1982 Peter Norton"
2050 PRINT
2060 PRINT "                Program 1 : Demonstrate all screen characters"
2999 RETURN

3000 REM  Subroutine to inquire about display type
3010 PRINT
3020 PRINT "Before we go any further, is this a color-graphics display? ";
3030 GOTO 3060
3040 PRINT
3050 PRINT "  (answer Y or N)  ";
3060 ANSWER$ = INKEY$
3070 IF LEN(ANSWER$) < 1 THEN 3060
3080 IF LEN(ANSWER$) > 1 THEN 3040
3090 SEGVAL! = 0
```

Figure 9.1 *A program to display all screen characters.*

notation was invented to make binary numbers more manageable. Don't think that hexadecimal numbers (or *hex* as hexadecimal is called) are different from binary digits inside the computer. Hex and binary are just different ways of writing numbers for human consumption.

In hex notation, 4 binary digits are represented by a single hex digit. If you take 4 bits and consider all the values that they can have, you will find 16 possible values. In numeric order they are 0000, 0001, 0010 and so on, through 1111. Sixteen different hex digits are used to represent each of the 16 4-bit sequences. The first 10 hex digits are the usual decimal digits, 0 through 9. Letters of the alphabet are used for the final six digits: *A* represents 10, *B*, 11, and so on, through *F*, which represents 15 (see Table 9.1).

Since there are 8 bits in a byte and each hex digit represents 4 bits, it takes 2 hex digits to represent a byte. (Since hex digits are half of a byte, they are sometimes called *nibbles,* but this term is used infrequently.) Four hex digits represent a 16-bit word and 5 hex digits are needed to represent the 20-bit address used by the PC's 8088 microprocessor.

Segmented Addressing

Most of the arithmetic that the 8088 does is limited to manipulating 16-bit words, which range from 0 to 65,535, or 64K. Since complete addresses are 20 bits long, a practical method had to be devised to control 20 bits, working 16 bits at a time. The solution was found in segmented addressing.

If you take a 16-bit number and add 4 binary zeros to it, you have a 20-bit number that can be used as a 20-bit address. By adding 4 zeros or shifting the number 4 binary places, you effectively multiply the number

```
3100 IF MID$(ANSWER$,1,1) = "Y" THEN SEGVAL! = &HB800 ' Color segment
3110 IF MID$(ANSWER$,1,1) = "y" THEN SEGVAL! = &HB800 ' Color segment
3120 IF MID$(ANSWER$,1,1) = "N" THEN SEGVAL! = &HB000 ' Monochrome segment
3130 IF MID$(ANSWER$,1,1) = "n" THEN SEGVAL! = &HB000 ' Monochrome segment
3140 IF SEGVAL! = 0 THEN 3040
3150 DEF SEG = SEGVAL!
3999 RETURN

4000 REM   subroutine to build the surrounding messages
4010 FOR HEX.DIGIT% = 0 TO 15
4020     LOCATE 6,HEX.DIGIT% * 3 + 14
4030     PRINT HEX$(HEX.DIGIT%)
4040     LOCATE HEX.DIGIT%+8,8
4050     PRINT HEX$(HEX.DIGIT%)
4060 NEXT HEX.DIGIT%
4070 LOCATE ,,0
4999 RETURN

5000 REM   subroutine to set the display array
5010 FOR ROW% = 0 TO 15
5020     FOR COL% = 0 TO 15
5030         POKE (ROW% + 7) * 160 + COL% * 6 + 26, COL% + ROW% * 16
5040     NEXT COL%
5050 NEXT ROW%
5999 RETURN

6000 LOCATE 25,1,1
6010 PRINT "Press any key to return to DOS... ";
6020 IF LEN(INKEY$) = 0 THEN 6020 ' wait for a keystroke
6030 CLS
6999 SYSTEM

9999 REM   End of program listing 1
```

Figure 9.1 *(continued)*

by 16, and its value can then be as high as 1,024K. Unfortunately, with 4 zeros, a 20-bit number can specify only 1 out of every 16 memory locations, the one whose 20-bit address ends in 4 zeros. None of the other locations with addresses ending in any of the other 15 possible combinations of 4 bits can be specified by that kind of addressing.

To complete the solution to the problem of 20-bit addressing, two 16-bit numbers are used. The first is considered to have 4 binary zeros tacked on to the end, which makes it 20 bits long. This number is called the segment part of the address. The second 16-bit number is used as is. This number is called the relative part of the address. Added together, the two numbers make up a complete 20-bit address that can locate any of the 1,024K bytes in the PC's address space. The segment portion specifies a location called a paragraph boundary that is a multiple of 16. The relative value specifies an exact location some relative distance from the paragraph. (Figure 9.2 shows how a segmented address is put together.)

The relative part of the address is needed only to specify the last 4 bits of the 20-bit address, but it can have any value from 0 to one less than 64K. Most manipulation of memory addresses is done with the relative part. In effect, the segment part of an address becomes a base location for a 64K working area addressed by the relative part.

A segmented address is expressed in a conventional way that you can see in the PC-DOS programming tool called DEBUG and in assembler listings such as the one that appears in Appendix A of the *IBM Technical Reference* manual. The segment part of the address is written first, followed by a colon and the relative part of the address. For example,

Value in decimal	Binary bits	Hex digits
0	0000	0
1	0001	1
2	0010	2
3	0011	3
4	0100	4
5	0101	5
6	0110	6
7	0111	7
8	1000	8
9	1001	9
10	1010	A
11	1011	B
12	1100	C
13	1101	D
14	1110	E
15	1111	F

Table 9.1 *A summary of hex.*

if you had a segment part that was 2222 (in hex) and a relative part that was 3333, the segmented address would be written 2222:3333. The following addition shows that the value of the resulting 20-bit address is 25553 (in hex):

```
  22220
+  3333
  25553.
```

To make use of these segmented addresses, the 8088 microprocessor has special segment registers dedicated to holding the segment part of addresses. Once a value is loaded into a segment register, any of the 64K memory locations that follow can be addressed by specifying the relative offset. Without changing the segment register, the computer has a temporary working address space of 64K located within its complete 1,024K address space. By changing the segment register, any location can be addressed.

First take a segment address word:	1234
Then add a zero to its end (4 binary zeros):	12340
Then take a relative address word:	1234
Add them together for a complete address:	13574

The finished address is 5 hex digits, or 20 bits.

Figure 9.2 *Assembling a segmented address in hex.*

A computer normally uses its memory for several purposes; some of it is used to hold a program and some is used to hold the data that the program is working on. The 8088 has four segment registers, each with a special use, which allows it to operate with more than 64K at a time. The program, or code, segment is located by using the CS register; for the data segment, the DS register is used; for a special use of memory known as the stack segment, the SS register is used; and to provide some extra capacity, an extra segment (ES) register is used.

When a program is prepared to be run, the operating system, such as PC-DOS, decides which memory locations will be used for the program code, data, and stack. The segment registers, CS, DS, and SS are set to point to those locations. When running, the program makes use of the segment register values to find its way through memory.

The memory locations referred to by the four segment registers don't have to be located far apart. The registers can point anywhere, even at the same segments. If only a few thousand bytes of program and data are needed, the code and data segments will be placed close together. Although the working portions of the code and data segments are distinct, the 64K spaces addressed by their segment registers can overlap. If a program doesn't change its segment registers, it is limited to using a total of only 64K for both data and program code. On the other hand, if a program manipulates the segment registers, it can work on data of any size up to 1,024K. If you use either IBM Pascal or the BASIC compiler, you will find that programs can become very big, even larger than 64K, but the data that the programs can work with is limited to 64K.

This limitation for Pascal and the BASIC compiler programs refers to data in the memory. If your programs are reading and writing from disk files, more than 64K of data can move through the memory. But only 64K of data can be in memory at one time, which is a limitation on the combined size of your program's data variables.

For the interpretive BASIC built into the PC, the interpreter is the actual program that runs, and what you think of as your BASIC program is actually part of the interpreter's data. So for interpretive BASIC, your program is limited to the 64K that the data segment register covers at one time, plus another 64K for the program's data.

The practical result of this situation places some limitations on how much memory you can use. If you use interpretive BASIC, no more than 64K of memory can be used for BASIC programs, plus 64K for their data, regardless of how much memory is in your computer.

If you use compiled programs in languages such as BASIC, Pascal,

Hex memory paragraph	Size in k-bytes	Use for the area
FE00	8 K	ROM BIOS (contained in one chip)
F600	32 K	ROM BASIC (contained in three chips)
F400	8 K	reserved for extra ROM socket
F000	16 K	reserved (presumably for ROM)
C000	192 K	future use (ROM/RAM/?)
BC00	16 K	possible expansion of color/graphics
B800	16 K	color/graphics display (all used)
B400	16 K	possible expansion of monochrome
B000	16 K	monochrome display (not all used)
A400	48 K	reserved for future displays
A000	16 K	reserved
1000	576 K	RAM (expansion boards)
0000	64 K	RAM (on system board)
Total:	1024 K	

Table 9.2 *Allocation of PC memory.*

FORTRAN, or COBOL, however, the programs can grow to any size, although the data is still limited to 64K. On the other hand, a program can have huge code and data areas if it uses the advanced addressing techniques allowed by assembly language and some other languages.

Memory Organization

With over a million bytes of address space, the PC has a generous supply of memory. This megabyte potential is organized in an interesting way. Designers of the PC reserved several ranges of the highest numbered memory locations for special purposes and kept all the low memory locations free. Table 9.2 shows the allocation of PC memory.

The top quarter of memory from segment C000 up to the end is informally reserved for use by read-only memory (ROM). (All references to memory addresses are in hexadecimal unless otherwise indicated.) ROM is used to store permanent programs that are always available for the PC to use. They can't be written over, and they stay in place when the computer is turned off. Ordinary memory, called random access memory (RAM), is used on a temporary basis. The contents of RAM changes, depending on the programs you run on the computer. To run programs stored on disks, you must copy them into RAM; when the computer is turned off, the information stored in RAM is lost.

When the computer is turned on, the ROM programs are ready to be used. Some of the ROM programs test the computer and load the operating system. The testing procedure is called Power-On Self-Test (POST), and loading the operating system is called bootstrap loading, or simply booting.

The highest part of memory is occupied by ROM. The first 8K of it, beginning at segment FE00, is occupied by the ROM BIOS (BIOS stands for basic input/output system). The ROM BIOS contains all the fundamental service utilities built into the PC, including the test programs executed when the computer is first turned on. Support programs for peripheral devices like the display, the keyboard, and the disk drives are also contained in the ROM BIOS.

The next lower 32K, beginning at segment F600, is used to hold the PC's built-in version of BASIC. BASIC goes into operation when the PC is turned on without a disk in the disk drive. This BASIC that works by itself is Cassette BASIC. The disk versions of BASIC are called Disk BASIC and Advanced BASIC, or BASICA. Essentially, the disk versions of BASIC add extra capabilities to the built-in BASIC.

The ROM BIOS and BASIC interpreter are located in five chips, each containing 8K, plugged into the PC's system board. A sixth chip socket has been left free so that extra ROM can be added. The memory location

```
Listing 2:

1000  REM                                    A program to scan for and report active memory
1010  REM                                           (C) Copyright 1982, Peter Norton
1020  REM
1030  GOSUB 2000   '   TITLE
1040  GOSUB 3000   '   SEARCH AND DISPLAY
1050  GOSUB 4000   '   RETURN TO DOS

2000  REM   Title subroutine
2010  KEY OFF : CLS : WIDTH 80
2020  REM
2030  PRINT "                          Programs for INSIDE THE IBM PERSONAL COMPUTER"
2040  PRINT "                                 (C) Copyright 1982 Peter Norton"
2050  PRINT
2060  PRINT "                                  Find and Display Active Memory"
2070  PRINT
2080  PRINT "                            Be patient—this program takes 65 seconds"
2090  PRINT "                    (Addresses given as segment paragraphs in hexadecimal)
2100  PRINT
2999  RETURN

3000  REM   Subroutine for the main search and display
3010  TRUE.%  =  -1
3020  FALSE.% =   0
3030  IN.MEMORY.% = FALSE.%
3040  FOR PARAGRAPH.! = 0 TO 65535! STEP 64 ' CHECK EACH 1K OF MEMORY
3050     GOSUB 5000   '   CHECK FOR ACTIVE MEMORY
3060     IF (IN.MEMORY.%=FALSE.%)  AND  (MEMORY.HERE.%=TRUE.%)   THEN GOSUB 6000
3070     IF (IN.MEMORY.%=TRUE.%)   AND  (MEMORY.HERE.%=FALSE.%)  THEN GOSUB 7000
3080     IN.MEMORY.% = FALSE.%
3090     IF MEMORY.HERE.% THEN IN.MEMORY.% = TRUE.%
3100  NEXT PARAGRAPH.!
3110  IF IN.MEMORY.% THEN PARAGRAPH.! = 65536 : GOSUB 7000
3999  RETURN

4000  REM   Subroutine to finish up
```

Figure 9.3 *A program to scan for and report active memory.*

for the extra chip is at segment F400. Any of the PC memory space can be used for additional ROM, but to follow the general ground rules for PC memory usage, any ROM should be located above segment C000.

Below ROM is a large block of memory space dedicated to the PC display. The display memory is part of the computer's overall address space, although it is physically located on the display expansion board, or adapter. Beginning at segment address B000, the display memory extends for 64K up to segment C000. The display memory is divided into two parts: the lower half, at segment B000, is used by the monochrome adapter, and the upper half, at segment B800, is used by the color/graphics adapter.

Neither of the two display adapters uses the full 32K of space allotted to it. The monochrome adapter uses only 4K, and the color graphics adapter uses 16K. With the IBM Monochrome and Color/Graphics Adapters, the leftover spaces remain unused, but other display adapters could use those areas for enhanced display formats. Such enhanced display formats might include a 132-column screen, high-resolution

```
4010 PRINT
4020 PRINT "Finished."
4999 SYSTEM

5000 REM   Check for memory present—sample the first four bytes
5010 DEF SEG = PARAGRAPH.!
5020 BYTE0.% = PEEK (0)
5030 BYTE1.% = PEEK (1)
5040 BYTE2.% = PEEK (2)
5050 BYTE3.% = PEEK (3)
5060 CHECK.COUNT.% = 0
5070 IF BYTE0.% = 233 THEN CHECK.COUNT.% = CHECK.COUNT.% + 1
5080 IF BYTE1.% = 233 THEN CHECK.COUNT.% = CHECK.COUNT.% + 1
5090 IF BYTE2.% = 233 THEN CHECK.COUNT.% = CHECK.COUNT.% + 1
5100 IF BYTE3.% = 233 THEN CHECK.COUNT.% = CHECK.COUNT.% + 1
5110 MEMORY.HERE.% = FALSE.%
5120 IF CHECK.COUNT.% <= 3 THEN MEMORY.HERE.% = TRUE.%
5999 RETURN

6000 REM   Subroutine to start an active block of memory
6010 IN.MEMORY.% = TRUE.%
6020 START.! = PARAGRAPH.!
6999 RETURN

7000 REM   Subroutine to end a block of active memory
7010 SIZE.! = (PARAGRAPH.! – START.!) * 16
7020 IF SIZE.! < 8 * 1024 THEN 7999   '   SUPPRESS SMALL-BLOCK FALSE REPORTS
7030 PRINT "Active memory begins at ",
7040 PRINT HEX$(START.!)
7050 PRINT "                                        ends at ",
7060 PRINT HEX$(PARAGRAPH.! – 1);
7070 PRINT SIZE.! / 1024;"K-bytes";" (";SIZE.!;"bytes   )"
7080 IN.MEMORY.% = FALSE.%
7090 PRINT
7999 RETURN

9999 REM   End of program listing to explore memory
```

Figure 9.3 *(continued)*

monochrome graphics, or additional character sets such as italics.

The 64K block below segment B000 is also reserved for display memory. According to IBM documentation, the A000 block is reserved as part of a full 128K area reserved for display memory. This large area is intended for higher resolution display adapters that require more memory than the original monochrome and color/graphics display adapters.

Below segment A000, 640K of address space is available for RAM. All of the ordinary RAM installed in the PC is located in the low address locations of the memory address space. You can have almost as much memory installed as you want, up to the limits set by the reserved ROM and display memory locations. Whether you have only 48K, or 576K, the RAM on your computer occupies the low memory locations, beginning at zero (segment 0000) up to the highest address of your RAM.

The lowest part of RAM, starting at memory location zero (0000) and extending for about 1500 bytes, is dedicated to fundamental operating information for the computer. The first part of this area holds interrupt vectors. Following the interrupt vectors is data for the BIOS, DOS, and BASIC. After these reserved parts of low memory, the ordinary

Active memory begins at	0	
ends at	8FFF	576 K bytes (589824 bytes)
Active memory begins at	B000	
ends at	B7FF	32 K bytes (32768 bytes)
Active memory begins at	F600	
ends at	FFFF	40 K bytes (40960 bytes)
Finished		

Figure 9.4 *Amount of active memory.*

part of RAM begins, where programs are loaded into memory and where the programs' working storage is placed.

In between RAM and ROM is the special-purpose display memory. There are gaps in the memory between the end of the RAM and the display memory, and between the display memory and the ROM area. These gaps are inactive parts of the PC's address space, ready to be used whenever more memory is installed.

Exploring Memory

You can explore the memory in your PC to discover how much is present and where it is located in the address space. One way to test memory is to try to read from each memory location and then check the results. When this test is carried out with DEBUG or Pascal programs, the result is that all the bits are set (or that each bit has the value 1), which is the same as hex FF, or decimal 255. This result isn't too surprising. The most likely result from reading missing memory is all bits off, or all bits on. For some reason, when the test is run with BASIC, the result is usually decimal 233.

We can take advantage of this quirk to check the entire PC address space for active memory. Figure 9.3 shows a simple BASIC program that reads a few bytes from each 1K of memory and checks them for the decimal 233 value. If you run this program on your system, it will show you how much active memory you have. Figure 9.4 shows the results from a sample run of this program.

Notice in Figure 9.4 that three blocks of memory were detected. The first block, RAM, begins at segment 0. In this example, the first block is 576K because the memory consists of 64K on the system board and an expansion board containing 512K.

The second block of active memory begins at segment B000, which is where the monochrome display memory is located. This information shows that the system has the monochrome display. Notice that the program interprets this memory as extending for 32K even though the monochrome adapter contains only 4K. The extra 28K detected by the program is probably a side effect of the circuitry that supports the 4K of real memory. Running this program on a system with the color graphics adapter also shows 32K of memory, although only 16K is present on the color graphics adapter. After the display adapter memory, the program detects the ROM at the high end of the address space. For this last block, like the first one, the program detected exactly what was present.

While this is a useful program for exploring your system's memory, it is also an example of what you can do to learn about your PC. IBM didn't advertise that BASIC finds the decimal 233 value in missing memory. But with a little exploration, the program shown in Figure 9.3 was produced. This is the sort of thing you should do on your own. Explore your system, poke around in its dustier corners, and you will gain a world of insight into how the PC works. Be forewarned that some non-IBM memory boards give curious results when this test program is run. That's another way that you can learn more about how your PC thinks.

Peter Norton has more than 10 years' experience in computing, as a programmer, designer, and author. He wrote and produced The Norton Utilities. *This article is included in* Inside the IBM PC: Access to Advanced Features and Programming. *It is used by permission of the Robert J. Brady Co., copyright 1983, Peter Norton. This article was originally published in* PC World *Volume 1, Number 1.*

Getting Started with an 8087

Walter Cooke

If you were ever curious enough to pull the cover off your PC and nose around, you might have wondered why there is an empty socket next to the 8088 processor. This socket is the designated landing pad for what IBM manuals vaguely refer to as a "coprocessor." It didn't take long to figure out that the intended occupant was Intel's high-speed 8087 Numeric Data Processor. But why add another processor when the 8088 is capable of math operations?

The 8087 is a specialized processor that quickly handles the computational chores that the 8088 labors over, thus freeing the 8088 for control functions. But the 8087 cannot perform control functions for itself or work without the presence of the 8088.

Since IBM's announcement of its support for the 8087, a number of rash claims have been made about its performance. Although the 8087 is fast, consider what it can and cannot do for you before you rush out to buy one.

Pinning It Down

The package that I bought contains a three-page installation pamphlet, a 5 MHz Intel 8087 chip, a disk with some programs for use with the Microsoft Macro-86 Assembler, and a copy of Intel's *8087 Software Support Library Reference Manual.*

The 40-pin 8087 chip is not the easiest object to maneuver into the tight quarters on the IBM PC system board. Wiggling a chip into a barely visible socket underneath your shaking fingers while you wonder how many pins are snapping off is not an activity I would recommend. As you gently push it into its socket, the 8087 emits squeaks and groans—not the most reassuring sounds to hear emanating from your PC. The instructions then tell you to remove the chip to make sure you did not bend any pins. Such a maneuver gives you an opportunity to bend the pins you missed the first time as you reinsert the 8087.

If you are purchasing an 8087 from an authorized IBM dealer, it is probably a good idea to save yourself the trouble and let them install the chip. If you must install the chip yourself, follow the usual precautions for handling integrated circuit chips. Any source of static electricity can destroy the chip while you are handling it. Leave the chip in its antistatic case until you are ready to install it. Avoid wearing polyester clothing, but make sure to wear rubber-soled shoes. Also, don't handle any plastic, vinyl, or Styrofoam while working with the 8087. Make sure you are well grounded by wrapping some wire around your wrist and securing the end of the wire to a household water pipe or other electrical ground.

The rest of the installation is straightforward. Removing circuit boards from the slots next to the 8087 socket may be helpful, providing you with some extra finger space during the installation procedure. The only modification to the PC itself is to turn DIP switch 2 on the motherboard from on to off. If the 8087 is later removed from the PC, the switch must be returned to its original on position.

Testing the 8087

Later, I turned on my PC and ran the 8087 demonstration program included on the disk. Saying that the 8087 is fast is a gross understatement. Square roots and quadratic equations are child's play for the 8087, and the answers, accurate to 17 digits, are displayed as fast as you can hit the <Enter> key.

The disk includes a library called 8087.MAC, which holds all the assembly language instructions necessary for the 8087's operation with the 8088. But a single assembly language instruction is usually insufficient to direct the 8087 in a task, so they are grouped together in various macros. Each macro can be named with a single word, called a mnemonic, and used when needed throughout the assembly language program. The macros extend the assembler to include the 8087 operation codes such as FCOMPP, for floating-point compare and pop, and FPTAN, for floating-point partial tangent (see Table 9.3).

The macros work with the standard *Macro Assembler* sold by IBM and are entered into an assembly language program on the first line of code using an **INCLUDE 8087.MAC** command. With the aid of the macro

Processor Control Instructions

FINIT/FNINIT	=	Initialize NDP
FDISI/FNDISI	=	Disable interrupts
FENI/FNENI	=	Enable interrupts
FLDCW	=	Load control word
FSTCW/FNSTCW	=	Store control word
FSTSW/FNSTSW	=	Store status word
FCLEX/FNCLEX	=	Clear exceptions
FSTENV/FNSTENV	=	Store environment
FLDENV	=	Load environment
FSAVE/FNSAVE	=	Save state
FRSTOR	=	Restore state
FINCSTP	=	Increment stack pointer
FDECSTP	=	Decrement stack pointer
FFREE	=	Free register ST(i)
FNOP	=	No operation
FWAIT	=	CPU wait for NDP

Comparison Instructions

FCOM	=	Compare real to ST(0)
FCOMP	=	Compare real and pop
FCOMPP	=	Compare real and pop twice
FICOM	=	Integer compare to ST(0)
FICOMP	=	Integer compare and pop
FTST	=	Test ST(0)
FXAM	=	Examine ST(0)

Data Transfer Instructions

Real Transfers:

FLD	=	Load real to ST(0)
FST	=	Store real
FSTP	=	Store real and pop
FXCH	=	Exchange registers ST(i) and ST(0)

Integer Transfers:

FILD	=	Integer load to ST(0)
FIST	=	Integer store
FISTP	=	Integer store and pop

Packed Decimal Transfers:

FBLD	=	Packed decimal (BCD) load to ST(0)
FBSTP	=	Packed decimal (BCD) store and pop

Arithmetic Instructions

Addition:

FADD	=	Add real with ST(0)
FADDP	=	Add real and pop
FIADD	=	Integer add

Subtraction:

FSUB	=	Subtract real with ST(0)
FSUBP	=	Subtract real and pop
FISUB	=	Integer subtract
FSUBR	=	Subtract real reversed
FSUBRP	=	Subtract real reversed and pop
FISUBR	=	Integer subtract reversed

Multiplication:

FMUL	=	Multiply real with ST(0)
FMULP	=	Multiply real and pop
FIMUL	=	Integer multiply

Division:

FDIV	=	Divide real with ST(0)
FDIVP	=	Divide real and pop
FIDIV	=	Integer divide
FDIVR	=	Divide real reversed
FDIVRP	=	Divide real reversed and pop
FIDIVR	=	Integer divide reversed

Transcendental:

FPTAN	=	Partial tangent of ST(0) $0 \leq ST(0) < \pi/4$*
FPATAN	=	Partial arctangent of ST(0)+ST(1) $0 \leq ST(0) < ST(1) < +\infty$*
F2XM1	=	$2^{ST(0)} - 1$ $0 \leq ST(0) \leq 2^{-1}$*
FYL2X	=	$ST(1) \cdot Log_2[ST(0)]$ $0 < ST(0) < \infty$* $-\infty < ST(1) < +\infty$*
FYL2XP1	=	$ST(1) \cdot Log_2[ST(0)+1]$ $0 < \lvert ST(0) \rvert < (2-\sqrt{2})/2$* $-\infty < ST(1) < \infty$*

Load Constant Instructions

FLDZ	=	LOAD +0.0 into ST(0)
FLD1	=	LOAD +1.0 into ST(0)
FLDP1	=	LOAD π into ST(0)
FLDL2T	=	LOAD $\log_2 10$ into ST(0)
FLDL2E	=	LOAD $\log_2 e$ into ST(0)
FLDLG2	=	LOAD $\log_{10} 2$ into ST(0)
FLDLN2	=	LOAD $\log_e 2$ into ST(0)

Other Instructions

FSQRT	=	Square root of ST(0) $-0 \leq ST(0) \leq +\infty$*
FSCALE	=	Scale ST(0) by ST(1) $-2^{15} \leq ST(1) < +2^{15}$ and ST(1) integer*
FPREM	=	Partial remainder of $ST(0) \div ST(1)$
FRNDINT	=	Round ST(0) to integer
FXTRACT	=	Extract components of ST(0)
FABS	=	Absolute value of ST(0)
FCHS	=	Change sign of ST(0)

ST(0) = current stack top
ST(i) = first register below stack top
*Functional conditions

Table 9.3 *8087 macros.*

library, the 8087 performs 77 different mathematical, store, and control functions out of a total repertoire of 146 machine instructions.

Coming to Terms

The advantage of using the 8087 in a PC involves three crucial factors: precision, range, and speed. Until the introduction of 16-bit microcomputers, performing complex mathematics on a personal computer was difficult. Eight-bit computers are limited by the size of numbers they can handle. Current 16-bit computers like the PC routinely manipulate numbers up to 64 bits long. These are referred to as double-precision numbers because they take up 8 bytes of memory, compared with regular, single-precision numbers that fit into 32 bits, or 4 bytes. In a 64-bit double-precision number, 17 digits of precision are possible, with values ranging from 10^{-38} to 10^{38}. These are "real" numbers since they have a decimal point and a fractional component. They're also known as floating-point numbers because the decimal point floats around inside the memory location where the number is stored.

Inside the computer, real numbers are stored in two parts: the exponent stores the magnitude of the number and defines where the decimal point will be placed; the mantissa stores all the significant digits that make up the number. But if you looked at the contents of the memory location, you would not see any indication of a decimal point in the mantissa.

Keep in mind that the accuracy of any calculation is limited. Rounding occurs when real numbers cannot be absolutely defined with a limited number of digits. For example, 1 divided by 3 results in the number .3333333333 . . . , which is accurately represented with an infinite number of digits. Such a number cannot be used easily in calculations. The least significant digit of the number must be rounded so that it can be stored in the limited memory of the computer.

Some calculations do not even round off the last significant digit but "chop off," or truncate, the result at the least significant digit. Great differences in magnitude further skew the accuracy of a result. For example, if you add 10^{-29} to 10^{33}, the answer may well be 10^{33}. With only 18 significant digits to store the result, the tiny addition is lost.

All these error-magnifying problems, while acceptable by themselves, are compounded when a calculation repeats a looping process to arrive at a final answer. By the end of a calculation the result contains a significant error and, as such, can be considered only an approximate answer.

Precision

Precision is the most important consideration in calculation. It relates to the accuracy of operations performed on a number, the decimal places of accuracy, and how long calculations can continue before an unacceptable amount of error through rounding, truncating, large differences in magnitude, or conversion operations significantly affect the answer.

Precision is controlled by the size of the mantissa, which holds the most significant digits of a number, regardless of where the decimal point is located. Precision is not a problem with integers. Each integer in a computer is precisely represented by using two's complement format. But even the smallest real number can have an infinite number of digits, so it must be approximated to fit into a finite amount of memory.

The 8087 with its 64-bit mantissa is accurate to 1 part in 2^{64}. Such accuracy is seldom needed for a final result, but it is important during the intermediate stages of a calculation with a large number of steps.

Range

Range determines how large or small a number can be represented. With integers, the range is controlled by the number of bits used. Using 16 bits, the smallest and largest integers you can represent are -32768 and +32767 (using two's complement). For real numbers the range is controlled by the size of the exponent. In the 8087 the exponent is 15 bits long, allowing a very wide range of numbers, from 10^{-4932} to 10^{4932}, to be represented.

Instruction	Precision	Execution rate with 8087	Execution rate without 8087
Multiply	Single	19	1,600
Multiply	Double	27	2,100
Add		17	1,600
Divide	Single	39	3,200
Compare		9	1,300
Load	Single	9	1,700
Store	Single	18	1,200
Square Root		36	19,600
Tangent		90	13,000
Exponentiation		100	17,000

Table 9.4 *Execution rates (in microseconds) for an IBM PC with and without an 8087 installed.*

Speed without Pain

Beyond the esoteric considerations of precision and range is the issue of speed. Those who are bothered by the sluggishness of the BASIC interpreter may not be willing to devote time to converting their BASIC programs into a faster-running compiled language such as Pascal or C. The 8087 may provide a possible way to speed up BASIC programs. You can either buy a BASIC compiler with 8087 support which will convert your entire BASIC program into 8087 machine code, or you can assemblespecialized 8087 math subroutines that can be called from inside a BASIC program.

Both these and many other methods of using the 8087 with BASIC programming are discussed in Richard Startz's excellent book *8087 Applications and Programming for the IBM PC and Other PCs.* Not only is this the clearest textbook written on the subject; it is chock-full of examples you can immediately use. A "tool box" diskette with all the example programs is available at extra cost. The hours of typing and proofreading you will save makes this diskette a worthwhile investment.

As Table 9.4 demonstrates, the 8087 far outstrips the 8088 in real number calculations of all kinds. For any type of scientific or calculation-intensive work the 8087 can provide speed improvements of 10 to 100 times what an ordinary 8088 machine language program can accomplish.

Animation and color graphics routines that calculate trigonometric and positional information can also benefit from the 8087. While graphics routines chug along when displaying complex shapes on the screen, graphics routines rewritten for the 8087 produce the final image on the screen almost instantly.

Another task that requires rapid and precise computing is data encryption, the science of transforming information into a secret or secure form unintelligible to anyone but the intended receiver. Data encryption is used with increasing frequency in industry and by the military. Large numbers called keys are typically used in the mathematical process of transforming data into unreadable "ciphertext." The 8087 makes using powerful encryption systems possible in telecommunications and data management with the PC.

One encryption package that does not utilize the 8087 suggests that when large files need decoding, the user start the program and leave the PC running for the weekend to complete the calculations. Programs that calculate the encryption keys are similarly demanding. In this area of "number-crunching," the 8087 is the clear choice.

Inner Workings

As a coprocessor the 8087 shares both the I/O bus and the instruction "stream" with the 8088, and it monitors all the instructions sent to the 8088 for processing. The 8087 instructions are like bottles floating in a stream. The 8087 plucks them out, while the 8088 channels the rest of the flow. When the 8087 detects a special code sequence in the instruction stream (which is transparent to the 8088), it prepares itself for work. The first five bits of the code are always 11011; the last three bits contain part of the operation code for the 8087 (see Figure 9.5).

Meanwhile, the 8088 processes the next byte in line, which contains three more bits of the opcode and addressing information. The 8087 now knows exactly what operation to perform and lets the 8088 get the first byte on which to operate. The 8088 then releases the bus to the 8087, which retrieves extra bytes of data if necessary, performs its computation, and sends the answer down the bus.

The 8087 stores data in eight 80-bit registers while performing calculations. The 8087 can deal with seven different data types, including

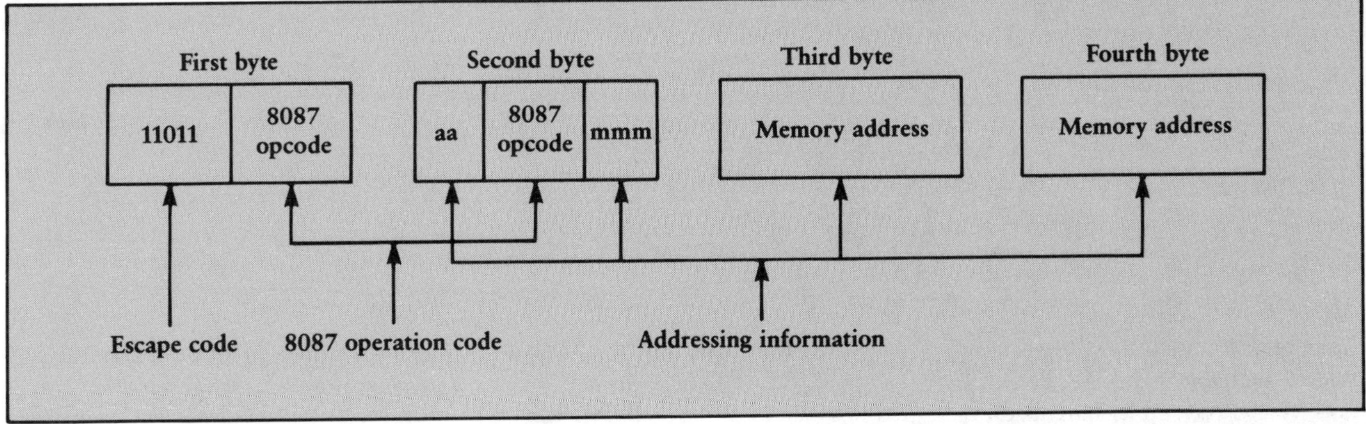

Figure 9.5 *A 4-byte 8087 instruction.*

three lengths of integers; one type of signed, packed, binary coded decimal (BCD) integer; and three types of floating-point representations.

The three integer types are word integers (16 bits long), short integers (32 bits long), and long integers (64 bits long). The packed BCD format has 18 decimal digits and a sign. Each digit is stored in 4 bits so that decimal precision can extend to numbers as large as

9,999,999,999,999,999.99

which is useful in commercial applications having large dollar amounts. Of the three floating-point formats, the most important to consider is "temporary real."

Before loading any type of number into the 8087's registers, it must be converted into an 80-bit format that Intel calls temporary real. Thus the 8087 has to operate on only one form of number when performing calculations. When a number is returned to memory, it is converted back to the desired format. These conversions are done inside the 8087, so a programmer need not be concerned with writing code. However, a programmer is responsible for modifying the location of the sign bit and the exponent value of all data entering or leaving the 8087 since the 8087 and PC-DOS do not use identical formats for storing data. Both the Intel *8087 Software Support Library Reference Manual* and the Richard Startz textbook provide the few steps needed for making these small changes.

The 80-bit temporary real format requires 1 bit for the sign, 15 bits for the exponent, and 64 bits for the mantissa. A bias is added to the exponent, allowing an equal number of large and small numbers to be represented. A bias is a way of indicating whether the exponent of the number is positive or negative without using a sign bit. A temporary real number can be as small as

2^{-16382} $(3.36*10^{-4932})$

or as large as approximately

2^{16384} $(1.19*10^{4932})$.

You can appreciate the magnitude of some of these numbers if you consider that about $2.0*10^{77}$ elementary particles would be needed to fill the entire universe. This number is tiny compared with the range of the 8087. Yet mathematicians can easily exceed the 8087's computing power. For example, the 8087 can compute factorials only as high as 1754.

The 8087 is not limited to "ordinary" numbers. It can work with conditions that do not correspond to normal floating-point operations. These conditions include denormals and unnormals (numbers usually too large or too small to process), infinites (such as a number divided by zero), indefinites (such as zero divided by itself) and NANs (not a number), which are involved in calculation error debugging.

8087 Limits

While the 8087 is preferable in most numeric processing, certain limits should be considered. The temporary real conversion process essential to the 8087's speed with large numbers is a hindrance with small ones. An 8087, 16-bit register-to-register addition using small integers is nearly 30 times slower than with the 8088. The 8087 is useful in this situation only when computations involve different types of numbers that require conversion to one format.

Write or Wait

It is important to realize that plugging an 8087 chip into your PC will not make your existing programs magically run faster. While the chip is fast and relatively cheap, few applications packages currently use the 8087.

If you want to write your own programs that support the 8087, you must make sure that the programming language you use has the 8087 links built in. Such software is now widely available in BASIC, Pascal, C, and Macro Assembler languages, or you can buy separate 8087 extensions for the language you choose.

A number of companies offer both Intel's 8087 and the extension software. If you buy the 8087 support for IBM's BASIC, for example, you receive a library of assembly language code, which is used in conjunction with the IBM BASIC compiler (not the BASIC interpreter). When you compile your BASIC programs, the library of 8087 functions replaces the slower 8088 algorithms of common BASIC functions.

When you are evaluating the 8087, remember that most software packages, such as *VisiCalc* or even the BASIC Interpreter, do not yet support the 8087. Be wary of salespeople who say that they think the particular program can use the 8087 but aren't really sure and have no documentation to prove it. When in doubt about using an 8087 for a particular application, talk to a reliable computer retailer who knows your work and system requirements.

Benchmarking

The best way to determine if a piece of software uses the 8087 is to test it. Run a benchmark program comparing two PC setups: one with and one without an 8087 installed. Use the software first on a machine that does not have an 8087, and run a program that takes several minutes or more to complete its calculations. Run the same program and data on a system that does have an 8087 installed. If the calculations are not completed in a much shorter time (10 to 100 times shorter), the software is not using the 8087's functions.

Choosing a calculation-intensive program for the test is, of course, important. A program that reads and writes data from one place to another is not going to run any faster with an 8087. As a wise programmer once said, "All computers, no matter how fast, wait at the same speed." If the 8088 is waiting for disk input and output to occur, the 8087 will not help it wait any faster.

As a final puzzle to ponder, there is the possibility of ending up with software that runs on a system with an 8087 installed but fails on a system without an 8087. It's most convenient if software using one algorithm for the 8087 would provide another in a system that does not have an 8087 installed. If you buy a program that uses the 8087, it is probably worth your while to see if it runs on a PC without an 8087. You may find out eventually if your 8087 or your PC fails.

If your PC is going in for repairs, you can pull the 8087 out of its socket and plug it into another PC to keep your special application running. If your 8087 chip goes "pins up," you will have to get another one before running any applications that require 8087 support. But unless you regularly run your PC without ventilation in 90-degree weather, it's unlikely that an 8087 will fail.

In the event that 8087-supported software fails to work in a properly configured PC, check the 8088 processor. Intel has discovered that older 8088 chips stamped "© 1978" cannot function with the 8087. Those stamped "© 1978, 1981" will function properly.

The popularity of the 8087 will be restricted until more applications programs are developed that put the 8087 to good use. Unless you are planning to use an application program designed for the 8087, a working knowledge of assembly language programming and engineering is advisable, along with a large reserve of patience.

Walter Cooke is a computer security specialist with the Investware Corporation in Vancouver. This article was originally published in PC World *Volume 1, Number 10.*

The Cassette Port Lives!

Michael A. Covington

The least-used standard feature of the IBM PC is surely the cassette port. IBM originally included a cassette port in order to compete with the TRS-80 Model I and the Apple II. What no one foresaw was that far less expensive machines such as the Commodore VIC-20 and the Radio Shack Color Computer would shortly take over the low-budget end of the market, and few people willing to pay for the higher performance of the PC would then want to economize by leaving out disk drives. Cassette-based PCs have become as rare as Cadillacs without air conditioning. In fact, the cassette port has been eliminated from the IBM PC XT, and it may soon disappear from the PC itself.

You can do much more with the cassette port than saving and reloading data on cassettes. The relay that controls the cassette recorder motor is easily manipulable from BASIC and can be used to switch almost anything on and off.

To use the relay all you need is a 5-pin male DIN connector to plug into the cassette port. The relay contacts are connected to the two DIN connector pins that are farthest apart (pins 1 and 3—they aren't numbered sequentially) and are rated to handle 1 amp at a low DC voltage (nominally 6 volts, but you can use somewhat higher voltages if you stay well below 1 amp). Both contacts are fully isolated from the circuitry of the PC. You can also use the relay inside the PC to control another, heftier relay, which in turn controls the load; Figure 9.6 shows how.

The relay contacts start out open ("off") when the PC is turned on. Their status can be changed using the MOTOR statement in BASIC. Specifically, the statement **MOTOR N** closes the contacts if *N* is nonzero, and it opens them if *N* is zero. *N* can be any expression that evaluates to a numeric value; in the simplest case, **MOTOR 1** closes the contacts and **MOTOR 0** opens them. Remember that logical expressions evaluate to numeric values (zero if false, nonzero if true), so that for example:

```
MOTOR A$="ON"
```

closes the contacts if A$ equals "ON" and opens them otherwise.

Once set, the relay retains its position until another MOTOR statement is executed or the PC is reset or turned off; resetting the PC or turning it off causes the contacts to open. You can leave and reenter BASIC as many times as you wish and run virtually any kind of software without affecting the relay.

A statement consisting of the word MOTOR without an expression after it causes the relay to swap states. If the contacts are closed, they open; if they are open, they close. Toggling is handled by the BASIC interpreter, which assumes that the contacts start out open. If you enter BASIC with the contacts closed, your first attempt to swap states will have no effect.

The cassette motor relay can control a wide variety of external functions. Using the relay alone or in combination with a larger relay, you can do such things as the following:

- Make your home look lived-in while you are away by turning lights on and off in as complex a pattern as you wish.
- Turn laboratory equipment on and off for specific periods of time or generate long pulses of accurately controlled length.
- Control lights or other equipment at the computer work station from the keyboard.
- Control a tape recorder or a slide projector for computer-run audiovisual presentations.
- Use the PC as part of the access control and user logging system for another piece of equipment.
- Key a ham radio transmitter to send computer-generated Morse code.
- Generate telephone dialing pulses.
- Turn a light on or sound an alarm at a remote location to indicate the status of the computer.

Timer

A program that enables the PC to be used as a timer can be as simple as the following:

```
10   IF TIME$="08:00:00" THEN
          MOTOR 1
20   IF TIME$="15:00:00" THEN
          MOTOR 0
30   GO TO 10
```

This sample program turns something on at 8 a.m. and off again at 3 p.m. It makes the computer repeatedly examine its internal clock. If the clock reads 08:00:00, it closes the relay contacts; if it reads 15:00:00, it

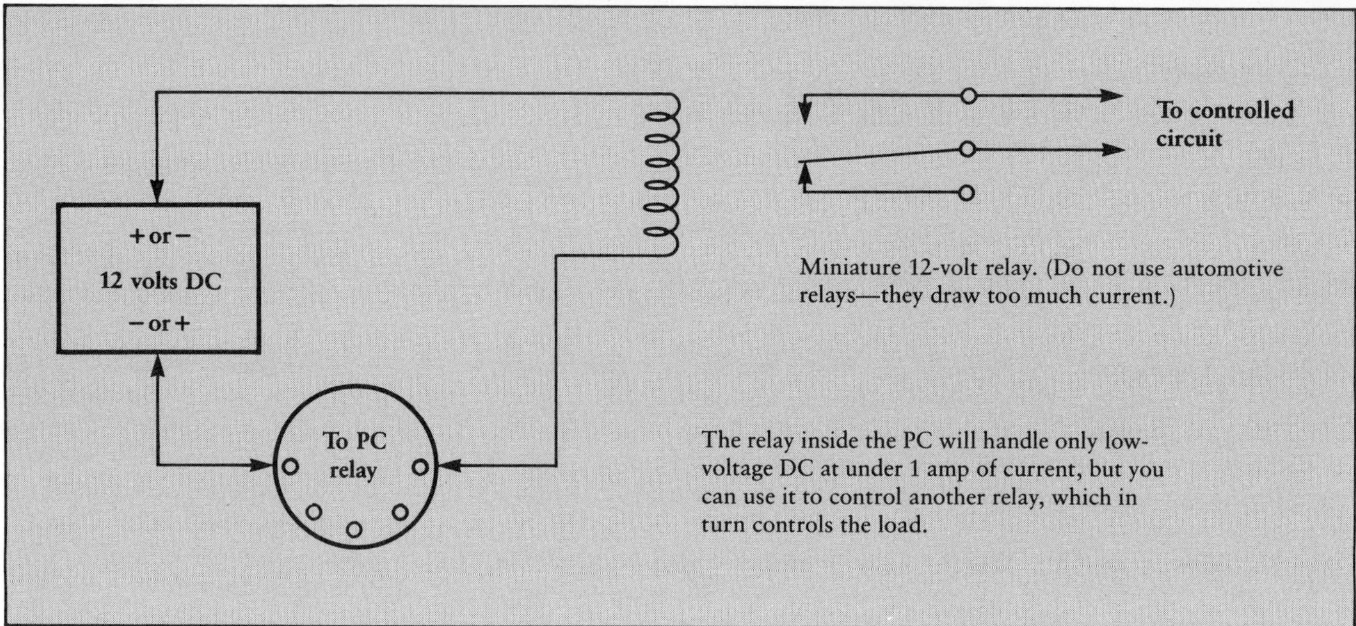

Figure 9.6 *Controlling another relay.*

opens them; at other times it does nothing. The computer checks the clock several times each second, and when it sees 08:00:00 or 15:00:00, it executes the accompanying MOTOR statement several times. Fortunately, this duplication of readings causes no problem—the computer is told to put the contacts into the position that they are already in, and so nothing happens.

Timing an interval, as opposed to waiting for a specific time of day, is a bit more complicated; Figure 9.7 shows how it's done. The main program, which begins at line 100, can be customized to give whatever timing pattern you want. Set the three variables— HR, MN, and SC—to indicate the length of the interval (in hours, minutes, and seconds), then put the motor relay in whatever state you want and GOSUB 10000 to wait out the interval. The subroutine at line 10000 calculates the time of day at which the interval will be over and waits for it; that routine in turn calls another subroutine, at line 20000, which returns the time of day as a number of hours instead of a character string.

Morse Code Generator

Figure 9.8 shows a program that generates Morse code and outputs it either by sounding tones in the PC's speaker, by closing and opening the relay contacts, or by doing both. In theory, the relay contacts can act as a telegraph key; in practice, they may be unable to handle the voltage or current. Check the specifications of your transmitter, and interpose a larger relay if necessary.

Burglar Alarm

Another intriguing possibility is to use the computer as its own burglar alarm. Close the relay contacts when the computer is to be left unattended and leave them closed; then run a program such as the following to open them when any key is pressed.

```
10  REM Open relay contacts when any
        key is pressed
20  MOTOR 1
30  IF INKEY$ = "" THEN 30
40  MOTOR 0
```

The contacts will also open if the computer is turned off or unplugged. Hence, an alarm that sounds when the contacts are open will protect the computer from theft or unauthorized use; it will, of course, also sound if someone simply unplugs the cable from the cassette port. Figure 9.9 shows a suitable circuit. An alarm that sounds when the contacts are closed is a far simpler affair: simply direct the PC relay to switch power to a small buzzer.

Data Output

You can even use the relay as a crude type of output port to transmit digital data to other equipment. To do this have the equipment on the receiving end count how many times the contacts close and/or measure how long they stay closed. You could, for example, transmit a string of ones and zeros, and hence an unlimited amount of data, by treating a brief closure as a zero and a longer closure as a one.

The main difficulty with such a method is that the relay contacts do not go cleanly and instantaneously

```
10 '    Interval timer program      (Michael A. Covington  1983)
20 '
30 '    Turns devices controlled by the cassette port relay
40 '    on or off for specified periods
50 '
60 '    Lines 100-9999 are the control program; modify it as
70 '    needed.  Essential subroutines begin at line 10000.
80 '
90 DEFDBL A-Z
95 '
96 ' This sample program turns the controlled device on for 1 min 30 sec,
97 ' then off for 2 min 45 sec, then on for 3 minutes, then off.
98 '
100 HR = 0
110 MN = 1
120 SC = 30             ' Set control variables to 0 hrs 1 min 30 sec
130 MOTOR 1             ' Turn controlled device on
140 GOSUB 10000         ' Wait out the interval
150 MOTOR 0             ' Turn device off
160 HR = 0
170 MN = 2
180 SC = 45             ' Set control variables to 0 hrs 2 min 45 sec
190 GOSUB 10000         ' Wait out the interval
200 HR = 0
210 MN = 3
220 SC = 0              ' Set control variables to 0 hrs 3 min 0 sec
230 MOTOR 1             ' Turn device on
240 GOSUB 10000         ' Wait out the interval
250 MOTOR 0             ' Turn device off
9990 END                ' Quit
9995  '
9999 '''''''''''''''''''''''''''''''''''''''''''''''''''''''''''''''''
10000 ' SUBROUTINE -- Causes computer to wait (in a loop) for the
10010 '                duration specified by HR, MN, SC .
10020 '
10030 DUR = HR + MN/60 + SC/3600    ' convert duration to decimal hours
10040 GOSUB 20000
10050 FINISH = TOD + DUR     ' compute time at which to finish
10060 WHILE TOD < FINISH
10070   GOSUB 20000          '  check time repeatedly
10080 WEND
10090 RETURN
19999 '''''''''''''''''''''''''''''''''''''''''''''''''''''''''''''''''
20000 ' SUBROUTINE -- Get time of day (TOD) in decimal hours.
20010 '                Add 24 hours for each whole day elapsed.
20020 T$=TIME$
20030 THR=VAL(LEFT$(T$,2))
20040 TMN=VAL(MID$(T$,4,2))
20050 TSC=VAL(RIGHT$(T$,2))
20060 TOD = THR + TMN/60 + TSC/3600
20065 '
20070 WHILE TOD < OLDTOD  ' (i.e., if date has changed since last call)
20080   TOD=TOD+24        ' (add 24 hrs. as many times as necessary)
20090 WEND
20100 OLDTOD = TOD        ' (On first run, OLDTOD = 0 .)
20200 RETURN
```

Figure 9.7 *Interval timer.*

```
10 '    IBM Personal Computer Morse Code Program
20 '
30 '    Michael A. Covington
40 '
50 '    This program produces Morse code by switching
60 '    the cassette motor relay on and off.  In addition,
70 '    the code can be indicated by sound from the speaker.
80 '
90 ''' Initializations
100 DEFINT A-Z
110 DIM CODE(128,7)
115 MSTART = 1 : MSTOP = 0   ' codes for motor control
120 PLAY "MB"     ' sound, if used, will run in the background
200 ''' Start-up screen
205 CLS : KEY OFF
210 LOCATE 10,18 : PRINT "IBM Personal Computer Morse Code Program"
220 LOCATE 12,18 : PRINT "Michael A. Covington                  1983"
230 FOR DELAY = 1 TO 1000 : NEXT
300 ''' Create an array with the code in it
310 READ I
320 IF I<0 THEN 1000
330 FOR J=1 TO 7
340 READ CODE(I,J)
350 NEXT
360 GOTO 310
400 ''' Each DATA statement contains ASCII code for the character
410 ''' followed by 7 numbers: 3 for dah, 1 for dit, 0 for null filler.
412 DATA 65, 1,3,0,0,0,0,0   :REM A
414 DATA 66, 3,1,1,1,0,0,0   :REM B
416 DATA 67, 3,1,3,1,0,0,0   :REM C
418 DATA 68, 3,1,1,0,0,0,0   :REM D
420 DATA 69, 1,0,0,0,0,0,0   :REM E
422 DATA 70, 1,1,3,1,0,0,0   :REM F
424 DATA 71, 3,3,1,0,0,0,0   :REM G
426 DATA 72, 1,1,1,1,0,0,0   :REM H
428 DATA 73, 1,1,0,0,0,0,0   :REM I
430 DATA 74, 1,3,3,3,0,0,0   :REM J
432 DATA 75, 3,1,3,0,0,0,0   :REM K
434 DATA 76, 1,3,1,1,0,0,0   :REM L
436 DATA 77, 3,3,0,0,0,0,0   :REM M
438 DATA 78, 3,1,0,0,0,0,0   :REM N
440 DATA 79, 3,3,3,0,0,0,0   :REM O
442 DATA 80, 1,3,3,1,0,0,0   :REM P
444 DATA 81, 3,3,1,3,0,0,0   :REM Q
446 DATA 82, 1,3,1,0,0,0,0   :REM R
448 DATA 83, 1,1,1,0,0,0,0   :REM S
450 DATA 84, 3,0,0,0,0,0,0   :REM T
452 DATA 85, 1,1,3,0,0,0,0   :REM U
454 DATA 86, 1,1,1,3,0,0,0   :REM V
456 DATA 87, 1,3,3,0,0,0,0   :REM W
458 DATA 88, 3,1,1,3,0,0,0   :REM X
460 DATA 89, 3,1,3,3,0,0,0   :REM Y
462 DATA 90, 3,3,1,1,0,0,0   :REM Z
464 DATA 49, 1,3,3,3,3,0,0   :REM 1
466 DATA 50, 1,1,3,3,3,0,0   :REM 2
468 DATA 51, 1,1,1,3,3,0,0   :REM 3
470 DATA 52, 1,1,1,1,3,0,0   :REM 4
```

(continues)

Figure 9.8 *Morse code generator.*

```
472 DATA 53, 1,1,1,1,1,0,0   :REM 5
474 DATA 54, 3,1,1,1,1,0,0   :REM 6
476 DATA 55, 3,3,1,1,1,0,0   :REM 7
478 DATA 56, 3,3,3,1,1,0,0   :REM 8
480 DATA 57, 3,3,3,3,1,0,0   :REM 9
482 DATA 48, 3,3,3,3,3,0,0   :REM 0 (ASCII 48, not 58!)
484 DATA 47, 3,1,1,3,1,0,0   :REM /
486 DATA 46, 1,3,1,3,1,3,0   :REM .
488 DATA 44, 3,3,1,1,3,3,0   :REM ,
490 DATA 63, 1,1,3,3,1,1,0   :REM ?
492 DATA 45, 3,1,1,1,3,0,0   :REM -
494 DATA 58, 3,3,3,1,1,1,0   :REM :
496 DATA 59, 3,1,3,1,3,1,0   :REM ;
498 DATA 40, 3,1,3,3,1,3,0   :REM (
500 DATA 41, 3,1,3,3,1,3,0   :REM ) (same)
502 DATA 43, 1,3,1,1,1,0,0   :REM +   representing AS ("Wait")
504 DATA 42, 1,3,1,3,1,0,0   :REM *   representing AR ("End of message")
506 DATA 35, 1,1,1,3,1,3,0   :REM #   representing SK ("End of contact")
600 DATA -1
700 ''' If restarting, clear away leftovers of previous run
710 MOTOR 0 : SOUND 32767,0 : RESTORE
1000 ''' Start-up parameters
1005 CLS : LOCATE 20,1
1010 PRINT "Do you want to hear the generated code through the PC speaker?"
1020 INPUT YN$ : YN$ = LEFT$(YN$,1)
1030 IF YN$ = "y" OR YN$ = "Y" THEN FREQ=880 : GOTO 1060
1040 IF YN$ = "n" OR YN$ = "N" THEN FREQ=32767 : GOTO 1060
1050 PRINT "Answer YES or NO." : GOTO 1020
1060 PRINT : PRINT "Do you want to use the cassette motor relay for keying?"
1070 INPUT YN$ : YN$ = LEFT$(YN$,1)
1075 IF YN$ = "y" OR YN$ = "Y" THEN 1100
1080 IF YN$ = "n" OR YN$ = "N" THEN MSTART = 0 : GOTO 1100
1085 PRINT "Answer YES or NO." : GOTO 1070
1100 PRINT : PRINT "Enter transmission speed (words per minute):"
1110 INPUT S!   ' (floating-point)
1120 TIMEUNIT = 2000/S!
1150 CLS
1160 PRINT "The following characters are supported:"
1170 PRINT
1172 FOR I=1 TO 128
1174   IF CODE(I,1)>0 THEN PRINT CHR$(I);
1176 NEXT
1180 PRINT : PRINT : PRINT
1200 PRINT "The following characters have special meanings:"
1210 PRINT "       __"
1220 PRINT "+ for AS ('Wait')"
1230 PRINT "       __"
1240 PRINT "* for AR ('End of message')"
1250 PRINT "       __"
1260 PRINT "# for SK ('End of contact')"
1270 PRINT
1280 PRINT "Unsupported characters are ignored and are not echoed"
1290 PRINT "as the message is sent."
1295 C = CSRLIN : LOCATE 25,1 : COLOR 0,7
1300 PRINT ".END     .RESTART              + Wait   * End msg   # End contact";
1310 LOCATE C+1,1 : COLOR 7,0
1320 PRINT "Type .END to end the program, .RESTART to restart it."
1330 PRINT:PRINT "Type one line in response to each question mark:"
```

(continues)

Figure 9.8 *(continued)*

```
1340 PRINT
2000 ''' Read a line and send it
2010 PRINT "? "; : LINE INPUT M$ : PRINT "   ";
2015 IF M$=".END" OR M$=".end" THEN CLS: KEY ON: MOTOR 0: SOUND 32767,0: END
2020 IF M$=".RESTART" OR M$=".restart" THEN 700
2025 FOR BYTE = 1 TO LEN(M$)
2030     ASCII = ASC(MID$(M$,BYTE,1))
2035     IF ASCII > 96 THEN ASCII = ASCII - 32   ' convert to upper case
2040     IF ASCII = 32 THEN GOSUB 5000 ELSE GOSUB 10000
2050 NEXT BYTE
2060 PRINT : PRINT
2070 GOTO 2010
5000 ''' Subroutine : Pause between words '''''''''''''''''''''''
5005 PRINT " ";
5010 FOR I = 1 TO 7*TIMEUNIT : NEXT : RETURN
10000 ''' Subroutine : Send a letter ''''''''''''''''''''''''''''
10005 IF CODE(ASCII,1)>0 THEN PRINT CHR$(ASCII);
10010 FOR I = 1 TO 7
10020     IF CODE(ASCII,I) = 0 THEN 10080
10030     MOTOR MSTART : SOUND FREQ,32767
10040     FOR J = 1 TO CODE(ASCII,I)*TIMEUNIT : NEXT
10050     SOUND FREQ,0 : MOTOR MSTOP
10060     FOR J = 1 TO TIMEUNIT : NEXT   ' pause between dits/dahs
10070 NEXT I
10080 FOR J = 1 TO 3*TIMEUNIT : NEXT    ' pause between letters
10090 RETURN
```

Figure 9.8 *(continued)*

from open to closed; they bounce against each other for a couple of milliseconds, moving together and then apart, and any attempt to count openings and closings directly will give inaccurate results. Figure 9.10 shows a possible remedy: a circuit whose output is a clean TTL-level signal, is free of bounce, and indicates the state of the relay accurately. Because of the time taken to open and close the contacts, the relay is quite slow—about 10 or 20 state changes per second is the maximum. This method is obviously not suitable for transferring files, but it could come in handy for controlling relatively simple equipment.

Sometimes the humblest parts (and ports) of a computer can be the most useful because of their simplicity. It would be a pity to spend hundreds of dollars on an interface board to encode your data if all you really need is a simple on-off. Besides the cassette motor relay, other underexploited features of the PC include the data lines in the cassette port, the joystick port (very handy for data acquisition), and the speaker (which can drive tone-decoding devices or produce single pulses). When you want to connect a custom-built, one-of-a-kind gadget to the PC, you may be able to save a good bit of money by using these neglected options instead of more conventional interfaces.

Michael A. Covington is a research associate of the Advanced Computational Methods Center of the University of Georgia, where he does research on artificial intelligence and supercomputer applications. This article was originally published in PC World *Volume 1, Number 10.*

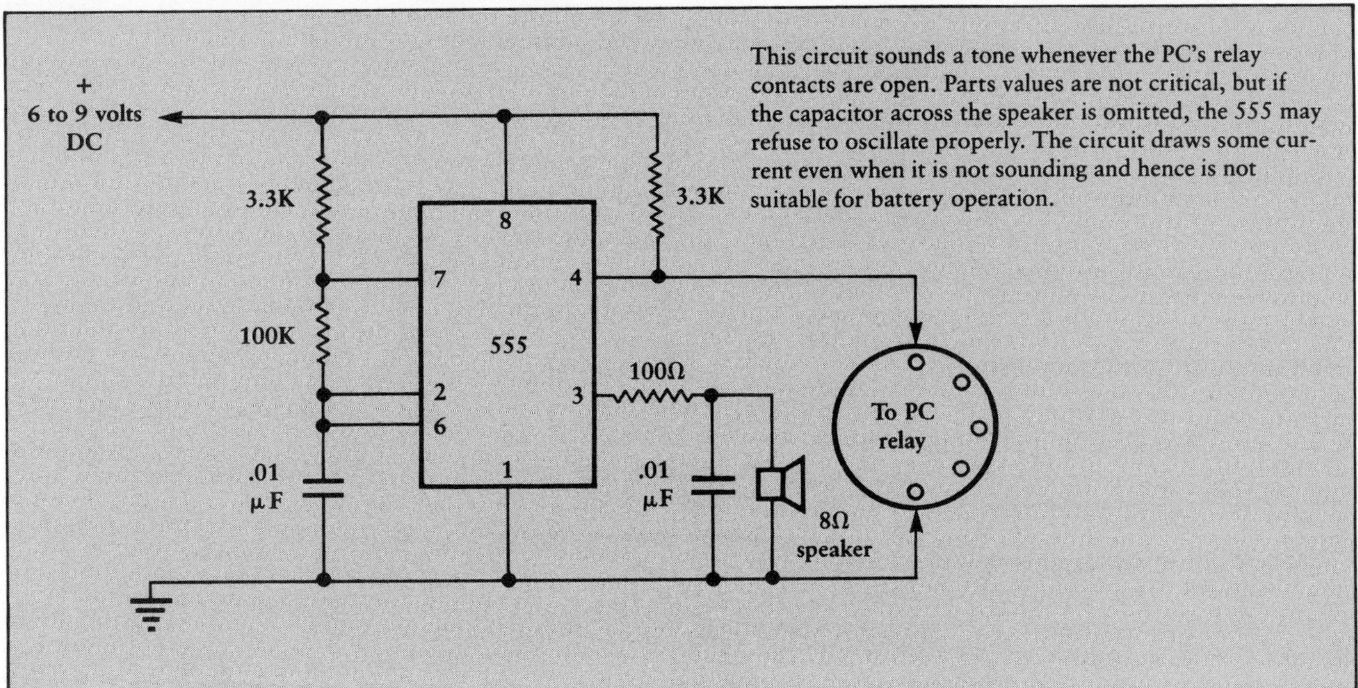

Figure 9.9 *Burglar alarm.*

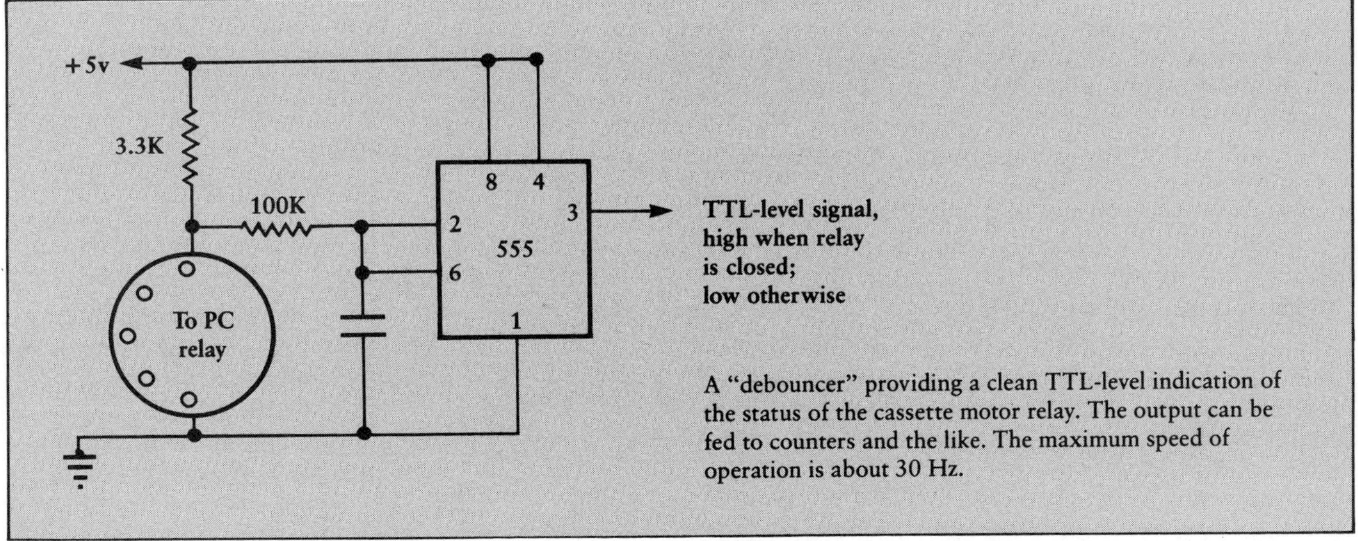

Figure 9.10 *Debouncer for data output.*

.

Star-Dot-Star

A popular joke in the computer industry asks "How many programmers does it take to change a lightbulb?" The answer, at least in some circles, is "None, that's a hardware problem." It does seem that whether you write programs or not, everyone who uses a computer must soon learn to cope with the hardware. In this section, "ProWriter Switches" shows how to set that printer's internal switches to make it work properly with a PC, and "Star Fix" offers a cure for the striped graphics that plague owners of Gemini 10X printers. Okidata owners (those without the "Plug and Play" option) will find "Okidata MODE Fix" just the trick for making their printer operate like the one sold by IBM, and almost everyone can use the technique from "Printer Check Perfected" to help out with that most troublesome of hardware problems, "operator error." For those who really enjoy working with hardware, "Half-Height Fix" tells what to do if you can't get your new Teac disk drive to work, and for tinkerers, "Cassette Port Control Compiled" shows another way to control the PC's cassette port.

ProWriter Switches

For three months I was frustrated in my efforts to get my ProWriter to print when I used the <PrtSc> key. The manufacturer, Leading Edge, finally answered my letter and told me the switch settings I could use. Perhaps you'd like to share those settings with your readers.

If you have a ProWriter, switch settings 2, 6 and 7 are closed on Switch 1, and switch setting 7 is closed on Switch 2.
Michael Trombetta
Manhasset, New York

Star Fix

I, too, have a Star Micronics Gemini 10X printer and was surprised to find that the printer, though the manufacturer claims it is Epson compatible, uses a different vertical step size than the Epson, causing horizontal stripes to appear in printed graphics.

I have seen many modifications published to solve the problem for various graphics-generating programs, including a patch to GRAPHICS.COM (see "Gemini Graphics," *.*, *PC World,* Vol. 2, No. 10), but I wanted a more permanent solution, one that would work for all programs. The routine EP2GEM.COM does the job nicely. It is a memory-resident program that examines characters as they are sent to the printer. When it finds a "set vertical spacing" command (Esc 3), it intercepts the next byte (the vertical spacing value) and converts that value to the equivalent Gemini value.

The routine is completely transparent to the printer and graphics software, works well with print spooling software, and can be included in an AUTOEXEC.BAT file so that it loads into memory whenever you start the computer.
Stephen Davis
Greenville, Texas

Editor's note: Load BASIC, type in the lines in XMAKER.BAS (see Figure 8.20 in Chapter 8), followed by the lines shown in EP2GEM.DAT (see Figure 9.11), then RUN the program to create EP2GEM.COM. To use the program, type **EP2GEM** *when you see the DOS prompt.*

Note that EP2GEM.COM will translate all "set vertical spacing" commands. Even programs that are already configured for the Gemini 10X printer will be affected, causing their output to be compressed. If this occurs, reconfigure the affected program to use Epson/IBM printer commands, or simply restart the computer without loading EP2GEM.COM into memory. Note also that the program will translate every occurrence of the Esc 3 sequence. There is a very slight chance that such a sequence would actually be part of the graphics data. This technique of using a memory-resident printer-translation program could be used to provide Epson compatibility to almost any printer.

Okidata Mode Fix

Users of the Okidata ML92 printer can easily patch the MODE.COM file to enable it to send the proper printer control codes for line length

```
1000 DATA "ep2gem.com"
1010 DATA 1,EB,51,90,0F,0F,90,D6,80,FC,00,75,42,2E,80,3E,04,-1,F6
1020 DATA 2,01,00,75,13,2E,F6,26,05,01,2E,F6,36,06,01,2E,C6,-1,49
1030 DATA 3,06,04,01,01,EB,26,90,2E,80,3E,03,01,00,75,11,B4,-1,D0
1040 DATA 4,33,2E,88,26,03,01,2A,E0,2E,88,26,04,01,EB,0D,90,-1,15
1050 DATA 5,B4,9B,2A,E0,80,E4,7F,2E,88,26,03,01,32,E4,EA,00,-1,25
1060 DATA 6,00,00,00,B0,17,B4,35,CD,21,BD,4E,01,2E,89,5E,01,-1,FB
1070 DATA 7,2E,8C,46,03,BA,07,01,8C,C8,8E,D8,B0,17,B4,25,CD,-1,0B
1080 DATA 8,21,BA,53,01,81,C2,00,01,CD,27,-1,14,-1
```

Figure 9.11 *EP2GEM.COM*

and number of lines per inch. Make a copy of the file MODE.COM, then type **DEBUG MODE.COM** <**Enter**>.

For DOS 1.10 type:

E863	<**Enter**>
1E	<**Enter**>
E873	<**Enter**>
1D	<**Enter**>
E89B	<**Enter**>
36	<**Enter**>
E8A6	<**Enter**>
38	<**Enter**>
W	<**Enter**>
Q	<**Enter**>

For DOS 2.00 type:

E855	<**Enter**>
1E	<**Enter**>
E865	<**Enter**>
1D	<**Enter**>
E88D	<**Enter**>
36	<**Enter**>
E898	<**Enter**>
38	<**Enter**>
W	<**Enter**>
Q	<**Enter**>

The same technique may be used for other printers, providing that the printer control codes to set normal or condensed printing consist of a single character, and the printer control codes to set the number of lines per inch consist of Escape followed by a single character. Simply substitute the printer control codes in the above procedure according to the following table:

1E	Control code for normal printing (80 characters per line, 10 cpi)
1D	Control code for condensed printing (line length of 132)
36	Control code for 6 lines per inch
38	Control code for 8 lines per inch

To eliminate possible confusion, rename the modified MODE.COM file to something appropriate. I call mine OKIMODE.COM.
Philip D. Ryals
Fremont, California

Printer Check Perfected

Many people will not be able to use the printer check program in "Easy Printer Check" [*.*, *PC World,* Vol. 2, No. 10] because it applies only to printers connected to the IBM Monochrome Display and Printer Adapter.

The PC can support three parallel printer adapters. When the system is started, it determines which adapters are present and creates a list of pointers to indicate the location (base port) of each one found.

The standard printer device designator, PRN:, is set to use the printer connected to the first adapter in the list (LPT1:). This may or may not be the Monochrome Display and Printer Adapter.

Rather than looking directly at a specific adapter, the printer check program should check the adapter indicated by the first pointer in the list. The program PRTRCHEK.BAS (see Figure 9.12) does exactly that. You can change the value of PRNTR in line 8000 if you wish to check the status of one of the other adapters.
James Lisson
Concord, California

Half-Height Fix

Here's a short problem-solver for those buying the Teac half-height disk drive for their IBM PCs. The drive may not come correctly configured for the IBM PC, resulting in a lack of response to any access command. After consulting my dealer, I discovered a solution. On the bottom of the drive (on the circuit board) in the rear near the control cable connection is a jumper block.

```
100 GOSUB 8000:END
8000 PRNTR=1 : DEF SEG=&H40 : BASE=(PRNTR*2) + 6
8010 IF PEEK(BASE)=0 THEN PRINT "No printer adapter present." : RETURN
8020 STAT=INP(PEEK(BASE) + PEEK(BASE+1)*256 +1) AND 160
8030 IF STAT = 128 THEN PRINT "Printer ready." : RETURN
8040 IF STAT = 0 THEN PRINT "Printer not ready."
8050 IF STAT = 32 THEN PRINT "Out of paper."
8060 IF STAT = 160 THEN PRINT "Printer not on."
8070 RETURN
```

Figure 9.12 *PRTRCHEK.BAS*

```
100 PRINT "MOTORing along at ";TIME$
110 '
120 OUT &H61,INP(&H61) AND 247   '-close relay contacts
130 '
140   SOUND 32767,(18.2*5)       '-start 5-second delay
150   SOUND 32767,1              '-suspend execution
160   SOUND 32767,0              '-clear timer
170 '
180 OUT &H61,INP(&H61) OR 8      '-open relay contacts
190 '
200 PRINT "MOTORing ended at ";TIME$
```

Figure 9.13 *MOTOR.BAS*

To configure the drive properly, two jumpers are needed: one at the HS position (first on the right) and another at the DSI position (third from the right). This usually entails moving the inner jumper one space to the left. Now, with the number one wire (the red one) of the control cable to the left of the drive (as you face the drive's front), the Teac half-height drive should operate properly.
Maurice White
Omaha, Nebraska

Cassette Port Control Compiled

I read with interest Michael Covington's "The Cassette Port Lives!" (Originally in *PC World,* Vol. 1, No. 10, and reprinted in this chapter.) I too have used the humble cassette interface to trigger external alarms.

However, the BASIC MOTOR statement is not supported by the BASIC Compiler. A little research in the Technical Reference manual (pages 1-9 and 1-25) reveals that the cassette motor relay is controlled by bit 3 of I/O port 61H. Setting this bit to 1 opens the relay, turning the MOTOR off, while setting the bit to 0 closes the relay, turning the MOTOR on.

The BASIC program in Figure 9.13, MOTOR.BAS, demonstrates this technique and works with any version of BASIC. Lines 120 and 180 are equivalent to MOTOR 1 and MOTOR 0 respectively. SOUND command "stacking" is utilized to suspend program execution for a specified amount of time.
Joseph E. Doran, Jr.
Carlisle, Massachusetts

Appendix: Products and Manufacturers

Following are products mentioned in this book. The software requirements represent the minimum needed to run each program.

Software

BASIC Compiler
IBM Corporation
P.O. Box 1328
Boca Raton, FL 33432
800/447-4700, 800/447-0809 in Alaska and Hawaii, 800/332-4400 in Illinois
Requirements: 64K, one disk drive

dBASE II
Ashton-Tate
10150 W. Jefferson Blvd.
Culver City, CA 90230
213/204-5570
Requirements: 48K, one disk drive

dBASE III
Ashton-Tate
10150 W. Jefferson Blvd.
Culver City, CA 90230
213/204-5570
Requirements: 256K, two disk drives, DOS 2.00 or later version

Grammatik
Digital Marketing Corporation
2363 Boulevard Circle
Walnut Creek, CA 94595
800/826-2222, 415/947-1000
Requirements: 64K, two disk drives or one disk drive and a hard disk

Microsoft Word
Microsoft Corporation
10700 Northup Way, Box 92700
Bellevue, WA 98004
800/426-9400, 206/828-8080
Requirements: 256K, one disk drive

Multiplan
Microsoft Corporation
10700 Northup Way, Box 92700
Bellevue, WA 98004
800/426-9400, 206/828-8080
Requirements: 128K, one disk drive

1-2-3
1-2-3 version 1A
Lotus Development Corporation
161 First St.
Cambridge, MA 02142
617/253-9150
Requirements: 192K; two disk drives; for graphics, color graphics board

PC-Talk III
Freeware/The Headlands Press, Inc.
P.O. Box 862
Tiburon, CA 94920
Requirements: 64K, (128K for compiled version), one disk drive, RS-232C serial port, modem

PC-Title
PC Resources, Inc.
62 Hobart Terrace
Santa Clara, CA 95051
408/243-4169
Requirements: 128K, one disk drive, color graphics board, RGB monitor (for color capability)

PeachText 5000
PeachTree Software, Inc.
3445 Peachtree Rd. NE
Atlanta, GA 30326
800/554-8900
Requirements: 128K, two disk drives

Personal Editor
IBM Corporation
Systems Products Division
P.O. Box 1328
Boca Raton, FL 33432
800/447-4700, 800/447-0809 in Alaska and Hawaii, 800/332-4400 in Illinois
Requirements: 128K, two disk drives

PFS: WRITE
Software Publishing Corporation
1901 Landings Dr.
Mountain View, CA 94043
415/962-8910
Requirements: 128K, one disk drive

ProKey
RoseSoft
4710 University Way NE #601
Seattle, WA 98105
206/524-2350
Requirements: 64K, one disk drive

Random House Proofreader
Digital Marketing Corporation
2363 Boulevard Circle
Walnut Creek, CA 94595
800/826-2222, 415/947-1000
Requirements: 64K, two disk drives or one disk drive and a hard disk

SuperCalc
Sorcim/IUS Micro Software
2195 Fortune Dr.
San Jose, CA 95131
408/942-1727
Requirements: 64K, one disk drive

VisiCalc
Software Arts
27 Mica Lane
Wellesley, MA 02181
617/237-4000
Requirements: 64K, one disk drive

Volkswriter Deluxe
Lifetree Software
411 Pacific St.
Monterey, CA 93940
408/373-4904
Requirements: 128K, two disk drives

WordStar, MailMerge
MicroPro International Corporation
33 San Pablo Ave.
San Rafael, CA 94903
415/499-1200
Requirements: 64K, one disk drive

Hardware

ADDS terminals
ADDS
Systems Division
100 Marcus Blvd.
Hauppage, NY 11788
516/231-5400

Advanced Programmer's Guide to dBASE II
Ashton-Tate
10150 W. Jefferson Blvd.
Culver City, CA 90230
213/204-5570

Anadex printers
Anadex, Inc.
9825 DeSoto Ave.
Chatsworth, CA 91311
213/998-8010

AST Combo-Plus expansion board
AST Research, Inc.
2121 Alton
Irvine, CA 92714
714/863-1333

Compaq computer
Compaq Computer Corporation
20555 FM 149
Houston, TX 77070
713/370-7040

Datasouth printers
Datasouth Computer Corporation
4216 Stuart Andrew Blvd.
Charlotte, NC 28210
704/523-8500

Diablo printers
Diablo Systems, Inc.
P.O. Box 5030
Fremont, CA 94537
415/498-7000

8087 Applications & Programming for the IBM PC and Other PCs
by Richard Startz
Brady Communications Company, Inc.
Bowie, MD 20715
800/624-0023

8087 Numeric Data Processor
Intel Corporation
1350 Shorebird Way
Mountain View, CA 94043
415/968-8086

Epson dot matrix printers
Epson America, Inc.
23530 Hawthorne Blvd.
Torrance, CA 90505
213/373-9511

14-16 CMOS Safe Inserter
OK Industries
3455 Conner St.
Bronx, NY 10475
212/994-6600

IBM Asynchronous
Communications Adapter
IBM Color/Graphics Adapter
IBM Dot Matrix printers
IBM Monochrome Display
IBM Corporation
Systems Products Division
P.O. Box 1328
Boca Raton, FL 33432
800/447-4700, 800/447-0890 in
Alaska and Hawaii,
800/322-4400 in Illinois

Dataproducts printers
(formerly Integral Data Systems)
Dataproducts, Inc.
Route 13 S.
Milford, NH 03055
603/673-9100

Intel *8087 Software Support Library Reference Manual*
Intel Corporation
1350 Shorebird Way
Mountain View, CA 94043
415/968-8086

Lear Siegler terminals
Lear Siegler, Inc.
Data Products Division
901 East Ball Rd.
Anaheim, CA 92805
714/778-3500

Microcom modems
Microcom
1400-A Providence Hwy.
Norwood, MA 02062
617/762-9310

Microsoft Macro-86 Assembler
Microsoft Corporation
10700 Northup Way, Box 92700
Bellevue, WA 98004
800/426-9400, 206/828-8080

NEC printers
NEC Information Systems, Inc.
1414 Massachusetts Ave.
Boxborough, MA 01719
800/343-4418

Okidata printers
Okidata
532 Fellowship Rd.
Mt. Laurel, NJ 08054
800/OKIDATA, 609/235-2600

ProWriter
Leading Edge Products, Inc.
225 Turnpike St.
Canton, MA 02121
800/343-6833, 617/828-8150 in
Massachusetts

Radio Shack Line Printer VIII
TRS-80
Tandy Corporation/Radio Shack
1800 One Tandy Center
Fort Worth, TX 76102
817/390-3700

Report Writing in dBASE II
SoftwareBanc
661 Massachusetts Ave.
Arlington, MA 02174

Hayes Smartmodems
Hayes Microcomputer Products, Inc.
5923 Peachtree Industrial Blvd.
Norcross, GA 30092
404/449-8791

Gemini 10x printer
Star Micronics, Inc.
70D Ethel Rd. W.
Piscataway, NJ 08854
201/572-9512

TEAC half-height drives
TEAC Corporation of America
7733 Telegraph Rd.
Montebello, CA 90640
213/726-0303

Tecmar expansion boards
Tecmar, Inc.
6225 Cochran Rd.
Solon, OH 44139
216/464-7410

TeleVideo terminals
TeleVideo Systems, Inc.
550 E. Brokaw
San Jose, CA 95112
408/971-0255

Texas Instruments 855
Texas Instruments Incorporated
P.O. Box 225012 M/S 84
Dallas, TX 75206
800/527-3500

To create this anthology, Joe Matazzoni pored over the entire set of articles that have been published in *PC World* magazine from its inception and made the preliminary selections. With the assistance of Steven Cook, Robert Eckhardt and Robert Gehorsam (Simon and Schuster Computer Book Division), Jeremy Joan Hewes, Karl Koessel and Art Wilcox, Joe made the final selections for the book. Joe has been associated with *PC World* from its beginning. He is currently a freelance writer and editor in Berkeley, California.

The following people contributed to this book:

Editors: Jeremy Joan Hewes, Larry J. Wilson
Project Editor: Joe Matazzoni
Consulting Editors, PC World: David Bunnell, Andrew Fluegelman
Consulting Editors, Simon & Schuster: Robert C. Eckhardt, Robert Gehorsam
Editorial Production Manager: Cynthia Mayer
Technical Editors: Steven Cook *with special assistance from* Karl Koessel, Seth Novogrodsky and Art Wilcox
Assistant Editor: Joanne Clapp
Editorial Staff: Valenta de Regil, Bill Grout, Vajeya Nagaram, Karen Payne, Curt Philips, Evelyn Spire, Otto Waldorf
Designer: Claudia Steenberg-Majewski
Typesetter: Design & Type, San Francisco

Each of the following products is a trademark, registered trademark, or service mark of the company listed in parentheses after the product name.

Software

dBASE II, dBASE III (Ashton-Tate); *Microsoft Word, Multiplan* (Microsoft Corporation); *Grammatik* (Wang Electronic Publishing, Inc.) *MailMerge, WordStar* (MicroPro International Corporation); *1-2-3* (Lotus Development Corporation); *PC-Title* (PC Resources, Inc.); *PC-Talk III* (Freeware/The Headlands Press, Inc.); *PeachText 5000* (PeachTree Software); *Personal Editor* (IBM Corporation); *PFS:* (Software Publishing Corporation); *ProKey* (RoseSoft); *Random House Proofreader* (Wang Electronic Publishing, Inc.); *SuperCalc* (Sorcim/IUS Micro Software); *Tron* (Walt Disney Productions); *VisiCalc* (Software Arts); *Volkswriter Deluxe* (Lifetree Software)

Hardware

ADDS (ADDS); Anadex (Anadex, Inc.); Apple II (Apple Computer, Inc.); Atari (Atari, Inc.); Avery (Avery Label); Combo-Plus (AST Research, Inc.); Commodore PET, Commodore VIC-20 (Commodore Electronics, Ltd.); Compaq (Compaq Computer Corporation); CompuServe (CompuServe, Inc.); Computerland (Computerland Corporation); CP/M, CP/M-80 (Digital Research, Inc.); Datasouth (Datasouth Computer Corporation); Diablo (Diablo Systems, Inc.); Ektachrome (Eastman Kodak Co.); Etch-a-Sketch (Ohio Arts); Epson (Epson America, Inc.); IBM, PC-DOS, Selectric (International Business Machines); Lear Siegler (Lear Siegler, Inc.); MCI (MCI Communications Corporation); Microcom PCS 2000 (Microcom); Microsoft Macro Assembler for MS/DOS (Microsoft Corporation); Okidata (Okielectric); PC World (PC World Communications, Inc.); ProWriter (Leading Edge Products, Inc.); Quadram (Quadram Corporation); Radio Shack Line Printer VIII, TRS-80, Radio Shack Color Computer, (Tandy Corporation/Radio Shack); RCA (RCA Corporation); Smartmodem (Hayes Microcomputer Products, Inc.); Spinwriter (NEC Information Systems, Inc.); Gemini 10x printer (Star Micronics, Inc.); TEAC (TEAC Corporation of America); Tecmar (Tecmar, Inc.); TeleVideo (TeleVideo Systems, Inc.); TI (Texas Instruments Inc.); The Source (The Source Telecomputing Co.)

Index

$ statement (BASIC), 234
/F: statement (BASIC), 249-50
/S: statement (BASIC), 249-50
/X commands (*1-2-3*), 20-21

1-2-3
  /X commands and, 20-21
  automatic execution, 100
  calculating with, 34
  cost-volume-profit analysis and, 12-19
  creating graphs, 112-14
  creating loops, 93-94
  creating macros with, 92-96, 99-100
  data entry macros, 92-93
  data query macros, 94-95
  designing templates, 90-91
  documenting macros, 100-101
  editing templates, 96
  entering data, 91
  extracting data from, 95-96
  graph legends and, 34
  graphics, 112-16
  macros and, 15, 20-27, 97-101
  printer codes and, 33-34
  printing graphs with, 115-16
  printing labels with, 97-99
  saving graphs, 114-15
  stop printing of, 34-35
  subdirectories and, 33
  subroutines and, 26
  templates and, 20-21
  using date functions, 91-92
  viewing graphs, 112-14
  wild-card characters and, 96
1.BAT, 202
2.BAT, 202
3.BAT, 202-203
4.BAT, 203-204
5.BAT, 204
6.BAT, 204
7.BAT, 204
8.BAT, 204
9.BAT, 205-206
10.BAT, 205-206
8087 coprocessor, 291-96
  8088 microprocessor and, 294
  Macro Assembler and, 291-93
  benchmarking, 296
  installing, 291
  limits of, 295
  macros and, 291-93
  precision of, 293
  range of, 293
  speed of, 294
  testing, 291-93
  writing programs for, 295-96
8088 microprocessor, 282-90
  8087 coprocessor and, 294
  BASIC compiler and, 253-55
  exploring memory of, 290
  memory addresses, 283-84
  memory organization, 287-90
  program size limitations and, 286-87
  segment registers, 286
  segmented addressing, 284-87

Adding data (*dBASE II*), 80-81
ADDNAMES.BAS, 218
Advanced BASIC. *See* BASIC
Advanced print enhancements (*WordStar*), 39, 45-46
Algorithm, 234
Alternate character fonts. *See* Character fonts
American Standard Code for Information Interchange (ASCII), 282-83
  extended character set, 207-208, 283
  graphics characters, 200-201
  graphics with, 148
ANSI driver DOS and, 208
Arithmetic, BASIC compiler and, 253-54
Arrays, BASIC compiler and, 254-55
ASCII. *See* American Standard Code for Information Interchange
Automatic execution (*1-2-3*), 100

BASCOM. *See* BASIC compiler
BASIC
  $ statement, 234
  /F: statement, 249-50
  /S: statement, 249-50
  block moves, 260-73
  CHAIN statement, 241
  checking cross-references, 274-76
  checking variables, 274-76
  CLOSE statement, 241
  CRLF$ statement, 119
  CTTY command and, 192
  CVD statement, 246
  CVI statement, 246
  CVS statement, 246
  differences between BASIC compiler, 251-52
  END statement, 241, 247
  EOF statement, 237-38
  ERL statement, 247
  ERR statement, 247
  FIELD statement, 245-46, 246
  GET statement, 120-21, 124
  GET # statement, 246-47
  history of, 233
  INPUT # statement, 236-37, 242-43
  INPUT # LINE statement, 242-43
  INSTR statement, 234-35
  LEFT$() statement, 122
  LEN statement, 245, 245
  LINE INPUT # statement, 236-37
  LMARGIN$ statement, 119
  LOAD statement, 241
  LOC statement, 247
  LOF statement, 247
  LPRINT statement, 121
  LSET statement, 246
  MKD$ statement, 246
  MKI$ statement, 246
  MKI$() statement, 121
  MKS$ statement, 246
  MOTOR statement, 297
  NEW statement, 241
  ON ERROR GOTO statement, 247-48
  OPEN statement, 240-41, 245
  OUT command, 182
  pausing programs, 276-77
  PLAY statement, 170-77
  PRINT # USING statement, 242-43
  PRINT # statement, 242-43
  programming, 234-38
  programming sound, 170-77
  PUT # statement, 246-47
  PUT statement, 256-58
  REPS statement, 122
  random-access files, 236, 240, 245-50
  RESUME NEXT statement, 247
  RESUME statement, 247
  RETURN statement, 247
  RIGHT$() statement, 122
  RSET statement, 246
  RUN statement, 241
  sequential-access files, 236, 240, 241-44
  SETCRLF$ statement, 119
  SOUND statement, 170-77
  STOP statement, 247
  string variables, 234
  SYSTEM statement, 241
  TOGRAPH$ statement, 119
  TOREG$ statement, 119
BASIC compiler, 251-59
  8088 microprocessor and, 253-55
  arithmetic, 253-54
  arrays and, 254-55
  cassette port (IBM PC) and, 306
  constants and, 253
  differences between BASIC, 251-52
  integer variables and, 252-53
  invoking, 252
  maximizing optimization of, 256
  MOTOR statement and, 306
  optimizing program size for, 258-59
  PUT statement and, 256-58
BASICA. *See* BASIC
Binary digits. *See* Bits
BLANK2.ASM, 223-27
BMOVE, 260-73
  Macro Assembler and, 260
  Screen Slinger and, 269-73
  string packing and, 264
Batch files
  creating menus with, 200-206, 220-22
  creating telephone directory with, 205-206
  redefining keys with, 207-209
  using disk emulator with, 222
Benchmarking, with 8087 coprocessor, 296
Bit graphics, 117-18
Bits, 282
  high-order, stripping (*WordStar*), 72-73
Blanking the screen, 223-27
Block graphics, *Personal Editor* and 56, 61
Block moves, 260-73
Blockbuster, 156-63
Boxes, drawing (*dBASE II*), 102-103
Break-even analysis, 12. *See also* Cost-volume-profit analysis
Burglar alarm, creating with cassette port (IBM PC), 298
Bypassing Volkswriter title page, 75
Bytes, 282. *See also* Kilobytes (K)

Calculating
  with *1-2-3*, 34
  file size, 240
CALSCR.BAS, 145-47
Cassette BASIC. *See* BASIC
Cassette port (IBM PC)
  BASIC compiler and, 306
  creating burglar alarm with, 298
  data output and, 298-302
  generating Morse code with, 298
  MOTOR statement and, 297
  timer for, 297-98
  uses of, 297

CHAIN statement (BASIC), 241
Changing
  file limits, 249-50
  output assignments (*ProKey*), 216-17
  reports (*dBASE II*), 89
Character fonts, 130-44
  constructing, 130-31
  downloading, 131-33
  Epson FX-80 and, 130-33
  TI 855 and, 130
  WordStar and, 130
Checking
  cross-references, 274-76
  printer, with PRTRCHEK.BAS, 305-306
  variables, 274-76
Clock ticks, 170
CLOSE statement (BASIC), 241
Closing sequential-access files, 241
Color
  graphics. *See* Graphics
  monitor. *See* Monitor
Command
  file (*MailMerge*), 50
  syntax (*ProKey*), 210
Communications. *See* Telecommunications
Compiled BASIC. *See* BASIC compiler
CONDENSE.BAS, 217
Configuring half-height disk drives, 305-306
Constants, BASIC compiler and, 253
Constructing character fonts, 130-31
Control codes for Okidata ML92, 304-305
Converting
  DOS files to *WordStar*, 71-72
  Microsoft Word files to *WordStar*, 70
Correcting errors (*dBASE II*), 79, 81
Cost-volume-profit analysis
  1-2-3 and, 12-19
  mechanics of, 19
Creating
  burglar alarm, with cassette port (IBM PC), 298
  files (*dBASE II*), 79
  graphs (*1-2-3*), 112-14
  loops (*1-2-3*), 93-94
  macros (*1-2-3*), 92-96, 99-100
  macros (*Personal Editor*), 56-59
  menus, with *ProKey*, 211-17
  menus, with batch files, 220-22
  reports (*dBASE II*), 82-83, 84
  telephone directory, with batch files, 205-206
CRLF$ statement (BASIC), 119
Cross-references
  checking (BASIC), 274-76
CTTY command (DOS), 191-93
  BASIC and, 192
  DEBUG.COM and, 194-96
  remote terminals and, 191-93
  Smartmodem and, 193
  STAT command and, 191
CTTYFIX.COM, 195-96
Customizing *WordStar*, 38-48
  advanced print enhancements, 39, 45-46
  with DEBUG.COM, 38-48
  function keys, 39-40, 46-47
  other options, 47-48
  printer options, 43-45
  screen display, 41-43
CVD statement (BASIC), 246
CVI statement (BASIC), 246
CVP analysis. *See* Cost-volume-profit analysis
CVS statement (BASIC), 246

Data base management systems (DBMS). *See 1-2-3*, *dBASE II*
Data
  files. *See* Files
  input macros. *See* Macros
DATAMKR.BAS, 277-78
dBASE II
  adding data, 80-81
  changing reports, 89
  correcting errors, 79, 81
  creating files, 79
  creating reports, 82-83, 84
  displaying records, 81
  drawing boxes with, 102-103
  formatting reports, 86-87, 87-89
  LIST command, 84
  modifying data base structure, 80
  planning data base structure, 78
  printing reports, 84-86
  quitting, 80
  record structure, 78-79
  reentering, 80
  REPORT FORM command, 84
  retrieving data, 81
  screen displays, 102-104
  sorting data, 81-82
  sorting records, 102
  totalling reports, 87
  tracking expenses with, 78-83
DBMS. *See* Data base management systems (DBMS)
DEBUG.COM
  bypassing Volkswriter title page with, 75
  CTTY command and, 194-96
  customizing *WordStar* with, 38-48
  Fill command, 38
  Quit command, 38
  reassigning keys with, 227-28
  Write command, 38
DEFINE, 130-44
Directories. *See also* Subdirectories
Disk BASIC. *See* BASIC
Disk files. *See* Files

Disk Operating System (DOS)
  ANSI driver and, 208
  batch files, creating menus with, 200-206
  commands, *ProKey* and, 211-17
  converting *WordStar* files to, 71-72
  CTTY command, 191-93
  FORMAT command, 226-27
  MORE command, 202
  placing on pfs:write disk, 74
  PROMPT command, 201, 207
Disks
  RAM. *See* Disk emulators
Display. *See* Screen
DOS. *See* Disk Operating System (DOS)
Dot matrix printers. *See* Printers
DOWNLOAD.ASM, 130-44
Data
  adding (*dBASE II*), 80-81
  entering (*1-2-3*), 91
  entry macros (*1-2-3*), 92-93
  extracting (*1-2-3*), 95-96
  file (*MailMerge*), 50
  merging with *MailMerge*, 51
  output, and cassette port (IBM PC), 298-302
  query macros (*1-2-3*), 94-95
  retrieving (*dBASE II*), 81
  sorting (*dBASE II*), 81-82
Date functions, using (*1-2-3*), 91-92
Declaring record structure of random-access files, 245-46
Defining
  dot commands (*MailMerge*), 51
  macros (*1-2-3*), 20
Dependency diagrams, 28-29
Designing
  games, 156
  templates (*1-2-3*), 90-91
Digital Deduction, 168-69
Directories, menus and, 200
Disabling function keys, 277
Disk drives
  configuring half-height, 305-306
  specifying with FORMAT, 226-27
Disk emulators
  using with batch files, 222
  using MORE with, 222-23
  using SORT with, 222-23
  Volkswriter and, 75
  WordStar and, 73-74
Displaying records (*dBASE II*), 81
Document
  file (*MailMerge*), 49-50
  structure (*Microsoft Word*), 62
Documenting macros (*1-2-3*), 100-101
Dot commands (*MailMerge*), 49
  defining, 51
Double-precision numbers, 293
Downloading character fonts, 131-33
Drawing boxes with *dBASE II*, 102-103
Drives. *See* Disk drives

Editing
  with *Personal Editor*, 53-55
  templates (*1-2-3*), 96
Electronic disks. *See* Disk emulators
ELITE.BAS, 217
End of file (random-access files), 247
END statement (BASIC), 241, 247
Enhancing *Personal Editor*, 52-61
Entering data (*1-2-3*), 91
EOF statement (BASIC), 237-38
EP2GEM.COM, 302-305
Epson FX-80
  character fonts and, 130-33
  extended ASCII character set and, 283
ERL statement (BASIC), 247
ERR statement (BASIC), 247
Errors
  correcting (*dBASE II*), 79, 81
  trapping (BASIC), 247-48
Exploring memory of 8088 microprocessor, 290
Extended batch files. *See* Batch files
Extended character set (ASCII), 207-208, 283
  Epson FX-80 and, 283
Extracting data from *1-2-3*, 95-96
Fields, 78
  files and, 239
FIELD statement, 245-46
  LSET statement and, 246
  RSET statement and, 246
Files. *See also* BASIC
  batch, creating menus with, 200-206, 220-22
  batch, redefining keys with, 207-209
  batch, using disk emulator with, 222
  buffers, files and, 240
  calulating size of, 240
  changing limits of, 249-50
  command (*MailMerge*), 50
  converting DOS to *WordStar*, 71-72
  converting *Microsoft Word* to *WordStar*, 70
  creating (*dBASE II*), 79
  data (*MailMerge*), 50
  document (*MailMerge*), 49-50
  fields and, 239
  file buffers and, 240
  locating with FIND, 220
  naming, 240-41
  random-access, 236, 240, 245-50
  records and, 239
  sequential-access, 236, 240, 241-44
  trapping errors, 247-48
  using, 240
Fill command (DEBUG.COM), 38
FIND, locating files with, 220
Find and Replace function (*WordStar*), 73
FLIP.COM, redefining keys with, 228-31
FlipLock
  ProKey and, 216
Floating-point numbers, 293
Fonts. *See* Character fonts

FOR APPEND statement (BASIC), OPEN statement and, 241
FOR INPUT statement (BASIC), OPEN statement and, 241
FOR OUTPUT statement (BASIC), OPEN statement and, 241
Form letters. *See MailMerge*
FORMAT, specifying drive with, 226-27
FORMATFIX2, 226-27
Formatting reports (*dBASE II*), 86-87, 87-89
FORMFEED, 216
Function keys
  customizing *WordStar*, 39-40, 46-47
  disabling, 277
FX-80. *See* Epson FX-80

Galleries (*Microsoft Word*), 63
Games. *See also* Blockbuster, Digital Deduction, Mine Field, Snake in the Glass,
  designing, 156
  modular programming and, 158
  programming, 158-62, 165-67, 168-69, 178
  top-down design and, 156
Gemini 10X
  graphics and, 304-305
Generating Morse code with cassette port (IBM PC), 298
GET statement (BASIC), 120-21, 124
GET # statement (BASIC), 246-47
Glossaries (*Microsoft Word*), 63
Graph legends (*1-2-3*), 34
Graphics. *See also 1-2-3*, BASIC
  1-2-3, 112-16
  ASCII, 148
  bit graphics, 117-18
  block (*Personal Editor*), 56, 61
  characters (ASCII), 200-201
  color, with OUT 985, 148
  Gemini 10X and, 304-305
  low-resolution color, 149-52
  screen dumps (BASIC), 117-29
Graphs (*1-2-3*)
  creating, 112-14
  printing, 115-16
  saving, 114-16
  viewing, 112-14
GRUMP, 117-29

Half-height disk drives, configuring, 305-306
Hard disk directories. *See* Subdirectories
Hayes Smartmodem 300. *See* Smartmodem
Hexadecimal notation, 283-84
High-resolution graphics. *See* Graphics

IBM PC
  cassette port and, 297-303
  memory. *See* 8088 microprocessor
  speaker, replacing, 175
IBM *Personal Editor*. *See Personal Editor*
IF functions (*SuperCalc*), 5
Ignoring delimiters of sequential-access files, 243
INPUT # LINE statement (BASIC), 242-43
INPUT # statement (BASIC), 236-37, 242-43
INS8250 LSI chip, Smartmodem and, 182
Installing 8087 coprocessor, 291
INSTR statement (BASIC), 234-35
Integer variables, BASIC compiler and, 252-53
Intel 8087 coprocessor. *See* 8087 coprocessor
Intel 8088 microprocessor. *See* 8088 microprocessor
Interpretive BASIC. *See* BASIC
Invoking BASIC compiler, 252

K. *See* Kilobytes (K)
Key redefinition programs. *See* Macros, *ProKey*
Keyboard. *See also* Keys
Keyboard macros. *See* Macros
Keys. *See also* Function keys
  <PrtSc>, using with ProWriter, 304
  redefining, with batch files, 207-209
  redefining, with DEBUG.COM, 227-28
  redefining, with FLIP.COM, 228-31
  redefining, with *ProKey*, 210-19
KEYDEFS.BAS, 277
KEYS.BAT, 207-209
Kilobytes (K), 282. *See also* Bytes

Labels, printing (*1-2-3*), 97-99
LEFT$() statement (BASIC), 122
LEN statement (BASIC), 245
  OPEN statement and, 245
Letter quality printers. *See* Printers
Limits of 8087 coprocessor, 295
LINE INPUT # statement (BASIC), 236-37
Linking worksheets (*Multiplan*), 28-32
LIST command (*dBASE II*), 84
LMARGIN$ statement (BASIC), 119
LOAD statement (BASIC), 241
LOC statement (BASIC), 247
Locating files with FIND, 220
LOF statement (BASIC), 247
LOOKUP functions (*SuperCalc*), 9
Loops, creating (*1-2-3*), 93-94
Low-resolution graphics. *See* Graphics
LOWRES.BAS, 149-52
LPRINT statement (BASIC), 121
LPTSWTCH, 216
LSET statement (BASIC), 246

Macro Assembler
  8087 coprocessor and, 291-93
  BMOVE and, 260
Macros
  1-2-3 and, 15, 20-27, 97-101
  8087 coprocessor and, 291-93
  Personal Editor and, 52-61
  creating (*1-2-3*), 92-96, 99-100
  creating (*Personal Editor*), 56-59
  data entry (*1-2-3*), 92-93
  data query (*1-2-3*), 94-95
  defining (*1-2-3*), 20
  documenting (*1-2-3*), 100-101
  subroutines (*1-2-3*), 26
  writing (*1-2-3*), 21-24
MailMerge, 49-51. *See also WordStar*
  command files, 50
  data files, 50
  document files, 49-50
  dot commands, 49
  dot commands, defining, 51
  merging data with, 51
Mainframe communication, PC-Talk III and, 194
MAKEBOX, 102-103
Maximizing optimization of BASIC compiler, 256
Medium-resolution graphics. *See* Graphics
Memory. *See also* 8087 coprocessor, 8088 microprocessor
  addresses (8088 microprocessor), 283-84
  bits, 282
  bytes, 282
  exploring (8088 microprocessor), 290
  locations, 282
  organization (8088 microprocessor), 287-90
  random-access (RAM), 287
  read-only (ROM), 287
  segmented addressing (8088 microprocessor), 284-87
  words, 282, 283
MENU.BAT, 202, 221
MENU.SCR, 201
MENU.TXT, 221
Menus
  creating, with *ProKey*, 211-17
  creating, with batch files, 200-206, 220-22
  directories and, 200
Merging data with *MailMerge*, 51
Micromodem PCS 2000, PC Talk III and, 194-95
Microsoft Word, 62-70
  converting files to *WordStar* format, 70
  document structure, 62
  galleries, 63
  glossaries, 63
  style sheets, 62-63
  style sheets, creating, 63-70
  usages, 63
Mine Field, 178
MKD$ statement (BASIC), 246
MKI$ statement (BASIC), 246
MKI$() statement (BASIC), 121
MKS$ statement (BASIC), 246
Modems, 181. *See also* Telecommunications
Modifying data base structure (*dBASE II*), 80
Modular programming, games and, 158
Monitor. *See also* Screen
  color, redefining with FLIP.COM, 228-31
  monochrome, redefining with FLIP.COM, 228-31
Monochrome monitor. *See* Monitor
MORE command (DOS), 202
  using disk emulator with, 222-23
Morse code
  generating with cassette port (IBM PC), 298
MOTOR statement (BASIC), 297
  BASIC compiler and, 306
MOTOR.BAS, 306
MOVARRAY.DEM, 268
Multiplan
  linking worksheets with, 28-32
Music. *See* Sound
MYKEYS.COM, 228-29

Naming files, 240-41
NEW statement (BASIC), 241
Numbers
  double-precision, 293
  floating-point, 293
  single-precision, 293
Numeric values, random-access files and, 246

Okidata ML92, control codes for, 304-305
ON ERROR GOTO statement (BASIC), 247-48
OPEN statement (BASIC), 240-41, 245
  FOR APPEND statement and, 241
  FOR INPUT statement and, 241
  FOR OUTPUT statement and, 241
  LEN statement and, 245
Opening
  random-access files, 245
  sequential-access files, 241
Operating system, 199. *See also* Disk Operating System (DOS)
Optimizing program size for BASIC compiler, 258-59
OUT 985, color graphics and, 148
OUT command (DOS), 182
  Smartmodem and, 182

Pausing programs, 276-77
PCBEEP, 194
PCS-TALK.PAT, 194-95
PC-Talk III
  mainframe communication and, 194
  Micromodem PCS 2000 and, 194-95
  Smartmodem and, 182-83

PeachText, subdirectories and, 74-75
Personal Editor
block graphics and, 56, 61
creating macros for, 56-59
editing with, 53-55
enhancing, 52-61
printer controls and, 55-56
pfs:write, placing DOS on disk with, 74
PHONE.BAS, 184-89
Photographing the screen, 145-47
Pixels, 119
Placing DOS on disk with pfs:write, 74
Planning data base structure (*dBASE II*), 78
PLAY statement (BASIC), 170-77
Precision of 8087 coprocessor, 293
PRINT # statement (BASIC), 242-43
PRINT # USING statement (BASIC), 242-43
Printer
checking with PRTRCHEK.BAS, 305-306
control codes for Okidata ML92, 304-305
codes (*1-2-3*), 33-34
controls, *Personal Editor* and, 55-56
options, customizing *WordStar*, 43-45
Printers
Epson FX-80, 130-33
TI 855, 130
screen dumps and, 117-29
Printing
graphs (*1-2-3*), 115-16
labels (*1-2-3*), 97-99
reports (*dBASE II*), 84-86
Programs
optimizing size for BASIC compiler, 258-59
pausing (BASIC), 276-77
speeding execution using BASIC compiler, 252-59
ProKey, 210-19
changing output assignments with, 216-17
command syntax, 210
creating menus with, 211-17
DOS commands and, 211-17
fixed field input and, 218
FlipLock and, 216
using Epson FX-80 printer with, 216-17
using NEC/SELLUM printer with, 216-17
variable field input and, 218
WordStar and, 217-19
ProWriter, using <PrtSc> key with, 304
Program size limitations, 8088 microprocessor and, 286-87
Programming, 234-38
games, 158-62, 165-67, 168-69, 178
modular, 158
sound (BASIC), 170-77
PROMPT command (DOS), 201, 207
PRTRCHEK.BAS, checking printer with, 305-306
<PrtSc> key, using with ProWriter, 304
PUT statement, BASIC compiler and, 256-58
PUT # statement (BASIC), 246-47

Quit command (DEBUG.COM), 38
Quitting *dBASE II*, 80

RAM. *See* Random-access memory (RAM)
RAM disks. *See* Disk emulators
RAMBATCH.BAT, 222
Random-access files, 236, 240, 245-50
declaring record structure, 245-46
end of file, 247
numeric values and, 246
opening, 245
reading from, 246-47
using, 248-49
using FIELD with, 246
writing to, 246
Range of 8087 coprocessor, 293
Read-only memory (ROM), 287
Reading
from random-access files, 246-47
from sequential-access files, 242-43
Record structure
declaring (random-access files), 245-46
dBASE II, 78-79
Records, 78
displaying (*dBASE II*), 81
files and, 239
sorting (*dBASE II*), 102
Redefining keys
with DEBUG.COM, 227-28
with FLIP.COM, 228-31
with *ProKey*, 210-19
with batch files, 207-209
Reentering *dBASE II*, 80
Remote terminals, CTTY command and, 191-93
REPORT FORM command (*dBASE II*), 84
Reports (*dBASE II*)
changing, 89
creating, 82-83, 84
formatting, 86-87, 87-89
printing, 84-86
totalling, 87
REPS statement (BASIC), 122
RESUME statement (BASIC), 247
RESUME NEXT statement (BASIC), 247
Retrieving data (*dBASE II*), 81

RETURN statement (BASIC), 247
RF modulator, using VCR as, 148-49
RIGHT$() statement (BASIC), 122
ROM. *See* Read-only memory (ROM)
RSET statement (BASIC), 246
RUN statement (BASIC), 241

Saving
- graphs (*1-2-3*), 114-15
- screens, with Screen Slinger, 269-73

Screen
- blanking, 223-27
- display, 119-20
- display, customizing *WordStar*, 41-43
- display, (*dBASE II*), 102-104
- dumps (BASIC), 117-29
- photographing, 145-47
- saving with Screen Slinger, 269-73

Screen Slinger, 269-73
- BMOVE and, 269-73

Segment registers (8088 microprocessor), 286
Segmented addressing (8088 microprocessor), 284-87
Separating values on sequential-access files, 242
Sequential-access files, 236, 240, 241-44
- closing, 241
- ignoring delimiters of, 243
- opening, 241
- reading, 242-43
- separating values on, 242
- using, 243-44
- writing, 242-43

SETCRLF$ statement (BASIC), 119
Single-precision numbers, 293
Smartmodem
- CTTY command and, 193
- INS8250 LSI chip and, 182
- OUT command and, 182
- PC-Talk III and, 182-83
- telephone dialing with, 184-89
- transmitting at 450 bps with, 182-83
- Xmodem and, 182

Snake in the Glass, 164-67
SORT, using disk emulator with, 222-23
SORT.DIR, 202
Sorting (*dBASE II*)
- data, 81-82
- records, 102

Sound, programming (BASIC), 170-77
SOUND statement (BASIC), 170-77
Speaker, replacing (IBM PC), 175
Specifying drive, with FORMAT, 226-27
Speed of 8087 coprocessor, 294
Speeding program execution using BASIC compiler, 252-59
Spreadsheets. *See 1-2-3*, *Multiplan*, *SuperCalc*
STAT command, CTTY command and, 191
STAT.BAT, 202
STD.PRO, 211-215
Stocks, tracking with *SuperCalc*, 4-11
Stop printing (*1-2-3*), 34-35
STOP statement (BASIC), 247
String packing, BMOVE and, 264
Stripping high-order bit (*WordStar*), 72-73
Style sheets (*Microsoft Word*), 62-63
- creating, 63-70

Subdirectories
- *1-2-3* and, 33
- PeachText and, 74-75

Subroutines, *1-2-3* and, 26
SuperCalc
- IF functions and, 5
- LOOKUP functions and, 9
- tracking stocks with, 4-11

SYSTEM statement (BASIC), 241

Telecommunications. *See* CTTY command, OUT command, PC-Talk III, Smartmodem
Telephone
- dialing, with Smartmodem, 184-89
- directory, creating with batch files, 205-206

Templates (*1-2-3*), 20-21
- designing (*1-2-3*), 90-91
- editing (*1-2-3*), 96

Testing 8087 coprocessor, 291-93
TI 855, character fonts and, 130
Timer for cassette port (IBM PC), 297-98
TOGRAPH$ statement (BASIC), 119
Top-down design, games and, 156
TOREG$ statement (BASIC), 119
Totalling reports (*dBASE II*), 87
Tracking
- expenses, with *dBASE II*, 78-83
- stocks, with *SuperCalc*, 4-11

Transmitting at 450 bps with Smartmodem, 182-83
Trapping errors, 247-48
Tree-structured directories. *See* Subdirectories

Usages (*Microsoft Word*), 63
Uses of cassette port (IBM PC), 297
Using
- date functions (*1-2-3*), 91-92
- disk emulator, with MORE, 222-23
- disk emulator, with SORT, 222-23
- disk emulator, with batch files, 222
- Epson FX-80 printer with *ProKey*, 216-17

FIELD with random-access files, 246
files, 240
NEC/SELLUM printer with *ProKey*, 216-17
<PrtSc> key with ProWriter, 304
random-access files, 248-49
sequential-access files, 243-44
VCR, as RF modulator, 148-49

VCR, using as RF modulator, 148-49
Variable field input (*ProKey*), 218
Variables, checking (BASIC), 274-76
Video games. *See* Games
Viewing graphs (*1-2-3*), 112-14
Volkswriter
bypassing title page, 75
disk emulators and, 75

Warnier-Orr diagrams, 184, 188, 190
Wild-card characters (*1-2-3*), 96
Word. See Microsoft Word
Word processors. *See Microsoft Word, Personal Editor, WordStar*
Words, 282, 283
WordStar. See also MailMerge
character fonts and, 130
converting DOS files to, 71-72
converting *Microsoft Word* files to, 70
customizing, 38-48
disk emulators and, 73-74
Find and Replace function, 73
ProKey and, 217-19
stripping high-order bit, 72-73
Worksheets, linking (*Multiplan*), 28-32
Write command (DEBUG.COM), 38
WRITE.BAT, 204
Writing
macros (*1-2-3*), 21-24
programs for 8087 coprocessor, 295-96
to random-access files, 246
to sequential-access files, 242-43

WS-EPSON.BAT, 217-18
WS-NEC.BAT, 218

XMAKER.BAS, 277-78
Xmodem, Smartmodem and, 182
XREF.BAS, 274-76

Other PC World Books

Getting Started with the IBM PC and XT

by David Arnold and the Editors of PC World

In *Getting Started with the IBM PC and XT,* David Arnold and the Editors of PC World have teamed up to give PC users a clearly written, authoritative guide to using the PC and its more powerful cousin, the XT. If you are new to the computer, you will value the tutorial approach to becoming familiar with the keyboard, the disks, and the disk operating system (DOS 1.10 and 2.00) and to learning how to set up and handle electronic files. You will appreciate the careful explanations of how to evaluate your software needs and the practical introduction to BASIC, which includes essential commands for file management as well as programming. If you are already working with the PC or the XT and want to explore further, you can count on *Getting Started* for detailed explanations and examples of advanced aspects of DOS 2.00 and special XT requirements, such as hard disk formatting. The book also includes a section on the maintenance and care of electronic equipment. Whether you're just beginning to use a PC or need a handy reference manual, this book will help you master the many facets of your computer and keep it running smoothly.

How to Buy an IBM PC or Compatible Computer

by Danny Goodman and the Editors of PC World

More people buy the IBM PC and PC compatibles than any other personal computers. But the PC and compatibles come in many configurations for many different tasks, and selecting an appropriate system is not always easy. This comprehensive, easy-to-understand guide is exactly what you need to save yourself hours of unnecessary effort and confusion. *How to Buy an IBM PC or Compatible Computer* answers all the common questions that frustrate buyers and also addresses many other issues that are often overlooked, such as matching the system to the work it must perform (including decisions about memory size, type of disk drives, displays and printers, conservation of expansion slots, and choice of essential software), evaluating dealers and salespeople, and selecting a maintenance organization and contract. The authors discuss the complex issue of PC compatibility and describe the most important PC-compatible computers. In today's crowded and confusing computer marketplace, *How to Buy an IBM PC or Compatible Computer* is the perfect guide to making sensible decisions about one of the most important purchases you'll ever make.

Essential Applications for the IBM PC and XT

by Patrick Plemmons and the Editors of PC World

Most people buy a personal computer for one activity, such as word processing, financial calculations, or information management. In doing so, they fail to use the computer's innate capacity to perform other types of tasks equally efficiently and effectively. *Essential Applications for the IBM PC and XT* demonstrates the amazing breadth and power of the PC and helps you take advantage of the computer's potential as both a personal and a professional tool. The book explains in clear and comprehensive terms the principal categories of professional computer applications: spreadsheets, word processing, data base management, accounting and financial programs, graphics, and integrated software, which is able to perform several applications and transfer information quickly and easily between applications. The authors show you how to make the best use of the computer to execute these tasks. You will learn about the major software packages in each applications category, and how to match tasks with the appropriate software. With *Essential Applications for the IBM PC and XT,* you'll never run out of practical uses for your personal computer and you'll always know how to get where you want to go.

Communications for IBM Personal Computers and Compatibles

by Lisa B. Stahr and the Editors of PC World

One of the truly exciting features of personal computers is their ability to exchange information with each other—and with distant mainframe computers—over the telephone lines. *Communications for IBM Personal Computers and Compatibles* provides a window to resources that extend beyond your PC. Clear, comprehensive, and thought-provoking, the book explains how to select the most appropriate communications software and peripherals for your PC and offers a nontechnical look at how computers actually communicate with each other. The authors explain how to use the different types of communications to best suit your professional and personal needs, including conducting research on commercial data bases; acquiring sofware—sometimes for free—directly over the phone lines; exchanging messages on an electronic bulletin board; and linking several PCs and XTs into a local area network so that you and your group can perform your work more efficiently than ever. No matter what your specific needs are, *Communications for IBM Personal Computers and Compatibles* will help you make the most of your computer's ability to join forces with other computers.

The Complete IBM Personal Computer

by Seth Novogrodsky, Frederic E. Davis and the Editors of PC World

The Complete IBM Personal Computer is an invaluable guide and reference that will help you make sense of the continually expanding and sometimes perplexing array of add-on equipment available for the PC, XT, and PC-compatible computers. If you're a newcomer to the PC, the general introductions to the entire array of peripherals—from such familiar devices as keyboards, game controllers, and monitors to more exotic possibilities such as voice recognition devices, bubble memory, and graphics plotters—will provide the basis for understanding each type of device and its uses. If you already know how you want to expand your system, you can consult the digests of major brand-name products to narrow your choices. Each product listing contains a complete description of the peripheral and its capabilities, as well as a discussion of the important criteria for evaluating features. *The Complete IBM Personal Computer* opens up new worlds of personal computing by helping you expand your system sensibly, efficiently, and precisely to your needs.

The Fully Powered PC

by Burton L. Alperson, Andrew Fluegelman, Lawrence J. Magid, and the Editors of PC World

Now that you own a PC and have been working with it for some time, are you starting to wish it had just a few more special features to help you do your job better? Perhaps a way to execute a command in one keystroke that now takes six? Or a way to make a section of internal memory act like a disk—but fifty times faster? Are you running out of expansion slots, even though you can think of a dozen more boards you'd like to add? Relax—and read *The Fully Powered PC*, the first and only guide devoted exclusively to ways of customizing the highly versatile PC with modestly priced software and hardware additions, including keyboard reconfiguration programs, spoolers, custom-designed menus, batch filers, and multifunction expansion boards (to squeeze even more capabilities into one expansion slot). With up-to-the-minute guidance from the experts, you'll be able to create a computer system exactly as you want it. When you're ready to take full advantage of your computing capabilities, shift into high gear with *The Fully Powered PC*.

The books in this series are produced by the editors of

PC W●RLD
The Comprehensive Guide to IBM Personal Computers and Compatibles

PC World is the monthly magazine of choice for people who use IBM Personal Computers and Compatibles. Each month, **PC World** delivers information designed to suit the needs of users at all levels. Regular features in **PC World** include:

- *Getting Started:* Articles for novice users covering the most popular computer applications.
- *Community:* Direct access to the people in personal computing and to the personal computing solutions other organizations have employed.
- *Review:* Independent evaluations of new products based on our exhaustive performance tests.
- *State of the Art:* Information about technologies under development and how these new inventions are likely to affect you.
- *Hands On:* "How-to" articles with valuable tips for making the most of popular products.

PC World is read by more IBM Personal Computer users than any other magazine. To find out how you can subscribe to **PC World,** please write the publishers at:

Circulation Department
PC World Communications, Inc.
555 De Haro Street
San Francisco, CA 94107

To save time, call our toll-free subscription information telephone numbers:
800/247-5470 (800/532-1272 in Iowa)